ENGLISH LOCAL GOVERNMENT

ENGLISH POOR LAW HISTORY
PART II: THE LAST HUNDRED YEARS
VOL. II

LONGMANS, GREEN AND CO. LTD.

39 PATERNOSTER ROW, LONDON, E.C.4
6 OLD COURT HOUSE STREET, CALCUTTA
53 NICOL ROAD, BOMBAY
167 MOUNT ROAD, MADRAS

LONGMANS, GREEN AND CO.

55 FIFTH AVENUE, NEW YORK
221 EAST 20TH STREET, CHICAGO
TREMONT TEMPLE, BOSTON
210 VICTORIA STREET, TORONTO

ENGLISH POOR LAW HISTORY: PART II: THE LAST HUNDRED YEARS. BY SIDNEY AND BEATRICE WEBB.

VOL. II

LONGMANS, GREEN AND CO.
LONDON ✦ NEW YORK ✦ TORONTO
1929

Made in Great Britain.

CONTENTS

VOLUME II

CHAPTER V

Why the Commission was Appointed—Its Constitution—
The Case presented by the L.G.B.—The Effect of Democracy
upon Poor Law Administration—The Internal Life of the
Commission—The Reports of the Special Investigators—What
were the Effects of Outdoor Relief ?—What happened when it
was Withdrawn or Refused ?—In what Condition were the
Children maintained on Outdoor Relief ?—How were the Sick
being Treated ?—What were the Causes that pressed People
into Destitution ?—The Views of the Problem taken by the
Commissioners—The Majority Report—The Minority Report—
The Cleavage in Spirit—The Change in Thought since 1834.

CHAPTER VI

How the Framework of Repression has been superseded
by the Framework of Prevention—What the Destitution is
that has to be Prevented—" Blocking the Downward Way "
by Factory and Mines Acts—The Legal Minimum Wage—The
Principle of the Common Rule—Communistic Services—The
Prevention of Sickness—Municipal Activities—The Campaign
for Infant Welfare—The Campaign against Venereal Disease—
Characteristics of Public Health Work—The Public Provision
for Lunacy and Mental Deficiency—The Prevention of Illiteracy
and Child Neglect—The School Medical Service—School Feeding
—Increase of Parental Responsibility—National Insurance—
Pensions for the Aged, the Widows and the Orphans—The
Evolution of Specialised Central Departments—International
Developments of the Framework of Prevention—Its Dependence
on Research and Knowledge.

CHAPTER VII

CHAPTER VIII

CHAPTER IX

Status ; (b) Registration ; (c) Charge and Recovery—What the Act will Accomplish—Nothing for the Unemployed !—The Need for a Specialised National Authority—The Development of the Ministry of Labour—What will remain under the Poor Law—The Old Principles and the New.

APPENDICES

CHAPTER V

THE Poor Law Inquiry Commission of 1832–1834 arose out of the intolerable scandals of the then-existing state of things ; and its revolutionary proposals were the outcome of a whole generation of abstract reasoning upon the misdeeds of the local administrators. The active members of the Commission and their staff of investigators all belonged to the then-dominant school of thought ; and the evidence was collected and arranged so as to bring into overwhelming prominence certain prejudged conclusions. The Report was immediately accepted by enlightened public opinion ; and, within a few months of publication, its recommendations were substantially embodied in an Act of Parliament.

The Royal Commission on the Poor Law and the Unemployed, which the Conservative Government appointed in December 1905, was in every one of these features the exact antithesis to its famous predecessor. It was not the outcome of any widespread or long-continued agitation against the existing system of Poor Relief. There had been no breakdown in the administration of the Boards of Guardians, which had become, on the contrary, under the continuous supervision of the Local Government Board, steadily more efficient and more humane. The " Principles of 1834 " were assumed to be in operation ; and they were professedly endorsed by the dominant philosophy and administrative experience of the time. Criticism there was, but it came from conflicting schools of thought ; and, owing to the consequent " cancelling out ", it had produced comparatively little effect on public opinion. The personnel of the new Commission differed radically from that of its predecessor. For good or for evil, the score of persons appointed to be Royal Commissioners in 1905 were far from homogeneous in opinion. Although the majority of them represented the views of those who approved of the existing order, they found themselves faced by able critics of the very basis of the Poor Law Amendment Act of 1834. Thus, the evidence collected by the Commissioners themselves, and by the staff of expert investigators whom they appointed, however accurate and comprehensive it might be, was used to support conclusions based on conflicting views of social expediency. The Majority and Minority Reports were both elaborate documents, alike more comprehensive in their scope and in their recommendations than the unanimous Report of 1834 ; they had a record sale, and attracted widespread attention ; but in spite of a large measure of agreement in their proposals, they ranged those who were interested in social reconstruction in two opposing camps. After many promises on the part of successive Cabinets, in the course of a couple of decades, neither the one Report nor the other has been embodied in legislation : and even the changes which the Majority and Minority alike advocated long failed to pass into law. The Royal Commission of 1905–1909 was, in fact, from a constructive standpoint, as big a failure as the Royal Commission of 1832–1834 was a success. What it achieved was a couple of discoveries, which, like many other new truths, discredited and disintegrated existing institutions, without providing any alternative that the the nation, at the moment, found practicable. The two discoveries were (1) that the " Principles of 1834 " had been, almost unawares, gradually abandoned in practice by the administration of successive governments, whether Conservative or Liberal ; and (2) that there had grown up, during the preceding half century, an array of competing public services which were aiming, not at the prevention of pauperism, but at the prevention of the various types of destitution out of which pauperism arose. We have accordingly to trace the emergence of these discoveries in the course of the three years' investigation of the Commission.

Why the Commission was appointed

At this point the inquisitive reader will ask : If there was no public demand for an inquiry into the working of the Poor Law, and no crying scandal, why did the Prime Minister (Mr. Arthur

Balfour), at the close of the session of 1905, announce in reply to an evidently prearranged question in the House of Commons,[1] that the Government had come to the conclusion that the time had come for a full inquiry into the whole question, adding with significance, that there had been no such inquiry since that of 1832–1834. Why did the Cabinet, on the very eve of its resignation, put itself to the trouble of choosing the members of a large and representative Royal Commission ; and charge it " to enquire (1) Into the working of the laws relating to the relief of poor persons in the United Kingdom ; (2) Into the various means which have been adopted outside of the Poor Laws for meeting distress arising from want of employment, particularly during periods of severe industrial depression ; and to consider and report whether any, and if so, what, modification of the Poor Laws or changes in their administration, or fresh legislation for dealing with distress, are advisable " ?

Who can read the hearts of Cabinet Ministers or discern their intentions, let alone the grounds of their intentions ? Our own impression at the time was that the Commission owed its creation to the coincidence of there being, as newly appointed head of the Poor Law Division, an energetic man of affairs (James Stewart Davy) intent on reaction ; and, as President of the Local Government Board, a philosopher (Mr. Gerald Balfour) who recognised the public advantage of a precise discrimination between opposing principles. Moreover, although the mean aggregate pauperism per 1000 of the population in successive cycles of eight or ten years, had continued steadily to decline,[2] those best acquainted with the detailed statistics noticed ominous features. From the beginning of the twentieth century the ratio of pauperism to population had, taking single years, started continuously to rise, whilst the total number was mounting rapidly. This was partly accounted for by an increasing willingness of the sick and the aged to accept the improved forms of Poor Relief which, as we have described in the preceding chapter, were now being offered to them. But there was a new feature in Poor Law statistics—a disquieting growth in the number of adult men claiming Poor

---

[1] Hansard, August 2, 1905.

[2] It fell from 31·2 per thousand in 1871–1880, to 26·6 per thousand in 1881–1888, 23·8 per thousand in 1889–1896 and 22·2 per thousand in 1897–1906 (Majority Report of Poor Law Commission, 1909, p. 36).

Relief—which was accompanied by a persistent agitation in and out of Parliament by the nascent Labour Party, which worried the Government into the enactment, during the session of 1905, of the Unemployed Workmen Act, opening up an alarming vista of local " relief works ", incompatible with the maintenance of a " deterrent " policy.   In contrast with the " Allowance System" of the Old Poor Law, which was almost entirely a rural problem, the impending danger seemed to arise wholly from ill-considered measures for the relief of the wageless workmen in the Metropolis and in the larger provincial towns.[1]   The position in London was regarded as specially disquieting.   There was, in fact, in official circles, an uneasy feeling that there had been, during the last two decades, an unwilling drift away from the " Principles of 1834 ", and one which, sooner or later, had to be decisively stopped.   The official objection to this policy of drift can be gathered, as we shall presently show, from the long and elaborate evidence of the Assistant Secretary and Chief Inspector of the Local Government Board, and his staff of inspectors.   A more direct, though less authoritative, confirmation of this suggestion is given in the following entry from the contemporary MS. diary of one of the Commissioners, jotted down a few days before the first sitting of the Commission in December 1905.   " I had extracted from Davy, the Assistant Secretary of the L.G.B., in a little interview I had had with him, the intention of the L.G.B. officials as to the purpose and procedure they intended to be followed by the Commission. They were going to use us to get certain radical reforms of struc-ture : the Boards of Guardians were to be swept away, judicial officers appointed, and possibly the institutions transferred to the county authorities—with all of which I am inclined to agree.   But we were also to recommend reversion to the " Principles of 1834" as regards policy, to stem the tide of philanthropic impulse that was sweeping away the old embankment of deterrent tests to the receipt of relief.   Though I think the exact form in which this impulse has clothed itself is radically wrong and mischievous, yet I believe in the impulse, if it takes the right forms.   It is just this vital question of what and which forms are right that I want to discover by [means of] this Commission to investigate.   Having settled the conclusions to which we are to be led, the L.G.B. officials (on and off the Commission) have predetermined the

[1] Majority Report of Poor Law Commission, 1909, pp. 37, 54.

procedure. We were to be ' spoon fed ' by evidence carefully selected and prepared ; they were to draft the circular to the Board of Guardians ; they were to select the Inspectors who were to give evidence ; they were virtually to select the Guardians to be called in support [of] this evidence. Assistant Commissioners were to be appointed, who were to collect evidence illustrative of these theories. And, above all, we were to be given *opinions* and not facts. . . . To-day at lunch I put Lansbury (the working-man on the Commission) on his guard against this policy ".[1]

The Constitution of the Poor Law Commission

In spite of ancient lineage and sonorous title, the British Royal Commission has no settled constitution, no single purpose, and no authoritatively imposed procedure.[2] There have been Royal Commissions which have resembled Courts of Justice in procedure or in function ; for instance, the Parnell Commission of

[1] MS. diary of Beatrice Webb, December 1905. Mr. Lansbury, of working-class origin, has retained throughout a devoted life working-class sympathies. He proved a most loyal and helpful colleague, and contributed much to the Minority Report. See *My Life*, by G. L., 1928.

The announcement of the intention to appoint the Commission—which was entirely unexpected by the public—had been received with some disquietude by the leaders of the Charity Organisation Society. " Politics " might intervene ! The scope must be limited. There must be no extension to " the problem of poverty ", or the possibility of a " reconstruction of society " (*Charity Organisation Review*, September 1905, pp. 140-143).

[2] It may be added that it was out of the difficulties encountered in obtaining a unanimous report, both from the Poor Law Commission and from the Welsh Church Commission, and out of the friction which had in some cases arisen, that arose the appointment, in 1909, of a Departmental Committee under Lord Balfour of Burleigh, " to consider what should be the procedure of Royal Commissions . . . with special reference to the duties and powers of the Chairman ". This Committee reported, in 1910, making various useful suggestions for securing both greater economy in the expenses of Royal Commissions and greater harmony in their proceedings. The Report has, however, not been given any sanction by statute, Order in Council or other authority ; and its suggestions, whilst naturally carrying weight with Chairmen and other members of Commissions, and with the Treasury and other Departments concerned, are not binding on them. Its principal novelty was the suggestion that Commissioners dissenting from the views of the majority were not empowered to address to the King a Minority Report unless they were at least equal to the number named in the Royal Warrant as a quorum of the Commission. Any smaller group of dissentients, or any individual Commissioner, was entitled, however, to present a " dissenting Memorandum ", giving the points of dissent and the reasons thereof, and " marshalling so much only of the evidence or facts which have been ascertained as may be necessary to support any alternative conclusion " (Report of Departmental Committee on the Procedure of Royal Commissions, 1910, Cd. 5235).

1888-1890, or the South African (Jameson Raid) inquiry of 1897, though this was a Select Committee of the House of Commons. There have been Royal Commissions which might just as well have been Committees of the Royal Society, so predominantly scientific were they in their personnel and their methods of investigation, such as the Royal Commission on Sewage Disposal. But the Royal Commission most typical of the past hundred years is that which is appointed to inquire into some existing institution, in order to prepare a scheme of reform that may afford a basis for legislative or administrative action. These " reforming Commissions " may be divided, according to their constitution, into those which are " impartial ", *i.e.* made up of persons assumed, by the Government, to be intellectually disinterested and without *parti pris* on the more obvious points at issue (*e.g.* the Samuel Coal Commission of 1926) ; and those which are intended to be representative of the interests or of the schools of thought concerned (*e.g.* the Sankey Coal Commission of 1919). Owing to the difficulty—a difficulty which is every day increasing—of finding " impartial " persons, or persons who will be deemed to be impartial by the classes or interests involved, the representative Commission is usually preferred for all questions which directly concern large or influential bodies of men having diverse or conflicting interests ; for instance, employers and wage-earners, consumers and producers, private traders and public corporations.

Now the Poor Law Commission of 1905-1909 was, to a marked degree, a " reforming Commission ", and a reforming Commission of the representative type. Many varieties of experience and the main schools of thought were represented, though, of course, not equally represented. Thus, unlike the Poor Law Commission of 1832-1834, that of 1905-1909 was largely composed of persons who had actually taken part in the administration of the Poor Law. There were on it no fewer than five Guardians of the Poor, four of whom were, or had been, Chairmen of their Boards.[1] Even more influential was the presence of the " Permanent Heads " of the Local Government Boards of England, Scotland and Ireland respectively, who were

---

[1] The Poor Law Guardians were F. H. Bentham, George Lansbury, T. Hancock Nunn, the Rev. L. R. Phelps, and F. Chandler (subsequently added to represent the Trade Union Movement).

personally directing the Poor Law administration of the three countries, together with the Senior Medical Inspector of the English Poor Law Division.[1] These nine experienced Poor Law administrators were reinforced by half a dozen prominent members of the Charity Organisation Society, all of whom began the inquiry as convinced adherents of the " Principles of 1834 ", notably the Society's General Secretary, C. S. Loch ; one of its founders, Miss Octavia Hill ; and two other distinguished exponents of its doctrines, Mr. Hancock Nunn and Mrs. Bernard Bosanquet.[2] There were two political economists, belonging to what was then called the " orthodox school " : Professor William Smart of Glasgow and the Rev. L. R. Phelps of Oxford. With the Rev. Prebendary Russell Wakefield, afterwards Bishop of Birmingham, the Church of England had three representatives, and the Roman Catholic Church in Ireland one (the Bishop of Ross).[3] This predominantly " stand pat " composition of the Commission was emphasised by the appointment of a Conservative ex-Cabinet Minister as Chairman (Lord George Hamilton). Out of the twenty members there were only three who belonged to the Labour and Socialist Movements—Mr. George Lansbury, Mr. Francis Chandler (General Secretary of the old-established Amalgamated Society of Carpenters), and Mrs. Sidney Webb. But the unique characteristic of this Commission was the inclusion in it of members who had proved their capacity for the work of social investigation. There was the Right Honourable Charles Booth,[4] who might be termed the inventor of one of the leading methods of sociological research ; there were the ablest

---

[1] Sir S. B. Provis, K.C.B., J. Patten-Macdougall, C.B., Sir Henry Robinson, K.C.B., and Dr. A. H. (now Sir Arthur) Downes.

[2] The C.O.S. members included the above-mentioned together with Rev. T. G. Gardiner and the Rev. L. R. Phelps.

[3] The Bishop of Ross (Dr. Kelly) was added to the Commission in place of the O'Conor Don, who died in 1906.

[4] The Right Honourable Charles Booth (1840–1917), shipowner and merchant, had devoted many years of thought and work, and large drafts upon his income, to statistical investigation of social conditions, for which he had a passion, and in which he became an inventor of new *technique*. Public recognition of his achievements came in a privy councillorship, a fellowship of the Royal Society, and doctorates of the Universities of Liverpool, Oxford and Cambridge. For his life, see *Charles Booth—A Memoir*, 1918 [by his widow]; and for an account of his great work, *Life and Labour of the People in London*, 17 vols., 1902 (of which the first volume in the original edition, had been published in 1889) see *My Apprenticeship*, by Beatrice Webb, 1926, chap. v., " A Grand Inquest into the Condition of the People of London ", pp. 216-256.

members of the Charity Organisation Society—a society whose activities were avowedly based, in a far-reaching survey of social results, on exhaustive inquiry into individual cases ; and there was one of the leading researchers of the Fabian Society. The Commission was, in fact, predominantly a body of experts, either in Poor Law administration or social investigation. Indeed, one of the few members of the Commission who had neither an extensive knowledge of the subject nor experience in research was its Chairman, Lord George Hamilton. Fortunately for the amenity of the Commission's internal life, and perhaps even for its efficiency as an instrument of research, this experienced politician and attractive *grand seigneur* combined exceptional personal charm and social tact with an open mind and a willingness to give free play to the activities of his fellow-Commissioners. Regarded as an instrument of reform, what the Commission seemed to lack was the guiding hand of an experienced lawyer, who might have kept the inquiry strictly within the terms of reference, and insisted on all evidence being brought before the Commission as a whole, and tested by some common standard of relevance and validity ; and who might, in the end, have " negotiated " a unanimous report on all those issues—and there proved to be many—upon which there was common agreement.[1]

[1] The Poor Law Commission of 1905-1909 exceeded, in the volume of published proceedings, memoranda, reports and (especially) statistics, even the Poor Law Inquiry Commission of 1832-1834. Besides the lengthy Majority and Minority Reports (Cd. 4625)—these were also published in three octavo volumes from which our quotations are taken—there were issued no fewer than 47 folio volumes of appendices ending with a specially elaborate " General Consolidated Index " of 1086 pages. For Scotland (Cd. 4922) and Ireland (Cd. 4630) there were also Majority and Minority Reports.

The Commission was greatly aided in its work by the ability and devotion of its secretariat, notably by its secretary, R. G. Duff, then an Assistant General Inspector, and subsequently a General Inspector, of the Local Government Board (now Ministry of Health) ; and by its Assistant Secretary, John Jeffrey, then in the Scottish Local Government Board and subsequently Secretary to the Scottish Health Insurance Commission (now Permanent Secretary of the Scottish Health Department).

Among the many books and pamphlets to which these official publications gave rise, we may mention specially *The Poor Law Report of 1909*, by Mrs. Bernard Bosanquet, 1910 ; *By What Authority ? the principles in common and at issue in the Reports of the Poor Law Commission*, by J. H. Muirhead, 1909 ; *The Poor Law Commission : what it proposes*, by C. B. Hawkins and J. S. Nicholson, 1909 ; *The Suggested New Poor Law : Knight's Synopsis of the Majority and Minority Reports*, 1909 ; *Unemployment : results of an Examination of the Report of the Royal Commission*, by (Sir) S. J. Chapman and H. M. Hallsworth, 1909 ; *Poor Law Reform : the Case for the Guardians*, by Sir W. Chance, 1910 ; *The Starting Point of Poor Law Reform*, by J. H. Muirhead,

The Case presented by the Local Government Board

During the first five months of the Commission's sittings the plea for a strict adhesion to " Poor Law Principles " was stated with considerable skill and exemplary discretion in the lengthy evidence of the principal officer of the Poor Law Division (J. S. Davy) ; and elaborated and illustrated by the shorter statements of his staff of Inspectors.

For the able-bodied and their dependents, the " Principle of Less Eligibility ", and the application of the Workhouse Test, was, Davy maintained, the accepted policy of the Local Government Board. On this policy rested the justification of the central control over the relief of destitution set up by the Poor Law Amendment Act of 1834. Through the Elizabethan Poor Law, as amended by that Act, the Government guaranteed the maintenance of destitute persons, but only " provided the condition of the person so maintained shall be, or shall appear to be, inferior to that of the poorest independent labourer " (Q. 2027) ; or, as he graphically expressed it, "that the hanger-on should be lower than him on whom he hangs " (Q. 2148). He and his staff " had to see that the machinery for carrying out what I believe to be the guarantee of the State is in working order ; and they have to see, as far as they can, that the conditions of relief are not such as to be mischievous to the Commonwealth" (Q. 2029). Seeing that the pauper had to be provided with a sufficiency of food, clothing and shelter—a sufficiency which did not always fall to the lot of the independent wage-earner—Davy held that ineligibility consisted of three main elements : " first of the loss of personal reputation (what is understood by the stigma of pauperism) ; secondly, the loss of personal freedom which is secured by detention in a workhouse ; and thirdly, the loss of political freedom by suffering disfranchisement " (Q. 2230). He wished that residence in the workhouse should be deliberately made unpleasant. Thus, he was strongly in favour of the Able-bodied Test Workhouse, as established at Manchester, Kensington and Sheffield. " If you

1910 ; *Principles of Poor Law Reform*, by Sir Arthur Clay, 1910. We are ourselves responsible for *English Poor Law Policy*, 1910 ; *The State and the Doctor*, 1910 ; as well as for a reprint of the Minority Report, with introductions, in two volumes, entitled *The Break-up of the Poor Law* and *The Public Organisation of the Labour Market*, both 1909 ; together with *The Prevention of Destitution*, 1911.

do not have a test house ", he declared, " you will have your
workhouse crowded up with loafers ; and you will have no means
of keeping in check that class of the population who positively
prefer an institutional life if it is given under anything like tolerable
conditions " (Q. 2365). " The work ", he said, " should be both
irksome and unskilled. . . . You have got to find work which
anybody can do, and which nearly everybody dislikes doing. . . .
You have got to give him something like corn-grinding or flint-
crushing, cross-cut sawing, or some work of that sort, which is
laborious and which is wholly unskilled " (Q. 2366). In addition
to unpleasant work, there must be a definite restraint on freedom
after work. Thus, he specifically objected to the " quite excessive " leave of absence customary in the General Mixed Workhouses of London, and he appealed to the Commission to help the
L.G.B. to discover " whether workhouses are ceasing to be
deterrent, and if they are, whether the change is not attributable
to a very large extent to the amount of leave which is given to
inmates " (Q. 2318). The Labour Test Order, under which the
Guardians were permitted to substitute employment in the stone-
yard for residence in the Workhouse, was, he thought, a source of
danger ; and he recommended that applicants should at any rate
be required to work a full six days' week, not for wages but merely
in return for the relief of their destitution (Q. 2443). The stigma
of pauperism should be maintained intact by a reversion to
complete Parliamentary and Municipal disfranchisement, as this
would deter " the high-class man who was on strike " from applying for relief, either for himself or for his dependents (Q. 2448).
Moreover, persons given work at wages by the Town Councils
under the Unemployed Workmen Act of 1905 ought to be struck
off the register for municipal elections, according to the principle
that no one should take part in the election of his own paymaster
(Q. 3179, 3224). For able-bodied men and women Outdoor Relief
was disastrous ; in some it destroyed the will to work ; in the
more industrious it led inevitably to a " rate in aid of wages ",
thus lowering the earnings of the independent poor. " I am
convinced, myself ", he said, " that the greatest wrong that is
done to poor people in England now is done by means of the
Outdoor Relief which is given to persons who are earning wages "
(Q. 2938). " If you give Outdoor Relief regularly—never mind
in how small sums—you will find a tendency to make a local

congestion of the worst-paid labour and of the poorest people "
(Q. 2942). But the Chief Inspector of 1906 went even further
than the Commission of 1834 and the official practice of the past
three-quarters of a century ; he, like the Inspectorate of 1871–
1892, wished to apply the " Principle of Less Eligibility " to the
aged, to the children, and even to the sick. The admission of the
aged to the modern Workhouse, he thought, with its material
comforts and leave of absence, even apart from doles in the home,
discouraged saving for old age ; and this generous provision for
the aged disinclined relatives to maintain their old people. The
steady growth in the number of children in Poor Law institutions,
together with the increased expense of their maintenance, was
due to the needless comfort and the extravagant cost of the new
" Cottage Homes " and other forms of residential provision for
children. The London Poor Law infirmaries erected during the
preceding half century, with their expensive equipment and their
staffs of skilled doctors and trained nurses, were attracting to Poor
Relief new sections of the population, and had become virtually
" State hospitals ", without any stigma of pauperism ; and they
would, he thought, if further multiplied over the country, arrest
the progress, and even threaten the continuance, of the present
voluntary hospital system (Q. 3393, 2891). The whole burden of
this impressive evidence, given as the outcome of official experience,
and as expressing the deliberate policy of the Local Government
Board, was that pauperism—meaning any form of dependence on
the rates and taxes—was a disease of society; and that its increase
was due, in the main, not to unemployment, sweated wages or
preventible sickness, but to the failure of the administrators to
adhere strictly to " Poor Law principles ", which were the
" Principles of 1834 ". " What is quite obvious is that, all over
England " (states this witness for the Local Government Board),
" you will find Unions with apparently the same social conditions,
the same rateable conditions, the same rate of wages, and in one
you will find pauperism is 30 per cent higher than in the other ;
and in every one of those cases you will find the proportion of
Outdoor Relief given is much greater" (Q. 3121). Davy did
not suggest that pauperism could ever be completely abolished.
"In any organised community", he declared, " there must be a
certain number of impotent folk, who must be kept in an institution ultimately " (Q. 2768) ; but the object of the Poor Law

should be to relieve only such of those belonging to this "irreducible minimum" as were not dealt with by private charity. Like Dr. Chalmers, the Chief Inspector preferred voluntary charity to any form of public provision : largely on the argument that charity not being a right of the poor, they could neither claim nor rely on it, and "therefore it does not enter into their calculations ; whereas if they knew that a State provision is waiting for them they are tempted to unthrift" (Q. 2781). He objected strenuously to "all the talk about desert and merit being a claim for relief, which has gone on since, we will put it, the year 1884" (Q. 2875), when the franchise was widened ; it was this talk that undermined "good administration".[1] Against it, he quoted John Stuart Mill as declaring that "What the State may and should abandon to private charity is the task of distinguishing between one case of real necessity and another. Private charity can give more to the more deserving. The State must act by general rules. It cannot undertake to discriminate between the deserving and the undeserving indigent" (Q. 2875). When questioned by Mr. Lansbury with regard to the suggested disfranchisement of men out of work through no fault of their own, the Chief Inspector replied " the unemployed man must stand by his accidents; he must suffer for the general good of the body politic. According to my view, what you have to consider is, not this or that pauper, but the general good of the whole community ; and the general good of the whole community is, I submit, that every obstacle should be put in the way of a man settling down into the status of a pauper—for pauper he is, whether he is disfranchised or whether he is not " (Q. 3219).

Undermining Poor Law Principles

The student of this elaborate exposition of the ideas of the Local Government Board will notice that the main complaint is not so much about a lax or foolish administration of the law by some of the Boards of Guardians, as about an undermining of the " Principles of 1834 ", by one relaxation after another, brought about by changes in the law, or by orders given by the President

---

[1] The Chief Inspector even added that " another reason for the preference of charity to Poor Relief is that a man who does an act of charity is doing himself good, whereas the Guardian who gives relief and thinks he is doing an act of charity is doing himself harm " (Q. 2782).

of the Board himself, very largely at the instance of the House of Commons. This tendency to relaxation began, so the Chief Inspector suggested, almost as soon as the Poor Law Board came to have its own Minister in the House of Commons ; but it became especially noticeable after the extension of the franchise in 1884, and, with the growth of public interest in Local Government, in the couple of decades since that date. "Members of Parliament," he said, " continually ask questions with regard to points of Poor Law administration, and they occasionally bring in and pass an Act of Parliament which is contrary to what would be generally considered the Poor Law principles as laid down by the original Commissioners. I will instance the Medical Relief Disqualification Removal Act, by which it is enacted that the man who is in receipt of purely medical relief shall not be disqualified from voting. I make this further point with regard to that Act—I suppose the intention of the framers was what appears on the face of the Act, namely, that the relief should be merely relief by advice or medicine. I am told—and this is a point which I think the Commissioners would do well to further consider—that some revising barristers now hold that inmates of Workhouses or Poor Law Infirmaries do not lose their vote, provided the first cause of their entrance into the Workhouse was their sickness, and not their destitution. This is an extension of the Act which would seem to imply that the framers of it did not quite see what the ultimate result of their action would be ". (Q. 2033). " A second Act ", he continued, " which was passed in 1904, went a step further, and enacted that the guardians were not to take into consideration sums received up to 5s. from a Friendly Society. That Act may have been right, or it may have been wrong, but it certainly was not in accordance with the Poor Law principles that had been worked on by the Department; for these reasons—It is giving relief to people who are not necessarily destitute; it is earmarking a certain sort of property for special treatment ; and it is restricting and curtailing the powers of Boards of Guardians in dealing with individual cases of relief—all of which is entirely contrary to the principles of the early Commissioners. Then there is a growing habit on the part of the House of Commons—I do not say it is not a useful thing to do—of referring Poor Law Bills to a Select Committee. The Select Committee makes a report, and you will find that in some of those reports there are

obiter dicta, which are not, as I should think, in accordance with
Poor Law principles. Then again, the fact that the President of
the Local Government Board changes with the Cabinet is not
conducive to continuity of administration " (Q. 2037).

The Effect of Democracy

How had this insidious emasculation of Poor Law administration during the latter decades of the 19th century been
brought about ? The answer of the Chief Inspector was as
self-assured as it was pessimistic ; pessimistic because it opened
out no hope of escape from social disaster. All this sentimental
laxness, directly contradicting the self-evident " Principles of
1834 " was due, so Davy said, to the inrushing tide of Political
Democracy. The Medical Relief Disqualification Removal Act
followed immediately on the lowering of the suffrage by the
Representation of the People Act of 1884 (Q. 3801). Then
came Joseph Chamberlain's Circular of 1886 recommending
public works for the Unemployed ; whilst the Local Government Act of 1888, by creating a widespread interest in Local
Government, started an " extraordinary increase in the cost
of relief" (Q. 3311). But the Chief Inspector suggested that
it was the Local Government Act of 1894, putting an end to
the property qualification for membership of Boards of Guardians
and dispensing with *ex officio* Guardians that opened wide the way
to a demagogic dispensation of relief (Q. 2059-2063). Meanwhile a series of Select Committees of the House of Lords or House
of Commons, together with the Royal Commission on the Aged
Poor, were constantly recommending this or that relaxation in
Workhouse discipline, differential treatment for aged persons of
good character, and the removal of the disfranchisement of persons
receiving relief on account of exceptional Unemployment. Owing
to the findings of these Select Committees, successive Presidents
issued Circular after Circular undermining the " Poor Law
Principles " professed by their own Department. From 1890—
" a year which forms a sort of epoch in Poor Law administration "
the Commission was told—these ameliorating Circulars or Orders
multiplied in number and variety. In 1891 a supply of books
and toys in Workhouses was recommended ; in 1892 tobacco and
snuff were to be supplied ; in 1893 Visiting Committees of ladies

were authorised, and every individual Guardian was given the right to inspect the Workhouse ; in 1894 an Order was issued permitting Guardians to give dry tea, with sugar and milk, so that the women might prepare their own afternoon tea ; in 1897 there was an Order instructing the Guardians to engage trained nurses for the sick ; finally, in 1900, there came Henry Chaplin's fatal Circular which positively recommended the grant of Outdoor Relief for the aged of good character, advice which, the Commission was assured, was taken by nearly all Boards of Guardians to be applicable to all persons of good character, whatever their ages !

With official discretion, the specific proposals of the Local Government Board witnesses were confined to particular points of law or practice. Medical relief should be given on loan, and should once more be made a ground of disfranchisement. All relief should be made legally recoverable as a debt within a certain period of its acceptance. Grants from the Exchequer in aid of any Poor Law expenditure should be restricted, if not abolished, as they merely encouraged extravagance (Q. 2052–2054, Q. 2207). Compounding for rates should be abolished.[1] Unemployed persons put to work by the Town Councils should be disfranchised for municipal elections (Q. 3224). Grandchildren should be made legally liable to maintain their grandparents (Q. 2477). Boards of Guardians should have power of compulsory removal to the Workhouse, wherever the state of the destitute persons makes this desirable (Q. 2485). They should have increased powers of detention in the Workhouse for bad behaviour or infectious diseases. Thus, the case of the Local Government Board, as presented by the principal officer of its Poor Law Division, did not include any far-reaching amendment of the constitutional structure of the Poor Law ; such as the abolition of the Boards of Guardians hinted at in the interview with one of the Commissioners. The only constitutional change expressly advocated was a suggestion that provincial Boards of Guardians

---

[1] J. S. Davy was strongly opposed to the landlord compounding for the rates of his weekly tenants : " In Poplar, where the compounding is compulsory, 80 per cent of the ratepayers of that Union compound, and the present rate of pauperism in Poplar is, I think, 66 per thousand, which is two and a half times that of London as a whole. I am told that in Whitechapel and Lewisham there is no compounding. The rate of pauperism in Whitechapel at that date was about 20 per thousand and Lewisham 22 per thousand " (Q. 2071).

might be " grouped ", as in London under the Metropolitan
Poor Act of 1866, with provision for throwing upon a local
Common Fund the cost of all relief other than Outdoor Relief,
in such a way as to encourage the " Offer of the House " as a
test of destitution (Q. 2449).

The evidence of the fourteen General Inspectors of the Local
Government Board followed so closely that of their Chief that
it is unnecessary to analyse it in detail.[1] Alike in its diagnosis

---

[1] When questioned on the following points they agreed with the Chief
General Inspector : that pauperism, beyond an irreducible minimum of disabled
persons, without relatives to maintain them, was a disease of society, brought
about, in the main, by lax administration ; that the General Workhouse had
ceased to be deterrent owing to the ameliorating Orders with regard to comforts
and separate accommodation for favoured classes, and the tendency to give
excessive leave of absence; that Outdoor Relief to able-bodied persons was
per se objectionable ; that the Chaplin Circular of August 1900 with regard to
the aged and deserving poor, was deplorable, because it had been interpreted
by many Boards of Guardians to apply to others besides the aged ; that disfranchisement should follow any kind of relief, even medical relief ; that Poor
Law infirmaries tended to become State hospitals, resorted to by non-destitute
persons, and that these departures from Poor Law principles were due to the
widening of the franchise for Parliamentary and Municipal elections, and to
the sweeping away of property qualifications for the office of Guardians. Two
of the ablest of the Inspectors, Philip Henry Bagenal and Herbert Preston-
Thomas, thought J. S. Davy's objection to any discrimination between the
deserving and undeserving both impracticable and undesirable. " I cannot
imagine any Board of Guardians in my district who, as a matter of practice,
would not treat the scamp differently from the industrious man " (Q. 12,274).
One additional fact was brought out by many of the Inspectors : the undesirability of relief being dispensed according to the individual Guardian's
knowledge of, or interest in, the person concerned. Hence the practice of some
large Boards of Guardians, of breaking up into committees dealing continuously
with the applicants from their own constituencies, was said to be the cause
of laxity and corruption ; and a similar objection was raised to cutting up the
Union into small electoral wards usually represented by resident Guardians,
who knew personally the applicants from their districts and brought their
cases before the Board. On the other hand, they favoured the rota system,
whereby committees of Guardians administered the relief of one district after
another, so that the factor of neighbourhood should be eliminated. All inquiries
should be made by the Relieving Officer, and the case for a particular kind of
relief stated by him, the Guardians to act solely as judges. Most of the
Inspectors did not venture to propose legislative reforms, but where they did,
these reforms followed the lines of the official proposals. Jenner Fust, the
General Inspector for the North-Western Counties, elaborated the proposal
for large rating areas for institutional relief, with smaller rating areas for
Outdoor Relief, so as to discourage the latter.
    On the other hand, Dr. Fuller, the Medical Inspector for the Provinces of
England and Wales, stated that " from the medical point of view ", to which
he confined himself, " it is not possible to make the condition of the sick
pauper less eligible than that of the independent wage-earner ; the patient
must be treated with a view to cure, and that means, in practice, extra comforts,
good nursing and skilled medical and surgical treatment ". Moreover, with

of the evil and in its implied or proposed remedies, the case presented at such length by the Local Government Board (the examination of its witnesses fills two closely printed volumes) [1] seemed hardly to differ from that of the Commissioners and Assistant Commissioners of 1834. The officials of the Poor Law Division seemed, in fact, to say to the Commission of 1905, " Here is the old evil back again, and we advise you to adopt the old remedies ". There was, for instance, no desire to prevent the occurrence of destitution, as distinguished from the resort to Poor Relief ; and no realisation that there had grown up, during the intervening seventy years, new public services, administered by rival and overlapping Authorities, concerned with supplying the needs, not of persons applying for relief, but of the whole body of citizens. On the other hand, there was, in much of this evidence by the Civil Servants, an undertone of criticism of the Ministers responsible for policy, and of the Parliament whose commands had to be obeyed. There was manifest an attempt to discriminate between the orthodox " Poor Law principles " of the Inspectorate, which were assumed to be those of 1834, on the one hand ; and on the other, not only much of the legislation of the preceding couple of decades, but also many of the decisions of the Local Government Board itself (as regards the aged), and even of the Poor Law Board of 1848–1871 (as regards the children and the sick). Thus it was not only, or even mainly, the maladministration of the elected Boards of Guardians that the Royal Commission was invited to investigate and condemn : it was also the whole trend of legislation of the preceding generation,

---

regard to such illnesses as phthisis (Q. 10,425) it is imperative to secure treatment on the first appearance of the disease, and therefore probably before the person is destitute ; and in that case there seemed to be no reason for disfranchisement. The same disinclination to accept the " less eligibility " principle appears in the evidence of Miss Mason with regard to the boarded-out children. That the children of independent labourers suffer from the itch and other dirt diseases, and are put to sleep together, or with other persons without discrimination of sex or age, is no argument for analogous treatment of the children for whom the Guardians are responsible. On the contrary, the foster-parents chosen by the Guardians should be persons of superior character, and of sufficient means to provide the requirements of physical health and good conduct for the children entrusted to their care, requirements which cannot be expected to be present in the poorest homes.

For all this evidence, see Appendix, vol. i. *Minutes of Evidence*, 1st to 34th days, 1909, and Appendix, vol. i.A., Appendices to the Minutes of Evidence, etc., 1909.

[1] Appendix, vol. i. and vol. ii.

and even the administrative policy of the Poor Law Board and the Local Government Board for over half a century, that were to be reviewed, considered and, if possible, set in a new and different direction, which, as the reader of our Chapter I. will realise, was, in its proposed deterrence, altogether above and beyond that embodied in the actual " Recommendations " of the Commission of 1832–1834.

The Views of the Guardians

The unhesitating and almost unanimous approval of the " Principles of 1834 " by the officials of the Local Government Board was not supported with anything like the same unanimity by those who gave evidence on behalf of the Boards of Guardians. It is true that the policy of a deterrent Poor Law and of a drastic restriction of Outdoor Relief was stoutly maintained, with able arguments from experience as well as from theory, by such representatives of " Poor Law Orthodoxy " as A. G. Crowder (Appendix, vol. ii. Q. 17,469-18,037), Sir William Chance (Appendix, vol. iii. Q. 27,059, 27,358, 29,095-29,389), Rev. Canon Bury (Appendix, vol. iv. Q. 48,031-48,223), and William A. Bailward (Appendix, vol. viii. Q. 78,703-79,023). Some of these went far beyond the discreet suggestions of the Government officials ; proposing, indeed, as the only way of ensuring the uniform application of a scientific policy of deterrence, that the administration should be taken out of the hands of elected representatives and entrusted to salaried officials who would be obedient to instructions from Whitehall. Many of the Poor Law Guardians who gave evidence expressed a similar approval of a deterrent Poor Law. But others were opposed to the application of the policy of deterrence to every class of recipients of Poor Relief. Many held strongly to the view that " each case should be dealt with on its merits ". A few of them felt that, as regards one or other class of paupers, the Poor Law was not a suitable agency. Some wished the care of the children transferred, some the medical treatment of the sick ; some would cut away from the Poor Law the whole provision for lunatics, whilst others wanted to be relieved of the vagrants. The Rev. C. J. Sharp, Chairman of the Edmonton Board of Guardians, was the chief witness who thought that all the classes of paupers, without exception, could be better dealt with by one or other of the existing public Authorities outside the Poor Law, which could, with advantage, be entirely dispensed with.[1]

Investigations by Individual Commissioners

During the six months taken by the Local Government Board to unfold its case against the existing administration, the Royal Commission had developed a life of its own, inspired in the main by the group of expert investigating members, among whom Charles Booth was pre-eminent. Early in February 1906 three committees were appointed : a Statistical Committee ; a Documents Committee, authorised to inquire into the policy of Parliament and the Central Authority; and an Evidence Committee, to arrange for witnesses, more especially from Boards of Guardians. Where the Commission was exceptional was in the favour that, during its first year, it showed to the investigations undertaken by individual Commissioners ; and in the extent and importance of the studies thus made, either at the request of the Commission or its Committees, or with their express sanction.[2] Thus Charles Booth, having at his disposal a secretarial staff accustomed to deal with figures, volunteered to present to the Commission an elaborate analysis of Poor Law statistics, broken up into geographical regions, so

---

[1] Appendix, vol. ii. Q. 17,254-17,274.

[2] The Commission issued to all its members a special warrant in the following terms : " Mr. A. B., a member of the above Commission, is hereby authorised to visit institutions and to attend meetings of Boards of Guardians and others, and generally to obtain information on the subject-matter of the Enquiry entrusted to the Commission by H.M. the King. In virtue, therefore, of the powers contained in the Royal Warrant dated 4 December 1905, the Guardians, their officers, and all other persons concerned, are hereby requested and enjoined to afford Mr. A. B. all reasonable facilities in the above respects. (Signed) George Hamilton, Chairman of the Commission ; R. G. Duff, Secretary to the Commission."

Among the reports and memoranda presented by Commissioners may be mentioned the voluminous " Reports of Visits to Poor Law and Charitable Institutions and to meetings of Local Authorities " (Appendix, vol. xxviii. p. 386) ; the very elaborate statistical tables and proposals for reorganisation and reform by Rt. Hon. Charles Booth (120 pages in Appendix, vol. xii.); seven historical memoranda by Professor W. Smart (Appendix, vols. xii. and xv., and Report on Scotland, Cd. 4922) ; and a memorandum on the Old Poor Law, 1601–1834, by C. S. Loch (Appendix, vol. xii.).

as to bring out the relation upon pauperism of the industrial or climatic environment. The secretary of the Charity Organisation Society, C. S. Loch, besides suggesting two inquiries to be undertaken by Special Investigators (on the overlapping of voluntary general hospitals with Poor Law medical relief, and on the relations between charity and the Poor Law), undertook himself to prepare a memorandum on the Old Poor Law prior to 1834. At an early meeting of the Commission it was suggested that individual Commissioners should investigate the relief policy of particular Poor Law Unions ; and Mrs. Bosanquet made an examination of the Outdoor Relief cases of Bermondsey, whilst Mrs. Sidney Webb set going an inquiry into the life-history for six months of all the applicants for Outdoor Relief in one urban and one rural Union. Early in March the Documents Committee, under the chairmanship of Professor Smart, authorised its Chairman and another member to undertake an analysis of all the Parliamentary Reports and Papers since 1834 dealing with the Poor Law ; and instructed Mrs. Sidney Webb to carry out an analysis of all the Poor Law Statutes, General and Special Orders, and other instructions issued by the Poor Law Commissioners, the Poor Law Board and the Local Government Board, from 1834 to 1906. The scope of the Commission's inquiry was in fact gradually extended—partly by the researches thus undertaken by individual Commissioners, and still more by those entrusted to the Special Investigators whom, usually at the instance of its members interested in investigation, the Commission successively appointed—far beyond the suggested maladministration of the Poor Law, so as to include the causes and effects, not only of pauperism, but also of destitution in all its ramifications.

The Internal Life of the Commissioners

A vision of the internal life of the Commission during the first year is afforded by the contemporary diary of one of the Commissioners, from which we print some extracts.

" December 10th, 1905. How interesting will be this conflict of wills. I will certainly describe it as it goes along. For instance, there are four big officials on the Commission, two from England, one each from Ireland and Scotland respectively. The

English officials think they are going to direct and limit the enquiry ; the Scotch and Irish officials told us pretty plainly that they did not want any enquiry, and they had already investigated the whole subject by Departmental Committees ! And, as there were no Irish and Scotch representatives of the anti-official view, the enquiry into Irish and Scotch Poor Law has been indefinitely postponed, and will probably hardly take place. On the other hand, Charles Booth and I want a real investigation of English administration, as well as an examination into pauperism, though C. B. is more concerned with the question of right treatment than of prevention by better regulated life. Lansbury, on the other hand, is willing and anxious to enquire into the initial causes of pauperism ; not so keen to investigate the effect of different methods of relief. C. S. Loch wants to drag in the whole question of endowed charity, in which he has the support of Mrs. Bernard Bosanquet. She and I, and possibly Miss Octavia Hill, may combine on the question of a rate in aid of wages to women workers, the need for discovering how far it actually obtains ; and there will be a good deal of common ground as far as the enquiry goes, between Loch and myself. Certain other Commissioners, such as Smart and Phelps, are going to look on, I think, and intervene as the spirit moves them."

"January 10th [1906]. Third meeting of Commission. I did not attend, as Adrian's evidence in chief consisted in his reading from copious notes a long legal disquisition ; which, as it was all taken down in shorthand and served to us in printed form in two days' time and before his cross-examination began, it was sheer waste of time to sit there listening to. On Monday (4th meeting) the cross-examination began; and on that afternoon and the following morning I tried to make him admit that we must see and study the general and special Orders, Circulars, etc., for ourselves, before we could understand the body of law and regulation under which the Guardians acted. In this endeavour I was stopped by the Chairman and Sir Samuel Provis ; and I had a little tiff across the table as to whether he or we should judge whether documents were important or not.[1] But I got a specific

---

[1] The day by day entries in a private diary necessarily record only the writer's hasty impressions of other personalities, and need revision when those personalities are better known. My diary records of Sir Samuel Provis are examples of this. In subsequent years, and indeed before the Commission had ended its work, I came to appreciate the accurate mastery of details, the open-

promise from the Chairman that all the documents that we needed
should be at the disposal of the Commission."

" 12th February 1906. There is one very pleasant feature
about the Commission. We are all of us after public objects,
however much we may disagree as to what these objects are and
how to arrive at them. There is hardly any personal vanity or
personal ambition, and no personal ' interest ' at work in the
Commissioners. A little jealousy of those who take the lead—
but very little of that. And we are getting fond of our Chairman
—who, like many a *Grand Seigneur*, can afford to be modest and
unassuming."

" 5th February 1906. The memo. I sent in on ' Methods of
Enquiry ' led the Chairman to ask all the other Commissioners
for memoranda. And some six or seven responded. Whereupon all have been referred to a Committee consisting of Lord
George, Provis, Booth, Bentham, Smart, Loch, Phelps, Mrs.
Bosanquet and myself ; and we meet on Monday 12th to consider
them. This morning I spent taking out all the questions which
the L.G.B. witnesses had told us we ought to enquire into,
with a view of trying to persuade the Committee to start on a
systematic survey of all the Unions with a view to more detailed
investigation of some. Yesterday Bentham—the ablest person
(except perhaps Provis) on the Commission—came here, and we
talked Poor Law from 5.30 to 11 o'clock. Result, bad headache
this afternoon ! "

" 12th February [1906]. I sent another memo. to the Chairman sketching out the work of three committees—on statistics,
local administration, and central policy respectively—a scheme
which in his gentlemanly way he pressed on the acceptance of
the Committee on Procedure. The Committee on Statistics was
agreed to, so was a Committee on Blue Books, etc., to which
the documents of the L.G.B. might be added ; and in the course
of the discussion it became clear that a Committee on Local

---

mindedness to new points of view, and the courtesy and generosity to colleagues
that characterised this eminent Civil Servant. I had the advantage of again
working with him on the Statutory War Pensions Committee, 1916–1917, and
on the Local Government Sub-Committee of the Reconstruction Committee
under Sir Donald Maclean, 1917–1918 (Cd. 8917 of 1918), when we found that
our proposals for reform, and even our points of view, were not so divergent
as my first impressions of him on the Poor Law Commission in 1905–1909 had
seemed to indicate.—B. W.

Administration would, in the end, be required. But most of the members were against taking any steps towards a positive scheme until after the Inspectors' evidence. Charles Booth wants one committee only ; Mrs. Bosanquet objects to any but temporary committees ; no member wants a systematic investigation but myself. I throw out the notion of a statistical officer and an assistant commissioner to undertake the investigation into local administration—but, as yet, it is not responded to. Meanwhile Sir Samuel Provis will not agree to anyone looking through the L.G.B. documents—insists that we must call for those we want to see and not have the run of the whole. In an interview we had at the L.G.B. he lost his temper and asserted that he ' would not have a roving enquiry into L.G.B. policy '. I kept my temper and we parted on friendly terms. Charles Booth blames me for having raised the hostility of the L.G.B. He may be right. . . . On the other hand, if one begins by being disagreeable, one may come in the end to a better bargain. It is, however, clear that I shall not have the support of the Commission in my desire for scientific research into the past seventy years."

" 11th March 1906. . . . Meanwhile my R.C. grinds slowly on. The three Committees that I pressed for on the Procedure Committee have been appointed and have set to work : Statistics, Documents (on Central Policy), Evidence (on Local Administration). I am trying to guide the Committee on Documents into making an analysis of all the documents of the Central Authority, statutes, Orders, reports, with a view of writing a memorandum on the attitude of the State towards each class of pauper. Lord George gives me unhesitating support ; my difficulty is with Sir Samuel Provis. But I had the most friendly chat with him this afternoon, and he comes to dine to meet a carefully selected party on Wednesday. Charles Booth has the Statistical Committee well in hand ; Bentham has elaborated and improved my questions as to the working constitution of the Boards of Guardians. I hope that investigations will be presently set on foot as to the life-history of paupers in different Unions. And I no longer find the association with my fellow commissioners disagreeable."

" 1st March 1906. At meeting of Tuesday 27th February of R.C., Charles Booth attempted the ' Method of the Interview ' which seemed to me illegitimate, and was hotly resented by

the Chairman, Sir S. Provis and others. He [C. B.] happened
to be in the Chair when Preston-Thomas (Inspector for South
Wales District) was to be cross-examined on his printed statement.
This statement concerned the district as a whole (I had urged
that the Inspectors should be asked to supply separate particulars about each Union, but, largely because C. B. backed
down, I was defeated, and the Inspector was asked to describe
his district as a whole). But Charles Booth insisted on taking
him right through the whole of the Unions—one by one—
asking him questions for which the man was not prepared, and
could only give hearsay evidence. Five hours were thus spent,
without the other members having a chance of asking questions
arising out of his printed statement. I had left after lunch,
but I hear that there was a hot dispute as to the relevancy of
the questions, and the Chairman seems determined to put a
stop to it. That sort of wholesale interviewing is all very well
if the man is prepared and is speaking of facts within his own
knowledge. But it is hardly worth the £100 which each weekly
[two days] meeting of the Commission costs the National
Exchequer.[1] I am inclined to think that a statement of the
cost of the different methods of investigation ought to be submitted to the Commissioners by the Chairman—it is a case
where efficiency would be actually promoted by some attention
to economy. A Royal Commission drifts into stupid, lazy and
costly ways through sheer inadvertence and lack of forethought
as to means and ways."

"5th March 1906. The Documents Committee, consisting
of Smart (Chairman), Russell Wakefield, MacDougall, Provis
and myself, met for the first time. I had circulated ' suggestions '
proposing to limit ourselves, in the first instance, to discovering
what policy had been laid down by the Central Authority as
to the relief of various kinds of paupers since 1834 ; and proposing that the work should be undertaken by an efficient
clerk under Jeffrey [Assistant Secretary to the Commission,
acting as clerk to this Committee], according to definite plans,

---

[1] This casual estimate was endorsed by the Departmental Committee of
1910. " Oral evidence is one of the most expensive methods ; it has been
known to cost as much as £50 per day for travelling expenses, shorthand-
writer's attendance and transcription of notes, printing ", etc. (Report of
Departmental Committee on the Procedure of Royal Commissions, 1910,
Cd. 5235, p. 9).

decided on by the Committee. To show what I meant, I circulated an analysis of the 1834 Report, the three first statutes and two General Orders, made by Mrs. Spencer [my secretary]. Prof. Smart, on the other hand, proposed that he and Wakefield should undertake the Blue Books, and that I and MacDougall should undertake the General Orders and Circulars, each selecting what we thought fit and doing it in the way we thought best. I was beaten, though Sir Samuel Provis supported my suggestion that the work should be done systematically under direction. The simple truth was that I had a majority against me on both counts. MacDougall, Wakefield and Provis did not want an historical retrospect—they desired only to enquire into the laws of to-day—and Smart, MacDougall and Wakefield did not want the work done systematically under a deliberate plan. Seeing myself beaten, I suggested that Smart and Wakefield should do their job first, and that, if that were satisfactory, we could then decide whether we would do the Circulars and statutes in the same way. So the Committee has adjourned for two or three months ; which has the incidental advantage of leaving my Monday mornings free for our own work. The longer the Commission delays the better for me. Meanwhile I will put Miss Longman on to the General Orders and Circulars. In all probability we shall have to do the work ourselves—a plan that has its advantages."

"15th May 1906. A baffling time divided between superintending two secretaries at work on the City of London records, and drafting a memo. on the Policy of the Central Authority of the Poor Law, 1834-47, from Miss Longman's notes. The R.C. lumbers along ; chaotic and extravagant in its use of time and money, each Committee doing as seems fit in its own sight. There is a lack of method and discipline, with which some of us get impatient ; and I fear I sometimes offend by my easygoing ways—intervening when I ought to hold my peace. ' You did not behave nicely yesterday ', said Lord George in kindly reproof, ' You should not have referred to current politics.' So I thanked him warmly for the hint, and I promised to be ' seen and not heard ' in future. I find it so difficult to be ' official ' in manner. However, I really will try. Dignified silence I will set before me, except when the public good requires me to come forward. Ah ! how hard it is for a quick-witted and somewhat vain woman to be discreet and accurate. One can manage to be both in the written word—but the ' clash of tongues ' drives both discretion and accuracy away."

" 22nd May 1906.   C. S. Loch completely lost his temper yesterday at my cross-examination of Lockwood.   He is always making *ex parte* statements in his questions, and yesterday he made Lockwood—a weak witness—advocate the prohibition of compounding, on the ground that the occupier, if he were con- scious of paying rates, would be more severe on expenditure. So I made Lockwood say that the landlord, whatever the arrange- ment, really paid the rates, and that the occupier would therefore prefer to pay [part of] the economic rent to the Local Authority, in the form of rates from which he received services, than to the landlord from whom he received nil.   Loch got white with rage and protested against my questions as misleading statements of economic doctrine.   All this dialectic seems to me a foolish business : but it is important to let the Commissioners know that we shall challenge all the current assumptions.   However, in the little tiff, the Commission was on my side.   What makes him angry is that the enquiry is drifting straight into the Causes of Destitution instead of being restricted to the narrower question of *granted destitution as inevitable, how can we best prevent pauperism ?*   And the answer that is being extracted by our enquiry into the causes of destitution takes the form of *More regulation and more public provision—without the stigma of pauperism*—probably compulsory provision which *must* be given and *cannot* be refused."

" 15th June 1906. . . . The Commissioners have, in fact, been run away with by those Commissioners who have been sufficiently pertinacious, without thought of the enquiry as a whole.   Charles Booth has scampered off with the Statistics of Today, I have seized upon the Historical Survey, and have secured the marking- off of Sweating as a cause of Pauperism.   Mrs. Bosanquet has captured her own little corner of Outdoor Relief as a rate-in-aid of wages to women.   Whether we three shall meet together in the same place at the end of our respective enquiries I do not know. Possibly other Commissioners feel that they are having their ' look in '. . . . But quite clearly there is no one directing purpose shaping the enquiry to a predetermined end.   Which of the many conflicting or diverging purposes will prevail remains to be seen. Meanwhile it means that, besides our own big task of the History of Local Government, 1689–1834, we have two investigations to direct—the Policy of the Central Authority, 1834–1906 ; and the connection between bad conditions of employment, or insanitary and overcrowded houses, with pauperism. All these investigations will have to go slow and be partially sacrificed the one to the other."

" 17th July [1906]. Yesterday we had a field day at the R.C. discussing our future procedure. Various memoranda had been circulated—conflicting, overlapping and irrelevant, from the Chairman, the Evidence Committee, the Secretary, C. S. Loch and myself—a fine confusion to serve instead of a compact agenda. The Chairman opened the proceedings by a long rambling statement : he had interviewed John Burns, who was willing to delay dealing with the Unemployed, otherwise than by an extension of the Act, until the Autumn session of 1908. From which Lord George deduced that our Report on the whole of our reference must be in the hands of the Government [by] August 1908. . . . After some preliminary sallies we settled down to consider evidence for October. Settled by lunch time. At the afternoon sitting we roamed over the whole field—spreading out our enquiry into the furthermost points that any individual Commissioner desired to reach ; Lord George always giving way with a weak protest against doing any one investigation ' too thoroughly '. I confined my effort to keeping open for further consideration questions which he or the Commission as a whole wished to close : Old Age Pensions ; the condition of the 200,000 children now receiving Outdoor Relief; the administration of relief by Boards of Guardians ; and more important than all, the Relation of Poor Law Medical Treatment to Public Health.

" This is a new hare that I have recently started. In listening to the evidence brought by the C.O.S. members in favour of restricting medical relief to the technically destitute, it suddenly flashed across my mind that what we had to do was to adopt the exactly contrary attitude, and make medical inspection and medical treatment compulsory on all sick persons—to treat illness, in fact, as a Public Nuisance to be suppressed in the interests of the community. At once I began to cross-examine on this assumption, bringing out the existing conflict between the Poor Law and Public Health Authorities and making the unfortunate Poor Law witnesses say that they were in favour of the Public Health attitude ! Of course Sidney supplied me with some instances, and I hurried off to consult M.O.H.'s—Dr. X. . . ., Dr. Y. (Infant Mortality expert). As luck would have it, Dr. Z. had to give evidence, and was puzzled to know what to talk about. He dined here, and I brought forward all my instances of conflict. In the witness-box he made this conflict part of his thesis, though taking the Poor Law attitude and complaining of the P.H. Authorities' pauperising tendencies. With S.'s help I drew up a memorandum emphasising all my points. . . . I am elaborating an enquiry of my own—with funds supplied by Charlotte Shaw [Mrs. Bernard Shaw]; so I merely said that I should, in the course of the next six months, present the Commission with a further memorandum. ' You might elaborate with a few more details the one you have already presented ', said Lord George in a frightened way. And so it was left. At present I am engaged in finding a medical woman to undertake the enquiry, and on rousing the interest of the M.O.H.'s throughout the country.

" Meanwhile, despairing of any action on the part of the Commission, I have undertaken, unknown to them, an investigation into the administration of the Boards of Guardians. I shall put Mrs. Spencer to analyse the documents that are pouring in to me by every post ; and Miss Bulkeley shall go through minutes.

" I therefore look forward to at least three memos. handed in by me—(1) Central Policy, (2) The Relation of Poor Law Medical Relief to Public Health, (3) Administration of Relief by Boards of Guardians, as well as the Report of the Special Investigators on the Relation of Bad Conditions of Employment to Pauperism. On these documents I shall base my report.[1]

---

[1] These memoranda developed into four that were published by the Commission (Appendix, vol. xii.), " The policy of the Central Authority from 1834 to 1907 ", which formed the basis of *English Poor Law Policy*, by S. and B. Webb, 1910 ; " The Medical Services of the Poor Law and Public Health Departments of English Local Government, in their relation to each other and to the Prevention and Cure of Disease ", which formed the basis of *The State and the Doctor*, by S. and B. Webb, 1910 ; " The History of Poor Law Administration in Bradford, 1838–1906 ", and " The History of Poor Law Administration in Poplar, 1837–1906 ". Other investigations, such as that into the by-laws made by some 300 Unions as to Outdoor Relief, that into 8500 births in 450 workhouses (as to legitimacy, mortality, etc.), and that as to the experiments with " Able-bodied Test Workhouses ", were offered to the Commission, but were utilised only for the Minority Report.

"My relations to my fellow Commissioners are now quite pleasant. I am completely detached from them, and yet on most agreeable terms. I just take my own line, attending for just as long as it suits me, cross-examining witnesses to bring out my points and conducting the enquiries that I think important independently of the Commission's work. The lines of reform, both in constitution and policy, are gradually unfolding themselves to me. Whether I shall embody them in a Report of my own, or give up part of my way in order to bring the whole Commission along, will be a question of expediency and delicate negotiation, about which nothing can at present be foreseen."

"22nd Sept. 1906. This day we begin our autumnal session, and, except for three or four days' visits, shall not be away from London until Christmas. I start Mrs. Spencer on Monday on her enquiry into Administration by Boards of Guardians : Miss [Dr. J.] Woodcock and Miss Phillips I have already started off on the Medical Relief and Public Health enquiry. Miss Longman is hard at it, preparing her memo. on the Central Policy (1847–1871) on the plan of mine. What I have to arrange is to oversee all this investigation without interfering with my own absorption in the second volume of our work which must come out this time next year."

"18th December 1906. . . . Meanwhile Loch has got on the scent of my various enquiries. He objected to my circularising the M.O.H.'s. I retorted that anyhow I had a perfect right to ask for information as an individual Commissioner ; and that as regards Public Health, I had actually been deputed to prepare a memorandum. 'We were not very wise when we put the matter into the hands of an individual Commissioner', Lord George sadly remarked. The odd thing is that now they are calling M.O.H.'s selected by me—four for Lancashire out of twenty witnesses ; and the whole enquiry is drifting in the direction of sickness as a cause of pauperism. But I shall be surprised if, sooner or later, I don't get into hot water over my 'special enquiries' and the means I am taking to get facts. Poor Lord George—what between Charles Booth, C. S. Loch and me, he is going to have a hard time ! "

Looking back on the proceedings of the Commission at the end of its first year, we may see that the investigating members were already unwittingly separating into two groups. One of these, taking substantially the standpoint of the Charity Organisation Society, seemed to be intent on discovering how far it might be possible, whilst maintaining the category of "the destitute ", to merge the work of the Poor Law Authorities in that of the various philanthropic agencies ; or, at least, so to amalgamate their functions that a new Public Assistance Board or Committee might emerge in each locality, which could not only co-ordinate, but also inspire, and so far as practicable direct, the work hitherto done by the elected Poor Law Guardians, as well as that performed by voluntary charity.   The other group of investigating members was apparently groping after the causation, not of pauperism but of the destitution from which sprang the applications for Poor Law Relief.   They seem to have been intent on discovering to what extent, and in what ways, the very occurrence of destitution could be obviated, possibly by further developments of legislative or administrative action along lines already empirically laid down in various parts of the field. Using these clues, the "industrious apprentice " who studies the forty-seven volumes of proceedings—especially the cross-examination by different Commissioners of the oral evidence of the innumerable witnesses, the reports of all the Special Investigators, and the memoranda submitted by individual Commissioners—will be able to trace the gradual development of two distinct schemes of reform.

The Reports of the Special Investigators

In the final pages of this chapter, we shall give a short summary of these two schemes of reform.   But seeing that neither the one nor the other was accepted by successive Governments, leaving the situation in 1927 substantially unaltered, what seems more important than the conclusions of the Commissioners is the series of reports presented to them by the Special Investigators whom they appointed.   These men and women were selected for a task of genuine investigation, irrespective of their political or economic opinions.   They were keenly interested in the discovery of the facts of the problem ; and most of them may not unfairly be described as experts in their task.   Thus their reports, founded not merely on extensive personal observation but also on statistics and documents, and illuminated by their inferences, are, in our opinion, of greater evidential value, though possibly less entertaining, than the verbatim accounts of the conversational opinions and smart dialectics bandied between Commissioners and witnesses, which figure as " Minutes of Evidence ", in the " proceedings " of this and other Royal Commissions.

In contrast with the Assistant Commissioners of 1832–1834, the Special Investigators of 1905–1909 found themselves, in the course of their inquiries, more and more minimising lax Poor Law administration as the main cause of pauperism. What forced itself upon the attention of all of them was the extent to which resort to Poor Relief was a direct result of genuine destitution. The investigation into the causes of pauperism thus became, very largely, an investigation into the causes of destitution itself.[1]

Outdoor Relief

The first of the inquiries into Poor Law administration was that entrusted to Mr. Thomas Jones and Miss Constance Williams, on the subject suggested by the representatives on the Commission of the Charity Organisation Society, namely, " the Effect of Outdoor Relief on Wages and the Conditions of Employment ".[2] The instructions given to these Special Investigators followed the lines of the principal Poor Law controversy of the past half-century. The investigators were specially to get information as to anything in the nature of a " Rate in Aid of Wages ", whether in supplement of actual weekly earnings, or for subsistence in the seasonal or " slack-time " intervals between wage-earning ; as to the differences between earnings and home conditions before and after the receipt of Outdoor Relief ; as to

[1] " The reports of the Special Investigators ", noted one of the Commissioners on January 18, 1907, " are all pointing away from bad administration as *the* cause of pauperism, and towards bad conditions among large classes of the population as the overwhelmingly important factor : conditions which, if we are to check destitution, must be changed. If we do not see to it that destitution is checked, it is, thanks to Democracy, too late in the day to check pauperism. That is the little lesson the C.O.S. will have to learn by this Commission." (MS. diary of Beatrice Webb.)

[2] Appendix, vol. xvii. (590 pages). Mr. Thomas Jones had been Lecturer on Political Economy at Glasgow University ; and became in 1912 Secretary to the Health Insurance Commissioners for Wales, in 1916 Acting Secretary to the War Cabinet, and since 1919 Assistant (later Deputy) Secretary to the Cabinet. Miss Williams was a C.O.S. worker.

whether any rise of wages had taken place in consequence of a
systematic discontinuance of Outdoor Relief; and as to any
migration of workers or of industries towards districts where
Outdoor Relief was freely given, or any retention in such districts
of decaying industries or inferior workers.

It is safe to say that the tenor of the voluminous reports made
by these Special Investigators, of their studies all over Great
Britain, extending over a couple of years, in Unions and parishes
of all descriptions, both urban and rural, was unexpected by any
member of the Commission. They found that there existed
practically no systematic Outdoor Relief to men who could
properly be classed as able-bodied and not mentally defective.
With exceptions too insignificant to be of any importance, the
whole of the persons in receipt of Outdoor Relief in 1906-1908
were the aged; the sick or crippled, or infirm of body or mind,
and those dependent on them; the mothers (whether widows,
deserted wives or wives of disabled men) burdened with young
children; and a certain number of cases temporarily relieved
owing to exceptional causes of distress. Therefore the question
of a " Rate in Aid of Wages ", in the ordinary sense—which the
Chief Inspector of the Local Government Board (J. S. Davy)
had stressed as the great wrong done to the wage-earning poor—
did not arise. What was frequent, and, in the case of adult
women not absolutely incapacitated, almost invariable, was that
the adults in receipt of Outdoor Relief, as they were expected
and even occasionally urged to do, earned something, in some
way, to supplement the admittedly inadequate dole which was
all that the Guardians allowed. " One [Relieving] Officer put
the common practice into a few words. ' We never bother
about what the women earn. We know they never earn ten
shillings. They can always find room for half-a-crown.' " [1]
What effect, on the paupers themselves and their relatives, or
on the wages of non-paupers, had this mutual supplementing of
inadequate Outdoor Relief and fractional casual earnings ? The
Special Investigators—hunting this hare up and down the
kingdom, in town and country ; following every sweated industry
and visiting the slum dwellings inhabited by these subsidised
families ; investigating the wage-books of employers and diving
into the uncharted sea of casual earnings—came to the con-

[1] Appendix, vol. xvii. p. 334.

clusion that nothing having the effect of a Rate in Aid of Wages could be said to exist. " Our investigation ", they report on the Metropolitan inquiry with which they began, " has convinced us that, whilst Out-Relief aggravates most evils, it is, in itself, a relatively unimportant influence in comparison with the other forces at work ; and that its withdrawal would hardly raise the level of unskilled women's wages in London." [1] As the investigation proceeded to the provincial towns, to the rural districts and to Scotland, the Special Investigators became even more decided in their judgment. " Whilst Out-Relief may tend to lower nominal wages in a particular condition of demand and supply, we believe that, in the present condition of the towns visited, the direct influence of Out-Relief in fixing the levels of wages, compared with the other forces at work, is *so small as to be negligible*. This is not to say that, if the number of occupied paupers were multiplied indefinitely, matters would remain the same. They would not. But we must distinguish between the tendency of a cause to produce an effect and the fact whether that effect has actually been produced. The tendency may have been opposed by stronger forces acting in an opposite direction, or accompanied by forces acting in the same direction so much more powerfully than itself that its own feeble influence may be neglected." [2]

" If the foregoing analysis is sound, it follows that the primary sources of ' sweating ' are the poverty, domestic afflictions, and physical infirmities of the workers, leading to industrial inefficiency and an incapacity to earn a normal wage. Low wages in turn perpetuate low earning power, and a vicious circle is established. The rates paid are of secondary importance compared with these primary disabilities. The employer's responsibility lies in his frequently doling out work as people dole out indiscriminate charity ; and in his desire to have a reserve of labour which costs nothing for upkeep, and which he can count on for a few hours, or days, or weeks, as it suits his convenience. This reserve is partly maintained by the Poor Law, but exists to a far greater degree outside its area. The great majority of the women paupers are not in the arena of labour at all ; for the few who are in it, the strain is eased a little by Out-Relief." [3]

[1] *Ibid.* p. 12.

[2] *Ibid.* pp. 344-345.   [3] *Ibid.* p. 342.

Accordingly the Investigators reported their complete and entire failure to discover any industries that could be said to be subsidised by the grant of Outdoor Relief, or maintained in existence when they had better have died. They could find no evidence of people being attracted to Unions where Outdoor Relief was granted, or of their migration away from Unions in which it was refused ; any more than they could hear of the location of new industries being in any way determined by the local policy as to Outdoor Relief. " We never met a Relieving Officer ", they report, " who could trace any appreciable connection between applications made for relief and seasonal slackness in any particular trade or firm. . . . In the rural Unions visited there was no proof that Outdoor Relief carried over the winter a supply of labour indispensable to the farmers in summer." [1]

But whilst decisively negativing the assumed influence of Outdoor Relief in directly lowering women's earnings, the Investigators found this method of treatment of the destitute open to great objection ; not necessarily in itself, but by reason of the failure of nearly all Boards of Guardians to take hold of the cases for effective treatment, by adequate inquiry, careful consideration of the probable effect on the health and character of the recipient and the provision of an income sufficient for proper maintenance. " We have said ", they continue, " that Out-Relief aggravates most evils, but is in itself a relatively unimportant influence in comparison with the other forces at work. Lax administration, however, undoubtedly harms many of the recipients. It damages character by inadequate enquiry and haphazard relief. It mixes the dissolute and the decent to the detriment of the latter. If Guardians think a woman is paying too much rent she is told to move to cheaper rooms. Sometimes this hastens deterioration, by withdrawing the support of a respectable street and placing women and children in an unfavourable environment. The help it affords is frequently insufficient for proper maintenance when all other resources are included. It deters women from entering the world of self-support." [2] But, usually, the effect on character of the Poor Law was deemed to be rather that of an intensifier than that of a cause. " As its direct contact (in Out-Relief) is usually with adults whose characters are more or less fixed, its action depends

[1] Appendix, vol. xvii. p. 329.   [2] Ibid. p. 14.

on what those characters are. It deepens tendencies already operative. The bad will turn its help into an instrument for deeper corruption, the good into a means of sustaining the Standard of Life through a period of struggle. . . . A few good are kept good, a few bad are made a little better, and some good are made worse. . . . But, generally speaking, and so far as our observation goes, what pauperism does, in the case of Out-Relief is to harden settled characteristics acquired in the outside world rather than to develop new ones." [1] We may end by giving the " remedies " suggested as the outcome of this wide-reaching and impressive inquiry.

" Remedies may be grouped roughly as : (1) Industrial. (2) Educational. (3) Administrative.

"(1) *Industrial.*—(*a*) Here the most urgent is the de-casualisation of men's labour and a better industrial training of boys and girls. This would attack the sources of supply in two ways ; by diminishing the number likely to be born at the casual level, and the number likely to sink to that level. The reform of industrial conditions is more urgently needed and more likely to be ' preventive ' than the reform of the Poor Law or the organisation of charity. (*b*) It is important to preserve the efficiency of the able-bodied worker in times of continued trade depression, both by insurance and by the provision of useful work during the depression.

" (2) *Educational.*—A bold and liberal policy towards widows and their children, on the lines of the Glasgow Special Roll. The maximum of good can be done by spending taxes to-day so as to raise the earning power of the rising generation. . . . This neglect of the children of outdoor paupers has been one of the greatest evils of the 1834 tradition of test and stigma. It is greatly to the public interest, whether from the standpoint of rearing good citizens or of swelling the national dividend, to have the children well-nourished and well-trained, whatever happens to the parents. . . . A bold expenditure now would at once permanently diminish the sources of pauperism and increase the sources of wages in the future. And inasmuch as the widow's work thus paid for would usually be in her household, harmful influences on wages in any particular market would be avoided.

" (3) *Administrative.*—The policy of deterrence should be given

[1] *Ibid.* pp. 2-3.

up for that of supervision. The obligation to assist in clearly defined cases should be openly undertaken, and the appropriate persons urged to apply rather than the reverse. But such a policy could be made effective and beneficial only if accompanied by a new classification and new machinery : (a) Aged persons should be dealt with by a pension system : a uniform and universal scheme, like Mr. Booth's, might have some harmful reaction on the national dividend, but it would probably be small. (b) Sickness should be treated as a problem in health, not as a problem in poverty. (c) The registration and organisation of charities ; the suppression of some ; and the co-operation of all with State agencies. In the case of widows, for example, the assistance of voluntary workers might be of great value. (d) If the above classes (the old, the sick, and the widows) were eliminated—and they are classes which admit of easily applied tests— then 'Out-Relief' as now understood, might be restricted to special cases of temporary distress, to be dealt with by a Poor Law board or a board of charities. The applicant should be called upon to make a written declaration of resources on pain of punishment for false statement (the North Witchford plan, pp. 179, 498) ; and employers should be compelled to make similar statements of earnings to accredited officials. Publicity in regard to wages is essential to a sound policy of relief. (e) For the able-bodied, the Workhouse Test should give place to an industrial test, applied through the Labour Exchange. Unworthy applicants should be offered help in disciplinary institutions." [1]

Refusal of Outdoor Relief

The inquiry into Outdoor Relief made by Mr. Thomas Jones and Miss Constance Williams, of which, in the preceding pages, we have given the barest outline, was supplemented by a minute analysis, by Miss G. Harlock, of the ascertained effect on the applicants of a Refusal of Outdoor Relief.[2] The Commissioners were well aware of the optimistic accounts of the general effect of a systematic refusal of Outdoor Relief in such Unions as Bradfield and Whitechapel. What was desired was an accurate description of the effect of the refusal in such particular instances as could be followed up in Unions where Outdoor Relief was not universally

---

[1] Appendix, vol. xvii. pp. 377-378.   [2] Ibid. vol. xxi. (72 pp.).

refused. In seven selected Unions—Metropolitan, urban and rural—the subsequent life-history was traced for a few weeks or months, by a painstaking personal investigation, of ninety cases (family groups) in which, whether under relatively strict administration or the reverse, particular applicants for Poor Law Relief had been only " offered the House ". In fewer than a dozen of these cases was this offer accepted. What happened to the others ? We give the Investigator's answer.

" Having given the above particulars with regard to the families visited, I am now in a position to discuss the results following the refusal to grant Out-Relief. These may be summarised as follows :

" (1) In no case was the support by relatives increased through the refusal of Out-Relief. In practically all the cases they were so poor themselves, that they were not in a position to give systematic assistance. If such additional help had been given, it must have been at the cost of the physical efficiency of the younger generation. (2) In no case has any charitable agency effectively dealt with the destitution. Occasionally I found that spasmodic gifts were made ; but, with one exception, no effort was attempted definitely to place the family upon a sound economic footing. (3) There was no evidence to show that the applicants themselves had been stimulated by the refusal of relief to greater personal efforts. On the contrary, the denial of assistance appeared to have discouraged and disheartened many whose energy might have been roused by wise guidance, accompanied by sufficient temporary aid to enable them to maintain physical efficiency. (4) Two of the cases found work. In one of these, the man went back to his old employment straight from prison, and in the other the man had got some irregular and possibly only temporary employment (Nos. 10 and 32). (5) In more than half of the cases the refusal of Out-Relief led to a gradual dispersal of the household furniture and wearing apparel, often not even excepting the most necessary clothing. There were also unmistakable signs of a marked physical deterioration of the members of the families, owing to lack of food, warmth, and proper clothing. If eventually the applicants are forced to enter the Workhouse they will do so with health gone, home gone, and spirit and courage shattered. This deterioration is, from the national standpoint, probably most serious in the case of the children. The homes which were being broken up were of two classes: firstly, respectable homes which have been in the past thoroughly comfortable (*e.g.*, Nos. 3, 6, 8 and 36) ; secondly, homes which possibly have never reached a high standard of comfort (Nos. 2, 7, 14, 26). (6) Six of the applicants accepted the order for the Workhouse. No. 5 died there shortly after admittance, and No. 15 remained an inmate for a few weeks, and died at the house of her grand-daughter soon after taking her discharge ".[1]

---

[1] Appendix, vol. xxi. pp. 60-61. We append some significant comments by the investigator.

" I was much struck with the hopeless condition of some of the cases at the stage at which I visited them. With these an earlier commonsense treatment would have prevented the development of destitution (and in some cases of degradation also) to its present acute form. Cases 8, 9, 10 and 20 illustrate this. To effectively suppress pauperism, cases of destitution should be dealt with at an earlier stage " (*ibid.* p. 61).

" I was particularly struck with the hardship of women with children, who are expected to be at the same time both the bread-winner and the housewife of their families (see Nos. 23, 25, 26, 27, 29). These women so often go under in their struggle to perform this impossible task, dragging their children down with them. Under more favourable circumstances this degradation would probably not have occurred. From the lowest standpoint, that of a merely commercial one, would it not be a better investment of the national resources to help these women *adequately*, while they are performing their duties as mothers, in order to assist them to bring up their children decently, instead of crushing them, and postponing the help until both the mother and the children are reduced to such a low state of mental and physical efficiency that no relief, when given, will be able to restore to them a decent home and their self-respect. The alternatives then are starvation or the workhouse, and the latter is now acknowledged to be a failure, at any rate so far as the children are concerned " (*ibid.* p. 3).

Another investigation, undertaken chiefly at the instance of (Sir) C. S. Loch, the Secretary of the Charity Organisation Society, was entrusted to Mr. A. C. Kay and Mr. H. V. Toynbee, on the Endowed and Voluntary Charities in certain places, and the Administrative Relations of Charity and the Poor Law (Appendix, vol. xv.). In eight selected towns of different sizes and eight rural parishes, the extent and effects of local charities were minutely investigated. They were found to be everywhere dispensed with even less discrimination than Outdoor Relief ; without co-operation or co-ordination with the work of the Poor Law Guardians ; with the result of relatively extensive over-lapping ; an actual increase both of pauperisation of the recipients and of applications for Poor Relief, and of mendicity and indiscriminate almsgiving. " ' Few charities, fewer paupers ' was the verdict of one of these Guardians, who were also of opinion that the charities had the effect of making people apply for relief at an earlier age than they otherwise would " (*ibid.* p. 66) . . . " producing a cadging and gift-hunting disposition among the poor " (*ibid.* p. 72). Thus the investigation gave no support to the idea that voluntary charity was superior, either in its administration or in its effects, to the work of the Poor Law Authorities. The only proposal of the investigators was that both voluntary charity and Poor Relief should be subjected to the control of a central representative council for each district.

A further investigation, into " the overlapping of the work of the voluntary

Children on Outdoor Relief

But the effects upon wages and employment of the grant of Outdoor Relief, and the effect upon the applicants of a refusal of Outdoor Relief, plainly do not exhaust the subject. How were the hundreds of thousands of destitute persons, whom the Boards of Guardians decided to maintain on Outdoor Relief, affected by this decision ? It was with some surprise that the Commission learned that the Local Government Board, which allowed the Outdoor Relief, had made no inquiry into, and had no knowledge of, the actual effects of this method of treatment of destitution.[1] The Commission chose, for investigation, as the most important class, the children (under sixteen) on Outdoor Relief, numbering, on January 1, 1907, in England and Wales alone, apart from those " boarded out ", and those obtaining medical relief only, no fewer than 157,919, being some 16 per cent of the entire pauper host.[2] This inquiry was entrusted to Dr. Ethel Williams, in conjunction with Miss Mary Longman and Miss Marion Phillips, assisted by the Charity Organisation Societies of Liverpool and Newcastle-on-Tyne. An extension of the investigation so as to include the condition of the " boarded out " children, of those in Poor Law Schools and of those in the General Mixed Workhouses, enabled useful comparisons to be made, especially as to the physical state of destitute children of the same age under different methods of treatment.[3] We cannot, in a brief summary, give the reader any adequate idea of the results of this extensive survey of the conditions of life of these hundred and fifty thousand recruits to the citizenship of the ensuing generation. The Investigators visited the children at home as well as at school ; they noted not only the

---

General Hospitals with that of Poor Law Medical Relief ", was entrusted to Miss Norah B. Roberts, whose report was published as Appendix, vol. xxii. (40 pp.).

[1] Research revealed that neither the Poor Law Commissioners nor the Poor Law Board, any more than the Local Government Board, had ever obtained reports, or made any systematic investigation, as to the conditions in which the Outdoor paupers lived, or as to the effect upon their lives of this method of dealing with destitution, which—far from being discontinued—was, in 1906, being applied to many more cases than in 1834 or in 1870.

[2] Four-fifths of these were the children of widows ; and one-eighth of wives deprived of their husbands by desertion, imprisonment or detention in asylum or hospital. Only in less than one-sixth of the cases was the husband at home, nearly always disabled.

[3] Appendix, vol. xviii. (285 pp.).

state of the room or rooms, and the dilapidations of the buildings, but also the character of the street, and the sanitary conditions amid which the children played. In many cases they measured the children and weighed them, and assessed their cleanliness and the state of their clothing. They ascertained the income on which the household had to be maintained, and the way the money was spent. The result of this Inquiry was to prove conclusively that, in a majority of cases, the amount allowed by the Guardians was not adequate. "The children", sums up the principal Investigator, "are under-nourished, many of them poorly dressed, and many barefooted. The houses are bare of furniture, for there is not money to buy sufficient food or boots, and any extra expense has to be met by selling or pawning furniture." . . . "The standard of Out-Relief must not be the least which will keep a widow and her children out of the House", continues Dr. Ethel Williams, "but the least which, added to her resources, will feed, clothe and house the family adequately. It cannot be expected that the Out-Relief mother will herself be ready to state the amount required. The decent mother's one desire is to keep herself and her children out of the Workhouse. She will, if allowed, try to do this on an impossibly inadequate sum until both she and her children become mentally and physically deteriorated. If she is lucky she struggles on till the children begin to earn. In many cases she gives up the hopeless struggle and drifts into the House. It must be remembered that semi-starvation is not a painful process, and its victims do not recognise what is happening. The under-nourished child is easily tired and usually slow, dull and listless, but he is often not to his knowledge hungry, and will refuse good food." [1]

Passing from the material conditions of the home to the moral character of the mother, the Investigators noted the same irresponsibility on the part of the Guardians for the present and future condition of these children of the State. With statistical ruthlessness the Investigators classified the mothers (more than five-sixths of the Outdoor Relief children being found to be, by death or absence, deprived of a father's care) into " Good and Capable " ; " Good but Incapable " ; " Slovenly and Slipshod " ; and " Really Bad " ; meaning, by the last class, " people guilty of wilful neglect, sometimes drunkards or people of immoral

[1] Appendix, vol. xviii. p. 88.

character ; no woman has been put into this class of whom it was not fairly evident that she was unfit to have charge of the children ". The Extra-Metropolitan and Urban Unions showed proportionately fewest mothers of the first class, and most of the fourth. In this respect the rural Unions come first with the highest percentage of good and the lowest percentage of bad mothers. A more striking divergence in results obtained was discovered between the well-administered Unions of Bradford and Paddington, where 81 per cent and 80 per cent respectively of the mothers fell into Classes I. and II. and the more casually administered Unions of Liverpool and Merthyr, where 22 per cent and 18 per cent of the mothers were placed in Class IV. It is happily true that these bad mothers—women guilty of wilful neglect, drunkards or people of immoral character— formed a small minority of the mothers in receipt of Outdoor Relief for their children throughout the whole country. But even the homes of mothers of Classes II. and III., women of weak character and slovenly and shipshod ways, were not considered as satisfactory. Their unfitness for their position, states Dr. Ethel Williams, " is largely due to the extraordinarily heavy burdens which their position has thrown on them. They have to take up the position of both parents, be bread-winner and housewife, keep house, often on an almost impossibly small sum, cook, clean, mend and bake when others are asleep. Little wonder that they break down in health and courage, become ineffective, colourless and whining." [1] Summarising this statistical investigation into the character and intelligence of nearly 60,000 mothers struggling to rear this not insignificant proportion of the citizens of the ensuing generation, Dr. Ethel Williams estimates that 6800 were in Class IV., " really bad mothers ", 10,300 in Class III., " slovenly and slipshod mothers ", 23,300 in Class II., indifferent mothers, and only 16,700 in Class I., above the latter level, capable and trustworthy, able to give their children an excellent training, to plan for their future well-being and to sacrifice a present gain to a future good. Thus no fewer than 51,000 children were being maintained at the expense of the Poor Rate in 17,100 homes of Classes III. and IV., which could not possibly be deemed satisfactory, whilst about 119,000 were in classes I. and II., few of which, we may note,

[1] *Ibid.* p. 61.

would have been thought good enough to be entrusted with boarded-out children.[1]

The Contrast with 1834

Let us now compare the reports on Outdoor Relief by the Special Investigators of 1905–1909 with those of the Assistant Commissioners of 1832–1834, alike in the range of their inquiries and in their conclusions. The Assistant Commissioners of 1832–1834 concentrated almost exclusively on the Outdoor Relief given to the able-bodied men ; and the evils on which they enlarged had relation to the effect upon the character and earnings of the recipients of a publicly subsidised livelihood. Further, they pointed out that these bounties operated also as an illegitimate subsidy to the employers of labour so assisted, to the disadvantage of employers and workers of less pauperised districts or industries. Hence they were unanimous in favour of the absolute refusal of Outdoor Relief, with the alternative " offer of the House ", to all able-bodied persons, however meritorious and whatever the cause of their Unemployment. About the non-able-bodied—the infants and children, the sick and the aged, the child-bearing and child-rearing mothers—the investigators of 1832–1834 were singularly unconcerned. They tacitly or explicitly acquiesced in a continuance of the then existing practice of staving off destitution by small money doles, which, in permanent incapacity or old age, became weekly allowances almost mechanically continued during life. There were, however, two requirements made by the Report of 1834 in respect of the administration of relief to the non-able-bodied, as well as to the able-bodied. " Uniformity in the administration of relief ", says the Report, " we deem essential, as a means, first, of reducing the perpetual shifting from parish to parish, and fraudulent removals to parishes where profuse management prevails from parishes where the management is less profuse ; secondly, of preventing the discontents which arise among the paupers maintained in the less profuse management from comparing it with the more profuse management of adjacent districts ; and thirdly, of bringing the management, which consist in details, more closely within the public control ".[2]   And

---

[1] Appendix, vol. xviii. p. 62.
[2] Report of Poor Law Inquiry Commission of 1834, pp. 279, 280,

the uniformity of treatment on which the Report of 1834 laid so much stress was held to apply in a special degree to the administration in respect of the character or past conduct of the applicants. The natural tendency of the relieving Authority, " to award to the deserving more than is necessary, or . . . to distinguish the deserving by extra allowances ", was denounced in that Report as an evil. " The whole evidence ", it was declared, "shows the danger of such an attempt. It appears that such endeavours to constitute the distributors of relief into a tribunal for the reward of merit, out of the property of others, have not only failed in effecting the benevolent intentions of their promoters, but have become sources of fraud on the part of the distributors, and of discontent and violence on the part of the claimants." [1]

The Special Investigators of 1905–1909 were not concerned with Outdoor Relief to able-bodied men, because it was ascertained or assumed that it no longer existed to any appreciable extent. How far the tenour of their Reports and character of their recommendations would have been altered or modified had they foreseen the outburst of unconditional Outdoor Relief to able-bodied men between 1920 and 1928 is an interesting speculation.[2] But the four millions sterling annually spent in Outdoor Relief in England and Wales in 1906 was distributed among the aged and infirm, the sick, disabled and mentally afflicted, the widows with children, and the wives of non-able-bodied men with or without children. In the preceding chapter we have described how, during sixty years of Poor Law administration, the principle laid down by the Report of 1834 with regard to the non-able-bodied—" uniformity in administration of Relief "— had been, without objection by the Ministry, not only disregarded but even deliberately departed from. But this rejection of one of the Principles of 1834 did not seem objectionable to the Investigators of 1905–1909 : indeed, any rigid uniformity would have

[1] *Ibid.* p. 47.

[2] One of the drawbacks of research entered on by temporary and *ad hoc* Commissions on topical questions is that those aspects of the subjects under investigation which are not *observable at that particular time* are almost inevitably ignored, alike in diagnosis and in proposed remedies. What is needed for good administration is continuous observation, verification and record, over long periods of time and in different places, so that no phase of organisation or the absence of organisation should be omitted from consideration.

contradicted their proposed preventive and curative treatment according to the character and circumstances of the recipient. What they brought to light and vigorously condemned was the absence of either the intention or the capacity to grant Outdoor Relief *in such a way as to raise the moral and material condition of the recipients.* The dole given was practically never adequate to the requirements of health subsistence. The sums awarded were almost mechanically doled out, according as the Relieving Officer reported the applicant to come into one or other wide category, as widow, sick husband, aged person, etc., without any real consideration of the sum that was required properly to maintain each household, and without any accurate ascertainment of its other resources. Along with the fact that the Outdoor Relief was practically never adequate for healthy subsistence, went the other fact, which was almost invariably found, namely, that Outdoor Relief was professedly not intended by the Guardians for those who were completely destitute, but for those who could, in one way or another, see their way to a few shillings a week. In many Unions the paradoxical position was reached that to those who were actually destitute, and had no resources whatsoever, deserving though they might be, Outdoor Relief was habitually refused ! But to the Investigators of 1905–1909 it seemed that the worst feature of the Outdoor Relief as they saw it practised was that it was wholly unconditional. With insignificant exceptions, Boards of Guardians gave these doles and allowances without requiring in return for them even the most elementary conditions of civilisation or citizenship. They were bound by statute to require that the children of school age should be in attendance at school ; and this alone was what the average Relieving Officer saw to. Many cases of gross insanitation and overcrowding were discovered, and not a few of indecent occupation. Homes thus maintained out of the public funds were in a state of indescribable filth and neglect, the abodes of habitual intemperance and disorderly living ; and this even in families in which Boards of Guardians were giving Outdoor Relief to enable children to be reared. So grave were these revelations that the Royal Commission, finding that the Local Government Board had never obtained any information on the subject, requested that all the Inspectors might be asked to report upon the character of the homes into which Outdoor Relief was being given. These reports bore out those of the Assistant Commissioners. " A not inconsiderable proportion of Guardians ", reported one Inspector, " take the view, first, that the disposal of the relief granted by them is a matter for which not they, but the recipients, are responsible ; and, secondly, that however small the relief given to a person with little or no other apparent means of subsistence, it is no one's business to inquire further if the applicant is satisfied ". " The first of these views ", continued the Inspector, " which I have heard expressed even by a Chairman of a Board of Guardians, is almost an incitement to a careless parent to waste on drink money which should be devoted to the nourishment and clothing of the children ; while the second may mean a bargain between a parsimonious Board of Guardians and liberty- or licence-loving paupers for the lowest terms on which they will keep out of the workhouse." [1] The same testimony was given with a special emphasis derived from his professional experience by the Medical Assistant Commissioner, Dr. M'Vail, whose report we shall presently deal with. " The worst kind of public policy ", sums up Dr. M'Vail, "is that under which an Authority representing a community confers personal benefits without any accompanying requirement of good order or obedience. I heard of a Relieving Officer in an urban Union who, reporting on an application, recommended that relief be refused because the applicant was a lazy loafer, continually to be found at public-house corners, and any money he received would be spent in drink. A Guardian listening to this report indignantly demanded to be told : What right has anyone to interfere with how a man spends his money ? The wrong policy is crystallised in the Guardian's query. It is surely obvious that if individuals or their dependants are to be selected for maintenance in whole or in part by local rates or Imperial taxes, they should in their maintenance be duly controlled by the Authority which supports them. The principle is so elementary as hardly to require setting forth, but under the Poor Law it is abrogated every day of the year and every hour of

[1] Summary of Reports on the Conditions of the Outdoor Poor by certain of the General Inspectors of the Local Government Board. The reports themselves were supplied to the Commission ; but it was thought better to print only a summary of them ; and therefore, in the quotations in the Reports, references to particular Unions were omitted. Ultimately not even the summaries were published, apart from a few extracts in the Commission's own Report. See Majority Report, pp. 199-201, vol. iii. ; Minority Report, p. 42.

the day. . . . Persons suffering from the most serious transmissible maladies are afforded relief without prevention of opportunities to inoculate the healthy or contaminate the next generation. . . . Phthisis cases are maintained in crowded unventilated houses where there is unrestricted facility to convey the disease to their own offspring. Diabetes cases live on the rates and eat what they please. Infirm men and women supported by the Poor Law are allowed to dwell in conditions of the utmost personal and domestic uncleanliness. Widows get money for the upkeep of their family without any advice or requirement as to the spending of it, or as to the healthy rearing of their children. . . . It is not worth while entering on any reform of the Poor Law unless this policy is changed. Beneficiaries must be compelled to obedience alike in their own and in the public interest." [1]

The Treatment of the Sick

The Commission of 1905–1909 stands in dramatic contrast with that of 1832–1834 in respect of its consideration of the sick poor. The Report of 1834 hardly mentioned the paupers who were sick. The Report of 1909 emphasised the fact that, after excluding lunatics in asylums, something like 30 per cent of all the paupers, indoor and outdoor, being more than a couple of hundred thousand persons in England and Wales alone, were at all times simultaneously under medical treatment. Hence the Commission, during its first year, decided to call, not only Medical Superintendents of Poor Law Infirmaries and District Medical Officers in attendance on outdoor paupers, but also Medical Officers of Health responsible for the health of the community as a whole. The evidence of these medical witnesses transformed the outlook of the Commission. In stating the case of the Local Government Board for stricter administration, the Chief Inspector and his staff had warned the Commission that medical relief was " the first step to pauperism ", and had insisted that medical treatment at the expense of public funds ought to be rigidly restricted to persons who were actually destitute, and accompanied by the stigma of pauperism through the disfranchisement

---

[1] Appendix, vol. xiv. ; Report . . . on the Methods and Results of the Present System of Administering Indoor and Outdoor Medical Relief, by Dr. J. C. M'Vail, 1907, pp. 148-149.

of the recipients. The weight of medical evidence was against this application of the "Principle of Less Eligibility" to the treatment of the sick poor. Witness after witness argued in favour of the Public Health principle of seeking out sickness among the poor, in order to give early treatment under the most advantageous circumstances, so as to prevent the continuance of disease as well as the spread of infection. Thus Dr. (now Sir) Nathan Raw, one of the ablest of the medical Superintendents of Poor Law Infirmaries, stated that " The great difficulty at present seems to be the reluctance, even in cases of dire necessity, on the part of the poor to enter a Workhouse or Workhouse Infirmary for the purpose of treatment. The very fact that no case of urgent sickness can be treated without the penalties and stigma of pauperism is, in itself, a sufficient reason to deter such people from seeking the aid of the Poor Law. To take an ordinary example :—A working man with a wife and family is attacked with an acute disease like rheumatic fever or acute pneumonia. His home is totally inadequate for the treatment of such a condition, and, moreover, he cannot afford proper nursing and proper food. He is reluctantly compelled to ask for Poor Law relief, when he will be removed to the Workhouse or the Workhouse Infirmary, and there treated until his recovery. He has, however, to be classed as a pauper. . . . He loses his parliamentary and municipal votes, and he is liable to be charged the full amount that he can afford to pay for his maintenance. . . . The strongest possible argument for the municipalisation of all hospitals is the present state of the Poor Law. . . . No man or woman should be punished because he is attacked by sickness or accident. . . . It is economic to give a poor man the best treatment so as to restore him to work quickly, rather than that he and his family should have to be supported by the rates for an indefinite period. . . . In my opinion, before the Poor Law can be made effective it will be necessary and desirable to dissociate from it the whole question of medical sickness." [1] The District Medical Officer of Aston Union (Dr. A. H. Bygott), who was responsible for the treatment of the outdoor paupers, was equally emphatic : " My department ought to be united with that of the Medical Officer of Health, and then our Poor Law infirmary and the treatment of

[1] Evidence of Nathan Raw, M.D., F.R.S. Edin., Appendix, vol. iv., Q. 37,927, paragraphs 12, 29 and 56 of Statement.

the sick should be entirely divorced from the giving of relief " ; [1] the reason he gave being that the poor do not come as soon as they ought to for Poor Law medical relief : " they put it off as long as possible ; in many cases they shrink from it ". [2]

When we turn from Poor Law medical practitioners to Medical Officers of Health, advocacy of early treatment and objection to the principle of deterrence was practically unanimous. " I look to a betterment of the personal factor as likely at the present time (now that environment has reached a high standard of excellence) to be most effectual in the betterment of physical life ", stated Dr. (now Sir) George Newman, then Medical Officer of Health for Finsbury. [3] " I would, if I could, bring to bear upon the homes of the people of Finsbury more suitable health visitation, by which we should gain (a) information as to the occurrence of illness, (b) information as to insanitary conditions, (c) advice on domestic hygiene, dietaries, cleanliness, etc., (d) direction and advice on the whole question of care of infancy and children, (e) counsel in carrying out of medical treatment, (f) special health work in the direction of phthisis prevention, physically defective children, invalid children, and so on. . . . I have no doubt at all that one of the necessary reforms in relation to the whole problem is *unification of the public medical services*. All infectious and infective disease should be looked upon as a ' nuisance ' to be prevented or removed, quite irrespective of poverty and destitution. What we need is an organisation of the existing authorities and powers under one authority. It cannot, it is evident, be under the Poor Law, for that is not sufficiently inclusive of the community. It would appear, therefore, that it should be under the Public Health Authority, which should be the direct teacher and aider of the poor, long before destitution, in all matters of physical concern, rather than, as at present, being confined in its operations so largely to external conditions. I should therefore view with satisfaction any provision for placing the Outdoor Poor Law medical officers under the Public Health Department of the Local Authority." [4]   The no less distinguished Medical Officer of

[1] Evidence of Dr. A. H. Bygott, Appendix, vol. iv., Q. 44,032.
[2] *Ibid.* Q. 44,004.
[3] Sir George Newman, K.C.B., is now (1927) Chief Medical Officer to both the Ministry of Health and the Board of Education.
[4] Evidence of Dr. (now Sir George) Newman, *ibid.* vol. ix., paragraphs 27 and 30 of Statement, and Q. 94,283-94,628.

Health for Brighton, Dr. (now Sir) Arthur Newsholme, lays stress on the importance of teaching people good habits not only in phthisis but in other diseases, diabetes, bronchitis, etc. To the astonishment of many of the Commissioners, he insisted that the giving of medical aid to the poor patient " has undoubtedly increased the patient's duties and responsibilities. . . . Take bronchitis, for instance ; a person who has a dusty occupation must take certain precautions ; he must wear a respirator or adopt certain means of getting rid of the dust. That is a great nuisance, and the workpeople do not like it, and they would almost rather have the bronchitis. Under a system of preventive medicine, pressure will be brought to bear upon them to use the respirators or other means that were needed." [1]

The Medical Investigation

Impressed by this and other testimony, and finding that no systematic medical survey of the hundreds of thousands of sick paupers had ever been made, and that no statistics of their diseases or of their mortality had ever been compiled, the Commission appointed a distinguished Scottish medical officer, Dr. John M'Vail, to " inquire into and report on the methods and results of the present system of administering indoor and outdoor Poor Law medical relief ".

The outstanding feature of Dr. M'Vail's report [2] was the extraordinary diversity that it revealed—in contrast with the national uniformity in Poor Relief on which the Commissioners of 1834 had insisted—between what was done for the destitute sick person in some Poor Law Unions and that done in others. Roughly speaking, about one-half of all the paupers needing medical treatment were being maintained on Outdoor Relief, and one-half in Poor Law institutions—this proportion differing, however, enormously, not only in town and country respectively, but also from Union to Union. The medical treatment of the "Outdoor" paupers, given by 3713 part-time medical practitioners as District Medical Officers, each having his own geographically

---

[1] Evidence of Dr. (now Sir Arthur) Newsholme, M.D., F.R.C.P., Appendix, vol. ix., Q. 92,784 and Q. 92,786. Sir Arthur Newsholme, K.C.B., was the Medical Officer of the Local Government Board, 1908–1919.

[2] *Ibid.* vol. xiv. Report on Poor Law Medical Relief in certain Unions in England and Wales (338 pp.).

defined district, was found to be hampered, in most Unions, by the "deterrent" character given to this form of Poor Relief, notably by access to the District Medical Officer having to be obtained through the Relieving Officer, whose duty it was to "restrict" the issue of "medical orders", however sick might be the applicant, to cases of genuine—that is to say, nominally complete—destitution.   In some Unions the deterrent policy had been carried so far by the Boards of Guardians as to reduce Outdoor Medical Relief to a minimum, with the result that many cases of disease—notably among the wives and children of able-bodied men—went entirely untreated, whilst a much larger number were so long delayed in treatment as to become incurable.[1] Dr. M'Vail gave case after case of neglected phthisis [2]—a disease asserted to be responsible for no less than one-seventh of the whole aggregate cost of Poor Relief—which it would have been of the utmost importance to have brought earlier to the notice of the Poor Law Medical Officer.   His report goes on to make the same criticism with regard to other diseases.   Any doctor dealing with the poor, he says, sees "many inoperable cancers and incurable Bright's disease, and overlooked rheumatic fever in children, causing heart disease later on." [3]

The inadequacy of the medical treatment of the sick pauper on Outdoor Relief could not be dissociated from the method in

---

[1] Incidentally, Dr. M'Vail found that the oft-repeated assertion that the grant of Poor Law Medical Relief—that is, of access to the District Medical Officer—was one of the high roads to chronic pauperism was devoid of foundation.   He reported that " Evidence given before the Commission shows it to be the opinion of authorities with special knowledge of the subject that medical Out-Relief may and often does lead to a life of pauperism. . . . The view is a perfectly natural one, and I had no doubt of finding abundant evidence of its soundness in the first Union to be inspected. . . . In reply to enquiry it appeared that in no single case had . . . pauperism begun by out-medical relief. . . . The replies were so unexpected that I asked the Master to continue cate-chising on the same lines. . . . He did so and the result was similar. . . . I accordingly had a tabular form prepared containing questions on this and on a variety of other points. . . . Summarising the facts, it appears that, as to indoor paupers, in a total of 490, 481 had had no medical Out-Relief, 5 had had medical and other Out-Relief simultaneously, and only 4 had begun with Medical Out-Relief apart from other Out-Relief." Investigation of Out-Relief cases led to a like result.   " In only 12 out of 1198 outdoor paupers . . . had general pauperism begun with medical Out-Relief only. . . . There is a some-what greater statistical possibility that in cities medical Out-Relief may be an inducement to general pauperism. . . . In short, I found it impossible to get, on a statistical basis, any evidence of the alleged evil influence of medical Out-Relief " (Appendix, vol. xiv. pp. 141-143).

[2] *Ibid.* pp. 92-102.   [3] *Ibid.* p. 108.

which the District Medical Officers were appointed and paid by
the Boards of Guardians : chosen, in many instances, because
they are prepared to do the work for the lowest remuneration,
paid often at a rate amounting to no more than fourpence or
sixpence per visit, and required to provide at their own expense
the bulk of the drugs that they prescribed.[1] Their work was
done under the most discouraging conditions. Over the greater
part of the country there existed no provision for the domiciliary
nursing of the patients whom they had to treat. " Quite unquestionably ", summed up Dr. M'Vail, " in some rural districts,
the want of sick-nursing of paupers is a serious defect in the
present system of Poor Law Medical Relief." [2]

But there had been, since 1867, an ever-increasing tendency,
with regard to the worst cases of illness among the persons
maintained on Poor Relief, as well as the large number of
" chronics ", to provide for them, not, as in 1834, on Outdoor
Relief, but by admission to the Poor Law institutions ; and to
these Dr. M'Vail accordingly gave systematic attention. Here
the diversity between one part of the country and another was
found to be, if possible, even greater than in Outdoor Medical
Relief. In the Metropolis and some of the larger towns the
sick ward of the Workhouse had been, in the course of the previous
forty years, developed into a specially erected, elaborately fitted,
separately administered, and extensively staffed " Poor Law
Infirmary ", which could sometimes claim to be little inferior to
a good voluntary hospital ; though Dr. M'Vail found even the
best of them markedly below the standard of the London hospitals
in the proportion of nurses to patients, and in the variety and
specialisation of the medical staff,[3] luxuries which even the most
enlightened Board of Guardians could not bring itself to believe
to be necessary for sick paupers.[4] In these separate Poor Law
Infirmaries something like a third of the institutional sick paupers
were being treated. In nearly 300 other Unions, largely urban
in character, Dr M'Vail found every grade of institution, some
of these Workhouses being only slightly inferior, as regards
provision for the sick, to the fifty or sixty separate Poor
Law Infirmaries, whilst others were no better than the General
Mixed Workhouses that have, since 1834, characterised the 300

[1] *Ibid.* pp. 119-121.   [2] *Ibid.* p. 112.
[3] *Ibid.* pp. 48-50.   [4] *Ibid.* p. 46.

essentially rural Unions. These latter, often the only institutions accessible to the sick poor of large areas, Dr. M'Vail found seriously defective from the standpoint of medical treatment of the sick. More than one-fourth of the wards that he measured " failed to comply with the requirements " as to minimum cubic space per inmate. In more than one-third of those he visited the hot water supply—" an absolute essential for the proper management of a Workhouse or Workhouse Infirmary "—was " more or less defective ". " Looking at the facts with regard to the individual rural Unions which I visited ", Dr. M'Vail reported, " I have concluded that the nursing staff is insufficient in the majority of them. . . . In one Workhouse the sick wards contain 24 beds, of which 16 were occupied, 9 of them by bedridden cases, and one of these with a bedsore. For all this work there was only a single nurse, both for night and day service, and her duty included attendance on confinements in the lying-in ward, though these, fortunately, were infrequent. . . . In only two or three of the rural Workhouses have I been able to form the opinion that the staff is sufficient." [1] The conclusions which this distinguished medical practitioner ultimately pressed on the Commission, as the outcome of his prolonged and extensive survey of every side of Poor Law Medical Relief, were as drastic as they were unexpected. He found the Poor Law Authorities and the Poor Law principles—in dealing with the sick poor—inept and dangerous to the public interest. As he journeyed from Union to Union pondering over what he had seen, the very existence of a Poor Law Medical Service, whether institutional or domiciliary, seemed to him of questionable public advantage. He found himself asking the question " Should the control of all the health conditions of the poor be put under a single health authority ? . . . Should this health authority supervise the work of the District Medical Officers, or, on the other hand, should there be two medical services supported by the State ? . . . Having no previous knowledge of the English Poor Law, I believe I approached the question with an open mind. . . . As my inquiry progressed, however, the conclusion has forced itself on me that transference of functions should take place if that be practicable." [2] " The reasons ", he said, " which can be advanced for combination of the medical services at present under the Public

[1] Appendix, vol. xiv. pp. 19, 22, 23, 28, 29.   [2] *Ibid.* p. 153.

Health Act and under the Poor Law respectively centre round the axiom that prevention is better than cure. The object of the Poor Law is to relieve existing distress and destitution ; to prevent death from starvation. The object of the Public Health service is to secure the individual and national efficiency which result from the living of a healthy life in healthy surroundings. . . . The new Health Authority ", which he thought should supersede the Board of Guardians so far as the sick poor were concerned, " would be both administrative and supervisory. It would have all the ordinary duties of water supply, drainage, scavenging, house sanitation, nuisance removal, food and drugs inspection, smoke prevention, sanitary supervision of workshops, prevention of rivers pollution, provision of isolation hospitals, disinfection, and control of infectious diseases. . . . The District Medical Officers would be under its charge. As regards disease, they would have duties not merely of cure or palliation, but of prevention. They would take note of and report defects in the health conditions of dwelling-houses visited by them. Their official work would be done under supervision by the principal officers of the new Local Health Authority. In the appointment of District Medical Officers heed would be given to their ac-quaintance with the preventive side of medicine. . . . Almost every disease can be dealt with from the standpoint of pre-vention ; and while phthisis is specially important, yet the early stages of disorders of all organs of the body, heart, lungs, kidneys, digestive system, brain, and the rest, often furnish indications for preventive measures. . . . The main policy of the new body would be to try to maintain the health of those com-mitted to its care, and to diminish the need for the curing of disease and the prescribing of drugs, but the treatment of disease in paupers would be included in its functions." [1]

The Environmental Causes of Destitution

The impressive series of reports by Special Investigators that we have so far described was completed by an elaborate and far-reaching investigation by Mr. (now Sir) A. D. Steel-Maitland and Miss Rose Squire [2] on what may be termed the environmental

[1] *Ibid.* pp. 153-155.

[2] Sir Arthur Steel-Maitland (created a baronet in 1917), after taking high honours at Oxford in classics and law, and pursuing his studies at the London

causes of destitution, and the consequent pauperism. These accomplished Investigators were instructed to inquire in what way and to what extent bad conditions of employment—notably what the House of Lords Committee of 1890 had defined as "sweating", insanitary workplaces, excessive hours of labour, and wages insufficient for healthy subsistence—together with "casual labour", seasonal unemployment and overcrowding in slum tenements, contributed to the pauperism among men, women and children respectively. The stream of reports which resulted from this inquiry, which extended over a couple of years and embraced almost every adverse environmental influence on the lives of the lower half of the manual-working population of the Metropolis, the ports and the manufacturing districts of England,[1] brought before the Commission, in convincing detail, the way in which numerous families in the less fortunate half of the wage-earning population were being brought down to destitution, either by involuntary interruptions or irregularities of their employment, or by the sickness and demoralisation resulting from the adverse conditions under which they had to work. This painstaking and lengthy inquiry amounted, in fact, to a study of the actual causation of destitution ; that is to say, into the manner in which occurred the constant new recruiting—possibly by some 50,000 families, or 200,000 individuals annually—of the four or five hundred thousand families, or a couple of million persons, who were perpetually either in or temporarily out of Poor Relief.

We cannot do more here than quote a few extracts from the Special Investigators' summaries. For the Metropolis, at least,

School of Economics, entered Parliament in 1910, and was made Chairman of the Unionist Party Organisation in 1911 ; Parliamentary Secretary of Overseas Trade Department in the Coalition Administration, 1917–1918 ; entered Mr. Baldwin's Cabinet as Minister of Labour, 1924.

Miss Rose E. Squire, O.B.E., served as Sanitary Inspector under the Kensington Vestry, and was appointed by the Home Office an Inspector of Factories in 1896, becoming in succession a Senior Inspector, Deputy to the Chief Woman Inspector, and finally a Principal in the Industrial Division. She served also on the Health of Munition Workers Committee, and as a Director of Women's Welfare in the Ministry of Munitions and of the Women's Training Department in the Ministry of Labour. After her retirement in 1926 she published an account of her official experiences, *Thirty Years in the Public Service*, 1927 ; and in chap. viii. she gives an interesting account of the Poor Law investigations.

[1] Appendix, vol. xvi. The Relation of Industrial and Sanitary Conditions to Pauperism, together with an additional memorandum on certain other points connected with the Poor Law System and its Administration (393 pp.).

they concluded that excessive hours of labour had, in themselves, no connection with pauperism.[1] Their "summary of causes leading to pauperism in London" emphasised the following six factors :

"1. Casual and Irregular Employment.—This is by far the chief cause of pauperism and calls for remedy. 2. Bad housing conditions.—These contribute to pauperism through disease and demoralisation. They are important causes of pauperism, but less so than the first. 3. Seasonal Fluctuations in Trade.—Such fluctuations cause pauperism to the extent that the seasonality partakes of a casual character. 4. Unhealthy Trades and In-sanitary Conditions of Work-Places.—There is a definite but very small proportion of pauperism distinctly resulting from such conditions. 5. Earnings habitually below what are required for healthy subsistence.—There is a distinct degree of pauperism in certain occupations which is due to this cause. 6. Dangerous Trades.—The aggregate effect of those investigated is limited by the small number employed. An undue proportion of pauperism is caused by them, of which the amount varies in each case with the degree of danger involved."

The greatest of these evil influences was found to be the system of casual labour which reaches its highest point in riverside London, as in other large ports. The report expressly declares that "Of industrial conditions, the most potent cause of pauperism to be found is casual labour. One other most efficient cause, however, which co-operates with casual labour to produce pauperism, deserves more than the brief mention given to it in an earlier place—the characteristics of boy labour under the conditions at present existing. There is no need to lay stress, as it is too well known, on the demand for boy labour for "vanguards", errand boys, and other purposes which combine a comparatively high present wage with an absence of any future prospects."[2]

"For the casual occupation offered, the casual character applies. Judged by their origin, these men are of two kinds, men bred to

[1] *Ibid.* p. 178 ; see also p. 52 and p. 72.

[2] *Ibid.* p. 47. The extent and influence of the system of boy-labour was specially investigated by Mr. Cyril Jackson. He found that "the evil is a very real one" (Appendix, vol. xx. p. 30), a large number of boys in urban centres all over the country being led "through a variety of jobs into casual labour and unemployment" (p. 32) ; often falling "into the lowest depths of immorality and criminality" (p. 25). We shall have occasion to deal, in our next chapter, with this valuable report.

unskilled work and brought up in the atmosphere of it, and men who have fallen either through fault or accident. The comparative proportions of such it is hard to determine. We have made several efforts to do so. Both come upon the Poor Law. The chief factors in producing men only capable of doing irregular work appear to us, beside the surroundings, to be the boy labour that leads to nothing . . . and the absence of any organised discipline-producing habits.

" Besides the master and the man there are the other circumstances which assist the result. The casual life exists in its worst form in the great centres of population. In a village it hardly exists. In a manufacturing town it is small. In a metropolis it is large. The probable reason lies partly in the ease with which the identity of the individual is lost and thus withdrawn from restraint. Women's labour, whatever be the opinion of it as a whole, co-operates to the same end ; so most powerfully does the presence of common lodging-houses and furnished rooms. Lastly the impossibility of adequate discrimination of poor relief at the present day is an important factor. In the revolt against a Poor Law treatment which is too bad for the good, it is very probable that such treatment now satisfies neither purpose and while still being too bad for the good is also too good for the bad." [1]

A very large share in the causation of destitution was attributed to continued ill-health, and the prevalence, among the poor, of specific diseases, notably phthisis. " Enough has been said in other passages to emphasize the importance of this disease in connection with pauperism. We have seen no reason in the course of our investigation to doubt the estimate of Dr. Nathan Raw that 40 per cent of paupers dying of phthisis have been reduced to pauperism through this disease, independently of other causes. Firstly, we recommend that a properly guarded power of compulsory removal to the infirmary should be established in the case of those applicants for relief who there is reason on examination to believe are suffering from tubercular phthisis. Under the present system a person whose home is totally unsuited for the treatment of a consumptive patient can, by persistent refusal to enter the infirmary, practically compel the grant of Out-Relief. From all classes of persons connected with the administration as well of the Poor Law as of public health we have

[1] Appendix, vol. xvi. pp. 179-180.

received repeated opinions of the harmfulness of a system under which this is possible. Of such opinions the following from the report of 1905 by the medical officer of health for Manchester is an example : ' The younger children, ill-nourished and remaining at home with their consumptive father, contract the disease and the plague is perpetuated '." [1]

Bad housing, and especially the one or two-roomed home, and the frequent overcrowding even of the three or four-roomed homes, was convicted of a large though an ill-defined share in the production of both sexual immorality and pauperism. " We believe ", conclude the Investigators, " that housing conditions must bear a large share of the blame for the fall of the women and girls who are thus made paupers. The shameful overcrowding of children of all ages and the life in one room to which the high rents in London condemn such large numbers of the people allow of no training in elementary decency, much less in modesty and self-respect. That it even causes vice of the worst type we have been assured by men who are officially engaged in vigilance work, and two cases have come under our personal knowledge." [2]

" Attention has been drawn in a previous part of the report to the pauperising character of various diseases. It is a matter for expert medical knowledge rather than for us to determine the proportionate share in the spread of each disease that should be assigned to bad housing conditions. One aggravating factor in the question deserves mention. The same poverty that helps so largely to cause the overcrowding helps also to diminish the vitality and power of resistance to the communication of the disease which overcrowding facilitates." [3]

" In any case the broad conclusion appears to be incontestable that bad housing conditions largely contribute to pauperism, not merely by their demoralising effects, but through the direct communication of disease, especially of phthisis, the most pauperising of all diseases." [4]

After convicting, as the main causes of urban destitution and pauperism, first casual labour, with its constant recruitment from the " blind alleys " of boy labour ; then the perpetual prevalence of disease, notably phthisis, among ill-fed and overcrowded men and women ; and thirdly the manifold effects of bad housing and

[1] *Ibid.* p. 184.
[3] *Ibid.*

[2] *Ibid.* p. 57.
[4] *Ibid.*

overcrowding, the Investigators found it difficult to assess with any assurance the influence of other contributory causes. Dangerous and unhealthy trades were not found to be directly responsible for more than a minute fraction of the total pauperism. But it was observed that " at the same time the unhealthiness of the trade means an early death. It is not, therefore, surprising that the clearest result of the effect of the occupation is seen when the class of younger widows and their dependents are considered." [1] The influence of intemperance in alcoholic drink was also found to be far from simple. " ' Drink ' ", the Investigators observe, " as the chief pauperising agent has been brought constantly before us throughout the inquiry, and there can be no doubt that it is one of the principal causes of pauperism. It is, however, for the most part, but the effect of causes which require to be sought out and removed. With some of these our report deals, such as dangerous and unhealthy conditions of work, excessive hours, low wages, and bad housing. Other contributory causes may be the too abundant facilities for drinking, and the paucity of easily accessible means of healthy and reasonable recreation. In all these respects further action seems necessary. ' Take away casual labour and drink, and you can shut up three quarters of the Workhouses ' is a sentence which typifies the opinion expressed by most officials of the Poor Law." [2]

Where employment was regular, and not too demoralising, even low wages, coupled with long hours, could not be identified as directly causing, by themselves, a relatively excessive amount of pauperism, even among women. But the Investigators observed "that the problems arising in the course of our inquiry from a consideration of the employment of women are too complex for us to attempt to offer any solution of them here. Unhealthy conditions of work, excessive hours and low wages have been found in certain occupations, and that poverty and suffering are caused by them is indisputable. That pauperism directly results except in individual instances, there is no evidence to show." [3]

" It is alleged that low wages of women are a direct cause of immorality. We do not find that this is sustained. In the course of our inquiry certain factories have attracted our attention by reason of several single women in the maternity wards of

---

[1] Appendix, vol. xvi. p. 180.

[2] *Ibid.* pp. 183-184.   [3] *Ibid.* p. 182.

workhouses having come from the same workplace. No direct connection between their circumstances and the wages or other conditions could be traced except in one instance. In that case there was reason to believe that there was a distant connection between the low wages and the conduct of the employés." [1]

Finally, we may add the comments of the Investigators as to the effects, noted by them, of different forms of Poor Relief and different methods of administration.

" If consideration is confined for the moment to persons of a wage-earning age, the most striking feature of the Poor Law, as at present administered, appears to us to be the equal failure of Indoor and of Outdoor Relief. Each appears equally inadequate to meet existing social conditions. Out-Relief appears to us, in the towns at least, to be either inadequate or demoralising. In one Union it was explicitly told us, and in many other cases we believe it to be the implicit principle, that the amount given in Out-Relief should be calculated on the assumption that the recipient enjoys earnings or other resources which are not disclosed to the Relieving Officer. Where, therefore, this is the hypothesis, the relief given will be wholly inadequate in those cases in which the recipient happens to have told the truth and really has not any undeclared source of income. Many such specific cases came before our notice. . . . Moreover, even where this assumption is not made, the same holds true, though in a less degree. This inadequacy strikes us as being particularly injurious in the case of widows who have young children dependent upon them. Yet the moment that the general scale of relief granted ceases to be inadequate, or even before that point, it begins to be mischievous. We have also observed a similar demoralisation in cases where the question has been one of contribution to the support of a parent, as in the actual application for relief.

" It has been stated in our report that the In-Relief given was too good for the bad and too bad for the good. . . . The chief reasons for this unsatisfactory state of affairs, as regards In- and Out-Relief, appear to be three. In the first place, social conditions have grown much more complicated than in 1834. That was the period when the immense expansion of trade had well begun, and when the difficulty of getting work for a man who wanted work

[1] *Ibid.* p. 182.

did not exist, or rather, if it existed, it would be hardly noticed in contrast with the advantage of getting rid of an old system of hampering regulations not suited to existing conditions." [1]

" In the present Poor Law system, being as it is one of haphazard accretions and alterations, no principle is discernible. . . . That the Poor Law reformers of 1834 had a clear idea of what they meant to do is known to members of the Commission better than to us ; but when their system became inapplicable to later circumstances and ideas, subsequent piecemeal tinkering has made of it a monstrosity." [2]

The Commission's Reports

As we have already indicated, the two streams of investigation set on foot by the Commission, yielding surveys of different ranges of fact and experience, resulted in conflicting judgments as to the proposals to be made to the Government. Notwithstanding agreement on certain fundamental reforms both in constitutional structure and in administrative policy, the Commissioners found themselves so much divided in spirit as to persist in two rival Reports, the one signed (though with reservations by five of them) by fourteen members, including the four Civil Servants and all the members of the Charity Organisation Society; whilst the other received the signatures of four members, including those belonging to the Trade Unions and the Labour Party.[3]

[1] Appendix, vol. xvi. p. 189.
[2] *Ibid.* p. 196.
Another series of investigations, entrusted to Cyril Jackson (who had had great experience in philanthropic work, had been a member of the School Board for London, and was afterwards successively Director of Education in Western Australia, Chief Inspector to the Board of Education for England and Wales, and a member of the London County Council) ; and the Rev. J. C. Pringle, since 1912 Secretary of the Charity Organisation Society. These investigations, relating to " The Effects of Employment or Assistance given to the Unemployed since 1886 as a Measure of Relieving Distress outside the Poor Law ", and resulting in separate volumes of reports for England, Scotland and Ireland (Appendix, vols. xix., xix. *a*, and xix. *b*), will be dealt with in a subsequent chapter on " Unemployment as a Disease of Modern Industry ".
[3] The majority consisted of Lord George Hamilton (Chairman), the Bishop of Ross, Sir Henry Robinson, Sir S. B. Provis, F. H. Bentham, Dr. Arthur Downes, Rev. T. G. Gardiner, C. S. Loch, J. Patten-MacDougall, T. Hancock Nunn, Rev. L. R. Phelps, Professor W. Smart, Mrs. Helen Bosanquet and Miss Octavia Hill. The Minority consisted of Rev. Prebendary Russell Wakefield (afterwards Bishop of Birmingham), F. Chandler, George Lansbury and Mrs. Sidney Webb. The Rt. Hon. Charles Booth had retired owing to

Both Majority and Minority Reports extended to such length, covered so many separate subjects, and indulged in so much detail, that it is not easy to give intelligibly their several proposals in summary form. We may usefully first extract those points on which they agreed. Both proposed a drastic revolution in constitutional structure : nothing less than the complete abolition of the Boards of Guardians, of the Union areas and of the General Mixed Workhouses, which had been the special products of the Poor Law Amendment Act of 1834. Both recommended the adoption throughout England and Wales, as the future local Authority, at least for finance and rating, of the directly elected County or County Borough Council, acting through committees to be appointed by these councils, with varying degrees of administrative autonomy in particular branches of the work, or in particular localities. Both of them agreed in the express abandonment of the conception of a deterrent Poor Law ; and also (at least so far as concerned the nine-tenths of the paupers who were not able-bodied wage earners) of the " principle of less eligibility ".[1] Both of them

---

ill-health in 1908, but not without presenting to his colleagues a remarkable statistical tabulation of all the Unions, with his own scheme of reorganisation (Appendix, vol. xii.), separately published under the title *Poor Law Reform : memoranda submitted to the Royal Commission*, by Rt. Hon. Charles Booth, 1910.

[1] It should in fairness be added that it seems to have been mainly this proposed abandonment of the conception of a deterrent Poor Law that inspired the reservations made by five of the signatories of the Majority Report. Dr. (now Sir) Arthur Downes specifically " detached " himself " from the schemes of new administrative machinery proposed in the Report ", which, in the memorandum that he added, he suggested would " be but a half-way step to the multiplication of relief Authorities advocated by the Minority, and to the very end which the whole argument of the Majority Report condemns " (separately published as *Memorandum on the Reports of the Royal Commission*, by (Sir) Arthur Downes, 1909). Miss Octavia Hill also added a memorandum recording her objection to " the municipalisation of the Poor Law ", to the increased Medical Relief, and, " emphatically ", to the " provision of special work in times of depression ", as well as to any removal of disfranchisement from recipients of any form of relief. C. S. Loch and Mrs. Bosanquet recorded their special objection to any form of relief to the unemployed remaining outside the sphere of the proposed new Public Assistance Authorities, and to any connection between such relief and municipal employment. T. Hancock Nunn added a lengthy memorandum advocating, as an alternative to much of the work of the Poor Law, a great development of voluntary " Councils of Social Welfare ".

It was due to the unfortunate retirement from the Commission of Charles Booth in 1908 that his proposals for reform were never adequately considered by the other Commissioners, and that they were relegated to one of the Appendix volumes (vol. xii.). He contemplated a development alike of national Old

agreed that whatever was done at the expense of public funds must, in future, in regard to the able-bodied as well as the non-able-bodied, be deliberately designed to be " preventive and curative " of the destitution which the Poor Law had heretofore professed only to " relieve ". So emphatic and decisive a condemnation, alike in structure and in function, of the English Poor Law system as it was devised in 1834, and as it has since been elaborated and improved by three-quarters of a century of central direction and control—a condemnation which it is safe to say had not been in the mind of any one of the Commissioners on their appointment—was entirely unexpected by the nation, and it produced a great effect on public opinion.

The two Reports agreed, moreover, in many of their specific recommendations for the new forms of public provision by which the Poor Relief devised by Nassau Senior and Edwin Chadwick should be replaced. Both Reports accepted (and even contemplated the enlargement of) the universal provision of national pensions for the aged of small means or none, which had been begun in 1908. Both proposed a vast extension of the best possible provision for the sick, from whatever disease they might be suffering, including not only free access to domiciliary treatment but also gratuitous hospital maintenance and treatment, together with any necessary maintenance of dependants calculated to induce an early acceptance of this provision. Both recommended the removal from the Poor Law, and the widest possible development of institutional treatment, of all the various grades and kinds of mental deficiency, from the dangerous lunatic down to the feeble-minded. Both contemplated an extensive development of residential schools and " boarding-out " with foster-parents, made freely available, not only for the orphans, but also for the children of parents who were either

---

Age Pensions, of voluntary general hospitals, and of municipal hospitals in so far as " public health " was concerned ; but always preserving Poor Law institutions as the " necessary complement to the whole system ", which must retain the conception of deterrence. Such a development of institutions would permit of a great restriction of Outdoor Relief. The Poor Law should be administered by boards formed, so far as urban districts were concerned, for very large new areas, of which he thought a dozen would suffice for half the population, whilst the other, or rural, half might retain its existing Union areas with minor improvements (see his separate publication, *Poor Law Reform : memoranda submitted to the Royal Commission*, by the Rt. Hon. Charles Booth, 1910).

financially unable to maintain them at a standard of civilisation which the community thought necessary for the public welfare, or were proved to be so neglectful or so incapable of the duties of parenthood as to cause, or even to allow, their children to fall below that standard. Even with regard to the most difficult part of the problem—the treatment of the unemployed able-bodied men — both Reports concurred in many specific recommendations. Both viewed with favour new and unprecedented forms of State intervention, such as the universal provision of Employment Exchanges ; the deliberate manipulation of the orders for goods and services given by Government Departments in such a way as to regularise the seasonal and cyclical volume of employment of labour ; [1] and a far-reaching reform of the conditions of the industrial employment of boys, so as to lessen the number of unhappy " blind alleys " in which these industrial recruits found themselves on reaching manhood. Both contemplated the development, under the auspices of the National Government, and partly at its cost, of a system of insurance against involuntary Unemployment, which should provide the " Out of Work Pay " that a certain number of the Trade Unions had already devised for their own members. In short, both Majority and Minority of the Commission found themselves concurring in the conception of a substitution of public provision, free from any association with " pauperism ", for at least certain forms of involuntary destitution to which individual culpability could no longer be imputed. Finally, both Reports agreed in definitely recommending penal measures— to be made as reformatory as the Prisons Department of the Home Office might find to be practicable—against those persons who should be judicially convicted of causing expense to the community by a persistent refusal to work for the livelihood of themselves and of any members of their family for whom they were legally responsible.

---

[1] The Commission was impressed by the evidence of (Sir) W. H. Beveridge, then a member of the Central Unemployed Body for London, as to Unemployment being caused, not by over-population at all, and far less by personal defects than by faulty organisation of industry ; and that of Professor A. L. Bowley, as to the statistical possibility of so rearranging the orders of public authorities as to smooth out the fluctuations in the total volume of employment from year to year (see Appendix, vol. viii., Q. 77,831-78,370, and Q. 86,111-88,366).

The Majority Report

We come now to the divergent proposals of the two Reports.
To escape any effect of bias against the Majority, we quote the
summary contributed by one of the principal signatories (Sir
C. S. Loch) to the *Charity Organisation Review* for February 1909.
" What is distinctive in the Report may be summarised in a few
paragraphs.   The Commissioners aim at unity in the administration of relief.   At present Poor Law relief is isolated from
charitable relief, and new statutory relief centres have lately
been created—as for instance under the Unemployed Workmen
Act and the Act for the provision of meals to school children
. . . . Next the Commissioners aim at the provision of large
means of variation in treatment.   In regard to indoor relief
they propose, instead of the General Workhouse, institutional
assistance of different kinds.   Thus, unemployed persons—
persons who require systematic work for their training and
improvement, and persons for whom detention is necessary—
might be properly dealt with.   Accommodation for the aged,
the sick and others, would in the same way be separately provided.
Where detention is necessary the institution would be under the
control of the Home Office, for detention would entail a magistrate's order and other conditions which lie outside the purport
of public assistance . . . Indoor or Outdoor Relief would
become different methods of treatment.   In great measure the
antithesis between them would disappear.

" From this conclusion there follows another, a readjustment
of administrative machinery.   The development of Poor Law
administration since 1834 has been from the parish to the Union.
Set aside in the Poor Law Amendment Act as the local centre of
organisation, the parish has become of less and less importance.
By the Report of the present Commission a further step is taken.
The Union is placed in a relation to the County or County
Borough.   The rate would become a County or County Borough
rate.   The County would be the area for institutional relief and
institutional and general supervision.   The Union or district
would be the area for the administration of relief at the home.
. . . Again, for the purposes of voluntary relief, the Union area
is taken as coterminous with the Poor Law or Public Assistance
area ; and the parishes, the usual areas for the administration

of endowed charities, are of service once more, being drawn into relation with one another in connection with a Voluntary Aid Committee for the Union. . . . In fact, a new Poor Law is proposed, governed by the following principles :—

" (1) That the treatment of the poor who apply for public assistance should be adapted to the needs of the individual, and, if institutional, should be governed by classification.

" (2) That the public administration established for the assistance of the poor should work in co-operation with the local and private charities of the district.

" (3) That the system of public assistance thus established should include processes of help which would be preventive, curative and restorative.

" (4) That every effort should be made to foster the instincts of independence and self-maintenance amongst those assisted.

" . . . It is recommended

" (1) That Out-Relief, or, as we shall call it, Home Assistance, be given only after thorough inquiry, except in cases of sudden and urgent necessity ;

" (2) That it should be adequate to meet the needs of those to whom it is given ;

" (3) That persons so assisted should be subject to supervision ;

" (4) That with a view to inquiry and supervision the casepaper system be everywhere adopted ;

" (5) That such supervision should include in its purview the conditions, moral and sanitary, under which the recipient is living ;

" (6) That voluntary agencies be utilised as far as possible for the personal care of individual cases ;

" Thus, Outdoor Relief becomes conditional, and is coupled with regularised supervision. . . .

" It is not proposed to repeal the ancient Poor Law of Queen Elizabeth. It already lies in the far recesses of administration. It remains ; but, what with changes introduced since the Elizabethan Act and the proposals now made, the adoption of a Public Assistance Law would become necessary, a law which being new in its characteristics would rightly entail a new nomenclature. . . . At the head there would be a Public Assistance Division of the L.G.B. In the Counties and County Boroughs there would be Public Assistance Authorities. The County or County Borough Councils would appoint the members of the Public Assistance Authorities, who would then become authorities similar to the local Education Authorities, acting in direct correspondence with the Central Public Assistance Division, to whom they would be responsible. The Public Assistance Authorities would in turn appoint the Public Assistance Committees for the Union or District areas, and the officers of these Committees. But, further, there would be under the Public Assistance Authority of the County or County Borough a Director of Public Assistance, and at the Public Assistance Committee—the local committee—there would be a Superintendent, who would be its chief responsible officer ; and under him the other officers—such as Relieving Officers—who would act as assistants. The whole service of the Public Assistance would thus become coherent and unified. . . . There would be an increase in the staff of central inspectors ; and they would deal not merely with the more general questions of the policy of Boards of Guardians and the visitation of institutions, but would be entitled and required to look into the details of the treatment of cases, so as to make sure that the administration is at heart sound and beneficial. The election of Guardians would be superseded by the appointment of members of a Public Assistance Committee ; for, rightly or wrongly, the separate election of Guardians appears to have become discredited, and it is desirable to free the administration from the incubus of political partisanship. As a substitute for election, therefore, the appointment of the Public Assistance Authority by the Council of the County or County Borough is proposed, on the express understanding that half the members of that authority be persons qualified for membership on the ground of experience, and chosen from outside the ranks of the members of the Council." [1]

The student will note in this authoritative summary of the Majority Report of the Commission of 1905-1909 a tacit abandonment of the main plank in the recommendations of the Commission of 1834 : the famous prohibition of " all relief whatever to able-bodied persons or their families otherwise than in the

---

[1] *Charity Organisation Review*, February 1909. An able exposition of the principles inspiring the Majority Report will be found in Bernard Bosanquet's article in the *Sociological Review*, April 1909 ; which is criticised in the Minority Report for Scotland (Cd. 4922).

well-regulated Workhouses ". The humane intentions of the
majority of the Commissioners of 1905-1909 amounted, in fact,
in many parts of their long Report, to a denunciation of a
deterrent Poor Law. The narrow category of the destitute was
to be replaced by the wider category of the necessitous. Even
the ancient term " Poor Law " was to be dropped. " It has
been impressed upon us in the course of our enquiry ", said the
Majority Report, " that the name ' Poor Law ' has gathered
about it association of harshness and still more of hopelessness,
which we fear might seriously obstruct the reforms which we
desire to see initiated." . . . " In our criticisms and recommendations we hope to show the way to a system of help which
will be better expressed by the title of Public Assistance than
by that of Poor Law.". . . "Help, prevention, cure and instruction [as contrasted with deterrence] " should each find its place
within the processes at the disposal of the new Authorities "
(Recommendations, pp. 189-190). And it is certainly significant
that, in their recommendations with regard to " *The Able-bodied
and Unemployment* ", the Majority should give the primary place,
not to the Poor Law at all, even as modified as they proposed,
but to newly devised preventive services such as " A National
System of Labour Exchanges ", under the Board of Trade ;
" The Education and Training of the Young for Industrial Life ",
to be undertaken by the Local Education Authorities in co-operation with the Labour Exchanges ; " The Regularisation of Employment ", to be devised by the Board of Trade, through all
the Government Departments and Local Authorities ; and,
finally, "A National System of Subsidised Unemployment Insurance ", to be established in co-operation with the Trade
Union Movement (Recommendations, pp. 265-266). So far as
the able-bodied were concerned, destitute merely by reason of
their Unemployment, there seemed, from these parts of the
Report, to be little left to be done by the once all-inclusive
Poor Law !

But the Majority Commissioners spoke with two voices. If,
on the one hand, the principal proposal of the 1834 Report, the
Workhouse System, seemed to be abandoned, on the other hand,
in other parts of the Report, the slogan of " Less Eligibility "
appeared in a new form. The " Home Assistance " to be vouchsafed to the necessitous able-bodied was to be " less eligible "—

not than the condition of the man in employment, but, curiously enough, less eligible than the aid that he might expect to obtain from the Voluntary Aid Committees that were to be set up alongside the Poor Law. " An essential principle ", the Majority Commissioners stated, " to be observed in connection with Home Assistance to the able-bodied, is that it shall be in some way less agreeable than assistance given by the Voluntary Aid Committee. Unless the superiority of the assistance afforded by the Voluntary Aid Committee is in some way secured, it is doubtful whether that Committee will be able to collect voluntary subscriptions for the purpose of helping deserving cases of Unemployment. Experience has again and again shown that the charitable public will not contribute to any extent towards a purpose for which they are also taxed or rated. It therefore follows that if, as is our desire, cases in the class we are considering should be chiefly dealt with by the Voluntary Aid Committee, it is necessary that the aid given by that committee should confer greater benefits, or have less onerous conditions attached to it, than the Home Assistance given by the Public Assistance Committee " (*Proposals as to Distress from Unemployment*, p. 542). Even " the registration of all cases assisted in the Union might ", we are told, " be better undertaken by the Voluntary Aid Committee than by the Public Assistance Committee. In these and other ways there would be built up a voluntary system of relief parallel to the public system, *which might take over the duty of giving relief at the home*, in co-operation with agencies and persons in the several parishes " (*Charities and the Relief of Distress*, p. 82).

"As we have shown," the Commissioners summed up, " by the inter-action of the Committee of Public Assistance and the Voluntary Aid Committee new forces will be brought into the field ; and *it will be the duty of the Public Assistance Committee to deal with no application that can be dealt with equally well or better by the Voluntary Aid Committee* ; and also, as we have shown, the persons who can be assisted by the Public Assistance Committee are those, and those only, who fulfil certain conditions. In this way, under proper supervision and subject to the proper training of those who take any responsible paid service with the committees, we think that *the burthen of Home Relief which now rests on the Guardians will become less and less*, and the responsibilities of the Voluntary Aid Committee will become greater. And thus we may hope that in the course of a few years Outdoor Relief [from public funds] will shrink to small proportions. In these circumstances we have recommended a policy of diminution and limitation instead of abolition " (*Charities and the Relief of Distress*, pp. 97-98).

In this constantly reiterated reliance on the personal service and pecuniary assistance to be voluntarily afforded by the rich to the poor we find the dominant faith of the Majority Commissioners of 1905–1909—a faith to which they seem to have sacrificed all their other prepossessions.[1]

In this ingenious but (as it must seem in 1929) somewhat fantastic proposal to replace Outdoor Relief by voluntary charity, to which the Majority of the Commission appended their signatures, we see a strange, and an entirely unexpected, reversion to the ideas of the Rev. Joseph Townsend and Dr. Chalmers, with which we dealt in the first chapter of this work. Or may we recognise in it a rescension of Goschen's much-belauded Minute of 1869 ? Unlike their predecessors, however, the Majority of the Commissioners of 1909 proposed to give the knots of local philanthropists, to whom the necessitous poor were to be handed over, a definite statutory authorisation ; to set them up in every locality as parallel in status to the public Authority ; to entrust them, in preference to the public Authorities, with the making and keeping of the authoritative register of applicants for relief ; to require all such applicants to apply, in the first instance, not to the public Authority but to the unofficial Voluntary Aid Committee ; and to have it laid down authoritatively that the public Authority should in no case presume to give any relief to those whom the Voluntary Aid Committee refused to help, other-

---

[1] The only other principle emphasised in this elaborate document of nearly 1000 octavo pages is the continuously repeated assertion that the Majority Commissioners, in contrast with the Minority, were in favour of one Authority, and one Authority only, for the relief of necessitous persons in each place. But this principle was not carried out in their specific recommendations. They did not suggest that the extensive activities of the Public Health and Lunacy Authorities, in the treatment and maintenance of sick and mentally afflicted persons, should be transferred to the new Public Assistance Authority that they proposed ; and they actually suggested that the Vagrants should be handed over to the Watch Committees and Joint Committees controlling the police, and that an entirely new form of public provision for the able-bodied should be established, under quite other Authorities, by a national system of Labour Exchanges, accompanied by a subsidised scheme of Unemployment Insurance, with which we deal in another chapter.

wise than in a form or under conditions "in some way less agreeable" than the Voluntary Aid Committee was accustomed to grant. By thus restricting the public Authority to the grant of relief in some "less eligible" form, the Voluntary Aid Committee, it was contemplated, would gradually get under its own control the bulk of the poor who now have recourse for Outdoor Relief to the Poor Law Authorities ; and would be able to restrict the new "voluntary system of relief" to whatever the charitable administrators thought wise, and subject it to such conditions as they might see fit to impose ; leaving to the tender mercies of the public Authorities—which would have always to make their assistance "less eligible" than that, for the time being, afforded by the Voluntary Aid Committee—only such applicants for domiciliary relief as these philanthropists thought proper to relegate to the Poor Law. In short, the Poor Law Authority that was to supersede the Board of Guardians was to maintain the Workhouse under a new name ; whilst the dispensation of Outdoor Relief was to be assumed by non-elected Voluntary Aid Committees, for which it was hoped to collect sufficient funds from the charitable, if not also to bring under their control the incomes of the existing charitable endowments.[1] In so far as these resources failed to suffice, or assistance was otherwise restricted, the applicants would be relegated to a "less eligible" Poor Law, practically offering only institutional relief.

[1] The Minority Report, whilst making equal recognition of the value of Voluntary Agencies and Personal Service, expressed an entirely different view as to their appropriate sphere. "It is one of the advantages", state the Minority Commissioners, "of the proposed distribution of the various services at present aggregated together under the name of Poor Law that it affords the opportunity for initiating a really systematic use of voluntary agencies and personal service, to give to the public assistance that touch of friendly sympathy which may be more helpful than mere maintenance at the public expense, and to deal with cases in which voluntary administration may result in more effective treatment than can be given by public authorities exclusively. . . . We think that it should be a cardinal principle of public administration that the utmost use should, under proper conditions, be made of voluntary agencies and of the personal services of both men and women of good will. . . . In the delimitation of this sphere, a great distinction is to be drawn between the use of voluntary agencies in the visitation of the homes of the poor, and the use of these agencies in the establishment and management of institutions. In the one case there should be absolutely no finding of money. In the other case, the more private money the better.

"With regard to the whole range of charitable work in connection with the home life of the poor, there is, in our judgment, nothing more disastrous, alike to the character of the poor and to the efficiency of the service of public assistance which is at their disposal, than the alms dispensed by well-meaning

The Minority Report

The scheme of the Minority Report was simpler in conception. " The dominant facts of the situation ", the Minority Commissioners stated, " are

" (i.) The overlapping, confusion and waste that result from the provision for each separate class being undertaken, in one and the same district, by two, three, and sometimes even by four separate Local Authorities, as well as by voluntary agencies.

---

persons in the mere relief of distress. This distribution of indiscriminate, unconditional and inadequate doles is none the less harmful when it is an adjunct of quite kindly meant ' district visiting ', the official ministrations of religion, or the treatment meted out by a ' medical mission '. . . . We are definitely of opinion that no encouragement whatever should be given to any distribution of money, food, or clothing in the homes of the poor by any private persons or charitable societies whatsoever. The only exception to this rule should be a regular pension to a particular person ; and this ought, in all cases, to be notified to the Registrar of Public Assistance. It is not that we undervalue the utility of the personal visits of sympathetic and helpful men or women. . . . But this service of visitation, to be effective, must be definitely organised, under skilled direction, in association with a special branch of public administration. . . . Thus, there are now a thousand or two of unpaid Health Visitors, acting under the direction of the Medical Officers of Health. Another example is afforded by the members of the Children's Care Committees . . . and the analogous committees of the Special Schools of the London County Council. . . . Such a band of volunteer helpers, acting within the framework of a specified municipal service, forms, in the densely populated districts of the great towns, an almost indispensable supplement to official activity. . . . It is, however, we repeat, essential that such domiciliary visitors should not have the distribution of money or relief in the homes, whether this be from public or private funds, their own or other people's."

. . . " On the other hand, there is still enormous scope for beneficent gifts of money, to be administered under voluntary management . . . new types of institutional treatment—whether it be the provision of perfect almshouses for the aged, or the establishment of vacation schools or open-air schools for the children ; whether it be the enveloping of the morally infirm, or of those who have fallen, in a regenerating atmosphere of religion and love, or some subtle combination of physical regimen and mental stimulus for the town-bred ' hooligan '—very large sums of money can be advantageously used, and are, in fact, urgently needed. . . . We should wish to see the several Committees of the County and County Borough Councils make full use of these voluntary institutions, entrusting to their care the special types of cases for which they afford appropriate treatment. But in this use there should be invariably two conditions. Any voluntary institution receiving patients from the Local Authority must place itself under the regular inspection both of that Local Authority and of the National Department having the supervision of that particular service. And if payment for treatment is required . . . even without other subsidy, the Local Authority must be given the opportunity of placing its own representatives on the actual governing body of the institution." (Minority Report, pp. 416-418 of 8vo edition, 1909.)

" (ii.) The demoralisation of character and the slackening of personal effort that result from the unnecessary spreading of indiscriminate, unconditional and gratuitous provision, through this unco-ordinated rivalry.

" (iii.) The paramount importance of subordinating mere relief to the specialised treatment of each separate class, with the object of preventing or curing its distress.

" (iv.) The expediency of intimately associating this specialised treatment of each class with the standing machinery for enforcing, both before and after the period of distress, the fulfilment of personal and family obligations.

" We have seen that it is not practicable to oust the various specialised Local Authorities that have grown up since the Boards of Guardians were established. There remains only the alternative—to which, indeed, the conclusions of each of our chapters seem to us to point—of completing the process of breaking up the Poor Law, which has been going on for the last three decades " (Minority Report, p. 395).

" This scheme involves ", we are told in the summary of their proposals, " that the services at present administered by the Destitution Authorities (other than those connected with vagrants or the able-bodied)—that is to say, the provision for

" (i.) Children of school age ;

" (ii.) The sick and the permanently incapacitated, the infants under school age, and the aged needing institutional care.

" (iii.) The mentally defective of all grades and all ages ; and

" (iv.) The aged to whom pensions are awarded—

should be assumed, under the directions of the County and County Borough Councils, by

" (i.) The Education Committee ;

" (ii.) The Health Committee ;

" (iii.) The Asylums Committee ; and

" (iv.) The Pensions Committee respectively.

" That the several committees concerned should be authorised and required, under the directions of their Councils, to provide, under suitable conditions and safeguards to be embodied in Statutes and regulative Orders, for the several classes of persons committed to their charge, whatever treatment they may deem most appropriate to their condition ; being either institutional treatment, in the various specialised schools, hospitals, asylums, etc., under their charge ; or whenever judged preferable, domiciliary treatment, conjoined with the grant of Home Aliment where this is indispensably required.

" That the law with regard to liability to pay for relief or treatment received, or to contribute towards the maintenance of dependants and other relations, should be embodied in a definite and consistent code, on the basis, in those services for which a charge should be made, of recovering the cost from all those who are really able to pay, and of exempting those who cannot properly do so.

" That there should be established in each County and County Borough one or more officers, to be designated Registrars of Public Assistance, to be appointed by the County and County Borough Council, and to be charged with the threefold duty of

" (i.) Keeping a Public Register of all cases in receipt of public assistance.

" (ii.) Assessing and recovering, according to the law of the land and the evidence as to sufficiency of ability to pay, whatever charges Parliament may decide to make for particular kinds of relief or treatment ; and

" (iii.) Sanctioning the grants of Home Aliment proposed by the Committees concerned with the treatment of the case.

" That the Registrar of Public Assistance should have under his direction (and under the control of the General Purposes Committee of the County or County Borough Council) the necessary staff of Inquiry and Recovery Officers, and a local Receiving House, for the strictly temporary accommodation of non-able-bodied persons found in need, and not as yet dealt with by the Committees concerned " (Minority Report, p. 430-431).

The Registrar of Public Assistance

The complete and final supersession of the time-worn Poor Law by the modern specialised Municipal Services, dealing separately with each category of non-able-bodied persons, would, it will be noted, involve one innovation of importance in the administrative machinery. The outstanding difficulty in the dispensation of money payments in the home, or any other form of domiciliary assistance, whether under the Old Poor Law or the New, had always been, not so much that of defining the principle on which the awards should be made, as that of ensuring, in the innumerable cases to be dealt with, anything like an even conformity with the principles determined upon.   In the grant of Outdoor Relief by such a " many-headed " tribunal as the Board of Guardians, or its constantly fluctuating committees, no elaboration of general rules or model scales, no departmental Orders or local By-laws, had been found to prevent a disastrous inequality of treatment between one applicant and another, due either to an inveterate desire to " deal with each case on its merits "—the " merits " being what can never be accurately assessed—or, even more frequently, to the partiality or favouritism that springs, almost inevitably, from the accident of personal acquaintance.   The Report of 1834 had endeavoured to solve this difficulty by repudiating all idea of assessing merits, and by imposing a rigid rule of relieving only persons actually destitute, to the extent only of providing the barest maintenance for all alike.   This rigid restriction, by which it was intended to secure not only a local but also a national uniformity of treatment of all cases, had never resulted in anything like the uniformity desired ;   and it was plainly inapplicable to the " preventive and curative treatment " which had henceforth to be substituted for the mere relief of destitution.   Moreover, the difficulty had become all the greater with the multiplication of public Authorities making allowances in money or food to the homes of the poor.   In 1909 it was found that the same family might be receiving, in respect of a grandparent, weekly payments from the Old Age Pensions scheme ; one child might be maintained in a Reformatory School, whilst others might be fed at the day school of the Local Education Committee ; an infant might have milk from the Local Health Authority ; whilst the father might be on the relief work of the Local Unemployment Authority (Distress Committee), and yet, perhaps in spells of sickness, be an applicant to the Board of Guardians for Outdoor Relief, without there being any machinery for ensuring that each of these Authorities knew what the others were doing, or had any means of ensuring that the aggregate subvention of the household from public funds was either accurately adjusted to its needs or within any maximum that had been prescribed. With this view the Minority Report proposed that there should be a salaried officer, the Registrar of Public Assistance, to whom should be reported every kind of public assistance awarded by any committee of any Local Authority (and, so far as their co-operation could be secured, by any philanthropic agencies) to any resident within the area. This Registrar would keep an accurate register of what each household was receiving from all sources, with the obligation, not of determining himself the sum to be given in each case—though there was much to be said for placing also this duty upon him—but of satisfying himself, first, that each dispensing Authority was aware of what the others were doing, and what was the financial position of the household ; and secondly, that the Orders and By-laws, general rules and model scales for the time being in force, were not being inadvertently infringed by any one of the committees or other bodies concerned. If the circumstances of any case were deemed to demand exceptional treatment, not authorised by the regulations of the Council, it would be open to the committee concerned to make a special recommendation to the Council for any exceptional treatment that the law allowed. It must be said that this proposal found little support, not only among those who desired to continue generous unconditional Outdoor Relief, but also—what seems more inexplicable—among those who were strongest in denunciation of lax administration, and loudest in their demands for complete registration.

A National Authority for the Unemployed

With regard to the class whom the Poor Law Authorities termed " the able-bodied ", and for whom Parliament was legislating as " the Unemployed ", the Minority Report suggested, as an alternative to their continued relief by Local Authorities (whether Boards of Guardians or municipal Distress Committees), a far-reaching scheme of prevention and curative treatment which could be successfully undertaken only by the National Government. An analysis of the Unemployed showed them to belong to three hopeful categories (" men from permanent employment ", men of discontinuous employment ; and casual labourers), requiring different measures for preventing, not so much destitution as the very occurrence of Unemployment itself; together with one unhopeful category ("the unemployable"), in which it was all-important that recruiting should be arrested, as well as desirable that the best available restorative training should be applied. We need not here describe the means—principally the systematic dovetailing of employment in seasonal trades, which were found, to a surprising extent, to alternate one with another; and the concentration of government orders in the "lean years" of the trade cycle—by which it was suggested that the National Government could, at least to a large extent, prevent the occurrence of both seasonal and cyclical unemployment; systematise the Unemployment of casual labour; and, by effective use of the national system of Employment Exchanges, reduce to a minimum the intervals between the jobs in those occupations in which intermittent employment could be not prevented. Yet, when all possible had been done to prevent the occurrence of Unemployment, there must still be cases in which, from one or other cause, the worker would find himself wageless. For many of these a system of national Unemployment Insurance could provide. For the rest, the Minority Report proposed that adequate maintenance should be provided out of national funds, but only conditionally on the unemployed man attending such day or residential training centres as might be required, in order to obtain whatever training —physical or mental, technological or cultural, usually in combination with each other—his condition might call for, or his faculties warrant. It is interesting to observe that the principal object of this proposed training was not any expected increased productivity, or immunity from future Unemployment, but merely the avoidance of the demonstrated evil result of maintaining able-bodied men in idleness. Those who were found to be unemployable owing to physical or mental deficiencies would be relegated to the Local Health or Lunacy Authority; whilst those judicially convicted of wilful idleness or contumacy would be committed to a reformatory colony to be maintained under the Home Office.

The Cleavage in Spirit

Where the Majority and Minority Reports differed most intractably was in the spirit in which they were conceived. The Majority might admit that the administration of what the community chose to provide for its citizens could not nowadays be deliberately made deterrent, where the recipients had not been judicially convicted of offences against the law. They might reluctantly consent to the exclusion from Poor Relief of the public provision of schools, hospitals and lunatic asylums, and even of Old Age Pensions and a national subvention of Unemployment Insurance. But they clung desperately to the maintenance, at least for some of the persons for whom the community had to pay, of a dyslogistic category, whether or not it was to be termed pauperism. This is expressed by an able apologist (Professor Bernard Bosanquet) : " The antagonism cannot be put too strongly. The Majority proceed upon the principle that where there is a failure of social self-maintenance in the sense above defined, there is a defect in the citizen character, or at least a grave danger to its integrity ; and that therefore every case of this kind raises a problem which is ' moral ', in the sense of affecting the whole capacity of self-management, to begin with in the person who has failed, and secondarily, in the whole community so far as influenced by expectation and example. This relation to a man's whole capacity for self-management, his ' moral ', is a distinctive feature, I take it, which separates the treatment required by the destitute or necessitous from anything that can be offered to citizens who are maintaining themselves in a normal course of life ".[1] It was in order that this class of persons might still continue to be separated from their fellow-citizens, and be dealt with, not simply according to their diseases or deficiencies, but according to their assumed common " defect in the citizen character ", that the Majority Report proposed that there should be established, under the County or County Borough Council, a non-elective and specialised " Public Assistance Authority " which should annex, from the existing Public Health and Education services, many of the activities of these non-pauper authorities, in order, on the one hand, to unite these accretions with the manifold activities to be taken over from the Boards of Guardians, and, on the other, to co-ordinate the whole with voluntary charity. Thus, there would still be a Poor Law—though " preventive and curative " instead of deterrent—and a specialised relief of the destitution of a pauper class. The Minority Report, on the other hand, emphasised the social importance of dealing with every

[1] " The Majority Report ", in *Sociological Review*, April 1909, vol. ii. No. 2.

case in which, from whatever cause, any person fell below the prescribed National Minimum of Civilised Life. The conception of the social advantage of a prompt administration of the wisest possible treatment replaced that of the benefit to the individual recipient of a charitable dole. Treatment could without danger be maximised ; whilst, in order to avoid demoralisation, charity had to be limited and even minimised. But some forms of treatment necessarily included the provision of food or money, which might, by its endowment of idleness, discourage thrift. It is an advantage of making the provision universal, as an attribute of citizenship—as against a policy of charitable gifts—that it leaves unimpaired the superiority in position of the thrifty man over the unthrifty. If the calamitous special subsidising of the unthrifty, together with the demoralising rivalry and overlapping of Authorities, was to be brought to an end, this could be accomplished only by the very conception of Poor Relief being abandoned, in favour of that of the provision, for the citizens, of whatever was called for in the public interest. To this conclusion the community had, in one field after another, empirically come. There had grown up, in fact, during the three-quarters of a century which separated the Commission of 1905-1909 from that of 1832–1834, a new Framework of Prevention ''—in supersession, it may be said, of the '' Framework of Repression '', out of which, as we have described in our preceding history, the '' Old Poor Law '' arose—which embraced, not '' destitute '' persons in respect of their destitution, but the whole population, in respect of their particular needs.

A Change in Thought

We end this chapter by an attempt to sum up the Royal Commission of 1905-1909, not according to the relative value of the two schemes of reform promulgated by rival groups of Commissioners, but as an episode in English Poor Law history, which brought into the limelight of an unprecedented publicity a radical change in thought with regard to the poverty of the poor. This change can be best shown by contrasting the philosophies that inspired, respectively, the findings of 1834 and those of 1909. The Commission that emanated from the reformed Parliament of 1832 embodied in its Report the two leading hypotheses of contemporary thought on poverty. It accepted unquestioningly the " discovery " by the Rev. Joseph Townsend and the Rev. Thomas Chalmers that the evil to be cured was pauperism ; and that pauperism was nothing more than an artificially created disease of society, which could be swept away by simply abolishing the Poor Law and the Poor Rate, whenever this became politically possible. This Commission accepted, too, a second hypothesis in the Malthusian Theory of Population, emphasised by the economists into the Theory of the Wage Fund, which led to the conclusion that any relief of destitution, in whatever form or by whatever agency, would, by causing an increase in the number of manual workers, actually operate to reduce the earnings per head of population, thus creating an ever-widening morass of destitution. Universally accepted by " enlightened opinion " up to the middle of the nineteenth century, and only slowly discarded by the " enlightened opinion " of the last quarter of the century, this so-called " Law of Population " inspired alike the findings of the Royal Commission of 1834, the administration of the Poor Law Commissioners of 1837–1847, and the policy of the Poor Law Board of 1847–1871 ; finding its last resting-place among the more dogmatic of the inspectorate of the L.G.B. from 1871 to 1906. Thus J. S. Davy, the energetic Chief Inspector, in his detailed indictment of the Poor Law administration by which he sought to guide the Commission in the way it should go, asserted and reasserted the " Principles of 1834 ", as if, in 1906, they still constituted the official policy of the Local Government Board. According to him, the various Circulars of successive Presidents of the Local Government Board departing from these principles had been but the weakness of politicians arising from the widening of the electorate. But, as the reader of our preceding chapter [1] will have perceived, the continuous series of "departures" from the "Principles of 1834"—the endless array of ameliorations of the conditions provided for the pauper children, the pauper sick, the pauper lunatics, the pauper aged, and even, here and there, for the pauper able-bodied who had begun to be called the Unemployed—had, for the most part, emanated, not from the politicians at all, whether Ministers or legislators, but from the permanent Civil Servants, notably the Inspectors and the Secretariat, and even more influential than

[1] Chapter IV., " Sixty Years of Poor Law Administration ".

these, the educationists and the medical experts. Nor had these " departures " been made wantonly or out of caprice. On the contrary, they had been successively forced upon the administrators, against their own prepossessions, by the scandalous results of the various applications of the " deterrent " policy in the actual production of illiteracy, disease, demoralisation, vagrancy and crime.

In contrast with its predecessor, the Commission of 1905-1909 was a mixed body, which, though preponderatingly revering the " Principles of 1834 ", started with no common doctrine with regard to the origin and treatment of pauperism, and had therefore, at the outset, no common view of the right direction of reform. It was accordingly all the more significant that the Commission ended, Majority and Minority alike, in the definite rejection of the notion that the main " disease of society " to be cured was pauperism—that is to say, the maintenance of the destitute out of public funds. What the Commission discovered was that the " disease " with which society had to grapple was destitution, of which " pauperism " was but one among many symptoms, such as mendicancy and vagrancy ; the physical ailments arising from under-nourishment, darkness and dirt ; the irregularities of life and degeneration of character that accompany casual labour and protracted Unemployment ; and all the evils of " sweating ". The mere relief of destitution, without adequate preventive treatment before and after its occurrence, may, indeed, actually intensify the social disease ; as we have abundantly seen in the "rate in aid of wages", in the daily doles of food and lodging to vagrants, and in the long-continued unconditional Outdoor Relief to unemployed healthy able-bodied men. Fundamentally, all this came back to the discovery by Charles Booth that, although the Poor Law statistics might register only two or three per cent of the population as applicants for Poor Relief in any one year, as many as thirty per cent of the whole population were always living under conditions that involved the majority of this considerable section passing, at one or other period of their lives, at least temporarily into the pauper class. It was plain that the " disease " which was annually creating so large a mass of new pauperism could not be cured merely by the abolition of the Poor Law and the cessation of the Poor Rate, even if this could be accompanied by an equally complete abolition of individual almsgiving, charitable endowments, " Lord Mayor's Funds " and the like.

Nor could the Commissioners, in 1909, be frightened by the " increase of population " spectre. Indeed, we ascribe the revolution in thought, alike in the Commission and in enlightened public opinion—apart from the influence of the gradual accumulation of objective studies from those of Edwin Chadwick to those of Charles Booth—mainly to the silent abandonment, by all the experts, both of the Malthusian Law of Population and of the Theory of a Wage Fund.[1] The Commission of 1909 realised, as that of 1834 could not do, that irregular employment, earnings inadequate for healthy subsistence, and housing below the level of civilised decency were accompanied, not only by chronic ill-health and preventible disease, but also by an entirely unrestrained birth-rate. If it was desired to arrest an unlimited

---

[1] It may be permissible to remind the reader unfamiliar with the writings of the economists that, except as a part of the history of economic doctrine, the " Theory of the Wage Fund " has long since ceased to appear in economic textbooks and treatises. After the exposure of its fallacies by F. D. Longe (1866), Frederic Harrison (1867), Fleeming Jenkin (1868) and W. T. Thornton (1869), it was unreservedly abandoned by John Stuart Mill in the *Fortnightly Review* for May 1869 (see *Wages and Capital : an Examination of the Wages Fund Doctrine*, by F. W. Taussig, 1896). The " Theory of Distribution " which has taken its place in the works of Marshall, Nicholson, Pigou, Gonner, Clay, Cannan, Chapman, Mavor, Smart and Symes—to name only British authors—does not afford even a presumption of the impossibility of a general rise in wages.

The employer of to-day asserts, as a limit to wages, not the amount of his capital, still less that of a fraction of it, but the amount of the product ; and he is concerned about the sufficiency of the share of the product that will be left to him. What has gone far to convert even the employer to the advantage of improving the condition of the manual-working class is the discovery that such improvement, whether in wages, hours of labour, the sanitation and amenity of the factory or regularity of employment, is often— we should ourselves say, usually—especially if made universally binding by law or Collective Bargaining as a " common rule " throughout a whole trade, *itself a cause of at least an equal increase in the product*, (a) by enabling more work and better to be got out of workers previously under-nourished, physically and mentally ; (b) by inducing and permitting the greater use of machinery, and the adoption of better organisation and new methods ; (c) by making it ever more unprofitable for each employer to have any but the most efficient workmen and technicians that he can obtain, causing, therefore, by incessant selection, a continuous increase in their aggregate productivity ; and (d) by similarly bringing into operation a continuous " selection of the fittest " among the employers and managers themselves, weeding out those unable or unwilling to rise to the higher professional standards made imperative by the increased concentration of competition upon quality, effected by the enforcement of the " common rules ". See our *Industrial Democracy*, pp. 603-632, 715-739.

increase of population, or to alter for the better the proportion
of wage-labourers to capital enterprise, this could be effected—
and apparently effected only—by measures deliberately taken to
raise the whole body of wage-earners to a higher level of civilisation. The more continuously comfortable the wage-earner's
home, the fewer the children. The popular discovery of birth-
control [1] had changed the conditions of the problem !

Another popular discovery was exercising scarcely less influence on public opinion. In the latter decades of the nineteenth
century the common acceptance of " Darwinism ", and of the
" struggle for existence ", leading to the " survival of the fittest ",
had operated in support of a restriction of almsgiving and personal charity, and of the strictest possible administration of Poor
Relief. Somewhat later, the common acceptance of the principles of Eugenics often tended in the same direction. But by
the end of the century it was realised by the thoughtful that any
such inference from the processes of organic evolution was wholly
fallacious. Samuel Barnett, in his work at Toynbee Hall, and
Charles Booth in his survey of the *Life and Labour of the People*,
had become no less deeply impressed than Dr. Southwood Smith
and Sir John Simon had previously been with the fact that the
destitution resulting from preventable disease or accident, impoverished Old Age or involuntary Unemployment did not result
in improvement, either of the individual, or of his contemporaries,

---

[1] For the modern statement of the " Law of Population ", which Malthus,
if he could read it, would hardly recognise, see *The Population Question*, by
A. M. Carr Saunders, 1922. The social expediency of a deliberate regulation
of conception, whether for preventing too short an interval between births,
or for limiting the size of families—the " Neo-Malthusianism " privately
advocated in 1823 by Francis Place and (as it is rumoured) the youthful John
Stuart Mill, together with Robert Dale Owen (1830), and Dr. Charles Knowlton
(1832)—is now (1928) widely accepted in Western Europe, Australasia and
America. Although its mere promulgation was criminally prosecuted in
England in 1877, in the persons of Charles Bradlaugh and Mrs Annie Besant
(and is still forbidden by law in parts of the United States), the practice is
widespread, and instruction in contraceptive methods is openly given, in some
places in public institutions by public officials. See the statistics given in
The Decline of the Birth Rate, Fabian Tract No. 131 ; *Industrial Democracy*,
by S. and B. Webb, 1897, pp. 636-642 ; and *Contraception, its Theory, History,
and Practice*, by Marie Carmichael Stopes, D.Sc., 1923 ; *Medical Aspects of
Contraception, being the Report of the Medical Committee appointed by the National
Council of Public Morals*, 1927 ; *Medical Views on Birth Control*, edited by
Rev. Sir James Marchant, 1927 ; and the interesting historical particulars
given in " The Birth Control Handbills of 1823 " (*The Lancet*, August 6, 1927,
p. 313); and "Charles Knowlton's Revolutionary Influence on the English Birth-
rate " (*New England Journal of Medicine*, Sept. 6, 1928), both by Norman E. Himes.

or of the succeeding generations. On the contrary, any lowering of the Standard of Life, and especially any reduction of families to destitution, whether due to misconduct or to misfortune, had, it was realised, its own inevitable effect, alike on the individuals themselves, and on the generations that followed them (for even if it were universally true that " acquired " characteristics are not inherited, there is the " heritage " of the home environment, which is unquestionably potent), of lessened physical vigour, increased liability to break-down and disease, disordered intellect, enfeebled will and every kind of degeneration. It was, in fact, discovered that those who failed in the struggle for existence were not necessarily or even usually " eliminated " as " unfit ". In many cases they continued at a lower level, sometimes even obtaining advantages enabling them and their descendants to survive in the competitive struggle against other less fortunate sections whom we might estimate to be superior. The more brutalising the condition, the lower the type that might be preferred. Evolution, in short, led indifferently either to progress or to degradation, according to the environment provided for each successive generation. The neglected infant, the child abandoned to illiteracy and destitution, the overworked factory operative, injured coal-miner, or half-starved labourer, did not necessarily die, and thus remove their individual degeneracy from the continual stream of the nation's life : they persisted in living at the lower level down to which they were pressed, and, by their mere existence in disease and squalor, vice, mendicancy and crime, infecting and contaminating the rest of the community. This result of destitution in the creation of new destitution was brought forcibly before the Poor Law Commission by nearly every one of its Special Investigators, whether lay or medical ; and it had a marked effect on the conclusions reached by Majority and Minority alike.

A Central Controlling Department justified

There was, however, one part of the philosophy that lay at the basis of the findings of the Royal Commission of 1832–1834 which was accepted and even accentuated by the Royal Commission of 1905–1909. It was the special merit of the famous Commission appointed by the Whig Ministry that it began to

press on an unwilling public opinion the Benthamite conception
of a series of central government Departments each directing and
supervising its own function as administered by one general
directly elected Local Authority for each area, whose special
task it was, in all branches of Local Government, deliberately to
change the environment of the bulk of the people in such a way
as not only to maximise their happiness, but also actually to
create improvement in their character and conduct. The one
Central Authority established by the Poor Law Amendment Act
of 1834 was, it is true, inspired by the principle of *laissez-faire* ;
that is, of actually reducing, and as soon as possible withdrawing,
the particular provision out of public funds which it happened to
consider injurious to the moral and material welfare of the
people. But Jeremy Bentham himself had been no worshipper of
laissez-faire. He had no faith in a natural order of society. His
dominant desire was to effect such alterations in this as in other
parts of " external nature " as would " maximise " human
happiness. To Bentham, as to the statesmen of to-day, it was
the very purpose of those communities of men that we call
nations or states, through the instrument of " government ", to
play on the wills of men, in order to harmonise the necessarily
conflicting interests of individuals among themselves, and also
the individual interests of all the citizens with that of the community as a whole. Thus, in his proposed machinery of government, Bentham included, as we have mentioned, with extraordinary prescience, not only an Indigence Relief Minister, but
also a Minister of Trade and a Preventive Services Minister,
the last-named dealing with unhealthy occupations, the fouling
of air and water, adulteration of food, and all the circumstances
of an industrial state that are inimical to the health of body and
mind. In the preceding chapters we have watched the emergence
of Bentham's Minister of Indigence Relief, and the steadily
improving organisation of the Local Authorities under his
supervision and control. But this was only part of the novel
conception of the functions of government that the Commission
of 1905-1909, Majority as well as Minority, unconsciously embodied in their far-reaching proposals for social reform. In the
development of the " Framework of Prevention ", which the
nineteenth century had been empirically building up, we see
emerging, not only the additional and separate Ministries of

Education, Labour, Transport, Mines and Health, along the lines of Bentham's suggestions, but also a new principle of social organisation in the progressive recognition and enforcement of the very condition of civilisation itself, the mutual obligation of service from the community to the individual and from the individual to the community. This " Framework of Prevention " we have now to describe.

CHAPTER VI

THE FRAMEWORK OF PREVENTION

IT is stated that it was the realisation, by the members of the Poor Law Commission, of the magnitude and varied range of the public administrations outside the Poor Law, that vitally affected the recommendations of Majority and Minority alike. These public administrations, which aimed at the prevention, not directly of pauperism, but of the destitution of which pauperism is only one of the manifestations, have a history of their own, extending over a whole century, that we cannot relate here. But in their upgrowth from the first quarter of the nineteenth century, and, still more, in their extraordinarily rapid extension and expansion during the first quarter of the twentieth century, they have so potently affected the development of the Poor Law itself, and they have, in 1928, so definitely become the predominant factor in the nation's treatment of " the poor ", that it is desirable to survey their varied developments, more particularly as they have severally impinged on the sphere of action of the older Destitution Authorities.

In our history of the Old Poor Law we described at some length the Framework of Repression, into which was fitted, right up to the Poor Law Act of 1834, the Elizabethan legislation concerning the relief of destitution.[1] This Framework of Repression, whether embodied in the Statute of Labourers (1350), or in the Law of Settlement and Removal (1662), or in the centuries old and continuously amended laws relating to Vagrancy, may be said to have been designed to regulate the behaviour of the propertyless man towards his social superiors, so that he should continue to serve his King and country in the subordinate station

---

[1] *The Old Poor Law*, 1927, particularly chapters i., iii. and iv.

554

of life in which God had placed him. Further, we suggested that this essentially penal legislation was, during the latter part of the eighteenth and the beginning of the nineteenth century, gradually being supplemented by the growing economic subordination involved in the machine industry and mass production. The loose and idle life and riotous living, about which we hear so frequently in the preambles of the " Laws relating to the Poor " from the fifteenth to the eighteenth century, became more and more impracticable under the disciplinary regimen of factory and mine. The task of holding down the common people to their " divinely " appointed duty of regular work for the masters directing their operations was, in fact, being slowly and silently transferred, from the Justices of the Peace and the King's Judges, to the keener brains and stronger wills of the new class of mill-owners, ironmasters, colliery proprietors and engineering employers, and the large wheat-growing and stock-breeding farmers (increasingly replacing the copyholders and commoners), whose energies had been released, and whose economic power had been indefinitely extended, by the theory and practice of free capitalist enterprise.

Coincidently with this ever-increasing pressure on the freedom of the bulk of the people, chiefly in the manufacturing districts, there came, as we have described in our previous history, a benevolent laxity in the County Justices' administration of the Poor Law ; a laxity culminating in the Speenhamland scale of Outdoor Relief to the able-bodied labourers and their families, amounting, in some cases, to complete and unconditional maintenance, but more usually to a " rate in aid " of wages falling below the starvation point. A less noted but more lasting outcome was the faint beginning of a comprehensive Framework of Prevention, which, after a century and a quarter of successive statutes, is still in process of completion—a series of social institutions designed for the prevention, not merely of pauperism, but of destitution itself.

The Meaning of " Destitution "

Let us begin by stating, as concisely as we can, exactly what we mean by the term destitution.

By destitution we mean the condition of being without one

or other of the necessaries of life, in such a way that health and strength, and even vitality, is so impaired as eventually to imperil life itself. Nor is it merely a physical state. It is indeed a special feature of destitution in modern urban communities that it entails, not merely a lack of food, clothing and shelter, but also a condition of mental degradation. Destitution in the desert may be consistent with a high level of spiritual refinement. But destitution in a densely crowded modern city involves, as all experience shows, not only oncoming disease and premature death from continued privation, but also, in the great majority of cases, the degradation of the soul. Massed in mean streets, working in the sweating dens, or picking up a precarious livelihood by casual jobs ; living by day and by night in overcrowded one-room tenements, through months of chronic underemployment, infants and children, boys and girls, men and women together find themselves subjected, in an atmosphere of drinking, begging, cringing and lying, to unspeakable temptations to which it is practically inevitable that they should in different degrees succumb, and in which strength and purity of character are irretrievably lost. Anyone acquainted with the sights and sounds and smells of those quarters of great cities in which extreme poverty is massed—especially anyone conversant with the life-histories of families habitually below the " Poverty Line "—learns to recognise a sort of moral malaria which undermines the spiritual vitality, the morals and manners, of those subjected to its direful influence. Whilst here and there a moral genius may survive, saddened but otherwise unscathed, this sort of destitution gradually submerges the mass of each generation, as it grows up, in coarseness and bestiality, apathy and cynical scepticism of every kind. When considerable numbers of people in such a condition are found together, still more when they are practically segregated in " cities of the poor ", this means that the community of which they form part is, to that extent, socially, as well as physically and mentally, diseased. It is in this sense that it is correct to say that " destitution is a disease of society itself ". It is this social disease against which a comprehensive but not yet complete Framework of Prevention has been erected.

Blocking the Downward Way

The principle of " Blocking the Downward Way ", that is, preventing any conduct on the part of employers injurious to the health and character of their " hired hands ", constitutes the foundation of the Framework of Prevention. Very much as the Framework of Repression was originally devised to regulate the behaviour of the peasant freedman to his lord, so the Framework of Prevention was first designed to regulate the behaviour of the industrial employer to his wage-earners. The small beginnings of this legislative regulation arose from simple humanitarianism. When the results of unrestrained competition in the employment of labour were gradually, and, very slowly, perceived by philanthropists, and made known by Robert Owen (1771–1858) and Lord Shaftesbury (1801–1885), successive Governments found themselves unable to resist the argument in favour of a new code of behaviour for the profit-making employer. The early steps in this legislative regulation of the conditions of employment, embodied in the Factory Acts of 1802, 1819, 1825 and 1833, and the Mines Regulation Act of 1842, were taken empirically, with the object of remedying patent abuses, and of giving to some of the weaker sections of the wage-earners, by the strong arm of the law, that protection against ill-usage which they had been unable to obtain for themselves. With the advent of political democracy in 1867 and 1884, and the rise of the " New Unionism ", in 1889, with its preference for legal enactment over collective bargaining, this legislative protection was extended from trade to trade, from one class of workers to another, and from one element in industrial life to another. The Mines Regulation Act of 1842 was followed by successive statutes, steadily increasing the extent and minuteness of the precautions required against accidents, of the provisions safeguarding the workers against being cheated in their wages, of the regulation of the work of women and boys, of the limitation of the hours of labour even of adult men, and, generally, of the public supervision of the methods of working. By the series of Merchant Shipping Acts analogous legislative protection was extended to the seamen, and to all others employed on ships. By the Regulation of Railways Acts of 1889 and 1893, the Board of Trade was charged with the prevention of excessive hours of labour among railway servants, and was enabled to insist on a reduction in the working day in all cases in which this was deemed necessary. By successive Truck Acts, Factory and Workshop Acts, and Shop Hours Acts, practically all manufacturing industries, and nearly all kinds of retail shops, were similarly brought under regulation and inspection. Meanwhile the statutory provision for the sufferers from industrial accidents, very partially secured by the Employers' Liability Act of 1880, was transformed by the more universal Workmen's Compensation Act of 1897, covering all accidents arising in the course of employment ; and by the inclusion, within the range of public investigation and regulation, and compulsory compensation, of an ever-increasing number of the diseases connected with the processes of particular industries.

But safety and sanitation in the workplace, and leisure after working hours, with compensation for accidents and occupational diseases, do not of themselves maintain the nation's workers in health and efficiency, or prevent them from being pressed down into destitution. This was eloquently pointed out as long ago as 1854 by the far-seeing Medical Officer of the Privy Council. " If such and such conditions of food or dwelling are absolutely inconsistent with healthy life, what more final test of pauperism can there be, or what clearer right to public succour, than that the subject's pecuniary means fall short of providing him other conditions than these ? It may be that competition has screwed down the rate of wages below what will purchase indispensable food and wholesome lodging. . . . All labour below that mark is masked pauperism. Whatever the employer saves is gained at the public expense. . . . It is the public that, too late for the man's health or independence, pays the arrears of wage which should have hindered this suffering and sorrow." [1]

In describing the economics of factory regulation in 1897, we urged that " just as it is against public policy to allow an employer to engage a woman to work excessive hours or under insanitary conditions, so it is equally against public policy to permit him to engage her for wages insufficient to provide the food and shelter without which she cannot continue in health. Once we begin to prescribe the minimum conditions under which an employer should be permitted to open a factory, there is no

[1] *Public Health Reports*, by Sir John Simon, 1887, p. 145.

logical distinction to be drawn between the several clauses of the wage-contract. From the point of view of the employer, one way of increasing the cost of production is the same as another, whilst to the economist and the statesman, concerned with the permanent efficiency of industry and the maintenance of national health, adequate food is at least as important as reasonable hours or good drainage. . . . The proposition of a National Minimum of wages—the enactment of a definite sum of earnings per week below which no employer should be allowed to hire any worker—has not yet been put forward by any considerable section of Trade Unionists, nor taken into consideration by any Home Secretary. . . ." [1]

The Legal Minimum Wage

Twelve years after this " intelligent anticipation ", the first Trade Boards Act (1909) was passed by a Liberal Government, to be so widely extended, in the Trade Boards Act of 1918, by a Coalition Government of Liberals and Conservatives, that by the end of 1921 over a million workers, of whom over 70 per cent were women, found their wages, whether calculated by time or by output, authoritatively safeguarded by a legally enforced minimum.[2]

[1] *Industrial Democracy*, by S. and B. Webb, 1897, pp. 773-774.

[2] The Trade Boards Acts are 9 Edward VII. c. 22, 1909 ; and 8 and 9 George V. c. 32, 1918. They arose immediately out of the Report of the Select Committee on Home Work in 1908 (H.C. 246 of 1908) ; that of Ernest Aves on the Wage-Boards and Industrial Conciliation and Arbitration Acts of Australia and New Zealand (Cd. 4167 of 1908) ; and that of a Sub-Committee of the Reconstruction Committee in 1917–1919 (Cd. 9239 of 1919, Appendix V.). Their operation down to the end of 1921 was examined by the Trade Boards Administration Committee, 1921, and by a Departmental Committee appointed by the Minister of Labour in that year " to enquire into the Working and Effects of the Trade Boards Acts " (Cmd. 1645 of 1922). Their history, with that of similar legislation throughout the world, is well given in the elaborate and painstaking *Wages and the State : a Comparative Study of the Problems of Wage Regulation*, by Mrs. E. M. Burns, 1926, which gives references to Dominion and Foreign sources ; and in *The British Trade Boards System*, by Dorothy M. Sells, 1923 ; *Trade Boards*, by W. Addington Willis, 1920. Among other English books we may cite *The Establishment of Minimum Rates in the Chain-making Industry*, 1914, and *The Establishment of Minimum Rates in the Tailoring Industry*, 1915, both by R. H. Tawney ; *The Establishment of Minimum Rates in the Box-making Industry*, by M. E. Bulkley, 1915 ; *Sweated Labour and the Trade Boards Act*, by Rev. Thomas Wright, 1911 ; *The Legal Minimum*, by J. Hallsworth, 1925 ; and two articles on Women's Wages by D. M. Barton, in *Journal of Statistical Society* for July 1919 and July 1921 (see also a Bibliography of Trade Boards in the *Bulletin of the British Library of Political and Economic*

The organisation and procedure of what, though not the first, is now the most important experiment in the Legal Minimum Wage in the world may be briefly described. In contrast with the general scheme of British Factory Legislation, the Trade Boards Act is applicable to trade after trade on the initiative and at the discretion of the Minister responsible to Parliament, before which his definitive Order is laid after it is made, when it may be annulled within forty days upon an Address to the Crown from either House. There is no limitation of sex or age, or the kind of trade or the method of remuneration; and the original restriction of the 1909 Act to trades in which wages are " exceptionally low " was replaced in the 1918 Act by the more general phrase requiring the Minister merely to have " regard to the rates of wages prevailing in the trade, or any part of the trade ". The Minister is empowered to make an Order in any case in which he thinks it expedient, and if he is " of opinion that no adequate machinery exists for the effective regulation of wages throughout the trade ". The Trade Board so established must consist of members representing employers and members representing workers in equal proportions, with some additional " appointed members ", of whom, in the case of a trade in which women are largely employed, at least one must be a woman. The representative members may be either elected or nominated by the Minister as may be provided by regulations made by him; whilst he is always to choose the " appointed members ", and to name one of them to be Chairman of the Board. In practice all the members of each Board are nominated by the Minister; but, as regards the representative members, only after suggestion by, and careful consultation with, the organisation and leaders of each side. The Board is empowered to fix not only the Minimum Time Rates and Piece Rates authorised by the Act of 1909, but also, by the Act of 1918, the Overtime Rates, Guaranteed Time Rates and Piecework Basis Time Rates which experience has shown to be required to safeguard and facilitate the working of the Minimum. The fixing of Overtime Rates involved defining the Normal Day. The determinations of the Trade

---

Science for May 1922). For the progress of the idea throughout the world, see *Minimum Wage-fixing Machinery : an International Study of Legislation and Practice* (International Labour Office, 1927) ; and " Minimum Wage Legislation in the United States ", by Rudolf Broda, in *International Labour Review*, January 1928.

Boards have the force of law ; and they are enforceable (like the provisions of the Factory, Mines Regulation, Merchant Shipping and Shop Hours Acts, and the Orders made by Ministers under those statutes) by criminal prosecution, usually instituted by the salaried Inspectors, in the Courts of Summary Jurisdiction. Employers convicted of breach of the law are punishable by fine, in addition to being required, if the Court so decides, to pay the arrears of wage due.[1]

At first the movement was slow. In the course of nine years from 1909 only eight Trade Boards were established in Great Britain, and five in Ireland, securing a Legal Minimum Wage to fewer than 600,000 workers. With the new provisions of the Act of 1918, and under the influence of the post-war mental climate, more than fifty additional Boards were set up in a couple of years, bringing the total number of workers affected up to more than a million. Moreover, there was a widening of scope. Industrial opinion, both among the employers and among the Trade Unionists, was coming round to the view that, in order to avoid trade disputes and secure continuity of working, it would be on the whole advantageous to both sides, as well as to the community, to settle the rates of wages by the authoritative determination of minima, not only for the lowest grades, but also for the higher, if not indeed throughout the whole establishment, and for all the establishments in each industry. Hence, whilst the proceedings under the original Act aimed almost entirely at determining a

---

[1] In 1912, by the Coal Mines (Minimum Wage) Act, provision was made for a compulsory minimum rate per shift worked by miners underground, the rate to be fixed for each coal-field, for men and boys respectively, by local Boards, appointed for this purpose, consisting of representatives of the local coal-owners and coal-miners respectively and a chairman appointed by the Home Secretary. In nearly all the coal-fields the chairman had, in 1912, to decide the rates, as the representatives failed to agree. This experiment, which gave a minimum to such among the million coal-miners as happened to be assigned to an " abnormal place ", differed from the Trade Board system in that the Legal Minimum Rates in the mining industry were made enforceable only by civil action for recovery of the sums due, at the suit of the aggrieved workers themselves—that is to say, as a private wrong—instead of by criminal proceedings instituted by the Inspectors, as an offence against the community. The Minimum Rates so fixed in 1912 for coal-mining became obsolete in the great rise of prices in the Great War, and have never been revised. The principle of a basic minimum, to be paid in all cases irrespective of the results of any piecework scale, had become so universally accepted that its legal prescription was apparently deemed unnecessary. The employers seem to have preferred to concede a Minimum by Collective Bargaining, whilst the miners have apparently not cared to appeal under the statute for new legal minima.

Minimum for the worst paid grade of workers, who were almost exclusively women, those under the amending Act were often directed to obtaining Legal Minimum Rates for men as well as women, and for workers in grades and at processes which could hardly be described as " sweated ".[1]

Then came, in 1920–1921, the sudden slump in prices, and a widespread industrial depression ; and with these a notable re-action in opinion, all along the line, alike among the employers and financiers, and among both Liberal and Conservative politicians. With regard to the legal regulation of wages, the outcome was the appointment in 1921 of a Departmental Committee to examine the working of the Acts of 1909 and 1918, before which em-ployers—very largely those in trades to which the Acts had not been applied—poured out their grievances against the Trade Boards. It is, however, significant that, even in this reaction, the great bulk of the employers did not ask for the repeal of the Acts, and disclaimed any objection to the prevention of " sweat-ing " by law. They confined their proposals to alterations of procedure which would, as they admitted, hinder any further extension of the activities of the Boards, and even hamper their effective working. The Committee itself, although it accepted the Trade Boards very coldly, did not recommend the repeal of the Acts ; and merely urged their restriction in scope. It " declared for a narrow interpretation " of the decision of the Legislature ; objected to any " coercive powers " being used to fix wages for " skilled work " ; and even deprecated the authori-tative fixing of piecework rates to any but outworkers.[2] The tone and spirit of this Committee, and the personal influence of its principal members, have been more effective than its specific recommendations. For seven successive years (although a Bill was introduced in 1923) the Government has, with regard to the Trade Board System, lacked courage to push through the reaction-

---

[1] With the fall in the value of money the wages fixed reached, in fact, in certain cases, as much as 2s. per hour for skilled operatives, whilst the piecework rates sometimes worked out at even higher earnings (Report of Committee to inquire into the Working and Effects of the Trade Boards Acts, Cd. 1645 of 1922, p. 26), or in the neighbourhood of £5 per week (these rates being fixed in the years of inflation, and being equal to about half these amounts at 1913 prices).

[2] Report of Departmental Committee to inquire into Working and Effects of the Trade Boards Acts (Cmd. 1645 of 1922) ; *Wages and the State*, by Mrs. E. M. Burns, 1926, p. 203.

ary legislation that the Federation of British Industries and other capitalist organisations have favoured. A more insidious method has been found in ministerial obstruction. The Ministry of Labour seems much less interested in maintaining and perfecting its part of the Framework of Prevention. The establishment of additional Trade Boards has been arrested ; the proposals of the Grocery Board have been refused sanction and the Board has been dissolved ; the glaringly inadequate staff of Inspectors has been kept down so that not more than ten per cent of the establishments subject to the Acts can be inspected each year, although it has been alleged that in as many as one-tenth, or, in some trades, even perhaps one-fifth of these establishments, breaches of the law are occurring; prosecutions are reduced to a minimum ; and when the Justices of the Peace occasionally deride the law and either refuse to impose penalties or neglect to require arrears of wages to be paid, the Government Department, whose duty it is to make the law effective, has not always found an effective answer.[1]

Here we must leave the story of the legal regulation of wages ; a story of which further chapters are plainly to come ! We may observe that there has been no explicit formulation of the idea of a National Minimum, common to all industries, below which no employer and no wage-earner is to be permitted to descend. This has no doubt been wise ; but it may be suggested that the time has come for the establishment of a Central Trade Board, as a tribunal of appeal, to which the Minister could refer any rate about which he is doubtful, and to which either side of any Board might appeal against its decision. In this way we might

---

[1] Report on the Administration of the Trade Boards Acts from January 1, 1921, to March 31, 1923 ; Reports of the Ministry of Labour for the years 1923, 1924, 1925 and 1925 ; *Wages and the State*, by Mrs. E. M. Burns, 1926. We may trace the reaction also in the great industry of agriculture, where a Legal Minimum Wage, to be determined by representative Local Boards, but with a statutory and instantly operative National Minimum of 25s. per week, formed part of the scheme of the Corn Production Act of 1920. This was, however, hastily repealed in 1921, on the slump in world prices. For the labourers there was substituted a compulsory scheme of conciliation, which, however, led to an agreed wage in only thirteen out of sixty-five districts, and failed to prevent a reduction of wages that was universally felt to be calamitous. In 1924, by the Agricultural Wages Act (which, in a greatly modified form, was passed by common consent), a Wage-Board system was again instituted, though with a minimum of coercive power ; and it may be said that even this simulacrum of a Legal Minimum Wage has at least prevented a further decline of wages.

safely advance towards a national and yet a flexible standard. The empirical groping of the Trade Boards System, as yet only nineteen years old in Britain, has been, like that of the successive Factory Acts, along the line of giving to each trade the wage-determination that the circumstances of the trade are thought to permit; of using the power of the law to raise the wage-practice of all the employers in each trade up to the level of the best and most progressive among them; and of bringing to bear, upon those who are backward in a continuous improvement of the conditions of labour, the public opinion of the trade as a whole in support of the successive innovations of its more enlightened members. The British Trade Boards have not committed themselves unreservedly to the Doctrine of the Living Wage, or to that of the Basic Rate, or to that of the " Wage that the Trade will bear "; but have, in characteristically British fashion, implicitly taken all three doctrines more or less into account in their wage-determinations. We may note also that the Trade Boards system is and has remained entirely different from that of the fixing of wages by Arbitration. What the British Trade Board determines, again in consonance with the British factory legislation, is only the Minimum to which all employers must conform. It confines itself simply to " blocking the downward way ". It does not prevent any employer from paying any worker, or paying all his workers, a wage in excess of the Minimum; and, equally, it does not forbid any wage-earner, or any class of wage-earners, from seeking a higher wage. Nor does the British Trade Board oblige any employer to engage or retain in employment any particular worker; or require any worker or any class of workers to accept engagement, or to continue in employment at any wage whatsoever. Finally, whilst the Trade Board system involves no prohibition of strikes or lock-outs, experience indicates that the determination of a Legal Minimum Wage by a Joint Board, and the Board's freedom at any time to vary the rate on the initiative of either the wage-earners or the employers, may well lessen the number and even mitigate the bitterness of such industrial dislocations. There is a change of attitude. The Trade Union finds a new form of corporate activity, and the Trade Union official exercises a new function, the advantage of which the whole body of members gradually recognise, namely, the preparation of cases for the

Board, and their advocacy before that tribunal ; an activity and a function which (supplemented by continuous research) may possibly forecast much of the future of vocational organisation.

The Old Way and the New

We can now appreciate the radical distinction between the two rival methods of dealing with the destitution arising in any industrial community suffering (to use the definition of the House of Lords Committee of 1890–1891) from the prevalence of " earnings barely sufficient to sustain existence, hours of labour such as make the lives of the worker periods of almost ceaseless toil, sanitary conditions injurious to the health of the persons employed and dangerous to the public ".

First the Poor Law method. The County Justices of the eighteenth century with their subordinate Overseers of the Poor, inspired by neighbourly benevolence or impelled by fear of revolution, not only took over the human wreckage—the crippled, the sick and the prematurely aged—but also systematically " made up " to subsistence level, out of public funds, the wages earned in particular parishes or paid by particular employers. This meant, in effect, subsidising the least efficient or the most grasping employers, who found themselves thereby freed from any obligation fully to maintain the persons whom they employed, or to provide for the rearing of a new generation to replace them. This form of industrial parasitism enabled the bad employer to put his product on the market on terms to which his rivals in the same trade were compelled to conform, or lose their customers. The adverse effect on the character and the conduct of the manual workers was even more obvious. The bread-winner discovered that he had no need to exert himself in his employment, seeing that, however little he earned, his weekly income would be automatically made up to the prescribed scale according to the number of his dependants. Even if he was dismissed from employment, and could find no other master, he and his family would be still maintained by the weekly dole out from the Poor Rate. Hence the discovery by Poor Law reformers, from Townsend and Malthus to Chalmers and Nassau Senior, that there was an artificially induced " disease of pauperism ", spreading from district to district and from industry to industry.

" Whole branches of manufactures ", declared the Poor Law Commissioners of 1832–1834, " may thus follow the course, not of coal-mines or streams, but of pauperism ; may flourish like the funguses that spring from corruption in consequence of the abuses which are ruining all the other interests of the places in which they are established, and cease to exist in the better administrated districts in consequence of the better adminis-tration." [1]

In short, the Poor Law method of dealing with destitution not only involved a constantly increasing drain on the National Income for unproductive purposes, but also, by this very expendi-ture, lessened the efficiency both of the employer and the employed, and actually diminished the output of industry.

The Common Rule

The rival method of Legal Regulation, stumbled upon unawares a century ago, and since continuously elaborated, which forms so large a part of what we have termed the Frame-work of Prevention, has had the very opposite effect alike on the employer and on the employed. Incidentally we may point out that this method of dealing with the misery of the poor involves the minimum of public expenditure : instead of subsidising the livelihood of millions of wage-earners in numerous industries, all that is called for from the rates and taxes are the expenses of the Trade Boards and the salaries of a few scores of inspectors ! When all the employers in a trade find themselves precluded, by the expedient of a legally enforced Common Rule, from worsen-ing the conditions of employment—when, for instance, they are prohibited from crowding an excessive number of operatives into their unventilated mills, and from keeping them at work for excessive hours ; or when they are prevented, by carefully elaborated and strictly enforced piece-work lists, from nibbling at wages—they are automatically impelled, in their competitive struggle with each other, to seek advantage by other methods. The downward way being blocked, they find an upward way. Experience proves that the legislative enforcement, upon all employers, of standard conditions of employment, positively stimulates the invention and adoption of improved processes of

[1] Report of the Poor Law Inquiry Commission, 1834, p. 76.

manufacture, and of a more intelligent (and therefore more economical) organisation of the industry. The beneficent effect of the Common Rule on the health and conduct of the wage-earners has been repeatedly demonstrated. Give the human being good ventilation, decent surroundings, adequate periods of rest and sufficient food, and, as with a well-kept horse, you can get much better work out of him. But the industrial worker is not a horse ; he is a human being, always seeking to adjust his conduct to surrounding circumstances. So long as the workers are " free " to take employment at any price, asking no question as to the length of the working day, and showing no troublesome fastidiousness as to the safety, sanitation and decency of the workplace, it positively suits the employer, if he can thereby get his work done at sufficiently low wages, to dispense with all references to character, and to turn a blind eye on coarse and brutal behaviour, and even on occasional lapses into disorder and dishonesty. The greatest scamp in London can get taken on as a casual labourer ; and the most dissolute woman can find a job in the workplace of some industry which has so far escaped the regulation and inspection of the Factory Acts. On the other hand, in a regulated industry, where every employer is compelled to equip his factory with all the comforts and conveniences and particular appliances prescribed by Parliamentary authority ; to pay to all his workers at least the prescribed standard rates of wage ; and to work regular, limited and relatively short hours, he finds himself impelled, whether he troubles about it or not, as the only way of recouping himself, to prefer workers of good character and regular habits, and to insist on a higher standard of order, honesty and skill.

Thus, the effect of a universally enforced compulsory minimum on the organisation of industry, like its effect on the manual labourer and the brain-working entrepreneur, is all in the direction of increasing efficiency. It in no way abolishes competition, or lessens its intensity. What it does is perpetually to stimulate the selection of the most efficient workmen, of the best-equipped employers, and of the most advantageous forms of industry. It in no way deteriorates any of the factors of production ; on the contrary, its influence acts as a constant incentive to the further improvement of the manual labourers, of the machinery, and of the organising ability used in the industry. Whether with regard to Labour or Capital, invention or organising ability, the mere existence of a uniform Common Rule in any industry, as contrasted with the irregularities of unrestricted individualism, automatically promotes alike the selection of the most efficient factors of production, and their combination in the most advanced types of industrial organisation. And these results are permanent and cumulative. However slight, within one generation, may be the immediately visible effect upon the character, skill or physical efficiency of the wage-earners or their employers ; however gradual may be the improvements in processes or in the organisation of the industry, these results endure, and go on intensifying themselves, so that the smallest steps forward effect, in time, an advance of the utmost importance.[1]

Finally, if further argument is necessary, we may find it in that sincerest form of flattery, the imitation and elaboration of this characteristically British sociological invention of factory legislation, forming part of a constraining Framework of Prevention, by all advanced industrial communities ; culminating, in 1919, in the " Labour clauses " of the international covenant embodied in the Treaty of Versailles, now being systematically applied by the International Labour Office of the League of Nations.[2]

Communistic Services

The blocking, by Legal Enactment, of the downward way in the competitive struggle constituted, as we have said, the foundation of the Framework of Prevention. The second, and more modern and more direct method of grappling with the problem of poverty in the midst of riches, is the provision, out of rates and taxes, of particular services and commodities open to use by all persons, whether propertied persons or not, who are found to be in need of them. This practical Communism—more extensive, we suspect, relatively to population and to needs, in the Britain than in the Russia of to-day—is " A House of Many

---

[1] The student will find the argument on this subject exhaustively set forth in *Industrial Democracy*, by S. and B. Webb, 1897, pp. 703-806 ; and, in another form, in *The Case for the Factory Acts*, edited by Mrs. Sidney Webb, with a preface by Mrs. Humphrey Ward, 1901, especially chapter i., " The Economics of Factory Legislation ".

[2] See *Draft Conventions and Recommendations adopted by the International Labour Conference at its Ten Sessions held 1919-27* (International Labour Office, 1928).

Mansions ", each mansion, with its staff of servants, being dedicated to a particular class of sufferers or potential sufferers : such as the physically sick, the mentally disordered or deficient, or the helpless infants ; the children to be rescued from illiteracy and ignorance ; and the aged, the widowed and the fatherless. We take separately each of these classes.[1]

The Prevention of Sickness

The application of a Framework of Prevention to the widespread and ever-recurring ill-health, which is so constant and so all-pervading a cause of destitution, arose out of a gradual realisation of the failure, as regards disease, of any merely penal attempt to " block the downward way ". Far into the eighteenth century the Government contented itself, so far as insanitary conditions were concerned, with seeking to punish, by the ancient and intricate legal procedure of presentment and prosecution at the Court Leet or in Quarter Sessions, all public nuisances—that is to say, conduct detrimental to the Public Health—a procedure which was slowly superseded by thousands of Local Act prohibitions, under pain of fine or imprisonment, in one place after another, of this or that practice injurious to the public. But mere punishment of bad behaviour proved hopelessly inadequate to stem the torrent of " nastiness " created by the massing of men and machinery in the rapidly expanding centres of industry. Some more direct and immediate course of action had to be found.

Municipal Services

We have described elsewhere the gradual rise, during the last half of the eighteenth century, among the well-to-do inhabitants of the towns, of voluntary associations of consumers for policing, paving, lighting, cleansing and generally improving the streets and squares in which they themselves resided. These voluntary organisations, maintained at first by subscriptions and voluntary rates, gradually obtained from Parliament powers of compulsory taxation, and were, in fact, the origin of most of the

---

[1] With the most difficult problem of all, the application of the principle to the able-bodied man or woman who fails to find employment by which to gain a livelihood, we deal in the following chapter, " Unemployment as a Disease of Modern Industry ".

modern municipal services.[1] Thus, during the nineteenth century, and especially after the Public Health Act of 1848,[2] we see developing a nation-wide network of Local Authorities providing sanitary services common to rich and poor, gradually becoming, in fact, substantially more and more uniform throughout each of the couple of thousands of separate jurisdictions established under the Municipal Corporations and Public Health Acts.

But there was a further stage. It gradually became apparent that, in this sphere, as indeed in others, uniformity was not equality. The circumstances of the citizens were in themselves so diverse that, quite apart from any theoretic conception of even-handed justice, the very protection of the public interest was found to call for a much closer adjustment of services to differing individual needs. Thus, the wealthy householder needed, almost as much as the slum dweller, a main drainage system, the paving, cleansing and lighting of the streets, and a

[1] For a description of these developments of voluntary associations of consumers into municipal Authorities see *English Local Government : Statutory Authorities for Special Purposes*, by S. and B. Webb ; more especially chap. iv. on " The Improvement Commissioners ", pp. 235, 349, and chap. vi., " The Emergence of the New Principles ", pp. 397, 486 ; and *Municipal Origins*, by F. H. Spencer, 1911.

[2] We may remind the student that the new municipal service of preventive medicine actually arose out of the investigations started by Edwin Chadwick whilst he was Poor Law Commissioner, 1832–1834, and secretary of the Poor Law Commissioners, 1834–1847, to which we made reference on p. 169. These investigations, carried out largely by Dr. Southwood Smith (*Dr. Southwood Smith*, by Mrs. C. L. Lewes, 1898, pp. 61-69), who had forerunners in such medical discoverers as Percival, Huxham, Ferrier and Haygarth in the preceding century, proved that sickness was one of the main causes of pauperism, and that much of this sickness was preventable. Hence Edwin Chadwick's long propaganda of " The Sanitary Idea ". The following quotation from the Report on the Sanitary Condition of the Labouring Population, 1842 (which he wrote) gives an indication of his argument, which (though he failed to foresee the discoveries of bacteriology) our present knowledge of the ravages of tuberculosis and " rheumatism " generally confirms : " The various forms of . . . disease, caused or aggravated, or propagated, chiefly amongst the labouring classes, by atmospheric impurities produced by decomposing animal and vegetable substances, by damp and filth and close and overcrowding dwellings, prevail . . . in every part of the Kingdom. . . . That such disease, wherever its attacks are frequent, is always found in connection with the physical circumstances above specified, and that where those circumstances are removed by drainage, proper cleansing, better ventilation, and other means of diminishing atmospheric impurity, the frequency and intensity of such disease is abated. . . . That the formation of all habits of cleanliness is obstructed by defective supplies of water. . . . That the annual loss of life from filth and bad sanitation is greater than the loss from death or wounds in any wars in which the country has been engaged in modern times."

good water supply ; but he needed in this department nothing more ; and too often, in the more backward municipalities, nothing else was done. The municipal supply of gas and electricity, and the municipal technical schools, are of greater advantage to those who can afford to pay for their use than to the very poorest class, which has often most need of them. Even the parks, the libraries, the museums, the art galleries, and the free concerts that the progressive municipalities gradually came to provide at the common cost, mainly profit those above the " Poverty Line ". To the slum dweller, the condition of the house drainage, the character of the water-closet accommodation, the laying-on of water to every floor, if not to every separate tenement, the state of the cisterns, the efficiency of the plumbing, the arrangements for removal of garbage, the position of the ashpit, the paving of the backyard, the ventilation, dryness and sunniness of each tenement, the extent to which it is allowed to be overcrowded, its periodical cleansing and disinfection, the internal provision for washing clothes, storing food, cooking meals, and bathing the children, and a hundred other things of that sort, are at least as important in maintaining health—whether of the slum dweller himself or of the city as a whole—as a street improvement or a main drainage system. In short, what is required is not, as some Radicals and Democrats long imagined, either uniformity or identity in the public services, but a further application in those services of the communist principle that was already supposed to govern the levying of the public revenue out of which the services were provided. " To each according to his needs " must be made to balance " from each according to his ability ". Very slowly and imperfectly even in the Britain of to-day, has this perfecting of the Framework of Prevention yet been accomplished. Only in some of the most advanced municipalities, and with regard to one or other of the communal services, has the Public Health Authority yet taken care that effectively as much shall be done for the sanitary environment of the slum dweller as for that of the villa resident, relatively to the particular needs of the well-to-do and of the poor. And in this respect the country is often as backward as the town, and even less conscious of the fact. In many a working-class village, inhabited almost entirely by miners, fishermen, quarrymen or labourers, even the main drainage and the common water supply are still lacking. Even in relatively well-administered towns there is still a tendency to do, at the public expense, only those things that are universally required, by rich and poor alike ; and to imagine that it is an ideally perfect administration which does them, in a measured way, uniformly all round. Yet it is plain that what is required, for municipal health, from the Framework of Prevention, is that no family, whatever its economic circumstances, shall be allowed to fall below the prescribed National Minimum of Civilised Life. Both the maximum of advantage to the citizens of all classes and the maximum of utility to the municipality as a corporate enterprise can be secured only by a maximum of effectiveness in the Framework of Prevention ; and this demands, it is clear, an adjustment of each service to the various needs of the individual householders, often inversely to their private wealth.

Very interesting has been the slow and gradual application of this idea of municipal provision according to need to the service of creating homes. During three-quarters of a century of legislation, from Lord Shaftesbury's Common Lodging Houses Act of 1851, down to the Rent Restriction Acts and extensive housing subsidies of 1921–1928, we see Parliament and the Local Government Board, and latterly the Ministry of Health, striving to erect a Framework of Prevention of the direst of all forms of urban destitution, inability to procure a sanitary residence. Penal statutes failed to prevent either overcrowding or the continuance, and even the increase, of slums. When capitalist enterprise would no longer produce dwellings at rents which the poorer wage-earners could pay ; and philanthropy, with all its utility in experimenting, plainly could not cope with the enormous need, the Local Authorities were empowered, by the long succession of Artisans' Dwellings Acts, to take the initiative and to erect the necessary buildings at the public expense ; but for a whole generation always on the tacit assumption that the rents charged would be high enough to cover, if not the annual value of the land, at least the interest on the cost of construction. Then came the War, the complete arrest of house-building, the soaring of the cost of repairs, and the rise of rents. Parliament could find, at first, no other expedient than a drastic legal prohibition of the raising of rents. Finally, under the successive Housing Acts of 1921–1927, the provision of dwellings for the wage-earning class, to the extent, already, of over one million houses, accommodating some five million inhabitants (one-ninth of the whole nation), at rents far below the aggregate cost for ground rent, interest, sinking fund and necessary repairs, has become recognised as a municipal obligation, from which there is no likelihood of the Local Authorities ever being relieved, and one needing to be heavily subsidised from the Exchequer. Attention is now (1928) being concentrated—inevitably with increasing dependence on public funds—not merely on completing the supply of houses for the annual increase of the population, but specially upon the provision of still cheaper dwellings for the poorest families, in substitution for the slums from which they are to be gradually dislodged.[1]

The Municipal Treatment of the Sick

So far we have dealt only with the application of Chadwick's " Sanitary Idea " to the improvement of the physical environment. But it soon became apparent to Chadwick, to his colleague Dr. Southwood Smith, and to Sir John Simon, that, for the Public Health, it was no less necessary to seek out the sufferers from disease themselves, with the view of providing for them, at the public expense, the medical treatment that they would otherwise fail to obtain. In 1834, it must be remembered, there was in no locality any treatment of disease out of public funds other than the meagre provision, meted out under deterrent conditions, by the Poor Law Medical Officers. To-day, alongside a greatly improved Poor Law Medical Service, we find, in every part of the Kingdom, an equally ubiquitous, at least as highly qualified, and practically as costly a service of public medical officers, maintained by the Local Health Authorities, with the

---

[1] The development of the municipal service of housing, together with " town planning ", may be most conveniently traced in such works as the *Handbook of Housing*, by B. S. Townroe, 1924 ; *Houses of the Workers*, by A. B. Sayle, 1924 ; *Housing*, by Harry Barnes, 1923; *The Housing of the Nation*, by F. E. Fremantle, 1927 ; and *London County Council Housing, a Record of Three Years' Work, 1922–5*, by C. B. Levita, 1925 ; *ibid., 1925–8*, by the same, 1928. See also *European Housing Problems since the War*, by the International Labour Office, 1924. For Town-Planning see *The Town-Planning Handbook*, by Richard Reiss, 1926 ; *The Law and Practice of Town-Planning*, by Sidney Davey and F. C. Minshull, 1923 ; *The Building of Satellite Towns*, by C. B. Purdom, 1925 ; *Town-Planning Theory and Practice*, by C. B. Purdom and others, 1925 ; and *Town-Planning in Practice*, by Raymond Unwin, 1924. *Ancient Town-Planning*, by F. Haverfield, 1913, has an interest of its own.

primary object of preventing alike the occurrence, the continuance, the recurrence and the spread of every preventable disease; and as we shall see, now a third even more extensive and costly medical service under the Health Insurance scheme. Throughout England and Wales, under the various Public Health Acts, the Municipal and District Councils are definitely charged (the latter with the co-operation of the Medical Officers of Health of the County Councils) with responsibility for the health of their several districts—that is to say, for the prevention of disease in all or any of the inhabitants thereof. To this end the Councils have been granted elaborate statutory powers, both of regulation and provision, some of them optional in character and others obligatory or compulsory. Accordingly, we find in England to-day nearly a couple of thousand Local Health Authorities, parallel with the Local Poor Law Authorities, actively engaged not only in extensive services of regulation and inspection, but also in the treatment and cure of the sufferers from whole ranges of diseases; amounting to the provision of medical attendance, medicine, and hospital maintenance for at least as many patients as are dealt with by the Poor Law Medical Service itself. And neither in legal theory nor in practical administration are the sick persons who are technically destitute excluded from the ministrations of the Public Health Authorities. We have, in fact, in every part of the Kingdom two Public Medical Authorities (including Insurance, indeed three) legally responsible for, and in many cases simultaneously treating, the same class of sick persons, sometimes for the same diseases. This costly duplication has arisen, partly from the gradual improvement of the Poor Law provision for the sick, but mainly from the almost continuous development of the Public Health work of the past half-century, of which we can here give only the briefest of summaries.[1]

[1] "In 1847 the Public Health connoted drainage, the removal of refuse, water supplies and the rudiments of epidemiology. But in 1927 it comprised work under a large number of Acts of Parliament concerned with personal health and disease, midwives and maternity, the vast field of infant and child welfare, a school medical service, the control of food supplies, sanatoria and hospitals, the conduct of clinics or dispensaries for tuberculosis and venereal diseases, the ways and means of dealing with an increasing variety of infectious diseases, rickets, nervous diseases, rheumatism, pneumonia and cancer, questions affecting the health of the worker in factories, industrial welfare as a whole, and the physical well-being of fourteen million insured persons in England and Wales" (*On the State of the Public Health :* Annual Report of

To take first the provision and maintenance of hospitals, we see the Local Health Authorities in 1928 maintaining out of the rates (including tuberculosis sanatoria) more than 900 public hospitals, having, in the aggregate, over 50,000 beds, being more than in all the endowed and voluntary hospitals put together. The municipal hospitals, the importance of which in the Framework of Prevention is only imperfectly indicated by their common designation of " Isolation Hospitals ", vary in size and elaboration from the cottage or shed with two or three beds, set aside for an occasional smallpox patient, up to such an institution as the Liverpool City Hospital, divided into seven distinct sections in as many different parts of the city, having altogether about 1000 beds, served by nearly a score of salaried doctors, half of whom are resident, and treating annually some 5000 patients for an average period of nearly eight weeks.[1] Such an institution is typical of what is being done, on a scale varying with the population, in all the great County Boroughs. In London the chief Hospital Authority is the Metropolitan Asylums Board, which has long ceased to have any but nominal connection with the Poor Law, and which, in its score of institutions, practically receives gratuitously any case recommended by any medical practitioner, irrespective of the patient's affluence. With few exceptions these Public Health institutions, whether in London or elsewhere, were originally established to provide for a limited number of diseases (namely, " fever cases ", chiefly smallpox, enteric and scarlet fever) ; but they are mostly under no such

---

Chief Medical Officer of Ministry of Health for the year 1927 (1928), p. 247). For further and more detailed accounts of the Public Health services, the student will refer to the Annual Reports of the Local Government Board down to 1918–1919, and thereafter those of the Ministry of Health, in both cases particularly the Reports of the Medical Officer, from 1908 to 1918, Sir Arthur Newsholme ; from 1919 the Annual Reports of the Chief Medical Officer of the Ministry of Health and of the Board of Education (Sir George Newman) ; *Memorandum in Medical Education in England*, by Sir George Newman, 1918, and the same officer's *Outline of the Practice of Preventive Medicine*, 1926 edition ; such descriptive volumes as *The Story of English Public Health*, by Sir Malcolm Morris, 1919 ; *The Ministry of Health*, 1925, and *The Evolution of Preventive Medicine*, 1927, both by Sir Arthur Newsholme ; and *Health Services and the Public*, by Dr. Stella Churchill, 1928 ; together with the Annual Reports of the Medical Officers of Health of the County Boroughs, of the Urban and Rural Sanitary Districts, and of the County Councils, an extensive collection of which will be found in the British Library of Economic and Political Science at the London School of Economics.

[1] See Report on the Health of the City of Liverpool during 1926 by the Medical Officer of Health (Dr. A. A. Mussen).

statutory limitation, and during the last few decades their range has steadily widened. They usually deal with diphtheria, and are available for the sporadic cases of typhus, cholera, yellow fever or plague ; in most towns of any size they accept cases of puerperal fever, or serious erysipelas ; here and there, at one or other time, children are admitted with chicken-pox, whooping-cough or measles, as well as scabies and pediculosis. In London whole classes of other suffering children are thus received, maintained and treated. Great work is being done for crippled children and for the blind. The after-consequences of poliomyelitis and epidemic encephalitis are treated. But the greatest development has been in the provision for tuberculosis, for which, by 1928 (in addition to wards in the above-mentioned institutions), no few than 160 special sanatoria and hospitals with 11,772 beds and 442 dispensaries for out-patients has been provided by Public Health Authorities.[1]

What might, in Poor Law parlance, be termed the Outdoor Medical Service of the Public Health Authorities has developed less systematically than its institutional provision. Throughout the Kingdom there is the characteristic preventive service, steadily widening in its range, of notification and registration of cases, inspection and arrangements as to isolation, the treatment of " contacts ", and the systematic disinfection of premises. From time to time, in this place or that, there is a public and gratuitous distribution, to all willing to accept it, of drugs and vaccines and serums : sometimes bottles of diarrhœa mixture, more frequently antitoxin serum in diphtheritic cases, for the universal injection of which, by any local medical practitioner, the Local Health Authority will (as the Fenton Urban District Council did in 1905) occasionally pay a fee. For the treatment of certain skin diseases (such as scabies and pediculosis), " baths

[1] On the State of the Public Health : Annual Report of the Chief Medical Officer of the Ministry of Health for the year 1926, p. 124.

It is only the Isolation Hospitals Act of 1893, permitting combinations of Public Health Authorities to establish joint hospitals for infectious diseases, that limits action to such diseases. The Public Health Acts do not prescribe the kind of disease to be treated in the hospitals that they authorise. In 1900 the Barry Urban District Council, with the express sanction of the L.G.B., established a municipal hospital exclusively for non-infectious cases, and intended principally for accidents and urgent surgical cases. The Widnes Urban District Council was definitely informed by the L.G.B. that it was free to start an accident hospital, and did so (*The State and the Doctor*, by S. and B. Webb, 1910, pp. 161, 170, 245).

and disinfecting chambers " are (as by the Marylebone Borough Council) gratuitously provided for the sufferers ; and rooms full of clothing, bedding, furniture are nearly everywhere gratuitously purified. Moreover, most Local Health Authorities now maintain a varied staff for domiciliary attendance, from the salaried Health Visitors now becoming universal in towns ; through the Home Nurses employed (as for particular classes of cases by the Brighton Town Council and the Barry Urban District Council, and by the Worcestershire County Council for all kinds of cases), and the Women Inspectors of the Liverpool Health Committee who, amid a wide range of other duties, " visit children suffering from ringworm, sore eyes, sore heads, skin diseases, etc." [1] This brings us up against the medical treatment of the child in attendance at school, with which we deal subsequently as a remarkable expansion of the education service.

The Campaign for Infant Welfare

Perhaps the most remarkable extension of the Framework of Prevention has been the creation, almost within a single decade, of a nation - wide organisation for the protection, against all injurious influences, of the 8·8 per cent of the population who are under five years of age. With this campaign for Infant Welfare, which may be said to have been started in 1900, the names of Sir George Newman and Sir Arthur Newsholme will always be specially associated. It is instructive to recall the successive stages in this development. Thirty years ago there was, it may almost be said, no technique of Infant Welfare protection. If the reformers had been required to state what was their plan of prevention they could not have convinced the public. Beginning with attempts to understand why there had been, during the preceding generation, little, if any, decline in the infantile death-rate, and with statistical investigations into its principal causes, the localities in which the several diseases were most prevalent, and the ages at which they proved most fatal, the first success of the campaign, and the necessary prerequisite of any public action, was the focussing of attention upon the

---

[1] Annual Report of the Medical Officer of Health for Liverpool, 1905, p. 89 ; Report on the Health of the City of Liverpool during 1926 by the Medical Officer of Health, 1927, pp. 104-109.

problem of child disease and child mortality. It had for some time been realised by various public health workers that the ordinary measures of environmental hygiene, which had so successfully been applied in other fields of preventive endeavour, were inadequate to afford effective safeguards for infant life. It had long been known that infant mortality was largely due to defective methods of infant feeding, and a considerable number of Medical Officers of Health had sought to teach better methods by the issue of advisory leaflets on infant care. In a few towns this had been supplemented by health visitation, notably in Manchester, where Health Visitors were at work as long ago as the eighties. These, however, were tentative efforts, and the impetus to the new movement began in France, where the declining birth-rate had forced the preservation of infant life to be regarded as a matter of national importance. The Infant Welfare Centre, which constitutes the most important feature of the modern preventive methods, originated in the " Consultation des Nourrissons " which Professor Herrgott founded at the Nancy Maternity Hospital in 1890, and the similar institutions which, in a more developed form, were founded a few years later in Paris by Professor Budin. The chief features of these institutions were the periodical medical supervision of the infants and the supply of suitably prepared food in cases in which artificial food was necessary. In 1899 the St. Helens Corporation, on the advice of a deputation that had studied French methods on the spot, opened an Infants Milk Depot, run on lines somewhat similar to the French institutions, from which the modern Infant Welfare Centre gradually developed. In 1906 public attention to the question was much stimulated by the first National Conference on the Prevention of Infant Mortality, which was held in that year under the presidency of Mr. John Burns, who did much to give the whole movement a wide publicity. In that year also the Huddersfield Corporation took an important step forward by obtaining power in a Local Act to require the notification, within thirty-six hours, of every birth that took place in the Borough. In the following year the Notification of Births Act permitted all Local Health Authorities to require a like immediate report of every birth—such early notification being made universally obligatory throughout the Kingdom by an amending statute in 1915—and also empowered them to make arrangements, in supplement of any already initiated by voluntary agencies, for the control of infant and child mortality. From 1914 onward this work has been encouraged by Grants in Aid distributed by the Ministry of Health. Little noticed by the public, the Maternity and Child Welfare Act, 1918, empowered all Local Health Authorities to make whatever arrangements might be sanctioned by the Minister of Health for attending to the health of expectant and nursing mothers, and of children under the age of five not in attendance at schools recognised by the Board of Education ; [1] making it obligatory, moreover, that if this work was undertaken, it should be directed by a separate Maternity and Child Welfare Committee. The " arrangements " thus made in the more progressive boroughs and counties are reported (1928) to be producing an almost miraculous change in the foundations of national health.

In the comprehensive campaign against infantile impairment, which has been organised within the last decade, the results of all the investigations and experiments have been utilised and combined. The Local Health Authorities begin with ante-natal supervision advice and treatment, for which there are now (in addition to nearly 300 voluntary centres) nearly 500 Municipal Centres, with a few special V.D. Centres, working in close conjunction with three score municipal (and as many more voluntary, mostly grant-aided) Maternity Homes and Hospitals, having, in the aggregate, over 2000 beds ; and occasionally (as at Birkenhead) with payment in suitable cases, of the whole or part of the midwife's fee for domiciliary attendance, and provision of sterilised outfits from Public Health funds. The most extensive development, however, has been in Infant Welfare Centres, of which there are now, besides over 800 under voluntary Committees, nearly all grant-aided), over 600 under County Councils, and nearly 900 under Town or District Councils. Whilst not normally supplying medical treatment beyond hygienic advice, a considerable proportion of these Centres have arrangements for dental treatment, and some for special treatment of sufferers from rickets and other ailments, a policy strongly encouraged by the Ministry of Health. These Centres are linked up by the widespread organisation of Health Visitors already referred to,

[1] 7 Edward VII. c. 40, 1907 ; 5 and 6 George V. c. 64 ; 8 and 9 George V. c. 29.

of whom, some whole-time and some part-time, there are now nearly 4000 at work ; and assisted by special "Babies' Hospitals", of which nearly a dozen are already established by Town or District Councils, with about as many more under voluntary committees.

In some of the most popular cities, the Health Visitor's services are accepted, to a greater or lesser extent, in 85 per cent of the births ; and as many as one-third of all the babies in the city are brought regularly to be seen and weighed at the Centres. An important part of the service of the Centres and of the Health Visitors, in many large towns (notably Liverpool) and in some counties (notably Durham) is the distribution of sterilised milk to expectant and nursing mothers, and to infants up to two years old, at a specially low price (varying from 1d. to 9d. per week, but mostly from 2d. to 3d.) fixed according to the circumstances of each family ; or, when necessary in exceptional cases, even gratuitously. In Liverpool, during 1926, nearly 18,000 mothers and infants were thus aided, for periods of two to eight weeks, about 5000 being at any one time on the books.[1] In the County of Durham, during the prolonged stoppage of coal-mining in 1926, nearly £100,000 worth of milk was thus supplied, mostly free of charge ; with the result that, in spite of the severe distress, the infantile mortality throughout the country continued to decrease.

In scarcely any other part of the Framework of Prevention can proof so convincing be given of its efficacy as in this case. In the decade 1891–1900 the average number of deaths under one year per thousand births was 153, whilst the average for the five years 1921–1925 was only 76, and that for the year 1925–1926 only 70 per thousand births. The death-rate had been, in a single generation, halved, with a great, though an incalculable, diminution of infantile disease.

The Campaign against Venereal Disease

We have still to mention another campaign of the Public Health Service, the establishment and quick development of the gratuitous and confidential treatment of Venereal Disease, adopted on the recommendation of a Royal Commission of 1916

---

[1] Report on the Health of the City of Liverpool during 1926 by the Medical Officer of Health (Dr. A. A. Mussen), 1927, pp. 102-104.

as the only effective way of dealing with what has been shown to be the cause of so many serious disabilities of a large proportion of the hospital, asylum and workhouse population. The proposals of this Commission, we are authoritatively told, constituted " a bold and far-reaching administrative scheme by which sufferers from these diseases might be cured and rendered non-infective. It was based upon the principle of rendering the necessarily costly means of diagnosis and treatment available, free of charge, to all. It assumed that, venereal disease once acquired, whether innocently or guiltily, it is both the duty and the interest of the State to see that it is promptly and effectually treated, so that the patient may cease to be a source of infection, may not be incapacitated from taking his due part in the nation's work, and may not become a charge upon the public funds. The Government was therefore advised to urge the local authorities to provide centres for gratuitous diagnosis and treatment throughout the land and to charge 75 per cent of the cost to the Exchequer, the remaining 25 per cent to fall upon the local rates. . . ." [1]

It is in this matter of Venereal Disease that the nation has, down to 1928, gone furthest in perfecting the Framework of Prevention. In contrast with nearly all the other provisions in this field, the establishment of V.D. Centres was made at once obligatory (by Order under the Public Health Acts, 1875 and 1913) on all Counties and County Boroughs. The principle of free medical treatment at the public expense for all comers, irrespective of race or nationality, age, domicile, residence, " place of

[1] *The Story of English Public Health*, by Sir Malcolm Morris, 1919, pp. 135-143 ; Report of Royal Commission on Venereal Disease, 1916 ; Annual Reports of the Medical Officer of the Ministry of Health since 1919. In some districts the travelling expenses are paid to and from the V.D. centre, so as to enable the very poorest person to come under treatment.

We have reason to believe that it was the adoption in 1916 of gratuitous treatment without " stigma of pauperism ", for the most personally discreditable of diseases, as indispensable in the interest of Public Health, that finally converted the Chairman of the Poor Law Commission of 1905-1909, who had been a member of the Venereal Diseases Commission, to the policy of also withdrawing from the Poor Law the whole of the treatment of the sick, the vast majority of whom suffer from diseases not personally discreditable to them. When in 1917-1918, Lord George Hamilton took part in the deliberations of the Local Government Sub-Committee of the Reconstruction Committee under Sir Donald Maclean, which considered, after nine years' interval, both the Majority and Minority Reports of the Poor Law Commission, he (together with Sir Samuel Provis) cordially assented to the complete supersession of the Poor Law administration by the other and newer branches of administration described in this chapter.

settlement ", or degree of affluence, was (with the assent, be it noted, of the British Medical Association) frankly and completely adopted—the only case in which, down to 1928, this can be said. Any person may apply for, and claim as of right, whatever treatment, whether institutional or as an out-patient, may be prescribed for him, at any Centre to which he chooses to apply. Following on the widely diffused establishment of such free Centres, the Local Government Board secured, in 1917, the passing of the Venereal Disease Act, making it illegal for anyone but a duly qualified medical practitioner to prescribe or treat for reward any case of venereal disease ; and prohibiting any public notices or announcements of quack treatments or remedies.[1]

The Cabinet, at the instance of the Local Government Board in March 1916, when Viscount Long was President and Sir Arthur Newsholme Medical Officer, took a bold step in adopting this far-reaching proposal, with the effect that, within a single decade, no fewer than 190 Venereal Disease centres have been established, now dealing gratuitously every year with over 80,000 new cases, with markedly successful results.[2]

The Characteristics of the Public Health Authority's Treatment of Disease

All treatment by the Public Health Authority has for its object, not the relief of immediate suffering, but the prevention of disease. What is sometimes forgotten is that this involves the treatment and cure of existing diseases in individual patients, if only because, as one Medical Officer of Health tersely puts it, " the cure of a sick person tends to prevent disease in that person ". But, unlike Poor Law medical practice, even of the best type, it involves much more. In the obviously communicable diseases, such as plague, cholera and typhus, smallpox, scarlet fever and enteric, it involves the securing of complete isolation of the patient, and even the isolation and medical observation of healthy " contacts ", sometimes with payments to them for their

---

[1] 7 and 8 George V. c. 21 ; *The Ministry of Health*, by Sir Arthur Newsholme, 1925, pp. 234-240. The absolute prohibition of practice by any but qualified persons has been applied, with some appropriate exceptions, also to midwifery and dentistry.

[2] *On the State of the Public Health :* Annual Report of the Chief Medical Officer of the Ministry of Health for the year 1926 (1927), pp. 140-147.

maintenance when prevented from working. In other infective cases, such as phthisis, trachoma, and chronic ear, throat and skin affections and venereal disease, it involves the education of the patient in a method of living calculated to minimise the recurrence or spread of the disease. But the special sphere of the Public Health Authority in the treatment of disease is not that of infectious or contagious but of *preventable* disease. It was, indeed, not to stop the spread of disease from individual to individual, but to prevent its arising from damp and filth, that the Poor Law Commissioners first made their Public Health investigations, and importuned the Government to give the Local Authorities Public Health powers. It was preventable disease which Chadwick found to be so great a cause of unnecessary pauperism. It was for the reduction to a minimum of this preventable disease that the Public Health Act of 1848 was passed ; and it is to preventable disease, whether communicable or not, that the powers and duties of Public Health Authorities to-day extend. The accident of the widely published advance of bacteriological science since 1880 has tended unduly to concentrate attention on the zymotic diseases, which, taken altogether, cause only 11 per cent of the deaths, and account, probably, for only a twentieth or a thirtieth of the persons ill at any one time. But as the Medical Officer of Health for Coventry remarks : " It is a great mistake to suppose that it is only infectious diseases that are preventable ". "Our activity as health officers", writes another Medical Officer of Health, " cannot be limited to the infectious diseases. There are indeed greater opportunities of preventing illness among the non-infectious ailments, *e.g.* ailments of the digestive system, almost, than in the case of infectious illnesses." To the long list of common infective diseases already given, we must add as plainly preventable : " Infectious eye diseases, such as conjunctivitis in most of its forms (trachoma, etc.) ; infectious ear diseases (abscesses, etc.) ; infectious nose and throat diseases ; abscesses of all kinds not due to tuberculosis ; parasitic skin diseases. . . . To these again we may add, as due to immediate environment, and preventable, the occupational (non-infectious) diseases ; chronic arsenical poisoning, chronic lead poisoning, chronic phosphorus poisoning, mercury poisoning, coal-miner's lung, steel-grinder's lung, the diseases due to dusty occupations, skin diseases, lung diseases, bowel diseases, and many others due

to special manufactures, as rubber works, chemical works, dry
cleaning, rag works, etc. etc. . . . Similar reasoning can be
legitimately applied to chronic bronchitis, which can usually be
prevented if the acute stage is properly treated ; to catarrhal
pneumonia, which is often the precursor of phthisis ; to the
heart diseases that are due to acute rheumatism ; to chronic
kidney disease, which often follows neglect of acute kidney
disease ; to some forms of cancer, which are curable if operation
is early enough."

Besides the preventable diseases brought about by environment, and by neglect of acute diseases, there are those now
recognised to be caused by bad hygienic habits of the individual
himself.   " The chief factor in disease production ", says Sir
George Newman, " is personal rather than external."   To quote
the epigram of a distinguished doctor : " We have pretty well
removed the filth from outside the human body "—unfortunately
a premature and far too optimistic a judgment [1]—" what we have
now to do in order to lower the death-rate is to remove the filth
from the inside ".   "Diseases spread not alone by infection and
contagion ", says another Medical Officer of Health.   " The
habits and practices of people are responsible in even greater
measure for the continuance of diseases.   These cannot be com-
bated by the popular panacea of a bottle of medicine.   It may
be said, in fact, that the Public Health method of treatment is
superior to that of the Poor Law because it is largely educative
and for the future."   Nor is this merely a matter of cleanly
living and the avoidance of excess.   The prevention of disease,
which, as the Medical Officer of Health always remembers, " is
far more effective and infinitely less costly than the treatment
of disease that is accrued, may depend on the adoption of a
particular mode of life.   Incipient phthisis, in particular, may
be thus curable ".   "Such conditions as diabetes, granular kidney
and aneurism ", says another authority, " are not necessarily
diseases.   If the condition is recognised early, and the patient
adopts the proper regimen, the symptoms which really constitute
the disease may be postponed for a considerable period."   We
come even to the study of individual proclivity or diathesis, as

---

[1] " There is ", states an eminent authority, " still an immense amount of
work to be done in the field of environmental hygiene : we must add personal
hygiene, not substitute the one for the other."

a branch of preventive medicine. " Thousands, nay, hundreds of thousands, of young men and women with hereditary or acquired tendencies to various diseases, are, *owing to want of knowledge*, brought up, enter upon occupations, and lead modes of life which inevitably result in disease and early death."

Thus the special characteristic of the treatment of disease by the Public Health Authority is, not to wait until the patient is so ill that he is driven to apply either by destitution or by collapse, but positively to search out every case, even in its most incipient stage. " An active Medical Officer of Health ", sums up one of them, " attempts anything and everything which promises to reduce death-rates or to prevent disease." The one recurring note of all the statements of the Medical Officers of Health is the vital importance of " early diagnosis ". " I am satisfied ", writes Sir George Newman, " that much illness is prolonged quite unnecessarily, and that there is a lamentable and disastrous amount of failure to deal with the *beginnings of disease*. Neglect of such things leads to mortality more than any other factors." The disastrous effects of failure to seek early treatment, in consumption, diphtheria and other diseases, are continually coming to the notice of medical men. It is a necessary condition of the Public Health medical service that there must be no delay in searching out and discovering all the cases ; there must be no delay in securing the necessary isolation ; there must be no delay in applying the necessary treatment ; there must be no delay in the adoption of the appropriate hygienic habits. It is the consciousness of the importance of this " early diagnosis ", the immense superiority in attractiveness of the incipient over the advanced " case ", the overwhelming sense of the dire calamities that may come from a single " missed case ", that mark the characteristic machinery of the Public Health Medical Service—its notification ; its birth, death and case visitation ; its bacteriological examinations ; its school intimations ; its house-to-house visitations ; its domiciliary disinfection ; its medical observation of " contacts ", and its prolonged domiciliary supervision of " recoveries " and patients discharged from institutions in order to detect the " return case ".

This all-pervading principle of " early diagnosis " and immediate treatment has important corollaries. The existence of preventable or communicable disease is of equal importance to the Medical Officer of Health, whether it is among the rich or among the poor. " In all this ", to use the words of the Royal Commission on Hospitals in 1882, " we suggest no distinction between rich and poor, pauper and non-pauper cases, except that between persons who can and those who cannot be isolated at their homes or in some place approved by the proper Authorities —an exception which, of course, will not extend to the official notification of disease. In default of which isolation the Hospital Authority (however constituted) should, we conceive, be bound and empowered to remove to the hospital every patient capable of removal without risk to life or serious aggravation of the disease." " The Public Health Acts ", says a high authority, " are not conditioned in their operation by any such irrelevant consideration as the possible patient's poverty or destitution. The authorities are bound to do what is possible to prevent disease whatever be the economic condition." Equally irrelevant to them must necessarily be the assumed Poor Law distinction between indoor and outdoor treatment which always implies some superiority in the indoor over the outdoor, as applying a deterrent test. And it is just because the Medical Officer of Health aims at dealing with every case in its incipient stage— even before the patient himself, or his family, recognises that he is ill, and long before the drug or the knife becomes requisite— that we find, in the public health curative treatment, the largest part played by hygienic advice, so that some of the more naïve witnesses before the Poor Law Commissioners of 1905–1909 declared that it was not medical treatment at all !

No " Pauperisation "

Passing from the characteristics of the Public Health Medical Service to its effects on its patients, there comes to light an interesting contrast with the Poor Law Medical Service. It was strongly urged upon the Poor Law Commission of 1905–1909 that Poor Law medical relief is not merely " deterrent " but that, when accepted, it breaks down the independence of the recipient and leads him frequently to become a chronic pauper. It is alleged that the labourer who begins by asking the Relieving Officer for a Midwifery Order or for medical attendance on his ailing infant is easily led on to apply for a Medical Order for himself and presently for Outdoor Relief. No such allegation is made with regard to submission to medical treatment by the Public Health Authority. On the contrary, there is absolute uniformity of testimony, from all sorts of witnesses in all parts of the country, that the medical attendance and medicine of the Public Health Department has no pauperising tendency. The fever-stricken patient who is removed to the isolation hospital, or the mother who receives hygienic advice about her infant, are not thereby induced to find their way to the Poor Law. Indeed, it has been repeatedly given in evidence by witnesses with practical experience that the essential characteristic of the Public Health Medical Service—that it is rendered in the interest of the community and not in order merely to relieve the suffering of the individual—actually creates in the recipient an increased feeling of personal obligation, and even a new sense of social responsibility. This sense of obligation is, we are informed, seen in a new responsibility as to not creating nuisances or infecting relations and neighbours ; in a deliberate intention to remain healthy, and therefore to control physical impulses ; and in an altogether heightened parental responsibility in the matter of the conscientious fulfilment of the daily, even the hourly, details of family régime necessary for the rearing of the infant or the recovery of the invalid. The very aim of sanitarians is to train the people to better habits of life. The main object of health visiting is to make the people understand that prevention is better than cure. It has, indeed, been strongly urged that actual experience of Public Health administration indicates that universal medical inspection and hygienic advice, and the offer of institutional treatment to those found out of health, might have as bracing an effect on personal character, by imposing a new standard of physical self-control, as it would have on corporeal health. Nor is this a mere figment of the imagination. " The form in which medical aid would be given ", stated Sir Arthur Newsholme, later principal Medical Officer of the Local Government Board, in the light of his actual experience with the hundreds of phthisical patients whom he had treated, " would be such as constantly to enforce on the minds of the patients their duty to the community and to themselves in matters of health. Though they would pay nothing, they would not be merely passive recipients of advice and attention. The influence of the doctor would demand from them habits of life and even sacrifices of personal taste in the interest of the health of the community, their families and themselves, which would leave them conscious of a sensible discharge of duty in return for the attention which they received. The discipline of responsibility into which the system would educate them should, in my judgment, suffice to avoid the loss of self-respect liable to arise from the merely passive receipt of gifts ; and it would introduce into the national life an attitude towards matters of personal health that would have an indirect influence on conduct while directly restricting disease."

The Public Treatment of the Mentally Disordered or Defective

It was the inability of the Poor Law Authorities of the several parishes to make any proper provision for persons of unsound mind that, as we have mentioned,[1] led, over a century ago, to the duty of establishing lunatic asylums being placed upon the County Authorities. It is needless here to describe the successive developments of this service, for which the County and County Borough Councils that are Lunacy Authorities now maintain 97 asylums, having, in 1926, 110,701 inmates, the great majority of them being paid for, as paupers (with the help of a Grant in Aid from the Exchequer of 4s. per person per week, and also of such sums as can be recovered from the relatives), by the Poor Law Unions to which they are chargeable.[2] These payments by the Boards of Guardians cover only the actual cost of maintenance in the asylums, at weekly rates now averaging about 22s. per patient ; and they leave as a charge upon the County or County Borough funds not only the interest and sinking fund on the loans incurred for capital expenditure, but also the maintenance of those patients whose Union of settlement cannot be ascertained. Thus, the total net charge upon the County and County Borough Councils for the lunacy service

---

[1] *The Old Poor Law*, 1927, p. 303.

[2] In addition there must be mentioned the provision made by the Metropolitan Asylums Board for idiots down to the lowest grade of intelligence. This, like the corresponding Metropolitan provision of Isolation Hospitals, though charged to the Poor Rates of the Metropolitan Unions, has passed from being a Poor Law service to becoming essentially a Public Health service, equalised throughout the Metropolis through the Common Poor Fund.

exceeds three million pounds per annum ; or not far short of that defrayed from the Poor Rate.

From our present standpoint, what is interesting is the development of this lunacy service out of a mere Framework of Repression of the lunatic as a common nuisance, if not a public danger, when he was merely, in the words of the Act of 1743, " to be kept safely locked up in some secure place, and if such Justices find it necessary, to be there chained " ; through a period when considerations of humanity led to these unfortunate prisoners being treated kindly, and sometimes even indulgently, but always on the assumption that their state was incurable and that their detention would be lifelong ; into the modern phase, scarcely a generation old, when the asylums are regarded and even described as " mental hospitals ", into which patients pass when " the world is too much " for their unstable mental equilibrium, and from which a steadily increasing proportion of them (commonly between 20 to 30 per cent of the admissions) emerge, after a longer or shorter course of curative treatment, restored to mental convalescence, and often to complete recovery of mental health. Indeed, one of the most significant features of the new conception of mental hospitals has been the organisation and development of investigation and research into the causation of all the various kinds of mental disorder, and into the regimen and curative treatment by which they can be prevented.

We see the same idea in the extension of the provision from cases of actual lunacy to those of that degree of mental deficiency which is now defined as feeble-mindedness. The victims of a congenital mental deficiency had long been a constant source of trouble and expense to the Poor Law Authorities. Unable to earn a complete subsistence, and often incapable of retaining any situation—the women, moreover, becoming the mothers of successive illegitimate children, who too frequently became lifelong paupers—these " morons " have, for generation after generation, steadily recruited, not merely the gaol population but also the great army of the destitute and of those chargeable to the Poor Rate. In 1904 a Royal Commission recommended that all those who could be certified to be mentally defective in the prescribed sense should be cut completely out of the Poor Law administration, which could only relieve their destitution ; and that they should be given not only maintenance and protection, but also the best possible treatment for their mental improvement and training, irrespective of whether or not they were destitute, under the direction of a distinct Central Department, the Board of Control, by those County and County Borough Councils that were Lunacy Authorities. What was recommended, in short, was that these unhappy victims should have the benefit of a Framework of Prevention, not only against their falling into destitution, but also against the worsening of their mental state, together with whatever ameliorative or remedial treatment, and whatever kind or degree of educational training, might prove practicable in each case.[1]

The Mental Deficiency Act of 1913, proceeding on the lines of the Commission's Report, placed this new duty of providing for what was then estimated to number one per cent of the whole population, or between four and five hundred thousand persons of either sex, and of all ages—the great majority of them being, at one or other period in their lives, either in receipt of Poor Relief, or existing precariously near to destitution—upon the County and County Borough Councils. Unfortunately, the years of war that ensued, and the years of financial parsimony that have followed, have prevented more being done, in the execution of this duty, than the provision of residential accommodation for the cases deemed to be urgent. It is estimated that the feeble-minded still constitute at least one-fourth of the total inmates of the Workhouses.

Entanglement with Poor Law

Unfortunately, too, the whole of the public provision for the mentally disordered and the mentally defective is hampered, and its efficacy as a Framework of Prevention of both destitution and pauperism injuriously affected, by its being still entangled in the Poor Law administration. The person found at large as a lunatic, or in trouble as a mentally defective, or merely wandering in a state of destitution, is, in the vast majority of cases, brought to the Workhouse, and thus straightaway made a pauper. He or she is detained in the " Observation Ward " (if the institution has such a place) under conditions, and in the custody of attendants, usually unsuited to such cases. Within a fortnight,

[1] Report of Royal Commission on Mental Deficiency, 1904.

two doctors and a Justice of the Peace certify such of the inmates
of the Observation Ward, or of the Workhouse itself, as can be
brought within the legal definition of " being of unsound mind " ;
and these are, or ought to be, transferred to a proper mental
hospital for appropriate treatment. But those who are merely
feeble-minded, and in many Unions also those certified lunatics
who are not dangerous or troublesome, are still retained in the
Workhouse, where they are, as we have already described, in
nearly all cases, neither separated from the other inmates, nor
given either the curative or remedial treatment, or the educational training that Parliament and the Board of Control have
intended them to receive. This is partly because the majority
of Poor Law Guardians resent having to pay the full charge for
maintenance, perhaps 22s. per week, made by the County or
County Borough Council ; and partly, as the Poor Law Commission was informed, because, in the absence of other able-
bodied men and women in the Workhouse of to-day, the labour
of the able-bodied lunatics and mentally deficients can be conveniently applied to the domestic service of the institution.[1]
The Royal Commission on Lunacy in 1926 emphatically demanded
the complete and entire " extrication " from the Poor Law administration not merely, as the Mental Deficiency Commission
had recommended in 1904, of the feeble-minded, but also of all
" persons of unsound mind " ; and their treatment exclusively
by the local Lunacy Authorities, on lines analogous to those
followed with regard to the sick by the Public Health authorities.[2]

[1] " We think we are not wrong," observed the Minority Commissioners,
" in attributing the retention of these 60,000 mentally defective persons in
the Workhouses to the fact that their labour is found useful—in the small rural
workhouses, indeed, actually indispensable to their administration on present
lines. We have ourselves been informed, in Workhouse after Workhouse,
that they had to rely on the imbeciles for practically all the manual work of
the establishment. We gather that it was principally on this ground that the
Local Government Board for England and Wales did not issue an Order requiring
compliance with the recommendation of the House of Commons Committee of
1899, and the removal of all imbeciles from the Workhouses (Q. 106). The
President seems to have been advised that, without the mentally defective
women in particular, the General Mixed Workhouses in the rural Unions could
not be carried on. " If ", said an objector, " you remove the feeble-minded
women from the Workhouse, who will do the scrubbing ? " (Q. 887). (Minority
Report of Poor Law Commission, 1909, p. 240 of octavo edition.)

[2] " We desire to see the treatment of mental disease freed as far as possible
from its present association with the Poor Law. . . . The problem of insanity
is essentially a Public Health problem to be dealt with on modern Public Health
lines. . . . The special provision already made for the treatment of infectious

What the Commission at all points specially emphasised was the preventive character to be given to the administration, alike by the earliest possible treatment ; by the attention to be given to improvement and cure ; by the organisation of " after-care ", even at the public expense ; by provision for the better safeguarding of the property of even the poorest patients ; by limiting the orders for repayment of part of the cost of maintenance to such amounts as the patient or the chargeable relatives might reasonably bear, without danger of reducing to destitution either the relatives or the patient after discharge ; and, above all, on the importance of developing, at the public expense, the provision already begun (notably by the London and Birmingham Lunacy Authorities) for systematic scientific investigation and research into the causation of mental enfeeblement, disorder and decay, with a view to the discovery of new means for its prevention and curative treatment.[1]

Thus, in our own day, the lunacy service, scarcely two centuries old, is at last fully recognised as, in the strictest sense, a Framework of Prevention of the mental disorder or deficiency which is so frequent a cause of destitution, and therefore of no small proportion of destitution itself.

The Prevention of Illiteracy and Child Destitution

This generation often fails to realise the fervour and the faith that inspired the campaign of successive generations of reformers, for the first three-quarters of the nineteenth century, in favour of a universal system of education. To Robert Owen and his disciples, on the one hand, and to such practical pedagogues as Bell and Lancaster on the other, the careful nurture and skilful schooling of every child was the one and only way of building up personal character. To James Mill and Francis Place, as to Brougham and Kay-Shuttleworth, and, in a later generation, Joseph Chamberlain and John Morley, the education of every child seemed as indispensable a condition of

---

diseases, tuberculosis and venereal disease affords some guidance " (Report of Royal Commission on Lunacy and Mental Disorder, 1926, p. 22).

" We conceive that lunacy administration will become part of the Public Health Service " (*ibid.* p. 145).

[1] *Ibid.*

national improvement as the extension of the suffrage. Indeed, the early enthusiasm of the Philosophic Radicals led them to believe that the combination of universal schooling and universal voting, with every man pursuing his own self-interest, would remove not only destitution but also all the other remediable evils of society. But it was to Jeremy Bentham, more than a century ago, that we owe the vision of a national system of education, administered by the local " sublegislatures ", and directed, as he before anyone else advised, by a Minister of Education responsible to Parliament, with a ubiquitous provision of publicly administered schools at which every child of school age would be welcomed, and which all such children would be required by law to attend, unless other adequate education was being provided for them. It is therefore not surprising that in 1832–1833 more than one of the Assistant Commissioners of the Poor Law Inquiry Commission should have emphasised the importance of a National System of Education as a means of preventing pauperism and destitution.[1]

We cannot here follow the long struggle to establish a national system of Education, whether regarded as a means of civilisation, as an expedient for increased efficiency in wealth production, or as an indispensable factor in the prevention of child destitution. To-day, in the twentieth century, it is hard to realise the fierceness and the long continuance of the opposition to any measures calculated to ensure the schooling, even of the most elementary kind, of the whole child population. Even if it were accepted that the mere teaching of the rudiments of secular subjects is of little effect in the building up of character without

---

[1] See Report of Poor Law Inquiry Commission, 1834, Appendix A, C. P. Villiers's Report and J. W. Cowell's Report, to which we have alluded at pp. 70-72 of the present work.

" The hope of curing the disease of pauperism lay in the education and separation of the pauper child," Dr. Kay " had seen, soon after his appointment as Assistant Commissioner " (*Life of Sir James Kay-Shuttleworth*, by Frank Smith, 1923, p. 52).

Historically it was directly from the Factory Act restriction of child workers to " Half Time " in the cotton-mills that sprang any universality in the provision of schools. The requirement that industrial employment of the " Half Timers " should be conditional on their attendance at school for the remaining half of their available time (and, therefore, in practice, on the provision of schools for the whole population of children from whom the employers could draw the " Half Timers " that they desired) was adopted by Parliament primarily as a device for ensuring compliance with the law limiting the children's working day.

the all-pervading influence of religion, a public-spirited citizen might easily not approve the jealousy which so long and so strenuously resisted any encroachment on the assumed monopoly of this influence by the Established Church. But the more widespread resistance to any systematic provision of schools throughout the whole Kingdom, with the threefold aid of public funds, municipal organisation and statutory compulsion, had also, as a motive, the underlying objection, which was occasionally openly avowed, of the upper and middle classes, to placing it within the power of the abler and more industrious children of the wage-earning class to compete with these classes for the better-paid places in commerce, the public service and the learned professions.[1] It is humiliating to look back on the three-quarters of a century of controversy, during which Germany, Switzerland and Scandinavia on the one hand, and the United States and some of our own Dominions on the other, not to mention also so near a neighbour as Scotland, surpassed England and Wales in nearly all forms of education, and particularly in the prevention, by universal schooling, of the child neglect that is the most characteristic symptom of child destitution. Generation after generation the really fruitful experiments of these countries were ignored, and the examples that they were affording were neglected. Not until the Education Acts of 1902 and 1903 can the long struggle in England and Wales be said to have been decisively settled, and the way opened for the truly remarkable progress of the past quarter of a century. To-day the Local Education Authorities are statutorily entrusted with the provision, throughout England and Wales, to any extent and in any way that they think expedient, not of elementary education

---

[1] According to Sir Joshua Fitch, the reactionary code of 1861, which crippled English education for a couple of decades, was actually based on a growing jealousy in the middle class. It was said that " the teaching in our National Schools goes too far. The children are receiving a better education than they need. Geography and Grammar have nothing to do with the life of the labouring man. It helps to make him conceited and discontented. The poor are being over-educated and the whole system requires a check." The contemporary opposition to the spread of popular education among the poor was due, he suggested, mainly to a mean jealousy on the part of the classes above them. " These poor children are getting a better education than my own sons are obtaining ", says the tradesman ; " I do not want a servant or a labourer to know history or mathematics " (*Public Education : Why is the new Code wanted ?* by J. G. Fitch, 1861 ; see in confirmation, *Life of Sir James Kay-Shuttleworth*, by Frank Smith, 1923).

only, but (without limitation of age or sex, affluence or social position, subject or grade) of anything and everything that can be deemed education, from the open-air Nursery School for mites of two, up to the Technical College and the University ; not, indeed, necessarily without fee, but mainly at the expense of public funds, and made widely accessible to the children of the poorest parents by numerous " free places ", as well as by bursaries and scholarships covering maintenance in addition to instruction.

We pause to notice the cynical contempt, often subconsciously entertained, and not infrequently expressed, for the " half-educated multitude ", resulting from the compulsory schooling of the whole population. To which social grade or " society set " the term half-educated is most accurately applied would be an amusing subject for intensive observation ! But, confining ourselves to the four-fifths of the community who are manual workers, there is indisputable evidence of the superiority, in habits of cleanliness and order, in high spirits and good manners, and in the faculties of attention, initiative and obedience, of the twentieth-century working-class children over the physically impaired and morally depraved child population described in the British Blue Books of 1832–1870. Further, it is worth considering how greatly the present universality of reading, writing and arithmetic, together with the rudiments of hygiene and physical training, domestic economy and manual dexterity,[1]

---

[1] For how much more than mere instruction in the Three R's, we are indebted to the elementary school, the following statement by the London County Council's Education Officer in 1927 indicates : " Admittedly the task which confronts teachers in schools in the poorest districts of London presents problems differing widely from those found in schools in more accessible and better-favoured localities. . . . In the poor school, a large part of the teacher's time must be spent—and rightly spent—in inculcating social and personal refinements, in making school a desirable and pleasant place before " schooling " begins, in winning the co-operation of parents who hitherto have been listless, indifferent or suspicious. The outstanding success of the infants' school was referred to by Dr. P. B. Ballard in last year's report. Reinforced by the school medical service and by the school care committees, by simple and more suitable forms of dress, by improvements in personal hygiene following upon the practice of cutting short the hair, the social changes achieved by the infants' schools are rapidly spreading to the girls' schools. The improvement is not so marked in boys' schools, although even here they are in progress. . . . The ' poor ' school is steadily becoming a purposeful and kindly martinet, one that can pleasantly enforce habits of dress, speech, manners and physical well-being despite its environment. . . . Moral and physical deterioration traditionally associated with the poorer quarters of the great town are being checked ;

contributes to the feasibility and efficiency of the Framework of Prevention upon which the nation now relies in the campaign against destitution. Neither Factory Legislation nor Legal Minimum Wage-rates could be made effective, even by the utmost prodigality of inspection, unless the whole body of workers could be acquainted with these statutory provisions by official notices and the newspapers ; and it may be added that without the common power of writing letters of complaint, however imperfect the composition, there would be but small means of making known the inevitable cases of oppression. Similarly, it is very largely on the dissemination of knowledge of what the Infant Welfare Centre and the Nursery School, not to mention the provision against tuberculosis and venereal disease, and other activities of the Public Health service, stand ready to do for the poorest and most friendless family, that the public efficacy of the whole preventive service depends.[1] When we come to such complicated and all-pervading contributory services as those of National Insurance for Health and Pensions (and, as we shall presently mention, also Unemployment Insurance), it must be clear that they could never have been started, still less generally taken advantage of, by a population unable either to read the notices, or to fill up the necessary forms of claim. Even as things are, many a sufferer from accident or industrial disease, or the

---

childhood is being safeguarded and enlivened by an organisation that marshals every child, and records with watchful care his social history " (London County Council Annual Report for 1926, vol. iv. Education, p. 16).

[1] " ' It is now something like half a century ', said the Medical Officer of the London County Council in his report for 1925, ' since elementary education became compulsory and universal in this country. Like the air we breathe, it is now regarded—or disregarded—as so much a part of our environment that its manifold reactions in all the affairs of life pass almost unnoticed and unrecorded. In common with every other aspect of social progress, that of Public Health has benefited also, both by the indirect and by the direct effects of the great education service. The indirect effects are those produced by the substitution of a reading and discriminating for an illiterate and ignorant public. Although intelligence has not necessarily been increased, knowledge has grown and spread. A public opinion has been created which stands behind the efforts of the sanitarian, without which his would still be a voice crying in the wilderness. A single example of the overwhelming importance of the indirect effects of the education system is seen in the remarkable fall of infant mortality and the saving of child life, which came about as a younger generation, after passing through the primary schools, became in due course the parents of a new generation. Thus the direct results of the education system are truly incalculable ' " (Quoted in London County Council Annual Report for 1926, vol. iv. Education, p. 16).

widow and orphans of such a sufferer, if unaided by any Trade Union or other protective organisation ; possibly even not a few State-insured persons, and ex-Service men with War disabilities, still fail, through ignorance or misunderstanding of the necessary regulations, to obtain all the provision that Parliament has made for them. Without the general spread of ability to read and write, and at least to understand simple money accounts, neither the Trade Unions nor the Consumers' Co-operative Movement, neither the Friendly Societies nor any political organisation of the working class—though they might have achieved some small local successes—could ever have enrolled their millions of members. Without a universality of common schooling there could not have developed the present extensive system of voluntary Adult Education under which several hundreds of thousands of young men and women in evening classes—often continuously, months at a time, in residential colleges of one sort or another—acquire additional useful knowledge, prepare themselves for University degrees, or obtain a certain measure of culture. The student has, indeed, only to reflect upon the impossibility of obtaining, from a people without either elementary education or culture, and practically unaware of any social organisation or institution beyond their own village, any universal appreciation of, and co-operation with, governmental measures, still less any intelligent participation in the public judgement of Government policy, upon which, in a Democracy, Parliamentary elections now turn, to realise how completely the modern industrial State depends, for its very existence as a civilised State, upon at least a limited measure of universal common schooling, and open access to further education in science and literature, for all who have the vote to use it with any measure of intelligence at all.

In this book we are concerned with the influence of the elementary school mainly as a factor in the national campaign against destitution. To the importance of this influence, even a generation ago, the testimony is significant of Charles Booth, a Conservative in politics, strongly anti-Socialist in temper and economic views, who emerged from his prolonged inquest into London poverty (1886–1902) with a profound admiration for the work of the London Education Authority. " Among the public buildings of the Metropolis ", he tells us, " the London Board Schools occupy a conspicuous place. In every quarter the eye is arrested by their distinctive architecture, as they stand, closest where the need is greatest, each one ' like a tall sentinel at his post ', keeping watch and ward over the interests of the generation that is to replace our own.   The School Board buildings, as befits their purpose, are uniformly handsome, commodious, and for the most part substantial and well arranged.   The health and convenience of both children and teachers have been carefully considered, and, in the later ones especially, have been increasingly secured.   They accommodate a little over 443,000 children, and have been erected at a cost of about four and a half millions sterling.   Taken as a whole, they may be said fairly to represent the high-water mark of the public conscience in this country in its relation to the education of the children of the people."   And, in summing up the influences for good among the denizens of the mean streets, he emphatically tells that " Of these general influences the greatest of all is elementary education. . . . Habits of cleanliness and of order have been formed ; a higher standard of dress and of decency have been attained, and this reacts upon the homes ; and when children who have themselves been to school become parents, they accept and are ready to uphold the system, and support the authority of the teachers, instead of being prone to espouse with hand and tongue the cause of the refractory child.   Schoolmasters need no longer fear the tongue of the mother or the horsewhip of an indignant father." [1]

Medical Inspection and Treatment

It is one of the curiosities of history that the governments and legislatures of the nineteenth century (perhaps owing to their exclusively masculine membership) conceived that it was practicable to train the intelligence of infants, children and young persons, while ignoring and neglecting the state of their bodies. To the tens of thousands of teachers (two-thirds of them women) employed by the Local Education Authorities, as well as to the more observant of the elected representatives and school managers themselves, it soon became apparent that many of the little ones were suffering from disabling disease ; they had upon them untreated cuts and sores ; they had adenoid growths requiring

---

[1] *Life and Labour of the People*, 1902, " Poverty ", vol. iii. p. 204, and " Religious Influences ", vol. ii. pp. 53-54 ; see *My Apprenticeship*, by Beatrice Webb, 1926, p. 245.

surgical removal ; their glands and tonsils were swollen and inflamed ; they had incipient spinal curvature needing remedial drill ; their eyesight was often defective and sometimes rapidly degenerating for lack of proper spectacles ; they had discharges from the ears, and inflamed eyelids, and skin diseases of various kinds—to say nothing of such gravely contagious conditions as ringworm and favus, and " dirty heads ". These hundreds of thousands of children were, from one cause or another, plainly destitute of the medical attendance that was necessary for them. According to law, it was the duty of their parents to provide this needed medical attendance, and, in case of inability to pay for it, to apply to the Relieving Officer for a medical order. It was the duty of the Board of Guardians to grant that medical order whenever necessary ; and they might prosecute the parents under various statutes (now summed up in the Children Act of 1908) if they failed to apply. How the Poor Law administrators, even from their own standpoint of keeping down pauperism, could ever have reconciled themselves to allowing so great a mass of destitution (with respect to medical attendance) to remain unrelieved requires explanation. We note that the earliest steps taken by the School Boards to ensure that every child detained at home through illness should be seen by a doctor were condemned by the Poor Law Authorities, and alternative courses suggested. Thus, the Chairman of the Atcham Board of Guardians (so widely known for its strict administration) demurred in 1890, to " the action of School Boards ", [which] " is telling upon the question of Medical Relief, as some School Boards insist upon medical certificates being obtained when the reason for non-attendance of the child at school is alleged to be sickness ; and thus many poor people, who would be able to provide for slight ailments by warmth, care and attention, are driven to the District Medical Officer for the sole purpose of obtaining this certificate, and thus becoming pauperised. This might be avoided by the School Boards engaging a medical man to visit, examine, and certify for these purposes, if not satisfied with their existing officers. It appears to be necessary for the Guardians to watch this most closely so as to prevent Medical Relief being abused. It is desirable to study what steps can be taken for this end." [1] It

[1] Report of Chairman of the Atcham Board of Guardians, June 24, 1890 ; see Minority Report of Poor Law Commission, 1909, p. 150.

must be admitted that there was common sense in the plea of the Chairman of the Atcham Board that, if it was desirable to inspect and treat all children disabled from attending school, the Guardians were the last body who ought to be asked to undertake the work. For if the Poor Law authority did the medical work it would be Poor Relief ; such relief being granted only to those who applied to the Relieving Officer ; almost necessarily made to depend, not on the gravity of the illness of the child, but on the status of the parent ; withdrawn as soon as the parents wished to be without it ; and, when given, given wholly unconditionally, and usually without even the necessary hygienic advice. On the other hand, the medical examination and treatment of school children by the Local Education Authority (or by the Local Health Authority at its instance) is not of the nature of Poor Relief at all, but rather of hygienic discipline. It is systematically applied, without any implication of pauperism, to all children who are found to need it, without waiting for application to be made for it.   It is continued as long as is found necessary, whether or not the parents actively desire it.   And it always takes the form, to a very large extent, of hygienic advice, obedience to which is strongly pressed both on the child and on the parent.   " This medical inspection ", so the Royal Commission of 1905–1909 was told, " has actually a tendency to increase parental responsibility."   When, for instance, under the London County Council, the School Nurse [1] visits a school to put in force the cleansing scheme, " she examines every child, noting all that have verminous heads. The parents are notified by a white card, on which is also printed directions for cleansing. . . . At the end of a week, if not cleansed, the child is made to sit separately from the rest of the class, and the School Attendance Officer serves a more urgent warning ' red card ' at the home. The Nurse, too, often visits to offer advice ; and then, if in another

---

[1] The duty of the School Nurse is thus described in the Annual Report of the Chief Medical Officer of the Board of Education for 1910, pp. 100, 101 : " (1) To assist the Medical Officer in the routine inspection of children at school ; (2) To visit the schools when authorised for the purpose of examining the scholars in respect to such conditions as uncleanliness, ringworm, etc. ; (3) To visit the homes of the children in order to follow up the work of medical inspection and to endeavour to ensure that adequate attention is paid to the advice of the doctor, and in many instances to assist the parent in carrying out the treatment prescribed for minor ailments ; (4) To assist the School Medical Officer in the examination and treatment of children at the school clinic should such exist.

week the child is still unclean, it is excluded, after having been
seen by the Medical Officer ; and the parent is prosecuted for
not sending the child in a fit state to school." [1] Under the
influence of such a system, now at work in all the large towns
and in many rural districts, the obligations of the parents in this
one matter of cleanliness have, in the course of the last two
decades, been so much increased that the number of verminous
children has, through the exertions of the mothers, been very
greatly diminished. In 1910 the proportion of " dirty heads "
was 30 per cent in rural districts, and as many as 50 per cent in
urban. In 1926 the percentage throughout the whole kingdom
was no higher than 6. An entirely new standard of cleanliness
has been set. The relatively small expenditure from public
funds upon this service, far from operating as Poor Relief to the
parents, has been actually the means of compelling the less
responsible among them to devote more of their own time and
money to their children's welfare. Being wise after the event,
we may now confidently assert that the provisions of the Act
of 1907,[2] requiring the Local Education Authorities in England
and Wales to provide for the medical inspection of all children
and empowering them to provide treatment for such as are found
suffering at school, have been, from every standpoint, thoroughly
justified.

We need not follow, in the admirable series of Reports on
the Health of the School Child between 1908 and 1927 by Sir
George Newman, Chief Medical Officer to the Board of Education,
the rapid development of the School Medical Service. These
Reports constitute, indeed, a sort of " Domesday Survey " of the

[1] Report of Medical Officer (Education) to London County Council, 1905,
Appendix III. p. 17 ; see Minority Report of Poor Law Commission, 1909,
p. 153.

[2] 7 Edward VII. c. 43, Education (Administrative Provisions) Act, 1907 ;
see Board of Education Circular, No. 576, of November 1907 (Memorandum,
on Medical Inspection of Children) ; and see *The Story of English Public Health*,
by Sir Malcolm Morris, 1919, pp. 93-94. It is worth recalling that this " was
foreshadowed some sixty years ago by the prescience of Edwin Chadwick, who
advocated not merely sanitary surroundings for school children, but medical
inspection and physical training. In connection with the Education Commission of 1861 he wrote that ' a special sanitary service applicable to schools is
needed, for the correction of the common evils of their construction and the
protection of the health of children therein ' " (*ibid.*). Much is due to the
energy and persistence in medical inspection of school children of Dr. James
Kerr, successively Medical Officer to the School Boards for Bradford and
London, and the first School Medical Officer to the London County Council.

physical condition of the English child for the last twenty years. From 1907, we are told, " the Board have made it perfectly clear that in the administration of the Education Acts Local Education Authorities were to be invited to take a wide and comprehensive view of their duties (see Circular 576, 1907, and Circular 596, 1908). And indeed it cannot be otherwise, for their purpose is *to prepare the child for education and for citizenship.* Merely to provide for the medical inspection of children, or even the treatment of those found to be suffering from one or more physical defects, would be to overlook the fact that the School Medical Service is fundamentally physiological in conception and preventive in purpose, one of the most far-reaching social reforms. In the interest of convenience and brevity, it may be said that the school medical service is designed : (1) To fit the child to receive the education provided for it by the State. But this must also mean to adapt educational methods to the natural physiological capacity and powers of the child. This involves a study and understanding of the sphere and compass of a child's physiology. (2) To detect any departures from the normal physiological health and growth, any impairments, aberrations, defects, or disease (physical or mental), and advise the remedy or amelioration of them (at the school or otherwise) lest worse befall. (3) To seek the causes and conditions (external and internal to the body of the child) of such defect and disease, and, as far as may be, prevent them. (4) To teach and practise personal hygiene in every school, so that a habit of hygiene may be contracted by the children, and the way of physiological life may be followed by each coming generation."

" The whole design ", Sir George Newman summed up in 1926, " *is an opening of the gates* of physical opportunity. Medical inspection is merely an arrangement to explore and unveil the condition of each child in order that the rest of the programme may be fulfilled with a correct regard to the facts of the case." [1]

" Formerly ", reported the Education Officer of the London County Council in 1911, " education was in the main confined to (1) the growth of character, and (2) the growth of the mind. Now education looks increasingly at the social problems that present themselves for solution in the case of the individual child,

[1] *The Health of the School Child :* Annual Report of the Chief Medical Officer of the Board of Education for the year 1926, pp. 6-7.

the problem of physical deterioration, of underfeeding, of impoverished homes and unsuitable employment. The State has come to see that it is not enough to impart knowledge, but that it must also see that the child is capable of assimilating that knowledge, and that his environment is not such that it will entirely undo the effect of the school training." It is not to be wondered at that the general acceptance of such a view took " Poor Law orthodoxy " by surprise. " This is a startling definition ", wrote W. A. Bailward in 1914, " of the scope of education." [1]

School Feeding

We now come to the most remarkable and, it must be admitted, the most controversial of the invasions by the Local Education Authority of the sphere of the Poor Law Authority. Established to provide schooling only, the School Boards were naturally averse from assuming responsibility for the home circumstances of their pupils. They were under no legal or even moral obligation to see that their pupils were properly cared for out of school. What forced them to realise the existence of child destitution was the manifest absurdity of wasting costly education on hungry or starving children.[2] When active physical exercises, which could not be shirked by the child, were added to mere sedentary listening to the teacher's lessons, which did not need to be learnt, this absurdity approximated to cruelty. To the keen educationist, as to many practical teachers, it became apparent that the semi-starvation from which, in " slum "

---

[1] *Some Recent Developments of Poor Relief*, by W. A. Bailward, 1914.

[2] A brief record of the previous experiments in school feeding is contained in the Annual Report of the Chief Medical Officer of the Board of Education for 1910, Section XIII. p. 245. Pioneer work was done, at the expense of voluntary funds, in Manchester, Bradford and London, in the last two decades of the nineteenth century. Public attention was arrested by the findings and recommendations of the Royal Commission on Physical Training in Scotland, 1902–1903, and especially by those of the Physical Deterioration Committee of 1903–1904. The Interdepartmental Committee appointed in 1905 was instructed to report not only on the Medical Inspection of children by the Local Education Authorities, but also " to inquire into the methods employed, the sums expended, and the relief given by voluntary agencies for the provision of meals to children at public elementary schools, and to report whether relief of this character could be better organised without any charge upon public funds, both generally and with special regard to children who, though not defective, are from malnutrition below the normal standard " (Cd. 2779 of 1905).

districts, whole schools were suffering, was producing two types of abnormality, both disastrous alike to the future welfare of the community and to the present efficiency of the school. These results of child destitution are graphically described by the medical expert who examined the children in the schools of the Liverpool Education Authority in 1907 :

" Starvation acting on a nervous temperament ", reported Dr. Arkle as to the children whom he examined, " seems to produce a sort of acute precocious cleverness. Over and over again, I noted such cases of children, without an ounce of super-fluous flesh upon them, with skins harsh and rough, a rapid pulse, and nerves ever on the strain, and yet with the expression of the most lively intelligence. But it is the eager intelligence of the hunting animal, with every faculty strained to the uttermost so as to miss no opportunity of obtaining food. I fear it is from this class that the ranks of pilferers and sneak-thieves come, and their cleverness is not of any real intellectual value. On the other hand, with children of a more lymphatic temperament, starvation seems to produce creatures much more like automata. I do not know how many children I examined among the poorer sort, who were in a sort of dreamy condition, and would only respond to some very definite stimulus. They seemed to be in a condition of semi-torpor, unable to concentrate their attention on anything, and taking no notice of their surroundings, if left alone. To give an example of what I mean, if I told one of these children to open its mouth, it would take no notice until the request became a command, which sometimes had to be accompanied by a slight shake to draw the child's attention. Then the mouth would be slowly opened wide, but no effort would be made to close it again, until the child was told to do so. As an experiment, I left one child with its mouth wide open the whole time I examined it, and it never once shut it. Now that shows a condition something like what one gets with a pigeon that has had its higher brain centres removed, and it is a very sad thing to see in a human being. I believe both these types of children are suffering from what I would call starvation of the nervous system, in one case causing irritation, and in the other torpor. And further, these cases were always associated with the clearest signs of bodily starvation, stunted growth, emaciation, rough and cold skin, and the mouth full of viscid saliva, due to hunger.

With such children I generally had to make them swallow two or three times before the mouth was clear enough to examine the throat. . . . I do not think I need say any more to show that the extent of the degeneration revealed by this investigation has reached a very alarming stage. . . . What is the use of educating children whose bodies and minds are absolutely unable to benefit by it. In my opinion, the children must first be taught how to live, and helped to get food to enable them to do it." [1]

Once the evil was officially recognised, the campaign against it was promptly organised and skilfully pursued. " Defective nutrition ", summed up the Chief Medical Officer of the Board of Education in 1910, " stands in the forefront as the most important of all physical defects from which school children suffer. . . . No class of child requires more careful ' following up ' and re-examination, even though no notice of ' treatment ' being required by a medical practitioner has been sent to the parent. Every endeavour, by means of questioning the parent, by a visit of the School Nurse to the home, or by fuller examination of the child, should be made in order to ascertain the probable cause or causes. Careful estimation of the height and weight of exceptional children should be made in the first instance by the Medical Officer himself, and all children noted as suffering from malnutrition should be weighed at regular intervals of 1-3 months, every care being exercised that such measurements are taken under comparable conditions. But weight is not the only index of nutrition. There is the ratio of stature to weight; the general appearance, carriage, and ' substance ' of the child ; the firmness of the tissues; the presence of subcutaneous fat; the development of the muscular system ; the condition of the skin and redness of the mucous membranes ; the expression of list-lessness or alertness, apathy or keenness ; the condition of the various systems of the body; and, speaking generally, the relative balance and co-ordination of the functions and powers of digestion, absorption, and assimilation of food." [2]

Unfortunately, nearly twenty years after these reports on the semi - starvation of many school children, the problem of

[1] *The Condition of the Liverpool School Children*, by A. S. Arkle, B.A., M.R.C.S. (Liverpool : Tinling and Co., 1907), p. 15.

[2] Annual Report of the Chief Medical Officer of the Board of Education for 1910, p. 26.

the child disabled through insufficient nourishment still confronts the administration. "What is a malnourished child?" asks the Chief Medical Officer of the Board of Education in his Annual Report for 1926. "It is not necessarily a hungry child, nor yet one in a condition of starvation. It is the child whose physical body falls seriously, or for prolonged periods, below that of sound balance, short of its full weight and wholesome capacity in relation to its size and build. The skeletal and bony framework of the malnourished child is unduly obvious and irregular; its musculature is weak, thin and flabby; its skin is pale, wax-like, or sallow in appearance, it is dry and inelastic to the touch, insufficiently supported by subcutaneous fat and therefore loose; the mucous membranes of the child are watery and colourless; the eyes may be unduly hollow-looking; the 'animal spirits' of the child are below par, and it is often listless or dull. These characteristics vary widely, sometimes the malnourished child is obviously emaciated and anyone can see it is under-nourished; at other times its malnutrition will only be detected by the expert and experienced eye."

The causes of this malnutrition are not always, so we are warned, the result of insufficient income. "It is commonly and correctly believed that poverty has much to do with it; sometimes it is a direct cause, but more often indirect in that poverty may bring with it *ignorance, unsatisfactory home conditions, lack of parental control*, and absence of influences favourable to nutrition. Many children would no doubt be better nourished if their parents had an income which would enable them to provide the necessaries of a full and replete life; but more often it is careless mothering, ignorance of upbringing and lack of nurture than actual shortage of food which results in a malnourished child. Insufficient sleep, chronic fatigue, absence of fresh air and lack of exercise are exerting a very great influence day by day on the well-being of multitudes of children. Magnificent schemes and expensive staffs are of no avail if mothers and teachers neglect these simple matters. It is important also to realise that usually malnutrition begins in infancy and has become a habit of the body before school age. . . ."

The second cause links up malnutrition with the school medical service, seeing that disease, and not an absence of food, frequently results in semi-starvation. "Enlarged tonsils or adenoids, debility, anaemia, decayed teeth, or chronic indigestion may lead to it. Even more degenerative are congenital syphilis, tuberculosis, heart disease and rickets. Tuberculosis is destructive of tissues, the result of heart disease is general incompetency of body, and rickets is well known as directly and indirectly contributory to faulty nutrition. Hence to provide more food, or even better food, is by no means the only answer to malnutrition. The whole child must be dealt with, and all the resources of medicine and hygiene, all the resources of the Home and the School, brought to its succour. For the malnourished child is incapable, susceptible to disease and mentally retarded." [1]

Whilst the primary object of school feeding is to enable even the poorest and most neglected children to take full advantage of the education provided for them, the service has broadened out in diverse ways. On the one hand, the provision of nourishment has been more closely associated with the School Medical Service. In some places, notably in London, the simple breakfast or dinner has been supplemented (and, with the extensive provision of Unemployment Benefit, even largely replaced) by meals of milk and cod liver oil ordered on medical grounds in particular cases, whilst careful studies have been made of the effect produced on the children's weight and health. On the other hand, facilities have been given for the provision of the midday meal at school by or at the expense of the parents themselves, either by affording means for heating or preparing food brought by the children residing far from the school, or by the institution of school canteens, supplying meals on payment. In London, to-day, a much larger number of parents pay for the meals thus provided for their children at the schools than there are meals served gratuitously ; and the dinner thus eaten by the children in common, without visible distinction between those who pay and those who do not, under conditions of decency and mutual courtesy, constitutes, in itself, not the least useful of the lessons of the day. [2]

[1] *The Health of the School Child :* Annual Report of the Chief Medical Officer of the Board of Education for 1926, pp. 16 and 17.

[2] The continued efforts of the Board of Education to ensure that none of the children, for whose schooling so large an expenditure has to be incurred, should be suffering from malnutrition are still hampered by the lack of definiteness of the statutory authority. The Act of 1906 is permissive only, and it contemplated mainly the application of voluntary funds. Many Local Education Authorities are reluctant to put the Act in operation, unless not merely

A further development of the Education (Provision of Meals) Act of 1906 and its amendments has been its application to occasions of widespread distress, arising from Unemployment or otherwise. Thus, on the occasion of the General Strike of May 1, 1926, coinciding with the closing down by the colliery companies of all the coal-mines in Great Britain, and the discharge of all their manual-working employees, the Minister of Health promptly issued a Circular to the Boards of Guardians in the distressed Unions, requiring them to co-ordinate their Poor Relief to the wives and children with the provision of meals made by the Local Education Authorities. The unexampled extent and duration of the dispute in the coal-mining industry led to an unprecedented rise in school feeding.

" As was to be expected, there was practically no difference in the number of children fed at school during the first week of the stoppage ; families were living on the last wages received. In the second week 8 additional Authorities began to feed and the number of children rose by 50 per cent to 88,070. In the third week 14 more Authorities started school feeding, and the number of children fed jumped up to 216,167 ; the additional areas commencing feeding were all mining and industrial areas acutely affected by the coal stoppage. The number of children fed continued to increase week by week until the ninth week (week ended 3rd July), when 262,495 children were fed by 157 Authorities. From the beginning of August the figures fell back to just over 200,000. This was due to the effect of the summer holidays on the normal feeding areas ; in nearly all the areas directly affected by the stoppage school feeding was continued during the holidays. By the end of August the numbers had risen again to 234,064 and remained fairly stationary between 230,000 and 240,000 until the end of the stoppage. The number of meals provided rose from 291,730 in the week ended 1st May to a maximum of 2,363,503 in the week ended 3rd July. This increase is not merely proportionate to the increased number of children ; it represents an average of 9 meals per child per week

---

some, but actually a large proportion of the children, are certified to be in need, and usually only when the need arises from some exceptional cause. The requirement of specific sanction from the Board of Education for the purchase of food tends to delay. Finally, the School Medical Officers differ in their views as to the need for such action, as well as in their judgement as to which children require feeding.

compared with an average of 5·4 in the week before the stoppage. As a rule Authorities undertaking school feeding provide only one meal a day, usually dinner, for the children. In the exceptional circumstances created by the coal stoppage many Authorities felt that the provision of one meal only was not sufficient, and two meals were provided by a considerable number, while a small number provided three, that is breakfast and tea as well as dinner. The average for the whole country, however (including the normal feeding areas), never rose above 9·2 per child per week. . . ."

Whatever may be thought of the merits of the dispute, there was, we think, no disposition to doubt that, so far as the children were concerned, the prevention of destitution by the free provision of school meals was in every way preferable to its treatment by Poor Relief. It was markedly successful in maintaining their health.

" The general tenour of the reports received, whether from School Medical Officers, the Board's Medical Officers or His Majesty's Inspectors, showed that with few exceptions the nutrition of the children was maintained unimpaired throughout the stoppage, indeed in some instances a higher standard of nutrition was obtained as a result of a long period of regular and wholesome feeding." [1]

The Gaps in the Framework of Prevention as regards Child Destitution

There are, however, besides the inevitable shortcomings in the working of the organisation, still two gaps by which the continuity of the public supervision and protection of the child falls short of completeness.

The first arises merely from the fact that two different Local Authorities are concerned. The difficulty of the Local Education Authority, observes Sir George Newman, is twofold : " (a) The child is under the Maternity and Child Welfare Authority from birth to five years of age, and then from five to fourteen comes to the Education Authority ; *there is no continuous supervision by the same Authority*, though the child itself lives a continuous

---

[1] *The Health of the School Child :* Annual Report of the Chief Medical Officer of the Board of Education for 1926, pp. 138-139.

life, and carries on its maladies from one stage to the next ; and
(b) the child coming to the Local Education Authority is all too
often physically defective, owing to the fact that there is no
systematic provision for the child under school age to be medically
treated.   Hence, the Local Education Authority had had to
receive, what one school doctor calls ' damaged goods ', and pay
out of the education rate for their repair.[1] . . . It is at present ",
he complains, " an unfair medical burden on the education rate
and on the school doctor, nurse and clinic.   Still more is it true
to say that by its present neglect the nation is imposing an unfair
burden upon itself. We allow disease to get ahead of us. Between
the years of one and five, as I have pointed out before, the seed
is sown which comes to fruit in school life and subsequently. The
maternity and infant welfare centres are at present our only
succour. They are doing extremely valuable work, but most
of it is, naturally enough, for the child under one year of age.
What seems to be needed is an extension of this work up to five
years of age, and the inclusion of definite medical inspection and
treatment." [2]

This gap could, however, be lessened in many cities and towns
exceeding 20,000 in population, by the Public Health and
Education Authorities both being committees of the same
Council, and by a closer co-ordination of the two services,
which is increasingly marked by the union in the same person
of the posts of Medical Officer of Health and School Medical
Officer.   " Effective arrangements become then merely a question of administration and the designing of suitable institutions for providing medical supervision for the child below
school age (e.g. the use of the school clinic for treatment or
the nursery school for nurture). Thus, in a city like Liverpool,
the pre-school child is dealt with by the same Authority as
that concerned with the school child, and it has post-natal
centres, health visitors, day nurseries, infant welfare centres,
a " toddlers " clinic, and a dental clinic—all for the pre-school
child." [3]

The other breach in continuity occurs at the school-leaving
age, when (except for what may be voluntarily arranged in the

---

[1] *The Health of the School Child :* Annual Report of the Chief Medical
Officer of the Board of Education for 1926, pp. 33-40.
[2] *Ibid.* pp. 113-114.   [3] *Ibid.* p. 37.

way of Continuation Classes and evening instruction) the child passes out of the jurisdiction of the Local Education Authority. At this point there is, as yet, no sufficient articulation with the organisation of the Employment Exchanges, Unemployment Insurance, Juvenile Training Centres and Trade Boards administered by the Ministry of Labour, to which we refer in the next chapter.

The Characteristic Influences of a System of Universal Schooling

From the standpoint of coping with destitution, we notice three distinctive characteristics of the application of the Framework of Prevention to the child, by means of universal and compulsory schooling, namely, the exceptional continuity of its influence ; the increased personal responsibility for the child's welfare which it imposes upon, and evokes from, the child's parents, and the amount of investigation and research into the causes of physical and mental deficiencies among infants and children that it has so far promoted.

We have already noticed how inevitably the Poor Law provision for children, alike institutional and domiciliary, has suffered from the irremediable flaw of discontinuity. Not until destitution had set in could the Relieving Officer or the Board of Guardians become even aware of the needs of the child. Immediately the parents chose to dispense with Poor Relief, their children passed suddenly and completely out of the ken of the Destitution Authority ; sometimes, as with the " Ins and Outs ", alternately entering and leaving repeatedly within a single year. The Public Elementary School, on the other hand, maintains a continuous supervision over the child from five (or even earlier) to the end of the school year in which the child attains fourteen years of age, and in some cases even longer. Not only is every one of the five million boys and girls on the school roll actually under the eyes of competent and responsible officers of the Local Education Authority for five hours on nearly every day of the year ; but even when they are not present at school the supervision is maintained. Registration begins, with the periodical " scheduling " of the child population by the School Attendance Officers, even before the age for compulsory attendance. If the child fails to enrol, or fails to attend when enrolled, the home is visited, and usually the child is seen, as well as the parent. If the child at school is found to be unwell, or to be inadequately clothed and booted, or to be below the prescribed standard of cleanliness, its home is visited, and personal influence is brought to bear on the parents in such a way as to get the neglect remedied. " Following up " has, in fact, become a recognised special technique in the daily activities of Local Education Authorities, to an extent of which the public are quite inadequately unaware.[1] For this work there has been built up an organised service, in which the School Attendance Officer, the School Nurse, the volunteer members of the Children's Care Committee, and often also some paid or unpaid specialist experienced in one or other of the dangers and troubles of child life, have all their parts to play. Three times at least during the years of school attendance, and oftener whenever required, the child is inspected by doctor and nurse, with a view to discovering any incipient ailments or any defects of sight or hearing, or any falling below the pre-scribed minimum standard of intelligence, in order that appro-priate remedial measures may be taken. Every child found to be needing treatment or attention is visited by the School Nurse, or by a member of the Children's Care Committee, or by both in succession, to ascertain whether matters have been put right, and often to show the mother how to put them right. If the child is found hungry at school, it is provided with one or more meals ; and if this is due merely to the neglect of the parents, they may be prosecuted and fined. But, as it has been wisely said, a child who has been allowed to go short of food is almost certainly lacking more than meals ; and it is for the visiting member of the Children's Care Committee to bring to notice what is amiss with the home, in order that the child neglect may be remedied.

---

[1] In the Annual Report of the Chief Medical Officer of the Board of Education for 1910, Section IV., no fewer than 23 pages are devoted to a description of the proceeding known as "following up". Sir George Newman emphatically declares that " a system of medical inspection, however complete in itself, will fall short of its practical value unless there is coupled with it an effective system of ' following up '. This is not only necessary in order to secure the treatment of individual children found to be defective, but it is necessary in order to obtain a wise and economic administration. Only by ' following up ' can a Local Education Authority control its medical inspection and make it complete and valuable, and only thus can it determine its measure of responsi-bility in securing from the parent of the child the treatment which it needs, and ensuring that the facilities for prevention and treatment existing in the area are sufficient, available, and actually used " (p. 96).

Finally, if the parents leave the district and the child ceases to attend, it is the duty of the School Attendance Officer in the one district to verify the departure, and of the corresponding officer of the other district to discover the new child's arrival and secure its enrolment.

Increase of Parental Responsibility

We have already incidentally alluded to the effect of the school influence—brought to bear alike by the teachers, the School Attendance Officer, the School Nurse and the Children's Care Committee—on the sense of parental responsibility. The working-class woman is as devoted to her children as any other mother. But it is one of the dire results of the poverty of the poor, manifested in overwork and wages insufficient for family requirements, especially in the conditions of overcrowding and dirt imposed by residence in the slums of great cities, that the standard of cleanliness, of clothing and generally of the watchful care required for healthy childhood, almost inevitably declines. In the ignorance and listlessness, and absence of standards, which characterise whole sections of slum-dwelling families, there was in the past, and but for influence of the elementary school there would be again to-day, the very minimum of fulfilment of parental responsibility. It is the watchful influence by inspection and visitation, advice and instruction, brought to bear on the mother of the children from infancy to school-leaving age that evokes the sense of responsibility, guides and assists its fulfilment, imposes continually the higher obligations of rising standards, and has, in fact, already resulted, as all evidence proves, in the working-class mothers of the present day devoting much more time and personal labour to cleansing, clothing and generally caring for their offspring than was given, in literally hundreds of thousands of cases, by the working-class mothers of the English industrial towns and the slum quarters of the Metropolis a century ago. Nor is this all. Far from resenting the compulsory absorption of more and more of the child's potential wage-earning years, a large proportion of the working-class parents of to-day are clamouring, in greater numbers than ever before, for further educational opportunities for their children. The demand and the competition for scholarships at secondary schools, even if these amount to nothing more substantial than free places, in spite of the very onerous burden that years spent in secondary schooling involve on working-class households, is far in excess of the steadily rising provision of such opportunities. This reaching-out of parental responsibility to new and extended burdens, willingly assumed for the benefit of the offspring, may be counted a direct result of universal and compulsory schooling. Whatever may have been felt in Scotland, in England the aspiration for extended years of education, notably in secondary or technical schools, is, among parents of the wage-earning class, in the main a new thing, quite definitely the outcome of the Education Acts of 1870 and 1902.

Unfortunately, the beneficent influence of the work of the Local Education Authorities in increasing and developing parental responsibility is checked and hampered by the widespread indisposition to take sufficiently drastic measures to prevent the large number of cases of culpable child neglect and wilful cruelty that still occur. It is true that, by the terms of the Children Act, 1908 (8 Edward VII. c. 67), Parliament purported to give complete protection against everything gravely harmful to child development. But all that was done was to enact that such acts of neglect or cruelty should be punishable as crimes ; just as, for several centuries, Parliament sought to prevent vagrancy by punishing it as a crime ! The Home Office, which took a lot of trouble to draft the statute, apparently overlooked the fact that no array of penal statutes will, in themselves, amount to a Framework of Prevention. The relatively few prosecutions, during the past twenty years, of parents guilty of child neglect, whether spasmodically undertaken, here and there, by exceptionally active Local Authorities, together with the assiduity with which the National Society for the Prevention of Cruelty to Children takes action in the cases discovered by its Inspectors, have proved far from adequate to prevent the constant occurrence of such neglect, especially by poverty-stricken, rather than by culpably negligent or positively cruel parents. The community cannot permanently continue to allow tens of thousands of its children to be thus physically and mentally damaged, whether the immediate cause be poverty or cruelty, many of them inevitably graduating into crime and its accompanying dissoluteness and destitution—even if the necessary Framework of Prevention proves to be a more drastic application of the law requiring the removal of children from parents who show themselves incapable of giving to children what is understood by parental care. For a terrible vision of the extent and injurious effect of this gap in the Framework, see the cases enumerated, on a sample inquiry at Birmingham, in the pamphlet *Parental Neglect and Juvenile Crime*, 1919, by Mr. Spurley Hey, Director of Education under the Birmingham Local Education Authority, who concludes by outlining the methods of " an immediate and sustained attack . . . against all conditions which either prevent or vitiate the attempts of the schools to educate the children of democracy under the best conditions and to the fullest extent of their capacity ". Practically none of the suggested measures have yet been taken.

National Insurance

At this point we have to bring in the effects, in our own country, of an entirely novel development of collective provision, definitely preventive of the destitution caused by sickness, accident and infirmity, which seems to us comparable, in its magnitude and far-reaching extension throughout the world, with the proposals of Juan Luis Vives and Martin Luther 400 years previously.[1] To the example of Prince Bismarck's legislation of 1880–1889 for the German Empire [2] must be ascribed the subsequent establishment, in more than a score of different nations, of national and compulsory systems of insurance, securing for practically the whole of the wage-earning population, and often also other sections, not only medical attendance and care in sickness, but also more or less provision for maintenance when thus prevented from working, and even universal life pensions from the age of sixty-five or seventy, to provide for the period

---

[1] See our previous volume, *The Old Poor Law*, pp. 35-40.

[2] A convenient account of Bismarck's experimental legislation will be found in *Social Insurance in Germany*, by W. H. Dawson, 1912, or in *Compulsory Insurance in Germany* (Fourth Special Report of U.S. Commissioner of Labour), by John Graham Brooks. For the gradual extension of the idea throughout the world, see *Social Insurance*, by I. M. Rubinow, 1913 ; or *State Insurance a Social and Industrial Need*, by Frank W. Lewis, 1909 ; or *Working Men's Insurance*, by W. F. Willoughby, 1898. But these have now been very largely superseded, so far as Health Insurance is concerned, by the elaborate world-survey of the International Labour Office of the League of Nations, entitled *Compulsory Sickness Insurance*, 1928, in which the systems of twenty-three nations are described, and their problems and tendencies authoritatively discussed.

at which pauperism is most widely prevalent, including, finally, pensions for the widows of the insured persons.

We cannot survey the extent to which this essentially modern development of the Framework of Prevention has already spread throughout the world, nor the varieties in its range and in its details. Confining ourselves to Great Britain, where the idea of Social Insurance on a national scale was not taken up for a whole generation after Bismarck's legislation, we note first that it is to the indefatigable energy and political courage of Mr. Lloyd George that must be ascribed the British following of the German example. Already in 1908, when the Old Age Pensions Act had given non-contributory Old Age Pensions at seventy, Mr. Lloyd George publicly promised to round off this measure by a general scheme of insurance against sickness. In 1908 he visited Germany to learn how it could be done, and in the two following years he sent a series of officials to that country to study the details.[1] In 1911, when he had become Chancellor of the Exchequer, the Cabinet, Parliament and the nation were induced to adopt a vast system of compulsory Social Insurance against Sickness and Invalidity, which, in magnitude of the financial transactions, exceeded at that date all the rest of the Framework of Prevention put together. To bring into a nation-wide organisation practically the whole manual working wage-earning class (and even all salaried workers below £250 a year), numbering, in all, over fifteen million persons ; to secure to all these employed persons free access to medical attendance and treatment, with the medicines prescribed ; to provide, at any rate partially, for their maintenance during sickness the sum of fifteen shillings per week, and for their chronic invalidity a weekly pension of half that amount ; to give, not only for every woman wage-earner so insured, but also for the wife of every insured man, a subsidy of £2 (and in some cases £4) for the expenses of childbirth, was a tremendous achievement. An annual expenditure under the Minister of Health now exceeding thirty million pounds represents a collective provision for individual ill-fortune outstripping in financial magnitude anything that the world had before seen. The question inevitably arises to what extent, and with what qualifications, this colossal

---

[1] *The Prime Minister,* 1920, p. 155 ; and *The Fire of Life,* 1925, p. 161, both by Harold Spender.

enterprise may properly be classed as part of the national Framework of Prevention of destitution.

Let us consider the National Insurance Scheme first as part of the campaign against ill-health—against the sickness to which, as Chadwick discovered three-quarters of a century ago, more than half of all the destitution is directly due. In spite of the ubiquitous provision of Poor Law Medical Officers, whose work is necessarily limited to persons who have already become destitute ; in spite also of the steadily extending range of the medical services of the Local Health and Education Authorities, which now provide, far from ubiquitously, only for certain diseases in the one case, and only for school children in the other, the mass of the manual working wage-earners have always been tempted, because of inability or dislike to pay the doctor's fee, to neglect the minor ailments from which they are always suffering. The National Health Insurance Scheme has removed that obstacle by giving every insured person the gratuitous service of a local doctor. What the scheme has done for the nation's Public Health organisation is to enrol at a cost of £6,000,000 a year 14,000 " general practitioners " in the public service, as " our first line of defence in the fight against disease and premature death ". The general practitioner may be inadequately equipped on the Public Health side. He is not giving his main thought to that side of his work. But he has this advantage over both the Poor Law doctor and the Public Health doctor, that the people spontaneously and trustingly come to him. " It is he who is first consulted by those in sickness. To him come the great host of patients with what are called 'trivial ailments'. Many of these are undoubtedly nothing more than unimportant deviations from normal health, but some are the first signs of grave disorders of body or mind. His skill must be the sieve that distinguishes the important from the unimportant. He must appreciate what is of moment in the beginnings of disease . . . for it is in its beginnings that disease can be most successfully controlled. The modern study of infectious disease has taught us the importance of ' missed cases ', *i.e.* cases which are either not recognised at all, or not until infection has had time to spread. A single ' missed ' case of smallpox may give rise to a serious epidemic. Early recognition is equally important from the point of view of the patient. It may mean the difference between life and death. Diphtheria recognised in time for antitoxin to be successfully administered is a very different matter from diphtheria unrecognised until it has reached a stage when the best therapeutic agents are of no avail. In the treatment of tuberculosis, cancer, kidney disease, to name only three examples, the recognition of the first signs of the disease is of vital importance." [1] We should be sorry to suggest that accurate diagnosis, any more than fully informed scientific treatment, has yet been secured for all the insured persons. The overworked general practitioner does his best, but little has yet been provided for his assistance, and even less has been made easily accessible to him, in the way of laboratory examinations, whether chemical, bacteriological or histological ; he is neither required nor paid, even when he is sufficiently equipped, to conduct such lengthy or intricate investigations himself ; and without such aids the diagnosis, in a certain proportion of cases, can be little better than guess-work. What has happened is that, in the Health Insurance system, a useful beginning has been made in the universal diagnosis of disease.

Similarly, a beginning has been made in the universal treatment of disease, notably with regard to the minor ailments which account for so large a proportion of ill-health and industrial disability. Pending the provision of a complete hospital system, covering all parts of the country, and of an equally ubiquitous nursing and midwifery service, universally available for all domiciliary cases—pending, too, the addition of the promised service of specialised consultants, together with the necessary dentistry, etc.—the general practitioner can often do no more than give the hygienic advice and prescribe the drugs that his experience suggests. We cannot prove by statistics by how much this great development of at least the rudiments of medical attendance and treatment has lessened the amount of ill-health or the loss by premature death, or by how much it has thereby diminished the destitution caused by sickness. But a gap in the previously existing Framework of Prevention has been at least partly filled.[2]

[1] Annual Report of Chief Medical Officer of the Ministry of Health for 1923.
[2] The British scheme is incomplete (a) in not providing for medical attendance for wives (not wage-earning), and for children under sixteen, or even beyond that age, so long as not employed ; (b) in omitting independent workers not " employed ", such as jobbing carpenters or gardeners, blacksmiths, small

And it is not only in its " Medical Benefit " that the Insurance Scheme operates in prevention of destitution. The cash payments in Maternity, in Sickness, and in Invalidity, amounting to nearly £20,000,000 annually, may be deemed, at first sight, to be preventive only in the sense of saving the recipients of these extensive " doles " from having to seek Poor Relief ; preventive, that is to say, only of Pauperism. This, however, is to ignore the important fact that the cost is provided to the extent of one-third directly by the insured persons themselves, besides as much more by levy on their employers (which cannot be deemed to have no effect at all upon the operatives' wage-rates), whilst less than one-third falls upon the National Exchequer. In this way the scheme amounts to one of compulsory thrift ; to the enforced saving, during health and employment, of millions of pounds annually, in order to prevent impoverishment in times of sickness and unemployment. This saving is clearly preventive of destitution, and none the less so because it is collective and enforced by law. And though compulsory thrift may not have the same beneficial influence on personal character as the thrift and insurance that spring from voluntary foresight and self-denial, yet even the conscious co-operation in a national scheme, and the sense of making payment for what is received, must be accounted a marked distinction between the " Insured Person " and the " Pauper ".

Yet more significant than all the beneficial effects upon the fifteen million insured persons and their dependants must be counted the fact that, at one stroke, the Government undertook in 1911 to provide, from the Exchequer, what has turned out to be no less than ten million pounds a year, in addition to everything else that was being done : a sum for prevention equal to one-half of the whole contemporary expenditure of the English Poor Law Authorities on all their varied forms of relief. It is

retailers, hawkers and pedlars, etc. ; (c) in not providing either skilled nursing or institutional treatment where one or other is required, or even pathological facilities for diagnosis, let alone specialist examination or treatment, however necessary ; (d) in confining the provision for maternity to a mere cash payment, instead of the requisite treatment, whether domiciliary or institutional ; and (e) in making insufficient provision (especially in the case of bread-winning heads of families) for maintenance at the present cost of living. (See, for instance, Report of Royal Commission on Health Insurance, 1926, chapters 4 and 5 ; Annual Reports of Chief Medical Officer of Ministry of Health for 1924, par. 359, and for 1925, par. 286 ; *Lancet*, March 3, 1928.)

characteristic of the chaotic condition into which British public administration had come, owing to lack of any general view, that this vast addition to the Framework of Prevention was made without any sort of co-ordination with the various other parts of that Framework. A huge new scheme was hastily contrived, without regard for the rest of the social services, and peremptorily ordered to start on a certain date, with the result that a great amount of novel social machinery had to be rapidly extemporised in a desperate attempt to get the scheme to work at all !

Pensions for the Aged and for Widows and Orphans

There is yet another extension of Social Insurance that has proved preventive of recruitment to the ranks of pauperism ; namely, the provision of pensions for the aged and for widows and orphans, classes from which a large proportion of the paupers have always come. Here the beginning was made in Great Britain in 1908, by the Liberal Government under Mr. Asquith, in the form of a direct pension from the National Exchequer to all persons who, at seventy, found themselves without any but the smallest resources. Under this scheme, as amended by subsequent Acts of 1919 and 1924, just under a million pensioners are now (1928) receiving £27,000,000 a year. In 1925, under the Unionist Government of Mr. Baldwin, a scheme was grafted on to the National Health Insurance System, under which insured persons, and the widows of such persons, would become entitled to Old Age pensions at sixty-five and at widowhood respectively, irrespective of their affluence or poverty. In this way the whole insured population, including nearly all the wage-earners and their wives, will obtain superannuation allowances of ten shillings per week each at sixty-five, without any reference to means, residence or nationality ; whilst any persons who fail to qualify by insurance will continue to obtain their superannuation allowances at seventy, on proof that they are qualified by residence and nationality and do not possess incomes of, roughly, £50 a year for one person or £100 a year for a married couple. Moreover, the widows of insured persons, whose widowhood occurs before they are sixty-five, will receive a widow's pension until remarriage or death, together with an additional weekly allowance for each child then under fourteen years of age, continuing up to fourteen, or, if still receiving full-time instruction at school, up to sixteen. All these benefits are now (1928) being paid to over three-quarters of a million new pensioners, whose numbers will, for some years, steadily increase, not from the National Exchequer, but from the Insurance Fund, formed, to the extent of over two-thirds, by the contributions collected by insurance stamps from employers and wage-earners.[1]

Here, too, as with the insurance against sickness, we have a form of compulsory thrift, a sense of having contributed throughout the working life, and even a feeling of co-operation in a national scheme, which enable the pension to be received without loss of dignity or stigma of pauperism ; and which warrant us in including the scheme in the Framework of Prevention.[2]

The Evolution of Specialised Central Departments

The development of the Local Authorities, during the past eighty years, in respect of the services of Public Health and Education, with all their ramifications, has been accompanied by a corresponding specialisation of the Government Departments concerned. The premature attempt of Chadwick and Southwood Smith to establish a Central Health Authority was summarily brought to an end in 1854 by an adverse vote of the House of Commons ; and for fifteen more years the various Local Authorities were left, with confused and fragmentary statutory powers,

---

[1] In this ingenious manner, it will be noted, the provisions of Mr. Asquith's Old Age Pensions Act of 1908 will be gradually superseded, in respect of all persons except those reaching seventy who have failed in some way to qualify for the new pension before reaching that age. The heavy financial burden will thereby be lifted from the Exchequer, to be borne by the Insurance Fund, towards which the Exchequer contributes less than a third of the annual requirements.

[2] We need do no more than note, at this point, the effect, in preventing destitution in thousands of working-class homes, of the tardily enacted obligation of employers to provide some imperfect compensation to such among their employees as are injured by accident or industrial disease arising out of, or in the course of their employment, and to the widows and children of those who thus lose their lives. It will, we think, be regarded in after ages as extraordinary that not until 1880 was this compensation required, even in the grossest cases (Employers' Liability Act, 43 and 44 Victoria, c. 42) ; and that not until 1897 was the obligation extended to the great bulk of employers (Workmen's Compensation Act, 60 and 61 Victoria, c. 37), to be made practically universal only in 1923 and 1925 (Workmen's Compensation Amendment Acts, 13 and 14 George V. c. 42, and 15 and 16 George V. c. 84). See *History of Trade Unionism*, by S. and B. Webb, 1920, pp. 364-366 ; *The Home Office*, by Sir Edward Troup, 1925, pp. 175-177.

to struggle, as best they could, against the insanitation of the ever-increasing slum areas. At last, in 1869–1871, a Royal Commission reported strongly in favour of the establishment of a Central Department of Public Health. The Cabinet of 1871 shrank from the re-establishment of anything like the unpopular General Board of Health of 1848–1854. It seemed easier to merge its surviving fragments, along with the Poor Law Board (which had recently found itself driven to develop, out of the mere relief of destitution, a " Hospital Branch of the Poor Law "), in a new Department, which was styled the Local Government Board. For nearly half a century the Poor Law side of that Department maintained its predominance. The Public Health activities of the Local Authorities were, however, increased and developed by the more enterprising Boroughs, often at the instance of their Medical Officers of Health, and spasmodically regularised by clauses inserted in their own Local Acts—presently to be accepted at Whitehall and made available, at least optionally, to all Local Authorities, by successive Public Health Acts, Isolation Hospital Acts, Artisans' Dwellings Acts, Sale of Food and Drugs Acts and various other statutes, under which the local expenditure grew apace. This aspect of the Local Government Board was developed after 1913, when the Board of Control (which then superseded the Lunacy Commissioners in the supervision of the provision for persons of unsound mind, and began a like work on behalf of the feeble-minded) increasingly emphasised the Public Health aspect of this service, and was brought into closer relation with the Local Government Board. Meanwhile there was growing up, from 1911 onward, under separate Boards of Commissioners for England, Scotland, Ireland and Wales, the vast new system of Health Insurance that we have described, which brought some fifteen million insured persons and fourteen thousand medical practitioners into direct relation with the Government. Immediately after the War these two branches (Lunacy and Health Insurance) of what is essentially Public Health work, together with some of the functions of the Privy Council, the Board of Education and other Departments, were absorbed (though the Board of Control was not abolished), with all the existing duties of the Local Government Board, into a comprehensive Ministry of Health. This final step involved the definite relegation to a subordinate position of the supervision of the relief of destitution, from which the Department had sprung in 1834, and which, until 1919, had remained the dominant part of the Whitehall administration.[1]

The concern of the Government for education took the form, as is well known, from 1833 to 1839, of mere annual grants of money, the distribution of which was left to the two rival societies that were at the time contending for the control of popular schooling.[2] This abstention of the Government from organisation, direction and control of what ought to become a national service was far from contenting the educational reformers ; and J. A. Roebuck in the House of Commons, with Lord Brougham in the House of Lords, persistently demanded the establishment of a central Education Department ; a " Board of Education ", said the latter, under a responsible Minister. Not until 1839 did the Whig Government venture on this step, and then only by administrative action, requiring no prior consultation of Parliament. In February of that year, Lord John Russell communicated to the Lord President of the Council the famous " Queen's Letter ", desiring him to form a Board or Committee " for the consideration of all matters affecting the Education of the People ". In April 1839 such a Committee of the Privy Council was appointed by Order in Council, consisting of the Lord President (Lansdowne), the Lord Privy Seal (Duncannon), the Home Secretary (Lord John Russell) and the Chancellor of the Exchequer (Thomas Spring Rice). To this " Committee of Council on Education " Dr. J. Phillips Kay, then an Assistant Poor Law Commissioner, was appointed Secretary.[3]

In 1847, we are told, " the business of the Education Committee has absorbed the greater part of the staff of the Privy Council Office " ; and the young branch counted a total establishment of forty ; but it was still not an independent Department.[4] After ten years' arduous work, incessantly disturbed by the constant feuds between the Churches, the health of the indefatigable

---

[1] *The Story of Public Health,* by Sir Malcolm Morris, 1919 ; *The Ministry of Health,* by Sir Arthur Newsholme, 1925 ; an article entitled " The Passing of the Local Government Board " in *The Local Government Chronicle,* July 19, 1919 ; *The Ministry of Health and the Poor Law,* by Sir W. Chance, 1923.

[2] The National Society for Promoting the Education of the Poor in the Principles of the Established Church (established 1811), and the British and Foreign School Society (established 1810).

[3] *Life of Sir James Kay-Shuttleworth,* by Frank Smith, 1923.

[4] *Ibid.* p. 216.

Secretary broke down in 1849, and he was succeeded by R. W. (afterwards Lord) Lingen. For the next couple of decades the Lord President of the Council remained nominally in control of the educational organisation of the nation, and it was he who answered for the nascent Department in the House of Lords, whilst a Vice-President of the Council was eventually appointed to defend it in the House of Commons.

The first real Minister of Education, though still nominally only Vice-President of the Council, was W. E. Forster in 1868 ; and in spite of the vast increase of the work after the Act of 1870, and the still greater extensions of the next thirty years, it was not until 1899 that the Department was cut adrift from the Privy Council and set up as an independent Board of Education, with its own President and Parliamentary Secretary representing it in Parliament.

By this time the Education and the Public Health services were already becoming entangled. The Local Health Authorities had begun, here and there, to make special provision for the younger children, whilst the Local Education Authorities were beginning to deal with the physical, as well as the mental, requirements of the children of school age. Both authorities were concerned about the crippled, the deaf and dumb, the blind and the mentally defective children. The Local Government Board found itself directing the inspection, not only of the Poor Law Schools, but also of residential schools under philanthropic management which were certified for the reception of Poor Law children, from which the Inspectors of the Board of Education were excluded. With the reorganisation of the central, as well as the local administration of Public Health, on the one hand, and of Education on the other, these difficulties have been very largely surmounted. In all the County Boroughs, nearly all the Municipal Corporations over 20,000 population, and those Urban District Councils that had over 10,000 population in 1901, the Local Health Authority and the Local Education Authority [1] are now both Committees of the same Council. What has been still more helpful is the arrangement by which, since 1919, the two posts of Chief Medical Officer of the Board of Education and Medical Officer of the Ministry of Health have been united in the person

[1] In municipalities which are not County Boroughs, only for elementary education.

of Sir George Newman, who is thus able to enter into direct relations with the local officers of both services.

We must for completeness add that a third specialised Ministry—that of Labour—was established in 1917, out of the Labour Department of the Board of Trade, in order to systematise and develop the administration of its own part of the Framework of Prevention, relating to the able-bodied unemployed. With this development of the Employment Exchanges, the Juvenile Advisory Committees, the great system of Unemployment Insurance, the incipient Training Centres and the beginnings of Organised Migration, we shall deal in the following chapter.

The International Developments of the Framework of Prevention

In contrast with the administration of the Poor Law, which has remained for a couple of centuries almost entirely insular and without connection with the corresponding administrations of other countries, neither learning from their experience nor offering anything that they thought worth copying, the central administrations of the modern preventive services have had interesting and important international developments. We need not dwell on the concerted action, during the nineteenth century, of the governments of all countries with regard to defensive measures against infection from plague and cholera, and the development of an international system of quarantine. For the last three-quarters of a century the interchange of ideas and projects has been continuous. In England and Wales the early educational reformers were very largely indebted both to the experiments of individuals and to the governmental administrations of Switzerland and Prussia, as well as to the examples of Scotland and the United States ; whilst, in later days, we have learned much—notably in technical education and continuation schools—from Saxony and Bavaria, as well as with regard to school feeding from France and with regard to infant schools from Rome. In return, the British experiments in the medical inspection and treatment of children attending school, and the whole range of work of the Children's Care Committees, have supplied ideas to the Dominions, to America and to the continent of Europe. If Britain led the way in factory legislation, which has since been adopted to a greater or less extent by every industrial community, it was New Zealand and Australia that showed us the possibility of a Legal Minimum Wage. Main drainage, the water carriage system, and a publicly managed supply of filtered drinking-water were contributed to the world mainly by Great Britain, but a great deal of preventive medicine has come from France and Germany ; and remarkable experiments of American philanthropists in Infant Welfare and the treatment of child delinquents have been imitated and improved upon in other lands. If the world owes Health Insurance and Old Age Pensions to Germany, that country has recently adopted Unemployment Insurance on the British model. There is, in fact, nowadays the utmost internationalism in the methods of prevention of destitution, alike in the infant, the child of school age, the adolescent, the sick and infirm, the widows and the aged, not to say also (as we shall presently describe) the able-bodied unemployed. This "internationalism of prevention" marks it out as a world-movement. It has now become common for conferences to be arranged among the leading Public Health, Education and Factory Legislation officials of all the important nations concerning new developments. The various parts of what we have termed the Framework of Prevention are now among the subjects dealt with both by the League of Nations and by the International Labour Office, with a view to the gradual formation of a uniform and mutually consistent body of law and practice among all the constituent nations.

The Advancement of Knowledge

There is, we think, a useful lesson to be learnt from the course of the progressive improvements in the Education, Public Health and Factory Act services from 1835 to the present day. In all the parts of what we have termed the Framework of Prevention the administration was started without the formulation of any comprehensive scheme of reform. When the Cabinet and the House of Commons were sufficiently convinced of the gravity and extent of the evil to be remedied, even without any clear vision of the means by which a remedy could be generally applied, the most promising measures were experimentally put in hand. *Knowledge came only with action.* Moreover, it is now plain that no great advance could be made, either in testing the experimental action or in the discovery of new methods of prevention, until each distinct part of the work had been committed to its own specialised administration. *Only from the specialised attention of those actually engaged in the work, whether as amateurs or as professionals, can we expect discoveries in technique.*[1]

It is, indeed, interesting in 1928 to look back to the scanty knowledge, although fervent faith, with which the educational reformers of a century ago sought to attack the problem. Almost ludicrous to-day are the feeble instruments and futile devices with which they sought to cope with the ocean of child neglect, which they saw to be engulfing the nation. We may count it fortunate that their courage and their faith were not daunted by any adequate vision of the difficulties which, notwithstanding all their efforts, their successors would still have to overcome. Fortunate, too, is it that Parliament and the Cabinet did not insist, in 1833, 1839, 1861 or 1870, on there being in existence a thought-out, comprehensive and generally accepted scheme, before consenting to take action.

Thus, it has been a feature of the continuous development of the English system of National Education, first in elementary schooling under the Act of 1870, and, secondly and more conspicuously, in the reaching-out of the school influence towards the whole physical and hygienic well-being of the child, that it has depended, step by step, on the scientific investigation and original research into the problems as and when they were encountered by the administrators ; investigation and research which the Central Authority, in close co-operation with the officials of the leading Local Education Authorities, has constantly promoted and assisted. Here theory and experiment have gone hand in hand. What has proved successful on a small scale has presently been officially commended for widespread imitation by the more progressive Local Education Authorities ; and finally prescribed as obligatory from one end of the Kingdom to the other. Whether it is manual training or

---

[1] We may contrast with the repeated successes of the Public Health and Education administrations the failure of the Boards of Guardians and the Poor Law Board, from 1834 to 1871, to make any discoveries in the *technique* of education or the treatment of disease, though they had hundreds of thousands of children and sick persons in their charge ; or the failure of the Home Office on the one hand, and the Boards of Guardians on the other, to discover how to put effectively in operation the provisions of the Children Act of 1908.

domestic economy to be included in the curriculum, or the addition of physical drill or lessons in hygiene ; what is the best method of teaching arithmetic or history ; how the provision of meals for children found hungry at school can be most usefully connected with the medical inspection ; what are the proper limits and the relative spheres of usefulness of the Day Nursery, the Open Air School for Infants and Young Children and the Infant Department of the Elementary School ; how far competitive examinations can be made the basis for the award of Secondary School Scholarships without encouraging cramming ; together with the various questions successively referred for consideration and report to the Consultative Committee appointed by the Board of Education itself—all represent a progressive advancement of knowledge and a constant improvement of the technique of educational administration of which it would be hard to overestimate the advantage.

At least equally remarkable have been the successive discoveries of the Public Health administration. The paucity of knowledge, and the vagueness as to the direction in which effective prevention would be discovered, out of which emerged Edwin Chadwick's "Sanitary Idea" of 1835–1842, afforded little promise of the remarkable developments to which it led. The " two-inch pipe ", on which so much of the drainage work of the General Board of Health was based [1]—justified, as it may have been, in contrast with the magnitude of the Roman sewer tunnels—appears almost ludicrous as the foundation of modern main drainage systems. Dr. Southwood Smith's treatment of " fever ", like the empirical dosing with quinine, gave no vision of the elaborate procedure of universal notification, compulsory isolation, preventive immunisation by inoculation, segregation of contacts, hospital provision, anti-toxin treatment and " after care " supervision by which the community of the twentieth century is protected from the spread of infectious disease. And when, even as lately as 1900, medical attention began to be concentrated on Infant Mortality, none of those concerned could have formulated the whole apparatus of prevention, from ante-natal supervision and immediate birth-notification, to

---

[1] See *Engineers and Officials*, 1854, an anonymous pamphlet in the British Museum.   For the subsequent development see *Outline of the Practice of Preventive Medicine*, by Sir George Newman, edition of 1926.

universal health-visiting, infant welfare centres, and milk distribution, by which the infantile death-rate has been, within a quarter of a century, actually halved. We are thus able to realise the importance of the fact—in marked contrast to the Poor Law Medical Service—that scientific investigation and research occupy a large part of the intellect and activity of the ideal Medical Officer of Health. We see him observing and recording the location and circumstances of diseases ; we find him applying logical methods to the discovery of the causes of the local outbreaks ; he brings statistics to bear on the problems of disease and makes them the foundation of local criticism ; he calls to his aid the microscope and chemical analysis. It is in the department of the Medical Officer of Health that (outside the hospital or the university) we find the bacteriological laboratory, with all its potentialities of scientific diagnosis. We are inclined to think that, in England to-day, there is more scientific research into the cause and treatment, as well as the prevention, of disease done by the medical officers of the Public Health Service, in proportion to their numbers (not to say their financial resources), than in any other branch of the medical profession outside the great hospitals.

It is seldom realised how much credit is due to the specialised Branch of the Home Office which has been responsible for the administration of the Factory and Workshop Acts,[1] for the successive developments of the very foundation of the Framework of Prevention. The legislation of 1802, 1819 and 1825 by which Parliament sought to protect the factory operatives was, for lack of administrative technique, almost inoperative. Nor could any reformer in that generation describe how any effective prevention of unduly long hours of labour, unhealthy conditions of work, and industrial oppression of women and children could be secured. But Michael Thomas Sadler and Lord Shaftesbury, with the pressure of Richard Oastler and the textile operatives behind them, induced Parliament and the Cabinet to set up an administration to make the attempt. This administration it is to which we owe the gradual creation, at the hands of a succession of devoted Inspectors and inventive central officials, of an

[1] And also to the Branch which, until the establishment in 1921 of the separate Ministry of Mines, was responsible for the administration of the Mines Regulation Acts (see *The Home Office*, by Sir Edward Troup, 1925).

elaborate technique of registration and periodical visitation, certifying surgeons and " labour certificates ", protective guards for dangerous machinery, codes as to " oversteaming " and ventilation, " dry rubbing " and working with lead, an ever-growing schedule of " industrial diseases ", devices such as the reporting of accidents and " particulars clauses ", and what not, by which, after generations of continued experiment, prevention has at last been made fairly, though still not completely, effective.

We may, we think, draw the lesson that, in the great problems of social administration, whilst it is to science that we have to look for success, yet neither the special discoveries of the laboratory, not their technical application to the industrial and social conditions in which they have to operate, can usually be discerned until after the necessary administrations have been started. Achievement in the field of social administration comes only by the method of " trial and error ". At the start, though the evil to be remedied may be recognised, there is never any adequate science formulated, never in existence any completely thought-out plan of reform. The administrative technique cannot be devised save only in the actual working of the administration itself. Only when we get a specialised organ set to do the work that Parliament or the Cabinet has commanded, will it be discovered, bit by bit, how the work can be done. Medicine and engineering have progressed in like manner. As it has been with the doctor's treatment and cure of ill-health in the individual patient, or the engineer's response to the order to construct a bridge over shifting quicksands, so it has actually been, in the England of the nineteenth century, with the prevention of disease in the community, with the prevention of child neglect and illiteracy, and with the prevention of industrial oppression in the factory and the mine. Not until Public Health administration, Educational administration and Factory Act administration had been actually started, each of them groping in the fog of ignorance as to how to accomplish their several purposes, have these purposes begun step by step to be accomplished.

CHAPTER VII

UNEMPLOYMENT AS A DISEASE OF MODERN INDUSTRY

WE cannot, in a work devoted to Poor Law history, deal adequately with either the history or the causes of Unemployment, any more than with those of physical or mental disease, each of which would require a treatise to itself. But in the present century the involuntary wagelessness of masses of workmen has exercised so great an influence on the evolution of the Poor Law that the subject cannot be omitted. In the following pages we describe how Unemployment has impinged upon Poor Law administration; and what suggestions are contributed by the extensive experiments of the past forty years towards the problem of the prevention of the large proportion of destitution that Unemployment directly causes.

The Rise of Unemployment

Though at all times some workers have found themselves wageless, massed destitution by reason merely of Unemployment is a comparatively modern phenomenon. It did not occur in slave civilisations, nor in mediaeval serfdom, nor is it found, even to-day, in countries in which any form of peasant agriculture remains dominant or widely prevalent. Slaves or serfs were normally given maintenance somehow, or else, exceptionally, were allowed to die. Their semi-starvation without being found work would have been a mere waste of their superior's income. The peasant agriculturist might be severely reduced by flood, pestilence, or failure of the harvest, by earthquake or fire, or by the destructive visitations of armed bands; but at least he always had his plot to dig, and the common waste or forest from

631

which to draw firewood and other necessaries. But when the slave
changed into the serf, and the serf into the freedman ; when the
copyholder and the cottier squatter on the waste became hired
labourers at money wages, then involuntary Unemployment
stood out as a new cause of destitution, and with it came an
aimless wandering in search of work. Yet, so long as the hired
wage-labourer was exceptional in a world of independent producers ; so long, too, as journeymen habitually became masters,
and carried on production to supply the needs of their own
neighbours, any widespread or continued destitution from lack of
employment was uncommon. Vagrancy, indeed, occurred at all
times, but it arose often from the wish to wander, or from the
desire to escape from some particular local oppression or personal
complication, or merely from a vague aspiration for better conditions. The severe statutes against Vagrancy, together with the
Law of Settlement and Removal, proceeded on the assumption
that there was no need for any migration or wandering as a
means of obtaining employment, and that such movements
were evidence, either of a wish to live without working, or, at
least, of an illegitimate attempt to exact more than the local
customary wage. The milder measures, which the Elizabethan
Poor Law applied to the homekeeping folk, took the form,
characteristically, of a primitive local Employment Exchange,
the Overseer allocating any wageless man to a master, or else
setting him to make up into useful commodities the parish stock
of flax, iron, hemp, etc.

We do not forget the economic dislocations that accompanied
the changes in the English agricultural economy at the close of
both the fifteenth and the sixteenth centuries. Nevertheless it
seems true to say that Unemployment of the modern type appears,
on any appreciable scale, first sporadically in the seventeenth century (as, for instance, in London on the disbandment of the armies
in 1646–1660) ; and it becomes a more frequently recurring trouble
with the gradual and ever-widening industrial transformations
of the ensuing couple of centuries.[1] Along with the successive

[1] " Unemployment, as we know it, is, comparatively speaking, a new
phenomenon. The introduction of steam power in the early years of the last
century, brought about a great change in the occupations of a large proportion
of the population, but during the expansion of trade which followed, there was
no Unemployment which gave rise to any social problem comparable to that
which subsequently emerged. Unemployment did, it is true, result first from

improvements in transportation and the growth of foreign trade ; the steadily increasing habit of producing for distant markets ; the rapid changes in industrial processes and the development of capitalist farming on a commercial basis ; and the massing together of large numbers of "hands" in the factories and mines, comes an almost continuous series of fluctuations in volume of this industry or that, in one place or another. With such fluctuations, however caused, appears involuntary Unemployment on a large scale, as the characteristic disease of the modern industrial system. Whether or not this disease has, during the last hundred years, increased in volume or duration, relatively to the magnitude of the population or the extent of the business transacted, is, in the absence of authentic statistics, not so certain as it seems. But the disease has made its appearance in all countries adopting the modern organisation of industry ; and it seems to prevail in such countries almost in proportion to the completeness of their Industrial Revolution.

This form of destitution has ominous new features. Unlike ill-health or old age, or other physical incapacity, the idleness due to inability to find employment deteriorates character as well as health, and gradually destroys both energy and skill. Further, involuntary idleness has a dangerous tendency, if it endures for any length of time, to turn into work-shyness. No man voluntarily becomes aged or mentally defective, and very few become voluntarily ill, merely in order to attract alms from the charitable or maintenance out of public funds ; but this voluntary pauperism is unfortunately a frequent outcome of quite involuntary wagelessness. And there is a third peculiarity of this characteristic disease of modern industry. When the mediaeval village suffered from destitution, more frequently than

---

the displacement of hand workers, and, later, as a consequence of over-production in particular directions. Towards the end of the century the evil became more manifest, notably in 1893 ; and in the first decade of the twentieth century it assumed still more serious proportions " (Report of the Unemployment Insurance Committee (Lord Blanesburgh's), 1927, vol. i. p. 23).

In this connection it is of some significance that the earliest use recorded in the New English Dictionary of the word " unemployed " is in Milton's *Paradise Lost* (1667) ; and that Yarranton (1677) was apparently the first to apply it to workmen (" a hundred thousand poor people unemployed "). Its use as a substantive seems to come only two centuries later (in 1882). The word " unemployment " appears to have been first used in 1888, and to have become common only in the following decade.

is usually remembered, from failure of crop, from flood or conflagration, or from the ravages of pestilence or war, all the folk in a common calamity hungered together. In a modern city, masses of men find themselves periodically wageless in the midst of plenty ; of plenty openly manifested in shops and warehouses full of food and other necessaries, in the flaunting luxury of a wealthy class, and in the regular work at good wages enjoyed by other workmen. Involuntary Unemployment is a concomitant of particular industrial change as well as of general industrial depression ; it exists, in some industries and in some places, even when business is brisk and the nation flourishing. There is, in fact, so both economists and employers agree, no necessary relation between the amount or range or intensity of Unemployment from time to time existing in a country, and the magnitude of its aggregate production, or the sum of profit of its capitalist class, or the amount of its accumulated wealth. This reduction of whole families to destitution in the midst of riches produces a peculiar psychological reaction. Though peasant revolts have usually arisen in periods of economic distress, the people's complaint was always against some political grievance. Against the "blight", by which a whole country-side used to be occasionally reduced to penury, no peasantry has ever rebelled. But when thousands of factory operatives or miners find themselves, without any obvious physical calamity, and merely by what seems an act of will on the part of those who own the instruments of production, denied even the opportunity to work for wages, and are thereby reduced to destitution through no fault of their own, they become bitter and angry, as well as a danger to the existing social order.

Involuntary Unemployment is now a world-wide constant phenomenon in every industralised state. But although it was certainly extensive in the Great Britain of 1826, and enormous in that of 1841 and 1879—although it has repeatedly reached a great height in the United States, as well as in many European countries and in Australia—it is only within the present century that its extent and duration has been accurately measured, and that only in a few countries. It is now known that Great Britain has had, at the best of times during the past half-century, at least 2 per cent of its wage-earners, or a quarter of a million workmen, unable immediately to find employment ; and that the proportion has periodically risen to 8 or 10 per cent, and the number to a million, whilst it has occasionally amounted to more than two millions. The duration of Unemployment in each case is apt to vary with its extent. When the number of the workless is at its lowest, very few of them need remain unemployed for long. On the other hand, Unemployment among many hundreds of thousands of men involves many thousands of them remaining without the opportunity of earning a subsistence for their families for long periods, even for several years at a stretch. For Germany, and a few smaller countries, there are statistics representing substantially a similar state of things. For the United States, such imperfect figures as exist indicate fluctuations in the total numbers at work, and both percentages and numbers unemployed, apparently as great as in Germany or Great Britain. Indeed, using all the information available, there seems no reason to suppose either that any industrialised community is free from this disease, or that it prevails to a greater extent, *relatively to the size of the wage-earning industrial population*, in the poorer nations such as Italy, Austria or Russia, than in those, such as the United States, Australia or Great Britain, in which the wealth and annual product per head is highest. To sum up, there is no reason to assume that the amount of involuntary Unemployment in any country at any time has any necessary relation to the amount of its accumulated wealth, the amount of its annual product, or the amount of rent or profit that is contemporaneously being received by its landlords and capitalists. The constant destitution of masses of wage-earners due merely to want of work is, in fact, the most sensational, we might even say the most scandalous, manifestation of poverty in the midst of riches.[1]

---

[1] The books, pamphlets, articles and reports about Unemployment—previously scanty—become after 1883 almost innumerable. *A Bibliography of Unemployment and the Unemployed*, by F. Isabel Taylor, 1909, enumerates, along with a few of earlier date, 700 such publications in Great Britain alone. Far more exhaustive for the period 1914–1925 is *The Bibliography of Unemployment* issued by the International Labour Office, 1926. We may mention specially the interesting but slight *Report on the Government Organisation of Unemployed Labour* (Fabian Society, 1884); *In Darkest England and the Way out*, by General Booth, 1890; Board of Trade Report on Agencies and Methods for dealing with the Unemployed, c. 7182 of 1893; Reports of House of Commons Select Committee on Distress from Want of Employment, 1895 and 1896; *The Problem of the Unemployed*, by J. A. Hobson, 1896, and *The Economics of Unemployment* by the same, 1922; *Unemployment: a Problem of Industry*, by (Sir) W. H. Beveridge, 1909; *The Remedy for Unemployment*,

Unemployment regarded as Inevitable, if not Desirable

Why then was involuntary Unemployment so tardily recognised as a disease of Modern Industry ? The very word Unemployment did not come into use until the last decade of the nineteenth century. Until well into the second half of that century, the periodical wagelessness of masses of men, as one of the principal modern causes of destitution, was either ignored, or, when recognised as an evil, was regarded as unavoidable. The idea that extreme penury and periodical semi-starvation was " the lot of man ", so far as the wage-earners were concerned, dependent on an inexorable law of population, and an equally imperative " Theory of the Wages Fund ", had not yet ceased to influence public opinion. To this lingering pessimism was added the opinion, on the part of many employers of labour, that—to quote the words once used by Charles Booth—" the modern system of industry will not work without some unemployed margin, some reserve of labour " ; [1] and that the constant existence of Unemployment was therefore necessary, and even advantageous to the community as a whole ; an opinion which was more than once reiterated before the Poor Law Commission of 1905–1909.[2] This

---

by A. R. Wallace, 1909 ; *The Public Organisation of the Labour Market*, by S. and B. Webb (Part II. of Minority Report of Poor Law Commission with Introduction), 1909.

[1] *Life and Labour of the People*, by Charles Booth, vol. i. p. 152 of 1892 edition.

[2] The special investigators, Mr. (afterwards Sir) Cyril Jackson and the Rev. J. C. Pringle (now Secretary of the C.O.S.), emphasise this in their Report into the Effects of Employment or Assistance given to the Unemployed. They state that in Liverpool and elsewhere the employers regard the permanent existence of a pool of unemployed labour necessary to " the Management of Men ". " By careful distribution of irregular work the margin necessary for the purpose can be kept up. The master porter, foreman, or other who has to get work done is much helped if he is always conferring a favour upon the man he employs, and a very marked favour upon those whom he employs frequently or constantly. This we believe to be the real objections to the schemes for diminishing irregularity of employment in the docks and warehouses of Liverpool by an association among the employers of this kind of labour, so ably and powerfully urged by the leading men of that city for many years. The men responsible for getting the work done are afraid to give the men security of tenure, for fear lest it should weaken their power over them. We made careful inquiries into the matter in Liverpool. In another town the manager of the gas undertaking informed us that to dovetail the unskilled labour needs of corporation departments into each other, in order to secure work for the men, would be absolutely subversive of discipline . . ." (Report of Poor Law Commission, Appendix, vol. xix., 1909).

Charles Booth, whilst stating the need for some margin of " reserve of labour ", added, in 1892, that " the margin in London seems to be exaggerated

led, subconsciously, to an impression, right down to the last
decade of the century, that those who found themselves without
employment were, if not the improvident and feckless, or the
indolent and the "work-shy", at best merely accidental sufferers
from transient ebbs in the tide of trade, due to improvements in
processes, or to changes of taste or fashion, or to recurrent
seasonal or cyclical fluctuations.[1]

in every department, and enormously so in the lowest class of labour. Some
employers seem to think that this state of things is in their interest—the
argument has been used by dock officials—but this view appears short-sighted,
for labour deteriorates under casual employment more than its price falls.
I believe it to be to the interest of every employer to have as many regularly
employed servants as possible ; but it is still more to the interest of the community, and most of all to that of the employed. To divide a little work
amongst a number of men—giving all a share—may seem kind and even
just, and I have known such a course to be taken with this idea. It is only
justifiable as a temporary expedient, serving otherwise but to prolong a bad state
of things " (*Life and Labour of the People of London*, by Charles Booth, vol. i.
pp. 152-153 of edition of 1892).

[1] How it seemed to a great business man, of exceptional intelligence and
knowledge, as late as 1903, may be seen from the following passage from
Charles Booth's *Life and Labour of the People* : " Looked at from near by, these
cycles of depression have a distinctly harmful and even a cruel aspect ; but
from a more distant point of view, ' afar from the sphere of our sorrow ', they
seem less malignant. They might then perhaps, with a little effort of the
imagination, be considered as the orderly beating of the heart causing the
blood to circulate—each throb a cycle. Even in the range of our lives, within
easy grasp of human experience, whether or not men suffer from these alternations
depends on the unit of time on which economic life is based. Those who live
from day to day, or from week to week, and even those who live from year
to year, may be pinched when trade contracts—some of them must be. There
are some victims, but those who are able and willing to provide in times of
prosperity for the lean years which seem inevitably to follow, do not suffer
at all ; and if the alternations of good and bad times be not too sudden or too
great, the community gains, not only by the strengthening of character under
stress, but also by a direct effect on enterprise. As to character, the effect,
especially on wage-earners, is very similar to that exercised on a population
by the recurrence of winter as compared to the enervation of continual summer "
(*Life and Labour of the People*, by Charles Booth, 1903, Second Series, Industry,
vol. v. pp. 73-74 ; see *The Decay of Capitalist Civilisation*, by S. and B. Webb,
1923, p. 160).

The economic student will be reminded of Nassau Senior's view of the
positive enjoyment of unemployment by the unemployed ! " But this evil
[of " anxious and desponding moments which the thought of so precarious a
situation must sometimes occasion "] is compensated, and in most dispositions
more than compensated, by the diminution of his toil. We believe, after all,
that nothing is so much disliked as steady regular labour ; and that the opportunities for idleness afforded by an occupation of irregular employment are so
much more than an equivalent for its anxiety [as] to reduce the wages of such
occupations below the common average." (*Political Economy*, by Nassau W.
Senior, sixth edition, 1872, pp. 207-208 ; *Seasonal Trades*, edited by Sidney
Webb and Arnold Freeman, 1912, p. 10 ; *Contemporary Theories of Unemployment and of Unemployment Relief*, by F. C. Mills, 1917, p. 14.)

This purely negative attitude among " enlightened " persons towards the misery and demoralisation directly traceable to Unemployment became difficult to maintain in the latter part of the century, in face of the magnitude and duration of the perpetually recurring cycles of trade booms and trade depressions. How could shipwrights and boilermakers, iron and steel workers, miners and cotton operatives be reasonably expected to regulate their weekly expenditure—not to mention the procreation of children—in such a way as to secure continuous livelihood for their households throughout months, and even years, of involuntary Unemployment affecting whole districts, and good and bad workmen alike ?   As early as 1857 we find an organ of orthodox Political Economy declaring that " The Poor Law is for the relief of a class who are unable to work ; not for the relief of men eager for work, and delighting in the sense of independence, but from some occasional cause unable to find the means of work. There would be nothing more fatal to the moral feeling of our working men than to reduce them in large numbers to a sense of pauperism and dependence at every temporary season of commercial distress. . . . This is a case where an economic law should yield to a social law ; and all the labour that can be employed, though it be without profit, or even at a prudent loss, ought to be employed, to avert, as far as possible, the terrible strain on one class of the community." [1]

This nascent consciousness in 1857 of communal responsibility for an incidental effect of mass production for foreign markets (one of the greatest sources of British riches) on the daily life of the wage-earner and his family was strengthened and confirmed by the economic circumstances of the ensuing decades. The acute depression of 1878–1879 was succeeded by only a brief and partial expansion during 1881–1883.   A period of prolonged though not exceptional contraction then followed, during which certain staple trades experienced the most sudden and excessive fluctuations.   In the great industry of shipbuilding, for instance, the bad times of 1879 were succeeded by a period during which trade expanded by leaps and bounds, more than twice the tonnage being built in 1883 than in 1879.   In the very next year this enormous production came suddenly to an end, many shipbuilding yards being closed and whole towns on the north-east coast

---

[1] *The Economist*, December 5, 1857, pp. 1343-1344.

finding their occupation for the moment destroyed. The total tonnage built fell from 1,250,000 in 1883 to 750,000 in 1884, 540,000 in 1885, and to the still lower total of 473,000 in 1886. Thousands of the most highly skilled and best organised mechanics, who had been brought to Jarrow or Sunderland the year before, found themselves reduced to absolute destitution, not from any failure of their industry, but merely because the exigencies of competitive profit-making had led to the concentration in one year of the normal production of two. " In every shipbuilding port ", says Robert Knight,[1] the able and conservative-minded General Secretary of the Boilermakers in his Annual Report for the year 1886, " there are to be seen thousands of idle men vainly seeking for an honest day's work. The privation that has been endured by them, their wives and children, is terrible to contemplate. Sickness has been very prevalent, whilst the hundreds of pinched and hungry faces have told a tale of suffering and privation which no optimism could minimise or conceal. Hide it—cover it up as we may, there is a depth of grief and trouble, the full revelations of which, we believe, cannot be indefinitely postponed. The workman may be ignorant of science and the arts, and the sum of his exact knowledge may be only that which he has gained in his closely circumscribed daily toil ; but he is not blind, and his thoughts do not take the shape of daily and hourly thanksgiving that his condition is not worse than it is ; he does not imitate the example of the pious shepherd of Salisbury Plain, who derived supreme contentment from the fact that a kind Providence had vouchsafed him salt to eat with his potatoes. He sees the lavish display of wealth in which he has no part. He sees a large and growing class enjoying inherited abundance. He sees miles of costly residences, each occupied by fewer people than are crowded into single rooms of the tenement in which he lives. He cannot fail to reason that there must be something wrong in a system which effects such unequal distribution of the wealth created by labour. . . ." [2]

[1] Some reference to Robert Knight, whose long and successful administration of the United Society of Boilermakers has passed out of memory, will be found in our volume, *History of Trade Unionism*, 1920 (pp. 322-324, 351-355, 378, 421 and 554), and *Industrial Democracy*, 1897 (pp. 30, 132, 204, 228 and 451).

[2] Quoted in *The History of Trade Unionism*, 1920, by Sidney and Beatrice Webb, pp. 277-279.

The Local Relief Funds

But, as had often been found when, for one or other reason, Poor Relief was not provided, the wageless workmen were not allowed to go without food. What was left undone by the statutory authorities was attempted, with even fewer safeguards, by voluntary charity. To supplement the individual almsgiving by which the actual starvation of the unemployed workmen had often been prevented, there grew up a custom of organising, in most industrial centres, temporary Relief Funds, the operations of which were elaborately investigated by the Poor Law Commission of 1905–1909. "The old system", so the Special Investigators reported, " was to ask the Mayor to open a Fund whenever there was an outcry as to unemployment. He issued an appeal in the Press or by letter, the response to which in the form of donations was of course very uncertain, varying with his personal popularity, as well as with the general opinion of the wealthier classes as to the existence of exceptional distress." [1] Innumerable Emergency Funds of this sort, varying in amount from a few hundreds to several hundreds of thousands of pounds sterling,[2] are to be found, in the records of the past century. The great distributions in London in 1861–1862 (at the East End Police Courts) and in 1886 (the notorious Mansion House Fund) are well known. In 1878–1881 such Emergency Funds were started in nearly all the large towns. In Sunderland, for instance, " in the early eighties there was great depression, and the grass was growing in practically every shipyard on the river. Men, women and children were literally starving. Private and sporadic efforts proved utterly inadequate to meet the requirements of the situation. At length the Mayor of the day set on foot an organisation to cover the whole borough. So widespread and acute was the excessive poverty that the numbers relieved by this Distress Committee reached, on one occasion, the huge total of over 17,000 individuals." [3] At Newcastle-upon-Tyne, the Poor

---

[1] Report on the Effects of Employment or Assistance given to the Unemployed, by Mr. Cyril Jackson and Rev. J. C. Pringle, p. 88, Report of Poor Law Commission, 1909, Appendix, vol. xix.

[2] Report of the Committee appointed at a Public Meeting at the City of London Tavern, May 2, 1826, to relieve the Manufacturers, by W. H. Hyett, 1829 (when £232,000 was raised).

[3] Evidence before the Poor Law Commission, Q. 52,708.

Law Commission was told : " Whenever serious distress has arisen here, say by severe winters, etc., public sympathy has always been evoked. Voluntary Distress Committees have been formed, money has flown in plentifully, and district or ward sub-committees have administered the necessary relief after investigation into the cases. Even then there has been a considerable amount of malingering, and caution has had to be exercised."[1] The general experience was, however, that "distress had become very acute before these funds had started and before any organisation could be formed and shaped untold miseries were endured by the sufferers. In the majority of cases these committees and officials were new to the work on each separate occasion, and had not the data and experience of previous efforts to guide them. The great part of the work of investigation and distribution had to be carried on at such time as could be spared to the work, and could not, from the very nature of the circumstances, be very thorough and complete. The test of willingness to work was not applied, could not, indeed, be applied, and the funds were distributed in money or kind, really as charities. The result of all these circumstances was that a very great amount of imposition was practised by thoroughly unworthy persons, in many instances the same persons over and over again, and the worthy and deserving generally kept themselves in the background and were overlooked."[2]   " It was found ", for instance, at Nottingham, in 1885–1886, " that there were a good many applications for relief from persons who gave false addresses and who could not be found when enquiry was made, and of those who applied others were not in need of or deserving of help ; whilst others in deep need were unwilling to apply, and their almost starving condition was only made known by friends and neighbours ".[3]   At Birmingham, " some of the local committees in 1905 adopted the system of giving one week's relief to the unsuitable cases rather than incur the odium of an entire refusal. In five districts, dealing with 2060 cases, 775 were discontinued at the end of one week. . . . The bulk of the one week cases

---

[1] Evidence before the Poor Law Commission, Q. 91,141, Par. 11 ; see also House of Commons Return of Circular Letters . . . with Reference to Pauperism and Distress, and of the Replies Received and also of other Papers on the Subject (1886, Session I. (6a), lvi).

[2] Report of South Shields Distress Committee, 1907.

[3] The Mayor's Relief Fund, 1885–1886, Nottingham Reports, p. 15.

may be taken to have been undesirables." [1]   Nevertheless, there can be no doubt that these Emergency Funds found many thousands of genuine cases in urgent need of relief.   " The reports of the investigators ", says a Chatham Report in 1905, " are pathetic documents, containing as they do tales of fearful want and of heroic efforts to avoid the workhouse.   There is no doubt that the regular help of this fund has already kept many from the fate they so much dread, thus preserving their sense of comparative independence and relieving the ratepayers of a serious burden." [2]   Experience indicated, too, that in the absence of any adequate public provision such Emergency Funds were never wanting in any season of distress.   Right up to the Unemployed Workmen Act of 1905—indeed, until the institution of National Insurance against Unemployment in 1911—popular newspapers rushed in, perhaps from somewhat mixed motives ; and raised tens of thousands of pounds for distribution in particular localities with hardly a pretence of investigation. [3]

Some of the more responsible of the administrators of these Emergency Funds were always trying to use them to start or subsidise Relief Works, either carried on by the Local Authorities out of charitable donations, or by various groups of philanthropists.   Thus, at Nottingham, in 1837, arrangements were secretly made with the Town Council to put selected men of the unemployed class upon sewer construction ; the difference in cost being made up from the charitable funds.   " If . . . a man with a large family applies for relief, whom Mr. B. [the Relieving Officer] knows to be industrious, who is not of pauper habits, but by the depression of trade is thrown out of employ, and obliged to seek temporary assistance . . . he gives him an order to the foreman of the work in hand, who sets him on by task work." [4]   In other cases, direct employment was afforded by philanthropy.   We find the " National Philanthropic Association " (founded in 1842) employing, winter by winter, 50 or 100 men in cleaning the streets,

[1] " Three Birmingham Relief Funds ", by F. Tillyard, in *Economic Journal*, December 1905.

[2] Report of Chatham, Rochester and Gillingham Unemployed Relief Committee, 1905.

[3] The more recent newspaper funds were described in Evidence before Poor Law Commission, 1909, Qs. 20,415-21,048, 78,638-78,702, 85,623-85,699. Further particulars of these " stunts " are given in *From the City to Fleet Street*, by S. Hall Richardson, 1927, ch. xi., " Charity at Large ", pp. 144-165.

[4] Mr. Gulson's Report to Poor Law Commissioners, April 23, 1837, p. 8.

" so that able-bodied men may be prevented from burdening the parish rates, and preserved independent of workhouse alms and degradation. . . . At one time upwards of 100 of these orderlies were employed at a weekly payment of 12s. each, under inspectors."[1] "During the year 1846–1847 . . . the Association has employed, at its own cost, 546 street orderlies."[2]

Innumerable examples of Relief Works of this kind are reported in the local newspapers between 1820 and 1880, at every period of depression. They had invariably three characteristics. The work was supposed to be restricted to sober and industrious men, not habitual paupers, thrown out of employment through no fault of their own. Married men with families were preferred. The amount earned was practically never more than a bare pittance, the work being paid for at low rates, and only provided for a few hours a day or a few days a week. The plan, in short, was always one of distributing small doles of " Employment Relief " to selected individuals. In 1878, an attempt by Francis Peek to systematise and develop this plan of endeavouring " to find partially remunerative employment for the Able-bodied ", under a central committee for London as a whole,[3] led to an objection from Sir Charles Trevelyan, from the standpoint of the C.O.S., in which the economic drawbacks of such a course were set forth. " Labour ", he said, " is an excellent thing. . . . But . . . it must be labour subjected to the true conditions of labour, the full market rate of wages on one side and severe privation on the other. Charity is also an excellent thing, but . . . when . . . labour and charity are mixed up together, great abuse and demoralisation are always engendered. . . . It was so in the Irish Famine. It was so in the Cotton Famine. It was so, to come nearer to the point, in the workrooms for women at the East End of London. . . . This should be left to the Guardians to do who have the law at their backs, and are fortified and guided by detailed instructions from the Local Government Board."[4]

[1] *The Charities of London*, by Sampson Low, 1850, pp. 149-150.
[2] Report of Progress in the Employment of the Poor (National Philanthropic Association), 1853. See also *Times*, December 26, 1845, and June 6, 1849 ; and *A Plea for the Very Poor*, 1850.
[3] *Times*, December 24, 1878.
[4] *Ibid.* December 25, 1878. It should, however, be noted that private relief works of this kind continued until the advent of municipal relief works under the Unemployed Workmen Act, 1905. The Liverpool Central Relief

The Advent of Political Democracy

In the very year that Robert Knight, as we have mentioned, was indicting the existing organisation of industry, the dividing line was reached in British constitutional history between the middle-class or plutocratic oligarchy, which had ruled since 1832, and the incoming wage-earning electorate. " Next year," declared Joseph Chamberlain, whom the rising tide of Radicalism had virtually forced Gladstone to admit to the Cabinet, to his working-class constituents at Birmingham in January 1885, " two millions of men will enter, for the first time, into the full enjoyment of their political rights. . . . To-day Parliament is elected by three millions of electors, of whom perhaps one-third are of the working classes. Next year a new House will come to Westminster elected by five millions of men, of whom three-fifths belong to the labouring population. It is a revolution which has been peacefully and silently accomplished. The centre of power has been shifted, and the old order is giving place to the new. . . . You are in the position of men who have suddenly come into a fortune of which a short time ago you had only a distant expectation. Almost immediately you will be placed in the full enjoyment of those political rights of which up to this time you have only had a trifling foretaste." [1]

The Radical leader was in no uncertainty as to the trend that the greatly enlarged electorate would and should give to the nation's policy. " I think ", he declared in the same year, " that we shall have to give a good deal more attention to what is called social legislation. We have a good deal to guide us, and much experience in that direction. Social legislation is not new. The Poor Law, for instance, is social legislation. It recognises that right to live which in some quarters is denied, and in itself is an endeavour on the part of a community to save themselves from the shame and the disgrace of allowing any of

---

and Charity Organisation Society, among others, long maintained workshops for the Unemployed, where respectable able-bodied men were enabled " to tide over a period of temporary lack of work ". They were employed at wood-chopping, bundling chips and making fire-lighters ; and " by making a proper effort, a man may receive from 1s. 6d. to 2s. 6d. daily ", on a scale of piece-work rates, with a bonus (Manual of Instructions . . . of the Liverpool Central Relief and Charity Organisation Society, 1906, pp. 19, 20).

[1] *Mr. Chamberlain's Speeches*, edited by Charles W. Boyd, 1914, pp. 131-132.

its members to starve. There are many people who propose to carry it further." " We are told ", he added, " that this country is the paradise of the rich ; it should be our task to see that it does not become the purgatory of the poor. It should be our task to strive, each according to his opportunity, to leave the world a little better than we found it." And he did not fail to warn the Liberal Members of Parliament and candidates at the Eighty Club that " because State Socialism may cover very injurious and very unwise theories, that is no reason at all why we should refuse to recognise the fact that Government is only the organisation of the whole people for the benefit of all its members ; and that the community may—ay, and ought to— provide for all its members benefits which it is impossible for individuals to provide by their solitary and separate efforts ".[1]

Hence it is hardly surprising that it was Joseph Chamberlain who, first among British statesmen, realised the bankruptcy of the Poor Law and the inadequacy of Voluntary Agencies as methods of dealing with the destitution caused directly by involuntary Unemployment. At the beginning of 1885 practically all the trades of Birmingham were in a state of extreme depression. " Hundreds of jewellers, silversmiths and electro-plate workers ", we read, " had been out or employment for months, if not years." [2] The result was the starting of a " Mayor's Fund " for the relief of the Unemployed, with the usual unsatisfactory features ; and an attempt by the Town Council to " make work " for as many men as possible. These resources were, however, limited, and the Birmingham Town Council implored the Birmingham Board of Guardians, in June 1885, at least to confer as to the measures called for by the continued distress. But the Guardians were " of opinion that no practical or useful result would be likely to follow ", and declined to confer, as they felt that the ordinary Poor Law was capable of dealing with the matter. The reluctance of the respectable craftsmen of Birmingham to condemn himself, his wife and his children to the evil promiscuity of the General Mixed Workhouse ; or, if he was unmarried, to subject himself to the penal conditions of the Able-bodied Test Workhouse, was known to Chamberlain. To the citizen of Birmingham, with its active political life, the

---

[1] *Mr. Chamberlain's Speeches*, edited by Charles W. Boyd, 1914, pp. 143, 150.
[2] *Birmingham Daily Gazette*, September 30, 1885.

disfranchisement entailed by Poor Relief may also have been specially deterrent. In October 1885 Chamberlain personally appealed to the Poor Law Guardians to reconsider their attitude. He explained the objections to the raising of special relief funds. He pointed out that the Mayor had declared that "it was not possible for the Corporation to find work for any considerable number *without displacing workmen already employed*". As the leading citizen of Birmingham, he urged upon the local Poor Law Authority that, in the then state of the law, "none but the appointed Guardians of the Poor" were in a position to perform the plain public duty of meeting the distress. And he concluded with the pregnant observation that "the law exists for securing the assistance of the community at large in aid of their destitute members ; and, where the necessity has arisen from no fault of the persons concerned, there ought to be no idea of degradation connected with such assistance. Those compelled to apply have probably paid rates and taxes in past time. The payment is, in part, an insurance against misfortune." But the Birmingham Guardians, firmly holding to the position of the Local Government Board during the previous decade, remained obdurate, refusing even to give Outdoor Relief in return for work in the Labour Yard. It was not long after this definite refusal of the Poor Law Authorities to make any special provision for the relief of distress from Unemployment, when a General Election had supervened, that Chamberlain found himself again in office. In the early months of 1886 it was forced upon his attention, as President of the Local Government Board,[1] that up and down the country there continued to be exceptional distress among "large numbers of persons usually in regular employment". The fact that this distress had not manifested itself in the statistics of pauperism did not surprise him. In the well-known Circular of March 15, 1886, the President of the Local Government Board recited as axiomatic that it was "not desirable that the working-classes should be familiarised with Poor Law Relief. . . . The spirit of independence which leads so many of the working-classes to

---

[1] Local Government Board Circular, March 15, 1886, in Sixteenth Annual Report of the Local Government Board, 1886–1887, p. 3 ; see also House of Commons Return of Circular Letters with Reference to Pauperism and Distress and of the Replies Received, etc. (1886, Session I. (6a), lvi). The long-continued influence of Chamberlain's Circular is noted in *Contemporary Theories of Unemployment*, by F. C. Mills, 1928, pp. 30-35.

make great personal sacrifices rather than incur the stigma of pauperism is one which deserves the greatest sympathy and respect, and which it is the duty and interest of the community to maintain by all the means at its disposal."

In Chamberlain's view, the " Ins-and-Outs " and the Vagrants might well be left to the Poor Law ; but for the persons normally in regular employment there was to be, in future, quite another provision, namely, work at wages under the Town Council. " His hope and belief was ", he told the House of Commons, " that the ultimate remedy for exceptional distress of the kind they had to deal with was to be found in the increasing activity of Local Authorities, which he believed had already been very considerably stimulated, and which he hoped to further stimulate." [1]

This municipal work at wages was to be given under two conditions : first, " that the men employed should be engaged on the recommendation of the Guardians as persons whom, owing to previous conditions and circumstances, it is undesirable to send to the Workhouse, or to treat as subjects for pauper relief " ; and secondly, " that the wages paid should be something less than the wages ordinarily paid for similar work, in order to prevent imposture, and to leave the strongest temptations to those who avail themselves of this opportunity to return as soon as possible to their previous occupations ".[2] Chamberlain did not remain in office long enough to carry out this incipient policy of Classification of the Able-bodied, with a twofold system of provision for their needs ; but successive Presidents adhered to the views which he had formulated, and continued their encouragement to Local Authorities, on the occurrence of any distress, to do their utmost to " employ the Unemployed ". Up and down the country hundreds of experiments were accordingly tried, and with results which were unconvincing to the experienced officials of the Local Government Board. But the Department, inflexibly bound up in the traditions of Poor Law administration, produced for its successive Presidents no alternative policy. Accordingly, what was substantially Chamberlain's Circular of 1886 was re-issued in 1887, 1891, 1892, 1893 and 1895.[3]

[1] Hansard, March 12, 1886, vol. ccciii. p. 356.
[2] Local Government Board Circular, March 15, 1886.
[3] Report of House of Commons Committee on Distress from Want of Employment, 1895, Q. 175.

The Socialist Agitation

This persistence in a policy in which, it is safe to say, neither the Ministers nor their official advisers put much faith, was due to the pressure of public opinion.   It was in these years that, in London and many of the large provincial cities, the popular Socialist organisations—at first the Social-Democratic Federation, and then the Independent Labour Party—made the question of Unemployment the centre of unceasing and vociferous propaganda.   To open-air meetings and processions through the streets there were added " Church Parades " and noisy deputations to Ministers and Local Authorities.   In the House of Commons, from 1893 to 1895, Keir Hardie, who stood out as the only avowedly " independent " Labour member, unceasingly pressed the claim of the wageless workman on the attention of the Government.[1] The demand for some specific relief of the Unemployed was, in fact, the centre of popular agitation for the fifteen years between 1883 and 1898.   The Unemployed were to be " organised " for productive work ;   as some imagined, with the expectation that such municipal farms and Government workshops would themselves develop into the public administration of all industry ;   or as others believed, that such developments would so undermine " the Capitalist System " that " nationalisation " would inevitably be the outcome.   The Government of 1892–1895 got out of its Parliamentary difficulties by relegating the whole problem to a Committee, which John Morley proposed in 1895,[2] and which tided over the agitation until

---

[1] In 1893, and again in 1895, Keir Hardie moved an amendment to the Address in reply to the Queen's Speech, in which the prevalence of Unemployment was emphasised—a step never before taken in the House of Commons (Hansard, Feb. 7, 1893, and Feb. 14, 1895).   On the former occasion, when he stated that 1,300,000 wage-earners were unemployed, he told the House that " all the horrors of sweating, of low wages, of long hours, and of deaths from starvation are directly traceable to the large numbers of people who are totally unemployed, or only casually employed.   The worker in the workshop is fettered by the thought that outside his workshop gates there are thousands eager and willing to step into his shoes should he be dismissed in consequence of any attempt to improve his position " (*ibid.* p. 726 of vol. viii.).   Keir Hardie's position was supported by Sir John Gorst, who declared that " the existence of the large bodies of unemployed, half-employed and casually employed in our great cities is a discredit to our civilisation, a standing danger to the maintenance of order, and a social evil which urgently demands the attention of Parliament and of the Government " (*ibid.* p. 754 of vol. viii.).

[2] Hansard, Feb. 13, 1895, p. 637 of vol. xxx. ; Report of House of Commons Committee on Distress from Want of Employment, 1895 and 1896.

trade improved. But after a brief spell of prosperity in 1900–1902, Keir Hardie's own campaign was resumed in the House of Commons, in favour of any practicable scheme of providing for the sufferers from the renewed Unemployment, by the newly elected knot of Labour Members by whom he was joined between 1900 and 1905. These were seconded, up and down the country, by the other candidates of the nascent Labour Party. The Radicalism to which Joseph Chamberlain had given expression in 1886 had become transformed into a form of Socialism, in which State provision for the Unemployed as such, a proposal which attracted much support from public opinion, was the central feature. The distracted Cabinet of those years could find no satisfactory policy with which to satisfy the clamour of Members of the House of Commons who were about to face their constituents in a General Election. But Walter Long, who had been since 1900 an able President of the Local Government Board, was as strongly moved in 1903 by compassion for the involuntarily unemployed workmen as Chaplin had been in 1900 by pity for the helpless aged. He energetically tried to get something done in London by concerted action among the Metropolitan Boroughs ; [1] and he drafted a Bill, which his successor (Mr. Gerald Balfour) carried into law in 1905, as the Unemployed Workmen Act.[2]

[1] London County Council : Minutes of Conference on Lack of Employment in London, February 1903 ; Minutes of Proceedings of a Conference of Representatives of Administrative Authorities in London, April 1903 ; Camberwell Borough Report of the Unemployed Central Committee, 1904.

[2] 5 Edward VII. c. 18. This Act may be said to have arisen from a Mansion House Committee in the autumn of 1903, in which a group of experienced administrators of charitable funds sought to devise schemes, particularly in respect of the East End of London, for limiting the social injury caused by the widely published advertisement and indiscriminate administration of newspaper and municipal funds for the relief of the Unemployed. The Committee emphasised (1) the great need for substantial assistance ; (2) the indispensability of systematic investigation, not merely of the distress, but also of the industrial status of every applicant ; (3) the selection, for relief work, only of men usually in settled employment, with prospects of resumption ; (4) the advantage of a rural colony ; and (5) the desirability of concert between the Poor Law Guardians and the Municipal Authorities. The President of the Local Government Board (then Walter Long) impressed by the value of the Mansion House Committee's proposals, got appointed, without statutory authority, in each Metropolitan Borough, a Joint Committee from the Board of Guardians and the Borough Council to undertake the investigation of cases ; and also a Central Committee for the Metropolis as a whole, made up of representatives of the local Joint Committees and of the County Council, to administer whatever funds could be obtained. The work, during 1904–1905, of the Central

The Unemployed Workmen Act, 1905

The uniformly unsatisfactory results of the experiments in Municipal Relief Work for the Unemployed between 1886 and 1904 were, it seems, so little realised by the Cabinet and the House of Commons that the same expedient was made the central feature of the new measure, which gave, indeed, by explicit statute, what was virtually approval and sanction of Chamberlain's Circular of 1886. The intention was that the " respectable Unemployed " should look for relief, not to the Poor Law Guardians, but to the new Joint Committees of Municipal Council and Board of Guardians. Only the locally resident men who had fallen out of definite situations were to be dealt with. " We propose ", said Mr. Gerald Balfour, " to deal with the élite of the Unemployed." The primary aim of the Act, it has been said, was " not to do anything new, but to do slightly better what had been done before ".[1] But the new authorities were to add to their provision of relief works various new devices. There were to be local Labour Exchanges to facilitate the finding of new situations ; and in connection with these there was to be an organised migration from congested districts, and emigration to the British Dominions overseas. And there were to be Farm Colonies in which men could be trained in agriculture, either for employment on British farms as labourers, or for settlement on the land as small-holders. Within a few months, not only was an elaborate organisation set up (the " Central Unemployed Body ") federating Joint Committees in all the Metropolitan Boroughs, but also similar " Distress Committees " in nearly a hundred of the other towns of the Kingdom.

The comprehensive experiment projected by Walter Long and Mr. Gerald Balfour and adopted by Parliament was only imperfectly carried out. In the provincial Boroughs, with insignificant exceptions, the Distress Committees had no other idea than a

Committee thus formed for the Metropolis, in establishing a co-ordinated series of Labour Exchanges throughout London, and organising the Farm Colony at Hollesley Bay to which unemployed men could be " rusticated " whilst their families were relieved at home, proved of the greatest value. The form as well as the policy thus adopted for London in 1904 by the Minister were embodied by his successor in the statute of the following year, and extended to all the large towns of the United Kingdom.

[1] *Unemployment a Problem of Industry*, by Sir W. Beveridge, 1909, p. 165 ; *Unemployment Relief in Great Britain*, by Felix Morley, 1924, p. 3.

continuance of the policy of municipal employment, which, as we have described, had been spasmodically carried out, here and there, during the preceding twenty years.   " The Labour Bureau" or " Labour Register ", set up under the new Act, was, in nearly every town outside the Metropolis, practically only as a means of registering the applicants for the " Employment Relief " dispensed by the Distress Committee.   Only the smallest use was made, except in West Ham and two or three other places, of the powers of assisting migration or emigration.[1]   What happened was that the provision of doles of work by the Municipal Authorities received a great extension, and became chronic. The simple device of anticipating works of paving, sewering and road-making, so as to begin them in the winter, before they were required, was adopted more widely than ever.   A certain ingenuity was shown in inventing special jobs on which to set the Unemployed at work ;   reclaiming part of Chat Moss,[2] planting trees in the water-catchment area of Leeds,[3] foreshore reclamation at Bristol, potato-growing at Oldham and Croydon, forming new recreation grounds or cleaning water-courses in many towns. Viewed as a whole, these provincial examples of municipal employment under the Distress Committees from 1905 to 1909, when rapidly improving trade brought them happily to an end, were marked by almost exactly the same characteristics as those under the Town Councils and Joint Committees from 1886 to 1905.[4]

[1] In 1906–1907, from all the provincial towns of England and Wales, only 268 persons were assisted to migrate, and 437 men (with 1232 dependants) to emigrate (House of Commons Return, No. 173 of 1908, p. 8).   Two-thirds of these were sent out by West Ham, Bristol, Birmingham and Leicester. No other Distress Committees did anything to speak of in this way.   In Scotland only four Committees did anything at all (Cd. 3431 of 1906).

[2] " The most that can be said of the experiment is that it provided wages for 252 men during a portion of the year.   The work was, however, attended by great expense, owing to railway fares, provision of shelters, etc., whilst no remunerative return was secured by the Distress Committee as a set-off against the wages paid " (Evidence before the Poor Law Commission, Appendix No. xcviii. (A) to vol. viii. par. 2 ; Report of Manchester Distress Committee, 1906–1907).

[3] Report of Leeds Distress Committee, 1906–1907.

[4] For almost contemporary records of the proceedings under the Unemployed Workmen Act—termed by one critic " this ill-considered, inadequate panic scheme " (*Insurance against Unemployment*, by Joseph L. Cohen, 1921, p. 165)—see *Unemployment a Problem of Industry*, by (Sir) W. H. Beveridge, 1909, pp. 162-191 ; the three reports of the Local Government Board for 1906, 1907 and 1908, entitled Proceedings of Distress Committees ; two similar

This quarter of a century of municipal experiment, in all parts of the Kingdom, under local administrations of different political opinions, and of varying degrees of competence, deserves to be studied by every Minister seeking to grapple with the problem of Unemployment, and by everyone propounding any views upon the subject. Unfortunately these experiments, like those which preceded them, were not made the subject of any systematic report by the Local Government Board. They were, however, exhaustively explored by the Special Investigators appointed by the Poor Law Commission, of which, indeed, we may suspect them to have been very largely the origin.[1]

The detailed reports of these Special Investigators, supple-

---

reports by the L.G.B. for Scotland, Cd. 3431 and Cd. 3830 ; the *Preliminary Report of the Central (Unemployed) Body for London*, 1906, and its *Second Report*, 1907 ; and many separate reports by local Distress Committees, 1906–1910. The Act was repealed in 1929.

[1] It is significant that, for the first time in Poor Law inquiries, the reference to the Commission of 1905–1909 expressly joined, to the inquiry into the Poor Law, that into " the Relief of Distress due to Unemployment by Agencies other than the Poor Law " ; about the effect of which the Department is known to have been uneasy, and the new President (Mr. Gerald Balfour) to have felt at least uncertain.

The principal among these Investigators, so far as Unemployment was concerned, were Cyril (afterwards Sir Cyril) Jackson, to whom we have already referred in Chapter VI. (pp. 523, 528), and Rev. J. C. Pringle, afterwards Secretary of the Charity Organisation Society. Their three Reports, " On the Effects of Employment or Assistance given to the Unemployed since 1886 ", in England, Scotland and Ireland respectively (Appendix, vols. xix., xix.a and xix.b), extend to 800 pages. To these may be added a separate " Report on Boy Labour ", by Cyril Jackson (Appendix, vol. xx.) ; " Replies by Distress Committees " (Appendix, vol. xxvii.) ; Reports of Visits to Foreign Labour Colonies (Appendix, vol. xxxii.), and two bulky volumes containing the Minutes of Evidence and oral examination of witnesses as to Unemployment (Appendix, vols. viii. and ix.). See also *Unemployment and Trade Unions*, by Cyril Jackson, 1910.

It is, we think, greatly to be regretted that so little is done by the Government in the way of recording and publishing the results of the experiments that are always being made in economic and political reorganisation. It should be the first consideration in every such experiment that a precise and detailed account of it should be compiled—perhaps several accounts by different observers—and that these should be published, after whatever delay is deemed advisable, for general information. We hazard the suggestion that had there been such descriptions available for Ministers' perusal of the experiments in " setting the poor to work " of the seventeenth and eighteenth centuries, of those in the employment of unemployed farm labourers and factory operatives between 1815 and 1886, and of those in Municipal Relief Works from 1886 to 1899, the Cabinet would not so confidently have made such municipal employment the basis of the Unemployed Workmen Act of 1905 ; or, as we shall subsequently describe, allowed so unconcernedly the development of a new series of " Relief Works " in 1921–1928.

mented and confirmed by the oral evidence to the Commission, give a vivid picture, not only of a couple of decades of social experiment between 1886 and 1905, but also of the proceedings under the new Act. They reveal the Local Authorities, at first reluctant to spend the ratepayers' money, gradually yielding to the pressure exerted by public opinion, by the House of Commons and by the Local Government Board, and striving to devise any form of useful work on which to employ the local unemployed. The old expedients are again employed. The Local Authorities again revert to hand labour on the roads, instead of sweeping and repairing by horse-power or steam-driven machines. They lay out more new parks and recreation grounds, and effect costly sewering schemes and street improvements. But one after another they find it as impossible as before to adhere to the idea that "the wages paid should be less than the wages ordinarily paid for similar work". Any such attempt to discriminate in wages between the ordinary municipal staff and the extra men taken on as "the Unemployed" not only produced disgust and angry rebellion, but also, when piece-work was made the basis, led to respectable and well-conducted men earning less than they needed for bare subsistence. Moreover, it was again found both inexpedient and impracticable to confine the municipal employment to men recommended by the Board of Guardians. It appeared neither desirable to compel the unemployed workman to come into contact with the Poor Law, nor practicable to give him such amount of employment as the Relieving Officer reported to be required by the number of children dependent on him, or other family needs. The only thing to be done was again to open a register at the Town Hall of all the local Unemployed, and take them all on in turn. This involved the renewed swamping of the lists, not by the men from permanent situations, but by men who had been at no time more than intermittently employed, whether these were dock or wharf or general labourers, or painters' and builders' labourers, and who were glad at any season to present themselves for odd days of work at current rates.[1]

---

[1] The Poor Law Commissioners found the employment given by the Distress Committee actually made to fit in with casual employment. At Liverpool, as our Committee notes, "the men, some of them, get dock work, and then, on their off days, they are allowed to work for the Distress Committees" (Reports of Visits by Commissioners, Poor Law Commission, No. 1, B, p. 4).

This meant, as before, only a series of short jobs for each man, with the result not only of positively increasing all the evils of casual labour, but also of creating a permanent dependence on an endless succession of these artificially manufactured municipal jobs, which it was impossible to maintain indefinitely. Moreover, as it was found impracticable to pay lower rates than were normally earned by the lowest grade of unskilled labourers, who swarmed into the Relief Works, there seemed nothing to be done but to restrict the jobs to a few days in the week, or to one week at a time, for each man taken on, during the whole course of the winter.[1] And every Local Authority in succession once more discovered, as their predecessors of the eighteenth and nineteenth centuries had done, that every such attempt to " set the poor on work ", even at the lowest possible wage, and even where safeguarded by systems of piece-work remuneration, was prodigiously costly. Every piece of work took longer to perform than had been expected, and involved considerably more expense than it was on any computation worth.[2] Nor did it all go to

---

[1] " It was decided to pay the workmen 4½d. per hour, and to employ them four days in succession, the time being nine hours per day " (Report of Distress Committee, Halifax, 1906). " Two gangs have work each week, one on the first three days, and one on the last three days " (Report of Dudley Distress Committee, 1907). At Ipswich, the Town Council refused to appoint a Distress Committee, preferring to let its Paving Committee execute extensive works of excavating and levelling on the Corporation land at piece-work rates, employing each man four days a week (Minutes of Ipswich Town Council, November 9, 1905).

[2] On one occasion thirty men, of whom the majority were young men, were discharged for laziness " (Report of the Effects of Employment or Assistance given to the Unemployed, by Mr. Cyril Jackson and the Rev. J. C. Pringle, Poor Law Commission, Appendix R, p. 363). At Newcastle-on-Tyne, in 1905–1906, " some site levelling, for which an item (£200) was on the city estimates, had been tendered by contractors. The lowest tender was £130, but this was probably too low—a fair price would have been £170. It actually cost by unemployed labour £415 : 6 : 3, of which the Corporation refunded £200. The great addition to the cost was due to the substitution, at first, of barrowing for carting, but this was given up after a short experience. The supervision was not strict enough, and the men got away to an unfortunately ' convenient ' railway arch. Some road work which was on the estimates had been tendered for at £1359 : 19 : 2, but with unemployment labour cost £1875 : 18 : 11 " (ibid. p. 129). " Our estimate as to the result is that it cost the Corporation 40 per cent more than if the work was done under contract " (Evidence before the Poor Law Commission, Appendix No. lxxvi. to vol. viii. par. 5). At Croydon it was reported " that digging upon some cemetery land—described as the easiest work at the time—cost £145 for 10½ acres. The surveyor estimates that similar work done with a plough would have cost about 25s. an acre " (Report on the Effects of Employment or Assistance given to the Unemployed, by Mr. Cyril Jackson and the Rev. J. C. Pringle,

the Unemployed. To supply the materials, provide the horses and carts and other necessary plant, and pay officers for direction and supervision of the work, to be carried out by unskilled, inefficient and not very strenuous labour, proved ruinously expensive. " It would really be cheaper to the ratepayers who have to find the money ", reported one Finance Committee to its Council, " if relief were given to the men themselves direct ", without bothering them to work. Finally, it came to be recognised, even among the workmen, that it was impossible, in this artificial manufacture of municipal work, to avoid anticipating the ordinary employment of the permanently engaged staff of labourers, or that of the contractors, so that the very employment of the Unemployed was creating, for the future, even more Unemployment.[1] In short, the lesson of the forgotten eighteenth-century experiments, repeated in those of 1886–1905, was again confirmed by those undertaken under the Unemployed Workmen Act. The Special Investigators could discover, in the municipal employment of the Unemployed, no sort of remedy for Unemployment, and not even any acceptable method of temporarily relieving the involuntarily Unemployed. In the end, neither

---

Poor Law Commission, p. 827). " We find, for example, that £3866 was paid for the construction of cricket fields, the normal value being £675 ; £2997 for levelling and excavating, instead of £1440 ; 16s. 10d. per ton for breaking slag and stone, instead of 11s. 9d." (Report by Town Clerk to the Bath Town Council as to the experience of the Unemployed Workmen Act by forty-five Municipal Corporations, 1907).

[1] " A few instances have been brought to our notice in which the regular staff of a Borough Council have been actually thrown out of work in the summer because the ' unemployed ' have already done certain jobs in the winter. . . . In many places we have found undoubted evidence of work which would naturally have been done by navvies or other workmen in the ordinary way being taken from them by being given to the ' unemployed.' . . . We have found actual evidence in a few places of men being displaced by the employment of the ' unemployed ' on relief works. In a Lancashire Borough, certain sewage works were in progress, and the Distress Committee offered to contribute £1000 in wages if the ' unemployed ' were taken on. It was, of course, found that the employment of a very large number of extra men expedited the work to such an extent that it was likely to be finished before the summer, and before the £1000 was expended. Of the permanent men some twenty-five were accordingly discharged. They were naturally indignant at being displaced by less competent men, and when told they might register as unemployed, and come back for three half-days a week at 5d. an hour (instead of full time at 5½d. an hour), they very properly refused to register as ' distressed ' workmen " (Report by Mr. Cyril Jackson and the Rev. J. C. Pringle, on the Effects of Employment or Assistance given to the Unemployed, Poor Law Commission, pp. 67, 117).

the Majority nor the Minority of the Poor Law Commissioners could find a word to say in favour of the expedient.

We cannot imagine a more conclusive test of the value of provision for the Unemployed by way of municipal relief works of the most varied kinds, in many different towns, under all sorts of administrators and in the most diverse circumstances, than that afforded—in succession to the previous experience between 1836 and 1880 and to that of the widespread and repeated series of experiments of 1886–1905—by the operations, between 1906 and 1909, under the Unemployed Workmen Act. The whole series ought to be studied by each succeeding generation. We must not, however, omit to mention the oft-quoted example of public employment during the Lancashire Cotton Famine of 1863–1866.[1] In so far as this was confined to a limited number of the skilled cotton spinners or weavers it must be regarded as successful. But the circumstances were exceptionally favourable. A few of the skilled cotton operatives could be employed upon public works at the current wages of unskilled men without disinclining them to take up their old occupation as soon as the mills were reopened. This outdoor work seems, in fact, to have served as a sort of physical training, and to have actually benefited the health of many of those who were accustomed to the confinement of a mill. But even here it was found necessary to supersede the ordinary machinery of the Local Authority by carefully devised organisation under specialised management, by which, at the cost of heavy loans charged upon the local rates, a limited number (never more than 4000) of the unemployed cotton spinners—not the labourers—were carefully combined with a large number of ordinary workmen accustomed to the work of sewering, paving and street improvements, engaged in the ordinary way, and many of them brought from a distance.

---

[1] The experiences in the relief of the Unemployed in the Lancashire Cotton Famine are most easily consulted in *The History of the Cotton Famine*, by (Sir) Arthur Arnold, 1864 ; *Lancashire's Lesson*, by W. T. M'Cullagh Torrens, 1864 ; *The Facts of the Cotton Famine*, by Dr. John Watts, 1866 ; *Public Works in Lancashire for the Relief of Distress*, 1863–1866, by Sir R. Rawlinson, 1898 ; and *History of the Poor Law*, by Thomas Mackay, 1899, pp. 398-424. See also the official papers, such as the series of reports by (Sir) R. Rawlinson, in Parliamentary Papers for 1864, 1865 and 1866 ; those of 1863 " on the Public Works required in the Cotton Districts and the Employment of Operatives thereon ", Nos. 293 and 361 of 1863 ; those of 1862–1864 " on the Distress in the Cotton Manufacturing Districts ".

This Lancashire experiment, which is frequently cited in support of the Muncipal Employment of the Unemployed, was, compared with the operations of the Municipal Authorities of the past twenty years, a relatively small affair. Its very success—so far as it can be considered a success—confirms the reason that we have assigned for the failure of Municipal Employment as a means of providing for the crowds that assail the Distress Committees of to-day. It was not the men living on casual employment in the Lancashire towns, it was not the general labourers, it was not even the labourers in the building trades for whom the Municipal Employment was found in 1863–1866. For the distress into which tens of thousands of these men were thrown, their chronic condition of Under-employment being aggravated as an indirect result of the Cotton Famine, provision was made by huge charitable funds, by soup kitchens and by the Poor Law. It was exactly because the Municipal Works organised by Sir R. Rawlinson were carefully confined, so far as concerned the " employment of the unemployed ", to the engagement of a limited number of spinners and weavers for whom it was known that situations in the cotton mills would be available as soon as the importation of cotton was resumed, that this small and costly experiment can be said to have been successful. *If adequate provision were made in some other way for the casual labourers in chronic Under-employment and those in trades in which employment is habitually discontinuous*, it is conceivable that the Municipal Authorities might successfully find work for the limited number of men whom some industrial dislocation had temporarily deprived of regular situations, and who needed only to be tided over until they got into regular situations again. Even then, the question arises whether, if financial considerations alone were regarded, it would not be found to be cheaper to give the men their wages without allowing them to spoil the material, wastefully use the plant, and necessitate the engagement of foremen and overlookers for the execution of the work, possibly not undesirable in itself, but of no real commercial value.

It should be noted that all these experiments of the past hundred years must be distinguished from what has not been tried, namely, an attempt not to employ the Unemployed as such, *but to prevent the occurrence of Unemployment*, even if only partially, by seeking to regularise the whole volume of wage-earning employment in the nation over a series of years, by deliberately reducing the amount of public orders given and public work undertaken in the years of " good trade ", and deliberately increasing them in the years of commercial depression.

Organised Migration

The Unemployed Workmen Act of 1905 introduced an interesting new form of assistance of the destitute. The Poor Law Amendment Act of 1834 had expressly forbidden the Destitution Authorities to make any payment, even by way of loan, to enable men to remove to another locality, although situations might be waiting for them. This fundamental principle of the New Poor Law was, in 1905, so far departed from as to enable public funds to be used (although not out of the Poor Rates, or by the Poor Law Authority) for paying the expenses of the removal of men and their families from places in which they could get no employment to other places in which there was an ascertained demand for labour. The Central (Unemployed) Body for London set itself diligently to utilise all the opportunities thus afforded. The other parts of England and Wales were scrutinised to discover situations for which no local candidates were available, and, contrary to the common expectation, such were found. It was discovered that some men in distress had family connections in other places, by means of which they could get along and become self-supporting, if only they could come within their reach. Care was taken that no removal was sanctioned until satisfactory assurances were obtained that definite situations were available, that the employment offered was of a permanent character, and that arrangements had been made for providing suitable homes in the towns or villages to which the families were transferred. In this way it was found possible to assist the removal of some scores of families, representing about 300 persons : one-half of them from Woolwich to South Wales and Lancashire, where there had been an unsatisfied demand for labour ; and one-half, being men who had been trained at the Farm Colony, to various situations in the country.

In addition to this newly authorised expenditure on migration within Britain, much was made of the chance to develop emigration to other parts of the Empire. Where men expressed a desire to emigrate, and were found, after careful investigation, in every way suitable, they were assisted to go to Canada, and, in a few cases, to New Zealand. In the first two years of its existence, the Central (Unemployed) Body thus enabled no fewer than 8000 persons to remove to new houses, in nearly all cases making arrangements which ensured the men employment immediately on arrival.

This policy of enabling selected men among the Unemployed to remove to new localities, whether merely from one county of England to another, or from one part of the Empire to another, was criticised as affording no real help. If, it was said, the men who wished to shift were strong and competent, the locality or country in which they were living could not afford to lose their services ; whilst if they were weak and incompetent, no other locality or country would wish to receive them, or would be able to provide a living for them. It was suggested, in short, that not only was there no unsatisfied demand for labour anywhere, but that, even if such an opening could be found, the best men would not need to go, and the worst men would not be allowed to come. This seems to have been the view taken by nearly all the provincial Distress Committees. But the Central (Unemployed) Body for London found that such a summary way of disposing of the possibilities of migration and emigration did not exhaust the question. Investigation and experience proved that, whilst a change of locality was not available as a method of assisting the bulk of unemployed workmen, there were some men for whose distress it was a successful, and even the most appropriate, remedy. At all times, and in all places, there are " industrial misfits "— men who have been thrown out of gear with their surroundings, it may be by the local stoppage of their industry, it may be by the loss of heart in themselves—who will never really be able to struggle to their feet in their old locality, but who, could they but get a new start, amid new circumstances, are likely to become permanently successful. To enable these men to change their environment may be, as the experience of the Central (Unemployed) Body for London proved—not, indeed, any panacea for preventing Unemployment, or any universal remedy for its dire effects—but the most really helpful, as well as the most permanently economical, way of relieving particular sufferers.

The Establishment of the Labour Exchange

It was the Unemployed Workmen Act that made the first trial in England of a public " exchange " for labour.[1] The scheme of the Act was that there should be, in every County and County Borough, an official organisation for ascertaining the local conditions of employment ; and this was intended to take the form of a universal network of Labour Exchanges covering the whole country, which would, when in full working order, show at once in what parts of the country there was any unsatisfied demand for labour. Where a Distress Committee was set up, the conduct of the Labour Exchange was entrusted to it. Wherever no Distress Committee was set up, there was to be a Special Committee appointed by the County or County Borough Council, and expressly directed to fulfil the same function. " The network of Labour Bureaus which the Unemployed Workmen Act *was intended to establish all over the country* " was, in fact, as Mr. Gerald Balfour described it to the Poor Law Commission, an integral part of the general scheme.

Unfortunately this part of the scheme was, outside the Metropolis, left practically inoperative. In spite of the mandatory terms of the Act the Special Committees were (except in London) nowhere appointed in England and Wales, and (except in Lanarkshire) nowhere in Scotland or Ireland ; and the Local Government Board, which, under Mr. John Burns, had no faith in Labour Exchanges, did not press for action to be taken.

Apart from the failure to set up Labour Exchanges in the places in which no Distress Committees were established, the Act was itself in fault, as we can now see, in associating one of these organisations with the other. The fact that the Labour Exchange was established by, or in close connection with, a Distress Committee, not only tended to make it regarded merely as an adjunct of the Municipal Relief Works, but also prejudiced it, from the start, in the minds of competent skilled workmen seeking new situations, and of employers desiring anything

---

[1] For the few voluntary experiments in Labour Exchanges in Great Britain, see the Board of Trade Report on Agencies and Methods for Dealing with the Unemployed, c. 7182 of 1893 ; Report on Labour Bureaux, by H. D. Lowry (Local Government Board, 1906) ; and (especially for the German experience) *Unemployment a Problem of Industry*, by Sir W. H. Beveridge, 1909.

better than the crowd of casual labourers and men downtrodden by misfortune or misconduct who make up the bulk of the applicants for Employment Relief. Nor did the Distress Committee make any attempt to create a network. We do not find that the different Labour Exchanges that professed to register the local demand for and supply of labour opened up communications with each other in order to make known the local position for each other's benefit. This needed organisation from a national centre, to which each Labour Exchange might have daily reported—even if it could report only that there were no unsatisfied demands for labour of any kind, and that there were so many men, of such and such occupations, out of work. Even this negative result would have been of use in preventing the aimless wandering in search of employment that was going on ; but no step was taken at Whitehall to create such a centre of communication.

In the Metropolis, however, the experiment of the Labour Exchange was tried with some success. The Central (Unemployed) Body took the view, after some discussion, that the Labour Exchanges contemplated by the Act of 1905 should have no connection with the temporary registers of applicants for Employment Relief that were opened each winter by the Distress Committees ; and that what was required, in good times and bad alike, was some permanent machinery for enabling employers and wage-earners to find out each other's whereabouts and each other's requirements more easily, more certainly and more quickly than would otherwise be possible. The Labour Exchanges that were set on foot in various parts of London were formed into a single organisation ; and after some careful experimenting as to what was and what was not practicable, the whole of the Metropolis was gradually covered by a network of public employment agencies, telephonically interconnected, and reporting to a common centre. These were resorted to by employers of labour of every kind, skilled and unskilled, male and female, manual and clerical, the number of situations offered through their agency being at the end of the year 1908 at the rate of 33,000 per annum, nearly two-thirds of which were professedly permanent. They were also increasingly applied to by wage-earners of every kind, not merely by those who were actually unemployed, but also by those who expected or desired to change their situations. It is interesting to find that the Trade Unions, at first suspicious, if not actually hostile, became steadily more friendly to the institution, which they found of positive advantage, not only to their members, but also to their organisation. By December 31, 1908, no fewer than thirty-two Trade Union Branches were already keeping their " vacant books " actually at the Labour Exchange itself.

The experience of the Labour Exchange in London indicated both its utility and its limits. It did not create work at wages where no employer offered it. But in all but the best organised trades it abridged the interval between one situation and another, during which no wages were earned. It reduced the weary tramp of the unemployed workman all over London, from one firm to another, in the attempt to discover, by actual application to one after another, which of them wanted another hand. It enabled the workman to ascertain, by calling at one office in his own neighbourhood, what inquiries had been made for his own kind of labour all over London. To the employer it offered, similarly, the choice among all the available workmen of the kind he required. But the Labour Exchange afforded a further contribution towards the solution of the problem of Unemployment. Experience proved that, even in London, at a time when thousands were unemployed, there were opportunities for the taking on of more hands, which employers forwent because they could not, in the absence of machinery of this kind, discover quickly and without trouble exactly the kind of labour that they required. By enabling these opportunities to be taken, instead of being let slip, the Labour Exchange may, to some slight extent, and with regard to certain specialised kinds of skill, even increase the volume of employment. Even to enable each employer to begin new jobs a day or two earlier than would otherwise have been possible, meant, by adding several days to the productive period of each year, an actual increase of production, and therefore an increased demand for labour. Finally, experience showed that the Labour Exchange offered the means of " decasualising " labour. Though one employer wanted a man for Monday only, there were others who wanted men for Tuesday only, others for Wednesday only, and so on. In so far as such employers drew their casual labour from a common Exchange, it might cease to be casual so far as the labourers were concerned, one job being " dovetailed " with another so as to give each man practically continuous employment.

In 1909, accordingly, the Government instantly acted on the unanimous recommendation of the Poor Law Commission in favour of the Exchanges, and promptly got passed the Labour Exchanges Act, enabling a National Labour Exchange to be set up, unconnected with any relief agency or the Poor Law Department, and under the direct administration of the Labour Department of the Board of Trade. This national organisation took over the London Exchanges of the Central (Unemployed) Body, and superseded the local registers of unemployed men which had been set up in other towns. During the next two years the network of Labour Exchanges gradually covered the whole Kingdom ; and an elaborate technique of registration, of mutual communication both of vacancies and of applications for situations, and of the experimental "dovetailing" of seasonal jobs and casual employment was hopefully worked out. By 1914 the National Labour Exchange was filling 1,116,909 vacancies a year; and in 1927, in spite of the long-continued severe depression of trade, the number had risen to more than a million and a half annually.

Unemployment Insurance

What has proved by far the most extensive, and, on the whole, the most nearly effective, of all the experimental fragments of a Framework of Prevention of the destitution of the able-bodied wage-earners was found, in 1911, in the device of compulsory insurance.[1] This application of universal insurance to Unemploy-

[1] For Unemployment Insurance, see the whole series of statutes from 1911 to 1927 ; the Reports of the Board of Trade, 1913 (Cmd. 6965), and those of the Ministry of Labour, 1923 and 1924, on the working of the scheme; the subsequent Annual Reports of the Ministry of Labour, 1925 to 1927 ; the Report of the Committee on Unemployment Insurance (Lord Blanesburgh), 1927 ; and other Parliamentary papers. Apart from such earlier examinations of the project, in the light of the local and voluntary experiments, as *Insurance against Unemployment*, by W. F. Willoughby, New York, 1898, and *Insurance against Unemployment*, by D. F. Schloss, 1909, the most comprehensive study is *Insurance against Unemployment*, by Joseph L. Cohen, 1921 ; see also his *Insurance by Industry Examined*, 1923, and *Social Insurance Unified*, 1924 ; and *Social Insurance, What it is, and What it might be*, by Alban Gordon, 1924. A concise account of the provisions of the State scheme is given in *A Guide to the Unemployment Insurance Acts*, by H. C. Emmerson and E. C. P. Lascelles, 1928, whilst the Acts themselves may be consulted in *The Unemployment Insurance Acts*, by Albert Crew and R. J. Blackham, 1928.

A discussion of the place of insurance will be found in *The Prevention of*

ment, unlike its application to Sickness and Infirmity, was not " made in Germany ". It had been omitted alike from Bismarck's legislation of 1880–1889, and, down to 1927, from all its successive amendments and extensions. Such a provision against Unemployment by continuous weekly subscriptions from the whole membership had, for a couple of centuries, been a feature of English Trade Unionism, and had, here and there, been adopted by English Friendly Societies, including members of diverse occupations. These relatively small experiments in insurance by voluntary associations, like the sporadic municipal experiments of subsidised voluntary insurance in various Swiss Cantons, at Ghent and in France, Norway and Denmark, afforded, however, but a small basis for any plan of compulsory insurance on a national scale, which could, indeed, scarcely be conceived as practicable without a network of offices constituting an Employment Exchange co-extensive with the population to be insured. It needed vision in 1907–1909 to transcend what had ever been attempted anywhere, and to work out a scheme for a National Employment Exchange ; still more to couple with this so daring a proposal as that the Government should engage to make definite payments to men who reported themselves as having been rendered idle merely through their failure to find anyone willing to employ them. The nation owes its present system of national, compulsory, State-aided and State-administered insurance against involuntary Unemployment mainly to the elaborate studies (and consequent inventiveness) of two of the ablest of our Civil Servants, Sir Hubert Llewellyn Smith and Sir W. H. Beveridge, both at the time at the Board of Trade, who found in Mr. Winston Churchill, in 1908–1911, a Minister sufficiently appreciative and courageous to adopt so novel and adventurous a scheme and to push it through the Cabinet and the House of

---

Destitution, by S. and B. Webb, 1911. It was officially classed as part of the Framework of Prevention in 1927. " The Code of Social Legislation.—Just as the Factory Acts aim at securing that work in factories shall be carried on under safe and reasonably healthy conditions ; just as the Trade Boards Acts aim at preventing sweating, and the Employers' Liability and Workmen's Compensation Acts provide for loss of earnings due to industrial accidents; just as the Health Insurance Scheme assists workpeople unable to earn wages through sickness, so the primary purpose of Unemployment Insurance is to provide a stand-by for workers thrown out of employment through no fault of their own " (Report of the Unemployment Insurance Committee (Lord Blanesburgh's), 1927, vol. i. p. 23).

Commons—a first instalment in the Labour Exchanges Act of 1909, to which we have already referred ; and when the network of Exchanges had been brought into operation, a second instalment imposing compulsory insurance on the employers and the workmen (two and a half millions in number) in seven industries selected for the experiment as being those most subject to recurrent periods of Unemployment.[1]

We need not recount in detail the successive developments of the Unemployment Insurance system, from its modest beginning in 1911, applicable only to certain industries, down to its latest amendment in 1927, readjusting the amounts and periods of benefit, now applicable (with the exceptions of agriculture and private domestic service, and certain exempted occupations) to all forms of employment of manual labour, and to all other employed persons paid up to £250 a year (the whole approaching twelve millions in number). Based on a triple series of contributions by the employers, the employed and the National Exchequer (the two former collected by stamps affixed weekly to an "Insurance Book", held by every insurable employee), this income amounting in 1927 to over 42 millions sterling, the National Insurance Fund undertakes to pay benefit at rates from 10s. per week for a young woman of 16, up to 36s. or so per week for a man with a large family, to insured persons between 16 and 65 who prove their involuntary Unemployment, arising otherwise than through sickness or accident, or their own misconduct or lack of due diligence in seeking situations. In good times the National Insurance Fund normally accumulates a surplus (which in 1920 exceeded £21,000,000), whilst in extremely bad times it incurs a debt to the Treasury (which in 1928 had risen to £30,000,000) ; a temporary overdraft repaid, with interest, by rates of contribution increased for this purpose. The huge administration that is involved, not only in registering and seeking new situations for an ever-fluctuating army of temporarily unemployed persons which has, at times, exceeded

[1] For convenience the Unemployment Insurance scheme, which was actually sponsored by Sydney (now Earl) Buxton, who had succeeded Mr. Winston Churchill as President of the Board of Trade, was combined in one Bill with Mr. Lloyd George's Health Insurance scheme, from which it was, and has remained, entirely separate and distinct. Both schemes became law as Parts I. and II. respectively of the National Insurance Act, 1911 (1 and 2 George V. c. 55) ; but they have since been successively amended by two separate series of Acts.

two millions in number, but also of awarding and paying weekly
benefits to so many persons dispersed through all trades, in all
parts of the Kingdom, is conducted, under elaborate regulations,
by the Ministry of Labour (into which the Labour Department
of the Board of Trade was, in 1917, developed), assisted by local
joint committees of employers and workmen, at the interconnected Employment Exchanges and other local offices of the
Ministry, about 1200 in number.

The scheme of Unemployment Insurance, combined with that
of an equally ubiquitous national system of Employment Exchanges, appears to promise—assuming that it could be completely and successfully carried out—to prevent the particular
kind of destitution arising by reason only of involuntary Unemployment of a transient nature, to which millions of the
population are continually being subjected. Within its limitations, the scheme has proved in the United Kingdom, even under
the severest trials, surprisingly successful in surmounting the
difficulties and in avoiding the evils that were apprehended.
So widely did it commend itself that the first international conference at Washington in 1919 of the International Labour Office
of the League of Nations imposed, on all the Governments that
ratified the Convention, the duty of establishing " free public
Employment Agencies under the control of a Central Authority ",
with Advisory Committees of employers and employed. It also
recommended each government to " establish an effective system
of Unemployment Insurance, either through a government system
or through a system of government subventions of associations
whose rules provide for the payment of benefit to their unemployed members ". By 1926 it could be reported that, whilst
Employment Exchanges had been established, more or less completely, in a score of States, compulsory systems of Unemployment Insurance were in operation in eight of them, whilst nine
others had State-aided voluntary schemes of greater or lesser extent.
It has accordingly become a world-wide permanent institution.
But everywhere it falls short of adequacy and completeness.
In Great Britain the Employment Exchanges, though they
now fill, gratuitously and promptly, and even in the worst of
times, more than a million vacancies every year, with a perceptible easing of the burden of discovering a new job, and
with some lessening of the average loss of working time between

successive jobs, do not yet hear of all the opportunities for employment throughout the whole Kingdom, owing to the failure of many employers to notify their vacancies, and their obstinate refusal to make a trial of the facilities for discovering the available candidates for employment which are gratuitously placed at their disposal.

The benefits payable during Unemployment, which amount to much less than the current wage-rates, are insufficient in themselves for complete family maintenance, for which they were never intended ; and they are necessarily terminable after a certain period of Unemployment has elapsed, even if no situation has been secured, seeing that no Insurance Fund can stand an unlimited drain. Moreover, as the scheme is based on deductions from wages or salary, it necessarily leaves unprovided for those workers, however intermittently employed, who are not under any " contract of service " : such as independent producers of all sorts, in agriculture or handicraft ; hawkers and pedlars ; working dealers and shopkeepers ; blacksmiths and chimney-sweeps ; hackney-carriage drivers, and others entering directly into relations, not with any employer, but with a series of customers. In all these cases involuntary Unemployment, in the form of a cessation of earnings though not of wages, still continues to furnish recruits to the great army of the destitute.

Finally, it must be said that the very magnitude of the benefit-distributing side of the work of the Employment Exchanges has, during the past few years, with a chronic inadequacy of staff, militated against the efficiency of the situation-finding service. Neither the work of "dovetailing" seasonal employments, nor that of popularising the Exchanges among the employers, has been successfully pursued in Great Britain during the past eight years of severe Unemployment.

Unemployment in the Years of War and After-War

In the unparalleled commercial prosperity of 1911–1914—transient as it was—the " Problem of the Unemployed " faded out of mind ; and with the outbreak of the Great War came new and unprecedented conditions. After a brief stress in the initial dislocation of trade, the continually increasing demand for fighters and munition workers found, for four years, continuous occupation for every available person of almost any age, of nearly every grade of capacity and of either sex. Regarded solely as an economic experiment, from the standpoint of an investigation of the problem of Unemployment, the Great War supplied a pretty conclusive demonstration of two negative propositions. It was made clear that there was, in the Britain of the period, nothing that could properly be described as a " surplus " population for which neither occupation nor wages could possibly be found. It was further demonstrated that the assumed category of the Unemployable had no definite boundary, seeing that a large proportion of those who had been classed as being either mentally or morally or physically incapable of any employment were, in fact, under conditions that actually existed for three or four years, usefully and even profitably employed.

It is, of course, merely of theoretic interest that—given a motive of sufficient intensity, shared by an enormous majority of the whole community—it was found to be neither physically impracticable nor actually beyond the financial capacity of the nation to organise employment at wages for practically the entire population, during a period of several years.[1] More relevant to our present subject is the lesser demonstration relating to the category of the Unemployable. During the ever-increasing demand for labour of all kinds, which nothing but such a war has ever yet produced, Unemployment, in practically all its forms, may be said to have ceased. Men

---

[1] It may be said that means were found for employing the Unemployed by drawing on the future. But the financial aspect of the war effort made by the British people may more correctly be put in the following way. In order to effect a nationally desired object, the families enjoying incomes greater than was required for subsistence to some extent voluntarily limited their personal consumption during the war, and also ceded in enforced taxation about a quarter of their incomes to pay the interest and sinking fund of the enormously swollen National Debt, and the greatly increased governmental expenditure that was judged necessary. As it happens, the property-owning class as a whole has been recouped by a rise in the rate of interest. There was no real forestalling of future production or consumption. The whole aggregate of persons who constitute the nation probably now possesses as much material wealth, and has for consumption annually as great a volume of commodities and services as it had before the war, and even nearly as much per head ; and, curiously enough, although individuals are differently affected, this " income " seems to be shared among social classes, taken as wholes, in much the same proportions as before, the increased taxation of incomes above the average having been made good by the rise in the rate of interest, and the loss of wages in exceptional Unemployment by the growth of social services.

whom the dislocation of industry deprived of permanent situations quickly found other opportunities of earning wages. The men in trades where employment is normally discontinuous found the intervals between jobs reduced to a minimum. Seasonal occupations became nearly continuous. Boys and girls were snapped up at almost adult wages. Elderly men and women ; the infirm ; even the halt, the lame and the blind—all were at work. But the most significant effect was that upon the pauper population.[1] The workhouses were largely emptied of all but those completely incapacitated, physically or mentally, for any kind of productive effort. The daily tide of vagrants along the roads, which had, for at least five hundred years, never before ceased to flow, came practically to an end. The Casual Wards stood empty, and were, in many Unions, closed. What no one had ventured to predict came actually to pass. Tens of thousands of men and women who had settled down in the workhouses to lives of listless idleness in chronic infirmity—even tens of thousands of professional tramps, habitual mendicants, begging-letter writers, and all the varieties of " the work-shy " in great cities—proved to be ready to accept manual working employment, and eager to labour, when employers were clamorous for additional hands, and when the terms offered were, not the scant and really insufficient subsistence of low-grade labour in peace time, but the doubled rate which such labour commanded during the war. What had been freely called " work-shyness " was found, in tens of thousands of cases, to be amenable to nothing more recondite than a keener demand for labour and a higher rate of remuneration.

After the war the whole circumstances underwent an almost instantaneous change, which presently took the form of the most violent slump on record.

[1] The total number of persons in Poor Law institutions of all kinds, and of pauper patients in lunatic asylums fell steadily from 365,233 at the beginning of 1914 to 266,282 at the end of 1918, a lower total than at any date since 1898. The total number in receipt of Outdoor Relief rose slightly during 1914, but fell from 394,707 at the beginning of 1915 to 287,244 at the end of 1918, a lower total than in any year since the beginning of the present statistics in 1849, and probably lower than at any date since the middle of the eighteenth century. The number in the Casual Wards fell from 7568 on January 1, 1914, to 1091 on December 28, 1918, a lower total than any previous record. The aggregate diminution of all classes of paupers was over 200,000, comprising practically all those between 14 and 70 who were not absolutely incapacitated by sickness or mental disorder.

The Industrial Depression of 1920–1928 in Relation to Unemployment

Whatever may be thought about the causation of the present depression, there is, we imagine, no dispute as to the circumstances in which it occurred. " Immediately after the war was over ", we are told, " there was an orgy of buying. Every country in the world wanted to replenish its stores of food, of raw materials and of manufactures. All the available purchasing power of the general public in neutral and late belligerent States was mobilised for this purpose. The war was ended. There was to be no more war. Psychologically this had an effect on sellers and buyers, tending to make them optimists—the former that they would be enabled to fulfil all orders ; the latter that they would be able to pay for all their needs. This world demand, acting on a market the supplies of which were bound to be short, produced a sudden and rapid rise in prices, accentuated doubtless by the inflation that had been characteristic of nearly all countries during the war." [1]

In Great Britain this " orgy of buying ", leading to a wild outburst of speculation, was made possible by the immediate abandonment by the Government in 1918–1919 of practically all the measures of control by which, during the war, production, distribution and investment had been, with steadily increasing efficiency, for four troublesome years, directed towards national ends. It was in vain that Reconstruction Committees and expert advisers warned Ministers and Parliament of the inevitable results of simultaneously removing all restrictions on the swinging-back of industry to the sole object of private profit-making. A thoughtless and unscrupulous Press campaign attributed every inconvenience from which the public had suffered to the manifold government interference with private enterprise. A House of Commons elected in the delirium of the Armistice, and overwhelmingly " capitalist " in composition, was blatantly eager for the full freedom of exploitation. The Ministers, who ought to have known better, ignored the recommendations made for " reconstruction " ; promptly " scrapped " all the restrictions of " control " and " priority ", and delighted in the immediate reversion to " freedom of enterprise " and

[1] *Unemployment as an International Problem*, by J. Morgan Rees, 1926, p. 171.

capitalist competition. But public complacency was short-lived. Within a little over eighteen months, as many economists had predicted (though none had given the date),[1] came the great slump, which turned out to be of greater severity and longer duration than could possibly have been imagined.

The resulting Unemployment has proved to be—in its magnitude, in its duration, in the wide range of its prevalence and the high percentage of the aggregate wage-earning class whom it has affected—the most serious that British industry has ever experienced. Moreover, it is, in 1928, not yet over. In its ninth year, it continues with unabated severity to confront the nation, and (as we shall presently describe) most seriously to distort the Poor Law Administration. Accordingly we cannot avoid a somewhat detailed description of what, in our judgment, takes rank with the greatest economic calamities in recorded history. Avoiding, on the one hand, all emotional colouring, and on the other all theoretic discussion of causes, we seek to state the bare facts of the Great Commercial Depression, particularly in its effect on Unemployment in Great Britain.[2]

[1] One of the most definite prophecies was put on record by Mr. B. Seebohm Rowntree early in 1918 :

" I think industry after the War will pass through three phases :

" (1) Great dislocation for a few months ;

" (2) Feverish activity for a year or two ;

" (3) A long period of depression, unless active steps are taken to avert it."

(B. Seebohm Rowntree, in *Labour and Capital after the War*, edited by (Sir) S. J. Chapman, 1918, p. 231.)

[2] We have not found any succinct and chronological description of the facts of the slump as an economic phenomenon. (*The Bibliography of Unemployment*, published by the International Labour Office in 1926, lists some 3000 articles, reports, books and pamphlets, in half a dozen languages, appearing between 1914 and 1925.) Most useful to us have been the series of studies in the two volumes issued by a small committee of economists under the chairmanship of Mr. W. T. Layton, entitled *The Third Winter of Unemployment* (1923), and *Is Unemployment Inevitable ?* (1924) ; together with the chapter on Unemployment in the second report of the Committee on Trade and Industry, entitled " Survey of Industrial Relations " (1926). The facts relating to business and finance may be best gleaned from the files of *The Economist* (weekly), or from its annual " Commercial History of the Year " ; and those relating to Unemployment from the numerous publications of the Ministry of Labour, especially the *Labour Gazette* (monthly). The course of events in other countries may be conveniently followed in *Unemployment as an International Problem*, by J. Morgan Rees, 1926, which is largely based on the valuable publications of the International Labour Office. For the crisis of 1926 in the United States, the articles by W. C. Mitchell and W. W. Persons in the *Supplement to the American Economic Review* for March 1922 may be consulted.

Other books of varying size and value are, *Unemployment, the Cause and a*

Though the advent of the depression appeared, at the time, to nearly every business man, remarkably sudden, precursory indications, as we can now recognise, were not wanting. Thus, "Japan began to feel the effect of trade depression in 1919, when trade in Great Britain was in full swing ".[1] Business in England was, indeed, not immediately affected. The transactions of the London Clearing House went on increasing, and reached their highest point in March 1920. Some anxiety was, however, already being felt, and we are told that in London, "informal conferences were held in the spring of 1920, at which the Government urged the banks to check the expansion of credit by definitely rationing their customers.[2] But though from November 1919, when the Bank Rate had risen to 6 per cent, the demand had been so great that the banks, for the sake of prudence, had to exercise restraint, no concerted action seems

---

Remedy, by A. Kitson, 1921; *Unemployment*, by F. W. Pethick Lawrence, 1922; *Unemployment in East London* (Toynbee Hall Report, 1922); *The Breakdown of the Minimum Wage and a Memorandum on Unemployment*, by A. A. Mitchell, 1922; *The Riddle of Unemployment and its Solution*, by C. E. Pell, 1922; *The Ebb and Flow of Unemployment*, by D. H. Robertson, 1923; *The Unemployment Problem*, by B. Seebohm Rowntree, 1923; *A Cottage and an Acre, the Remedy for Unemployment*, by Alfred Smith, 1923; *Unemployment*, by W. A. Appleton, 1923; *Control of Credit as a Remedy for Unemployment*, by J. R. Bellerby, 1923; *Out of Work*, by G. D. H. Cole, 1923; *Our Unemployment Problem*, by R. B. Crewdson, 1923; *International Aspects of Unemployment*, by W. Kirkconnell, 1923; *Unemployment, its Cause and Cure*, by A. Hook, 1924; *Unemployment, its Cause and Cure*, by T. Dickson, 1924; *Trade Recovery and the Relief of Unemployment* (Anon.), 1924; *The Solution of Unemployment*, by W. H. Walkinshaw, 1924; *Industrial Fluctuations*, by A. C. Pigou, 1925; *Unemployment*, by G. D. H. Cole, 1925; *Unemployment among Boys*, by W. M'G. Edgar and H. A. Secretan, 1925; *The Regulation of Unemployment*, by H. Feldman, New York, 1925; *The Inwardness of Unemployment*, by G. Wells, 1925; *Unemployment under Capitalism*, by Samuel Smith, 1925; *Unemployment: a Suggested Remedy*, by J. W. Scott, 1925; *Unemployment, its Causes and Cure*, by J. L. F. Vogel, 1925; *Industry and Politics*, by Sir A. Mond (Lord Melchett), 1927.

[1] *Is Unemployment Inevitable?* by W. T. Layton and others, 1924, p. 11. "Japan suffered first in the world crisis . . . the bankers tried to stop the period of instability and the wild speculation of 1919, but without much effect. . . . Prices began to break in the January of 1920 . . . by March there was a panic " (*Unemployment as an International Problem*, by J. Morgan Rees, 1926, p. 707).

[2] *Is Unemployment Inevitable?* by W. T. Layton and others, 1924, p. 16. The avowed intention of the Government, it should be said, was merely to try to preserve its market for Treasury Bills, which it needed to be constantly selling to the banks. The Treasury had thus a direct pecuniary motive for wishing to restrict the amount of even the best commercial paper coming on the market.

to have been taken, nor did the Bank of England think it right to take the initiative. A note of warning had, however, been struck by the issue, in December 1919, of a Treasury Minute to the effect that the policy of the Government was to allow no further increase in the currency note issue ; but that, on the contrary, the fiduciary issue would be restricted by making the highest total actually issued in any one year the legal maximum issue of the next. In other words, the legal tender in the country would be slowly contracted unless it were replaced by gold. The turn of the tide dates from the further rise of (the) Bank Rate (to 7 per cent) which occurred in the third week of April 1920." But there was still no obvious sign of collapse in Great Britain, though the rise in wholesale prices slackened, and presently stopped. In the United States, indeed, as late as April 1920, it could be testified before the Committee of the House of Representatives that there was then a positive dearth of workmen required for industry : a " labour shortage in practically every industrial activity ", amounting, it was seriously estimated, to five million men.[1] From that very time, however, there began to be signs in the United States of the appearance of a surplus of unwanted workers, which grew steadily and even rapidly.[2]

It was in June 1920 that the first clear signs of the coming collapse were to be detected by the business community in the United Kingdom. In that month wholesale prices began actually to fall, if only very slightly ; especially those of cotton and other textile materials, whilst the price of iron and steel fell only from August. This proved to be the beginning of a catastrophic and probably an unprecedented slump in prices generally, which continued for two and a half years. In October 1922, the general Index Number of wholesale prices stood at less than one-half that of May 1920.[3]

[1] *Migration and Business Cycles*, by Harry Jerome (National Bureau of Economic Research), 1926, pp. 24, 248.

[2] So enormously, indeed, did it grow that in September 1921, " the President's Conference on Unemployment met in Washington to consider measures for the relief of from four to five million men, resulting from the business slump " (*Ibid.*). The peak of wholesale prices in the U.S. was in May 1920, and June registered a slight fall. But such statistics as exist with regard to Unemployment indicate that this did not begin to rise until July.

[3] We cannot here examine, or even adequately describe, the various causes to which the great slump of trade, with the consequent Unemployment, have been attributed. Thus, the precipitation of the collapse in prices, production and employment—if not its ultimate cause—has been very definitely attributed

The collapse of business was, from the first, most apparent in the export trade. The exports of produce and manufactures of the United Kingdom, which had risen in 1920 to the unparalleled value of £1,334,469,269, fell in the very next year (1921) to no more than £703,399,542, or little more than one-half. Nor was this merely, or even mainly, due to the fall in prices. The exports of the different kinds of iron and steel that are recorded by weight sank from over three and a quarter million tons in 1920 to little over half that amount (1,696,000 tons) in 1921 ; and the exports of various kinds of cotton manufactures recorded by superficial extent sank from over four and a half million yards in 1920 to less than three million yards in 1921.[1]

The extension, in the autumn of 1920, of Unemployment Insurance (a measure regrettably delayed, so that it came only just in time) to all but a quarter of the wage-earning class—

---

to the decision of the United States Federal Reserve Board (which had raised its Rate of Discount to 6 per cent in November 1919), early in 1920, to arrest the increasing expansion of credit, and actually to reduce its aggregate volume, in order to forestall and prevent a disastrous financial crisis. This decision was presently followed by the raising in April 1920 of the British Bank Rate from 6 to 7 per cent. (It should, however, not be forgotten that the ending of the boom in trade and prices, and the raising of the rates of discount, may both have been the results of some common cause.) Allied with this view of the causation of the slump may be that which ascribes its long continuance and spasmodic aggravation to an actual insufficiency in the volume of currency and credit to supply the needs of the world's business at a level of prices still considerably above that prevailing before the war. But the position may be otherwise described. Thus, it is said that " the downward movement in 1920 started not as a result of a deliberately deflationist movement, but on account of the fact that the expansion could only have been financed by colossal inflation : and neither the Japanese, the American, nor the British Government—to take the order in which each faced the problem—was prepared to embark upon such a policy" (*Is Unemployment Inevitable?* by W. T. Layton and others, 1924, p. 83).

Again, the prolongation of the slump beyond 1926 in Great Britain, and much of its aggravation since that date, has been ascribed to the decision of the Bank of England and the British Government (come to in the honest belief that the result would in the long run be financially advantageous to Britain) at a time when the pound sterling was still depreciated in terms of the dollar, and when British prices were generally still about 10 per cent below those of the United States, to force the foreign exchange value of the pound to its pre-war parity with the dollar ; foreseeing and intending that this action would cause a further check to the British export trade, and a consequent increase in British Unemployment—not to say also a further reduction in the rates of wages of British workmen. " You will all have to reduce your wages " was the hasty expression reported (and, in spite of official denial, persistently believed) to have been used by a British statesman to a Trade Union delegation.

[1] Statistical Abstract for the U.K., 1927, pp. 337-339.

omitting, too, only the quarter which is least subject to Unemployment—enabled the nation, for the first time, to measure with some accuracy, month by month, the effect of business depression on the wage-earners' opportunities for earning their bread. It was in June 1920 (the month in which wholesale prices began to fall) that the percentage of insured persons who were unemployed, which had previously been steadily declining—it had got down in that month to no more than 2·6—started to rise. For several months the rise, though continuous, was slow. But "in August [1920] a decline in employment, beginning in boot and shoe manufactures, leather tanning and currying, cotton-weaving and the hosiery and jute trades, spread gradually to other industries." [1] By December 1920 the percentage of Unemployed in Great Britain had reached nearly three times the figure of June 1920, with 857,840 persons actually registered as Unemployed ; and in January 1921 it was more than four times what it had been only seven months earlier, with 1,213,386 so registered. In April 1921 the percentage was nine times as great as twelve months before, and the number had risen to 2,549,395 in addition to hundreds of thousands on short time, and a considerable number in receipt of Poor Relief. This colossal figure, representing (with wives and children) not less than one-fifth of the entire population of the Kingdom, registers an economic calamity of absolutely unparalleled magnitude. No previous Unemployment in the records of capitalist industry in Great Britain, not even the widespread collapses of 1879, 1841 or 1826 (though accurate statistics are lacking), can have come anywhere near it in the extent of its range. [2]

The unbroken continuity and long duration of the Unemployment resulting from the slump has been as remarkable as the suddenness of its advent and its universality. Though the registered Unemployed only remained over two millions during the three calamitous months affected by the stoppage of the coal-mining industry (April-June 1921), the total (including Northern Ireland) has, during eight long years, never once fallen

---

[1] "Commercial History" of 1920, in *The Economist*, 1921, quoted in *Is Unemployment Inevitable ?* by W. T. Layton and others, 1924, p. 20.

[2] The student will be reminded of the numerical magnitude of the economic results of the Black Death of 1349.

below one million.[1] Though the general level of wholesale prices has now been for several years fairly stable, and the aggregate volume of British imports and exports has considerably increased since the disastrous year 1921, the total number of the registered Unemployed seems unable to get below a million, with repeated rises to a million and a half.

Unfortunately, the Unemployed registered as in receipt of Insurance Benefit, or even as known to the " live registers " of the Employment Exchanges, do not include all those who (though able and willing to work) are actually wageless. The benefits of the Insurance Scheme do not, in many cases, last as long as the Unemployment, whilst other workers find themselves disqualified for benefit through inability to comply with the complicated regulations ; and some four or five millions of others, again, fall outside the Insurance Scheme altogether, either as being too young (under 16) or too old (over 65) for eligibility ; or as belonging to the excluded occupations of agriculture and private domestic service ; or as outworkers or homeworkers (mainly in the clothing industry) ; or as possessed of independent means, or as gaining a living otherwise than under a contract of service, or as engaged in the vocations excepted by reason of their habitual permanence of employment, which is yet not invariable or universal. For all these reasons many tens of thousands of workers, for whom Insurance Benefits are unavailable, have to be added to the aggregate numbers of Unemployed reported by the Minister of Labour. Of the magnitude of this addition to be made to the number of the recorded Unemployed from time to time not even any estimate can be formed. But the Poor Law returns during the past eight years show large numbers of these families, by reason of destitution caused merely by Unemployment and ineligibility for any Insurance Benefit, actually driven to Poor Relief ; to the number, at different dates during the past eight years (apart from those in receipt of Insurance Benefit inadequate for the support of their families), of between one and two hundred thousand manual workers, comprising, with their dependants, between three and six hundred thousand persons.

On the other hand, it must be noted that the Unemployment has differed very much in its duration in particular

---

[1] Nineteenth Abstract of Labour Statistics, 1928, p. 75 (Cmd. 3410).

cases and has fallen far from evenly upon the wage-earning population. "It is 'important', so the Minister of Labour tells us in 1926, "to bear in mind that the personnel of the Unemployed is constantly changing. There is a wide range in the spells of Unemployment, during which registration is maintained, varying from those of the skilled building trade operative, for example, whose name may appear on the register only for an hour—through the variety of intermittent periods of work inherent in such occupations as dock labourers and seamen, and the well-defined times of slack employment in seasonal trades—to the long and continuous idleness which during these years has been endemic in certain industries, and in the areas where those industries are chiefly placed." [1] The statistics indicate, indeed, that about two-thirds of all the insured workers have been, throughout the whole eight years (apart from the periods of illness, holidays and brief intervals between situations, which happen to all wage-earners, involving them, on an average, in a loss of income of possibly 10 per cent per annum), pretty continuously employed. Any long-continued Unemployment seems to have fallen to the lot of no more than about one million, out of some seventeen millions of manual workers.[2]

This extreme "patchiness" in the incidence of Unemployment has been caused only to a relatively small extent by the shortcomings and defects, physical, mental or moral, of individual men and women. The workers in the least fortunate "heavy" industries have been no more lacking in the social virtues than the workers in the trades that have suffered scarcely at all. Though nearly every occupation is believed to have had, at one or other period in the past eight years, rather more Unemployment than in the quinquennium that immediately preceded the outbreak of war, the extreme Unemployment has, on this occasion, been concentrated, probably more than in any previous depression, upon a limited number of industries, and these of a particular class. Unemployment has been markedly greatest and most continuous in what are termed the "heavy" industries,

---

[1] Report of the Ministry of Labour for the year 1925 (Cmd. 2736), p. 27.

[2] Thus, between October 1923 and April 1926, "out of 11½ million work-people insured . . . nearly 8 million drew no Unemployment Benefit at all, and of the remaining 3½ million, the Benefit drawn by 2½ million in no single case exceeded 100 days in all" (Industrial Transference Board Report, 1928, p. 4).

and in those producing mainly for export.[1]   Thus, the workers
in shipbuilding have had as many as 45 per cent of all their
number registered as Unemployed, and the percentage has never
fallen below 27.   The relatively few miners of iron ore, lead,
tin and copper have for eight years constantly had 17 to 25 per
cent of all their number Unemployed ; and during the last
three years they have been joined in this melancholy pre-
eminence by the hugely greater number of the coal-miners.   The
iron and steel workers and the glass bottle makers have suffered
nearly as severely as the miners : whilst the makers of marine
engines and various other kinds of engineers (other than electrical),
have been in little better case.   It is the great staple industries
of the nation which have suffered most.

The result has been an equally exceptional geographical
" patchiness " in the local distribution of the Unemployed,
which has aggravated the economic distress.   Geographically,
we may say, Unemployment has been largely concentrated in
the districts within which coal is worked.   These districts
include also the places in which the great bulk of the production
of iron and steel is carried on ;   the ports at which most of the
ships are built and nearly all the marine engineering is done ;
the homes of the greater part of " heavy engineering " generally ;
the principal seats of both cotton and woollen manufacturers ;
and generally the areas specially chosen for the commodities
making up the mass of the export trades.   The Clyde Valley,
the North-East Coast, South Lancashire and the West Riding,
South Wales, the " Black Country " around Birmingham, and
North-Eastern Ulster have all recorded, throughout the whole
period, exceptionally high percentages of wageless workpeople.
On the other hand, the Metropolitan area, which at previous
periods of depression has often suffered more acutely than other

---

[1] " The outstanding feature of Unemployment in the heavy industries is
that it is ' frozen ' by its close concentration in or about the coalfields in areas of
comparatively small extent.   Industrial development within these areas in the
past has been highly specialised.   In the inland districts many large communities (e.g. the Rhondda in South Wales with a population of 162,000) are
dependent on one industry only, the coal industry ; in others the only alternative employment outside coal-mining is in the iron and steel industries and, to
some extent, in shipbuilding " (Industrial Transference Board Report, 1928,
p. 15).   Exceptional concentration of Unemployment might be seen in May
1928 in South Wales at Merthyr Tydfil (62·3 per cent), Blaina (48·6 per cent),
Dowlais (38·8 per cent) ; and in Durham at Bishop Auckland (42 per cent),
Gateshead (30 per cent) and South Shields (24·9 per cent).

parts of Britain, and which, as a whole, had, in 1910–1913, usually more Unemployed than these, has been, during most of the eight years between 1920 and 1928, comparatively a bright spot. The Eastern and South-Eastern Counties and the Eastern Midlands, which had, in 1920, a relatively small share in the "heavy" industries, have benefited, together with " Greater London ", by the development of such new or expanding industries as those connected with artificial silk, " wireless " broadcasting, the generation and supply of electricity, automobile transport, the gramophone and the cinematograph, together with furniture-making, printing and publishing. Thus, large parts of Great Britain have had relatively slight Unemployment. In fact, south of the historic line " from the Severn to the Wash ", except for a few local pockets of Unemployment, business has been, on the whole, relatively " good ", plainly not by reason of any personal superiority either in the local employers or their workpeople, but owing to some cause independent of personal qualities.

This remarkable localisation of the bulk of the Unemployment, and its coincidence with the exporting, and especially the " heavy " industries in which coal and iron are concerned, prepares us for the conclusion that although it has been aggravated by some calamitous labour troubles, it cannot fairly be attributed, either to a stubborn refusal of Trade Unionists to submit to a reduction of their wages, or to any unusual prevalence of industrial disputes. In the course of the first two years of the slump (1921 and 1922), close upon two million workmen in the metal, engineering and shipbuilding trades accepted, almost invariably without stoppage of work, successive reductions of wages amounting, on an average, to more than thirty shillings per man per week, involving a saving to the employers, in these industries alone, of £150,000,000 per annum. The million miners, in the same two years, saw their rates of wages reduced, without stoppage of work (though there was, in 1921, one calamitous stoppage arising out of a claim for an improvement in conditions), by a similar amount, which saved the colliery companies over £75,000,000 per annum.

Altogether, the Minister of Labour reports a net decrease during 1921 and 1922 in the rates of wages, among all industries for which he has statistics, amounting to $10\frac{1}{4}$ million pounds per week, thus reducing the employers' expenses of production by more than £530,000,000 per annum ; and of these decreases in weekly wage rates, 9¾ millions were accepted without stoppage of work, and only half a million after stoppage of work.[1] Thus, for the two crucial years of the slump (1921 and 1922), it must be said that it was neither the wage-earners' resistance to necessary reductions, nor their wanton resort to strikes, that brought about the collapse of business enterprise. The number of disputes begun in 1921 and 1922 was, in fact, in each year, less than half the number begun annually during the two preceding years (1919 and 1920).[2] There had been, it is true, in the latter part of 1919, a prolonged dispute with the iron-founders ; and there was in the same year a short but extensive stoppage of the railways. In 1920 and 1921, as we have mentioned, there were serious stoppages of the coal-mines ; and in 1922 a dispute between employers and workmen among the engineers, all of which entailed serious dislocation of business in all directions ; but with these grave exceptions, industry was in these two years, in face of the enormous reductions in wage rates on which the employers in nearly all trades were insisting, no more disturbed by industrial disputes than in the five years 1910–1914, when British industry was at the height of its prosperity.[3]

The relative incidence on different industries of the Unemployment of the past eight years has, we suggest, a further significance. It can hardly be a mere coincidence that the four great industries which directly account for two-thirds of all the wageless men are exactly those in which the war needs enormously increased both productive capacity and the enrolment of labour, not in this country alone, but among all the belligerents. The war demand for shells and guns and armour-plate probably doubled the productive capacity and the output of the British forges and furnaces ; increased by 50 per cent those of the United States ; and similarly enlarged those of France, Belgium,

---

[1] Nineteenth Abstract of Labour Statistics, 1927 (Cmd. 3140), p. 137.
[2] *Ibid.*, 136-137.
[3] In 1921, whilst there were fewer disputes, that in the coal-mining industry was extensive and prolonged, so as to make the " days lost " far in excess of any previous year. In 1926 came the calamity of the seven months' stoppage of all the coal-mines, together with the ten days " General Strike ", which gravely aggravated the depression in trade. But these serious interruptions cannot be supposed to have caused the depression which began in 1920, though they have of course militated against recovery.

Germany, Czecho-Slovakia, Italy, and other countries. With the cessation of war, the world's absorption of steel, after a brief spurt of shipbuilding, and other forms of repairing war damage, reverted to something like its pre-war need, or even less.[1] Much the same may be said of coal. From the British pits the miners in 1914–1915 voluntarily enlisted in such streams that, presently, in order to maintain the necessary output, many thousands of them had to be returned to coal-mining, and other tens of thousands of workers enrolled, including Irish and Belgians, but also many English who, on account of age, physique or other grounds, had escaped the earlier drafts. When the war was over, and the surviving miners resumed their civil occupation, the newcomers were not wholly extruded, so that the total recorded as employed in 1920 (1,248,224) was actually 120,000 in excess of that in 1913 (1,127,890).[2] Meanwhile the world's need for British coal had shrunk, partly owing to lessened purchasing power in the European countries, partly through the ever-increasing sub-stitution of internal combustion engines fed by oil for steam engines fed by coal; partly through the substitution of oil for coal as fuel; partly through the continuous development of hydro-electricity ; and partly (as with iron and steel production) in consequence of the increased efforts of nearly all countries to make themselves as far as possible independent of foreign coal. For the builders of ships and the makers of their manifold equip-ment, among whom there prevailed in 1919–1920 a frantic and largely speculative activity, the fact is grimly eloquent that the world's shipping in 1928 is reported to be some 20 million tons in excess of what it was in 1914, whilst the aggregate amount of commodities now conveyed from country to country is some 20 per cent less than it was before the war. It must clearly be many years before so many new ships will be required in all the world as would employ all the workers who were attracted into

---

[1] It was pointed out in 1923 that, in addition to the Unemployment resulting from an ordinary trade depression, " there is the special problem of Unemploy-ment due to the abnormal twist that the war gave to the country's industry . . . in the engineering and metals group the numbers have increased by a third " or, including shipbuilding and vehicles, 575,000 men (between the Censuses of 1911 and January 1922). " The war, it would seem, attracted to industries an enormous number of men for whose work there is at present no demand ", and there was a " simultaneous over-development of their foreign competitors " (*The Third Winter of Unemployment*, by W. T. Layton and others, 1923, pp. 7-8).

[2] Annual Report of the Minister of Mines for 1927 (1928), p. 92.

the industry either during the war, or by the excessive speculative activity that marked the first fifteen months of peace.   Thus,
it is impossible to avoid the conclusion that a large part of the
Unemployment from which the nation has been suffering is a
direct result of the world-wide hypertrophy of these great industries, due to the imperative necessity of instantly meeting
the colossal but necessarily transient needs of the belligerent
nations during the war.   In this view, the greater part of the loss
and suffering of the present slump is only a share of the immense
cost of carrying on the war from 1914 to 1918—expenses not met,
or even foreseen, when they were being incurred, for which, in
fact, the bill is only now being sent in !   The tragic unfairness
is that the loss and suffering involved in these " expenses "
incurred by the Governments of 1914–1918 is being allowed to
fall, in the main, not on the " war profiteers ", not even on the
whole community in proportion to ability to pay ;   but mainly
on the 15 to 20 per cent of the manual-working wage-earners
living in the distressed areas.

Finally, we must add the reflection that the present condition
of colossal and continuous Unemployment differs from every
previous experience of the kind in that public opinion (and
particularly that of the two-thirds of the whole population who
are dependent on wage-earning) is far less willing than before to
accept as conclusive the explanation that, given the universal
desire for pecuniary gain and the state of " private war " in the
production and distribution of commodities, successive booms
and slumps are inevitable, and must be considered as part of
the nature of things ! [1]   An even more momentous alteration is
the fact that the wage-earners—the Unemployed as well as the
others to whom long-continued Unemployment is no more than

---

[1] It is only thirty-five years ago that Gladstone, then Prime Minister, was
horrified at the notion of the subject Unemployment being even raised in the
House of Commons, which he regarded as both unconcerned with, and entirely
unfit to deal with, such issues.   That Parliament should ever legislate on the
subject was entirely beyond his vision.

The wage-earners are at least entitled to say that a great deal of economic
opinion has, rightly or wrongly, come round to the view that—to use the words
of Professor Cassel's Memorandum to the Financial Conference of 1920—the
collapse of business " *was not merely a spontaneous result of forces beyond our
control, but was the result of a deliberate policy of deflation of currency and credit* ",
which may possibly have been advantageous in the long run, but for which
Ministers must be prepared to answer in Parliament, and for which there seems
no reason that the wage-earners in particular should have to pay.

an apprehension—now possess both the Parliamentary and the Local Government franchise ; and that they return members of their own to the House of Commons and the Municipal Councils.

How the Governments of 1921–1928 dealt with Unemployment

During these eight years of severe Unemployment, when in session after session the House of Commons has resounded with demands that systematic and adequate provision should be made for the million or more of wageless workers, Government after Government has failed, as is now clear, to devise and put in operation any satisfactory way of meeting the unprecedented national emergency. After eight years of effort, the close of 1928 finds the situation statistically no better than in the latter part of 1920 ; with the poorest quarter of the whole population —and, indeed, nearly the whole wage-earning class—more impoverished, the Unemployment Insurance scheme more heavily indebted, and (as we shall describe in a subsequent chapter) the organisation of the Poor Law so strained and demoralised by the demands upon it as to be, perhaps, in as bad a plight as it was found by the Royal Commission of 1832–1834. Our interest in the record of the measures taken during this period, with regard to the Unemployed, necessarily lies less in the palliatives themselves than in the general conception on which the Government acted ; in the effect of the Government's action or inaction upon the Poor Law, and in the lessons to be drawn from the experience gained.

An Obstinate Optimism

Looking back, in 1928, on the whole course of action of the successive Cabinets since the beginning of the slump in 1920, the deepest impression is that of a reluctant slowness of comprehension—an almost invincible optimism—which prevented the nation from realising the gravity of the situation. Year after year, Ministers, financiers and " captains of industry " alike persisted in believing that the blight which had fallen upon British industry was, as on previous occasions, only transient ; that the trade depression would gradually pass away, and with it once more the clamours of the Unemployed ; that even as they spoke signs of improvement were already visible, and that—

so it was suggested—nothing drastic, and especially nothing costly to the tax-payer, or inconvenient to the private profit-maker, needed to be undertaken. It is, for instance, possible to construct, from the annual speeches to their shareholders of the various chairmen of the principal banks, a *catena* of comforting prognostications, based on actually observed indications of an improvement in the commercial weather—prognostications that have proved, one and all, delusive. Already in 1923, one of these financial magnates saw "signs that the worst period of depression has passed ". In 1924, two of them testified that there was a " definite improvement in trade and [that] Unemployment is declining ", and that there prevailed in the business world " a definite feeling of confidence and hope for the coming year ".[1] In 1925, some of them actually saw " notable improvement in many directions, for instance in the cotton trade " ; or declared that " prospects for increased trade throughout the world are, I believe, favourable ". In 1926, it was boldly testified by one that " our feet are now on the road to recovery " ; and by another that " our trade is not only holding its own, but shows fair promise of considerable improvement." Yet another —not a young man—went so far, in 1927, as to say, " I do not remember the time when, throughout the industries of the country, there has been such a feeling of expectation, and indeed optimism ". Finally, in 1928, we are told that " both industry and trade in this country are showing indications of a substantial revival at the present time." [2] Yet throughout all these years the number of the registered Unemployed has continued to move spasmodically up and down between the enormous figures of one and two millions, representing, with wives and children, between one-tenth and one-fifth of the whole population of the nation.

[1] Economists seem to have had a similar feeling in that year. " The situation as regards employment has immensely improved in the last two years ; and whether we look at the near future or further ahead we see no reason for taking a pessimistic view of Britain's possibilities " (*Is Unemployment Inevitable ?* by W. T. Layton and others, 1924, p. 85).

[2] These interesting *dicta* were collected by an enterprising official of the London County Council ; and given (with names) in the *L.C.C. Staff Gazette* for July 1928. It may be said (though by way of explanation rather than excuse) (*a*) that the banks themselves were able, throughout, to maintain their dividends and to increase their reserves ; (*b*) that the bank chairmen and most of the shareholders had no personal knowledge of the condition of the Unemployed ; and, as we fear we must add, (*c*) they were strangely lacking in imagination !

We do not reproduce these current optimisms (which might be paralleled by similar remarks by Cabinet Ministers in Parliamentary debate) out of any complacent " after the event " wisdom. They enable us to understand the inability of successive Governments to rise to the height of what was really a desperate situation. Not until the publication, in July 1928, of the report of the Industrial Transference Board [1]—of a tenor and in a phrasing reported to have been unexpected by the Cabinet— does the essential nature of the problem appear to have been realised. This report (which had, after six months, practically no achievements in transference to record) emphasised the folly of supposing that the long-continued slump in half a dozen basic industries (which accounted directly for the greater part of all the Unemployment) could be attributed to any " cyclical " depression of trade, or could be expected, in any reasonable period, simply to pass away. The most serious feature of the Unemployment of 1920–1928, so the Transference Commissioners insisted, and the one in which it differs markedly from any previous period of trade depression, is in its not being attributable to the " trade cycle ", or to any passing cause : in its revelation, perhaps for the first time in British history, of a genuine " surplus " of manual workers, largely skilled operatives, running into many tens of thousands, almost entirely confined to certain " basic industries "—coal-mining, iron and steel production and shipbuilding, with marine and other " heavy " engineering— an unwanted labour force which is thought never likely again to find employment in its once prosperous occupations. This surplus, the Government was authoritatively informed, could not be put at less than a quarter of a million men (four-fifths of them being coal-miners), comprising, with their dependants, about one million persons, *or more than 2 per cent of the whole population*. " The moral to be drawn ", emphatically reports the Industrial Transference Board, " is . . . that in many of the districts concerned the idea of a cyclical or transient

[1] The Industrial Transference Board, consisting of Sir Warren Fisher (Permanent Secretary of the Treasury), Sir John Cadman and Sir David Shackleton, was appointed by the Cabinet on January 6, 1928, not to advise or report, but " for the purpose of facilitating the transfer of workers, and in particular of miners, for whom opportunities of employment in their own district or occupation are no longer available " (see *Labour Gazette*, January and August 1928).

depression must now be recognised, quite unflinchingly, as no longer tenable. . . . We are definitely led to the belief that it would be unwise to count upon the recovery, by certain areas dependent upon the basic industries, and particularly coal-mining, of the position they occupied before the War." [1] What-ever may be done by or for the surplus of man-power in these areas, " the first aim of policy must be the dispersal of the heavy concentrations of Unemployment ". As one Minister has put it, the view to which the Cabinet was pressed to come in 1928 was that they had at all costs—costs, that is, of personal suffering to the poor, not of the Chancellor of the Exchequer's money—" to break up the ice pack ".

The Wavering of Policy

It was, we think, owing to this long-continued optimism that the policy of the Government throughout the eight years was marked by uncertainty and wavering, in the course of which a dozen different " remedies for Unemployment " were, simultane-ously or alternatively, advocated and adopted.

Insurance

The first expedient was to extend the 1911 experiment of contributory insurance ; and then, in order to admit to benefit as large a proportion as possible of the Unemployed, to weaken considerably the contributory element. The rapid development of the slump in the summer of 1920 gave the Government at last both the strength and the courage to carry through a somewhat sceptical House of Commoms the long-projected Bill which widened the range of Unemployment Insurance from $2\frac{1}{2}$ to over 11 million wage-earners.[2] The very month after this great

---

[1] Report of Industrial Transference Board, 1928.

[2] Unemployment Insurance Act, 1920. The successive expansions and other changes in Unemployment Insurance can be best followed in the severely critical *Unemployment Relief in Great Britain*, by Felix Morley, 1924. Between 1919 and 1928 there were no fewer than fifteen Unemployment Insurance Acts amending the original Act of 1911, and those of 1914 and 1916. See Report on Unemployment Insurance (Cd. 6965 of 1913) ; Report of Ministry of Labour on National Unemployment Insurance to July 1923 ; the Annual Reports of the Ministry of Labour for 1923 and 1924 (Cmd. 2481 of 1925) ; for 1925 (Cmd. 2736 of 1926) ; for 1926 and for 1927 ; Report and Evidence of the Committee on Unemployment Insurance of which Lord Blanesburgh was chairman (Stationery Office, 1927).

measure came into operation the situation was found so menacing that the Act had to be hastily amended, so as to admit to Benefit many thousands of wageless workmen who had not even four weekly contributions to their credit. In the following years further amending Acts were passed, increasing the amount of Benefit ; providing for two " special periods " during which the limitation of Benefit to one week for every six contributions was, under certain conditions, suspended ; and empowering the Treasury to advance to the Insurance Fund up to £10,000,000— subsequently increased to £30,000,000—to enable the Fund to meet its ever-growing liabilities. We need not follow the further amendments introduced into the scheme by the later Acts, of which each session had at least one, whilst several had two or more, making altogether 19 statutes in the eighteen years 1911–1928. We shall not attempt to enumerate these changes—the successive additions of " uncovenanted " or " extended " Benefit, to be enjoyed by those (presently numbering more than one-half of the whole) who had exhausted all the rights that their prior contributions had given to them ; of " dependants' allowance " for an ever-widening circle of recognised dependants of the contributors ; of the " bridge " by which many of the irregularly employed men were enabled by " spread overs " of intermittent employment to mitigate the hardship of the " waiting period " at the beginning of each spell of Unemployment, during which no Benefit is payable ; and of various other modifications designed to make the Benefits more nearly co-extensive with the growing host of the Unemployed.

Under these developments, the character of the Insurance scheme was subtly changed. " It would seem ", it could be said as early as 1923, " that the Benefits paid under the Insurance Scheme have lost to some extent the character of insurance. The Scheme provides a convenient form for providing relief, and the effects . . . have been almost wholly good. But it has two grave defects as a relief scheme. The first is that it places on the shoulders of the employer and the employed worker in industry the greater part of the cost of maintaining, not only the Unemployed whose condition may be regarded as a normal risk of industry, but also the abnormal burden of Unemployment due to the present abnormal political and economic situation. This is a burden that would seem more properly to belong to the community as a whole ; and the placing of it on industry when trade is depressed and wages low may be hampering trade recovery. The second defect is that, even with its present wide extension, the scheme is not a complete relief scheme. Not only the Unemployed in uninsured trades are unprovided for, but in the insured trades the ' gap week ' [since abolished] and the waiting period leave a proportion of the Unemployed without relief from this source." [1]

The Execution of Public Works

The Government had, however, another remedy for Unemployment in the shape of the execution of public improvements on a large scale. The Chancellor of the Exchequer found money, to the extent, in the eight years 1921–1928, of no less than eighty-six millions sterling, with which to aid Local Authorities and Public Utility Companies to carry out public works of various kinds.[2] These were to be either works of magnitude which could not otherwise be undertaken, or else works which could be expedited for the relief of existing Unemployment. This scheme was administered by a nominated " Unemployment Grants Committee ", in conjunction with the Ministry of Labour. The Government grants took the form, either of the payment of a proportion of 50 to 65 per cent, and in some cases even 75 per cent, of the interest and sinking fund upon the loan raised by the Local Authority, for a period of from five to fifteen years, according to the nature of the work to be executed ; or of the grant of as much as 75 per cent of the wages paid in works carried out by direct employment.[3] Under this scheme several thousands of widely scattered public works were carried out by several hundred Local Authorities and Public Utility Com-

[1] *The Third Winter of Unemployment*, by W. T. Layton and others, 1923, pp. 39, 40. See, on these points the very critical *Unemployment Relief in Great Britain*, by Felix Morley, 1924.

[2] " The Government policy is, in effect, to relieve the burden on the localities by national schemes of insurance and by grants made by the Unemployment Grants Committee and by other grants for the acceleration of Relief Works " (Third Annual Report of Minister of Health, 1922).

[3] Ministry of Health Circulars, Nos. 245 of September 22, 1921, and 251 of October 12, 1921 ; August 19, 1924 ; March 30, 1925. The Circular of December 15, 1925, announced a drastic limitation of the assistance previously offered. The offer was renewed in 1928.

panies, often by the direct employment of selected wageless men by the Local Authority concerned, consisting mainly of the making and widening of roads, the laying out of recreation grounds and cemeteries, the erection of public buildings, the provision of sewers and sewage works, the paving and repaving of streets, the extension of docks, quays and harbours, water, gas and electricity works, the extension of tramways, land reclamation and drainage, and similar improvements.[1]

Much the same scheme appeared in a different form in the extensive grants made to Local Authorities between 1920 and 1928 by the Minister of Transport out of the Road Fund, to which the annual licences on automobile vehicles were credited. With the aid of these grants, amounting in the aggregate to thirty-seven millions sterling, in addition to a further twenty millions from local rates, an enormous improvement has been made in the principal roads throughout the country, and a certain increase in the aggregate volume of employment has been caused.

From the standpoint of provision for the Unemployed, both these forms of Government grants to Local Authorities appear to have had practically the same advantages and disadvantages as the previous provision of work by the Municipalities. The operations were always more costly when carried out by the Unemployed than they would have been if they had been undertaken by the contractors' ordinary staffs, whose own opportunities of employment were thereby diminished. Those among the Unemployed who were fortunate enough to be selected for a job enjoyed only a few days' or a few weeks' wages, and then had to give place to others. The work was only partially a real increase in the aggregate volume of employment, as many of the enterprises would anyhow have been undertaken, and Local Authorities used a certain ingenuity in getting defrayed out of Government grants the cost of works that they would otherwise have executed, sooner of later, at the expense of the local rates. The diminution in the mass of a million or so wageless men, even by the expenditure of millions of pounds,

---

[1] First to Sixth Reports of the Unemployment Grants Committee, 1922–1928; see also Appendix VI. in *Unemployment Insurance in Great Britain*, by Felix Morley, 1924, pp. 189-191 ; Memorandum on the Provision of Work for Relief of Unemployment (Cmd. 2196 of 1924).

was relatively trifling. The result was a very general sense of disappointment. On the other hand, the public got the benefit of the roads, etc.[1]

Emigration

One result of the war was the temporary cessation, and, as it seems, a lasting discouragement to migration overseas. In the three pre-war years 1911–1913, the net outward flow from the British Isles amounted to nearly one million persons, about one-half of these proceeding to Canada and the United States. In the whole five years, 1914–1918, into which the war entered, the total net outward flow did not reach 60,000 persons. Thus the number of persons retained at home, who might otherwise have emigrated, considerably exceeded the total number of British deaths on war service. After the Armistice special efforts were made to facilitate the emigration, to other parts of the British Commonwealth of Nations, of ex-service men and their families ; and in 1922 similar facilities were offered to all British residents by the Empire Settlement Act. These efforts have had only a limited success. In spite of all the expenditure, British emigration has not, so far, attained anything like its pre-war dimensions. In the seven years 1919–1925, the net outflow, far from taking off half a million a year, as might not unreasonably have been hoped for, averaged only about 130,000 per annum, or not much more than one-third of the pre-war rate.

The causes of the failure of the Government to make emigration an effective outlet for the Unemployed seem to have been threefold. From this standpoint the financial assistance has been unduly niggardly. To make any perceptible effect upon an overstocked Labour Market nothing less than the removal of large numbers of adults and young people could be of use ; and the number of families who found it possible to move, on the terms that the Government offered, has hitherto been disap-

---

[1] In November 1928 the Government made a new offer to *Local Authorities for areas not specially depressed* of substantially half the cost of " accelerated " works, provided that not less than half the men employed are drawn from depressed areas—for whom there is usually no housing accommodation available in the district into which they are to be attracted, nor is any assistance offered for their transportation ! (Circular of Unemployment Grants Committee of November 9, 1928.)

pointingly small.[1]   To be within reach of the ordinary family in
the Unemployed class, emigration, it seems, must be rendered
almost costless to the emigrant. " The passage rates ", euphe-
mistically observed the Industrial Transference Board, " must be
within the reach of the ordinary man."   He must have, in
addition, " the minimum of outfit necessary for his start in a
new country, and a small sum of money to fall back upon after
arrival ".   Not many of the Unemployed, by the time they had
brought themselves to be willing to emigrate, were able to find
the share of the passage money on which the Government insisted.

Scarcely less deterrent have proved the limitations which the
United States on the one hand, and the Dominions Governments
on the other, have placed upon the total number of immigrants
to be admitted or assisted.   It is true that it does not seem to
be established that the maximum number allowed to enter the
United States from Great Britain has been actually attained in
every year ; or that the number fixed for particular categories
from time to time by the Australian Governments have always
been reached.   The very apprehension of a restriction of numbers
has apparently sufficed to prevent quite all the permitted quotas
being recruited or despatched.

But an even greater obstacle to the success of the policy of
assisted emigration, as a remedy for the situation in which the
Government found itself with regard to Unemployment, has
proved the coil of complications in which the Home and Dominion
Governments between them enveloped the transaction.   The
effect of this " formidable tangle of procedure " which involved
applicants in delay, expense and often an embarrassing publicity,
was seriously to hamper the scheme.   The Industrial Transference
Board, in July 1928, were emphatic in declaring that, if emigration was really going to be promoted in such a way as to affect
the overstocked Labour Market in Great Britain, a drastic change
was required.   " All the controversial talk about emigration ",
they observed, " all the complications and delays and disappoint-
ments at present attendant upon the schemes of assisted passages
under the Empire Settlement Act . . . have undoubtedly induced a general mood of doubt and reluctance that may get into

---

[1] During the whole seven years, 1922–1928, the total number of families
emigrating by passages assisted under the Empire Settlement Act, 1922, does
not seem to have reached 80,000 (about 300,000 persons).

a definite unwillingness . . . unless migration can be promptly made cheap and easy." [1]

The Provision of Training for the Unemployed

A far-sighted section of the original Insurance Act of 1911 provided for the requirement, in any cases in which it was thought desirable, that men in receipt of Unemployment Benefit should submit themselves to industrial training.   For a whole decade no action was taken in this direction.   When in 1921 it became apparent that there was no likelihood of the Employment Exchange being able to find situations for hundreds of thousands of the men and women still unemployed, there were demands from all sides that training should be provided.   Some wished for training in order to fit the men and women for other kinds of employment.   Others saw in training a means of getting off to Canada or Australia some of the " surplus population ".   To others, again, the offer of admission to a Training Centre appeared a happy substitute for the " offer of the Workhouse " as an instrument for " deterring " men from continuing idly to draw Unemployment Benefit.   To few, perhaps, did it seem anything like the adoption of a proposal made by some of the members of the Poor Law Commission of 1905–1909, that Un-employment Benefit should, systematically and normally, be made conditional on daily attendance at a Training Centre, not as an educational device, but as the only practicable way of preventing the Unemployed from suffering the demoralisation of idleness.

The Training Centres experimentally established by the Minister of Labour during 1925–1928 did not, perhaps, correspond exactly with any one of these ideas.   Those at Brandon and Claydon, in Suffolk, were residential establishments at which a couple of hundred carefully chosen young men were given four months' training in elementary farm work, calculated to fit them to obtain employment in agriculture in Canada or Australia.   A small number of men were also trained for home employment, on the lines described in the next paragraph.   Out of 1500 who, by November 1927, had completed their course, nearly 1100 had been found employment in Canada or Australia, whilst over 300 had been placed in situations at home.

[1] Report of Industrial Transference Board, July 1928.

The Training Centres at Wallsend and Birmingham had a wider outlook. Here the young men are put through an intensive course, extending over about six months, in various handicrafts, such as bricklaying, carpentering and metal-work, including the execution of minor repairs to walls, roofs and furniture, and even to motor-cars. The principal result of the training, whether or not this was the intention, is not to make the trainees into skilled craftsmen, for which, apart from other difficulties, the time is too short, but to accustom the men to factory hours, factory speed and factory discipline, and to build up their strength and *morale*, which will make them eligible for employment when situations can be found. Out of 4000 men admitted to these Centres down to August 1927, some 2850 had completed the prescribed course, and of these 91 per cent had been found situations in a variety of occupations in which they appeared to be giving satisfaction. During 1928, additional Centres on these lines were opened at Derby, Bristol and Glasgow, specially for young miners.

Meanwhile, over 30 non-residential centres for training young women for domestic service had been established through the agency of the Central Committee for the Training of Women, to which Government subventions were made. In these Centres the shop assistants or factory operatives who found no employment at their former occupations were converted, by carefully planned courses in every branch of household work, into competent domestic servants, for whom it was possible promptly to find residential situations at substantial wages.[1] The Committee has also established at Market Harborough a Centre financed jointly by the British and Australian Governments, where 40 young women at a time receive a course of training lasting about two months, designed to prepare them for domestic service in Australia.

With these small experiments in training must be named the somewhat different Juvenile Training Centres, for the admission, up to the age of eighteen, of boys and girls who had left school, but who were, for the time being, unemployed. Of

---

[1] It is not generally appreciated that, in this way, " the pronounced shortage of domestic workers has, since 1921, led the Ministry to train in domestic duties 33,000 unemployed women " (Report of Unemployment Insurance Committee (Lord Blanesburgh's), 1927, vol. i. p. 59).

these, in London and several dozen large towns, about 80 had been established by 1928, dealing in the aggregate, for longer or shorter periods, with something like 10,000 young people annually.

The numbers in all these experiments must appear ludicrously small in comparison with the aggregate number of men, women and youths receiving Unemployment Benefit, varying between one and two millions.   All that can be said is that the apparent success of the experiments, coupled with the widespread public demand for more training, induced the Government, in the Unemployment Insurance Act of 1927, to insert a section definitely providing for such training ; and that the Minister of Labour announced, at the beginning of 1928, the projected establishment of some dozens of additional Juvenile Training Centres.

What has stood in the way of the provision of training as an important factor in the treatment of the Unemployed, for whatever reason this is advocated, has been primarily the cost. The Government has been painfully aware that, as every experiment has demonstrated, it is far cheaper, in each individual case, to pay what will be accepted as subsistence, whether as Unemployment Benefit or Poor Relief, than to make provision of any sort in an institution, or to set the Unemployed to work in any way whatsoever, or to give them training as well as maintenance, or even to put them under educational discipline whilst they are maintained.   This reluctance to spend, say two or three pounds per week, on maintenance under training, instead of eighteen shillings per week on maintenance alone, is, of course, usually disguised as scepticism about the possibility of finding durable situations for the trainees—as if the object of the training was merely, or even mainly, to equip the men for situations ! We do not feel sure that the Government has yet discovered, as the more clear-sighted of the Poor Law Authorities have done, that, whilst the unconditional gift of money week by week appears the cheapest device, this cheapness is in the long run delusive, both because of the physical and moral degeneration to which, in a certain proportion of cases, it inevitably leads, and because of the swollen number of applicants that such a dole invariably attracts.   Our own inference is that, whilst money payments contributed by way of insurance have proved less harmful than we in 1911 anticipated,[1] they have not been entirely free from

---

[1] *The Prevention of Destitution*, by S. and B. Webb, 1911.

injurious results ; and that it is imperative, even at a higher money cost, and quite irrespective of whether or not the trainees can be ensured future employment, that at least all cases in which the unemployed man has " run out of benefit ", and probably all cases whatever of young men or women—possibly even all single men and women under thirty—whether in benefit or not, should be dealt with in *some other way* than the mere unconditional provision of a weekly dole in idleness.

The Ministry of Labour

The intervention of the Government for the prevention of the destitution arising from Unemployment—apart from the Poor Law and its administration—has, it will have been noticed, for a quarter of a century been extensive and continuous. With the administration of the Trade Boards Acts, the main-tenance of the Employment Exchanges, the conduct of National Unemployment Insurance and the provision of a whole series of Training Centres, the new service has compelled the Government to enter into direct and continuous individual relations with nearly twelve million employees, being 75 per cent of the whole wage-earning population of the Kingdom ; and to undertake the dispensing, to a shifting million or two among them, week by week, of a sum of money which has (in 1926) reached no less than fifty millions sterling in a single year, representing an aggregate volume of centralised administrative detail greater than the entire business of the 625 Boards of Guardians in addition to that of the Poor Law Division of the Ministry of Health. This complicated novel service, handled at first by the Labour Department of the Board of Trade, was set up in 1917 as an independent Ministry of Labour, to which was committed also the duty of inquiry and of conciliation in disputes between employers and workmen, and (from 1920) certain important functions relating to Labour in connection with the International Labour Office of the League of Nations. This official recognition, arising as it did, not from any theory, but as the outcome of experience, of the practical distinction between the social problem of the able-bodied workman without employment, and that of " the impotent poor " in their several classes of infancy, child-hood, sickness or chronic infirmity of mind or body, and old age, seems to us full of significance. More and more, during the past decade, so far as the able-bodied wage-earner is concerned, has the service of the Ministry of Labour been substituted for that of the Poor Law Division of the Ministry of Health. It must, however, be admitted that successive Cabinets have so far shown little consciousness of its being the duty of the Minister of Labour to construct and administer anything like a complete Framework of Prevention of the destitution due to Unemployment, in extension of that of the Minister of Health with regard to sickness, that of the Minister of Education with regard to illiteracy, and that of the Home Secretary, the Minister of Mines and the Minister of Transport with regard to bad conditions of employment ; nor has he been able even to bring to an end, in the relief of the Unemployed, the constant overlapping of the work of his Ministry with that of the Poor Law. This " stopping short " on the part of the Government is marked, at the end of 1928, by its obstinate refusal even to consider the proposal, now pressed on it by an ever-growing section of public opinion in all three political Parties, as well as among Poor Law Guardians, that the Ministry of Labour should take upon itself the entire responsibility for dealing with the Unemployed, with the consequent exclusion of the able-bodied men in health from the sphere of action of the Poor Relief Authorities.

The Export Credits Scheme

But there were yet other expedients to which the Government was successively driven. In 1919, when it was realised that the British export trade was not at once recovering its pre-war volume, the then Chancellor of the Exchequer had propounded an Export Credits Scheme, under which the Treasury would guarantee the payment, by accredited foreign purchasers, of a portion of their indebtedness on new orders to British exporters. The necessary precautions and limitations of such a scheme prevented any considerable advantage being derived from it in its first form ; [1] but improvements were introduced, largely upon the suggestion of the Bradford and Huddersfield export merchants, under which the Government, in return for a small premium, in most cases simply "backed" the exporter's accepted

---

[1] Out of £25,000,000 offered, less than £4,000,000 was accepted.

bill of exchange, the risk of ultimate loss being usually shared between the Government and the exporter. In this form the Export Credits Scheme, extended to practically all countries except the Union of Socialist Soviet Republics, has been found of considerable use. By September 1922 the maximum credit to be thus guaranteed at any one time had been raised to £22,000,000, whilst the losses, so far, had been inconsiderable. It was accordingly decided, in July 1928, to continue the scheme in a form still further improved.

The Trade Facilities Acts

In 1921 the Government found another way of assisting the British employers to extend their enterprises. After more than a year of depression, when Unemployment had become extensive, the Ministry became seriously alarmed. " The state of Unemployment in the country at the present time ", said the Chancellor of the Exchequer in October 1921, " is grave, so serious, indeed, that in not inconceivable circumstances it might prove a menace to the social fabric of the State. Distress is acute, and innumerable households are confronted at this time with a position which is almost desperate." [1] The Government accordingly induced Parliament, in the Trade Facilities Act, to place at the disposal of British entrepreneurs, whether in public enterprise or private profit-making ventures, a large amount of capital (the limit of which was, within six years, successively increased to £75,000,000), by giving the Government guarantee for interest and sinking fund on the loans that could be floated in the London market. Under this scheme, as renewed by successive statutes in the ensuing six years, capital was obtained at about 5 per cent, instead of nearly twice that rate, even when it could be obtained at all ; and many business enterprises were able to erect and equip additional factories and warehouses, to install the newest machinery, to extend and re-equip docks and harbours, to open new mines and quarries, and to build new steamships—all with the double object of rapidly developing British trade and of immediately increasing the employment available for British workmen.

[1] Sir R. Horne, Chancellor of the Exchequer, Oct. 25, 1921, Hansard, p. 656 of vol. cxlvii.

This gift of Government credit to profit-making capitalists, as a means of providing for unemployed workmen, was skilfully administered by a nominated committee of experienced business men, so that the losses directly incurred were small. The indirect cost to the Exchequer, in the higher rate of interest on the large floating debt, and on renewals of bonds falling due for redemption, which the increase of Government liability may have entailed, cannot be accurately computed. The advantage of the scheme to the wage-earning class in actually diminishing the amount of Unemployment was less than had been anticipated, because the wealthiest and most solvent capitalists did not scruple to accept the Government gift for enterprises which, either by reason of their urgency, or because they promised to yield exceptional profit, would anyhow have been undertaken without Government help. Moreover, as the committee dispensing the credits was naturally unable and unwilling to discriminate between one project and another, otherwise than in respect of the solvency and credit of the entrepreneurs, it presently appeared that factories were being multiplied, and ships launched, in industries or for purposes already sufficiently provided for. The owners of the existing factories and of the ships already at sea naturally protested against this artificial manufacture of new rivals, by whose coming into operation both existing profits and existing employment would be lessened. By the time that the Government had in this way lent its credit to the extent of over seventy million pounds, the favour shown to this method of relieving the Unemployed had evaporated ; and the Trade Facilities Acts were, in 1927, allowed to expire without renewal.

Protective Customs Duties

It was inevitable that the fanatical believers in the advantage of a Protective Customs Tariff should, as they had done on previous occasions, once more take the opportunity presented by the prevalence of Unemployment to denounce foreign imports as its principal cause, and to advocate Fiscal Protection as its only effective remedy. This time they succeeded in persuading the Government (except during the brief term of office in 1924 of the Labour Party's administration) avowedly to adopt Protective Customs Duties as an important part of its policy for dealing with Unemployment. This was certainly part of the reason for the maintenance, after 1919, of the " key industry " duties on fine chemicals and magnetos, which had been intended only as a means of getting certain new industries started during the war; and also of the so-called "M'Kenna Duties" on motor-cars, musical instruments, watches, etc., which had been imposed in 1916 deliberately in order to reduce imports, but exclusively as a war measure, for the purpose of temporarily economising both our shipping and our purchasing power in foreign exchange.[1] After the business depression had lasted two years, Mr. Baldwin announced, in 1922, that he could find no way of coping with the problem of Unemployment other than the imposition of a Protective Tariff, a remedy, however, which was not to include in its wide scope the staple foodstuffs which made up so large a proportion of British imports. Notwithstanding this promised exclusion of any important " tax on food ", the electorate, at the General Election that followed, voted emphatically against a Protective Tariff and incidentally put the Labour Party in office for eight months as a Minority Administration. When the Unionist Government resumed office in 1925, it felt itself precluded from a Protective Tariff as such, which was popularly termed a General Tariff ; and it fell back on the policy of the special " safe-guarding of industries " which could be shown to have suffered seriously from a new or an exceptional flooding by importations from foreign countries with which the British manufacturers were unable to compete in price. Between 1925 and 1928 such " safe-guarding duties " of 33⅓ per cent *ad valorem* were imposed on foreign lace, gloves, cutlery, gas mantles, wrapping-paper, translucent china, buttons and enamelled hollow-ware. We are, of course, unconcerned here with the Fiscal Controversy ; but the grave new departure in British policy represented by so extensive an adoption of Protectionist Customs Duties is avowedly justified and defended, by the Ministers themselves, as part of the Government policy with regard to Unemployment. As such it has to be included in our survey.

It will be seen that the new Protective Duties, which are

[1] These latter duties, the abolition of which on the cessation of the war had been expressly promised, were removed by the Labour Government in 1924, but reinstated by the Unionist Government of 1925, and somewhat extended by that of 1927.

unaccompanied by any countervailing Excise Duties, do not touch the industries (coal-mining, shipbuilding, iron and steel production and " heavy " engineering) which directly account for two-thirds of all the Unemployment ; nor can they, by their very nature, improve matters in other industries working mainly for export, such as that of cotton spinning and weaving.   Apart from the manufacture of motor vehicles of different kinds, which has been, for a couple of decades, and whether " protected " or not, a rapidly increasing industry,[1] the protected trades are relatively small in extent, employing in the aggregate—on dye-stuffs and other fine chemicals, magnetos, musical instruments, watches, lace, gloves, cutlery, gas mantles, wrapping - paper, translucent china, buttons and enamelled hollow-ware—certainly not more than a few hundred thousand workers, among whom Unemployment has, in nearly all cases, been less severe than in the great basic industries ; and, taken as a whole, has apparently not been above the general average.   Unfortunately, official statistics, or indeed any trustworthy statistics, do not exist, from which it might be confidently concluded whether, even in these specially favoured industries, there has been any diminution of Unemployment since the imposition of the protective duties.[2]

The Sugar-Beet Subsidy

Another of the measures taken in connection with Unemployment—demanded and justified also on other grounds—has been the attempt to establish in England the cultivation of the sugar-beet, and the production of sugar.   The vast production of beet sugar on the Continent, which, after a century of effort, had made itself independent even of the aid afforded by the so-called Sugar Bounties, had long excited the interest of English agriculturists and financiers.   Various attempts to set going a

[1] Another rapidly expanding industry is that of artificial silk, which has perhaps enjoyed, since 1926, a slight degree of fiscal protection, in that the countervailing Excise Duty is alleged to be somewhat smaller than the Customs Duty, and the latter is rigorously imposed also on manufactures of silk.

[2] See Lord Arnold's analysis of the position down to the end of the session of 1928 (Hansard, House of Lords, July 18, 1928).   The same absence of evidence applies also to the alleged effect of the Duties in bringing about " production on a large scale ", or up to maximum capacity, with a consequent lessening of " overhead charges ", on which the newest protectionists rely for their astonishing claim that such Duties do not, in fact, lead to any increase in the retail price of the commodity over what it would have been under free imports.

similar industry in England had failed to overcome the difficulties of the first few years of such an innovation. Without an assurance that a sufficiently large area would be put, year after year, under sugar-beet, no sugar factory of adequate size could be made a commercial proposition. Without the assurance that such a factory would be provided and kept at work, no farmer would venture on the new crop. The inconvenience of dependence on foreign supplies of beet sugar had been immediately made manifest on the outbreak of war in 1914. When, in the slump that began in 1920, the desire to come to the rescue of the British farmer was reinforced by the pressure to increase the opportunities for employment of the British workman, the long-maintained objection of the British Treasury and the habitual prejudice of British statesmen against the barefaced grant of subsidies to capitalist employers at last gave way. In 1925 the Sugar Beet Industry Act authorised the grant of a subsidy from public funds to manufacturers of beet sugar in Great Britain, hedged round by numerous safeguards, and limited in duration for ten years, at so much per ton of sugar produced, the amount falling year by year until its complete cessation at the end of the decade.

The " Derating " of Productive Industries

In 1928 the Government found yet another remedy for Unemployment in its proposal to stimulate an expansion of production by what amounts to a subsidy from public funds in the form of " derating " the land and buildings used in manufacturing industries, or in agriculture, together with the railway tracks and stations on freight-carrying lines. From April 1, 1930, the farmer is to have his land and his farm buildings wholly exempted from local rates ; the manufacturer of any commodity whatsoever, the colliery company and the iron and steel producer, is to have the premises used in actual production excused three-fourths of the local taxation they would otherwise bear ; whilst the railway companies are to allocate the amount by which they are being similarly relieved from October 1, 1928, entirely to a reduction of their freight charges on the carriage of coal, and of iron and steel (but only such as is destined directly for export), and on the carriage of agricultural requirements or produce for sale. The Chancellor of the Exchequer undertakes to make up to the Local Authorities, by increased Grants in Aid, the whole amount of the loss of revenue—estimated at some twenty-four millions annually—that they will suffer by this " derating ".

It will be seen that this proposal, which Parliament voted with some misgivings, amounts to an annual subsidy from national funds, payable through the medium of a diminished rate demand by the various Local Authorities, to manufacturers and farmers as such. It is certainly an extraordinary kind of subsidy that is given to all employers engaged in production,[1] irrespective of which commodity they produce, or whether their industry (like that of brewing, or making artificial silk) is exceptionally prosperous, or (like the production of iron and steel) in nearly all cases unprofitable ; and whether the premises are situated in a specially distressed or necessitous area where the rates are high, or in another part of the country where the rates are low. It appears that the subsidy will be payable in equal sums for premises of the same rateable value within the same rating area whatever the amount of commodities produced, whatever their aggregate value, whatever the efficiency of the establishment, and whatever the number of persons now or hereafter employed. On the other hand, the amount of the subsidy will vary, for establishments of the same efficiency, in one and the same industry, employing equal numbers of workers, occupying premises assessed at equal sums, and producing the same value of product and identical profits, according as they happen to be situated in different rating areas, in one of which the amount of rate in the pound is actually several times as great as in the other.

It seems to us beyond the powers of economic science or of business shrewdness to come to any conclusion as to the effect of such a subsidy either on the net cost of production by the marginal establishment making any commodity whatsoever, and

---

[1] To the exclusion, be it noted, of any " productive " enterprises conducted by the Local Authorities though including those of the State ; to the exclusion, also, of the large aggregate of educational, sanitary, eleemosynary and other social services ; most remarkable of all, to the exclusion of any sort of " distributive " service, whether wholesale or retail, even to the extent to which actual manufacturing is carried on upon the same premises, however many " productive " workers are therein employed ; and, finally, also to the exclusion of the whole range of employers in merchanting, banking, insurance, and ship-owning with their extensive staffs.

therefore on its price in the market ; and, consequently, there
appears no basis for any prediction as to its effect on the volume
of business in each commodity, or on the amount of its aggregate
production, or on the total number of persons employed therein.[1]
A subsidy so strangely graduated, and amounting on an average
to less than 2 per cent of the total cost of production of commodities generally, appears likely, indeed, to have more result
on the net profits of particular employers than on costs and
prices. We cannot think that it will be possible, even after
several years, to trace any appreciable influence upon the volume
of Unemployment of a subsidy given to employers, irrespective
of their use of labour, merely to dispose of as they choose. It is
curious to speculate on the amount of improvement in ventilation and cubic space, in sanitation and safety appliances for
dangerous machinery, that would have resulted from nothing
more than a Government subsidy to mill-owners and mine-owners,
when the Governments of 1850–1880 had become convinced that
all these readjustments of industrial organisation were required
to prevent the evils of Insanitation and Accidents. The Governments of those years came to the conclusion that the necessary
reorganisation of conditions in the mill and in the mine would
not take place without something more coercive than an unconditional subsidy. In view of the fact that the alternation
of boom (1919) and slump (1920–1928) came about largely through
the unco-ordinated eagerness of the whole crowd of employers
to increase production as much as possible in good times, and to
restrict it as drastically as possible when business became unprofitable, there seems something ironical in entrusting the same
crowd of employers, still unorganised and unco-ordinated, with
twenty-four million pounds a year of money for their private
use, free from conditions or directions, in the hope of thereby
producing, out of the chance-medley of competitive profit-

---

[1] The temporary subsidy to the coal-mining industry in 1925 (conceded by
the Government in an emergency in order to stave off the threatened complete
closing of the mines by the coal-owners for such period as might prove necessary
to compel the miners to accept a great reduction of wage-rates) was, at any rate,
proportionate to the number of men thereby retained in employment. That
for ten years conceded to the sugar-beet industry in the same session was fixed
in exact proportion to the output of sugar, which was a pretty exact measure of
the new employment to be afforded. The subsidy of 1928–1929 by the method
of " derating " offered to all private employers engaged in production bears no
relation to the number of workers indirectly affected.

making, that better adjustment of production to demand, or of purchasing power to output, on which continuity of employment depends.

Poor Relief

Notwithstanding the variety of expedients and remedies by which the successive Governments sought to cope with Unemployment during 1920–1928, their efforts failed, as we have seen, to relieve the nation of its burden of between one and two millions of wageless men. They failed, even—if this was ever seriously intended—to keep the Unemployed from pauperism. From the very beginning of the slump, the numbers in receipt of Poor Relief went up ; and presently there came to be between one and two hundred thousand able-bodied men in health, destitute only by reason of Unemployment, together with dependent wives and children numbering thrice as many, on the hands of the Board of Guardians. How, in more than a hundred Unions, this sudden swamping of the local administration strained and distorted, and to a large extent also demoralised, the whole organisation of the Poor Law in the industrial districts we shall relate in a subsequent chapter.

A Survey of Policy

It may be expected that the economic historians of the future, in surveying the action of the British Government for the past decade with regard to Unemployment, will not credit Ministers with any clear understanding of the problem, or any high degree of economic statesmanship. We limit ourselves to a few comments.

The Government's expedients during the decade seem to fall into two classes. On the one hand are those which, accepting the necessity of making some immediate provision, other than Poor Relief, for the mass of wageless workers, provided, year after year, millions and millions of pounds by way of Out of Work Donation, " extended " Insurance Benefits, " Employment Relief ", maintenance at Training Establishments, or gratuitous passages overseas and a new start in life in the British Dominions, together, as we shall presently relate, with a lax and swollen distribution of Outdoor Relief for all those whom the other expedients fail to keep from starvation. We estimate the total public expenditure in Great Britain, in the decade that has followed the Armistice, on all these forms of the " Relief of the Unemployed " at something like three hundred millions sterling. Some such provision, even on a huge and quite unprecedented scale, was doubtless inevitable in the terrible emergency, which found the nation unprepared for a slump which had clearly been predicted. We may rightly deplore the failure to heed the warnings and adopt one or more of the recommendations of the innumerable committees and sub-committees on " Reconstruction ", which found, in the Cabinets of 1917–1919, so little favour—even so little comprehension.[1]

But even when the emergency had come, and anything between one-tenth and one-fifth of the population were wageless and had to be fed, the Government hardly ever got beyond the conception of what were, in one form or other, under more or less suitable conditions, mere subsistence doles. To the Cabinet, as to the House of Commons of 1918–1922, such subsistence doles seemed the cheapest expedient—in fact, the only one that the nation could afford! The result of such a system (as with charitable donations) is that no lasting improvement is effected. It is not economy, but extravagance. After a whole decade of doles the number of persons needing to be fed is undiminished ; and the problem remains.

It is only fair to say that, to some relatively small extent, the expedients adopted went beyond the mere subsistence dole. A certain amount of additional employment was created in the execution, at regular wage-labour (and thus largely free from the evils of " Employment Relief "), of Public Works that would not otherwise have been undertaken. A certain number of families were successfully set up as small-holders in British agriculture, or as emigrants to the Dominions ; and in the last few years a small but slowly increasing number of young men

---

[1] In particular, it is difficult to understand the delay in making universal the successful Unemployment Insurance Scheme of 1911. Ministers came bitterly to regret that this had not been done in 1915, when the whole population was employed at high wages, and practically all employers were (as the Excess Profits Duty proved) making exceptional profits. In November 1918 it was officially announced that " universal contributory insurance " had actually been decided on (*Labour Gazette*, p. 437). But even then the Bill was not introduced until November 1919 ; to be then postponed and reintroduced in February 1920 ; and then so delayed as not to become law until August 9, 1920 ; and not to come into operation until November 8, 1920—by which date all the golden years had passed away ! (see *Unemployment Relief in Great Britain*, by Felix Morley, 1924, pp. 25-33).

and women have been given training in addition to maintenance. The defect of these expedients—considered as remedies for Unemployment—has been their painful minuteness of scale. In their effect on the character of their direct beneficiaries they have proved immeasurably superior to the gratuitous dole—so much so, indeed, as to confirm the view expressed in the Minority Report of the Poor Law Commission in 1909 that some such treatment or training should, *for this reason alone*, accompany all provision of maintenance for the Able-bodied. Moreover, to a few thousands of men and women such expedients have been an effective means of rescue from the slough of involuntary idleness. But regarded as anything like a remedy for the disease of Unemployment from which British industry is suffering, the very minuteness of the scale on which they have been tried has rendered them of no avail whatever. " When the object ", observed John Stuart Mill three-quarters of a century ago, " is to raise the permanent condition of the people, small means do not merely produce small effects : they produce no effect at all ".[1] If industrial training, or emigration, or establishment on the land is intended as even a partial remedy for Unemployment— as a means, that is to say, of curing or preventing Unemployment—it would have to be tried on a large scale. If, for instance, emigration is proposed, we suggest that the removal, not of ten thousand, but of at least a hundred thousand families annually for several years would probably be required to produce any appreciable effect on an overstocked Labour Market.

Movements on this scale are, however, seldom practicable, even if Parliaments would vote the necessary expenditure. Substantially, therefore, we think that the experience of the decade has amply confirmed what Sir William Beveridge told the world in 1909, namely, that " the problem of Unemployment—this is a point that cannot be too strongly emphasised—is insoluble by

---

[1] *Principles of Political Economy*, by J. S. Mill, bk. ii. ch. 13, sec. 4, p. 232 of edition of 1867.

To those who do not see how this paradoxical statement can be true, as physicists teach us that even the smallest cause must have its exactly equivalent effect, it may be suggested that Mill meant that from small causes there would be no effect *on the sociological plane*. Even the slightest mechanical friction between two substances produces some mechanical effects, but it must be friction of a considerable amount to create any noticeable heat, and of still greater amount to produce light or to generate electricity.

any mere expenditure of public money. It represents, not a want to be satisfied, but a disease to be eradicated. It needs not money so much as thought and organisation." [1]

Now the efforts at " organisation ", which constitute the second class of the Government's expedients of the past decade, have all been of a peculiar kind. They have all taken the form, in one or other varieties, of a subsidy from the public to the profit-making employer, not dependent on his actually taking on at wages so many additional men, or any men at all, but simply in such a way as to increase his profits. In this manner, it has been argued, a stimulus will be given to business, to productive industry and to the employment of labour. Thus, in the Export Credits Scheme ; in the valuable guarantees accorded under the Trade Facilities Acts ; in the various series of Protective Customs Duties accorded to trade after trade ; and (in 1928), finally, in the substitution of additional Grants in Aid to the Local Authorities for the rates that the employers would otherwise continue to have had to pay to them, " private enterprise " has been—almost as nakedly as in the temporary Coal subsidy of 1925 and the ten years Sugar-beet subsidy of the same year—bribed by gifts to continue functioning, in order that fewer wage-earners may be left in involuntary idleness. Unfortunately, it does not seem possible to test by statistics to what extent this peculiar form of " organisation " has proved a remedy for Unemployment, or whether it has even temporarily lessened the aggregate number of the Unemployed. What is clear is that some at least of the *largesse* has been enjoyed in enhanced profits by employers who have not opened up any new business at all, or created any additional employment, just as some of the valuable privileges of the Trade Facilities Acts have been obtained by capitalists who stood in no need of assistance, and who merely executed, with a Government guarantee, enlargements and improvements that they would anyhow have carried out without assistance.

For any other form of " organisation " to repair the mal-adjustments of the Labour Market, whether by way of directly increasing the aggregate demand for wage-workers or by way of providing new kinds of employment for the men whose hyper-trophied war-time industries had suddenly shrunk, the Government appears to have had no liking. It was prepared, under

[1] *Unemployment a Problem of Industry*, by (Sir) W. H. Beveridge, 1909, p. ix.

extreme pressure, to assist the Local Authorities with grants and loans that were presently stopped, to carry out Public Works ; and even to let these be used as a basis of " Employment Relief ". But without central organisation and control, and some clear insight into the conditions, which might have been gained from past experience, this was only to start once more the weary circle of " Relief Works ", differing only slightly from those of 1886–1898, or those under the Unemployed Workmen Act from 1905 to 1910. It can only be concluded that " the elementary lesson that effective treatment of the Unemployment problem is utterly beyond the power of Local Government had not been learned ".[1] Even with regard to the provision of maintenance, the Government refused to realise " the difficulties inherent in the use of a local system of relief to cure a depression national in its scope, and due to causes that are national and even international rather than local in their character ".[2] The Cabinets of these years, presumably under the advice of the Treasury, were averse from any national effort at the organisation of labour which might have been more effective in restarting the wheels of trade than the sporadic attempts of the Town Councils to give " Employment Relief " to the local wageless men ; and possibly neither more costly to the Chancellor of the Exchequer than his dispensation of subsistence doles, and no more injurious to his credit " in the City " than the multiplication of State guarantees under the Export Credits Scheme and the Trade Facilities Acts.

It need hardly be said that, in the whole decade, practically nothing has been effected in the prevention, not so much of the destitution that arises from Unemployment—on which so much money has been spent year after year—as of the occurrence of involuntary Unemployment itself. The various suggestions to this end, made in both the reports of the Royal Commission on the Poor Law and Unemployment in 1909, and those embodied in the numerous reports of the Reconstruction Committees of 1918–1919, have neither been exhaustively explored nor effectively tried. The decasualisation of casual labour by the systematic organisation of dock and market employment, possibly involving the compulsory notification of vacancies to the Employment

---

[1] *Unemployment Relief in Great Britain*, by Felix Morley, 1924, p. 3.
[2] *The Third Winter of Unemployment*, by W. T. Layton and others, 1923, p. 48.

Exchange; the "dovetailing" of the various "seasonal" occupations, which are believed, on fairly good evidence, to show, in the aggregate, no seasonal fluctuation at all; and the still more ambitious "regularisation" year by year through each trade cycle of the aggregate volume of wage-earning employment, by means of aggregating in the "lean years" of the cycle a large part of the orders for commodities required over the whole decade by the Public Authorities, central and local—none of these seem yet to have been taken seriously in hand by the Minister of Labour or the Cabinet.[1]

The Outcome of Forty Years of Experiment

What emerges from the experiments of the past forty years with regard to the Unemployed is the necessity, on the one hand, for classifying the wageless men, with a view to an appropriate treatment for each of the several types, and, on the other, for distinguishing between different causes of Unemployment, in order to discover in what way, and to what extent, each of them may be prevented. And practical experience shows that the principal classification of the Unemployed must be based, not on their trades or ages, and not upon their personal character, but upon the nature of the industrial position just vacated by each person. The Unemployed, on this view, belong to one or other of six classes, each requiring distinct and separate treatment.

There are, first, the men from permanent situations, in occupations in which re-employment may reasonably be expected, such as the engineers, the boot and shoe operatives or the gardeners. Next to these, but offering a problem of much greater difficulty, are the men who have dropped out of situations in occupations formerly regarded as permanent, but which are now decaying or

---

[1] Some promising beginnings were made before the war in regularising and decasualising the Liverpool Dock Labourers, the Bristol Channel Trimmers and Teamers, and the Manchester Warehouse Porters. A new committee (Dock Transport Workers' Registration and Guaranteed Week) was set up in 1924. See, on this subject, *Dock Labour and Decasualisation*, by E. C. P. Lascelles and S. S. Bullock, 1924.

At the beginning of 1914 a Government Committee was actually beginning to consider what could be done to equalise the aggregate volume of employment throughout each trade cycle by a better distribution of Government orders. We cannot learn that this exploration has been resumed.

dwindling to such an extent as to make it certain that a considerable proportion of the men will not regain employment in their old trades ; such, for instance, as (in 1910–1920) the men working with horses, or (in 1927–1928) the coal-miners. A third class is made up of men from situations in occupations which are normally discontinuous, involving always a series of passages from job to job ; such, for instance, as the various kinds of operatives in the building trades. In a fourth class are the casual labourers, who never hold any situation of even a week's duration, but serve only on a succession of jobs, each lasting a few hours or a few days, often for a whole series of separate employers ; of these the best-known types are the dock or wharf labourers and the market porters. Then there are the juveniles, and the boys and girls who have left, not employment, but school, and find it difficult either to find any employment, or any but short and shifting jobs. Finally, there is a mixed residuum constituting a sixth class, whom we may call the Unemployable, including those who, by reason of physical, mental or moral deficiencies, have great difficulty in discovering any employer willing to engage them at any price ; and also those who, finding other ways of picking up a meagre subsistence, are not, with any reality, seeking employment at all.

This classification of the Unemployed according to their industrial status has to be supplemented by a cross-classification according to the direct and immediate cause of their Unemployment. These causes are, first, the cyclical fluctuations in the general volume of business, to whatever ultimate cause such fluctuations may be ascribed. Secondly, there is the dwindling or decay of particular occupations, which may be relatively small or transient, but may in other cases (as in the post-war years) be colossal and lasting, whether due to changes of fashion or habit, to changes in industrial processes or methods of business organisation, to the substitution of new commodities through invention or discovery, or to an extensive change in the course of international trade. Thirdly, there are recurrent seasonal fluctuations in the volume of particular industries affected principally by harvests, changes in temperature, or holidays ; fluctuations which often occur simultaneously in different directions within each community, and thus may, to a great extent, be capable of removal by organised "dovetailing" of occupations. Fourthly, there are what may be called the accidental vicissitudes of particular undertakings, such as bankruptcies, absorptions, amalgamations and technological transformations, each of them usually involving the discharge of employees of exemplary conduct and long standing. Finally, there is the whole range of personal grounds for termination of engagements, including not only ill-health, infirmity or advancing years, but also the clash of temperaments, from the mere " words with the foreman ", or refusal to obey orders, up to serious neglect or misconduct on the one hand, or caprice or tyranny on the other.

It may confidently be inferred, in view of the very different classes to which the Unemployed belong, that any successful treatment of the individuals among them must necessarily have regard to their several positions and circumstances. Any mass treatment of all alike, whether unconditional dole or common employment on Relief Works, stands condemned in advance.[1] Moreover, the community cannot safely or economically stop at mere provision for the individuals, however successful their treatment may be. It is necessary to consider the causes of the Unemployment, in the hope of finding some means of either preventing or mitigating such injurious influences. An interesting analogy may be found in the history of Public Health. The earliest communal attempts to deal with sickness as a cause of destitution—such as the provision made in the seventeenth and eighteenth centuries of drugs and fumigation for plague and fever patients—may or may not have relieved the sufferers, but was certainly ineffective in stopping the destitution due to plague or fever. Not until well into the nineteenth century do we find Southwood Smith and Chadwick drawing the inference that, whatever might be required for each individual patient, one social cause of the destitution-bearing disease was to be traced to some maladjustment of the environment of the population in the district, which needed to be separately dealt with. Hence Public Health has developed concurrently along two different lines : on the one side, the improvement of the environment (water supply, purity of the atmosphere, unadulterated food, healthy dwellings, paved backyards, open spaces, and so on) ;

---

[1] Keir Hardie vainly urged, in his motion upon the Address in 1893, that " any remedy proposed would require to meet all three cases "—the threefold classification which is now represented by a sixfold—" *and deal with them separately* " (Hansard, February 14, 1893).

on the other side, the improvement of the individual so as to prevent the continuance, the recurrence or the spread of the disease (isolation, medical treatment, personal hygiene, etc.). It may be found that the same is true of Unemployment !

Apart from a more accurate diagnosis of Unemployment, what has the nation learned from these forty years of experiment ? Since Joseph Chamberlain's Circular of 1886, down to the end of 1928, the Government give the impression of having been empirically groping after something which they could neither perceive nor describe.   We suggest that what they had to construct was a Framework of Prevention as closely applicable to the destitution of involuntary Unemployment as those of the Ministries of Health and Education are to the destitution of the impotent poor.   Such a structure is, in fact, in 1928, scarcely in view. It has, indeed, once more been learned by experience that the " provision of work " for the Unemployed, like the " profitable employment of the poor "—whilst it may usefully find a limited utility as one of the devices in any comprehensive scheme of treatment—will certainly prove neither productive of commercial goods nor financially profitable ; but, on the contrary, definitely more costly (if, presumably, less demoralising) than mere doles of Poor Relief.   Nor has it been found possible, otherwise than at great cost, and only in a relatively few carefully selected cases, to " bring the landless man to the manless land ", as General Booth and many others have advised.   As a measure applicable to the hundreds of thousands of unemployed men requiring maintenance, neither emigration to the Dominions or to North or South America, nor the provision of Small Holdings in Great Britain ; neither employment in spade labour, nor segregation in Rural Colonies, is a practicable measure for the prevention of able-bodied destitution.   On the other hand, the establishment of a national network of Employment Exchanges has proved, within its limited scope, though terribly hampered by the extraneous duties cast upon it without adequate increase in its staff, entirely successful ; whilst the creation of a system of Unemployment Insurance which the Employment Exchanges have made possible—supplying as it does to three-fourths of all the breadwinners in working-class families a certain, though not a complete, measure of protection against the worst evils of the failure of industry to maintain its wage-earners—has been, within its own range, of untold advantage in staving off destitution, with unexpectedly little of the injurious reaction that was feared. But, unfortunately, these various parts of a Framework of Prevention have remained isolated, fragmentary and incomplete. Thus, Unemployment Insurance leaves altogether outside its scope not only all the workers under 16 and over 65 years of age, and all those working otherwise than under a contract of service, but also something like a couple of million persons employed either in agriculture or in private domestic service, and a million or more of persons employed in various exempted occupations or individually " excepted ". The benefits that Unemployment Insurance provides are never adequate for complete family maintenance, and do not necessarily last as long as the Unemployment continues. The strictness and rigidity of the administration—absolutely necessary in such a system—result in many tens of thousands of wageless workers being, sooner or later, refused the benefits that their condition requires. Moreover, Unemployment Insurance has hitherto been administered without the help that might be derived from a judicious use of Municipal Employment—not, as in Relief Works, as a panacea, or a remedy, or even as a form of relief of distress, but as a valuable device both for testing and for assisting selected claimants. In the same way the smallest use has yet been made by the Unemployment Insurance administrators of the device of demanding, in return for maintenance, the whole time of the workless men, for educational training, partly as a test of the involuntary character of their worklessness, but mainly as a means of preventing their demoralisation by idleness, quite irrespective of the possible advantage of fitting them for other and better employment than that from which they have been discharged. In short, the greatest drawback of the system of Unemployment Insurance, as it is at present administered, is its practical isolation. It stands revealed, in practice, as not " joined up " with other parts of the Framework of Prevention, being properly articulated neither to the Health Insurance system, nor to the beneficent activities of the Public Health and Education Authorities ; neither to the arrangements for Workmen's Compensation for accidents and industrial diseases, nor to the vast provision that is temporarily being made for ex-Service men and their dependants suffering from the war ; neither to the national pensions in old age nor to those for widows and the blind. Even if the Government cannot see its way to a comprehensive Framework of Prevention, it might at any rate " close these gaps ", which now allow thousands every year to fall through into destitution.[1]

It would be out of place, in this historical work on the Poor Law and its administration, to propound any " Remedy for Unemployment ", or to advocate any positive scheme for the relief of the Unemployed as such—even if we had any panacea that could be stated in a paragraph![2] At the end of this book we shall have something to say with regard to what is within the scope of our work, namely, what experience shows can, and what cannot, wisely be done in the treatment of the destitution of the Able-bodied. At this point we need do no more than emphasise, with regard to Unemployment as a Disease of Modern Industry, what we have already noted in connection with the other parts of the Framework of Prevention, and the measures taken to deal with Sickness and Infirmity of every kind, and with Child Neglect. For Unemployment — in Sir William Beveridge's sense of " a disease to be eradicated ", not by relief of any kind, but by "thought and organisation"[3]—there will, in our opinion, be discovered and recognised nothing that can be proved to be a remedy until the nation has already set to work a Department charged to devise the necessary social and industrial adjustments that promise gradually to prevent the very occurrence of widespread or long-continued involuntary wagelessness, and to put them one by one tentatively in operation. The

---

[1] This shortcoming was reported on, without much sympathy with the need for closing the gaps, and without adequate appreciation of the importance of making a complete Framework of Prevention, by the " Committee on the Co-ordination of Administrative and Executive Arrangements for the Grant of Public Assistance on account of Sickness, Destitution and Unemployment " (Cmd. 2011), 1925.

The Government Actuary (Sir Alfred Watson) pointed out that " the two systems of compulsory State Insurance cannot be said to be properly articulated if a person who has been in receipt of Sickness or Disablement Benefit for many weeks is subsequently refused Unemployment Benefit on the ground that in those weeks or some of them he did no work "—having, in fact, been then forbidden to work ! (Report of Committee on Unemployment Insurance, 1927, vol. ii. pp. 202, 208).

[2] The suggestions in the Minority Report of the Poor Law Commission, 1909, might be considered. See *The Public Organisation of the Labour Market*, by S. and B. Webb, 1909.

[3] *Unemployment a Problem of Industry*, by Sir W. H. Beveridge, 1909, p. ix.

nation, as we have remarked, did not wait, before taking action to deal with dangerous diseases, or even with child illiteracy, until someone had produced a complete scheme, commanding universal assent, for the prevention of all sickness whatsoever, or for the provision, for the entire population, of every kind of education. When " enlightened public opinion ", and Cabinet wisdom, had, perhaps under electoral pressure, become sufficiently awake to the fact that a patent evil had to be grappled with, the machinery of administration was so directed as to utilise all the knowledge and science available at the moment (a sadly inadequate amount), and to apply experimentally one device after another—this or that variety of medical treatment, this or that Public Health expedient, this or that type of school, this or that scheme of educational administration—until, by a continuous process of " trial and error ", the safe and effective prophylactic methods had been discovered and demonstrated.

In the history, during the past hundred years, of what has grown into the universally approved edifice of Factory Legislation, Public Health and Public Education, we see how closely science has waited on administration, and administration on experiment. It is only by the application, to specific social problems, of the scientific method, and, by the use of specialised administration, both to discover and to put in operation the necessary social adjustments, that the nation will be able, as soon as it chooses to do so, to build up, piece by piece, a Framework of Prevention in relation to the social disease of Unemployment, as comprehensive and as successful as that already achieved—but still in progress of improvement—in relation to the Conditions of Industrial Employment, Sickness and Illiteracy.

CHAPTER VIII

THE GUARDIANS ON THE DEFENSIVE (1909-1918)

For a whole decade after 1909 English Poor Law administration lived in a cataclysmic environment. For the first five years (1909-1914) after the Report of the Royal Commission—a time of good trade and lessened demand for Poor Relief [1]—the Boards of Guardians were distracted by an incessant public agitation for drastic reforms, and disturbed by the continuous upgrowth of gigantic rival systems of national provision for the aged, the sick and the Unemployed, which caused a feeling of uncertainty as to the extent of their effect on Poor Law work.[2] During the second five years (1914-1919) the Guardians could think of nothing but the Great War and the subsequent demobilisation, the whole period being marked, on the one hand, by the temporary absorption into employment at high wages of 200,000 of the less impotent of the paupers; and, on the other, by the sensational distribution of public money to literally millions of homes, first in separation allowances to soldiers' families and in pensions to widows and to wounded warriors, and then as gratuities on demobilisation, and yet more pensions.

An Agitation that failed ?

To whatever influences it may be ascribed, the Reports of the Poor Law Commission were not favourably received by the

---

[1] " During the period 1895–1910 the numbers in receipt of domiciliary relief seldom fell below 500,000. Their range during the period 1911–1914 was round about 400,000, and during the period 1917–1920 was round about 300,000 " (First Annual Report of Ministry of Health, 1920, Part III. p. 13). On January 1, 1913, the total number of paupers (apart from the insane in asylums) had sunk to 21·7 per 1000 of the population, " a rate lower than that of any previous year " since records began (Forty-second Annual Report of Local Government Board, 1913, p. vii).   [2] *Ibid.*

Liberal Cabinet of 1909. Mr. John Burns, who had been President since 1906, openly declared that no such legislative changes
were required, and that he would be able, by administrative
measures, to effect all the needful reforms. Other Ministers
had rival projects unconnected with the Poor Law ; and the
Government as a whole presently became absorbed in the political
campaign against the House of Lords, which Mr. Lloyd George's
Budget of 1909 had inaugurated.

The indifference of Downing Street was not reflected in the
country. The two Reports of the Royal Commission had an
unparalleled sale. The evidence, the allegations and the proposals were, for a couple of years, discussed, not only by every
Board of Guardians and at every Poor Law Conference, but also
in the local newspapers ; among people who had seldom concerned
themselves about Local Government ; in the Churches, and in
both official and academic circles. So widespread an interest
was due largely to the thoroughness of the investigations of the
Royal Commission, the great scope of its reports and the drastic
nature of the changes that both Majority and Minority recommended. But the considerable public education that resulted
is to be ascribed, as we think, mostly to the energetic propagandist efforts made by those who favoured the adoption of one
or other of the rival schemes of reform : propagandist efforts in
connection with a Royal Commission that, in their magnitude
and in their educational effect on public opinion, recall to the
student the like efforts made, according to the methods of the
time, in connection with the Report of the Commission of
1832–1834.

In this work of public propaganda the lead was taken by the
Minority Commissioners, who (in order to counteract the superior
influence naturally attaching to the proposals of a majority of
the Commissioners, headed by the Chairman) promptly formed
an organisation to make known the Minority Report.[1] The

---

[1] This organisation, which began August 1909, and was styled at first the
National Committee for the Break-up of the Poor Law, but after its first
Annual Meeting on May 31, 1910, the National Committee for the Prevention
of Destitution, had for President the Rev. Russell Wakefield (one of the
Minority Commissioners), who became successively Dean of Norwich and
Bishop of Birmingham. The large Executive Committee included Members
of Parliament of all three Parties, representatives of the principal religious
denominations, County and Borough Councillors and Poor Law Guardians,
employers of labour and Trade Union officials, doctors and professors. Its

activities of this body during the next four years afford an interesting study in the methods of propaganda. Although its object was to induce the Cabinet to prepare and recommend to Parliament the sweeping measure that was required, the very smallest attention was paid to the political aspect of the subject, or to the political Parties. Practically the whole effort was directed to the education of the nation in the working of the Poor Law, its defects and its shortcomings, and in the methods of preventing the occurrence of destitution which might be substituted for its mere " relief ". Means were taken to secure a large sale for a cheap edition of the Minority Report without footnotes or references ; whilst owing to the methods of advertisement, which were " extensive and peculiar ", the official editions of the Report obtained an unprecedented sale, actually more copies of the Minority Report being sold by the Stationery Office than of the Majority Report.[1] A varied and widely dispersed membership of 25,000 men and women was individually enrolled. For four years many thousands of lectures were given by a staff of no fewer than 400 volunteer lecturers, to all kinds of audiences, from Inverness to Penzance. Wherever possible, public debates with competent opponents were arranged. Everywhere it was made a feature that unlimited questions from the audience should be invited and encouraged, in order that difficulties might

activities may be followed in its monthly journal, *The Crusade*, 1910–1913, with frequent supplements ; and in the scores of pamphlets and leaflets published during these years.

[1] Of the National Committee's own edition of the Minority Report over 12,000 copies were sold ; in addition to over 33,000 copies of one or other of nine separate chapters, and 10,000 copies of the Minority Report of Scotland. There was also an edition of the Minority Report for England, with introduction and appendix by S. and B. Webb, published by Longmans Green & Co. in two volumes, entitled respectively *The Break Up of the Poor Law* and *The Public Organisation of the Labour Market*.

Meanwhile the Stationery Office issued two separate editions of the whole Report for England, namely, one in folio, in one great volume, of which 7110 copies were sold to the public and 2298 issued for official use ; and a specially cheap octavo edition, the Majority Report in two volumes, and the Minority Report in one. Of this octavo edition about 2800 copies of the Majority Report were sold to the public, and some 600 supplied for official use ; whilst of the Minority Report 3296 copies were sold to the public and some 600 supplied for official use. The Stationery Office sold also 2242 copies of the Report for Scotland, and supplied 1882 for official use.

It is interesting to note that altogether five separate editions of the Minority Report were thus, between 1909 and 1914, simultaneously on the market, at widely differing prices, and they did not, apparently, interfere with each other's sales.

be explained and information supplied. This extensive apparatus of oral tuition was supplemented by a continual stream of articles and letters on particular aspects contributed to the local news-papers in practically every county in the kingdom ; by a large output of more substantial articles in the magazines ; by the sale or gratuitous distribution of hundreds of thousands of specially written pamphlets and leaflets ; and by the publication of a monthly journal (*The Crusade*) devoted exclusively to the means of actually preventing destitution. " A great number of persons ", complained one of the Majority Commissioners at a Poor Law Conference in July 1910, " have aided the pro-pagation of the Minority Report in sheer and utter ignorance of its provisions, under the impression that it contained the only proposals before the country for the ' prevention of destitution '. A neighbour of mine, who had undertaken to hold a drawing-room meeting for its propaganda, asked me (of all people) to take the chair, knowing my views, not knowing the Minority Report, but believing that, like every sane man, I must be in favour of ' preventing destitution '. A most distinguished Medical Officer of Health in London, an avowed supporter of the Minority, was staggered to learn from me quite lately that the Health Authority, under the provisions of the Minority Report, would be responsible for the relief of all sick persons needing assistance, unless they were of school or of pension age." [1]

Those who favoured the proposals of the Majority were naturally stirred to activity by so extensive a propaganda ; [2]

---

[1] *Poor Law Conferences, 1910–1911,* p. 181. It is significant of the change of opinion that the unification, under the Local Health Authority, of all the public provision for the sick (which in 1910 could be honestly regarded as " Socialism ") should, in 1926–1928, form the central feature of the legislative proposals of the Conservative Minister of Health (Mr. Neville Chamberlain), as being only obvious common sense.

[2] The reader will excuse a quotation from a contemporary diary giving a glimpse of this activity :

" As I sat in my office this morning—the three rooms crowded with volunteers —Bentham [a member of the Majority of the Commission] was announced. I gave him the warmest welcome, introduced Colegate [the secretary] to him, and asked him ' What we could do for him '. He seemed almost dazed with the bustle of the office. ' I wanted to see your literature,' he said. ' You seem as busy here as if it were a General Election.' ' Perhaps it is,' I laughingly replied. ' I wish we had someone to organise our side, like you ; no member of the Majority cares enough about it.' He seemed much perturbed by Willis Bund's leaflet [the Chairman of the Worcestershire County Council had become a convert to our Report], and Shackleton's adhesion [a Labour M.P.] ; collected all the literature he could get hold of, paid for it, and retired, after I had

and a second organisation was presently created to counteract its effects. It is, perhaps, significant that this organisation was formed, in February 1910,[1] not on the basis of the Majority Report, nor specifically to advocate its proposals—these had, indeed, within a few months of their issue, fallen largely out of mind as being, as a scheme of reorganisation, both impracticable and almost universally objected to [2]—but on a platform of opposition to the Minority Report, on which those who objected to any substantial change in the Poor Law joined hands with those who wished to see carried out any one part of the Majority Scheme. This organisation had its own meetings and lectures, its own publications and newspaper correspondence, the rivalry, and especially the clash of opinions, of statements of fact, and of arguments, adding considerably to the public interest, and to the educational effect of the agitation.

Within half a year, at the beginning of 1910, it became clear

---

shown him our third room full of stock and literature. Now they have realised we are at work, what will the Majority do ? Will they start a rival organisation ; or will they issue a manifesto warning the world against us ; or will they subside into apathy ? " (MS. Diary of Beatrice Webb, July 23, 1909).

[1] This was styled the National Poor Law Reform Association, and had for its President Lord George Hamilton, who had been Chairman of the Poor Law Commission.

This organisation should not be confused with " The National Committee for Poor Law Reform ", a short-lived offshoot of the " British Constitutional Association ", which obtained the adhesion of the best known of the advocates of the " strict " administration of the Poor Law. It was avowedly " established, not only for the purpose of opposing the only recommendation as to which the Majority and Minority of the Poor Law Commission seem to be in entire agreement, but also of promoting and supporting such reforms as are generally considered to be desirable ". (See *Poor Law Reform—Via Tertia—the Case for the Guardians*, by Sir W. Chance, 1910.)

[2] " The Majority Report, in fact, was still-born " (Rev. P. S. A. Propert, of the Fulham Board of Guardians, in *Poor Law Conferences, 1909–1910*, p. 727).

" Speaking generally," stated a leading Poor Law administrator of the old school, " the Majority Report would enormously extend the functions of State relief, and it would, in fact, bring about a sort of system of State-organised charity which would probably eventually be almost wholly dependent upon public funds. . . . I end as I began, by saying that there are, in my opinion, only two possible policies for the future. The one is that of independence, upon which the reforms of 1834 were based. The other that of the Minority Report, which frankly adopts universal provision by the State. The Majority try to steer a middle course. I think that they will fail. I cannot help thinking that the majority of Guardians will prefer the old policy, under which this country has made such enormous strides, under which the great friendly societies have been born and flourished, under which rural able-bodied pauperism has practically disappeared " (*Poor Law Conferences, 1911–1912*, pp. 183, 187, address by W. A. Bailward).

to the propagandists of the Minority proposals that the frontal attack on the very existence of the Boards of Guardians, bound up with so ancient an institution as the " relief " of destitution, was, in view of the prepossessions of the Liberal Cabinet of the time, unlikely to achieve any immediate success in the political field.[1] More effective results might be obtained, in the long run, by promoting, through an unsectarian organisation, the growth and development of the various parts of the Framework of Prevention, which, as we have already described, was gradually superseding particular departments of the Poor Law. In this work it was possible to go beyond the Minority Report and its supporters, and to enlist the sympathies, not only of distinguished medical and educational experts, but also of the officials engaged in the various public services, the three political Parties, and even of Lord George Hamilton (Chairman of the Poor Law Commission) and some of his Majority colleagues. Thus, at the opening meeting in the Albert Hall of the first " National Conference on the Prevention of Destitution ", in Whit-week 1911, presided over by the Bishop of Southwark (Talbot), Mr. Arthur (now the Earl of) Balfour, Sir John Simon (at that time Solicitor-General), Mr. J. Ramsay Macdonald, proposed, seconded and supported " the formation of a National Conference of a non-party and nonsectional character, to promote the working of the various agencies for the prevention of destitution . . . as a valuable means of bringing together municipal representatives and social workers from all parts of the country ".

The two substantial volumes in which are enshrined the proceedings in 1911 and 1912 of this National Conference for the Prevention of Destitution are, we think, worth the attention of students, both for the extensive and varied information that they contain, and as throwing light upon the public opinion of the time.[2] Each year the week's proceedings (in which from 700

---

[1] The whole scheme of the Minority Report was brought before the House of Commons on Friday, April 8, 1910, by Sir Robert Price, where it attracted an unusually large attendance of Members, and elicited speeches from the Prime Minister (H. H. Asquith), the President of the Local Government Board (Mr. John Burns) and the Leader of the Opposition (Mr. Arthur Balfour). No division could be taken (Hansard, April 8, 1910).

[2] *Papers and Proceedings of the National Conference for the Prevention of Destitution*, 1911 (766 pages, P. S. King & Son) ; ditto, 1912 (593 pages). These Conferences had, as Honorary Secretaries, Mr. J. W. Hills, Conservative M.P. for Durham, and Mr. Robert Harcourt, Liberal M.P. for

to 1100 delegates, representing some 200 Local Authorities, 150 voluntary associations and several Government Departments, took more or less part) were elaborately organised in five sections, each meeting separately, or, for particular questions, jointly with another. Each section had its own chairman of some eminence or repute, and attracted its own interested audience, which discussed papers contributed by expert specialists in Public Health or Education, the care of the Mentally Defective or the Provision to be made against Unemployment, the Organisation of Housing or the Treatment of Crime and Inebriety. The leading idea was to get the persons actually concerned with Public Health, Education, Mental Deficiency and Unemployment respectively, to envisage their own work, not merely as an isolated effort, but as part of the nation's organisation for the Prevention of Destitution, engaged in stopping the several roads down which men and women travelled to that morass. The Conference, including a hundred or more of the leading Poor Law Guardians,[1] was thus led to visualise these several branches of work of the National and Municipal Government as actually constituting, in combination with each other, the Framework of Prevention of which we have, in a previous chapter, described the gradual erection.

The agitation, powerful as it became, was destined to be unfruitful in the political field. The Liberal Cabinet remained unfriendly to any legislative reform of the Poor Law, to which the Minister primarily concerned (Mr. John Burns from 1906 to 1914) was resolutely opposed. Meanwhile Mr. Lloyd George,

---

Montrose Boroughs; whilst the organisation was carried out by Mr. Clifford Sharp.

Among the other publications of these years we may cite *Poor Law Reform*, by Charles Booth, 1911; *The Poor Law Enigma*, by M. F. Robinson, 1911; *Circumstances or Character : Studies in Social Work*, by C. F. Rogers, 1911; *Two Schemes to Prevent Pauperism*, by L. B. Stearns, 1911; *Unemployment, a Social Study*, by B. Seebohm Rowntree and B. Lasker, 1911; *The County Councils' Association's Proposals for Poor Law Administration*, by J. W. Hills and M. Woods, 1912; *The Destitute of Norwich : how they live*, (Anon.), 1912; *Poor Relief and the Church*, by H. T. Knight, 1913; *Poverty*, by B. Seebohm Rowntree, 1913; *Poverty as an Industrial Problem*, by R. H. Tawney, 1914; *Poverty and Waste*, by Hartley Withers, 1914; *The Poor Law Indispensable*, by Gladstone Walker, 1914; *Some Recent Developments of Poor Relief*, by W. A. Bailward, 1914.

[1] Whether it occurred to anyone as strange that, in a Conference on the Prevention of Destitution, there was no section devoted to the Poor Law (which was empowered only to relieve it) is not recorded.

the most powerful force in the Government, had become en-
amoured of an entirely distinct method of dealing with poverty,
and was pressing forward the vast scheme of Sickness Insurance,
to which the initial experiment in Unemployment Insurance
promoted by Mr. Winston Churchill was eventually attached.
Although these schemes of Social Insurance left untouched both
the evils and the cost of the Poor Law, and thus gave the go-by to
all the proposals of the Royal Commission, they presently absorbed
the whole attention, not only of the Cabinet and the Legislature,
but also of the public. All the steam went out of the movement
for extinguishing the Boards of Guardians and transferring their
powers to the County and Municipal Authorities and to the
National Government, whether according to the prescriptions
of the Majority or those of the Minority.[1]

POOR LAW ADMINISTRATION PRIOR TO THE WAR (1909–1914)

A. THE CENTRAL AUTHORITY

As soon as it became apparent that the Cabinet would not
insist on legislative action being taken on the Commission's
Reports, the Local Government Board proceeded to set its own
house in order. It opened action in March 1910 by a lengthy
Circular [2] to the Boards of Guardians stating that it had " had
under consideration the recommendations of the Royal Commission . . . with regard to the methods and principles which
should govern the administration of Public Relief " ; and—
without saying whether or not it agreed with these recommendations—that it would " set out briefly the main principles

---

[1] " Lansbury told us that Masterman [the Liberal Minister] came up to
him, after Lloyd George's triumphant exposition of his scheme, with a pleasant
jeering expression, ' We have spiked your guns, eh ? ' showing that he is hostile
to the whole conception of the Minority Report, and that the Government
schemes are intended as an alternative method of dealing with the question of
destitution. J. B. also goes about saying that insurance has finally ' dished
the Webbs '. All of which is interesting " (MS. Diary of Beatrice Webb,
May 26, 1911).

[2] Circular of March 18, 1910 ; Thirty-ninth Annual Report of Local
Government Board, 1910, p. xix ; see " The Recent Circular Letter of the
L.G.B. relating to the Administration of Outdoor Relief ", by J. E. Moulding,
in *Poor Law Conferences, 1910–1911*, pp. 580-602. The Circular was characterised by the Inspector for South Wales as " a most helpful guide to sound
administration " (First Annual Report of Ministry of Health, 1920, Part III.
p. 125).

on which relief to the poor in England and Wales is based, together with some suggestions for improving the machinery of administration ".

This momentous Circular was specially directed to the subject of Outdoor Relief ; and (in conjunction with the Circular of December 29, 1911, relating to the codification in that year of the Outdoor Relief Orders) it constituted an authoritative pronouncement of the Department's own policy. As such it demands a somewhat elaborate analysis.

We note, to begin with, that the Circular made no mention either of the " Principles of 1834 ", or of the " Workhouse Test ", or even, in so many words, of " Less Eligibility ", all of which had for so long been prescribed as the principles of Poor Relief. The whole Circular was devoted to the methods of administering Outdoor Relief, and was far from suggesting that there was anything unsound or objectionable in this form of relief, even for the Able-bodied. Indeed, by avoiding any condemnation of Outdoor Relief as such, and by confining the criticism to various imperfections in the manner in which many Boards of Guardians had administered it, the Circular was not unnaturally construed as definitely sanctioning this form of relief in all " suitable cases ". What was condemned was the " indiscriminate " or " unconditional " grant of Outdoor Relief, and—as Chadwick and Nicholls would have thought most remarkable—also the failure to grant Outdoor Relief upon some uniform principle, and in amounts sufficient to meet " the actual necessities " of each case. Instead of deprecating the grant of Outdoor Relief as such, the Circular emphasised that it should " be carefully adapted to the needs of the case *and adequate in amount*. The Board regret that it is sometimes the practice to get rid of an applicant by giving him a small amount of relief, which on the face of it is insufficient for his support, on the assumption that he has other resources available which have not been declared. The injustice of such a method is evident, for, if the applicant is honest, the relief given is not enough for his proper support, while if he can successfully conceal his means of subsistence he may get more than he actually needs. *It is the plain duty of the Guardians to take precautions to ensure that the relief is adequate, and that the pauper is sufficiently fed, clothed and lodged.*" It is not surprising that this new phrase was taken, in some quarters, as sanctioning a new standard, in supersession of the former measure of the mere " relief of destitution ". On the other hand, the Guardians were told that any grant of Out-door Relief should be made only after full investigation, with the adoption of the Case Paper System,[1] and should be constantly revised ; that it should be accompanied by careful supervision of the homes and the conduct of the recipients ; and that their continuance in insanitary conditions should not be tolerated, and should, in particular, be prevented by calling the attention of the Local Health Authority to each case.

It must be said, in fairness, that the references in the Circular to Outdoor Relief can be properly interpreted only as applying to Outdoor Relief which could lawfully be granted under the Statutes and Orders then in force. It was such Outdoor Relief only that was always to " be carefully adapted to the needs of the case and adequate in amount ". It was the paupers so relieved for whom the Guardians were " to take precautions to

---

[1] For the "Case Paper System"—the substitution, for the old separate record of each application for relief, of a continuous record of all the successive applications and decisions with regard to each family coming within the scope of the Poor Law—see *The Better Administration of the Poor Law*, by Sir William Chance, 1895, pp. 30-32 ; *Poor Law Conferences, 1894–1895*, pp. 214-217 ; and especially the discussions in successive Conferences from 1902 to 1909, separately republished as *The History Sheet or Case Paper System*, 1909 ; and also *Practical Treatise showing how the Case Paper System can be worked*, by H. B. Everest, 1912.

Its history is given in a valuable paper in *Poor Law Conferences, 1912–1913*, by J. J. Simpson (Clerk to the Bristol Union), p. 147, etc. "There is one Union in this Conference District (Atcham), in which a system of keeping a Book Register of Cases (with proper indexes) has been in operation since the establishment of the New Poor Law in 1834, the first Chairman of that Board —a name still remembered with respect by some present-day administrators (Sir Baldwyn Leighton, Chairman from 1838 to 1871)—having introduced that system. But the credit of inaugurating the Case Paper System, in the form now adopted by the Local Government Board, is due to the Paddington Guardians and their able Clerk, M. H. F. Aveling, who have had it in successful operation since 1890. Since then the Eastbourne Union, Eccleshall Bierlow, Kensington, Bethnal Green, Bristol, and some few other Unions have adopted the system ; and I have no hesitation in saying that in a few years' time the advantages of its general adoption will be plainly apparent."

The advantages of the Case Paper System were succinctly stated by P. G. Bagenal, an able Inspector : "The Case Paper System should be adopted in every Union because : (1) it provides a complete history of every case, which is thus preserved in record in an accessible manner for all Relieving Officers old and new ; (2) it shows at a glance the decisions of the various relief com-mittees in consecutive order ; (3) it is useful at the police courts as evidence as to who are liable to maintain their relatives ; (4) it assists the Settlement Officer by giving details as to the applicant " (Thirty-ninth Annual Report of Local Government Board, 1910, P. G. Bagenal's Report, p. 84).

ensure " that they were " sufficiently fed, clothed and lodged ". These are sometimes assumed to have been, at that date, exclusively the non-able-bodied. This, however, was not the case. As had been pointed out in the previous year by the Minority Report of the Poor Law Commission,[1] no small number of able-bodied men (and many women) were at all times being lawfully relieved under the various exceptions to the prohibition specified in the Orders in force. The reasons adduced in the Circular against inadequate relief plainly applied equally to the relief lawfully granted to the families of which the head was technically "able-bodied", and to the relief lawfully granted to those without such a head.

With regard to able-bodied men in health, the Circular quoted with approval the objection taken in Goschen's Minute of 1869 to the supplementing of their wages or earnings (the " Rate in aid of wages ") ; but, significantly enough, the Circular made no reference to the more fundamental objection of the 1834 Report to any Outdoor Relief at all (apart from sickness, and sudden or urgent necessity) to the entirely wageless workmen (the Unemployed). With regard to the latter class, the Circular observed that " the number of able-bodied men in receipt of Outdoor Relief is now, generally speaking, comparatively small ; but occasionally in times of exceptional distress the Guardians find it necessary to relieve members of this class. The plan usually adopted on these occasions is to give the relief under a Labour Test. This expedient is always open to objection, but when the Guardians are obliged to resort to it they should bear in mind that the men should be kept employed for at least eight hours a day during the whole time they are receiving relief, not so much for the purpose of testing whether they are in need of relief as for the purpose of preventing them from loafing idly about the streets, or competing for odd jobs with independent workmen." And the Circular concluded with a vague commendation of Goschen's suggestion of 1869 in favour of co-operation between Poor Relief and private charity ; stressing in particular the desirability of a complete register of all persons receiving assistance of any kind.[2]

---

[1] Poor Law Commission, Minority Report, pp. 446-451.

[2] We may note, as issued on June 21, 1910, a useful Circular deprecating the appointment by a Board of Guardians to any paid office of any member

The Relief Regulation Order, 1911

In the following year (1911) the Circular was followed by the revision and consolidation of all the previous Orders relating to Outdoor Relief;[1] a simplification which the Majority Report of the Commissioners had recommended. This revision and consolidation, made by an expert committee of officials under the chairmanship of Sir Samuel Provis, resulted in the Relief Regulation Order, 1911, which, unlike its predecessors, was issued simultaneously to the whole of the Unions. The new Order adopted the form, and purported to follow, in the main, the prescriptions, of the strictest of the Orders which it superseded, namely, the Prohibitory Order of 1844.[2] But, as the Report itself stated,

---

or ex-member of the Board, unless the latter had ceased to be a member for at least twelve months. It was announced that, unless very special grounds were shown, the Local Government Board would not approve or acquiesce in such an appointment. This was made law, fourteen years later, by the Poor Law Officers (Qualification) Order, 1924, which provided that " no person should be appointed or eligible for appointment to any paid office under a Board of Guardians who was or had been within twelve months the Chairman or a member of the Board of Guardians " (Sixth Annual Report of Ministry of Health, 1925, p. 115).

[1] The Outdoor Relief Prohibitory Order of 1844 ; the Outdoor Relief Regulation Order of 1852 ; and the various forms of the Labour Test Order (see pages 149-151 of Vol. I.) ; together with the Modified Workhouse Test Order (*ibid.* p. 464) first issued in 1887 to the Whitechapel Union, and subsequently only to such Unions as pressed for it (Report of the Departmental Committee on the Administration of Outdoor Relief, Cd. 5525, February 1911 ; *The Outdoor Relief Orders*, by the Editors of the *Poor Law Officers' Journal*, 1912 ; " The Report of the Departmental Committee ", etc., by J. J. Simpson, in *Poor Law Conferences, 1911-1912*, pp. 34-40 ; *The Ministry of Health*, by Sir A. Newsholme, p. 178).

[2] The use of the Case Paper was made compulsory. No Outdoor Relief was to be granted for more than fourteen weeks at a time ; and revision at least every five weeks was required. But the general effect of the new Order was towards relaxation. Non-resident relief was expressly sanctioned to persons liable to removal to the Union. The grant of Outdoor Relief to the wife and children of men otherwise ineligible was allowed, upon the passing of a special resolution of the Guardians, if the man entered the Workhouse (the old Modified Workhouse Test). It was made clear that the amount of Outdoor Relief might (and, indeed, should) include what the recipient had necessarily to pay in rent. The exceptional grant in cases of " sudden or urgent necessity " (which was required by the 1834 Act and which may not be made " on loan ") was not referred to in the Order, and therefore continued as a duty of the Relieving Officer, irrespective of any decision of the Board of Guardians without any regulation by Order.

The Departmental Committee had recommended, and the Local Government Board had decided on what would have proved, in practice, a severe limitation on the Guardians' liberty to grant Outdoor Relief to the various classes of the " impotent " poor ; namely, the requirement that, in each case, there should first be produced " a certificate by a Medical Officer stating the

" the change is one of form only, and not of substance " ; and, in fact, the new Order was so worded as to incorporate, as express exceptions to the prohibition, all the classes of cases in which Outdoor Relief had been allowed by the laxer Regulation Orders ; and also, with regard to the rest—the term " able-bodied " being for the first time abandoned—the permission accorded by the old Labour Test Order for the grant of Outdoor Relief (at least one half to be in kind) to " any male persons ", conditional on a test of work ; subject only to the Guardians passing a general resolution of " exceptional circumstances ", and reporting it to the Local Government Board. This new requirement of a special resolution and report on the introduction of a Labour Test, whilst making the renewal of such a resolution subject to the specific approval of the Local Government Board, was, we gather, a measure of restriction, aimed at a limited number of Unions which kept their Labour Yards perpetually open. The most important loophole for evasion of any prohibition of Outdoor Relief was—doubtless because it had been embodied in statutory form in the Poor Law Amendment Act of 1834—left unclosed, with momentous results that we shall presently have to describe. Under the Relief Regulation Order, as under its predecessor, it remained open to any Board of Guardians, " upon consideration of the special circumstances of any particular case ", to depart from any or all of the regulations, and to grant any relief in any form that the statute-law permits, subject only to promptly reporting the matter to the Local Government Board, and to the Board thereupon not formally expressing its disapproval of the Guardians' action.[1]

nature of the disability ". This was hotly resented by Boards of Guardians, and when the new Order was finally issued this requirement, because it was realised that it might cause undue delay in cases of sickness, was so limited as to be practically abandoned (*i.e.* it was not to apply to any existing cases, nor to any cases of old age, nor to any permanent disability which had once been certified, nor to any case whatsoever on a first application).

Moreover, the Local Government Board accepted the enlargement pressed for by the Poor Law Unions Association, allowing Outdoor Relief without limit of time to a widow without illegitimate child, and to a deserted or separated wife, resident within the Union or without ; including any wife living, in fact, geographically separated from her husband (which had been, in fact, prescribed by sec. 18 of the Divided Parishes and Poor Law Amendment Act of 1876), and therefore the wives of all men detained in prison.

[1] The Out-Relief Order, 1911 ; Forty-first Annual Report of Local Government Board, 1912, p. xix, Appendix, pp. 27-43 ; *The Relief Regulation Order, 1911, and the Boarding-Out Order, 1911,* by H. Jenner Fust, 1912.

Children under the Poor Law

In view of the special attention that the Poor Law Commission had devoted to the condition of the 150,000 children on Outdoor Relief, and the evils which had been revealed, it seemed surprising that this part of the problem should have been ignored in the Circular on the administration of Outdoor Relief. For some reason the Local Government Board reserved the treatment of the children for a separate Circular, which was issued three months later.[1] This Circular, even more definitely than its predecessor, abandoned the phraseology of 1834–1890 ; and expressly recognised that " the considerations which apply to other cases of relief are not applicable in their entirety to the case of children, whose pauperism is always due to misfortune and for whom the preventive and curative processes of help recommended by the Royal Commission offer the surest prospects of success ". There was no depreciation or discouragement of Outdoor Relief ; " but if Guardians give relief to the parent, they are bound to see that the relief is properly applied, and that the child is not neglected ". This would involve greatly increased supervision of the homes into which Outdoor Relief is given ; and the appointment was suggested of additional officials, who might with advantage be women. What was expected from such additional officials was more explicitly stated by an Inspector. The duties of the woman Assistant Relieving Officer appointed by the Bury Board of Guardians were described as follows :

" In the visitation of the homes of persons in receipt of relief in respect of children she must, by personal enquiry and observation, obtain such particulars as may enable her to report for the information of the several Out-relief Committees on the following matters :

" (a) As to the appearance of the children in relation to health, nourishment and personal cleanliness ;

" (b) As to the general condition of the house in respect of ventilation, cleanliness and tidiness, and the provision of necessary bedding, etc. ;

" (c) As to any apparent lack of means to provide the

---

[1] Circular on " Children under the Poor Law ", of June 16, 1910 ; Fortieth Annual Report of Local Government Board, 1911, p. xix.

ordinary necessaries of life in the way of food, clothing and bedding ;

" (*d*) In the case of very young children as to whether the diet contains a reasonable amount of milk." [1]

When the children were of school age, it was suggested that arrangements might be made with the Local Education Authority to communicate to the Guardians regular reports on the school progress of the children, and particularly the reports of their periodical medical inspection by the School Medical Service ; whilst the Guardians might usefully get (and pay for) special reports from their own Medical Officers on individual children.[2] Contrary to the principle laid down in the Goschen Minute of 1869 and in Sir J. S. Davy's evidence before the Poor Law Commission in 1906, that Outdoor Relief should not be given in aid of wages, the Local Government Board suggested that widows with children should not necessarily be debarred from earning money whilst in receipt of Outdoor Relief ; but " the circumstances in each case should be carefully considered and watched ; and the mothers should not be expected to earn unless satisfactory arrangements can be made for the children ". With regard to parents, who, whether " by reason of mental deficiency, or of vicious habits or mode of life ", are unfit to have charge of their children, the Board suggested the formal adoption of such children by the Guardians, when they could be provided for as if they were orphans. The practice of Boarding-Out was also commended, but it was recognised that further and better supervision was called for ; and attention was drawn to the new Boarding-Out Order recently issued,[3] which aimed at

---

[1] Fortieth Annual Report of Local Government Board, 1911, A. B. Lowry's Report, p. 80.

[2] This feeble suggestion fell far short of the systematic national co-operation between the Guardians and the School Medical service that had been called for. One of the L.G.B. Inspectors had to report in 1912 that " it must, however, be confessed that a system is required for the whole country whereby Guardians should be kept informed of the School Medical Inspections of children for whom they are to some extent responsible in that they are supposed to give such relief as may meet their needs " (Forty-second Annual Report of Local Government Board, 1913, Wethered's Report, p. 49).

[3] The Boarding-Out (within Union) Order, December 31, 1909 ; Thirty-ninth Annual Report of Local Government Board, 1910, pp. xxiii-xxiv, and Appendix, pp. 1-14. This Order was superseded in 1911, as we shall presently describe, by one applying the same code to all Boarding-Out whether within or without the Union (The Boarding-Out Order, 1911 ; Forty-first Annual

ensuring a systematic inspection of every child boarded out
within the Union to which it belonged by members of a special
Ladies' Committee, as well as by the Guardians' medical officers
(to the exclusion of the Relieving Officer), to be supplemented
by the supervision and sample inspections of the Local Government Board's Lady Inspectors. For the children under institutional care, the Board left open to the several Boards of Guardians
the choice between the Poor Law Schools, the Cottage Homes
and the Scattered Homes, on the one hand, and the Certified
Schools, the Training Ships and organised emigration to Canada
on the other. But, above all, the children over three had to
be everywhere got out of the Workhouse, maintenance in which
could no longer be recognised " as a legitimate way of dealing
with them ". For the children under three, the Workhouse
Nurseries were to be reorganised, particular attention being
paid to " a sufficiency of light and ventilation, a good supply
of hot and cold water, means of airing and exercise, proper
floor-covering, means of sterilising milk, etc.". It was remarked
that " more trained nurses are required " for the Workhouse
Nurseries ; but there was no suggestion that the employment
of pauper women to look after the infants should be abandoned.
With regard to the placing out of children, the Board urged
that endeavours should be made to start them, not in " blind
alley " occupations, such as that of errand boy, but in skilled
employments ; and that training for domestic service should
be provided for girls.[1]

Four years later the Local Government Board returned to
the subject in another Circular, dealing particularly with relief

Report of Local Government Board, 1912, pp. xxiii-xxiv, Appendix, pp. 3-23 ;
The Relief Regulation Order, 1911, and the Boarding-Out Order, 1911, by H.
Jenner Fust, 1912).

[1] Unfortunately this reference to " placing out " was relegated to the part
of the Circular dealing with children on Indoor Relief ; and nothing was said
on the subject with regard to the much larger number on Outdoor Relief,
thus tending to perpetuate the common impression that the Guardians had
no concern with, or responsibility for, the apprenticeship of the latter. This
misunderstanding, left uncorrected for four years, was expressly referred to in
a later Circular (October 8, 1914) described in the following pages, in which the
Guardians were plainly told (we think, for the first time) that " similar considerations apply to children of women in receipt of Outdoor Relief ". These
children, also, should be placed out in permanent occupations, and therefore
given " some training after leaving school ", and kept under the same supervision
" as in the case of those children who are placed out by the Guardians directly
from their own institutions ".

to widows with children, in which the advice given in the Circular of 1910 was repeated, with some significant variations.[1] Again the emphasis was laid on the need for close supervision of the home into which Outdoor Relief is being given, and on the Guardians' responsibility for imposing the conditions necessary to secure that the money is properly applied. The importance of appointing women officers was insisted upon, together with the advantage of placing the children under the care of a " specially constituted committee ", including women other than Guardians. In order to secure its adequacy the Outdoor Relief might advantageously be based on " the normal standard of income on which a woman may reasonably be expected to bring up her family "—*not necessarily, be it observed, so as to be less than the rate of wages of the lowest-paid independent labourer*—but " regard being had to the cost and general standard of living, rate of wages, etc., in the locality ". The widow need not be prevented from obtaining employment provided " the home and the children are " unlikely to suffer thereby. What the Guardians are to seek to prevent is, not her working, but her getting low wages ; and (a remarkable innovation) " they might, for instance, make it a rule that women in receipt of relief should not accept employment at a rate of remuneration below the current rate of wages received by the independent workers in the locality ".[2] Another suggestive innovation was that Outdoor Relief should not necessarily be refused to mothers of children " in the early days of widowhood whilst the actual resources of household are still unexhausted ". The Guardians were informed in significant phraseology, that, " as the Board have frequently stated, a person may be entitled to relief though not destitute in all respects, nor entirely devoid of the means of subsistence ; and the Board desire it to be clearly understood that, in the case of widows with children, who will obviously require assistance from the Poor Law in the near future, the Guardians would not only

---

[1] Circular on " Relief to Widows and Children ", October 8, 1914. How much such a new stirring-up of the Guardians was required may be inferred from the valuable *Report on the Condition of Widows under the Poor Law in Liverpool*, by Eleanor F. Rathbone, presented to the Liverpool Women's Industrial Council on December 11, 1913. This sample inquiry during 1913 revealed the very smallest improvement on the Poor Law Commission's inquiry during 1907–1908.

[2] The Guardians, it was suggested, might also make a rule prohibiting the employment of Outdoor Relief children in any form of street-trading.

be within their rights " (this, we suggest, was novel doctrine), " but would be acting with wisdom and foresight, in affording relief *before the family resources, such as the stock of clothing, bedding, etc., are so depleted as to render it impossible afterwards to deal with the case without making good the deficiency* ". This suggestion was criticised by some doctrinal purists as sanctioning, for the first time, Poor Relief prior to destitution, in order to prevent destitution from setting in at some future time.

The New Order as to Institutions

The series of reforming Circulars of these years was completed by that of 1913 transmitting a new Order [1] relating to the administration of the Workhouses and other institutions of the Guardians, in supersession of the antiquated General Consolidated Order of 1847. This Order, with a complementary one on nursing in Poor Law Institutions, had taken the expert Departmental Committee two years to prepare. Covering, as it did, the whole administration of more than a thousand institutions of different kinds and sizes, the Order included a mass of detailed prescriptions, which it is impossible to enumerate or even to summarise. Perhaps the most striking feature of this comprehensive Order (following the precedent silently set in the Out-relief Order of 1911) was the complete omission of the words " Workhouse " and " pauper ", which thus, after several centuries of unquestioned usage, finally passed out of the official vocabulary.[2] In their stead, we have " inmates " of various

---

[1] The Poor Law Institutions Order, 1913, and the Poor Law Institutions (Nursing) Order, 1913, transmitted in Circular of December 31, 1913 ; Forty-third Annual Report of Local Government Board, 1914, pp. 3-10 and xxxix-xli ; *The Poor Law Institutions Order, 1913, and the Poor Law Institutions (Nursing) Order, 1913*, by W. H. Dumsday, 1914 ; *Shaw's Annotated Edition of the Poor Law Institutions Order, 1913* (1914) ; *Letter to the President of the L.G.B. on the New Poor Law Institutions Order*, by J. Theodore Dodd, 1914 ; *The Ministry of Health*, by Sir A. Newsholme, 1925, pp. 181-182.

[2] For comments on this change see *First Report of the Departmental Committee . . . with respect to the Poor Law Orders*, etc., edited by the Editors of the *Poor Law Officers' Journal*, 1913, p. vii. It should be stated that the Institutions Order, whilst applying to all ordinary Workhouses, and other premises administered by Poor Law Guardians or by Joint Committees of Guardians, did not apply (1) to Casual Wards, (2) to Poor Law Schools or Cottage Homes or Scattered Homes ; or (3) to Poor Law Infirmaries, Sick Asylums, Mentally Defective Homes, or any other " institutions for persons suffering from disease of body or mind carried on under separate administration

kinds of "institutions" . . . "for the reception and maintenance of poor persons ". But the most important innovation
was the. definite prohibition, after 1915, of the maintenance in
the Workhouse, or rather in " any institution containing adults ",
of any children over three years of age, for a longer period than
six weeks ; exception being made only for children in sick wards,
or detained on Medical Officer's certificate for medical reasons,
or by reason of an outbreak of infectious disease. The original
proposal had been to exclude from the Workhouse all healthy
children over three years of age ; but this limit had been changed,
in the Draft Order, on the representations of the Guardians, to
five years ; and even as modified it was freely predicted that the
prohibition would be found to be ineffective.[1] Under strong
pressure from those most interested in the children's welfare,
the President of the Local Government Board reinserted the age
of three years as the limit for residence in a Workhouse ; with
the result that, notwithstanding the troubles caused by the war,
the majority of Boards of Guardians gradually established small
" Scattered Homes ", or made use of their opportunities of
placing children either in Certified Schools or in the Poor Law
Schools of other Unions.

Another important innovation in the Order of 1913 was the
final abandonment, after three-quarters of a century of attempted
enforcement, of the elaborate sevenfold classificatory scheme
which the Poor Law Commissioners of 1834–1847 had imposed,
with the force of law, on all Workhouses, great or small, urban
or rural. In its place the new Order required only that (1)
" Males and females above the age of eight years shall not be
included in the same class ; (2) except in the sick wards, children
shall not be included in the same class with other inmates ; and

---

in pursuance of a Special Order ". (See the official Report of Departmental
Committee, etc., issued as Cd. 6968, in January 1913 ; see also *Suggestions for
Amendment of the Consolidated Orders and for Improvements in Poor Law
Administration*, by J. Theodore Dodd, 1913).

[1] *The First Report of the Departmental Committee*, etc., by the Editors of the
Poor Law Officers' Journal, 1913, p. viii. Unfortunately this prediction has
been, to a great extent, justified. In 1928, after fifteen years of effort to
enforce the prohibition, the Ministry of Health has to confess to several
hundred healthy children over three being found by its Inspectors, by dozens,
in breach of the Order, permanently living in General Mixed Workhouses,
notably in Cornwall. (See " Children in Workhouses ", by Lovat Fraser, in
Nineteenth Century and After, February 1928.)

(3) in forming classes to include inmates who are infirm, or who suffer from disease of body or mind ; women who are advanced in pregnancy, or suckling infants, or have recently been confined ; or infants, the Guardians are to have regard to recommendations to be obtained in writing from the Medical Officers ". Otherwise the classification of each Institution was henceforth to be determined by the Guardians.[1]

An administrative reform to which great objection was taken by many Boards of Guardians—one which the Departmental Committee described as among " the most important departures from the existing system of regulations "—was not only the express permission for the appointment of Women's Committees, wholly or partly of non-members of the Board, but also the specific requirement of a separate House Committee to administer " each Poor Law Institution ", to consist of a limited number of members, not exceeding twenty-four, or in the case of a large Union, not more than one-half of the Guardians.[2] This proposal to put a limit to the number of the House Committee—and thus to prevent its object being defeated by the appointment of the whole Board to be the House Committee—excited the strongest opposition ; and it was eventually withdrawn from the Draft Order. The result has unfortunately been, as was foreseen, that some Boards of Guardians have declined to adopt the suggested improvement of constituting a small Committee, responsible to the Board as a whole ; and have thus, by merely calling the whole Board the House Committee, incidentally destroyed the separate Visiting Committee that formerly existed.

The Nursing Order, complementary to the Institutions Order, made what the Circular described as "a further step forward " in the provision of trained nurses for all the sick and infirm inmates. It was not, indeed, thought expedient absolutely to prohibit the employment of inmates in the sick wards—a reform pressed for during half a century—but the new Order forbade any inmate to be employed actually " in the nursing of the sick ",

---

[1] For the first time it was noticed in an Order that, despite all systems of classification, Workhouse inmates normally dined together, and attended Divine Service together. Express provision was made in the Order for a mother to see her infants at least daily, and for other inmates to see any members of their families at reasonable intervals (*The First Report of the Departmental Committee*, etc., p. 64).

[2] *Ibid.* pp. ix-x, 115-117.

and made the employment of inmates in the sick wards, the lunatic wards or the nurseries, " in any capacity ", dependent on the approval, for the particular employment in each case, of the Medical Officer, and for such employment being under the immediate supervision of a paid officer. Moreover, though it was still deemed impracticable to require that every Poor Law Institution without exception should have among its resident staff at least one trained nurse (even if she acted also as Matron, or as Midwife, or as Nurse for the sick on Outdoor Relief), the Order definitely required the Guardians everywhere somehow to make " skilled nursing attendance (including provision for cases of emergency) . . . available for the inmates of every institution ". If there was on the staff no trained nurse, and the Guardians refused to appoint one, they might propose arrangements with a local District Nursing Association, under which the District Nurse could be sent for when required. For the larger institutions a Head Nurse, or a Superintendent Nurse, would be placed in charge of the nursing staff under the Medical Officer. The reader who has in mind the whole history of Work-house Nursing, from the efforts of Dr. Joseph Rogers and the philanthropic pioneers of 1860–1871, through the lifelong propaganda and munificent endowment of William Rathbone, down to the official struggles of 1895–1913 by Sir Arthur Downes together with the later work of Sir Arthur Newsholme and Sir George Newman, may find the progress slow.[1] But in probably as many as four-fifths of the Unions a great, and usually a continuous improvement has taken place. It is no small contribution to the general improvement of the nursing service of the country that the larger Poor Law Unions have made in training, in their own institutions, a large proportion, possibly even one-half, of all the trained nurses and midwives now at work. Every year over 3000 now gain, from Poor Law institutions, either the

---

[1] The number of salaried nurses in Poor Law institutions had failed in thirty years to reach even 3 per cent of the number of inmates (which rose from 178,000 in 1891 to 278,000 in 1911), whilst the proportion of the total who were actually under medical treatment had been steadily increasing. In 1883 there were 2385 salaried nurses ; in 1893, 2994 ; in 1907, 4106 ; in 1910, 5674 ; in 1913, 7652 (Forty-second Annual Report of Local Government Board, 1913, p. lv), and in 1928 some " 10,000 nurses and probationer nurses, nearly 4000 of whom are fully trained " (Ninth Annual Report of Ministry of Health, 1928, p. 166). These numbers include Matrons or Masters' wives with nursing qualifications.

preliminary or the final examination certificate of the General Nursing Council. If some Boards of Guardians are slow to be convinced, and a few are still scandalously neglectful of the sick poor, the Ministry of Health may well reply that not even the most stringent Orders, not even the repeated complaints of Inspectors and District Auditors, can prevail (at least in the absence of a specific Grant in Aid) against a system which confers a practical autonomy on elected bodies too unenlightened to realise the extravagant waste involved in improperly treated sickness.

We must, further, mention the passing of the Mental Deficiency Act of 1913, to come into operation on April 1, 1914, which led to a Circular dated March 31, 1914, pointing out that the new Statute provided for (and contemplated) the removal to more suitable institutions of the persons who might be certified under the Act.[1] No definite instructions for any such removal were, however, given by the Board ; the whole initiative was left to the Board of Guardians in each case ; and what with the war and then the attempts to reduce expenditure, what with the continued neglect of the Lunacy Authorities to make the necessary provision, and the Guardians' indisposition to part with any person whatever, it does not seem that much has yet (1928) been done to carry out the law.

The subject of Vagrancy continued, too, to occupy the thoughts of the Central Authority, especially as the number of persons resorting to the Casual Wards persisted in rising—it reached 14,757 in June 1909, but declined to 8882 on January 1, 1913—in spite of prosperity and a reduction in the total pauperism. The current panacea for reform was the constitution of Joint Vagrancy Committees of the Boards of Guardians within each geographical County, for the adoption of a common Vagrancy policy, and the " pooling " of the expenses incurred by each of the constituent Unions, with an equitable sharing of the total sum among all the Unions concerned, according to

---

[1] A special return of December 1912 had indicated that as many as 31,824 persons in Poor Law institutions might be eligible for certification under section 17 (2) of the Mental Deficiency Bill then before Parliament ; namely, 1766 as idiots, 4887 as imbeciles, 14,172 as feeble-minded, 727 as moral imbeciles, and 10,272 as mental imbeciles. The number of feeble-minded women giving birth to children in the Workhouses had averaged 509 per annum during the preceding five years (Forty-second Annual Report of Local Government Board, 1913, p. xv).

their rateable value. By the end of 1912 such Joint Vagrancy Committees had been voluntarily formed in twenty different Counties (though not always securing the adhesion of all the Unions, and being variously limited in the scope of their functions). The Local Government Board, which had, from the first, been friendly to the experiment, then issued an Order on February 13, 1913, officially sanctioning the formation of these Joint Vagrancy Committees outside the Metropolis.[1]

The outbreak of war delayed any real trial of this experiment, to which we shall recur.

B. THE GUARDIANS ON THE DEFENSIVE

We pass now from the Orders of the Central Authority to the activities of the Boards of Guardians, as these are portrayed, between 1909 and 1914, in the detailed reports of the Local Government Board Inspectors, and in the informative papers and discussions by Guardians and officials at the twelve Poor Law Conferences held each year in different parts of England and Wales.[2]

The general impression yielded by these documents is that the abler and more energetic Guardians, once they had got over their indignation at the unfavourable reports of the Poor Law Commission, showed a lively intention of justifying the existence, consolidating and extending the powers, widening the scope and, where practicable, increasing the autonomy of the *ad hoc* democratically elected Destitution Authority.

---

[1] Vagrancy (Joint Committees) Order, February 13, 1913 ; Forty-second Annual Report of Local Government Board, 1913, p. lxx.

[2] For this section we have drawn chiefly (1) on the successive Annual Reports of the Local Government Board from 1910 to 1914, which give, in extracts from the detailed reports of the Inspectors, an illuminating vision of the proceedings of the Boards of Guardians ; (2) on the voluminous reports of the papers and discussions at the sixty or seventy Poor Law Conferences of these years ; and, to a small extent, (3) on the scanty printed reports and accounts—occasionally the MS. Minutes, etc.—of the Boards of Guardians themselves, with the imperfect reports of their meetings in the local newspapers, and in the *Poor Law Officers' Journal*. Wherever possible, we have quoted the actual words of the Inspectors' reports, and those of the papers or addresses of Guardians who were delegates to the Poor Law Conferences.

Outdoor Relief

To take first the administration of Outdoor Relief, " the most vital as well as the most complicated problem of the Poor Law " (to quote the words of an Inspector), we watch many Boards of Guardians, in constant consultation with the Inspectorate, introducing the " Case-Paper System ", abolishing or diminishing Pay Stations in favour of payment in the homes, and appointing supervising Relieving Officers and Cross Visitors, many of them women.   More important than these improvements in machinery was the readiness with which many Boards of Guardians accepted the axiom that, when Outdoor Relief is given, it should be " adequate " for full maintenance under healthy conditions : a doctrine which, as we shall see, led in the post-war period to acute controversy between Whitehall and some Boards of Guardians as to what ought to be considered a decent subsistence for paupers living in their own homes.

" The Relieving Officers," reported in 1911 the Inspector for the Eastern Counties, " now visit every case on relief once in six weeks, and though it has been considered that an entire adoption of domiciliary payment will not be justified, owing to its cost, the officers pay all recipients of relief suffering from sickness, and other suitable cases, at their own homes. A proposal to lay down a Scale for the granting of relief was rejected by the Guardians, who considered that each case should be decided on its merits. The relief now granted is higher per individual than hitherto, and has a distinct tendency to rise. A very large amount of time is given to the consideration of applications, many being brought before the full Relief Committee. . . . The best-administered Unions continue to apply the necessary tests to doubtful applicants for assistance. As a whole, there is a tendency to increase the Scale of Out-relief to aged poor persons on the Relieving Officers' books, so as to bring them nearer the level of Old Age pensioners." [1]

" As the Guardians become more convinced," stated the Inspector for Wales and Monmouthshire in 1912, " of the need of granting relief that is adequate, so also do they realise the necessity in most cases of seeing that only those who are helpless

---

[1] Forty-first Annual Report of the Local Government Board, 1912, G. A. F. Hervey's Report, pp. 80-81.

and destitute are given assistance. Generally speaking there is now much better supervision over relief cases than was formerly exercised [1] . . ." The administration of relief, " both Indoor and Outdoor, continues to improve, and it is due to the Boards of Guardians, all of whom have just terminated their three years' term of office, to record that in no similar period in the history of Poor Law, has greater progress towards sound and sane administration been attempted and secured ".[2]

There was, however, one instruction of the Central Authority that the Guardians resented, and in many cases refused to adopt—the Local Government Board's objection to a Guardian for a particular parish or ward adjudicating on applications for relief from his electors or potential electors. " In most Unions ", stated the Inspector for the North-Western Counties, " the system remains as before ; the Committees consisting of the representatives of the areas from which the applicants come. As a rule, the Committees are in theory bound by general rules made by the Board of Guardians, but generally it is nobody's business to see that the rules are enforced ; and, even when departures from the rules are formally reported to the Board of Guardians, they are usually passed without comment. The practical result is that there may be, in a Union, half a dozen virtually independent bodies, performing, without check by the Board of Guardians, the most important of the functions of that body ; and expending, each in a particular portion of the Union, money drawn from the rates of the Union as a whole. The disadvantages of such a system are obvious, but when they are pointed out, the individual Guardian is inclined to feel that a reflection is made upon his personal integrity. Where the system prevails, it is not the discretion of the Board of Guardians which is threatened by any proposed restriction of the power of granting Outdoor Relief, but the discretion of the irresponsible Relief Committee." [3]

" The objection which most Guardians have to this suggested prohibition to adjudicate on their own cases ", observed the Inspector for Wales and Monmouthshire, " is that they claim to be in possession of the whole facts ; but they forget that it

[1] Forty-first Annual Report of Local Government Board, 1912, p. 133.
[2] Forty-second Annual Report of Local Government Board, 1913, p. 85.
[3] Fortieth Annual Report of Local Government Board, 1911, A. B. Lowry's Report, p. 81.

is the duty of the Relieving Officer to investigate fully into every application, and to report in sufficient detail all the circumstances, in such a manner as to enable any Guardian, whether personally acquainted with the applicant or not, to order what relief is necessary for the applicant, with due regard to the best interests of the applicant and the community. . . . I am convinced that were it possible to make it unlawful for a Guardian to adjudicate upon applications for residents in his own parish or ward, there would result a much more uniform and equitable administration of Outdoor Relief." [1]

Out-relief on Behalf of Children

The most scandalous cases of inadequate Outdoor Relief revealed by the Poor Law Commission of 1905–1909 were those of widows with children, and it is in this sphere that Boards of Guardians were most persistently pressed by the Poor Law Division and its Inspectorate to mend their ways. " As regards children in receipt of Outdoor Relief with their parents," stated the Local Government Board Report for 1910–1911, " we drew attention to the necessity for constant supervision over the condition and interests of the child ; and we pointed out the means, such as the utilisation of charitable agencies or of individual visitors, and the information obtained as the result of the medical inspection of school children, by which this could be secured." [2] Many of " the most progressive Boards of Guardians ", reported an Inspector in the same year, " consider it the wisest economy to allow sufficient relief to enable the widowed mother of a family to remain at home to look after her children, make and

---

[1] Fortieth Annual Report of Local Government Board, 1911, H. R. Williams' Report, p. 104.

It must be said that during these years (1909–1914) pauperism was steadily declining, and Outdoor Relief was generally lessening year by year—that to Able-bodied applicants becoming, in nearly all Unions, merely exceptional. In all the English Counties, with the exception of Dorset, Lincoln and Cornwall, the expenditure on Outdoor Relief sank to less than that on the Poor Law institutions. This was not the case in Wales, where Outdoor Relief remained predominant in the expenditure—the Unions in North Wales (notably those in Anglesey), and those of Pembroke and Carmarthen in South Wales, spending relatively little on their institutions, which remained in most cases at a low level of development. (See Forty-second Annual Report of Local Government Board, 1913, p. xxv.)

[2] Fortieth Annual Report of Local Government Board, 1911, p. xix.

mend their clothing, prepare proper meals, and attend herself
to those under school age, rather than entrust them to the care
of a neighbour while she goes out working. Formerly, when
the relief was inadequate, the poor widow was compelled to turn
out and eke some little addition to her slender means, and consequently the children were perforce left to the care of a neighbour
or to one of the elder children. It should be added that it is
only when Guardians have appointed a lady visitor, or a female
visitor under the Children Act, who is deputed to visit the homes
of women with children receiving Out-relief, or when the cases
are carefully watched by the Relieving Officer, that there is the
necessary security that every widow with children who receives
this adequate relief expends it properly for the welfare of herself
and the children. . . . The increase in the number of children ",
this Inspector added, " is no doubt attributable to the more
generous relief now administered to widows with children. In
most of the larger Unions a fixed sum is allowed in respect of
each child, and I am afraid that it is becoming a rule in some
Unions to give this fixed sum with very little regard to the
earnings or other income going into the house. This policy
removes all incentive to self-effort, and many women are in
consequence more ready than formerly to accept Out-relief,
and thus pauperise themselves as well as their children." [1]

" Considerable progress has been made ", reported the
Inspector of the Midland Counties, " in the treatment of widows
and women with families, who are in receipt of Outdoor Relief.
More exhaustive enquiries are made ; relief is refused in those
cases where such enquiries show that a considerable sum is
coming into the house from hitherto unsuspected sources ;
while relief, when given, is much more frequently adequate to
the circumstances of the case. The appointment of female
Relieving or Visiting Officers is likely to be of great assistance
in this respect." [2]

---

[1] Fortieth Annual Report of Local Government Board, 1911, H. R. Williams'
Report, pp. 102-105.

[2] Forty-second Annual Report of Local Government Board, 1913, C. F.
Roundell's Report, p. 22.

After the war (1919–1928) the practice of employing women officers continued
steadily to increase in most of the populous Unions, the total number in
England and Wales—usually with the title of Assistant Relieving Officer—in
1928 being estimated at several hundreds. The effect of the Widows, Orphans
and Old Age Contributory Pensions Act, 1925, was nearly to halve the numbers

Confronted with the peremptory Order to take out of the General Mixed Workhouse all children over three years of age, many Guardians fell back on the method of Boarding-out, within or without the Union. Hitherto, as was pointed out in 1911 by the Inspector of the North-Western Counties of England, Boarding-out had, in the practice of the Unions in this area, taken two different forms : " The case of a child who is placed in a carefully selected home with a foster-parent of known respectability, and the case of a child given into the care of a person whose chief qualification for the duty is that she is some relation of the child's dead parent. There is no doubt that in many instances of the latter kind the home provided for the child, and the influences which surround it, fall far short of the standard which the Guardians would rightly require in the home of a foster-parent selected by them." [1]

" Other Boards of Guardians ", reported another Inspector, " are too much disposed to adopt the Boarding-out system as the cheapest method of dealing with the children. Where an adequate amount is paid for the child's maintenance, and a suitable home is obtained, the results justify the system. But where cheapness is the chief consideration, or there is insufficient inquiry into the suitability of the home, the results are not satisfactory. Generally speaking, people do not become foster-parents from actual love of the children ; the object is to increase the family income by the pay which the Guardians allow. This pay is sometimes not more than 2s. 6d. a week, with an allowance of 10s. a quarter for clothes ; but this latter amount is not always given. It is only right, however, to say the allowance of 2s. 6d. a week is sometimes given to relatives when they act in the capacity of foster-parents ; but I hold that such an arrangement

---

of widows with children (and possibly also of doubly orphaned children) in receipt of Outdoor Relief ; and thus, incidentally, to withdraw such children from whatever supervisory care they had received when they had been maintained on Poor Relief ! (" The number of widows with dependent children in receipt of relief on the 1st January 1927, and the number of those children, was 30,671 and 64,490 respectively. These figures show decreases of 29,946 and 61,185, as compared with the corresponding number in receipt of relief on the 1st January 1926. . . . The number of orphans receiving domiciliary relief was, on the 1st January 1926, 10,761, and on the 1st January 1927, 9116 " (Eighth Annual Report of Ministry of Health, 1927, p. 115).)
[1] Fortieth Annual Report of Local Government Board, 1911, A. B. Lowry's Report, p. 80.

is not to be countenanced, except in cases where the relatives live under favourable surroundings, and are fit and proper persons to have charge of the children." [1]

To remedy these defects the Local Government Board issued, as has already been stated, a new Boarding-out Order. " Until the 1st January, 1912, the Boarding-out of pauper children was regulated by different Orders according as a child was placed within or beyond the Union to which he was chargeable. The most recent orders of either kind were the Boarding-out Order, 1905, and the Boarding-out (Within Unions) Order, 1909. The question of replacing these Orders by a single code of regulations had for some time been under our consideration, and on the 16th October, 1911, we issued a new order . . . under the title of ' The Boarding-out Order, 1911 ', which has this effect.

" Under the new Order the distinction between Boarding-out within and beyond the Union practically disappears, the same procedure being applicable in all cases. It is, however, replaced by a distinction based on the nature of the Committee under whose care the child is placed. The Committees may derive their authority either from an appointment by a Board of Guardians or from an authority given by us. So far as the care of the children is concerned, the regulations and conditions to be observed are now universally the same, but the relations between the Guardians responsible for a child, and the Committee supervising it, may be of different kinds. The ground for the distinction is that while an authorised Committee is practically an independent body, not subject to any periodical reappointment, and in the last resort controlled only by our power of altering the area assigned to it, or of withdrawing the authority given by us, an appointed Committee is, like other committees of the Guardians, appointed only for a defined period, and its acts are, within the compass of the Order, subject to regulation by the Guardians by whom it is appointed." [2]

The result of this Order was slightly to increase the use of the device of Boarding-out as a way of getting the children out of the Workhouse. " There would have been a still further

---

[1] Fortieth Annual Report of Local Government Board, 1911, E. B. Wethered's Report, p. 62.

[2] Forty-first Annual Report of Local Government Board, 1912, p. xxiii.

increase ", reported the Inspector for Berks and Bucks, " in the number receiving Indoor Relief, but for the Guardians having taken more advantage of their powers under the Boarding-out Orders to deal in this manner with those that are eligible. A further increase in the number of children boarded-out is likely to occur, as since the new Boarding-out Order was issued this system has been adopted by several Boards of Guardians who had not done so before." [1]

Under this pressure the number of children whom the Boards of Guardians consented to board-out increased from 8620 in 1905 to 11,596 in 1914. Unfortunately, the reports indicate that, whether the Boarding-out was within the Union or without, the supervision of the children was far from satisfactory. " All the Inspectors," stated the Superintendent Lady Inspector in 1912, " report numerous instances of a grave laxity on the part of those acting on behalf of committees, in cases of children, boarded-out within the Union to which they are chargeable, in supervising sleeping accommodation in the homes in which children are placed. The conditions found are not infrequently seriously objectionable, and the consequent overcrowding is injurious to health and morals ; it is, moreover, impossible to inculcate decency where decency cannot be practised. It is of course true that in many country cottages the bedrooms are small and badly planned, but a minimum standard of decency should be imposed, in order to secure the proper separation of the sexes in the sleeping rooms. Miss Jones expresses the opinion that no child should be boarded-out where there is a family of boys and girls, unless there are at least three bedrooms in the house."

" The following typical case of overcrowding is reported by one of the Lady Inspectors : A.B., girl, 15-16 years of age ; C.D., boy, 12-13 years of age, living with uncle, Mr. F. Foster-father casual labourer. Three sons, aged respectively 16, 12, 6 years of age. Two small bedrooms. The Inspector had every reason to believe that the girl shared a mattress on the floor in the foster-parents' room with her cousin, a boy of 6-7 years of age ; the girl was suffering from acute anaemia, and as no windows or bedroom chimneys were open, this was not to be

[1] Forty-first Annual Report of Local Government Board, 1912, Herbert's Report, p. 69.

wondered at. The foster-mother was said to drink. Many of the conditions reported by the Lady Inspectors relating to the sleeping accommodation and personal cleanliness of children boarded-out within the Union to which they are chargeable would, had they occurred in Poor Law institutions, have involved a public scandal." [1]

Nor did the Guardians succeed much better in boarding-out beyond the Union. " The reports of Inspectors ", stated the Superintendent Lady Inspector in 1914, " show an unfortunate indisposition on the part of Guardians to take any advantage of their power to make an agreement with a Committee beyond the Union of their chargeability. Appointed Committees, however, are sometimes reluctant to undertake supervision of cases not chargeable to the rates of the particular Union in the area of which they act ; and cases have been known of Boards of Guardians refusing to undertake supervision of cases not chargeable to the rates of their Union, whilst in other cases the oversight given is of a very indifferent kind. In one non-settled case, relieved as boarded-out beyond the Union of chargeability under an Appointed Committee, the child was found, when visited, to be living under conditions of such dirt and squalor that the relief was withdrawn. Thereupon the quondam foster-parents applied for Outdoor Relief to the Guardians of the Union of residence. Some Boards of Guardians do not receive, from the Union in which the boarded-out child is resident, copies of the visitors' and school teachers' quarterly reports on the case, and are consequently not kept acquainted with the progress of the child and state of the home. Where the maintenance money is paid by the Union of chargeability direct to the foster-parents, and there is no local visitor to watch the child's progress, there is a real danger that monies may be paid by the Union of chargeability after a child has gone to work and should have ceased to be chargeable. In one Union payment was made to the foster-parent direct by the Union of chargeability for a period of some months after the girl had gone to service and was keeping herself. In extra-metropolitan districts there seems to be considerable difficulty in arranging for the transfer of children suitable for Boarding-out to districts in which suitable foster-homes are available, outside the Union area to which they belong.

---

[1] Forty-first Annual Report of Local Government Board, 1912, p. 139.

To illustrate the dangers of Boarding-out children whose relatives are undesirable in proximity to the Unions of chargeability,
the following instances may be cited : ' (1) A girl waylaid by
her father on her way to and from school and frightened by his
threats ; (2) Two boys boarded-out in a village some three
miles from a town in which their immoral mother resides.   The
latter escorted them one day from the village school to their
home at which, in the presence of an assembled crowd, she
subjected the foster-mother to gross abuse.' " [1]

[1] Forty-third Annual Report of Local Government Board, 1914, pp. 80-81.
During the war and for the first two years of peace the number of children
boarded-out steadily declined, being 12,019 in January 1915 to 9354 in January
1920.   To counteract this decline (which had been latterly attributed to the
authorised payments having become insufficient to cover the increased cost of
maintenance), a Circular (May 3, 1920) rescinded the article in the Boarding-
Out Order of 1911 which fixed the maintenance allowance that might be paid
to foster-parents.   The Guardians in the more energetic Unions thereupon
raised the amount to seven, and even to ten shillings or more per week ; but
the difficulty of finding suitable foster-parents was apparently not greatly
lessened ; and it was reported in 1923 that " the number of independent
Boarding-out Committees continues to decrease ", being only 126 in 1924 and
122 in 1925.   The total number of children boarded-out rose very slowly from
9315 in 1920 to 10,489 in 1925, but then dropped to 10,461 in 1926 and 9253
in 1927—a decline attributed to the removal of children from Poor Relief on
being awarded pensions under the Widows, Orphans and Old Age Contributory
Pensions Act of 1925.   It is significant that the total number boarded-out
beyond the Union, which advocates of the system regarded as its best form,
sank to no more than 1616, and has never, at the highest (in 1915), exceeded
2370.   Half a century of experience seems to indicate the impossibility of
persuading the average urban Poòr Law Guardian to be very zealous in placing
children in country cottages ; and also the failure of philanthropic effort
either to discover a sufficient number of suitable foster-parents, or to maintain
continuously the requisite voluntary supervision of the homes that are chosen.
Moreover, it was realised that not all the children boarded-out were suitable
for that method of provision.   "It is found ", it was said in 1927, "that
children suffering from arrested development or lowered vitality, or even with
a tendency to phthisis, precisely in fact such children as require careful supervision, medical and otherwise, and special teaching, are too often entrusted to
foster-parents who, with the best will in the world, could not be expected to
provide for their special needs.   Children who are actually feeble-minded or
on the border-line are sometimes found with foster-parents " (Sixth Annual
Report of Ministry of Health, 1925, p. 114).   The Roman Catholic Guardians
never ask that Roman Catholic children should be boarded-out.   " Boarding-
out, owing to the difficulty of finding suitable foster-parents, has proved a
failure in so far as Catholics are concerned.   We are therefore reduced to the
one system which I consider, after many years' experience, to be the best we can
possibly provide for our healthy Catholic children, viz. the Catholic Certified
Schools and Homes " (*What Catholics have a right to expect under any Reform
of the Poor Law*, by Thomas G. King, Catholic Guardians' Association, 1926).

The Overlap with the Education Authority

The increasing provision, by Local Education Authorities, of meals to children found hungry at school, and the treatment for those in whom the Medical Inspection revealed remediable defects, inevitably produced an overlap with the work of the Boards of Guardians in so far as their Outdoor Relief was concerned. This intrusion of the Framework of Prevention into the very texture of the Poor Law was hotly resented by some Boards of Guardians.

" I feel very strongly ", stated Sir William Chance at a Poor Law Conference in 1912, " that the work of relieving the wants of necessitous children, whether it be in feeding, clothing, or medical treatment, is and ought to be strictly Poor Law work, and that the Boards of Guardians would carry it out more effectively in co-operation with the Education Authorities than can be done by the latter Authorities alone. Indeed, the arguments for the medical treatment of school children under the Poor Law apply equally to the supply of their food or clothing. The danger which underlies the undertaking by the Education Authorities of this relief work is that, like education itself, it may become *free.*" [1]

According to many Guardians the removal of the stigma of pauperism from children fed or medically treated out of public funds was wholly disadvantageous. . . . " Many parents ", it was urged, " who now refuse to get the necessary treatment for their children, although they can afford to do so, would be led ", if the stigma of pauperism were retained, " to do their duty in the matter, from the sense of shame at getting it done for them through the agency of the Poor Law, and then having to pay after all for the cost." And with a curious inconsequence, the speaker added, " it would, on the other hand, be no more disgrace, to a parent who was not able to pay for the treatment, to be helped through the Poor Law rather than by the Education Authority ".[2]

" ' London, with its ill-considered and wholesale feeding of school children, ' " wrote in the same year a leading member of the C.O.S., " ' set the country a bad example, and has made the work, the " care " of school children, much harder than it

---

[1] *Poor Law Conferences, 1912–1913*, p. 12.   [2] *Ibid.* pp. 16-17.

might have been ; for in this neighbourhood I have, as it were, been on guard night and day with a pistol in one hand and a bayonet in the other, to prevent the starting of feeding out of the rates ; and, in addition, have been hampered in finding the requisite help for legitimate case-work, as so many people were prejudiced, thinking that it merely meant free food and the giving away of boots. Now comes the further danger of rate-paid and State-subsidised medical treatment.' " [1]

The situation was, in fact, as perplexing as it was paradoxical. If Boards of Guardians were fulfilling their obligation adequately to relieve destitution, there should be no occasion for the Education Authority to step in and provide, not only medical inspection and treatment, but actual food for starving children. But as an experienced Guardian observed, " If they were to give food to the children through the Poor Law, it would disfranchise the fathers, which was not the case with the new Act for the Education Committees. In Coventry the first thing the Education Committee did was to get members of the Board of Guardians to assist them in their work, and where the parents of children were found to be receiving Outdoor Relief, that relief was made adequate so as to enable them to feed their children. In those cases the Education Authority were asked to discontinue feeding the children." [2]

" The new Children's Care Committees are springing up everywhere in connection with the Education Authority," stated another delegate, " and as they make neglected or underfed children their special care they frequently interest themselves in the children on Outdoor Relief. It is this encroachment of the Education Authority on to the duties of the Guardians which has led a certain school of Poor Law reformers to advocate the taking of the children who need relief right out of the hands of the Guardians and entrusting them to the Education Authority. The latter would maintain in schools the orphan and deserted children, and would grant maintenance allowances to those living at home with their parents, through the Attendance Officers, as is now done by the Guardians through the Relieving Officers. This would undoubtedly be a simplification in that we should only have one Authority directly dealing with the children instead of two,

---

[1] *Poor Law Conferences, 1912–1913,* p. 18.
[2] *Poor Law Conferences, 1909–1910,* p. 729.

and we should remove from them what has been called the stigma of pauperism." [1]

Institutional Treatment

The movement towards a wisely generous treatment of the applicants for relief was, as might have been expected, far more marked and continuous in the administration of the Poor Law institutions than in Outdoor Relief. "A new era had arisen in Workhouse management ", explained a Manchester Guardian at a Poor Law Conference in September 1912 ; "the 'Labour Master ', formerly a synonym for a tyrant of the worst type, had gone, and given place to men of a more humane and merciful temperament. The increase of wealth in this country during the last forty years had been enormous. And surely it was only equitable that whilst the fortunate ones had gained increased comforts and enjoyment, some crumbs of comfort should fall to the less fortunate inmates of Poor Law institutions. Everywhere everybody wanted a better place in the sun, and it was but right that they should get it. The present-day Workhouse as a deterrent had become largely a spent force. It was formerly the practice to make everything and everybody about the Workhouse as disagreeable as possible. But a wave of humanity had come along and swept that noxious spirit out of existence. Humane sympathy, compassion for the afflicted and the feeble, had taken the place of the early harsh methods. The spirit of 'brotherhood ' had been largely adopted by all present-day Guardians, so that politeness, kindness, and increased comfort all round were the order of the day in workhouse administration." [2] Anyone who visits the Tame Street (Manchester)

---

[1] *Poor Law Conferences, 1912–1913*, p. 235.

[2] *Ibid.* pp. 508-509.

With the improvement in trade and the reduction to a minimum of able-bodied pauperism after 1909, the Able-bodied Test Workhouse passed out of the picture ; with the exception of Belmont (maintained by the Fulham Union, London), which apparently had a chequered career. In 1910 it was made available also for adult male epileptics, otherwise healthy, and not of unsound mind, adjudged capable of light work ; although not for the "in and out" class. "The epileptics at Belmont ", we read, " are located in the old infirmary buildings, and are kept quite distinct from the other inmates. They have a plot of ground at the back, on which they are employed at such light work as they are able to perform. A very careful record is kept of all the cases, and their change to Belmont [from the General Mixed Workhouse] has proved very beneficial to many of them."

Whether or not the presence of epileptics was distasteful to the unemployed

Able-bodied Workhouse to-day (1928), and compares its kindly administration, cleanliness and good food, its club-rooms and its easy tasks, with the grim penal establishment (far harder in its disciplinary regimen than the modern prison) inspected by the Royal Commissioners of 1905–1909, will not deny the humanitarian hospitality displayed by some Boards of Guardians in densely populated industrial areas.

The effect upon the minds of the Poor Law Guardians of the unanimous and almost vehement denunciation of the General Mixed Workhouse, alike by the Majority and Minority of the Poor Law Commissioners, 1905–1909, may be seen in the increased use made of specialised institutions. The Local Government Board's peremptory Order of 1913, that all children over three were to be removed from the Workhouse, was accepted without revolt. At the same time, we are told by the Local Government Board, " we indicated at length the various methods by which children could be provided for outside the Workhouse, and while drawing attention to the relative merits of the larger or smaller ' grouped Cottage Home ' system, the plan of ' Scattered Homes ', the placing of children in Certified Institutions and on Training Ships, and finally the system of Boarding-out, we impressed on Boards of Guardians the duty of giving first consideration to the needs of the individual case in determining the method of treatment to be adopted ".[1] But, although the Boards of Guardians in the large towns were active in improving their own Separate Schools, or in starting Cottage Homes or Scattered Homes, reform came slowly and reluctantly in smaller rural Unions. Thus, it is reported in 1911, that steps have been taken by urban Guardians

---

workmen drawn from " about twenty different Workhouses of the Metropolis ", or whether it was, as they asserted, a question of diet, the discontent culminated towards the end of 1910 in riots resulting in more than eighty men being sentenced to various terms of imprisonment. The Inspector attributed " this disorderly conduct to the difficulty of providing work on the land in wet weather, and the opportunities for conversation with regard to the different treatment in the various institutions from which they come. . . . The Belmont diet is well above the recognised standard," he added, " and although it may not be very appetising, it contains ample nourishing properties. It is very difficult to arrange a dietary that contains all that is sufficient, and yet is not so much more palatable than the diet that this class of inmate is used to outside the Workhouse, as to make him desire to remove himself from the rates " (Fortieth Annual Report of Local Government Board, 1911, Report of Inspector for the Metropolis, etc., p. 34).

[1] Fortieth Annual Report of the Local Government Board, 1911, p. xx.

to remove children out of the Workhouse, but " a regrettable number of the larger semi-urban Unions, such as, *e.g.* Ludlow (25 children), Macclesfield (50 children), and Wellington (35 children), and practically all the smaller rural Unions still refrain from providing separate accommodation for the young people.

" The main causes of this adherence to obsolete methods appear to be :

" (1) The recent decrease of pauperism has lessened the pressure on the Workhouse accommodation, and has consequently weakened the motives for making available, for other classes of paupers, the quarters at present occupied by the children.

" (2) An insufficient appreciation by Guardians of the evils of Workhouse life for the children, notwithstanding an unanimous adverse verdict by Commissions, Poor Law Conferences, and educated public opinion.

" The combined results of (1) and (2) is, that Guardians do not feel called upon to face the, in some cases, considerable expense of providing separate accommodation for their children.

" It is not a little lamentable to find that according to a special census taken by me this year, there were in the Workhouses of my district nearly a thousand healthy children above the age of three. This represents 35 per cent of the children above three years of age receiving Indoor Relief." [1]

This inertia on the part of the rural Guardians unfortunately long continued. " Andover and Malmesbury," said the Inspector of the South of England, " having referred the question to committees of their respective Boards, ultimately refused to adopt the recommendation of their committees in favour of the removal of the children from the Workhouse, several members of both of these Boards of Guardians expressing the opinion that it was an unnecessary waste of the ratepayers' money to incur the expense of making provision for them in a separate institution. . . . Some of the Boards of Guardians are faced by the difficulty that the number of children for whom they would, under normal conditions, have to provide is too small to enable them to have a home for boys and another for girls, or even one home so adapted that it might serve for both sexes. The diffi-

[1] Fortieth Annual Report of the Local Government Board, 1911, R. G. Duff's Report, pp. 68-69.

culty is a real one, but it appears to me that it could quite well be met by a combination of small Unions for the purpose of providing homes for the children ; or by an agreement for the reception into the homes of one Union of children belonging to another ; or by placing the children in Certified Homes or other similar institutions." [1]

In about half the fifty Unions in Cornwall, Devon and Somerset no decided step had been taken in 1914 for removing children from the Workhouse. " This removal will, under the Poor Law Institutions Order, 1913, be generally compulsory after March, 1915, and a number of Boards of Guardians, who had been unwilling to move, are now giving the provision of outside homes their serious attention." [2]

The Workhouse Nurseries

The members of the Royal Commission had been shocked in 1906–1908 at the condition in which they found the nurseries [3]

[1] Forty-third Annual Report of the Local Government Board, 1914, Report of J. W. Thompson, p. 40.

Meanwhile the number of children on the hands of the Guardians was, in some cases, increasing ; owing, partly, to an increasing use of the powers of adoption under the Acts of 1889 and 1899 ; partly to the activities of the Society for the Prevention of Cruelty to Children ; and partly, it must be added, to an increasing willingness, among parents and Guardians alike, to give children the " advantages " of a Poor Law education. Thus, the Inspector for the Counties of Berks, Bucks and Oxford reported in 1911 as follows : " It must be remembered that as a result of the removal of the children from the Workhouses to Cottage Homes, and the more kindly treatment they receive, many parents are glad rather than otherwise, when the Guardians offer to take charge of their children.

" When applications for the relief of children are made, most Boards of Guardians cause very thorough enquiries to be made as to the conditions under which the children are likely to be cared for should Out-relief be granted, and whilst there is every desire on their part to allow a mother to have the care and training of her children, the Guardians do not hesitate to offer Indoor Relief, if they think that such relief is in the best interests of the children themselves.

" The increase in the number of children receiving Indoor Relief has been going on steadily for the past 11 years. On January 1st, 1901, there were in this district 1626 children in receipt of Indoor Relief, and on January 1st, 1912, 2483, a rise of 857 in numbers, and equal to an increase of 52·7 per cent during the eleven years " (Forty-first Annual Report of Local Government Board, 1912, pp. 68-69).

[2] Forty-third Annual Report of Local Government Board, 1914, Report of E. D. Court, p. 44.

[3] Majority and Minority Reports of Poor Law Commission, 1909 ; see, in particular, the special inquiry made by certain members of the Royal Commission into the mortality in Workhouse Nurseries given in Minority Report,

in the Workhouses, where the Boards of Guardians were attempting to rear the four or five thousand infants under three years of
age, who had either accompanied their parents into the Institution,
or had been brought as orphans or foundlings.   In the worst of
these Workhouse Nurseries, where the care of the infants was
practically left to pauper inmates, with the very minimum of
supervision either by the Workhouse doctor or the Guardians
themselves, the mortality was admittedly " higher than in the
general population ", and the health of those who survived
left much to be desired.   From 1909 to 1914 there seems to
have been a steady improvement in the administration.   The
Inspectors gave the Nurseries more attention on their visits ;
and their criticisms were presently reinforced by the appointment
of an increasing number of Assistant Inspectors, some of them
women with nursing qualifications and experience, who (besides
accompanying the Inspectors) made independent inspections.
In 1910 the attention of the Guardians was officially directed
to the need for drastic reorganisation of these Workhouse
Nurseries ; and in the Circular on " Children under the Poor
Law ", of the 16th of June of that year, the necessity was emphasised of such elementary requirements as "a sufficiency of light
and ventilation, a good supply of hot and cold water, means of
airing and exercise, proper floor-covering, means of sterilising
milk, etc.".   It is to be feared that few among the 24,000 Guardians
took very seriously such general remarks, and they were certainly
slow to act on the further hint that " more trained nurses are
required " for the hapless infants.   More effective was perhaps
in 1913 the new Institutions Order.   This made the employment
of pauper inmates in the Workhouse Nurseries "in any capacity "
dependent on the approval, for the particular employment in
each case, of the Medical Officer, and for such employment being
under the immediate supervision of a paid officer of some sort.
But the decisive reform was, we imagine, the specific new duty
imposed on the Workhouse Medical Officer of keeping a separate
record paper for each infant ; and of personally examining each
of them once a fortnight during the first eighteen months, and

pp. 83, 84, 85.   This statement of the excessive mortality of infants in Workhouses was criticised in a " Memorandum by the Local Government Board
on Deaths among Infants in Poor Law Institutions ", April 7, 1909, H.C.
No. 99.

once a month for the second eighteen months, in order that
any defects might be promptly detected and dealt with.   Gradually, it seems, the Workhouse Medical Officer undertook the
special responsibility thus cast upon him for securing proper
conditions of nurture for each separate infant in the Workhouse ;
and, often with the zealous co-operation of the women members
of the Boards of Guardians, detailed reforms were quietly made.
"One or two Boards", it was reported in 1914, "have joined the
number of those who employ an officer specially to look after
the children in the Nursery ; and in these cases the improvement
in the appearance of the children has been most marked.   Great
improvements in recent years have taken place in the Nurseries." [1]

Few were the Unions, however, which got so far as to "take
the infants out of the General Mixed Workhouse ".   In 1912
the Nottingham Board of Guardians were reported as having
established, in a house adjoining the Workhouse grounds, a
" Nursery for Indoor Babies ", where some fifty infants were
accommodated under a special woman officer.[2]

The Treatment of the Sick

If to the children the General Mixed Workhouse was injurious,
to the sick it was fatal.   The senile and hopeless cases in the
Workhouse wards, who, in spite of the Nursing and Workhouses
Order of 1897 (which prohibited actual nursing by paupers), were,
in many small Workhouses still largely left to the sometimes
kindly but always inept handling of fellow-paupers, could but die ;
at worst a little sooner or with less comfort than was humane.
But men and women in the prime of life, and children at the
healthiest age, suffering from curable complaints which had compelled their removal to the General Mixed Workhouse, were, in

---

[1] Forty-third Annual Report of Local Government Board, 1914, G. Walsh's
Report, p. 62.
[2] Forty-second Annual Report of Local Government Board, 1913, G. Walsh's
Report, p. 62.
Whilst the persistent efforts of the Inspectors (and especially the scrutiny
of the women Assistant Inspectors), which were resumed after the Armistice,
have, we believe, resulted in a continuous and almost universal improvement
in the conditions of the Workhouse Nurseries, we cannot learn of any successful
attempts, apart from those made in the Nottingham, Birmingham, and a very
few other Unions, to remove the children under three years of age—even if
without mothers—from the General Mixed Workhouse.   There are now (1928)
still some 3870 children under three, not being sick, in the Workhouse Nurseries.

three-fourths of the Unions, being denied the specialist medical skill and often the continuous trained nursing that would alone enable them to return to the ranks of productive citizenship. Hence the movement initiated in the latter half of the nineteenth century to separate the sick-wards from the General Mixed Workhouse, and, better still, to establish distinct Poor Law hospitals, under medical superintendence in place of the Workhouse Master, and replacing the pauper attendants by a staff of trained nurses. During the period 1909–1914 this deliberate separation of the sick from other classes of paupers became increasingly general.[1]

" The arrangements for the nursing of the sick in the Workhouses ", stated in 1913 the Inspector for some Midland Counties, " show a steady and most gratifying improvement. Excluding the Separate Infirmaries and sick-wards under separate infirmary control, in 50 Unions the average number of beds per nurse is 14. Of the cases in these wards 30 per cent only were bed-fast. The services of pauper inmates in the sick-wards are steadily being dispensed with, and the actual nursing services rendered by such inmates are very small." [2] The total number of nurses in the Workhouses throughout the Kingdom did, indeed, increase steadily, if, in the rural Unions, extremely slowly. But it cannot be pretended that these rural Unions,

[1] In these years the official conception of the essential difference between the Workhouse and the Poor Law hospital became clarified. " In previous reports ", we read in 1914, " ' Separate Infirmary ' has been used to denote a separate building or a separate block of the Workhouse, whether separately administered or not. This definition has now been abandoned and the term restricted to those cases where the administration of the Infirmary is governed by a set of regulations distinct from those relating to the Workhouse " ; the Infirmary becoming, in fact, an entirely distinct institution, invariably under a Medical Officer. In such Infirmaries there were, on January 1, 1914, 27,649 inmates, in contrast with 66,285 in special wards of Workhouses, and 108,240 in other wards of Workhouses (Forty-third Annual Report of Local Government Board, 1914, p. ix).

" To-day," it could be said in 1928, " apart from buildings administered as one with the Workhouses to which they are attached, there are 60 Poor Law Infirmaries under separate regulations . . . the chief control is vested in the Medical Superintendent with a Steward and Matron as his chief assistants. In addition there are 33 Infirmaries separately administered but not under separate regulations, which include 19 used solely for mental cases. On the night of February 11, 1928, these 93 hospitals had 35,864 inmates, and there were 5125 vacant beds " (Ninth Annual Report of Ministry of Health, 1928, p. 165).

[2] Forty-second Annual Report of Local Government Board, 1913, Report of C. F. Roundell, p. 24.

numbering more than half the whole, were making any real attempt to provide suitable institutional treatment for the inmates who were sick, let alone for the wage-earning population. Although the General Mixed Workhouse was (as it remains in 1928), in many districts, the only available institution for the sick poor, the Board of Guardians simply could not think of itself as the Hospital Authority even for the destitute. It is only fair to the Guardians to say that the Local Government Board never brought itself to explain to them that, according to the law, the Poor Law Authorities are empowered and required to make this hospital provision. The persons (probably nine-tenths of the population) who, though able to support themselves in health, are unable to provide for themselves in illness the expensive institutional provision, the skilled nursing, and the expert medical and surgical treatment that their illness required, " in order to obviate, mitigate or remove causes endangering life, or likely to endanger life or bodily fitness for self-support ", are—as the legal adviser of the Local Government Board explained to the Poor Law Commission in these very words —within the category of the " destitute ".[1] The Boards of Guardians of 1909–1914 were accordingly both empowered and required to provide what these illnesses called for ; and in a small minority of Unions this provision was being made at great expense, without objection being taken. It would, of course, be unfair to comment adversely on the failure, in 1909–1914, to provide what might properly be expected in 1928, when the Ministry of Health has actually sanctioned a Poor Law Authority (the Metropolitan Asylums Board) providing and equipping a most costly " Radium Treatment Ward " for the reception of female paupers suffering from uterine cancer ; and, in the same year, has allowed a single Board of Guardians (Edmonton) to spend £6000 on radium for the same purpose. Yet even in 1909–1914 it would have been in consonance with contemporary public opinion, as well as within the law, that sick Workhouse inmates should everywhere be given medical treatment and nursing equal to that obtained in country districts by comparatively well-to-do persons living in their own homes. But neither the Local Government Board nor its Inspectors in these years published

[1] See the evidence of A. D. Adrian, Poor Law Commission, Appendix, vol. i. Q. 973.

to the world, or attempted to enforce on the minds of the Guardians generally, what was officially held to be their lawful function and duty.

With regard to one disease, namely, tuberculosis, a certain number of Unions must be credited with attempts to make the required institutional provision. " For some years ", reported in 1913 the Inspector for Wales and Monmouthshire, " the Guardians in this district have been very active in making suitable provision for the institutional and domiciliary treatment of phthisical cases, and for the proper maintenance of the families of the bread-winner. Inexpensive sanatoria, or shelters and chalets have been constructed for their use for some years, at the following places : Cardiff, Llanfilo-fawr, Merthyr Tydfil, Newport, Pontypool, Pontypridd, Swansea, Bangor and Beaumaris, Carnarvon, Hawarden, Holywell, Pwllheli." [1]

In most of the larger County Boroughs the Boards of Guardians —in contrast with those of the rural Unions, but with no greater statutory powers or duties—made steady progress in the development of their Poor Law Infirmaries, not only into institutions entirely distinct from the Workhouse, but into General Hospitals. The buildings and equipment were repeatedly improved, the nursing staffs became steadily more adequate and better trained, the number of resident Medical Officers was increased, and their ministrations were increasingly supplemented by specialist consultants. Where (as was in many places the case) the Voluntary Hospital was either lacking, or inadequate to the demands for admission, the Poor Law Infirmary became more and commonly resorted to by the whole wage-earning class, and even by the less well-off of the middle-class, frequently even on payment of a part or the whole of the estimated cost of the maintenance and treatment of the patient. The Local Government Board, whilst helpfully critical as to the plans and estimates, and often making useful suggestions for securing both greater efficiency and greater economy, never objected, in principle, to this steady but

---

[1] Forty-second Annual Report of Local Government Board, 1913, Report of H. R. Williams, p. 87. It need scarcely be said that these Boards of Guardians admittedly had no more and no other legal powers, or statutory duty, with regard to tuberculosis than with regard to rheumatism and heart disease, pneumonia and cancer. With the adoption by the Local Health Authorities of the duty of providing for tuberculosis, under the Public Health (Tuberculosis) Act of 1921, these Poor Law sanatoria were everywhere abandoned to the Borough or District Councils.

sporadic elaboration of the Poor Law Infirmary into the General Hospital.[1]

It was, however, in the Unions of the Metropolitan area that most progress continued to be made in what had been, as long ago as 1870, officially termed " the hospital branch of the Poor Law ". In addition to the great hospitals for infectious diseases maintained by the Metropolitan Asylums Board, which (although provided at the expense of the Poor Rate) had long ceased to be typical Poor Law institutions,[2] each of the London Unions had its own separate Poor Law Infirmary, serving, in its own district, as a General Hospital, which presently came to be used, with little feeling of pauperism, by nearly the whole of the sick poor.

" Of the 33,717 paupers under medical treatment or care in separate poor law institutions for the sick throughout England and Wales on 4th November, 1911," we are told that " 13,727 or nearly 41 per cent, were relieved in institutions in London " ; [3] being more than three-fourths of all the paupers under medical treatment, and actually 28·8 per cent of all London's pauperism. Moreover, between 1909 and 1914, special efforts were made to get as large a proportion as possible of the sufferers from tuberculosis in the Metropolis into institutions, with a view either to a cure or at least an arrest of the disease in its early stages *before destitution in a pecuniary sense had set in* ; or, on the other hand, to the isolation and treatment of patients in the advanced stages. This campaign was undertaken wholly at the expense of the Poor Rate. The Metropolitan Asylums Board, acting as a Poor Law Authority, opened five institutions with 2872 beds principally for the open-air treatment of tuberculosis in its early stages. These, in 1911–1912, received, for a longer or shorter stay, 1732 men, 832 women and 308 children. The twenty-seven Separate

---

[1] This was, indeed, only a continuation of the policy initiated by the Poor Law Board in 1867 ; and (we believe) uninterruptedly pursued by the Local Government Board, at least in the Unions comprising any large town.

[2] " The patients in the fever and small-pox hospitals [of the Metropolitan Asylums Board] on the 1st January, 1914, numbered 5042. They are not included in this table [of pauperism] as it is provided by Section 80 (4) of the Public Health (London) Act, 1891, that the maintenance in such hospitals of a person suffering from infectious disease shall not be considered to be parochial relief " (Forty-third Annual Report of Local Government Board, 1914, p. ix).

[3] Forty-second Annual Report of Local Government Board, 1913.

Infirmaries of the several Boards of Guardians ; the two remaining " Sick Asylums " maintained by Joint Committees of such Boards ; [1] and even eleven of the General Mixed Workhouses in which separate sick wards could be allocated to the cases, were all made available, on the advice, and even the pressure, of the Local Government Board, for the gratuitous treatment of as many of the patients suffering from this particular disease as their medical attendants, or the Poor Law doctors, could be induced to recommend for admission. It is interesting to note the complacency with which the Local Government Board of these years records this extreme widening of the scope of Poor Relief, very largely to persons who were pressed to accept it, many of them not " destitute " of anything but such costly institutional provision.[2] Yet the legal powers and statutory duties of the Metropolitan Boards of Guardians were no different with regard to persons suffering from tuberculosis than with regard to those suffering from other kinds of ill-health.

There were, however, certain permanent discouragements in respect of the better provision for the sick under the Poor Law, which are constantly referred to in the reports of the Inspectorate or by the speakers at Poor Law Conferences. Boards of Guardians were not authorised to " seek out " persons needing treatment in the early stages of disease. They could not treat them unless they were destitute, and the average Guardian failed to understand, what even the Inspectors did not explain, that to be " destitute " was now held to mean nothing more than to be unable to pay for the expensive treatment required. The Guardians were, in fact, bound hand and foot by the long tradition of actually deterring persons from applying for relief, even for medical relief only, unaccompanied by maintenance.[3] And they were not empowered, or even recommended, to insist on

---

[1] The "Central London" and the "Poplar and Stepney" Sick Asylum Districts.

[2] Forty-second Annual Report of Local Government Board, 1913, pp. lxii, 202-203.

[3] This tradition endured even after the Reports of the Poor Law Commission of 1905-1909 ; and we find experienced Guardians regretting that Medical Relief " no longer disenfranchises the recipient ; it is better that one man should lose his vote than that one single mark of the inferiority of the State-supported man to the self-supported man should be removed. It is independence, not dependence, that we want ; and everything that is being done for us by State provision, and not by our own effort, tends to degrade and demoralise us " (*Poor Law Conferences, 1910–1911*, p. 124).

the patient staying until he was completely cured. Thus the Medical Officer of the King's Norton Workhouse stated in 1911, " The most striking points brought out by analysis of the cases of Pulmonary Tuberculosis treated in our ' open-air ' wards are the preponderance of male over female patients and the extremely high death - rate. The preponderance of male over female patients is, I think, in some measure due to the fact that the men, being bread-winners, relief is quickly sought *on their becoming too ill to work* ; they are then advised to come into the ' open-air ' wards for treatment. The death-rate among males was $37\frac{1}{2}$ per cent, the average age being a little over 44 years. Among females the death-rate was $27\frac{7}{9}$ per cent, the average age being a little over 33 years. Death occurs, therefore, just at the prime of life in both sexes, the women dying at a younger age than the men. The high death-rate is due to the fact that the majority of our cases are in an advanced stage of the disease on admission, and although with open-air treatment, rest, good food, etc., they often improve considerably, a cure cannot be anticipated." [1]

" Frequently," stated in 1911 the Inspector for the West Midland District, " when a patient improves in health he takes his discharge before he should ; he returns to his usual occupation, which is often unsuitable considering his complaint, and the result is a relapse ; finally he returns to the Workhouse or Infirmary to die. In the meantime he has often been living with his family, with the risk of infection to his wife and children."[2] Hence the conception of the Poor Law Infirmary, not as a curative establishment, but merely as an isolation hospital to prevent the dying person from contaminating the healthy inmates of his home ! " A vast majority of hopeless cases that come under the administrative control of the Poor Law are hopeless cases," reported in 1911 P. H. Bagenal, one of the ablest of the Poor Law Inspectors of that time, " that is to say, cases which no amount of outdoor treatment or improved diet can cure. It follows, therefore, that *the main task of Boards of Guardians must be to benefit the community by diminishing the centres of infection* ; and this is best done by providing accommodation for the hopeless

---

[1] Fortieth Annual Report of Local Government Board, 1911, Report of Dr. Ellis, p. 63, included in Report of E. B. Wethered.
[2] *Ibid.*, E. B. Wethered's Report, p. 62.

cases on the Workhouse site. The small number of curable cases which come under the Poor Law can best be dealt with by sending them to sanatoria, where they can have the full benefit of modern treatment. Guardians should, however, grasp the fact that *the problem of phthisis, as far as they are concerned, mainly consists in the treatment of the bedridden consumptive* ; and that by dealing with these they are diminishing the total mass of infection throughout the Union." [1] Truly a counsel of despair, which would hardly encourage any high standard of efficiency in hospital administration !

With institutions working under circumstances so discouraging to the doctors and nurses, it was natural to look for low standards of hospital efficiency. This, in itself, made advance difficult. " Except in the larger Separate Infirmaries " [existing in less than 10 per cent of the Unions], reported an Inspector in 1914, " which are in no way inferior to the best general hospitals, neither the conditions of life, the prospects, nor the class of case in a Poor Law Institution are likely to attract the trained nurse who has an ambition to excel in her profession. There are an increasing number of openings for a good nurse where her work is more interesting and her prospects brighter than under the Poor Law ; and in the smaller country institutions, even when trained nurses are obtainable, they do not remain long." [2]

Another cause of discouragement in the Poor Law treatment of sickness was the inability of Boards of Guardians to exercise any control over the environment of the sick person, past, present or future. When the Local Health Authority was required to provide Isolation Hospitals for cholera and typhus, scarlet fever and smallpox, it acquired and exercised the power to *prevent the*

[1] Fortieth Annual Report of Local Government Board, 1911, P. H. Bagenal's Report, p. 91. Under the Public Health (Tuberculosis) Act, 1921, the duty of providing for tuberculosis patients at all stages of the disease was assumed by the Local Health Authorities. Venereal disease presents an equally strong case for early treatment, before destitution has set in ; and this led the Venereal Disease Commission in 1916 to recommend that the action urgently required to cope with its ravages should be taken, not by the Poor Law Authorities (although a large proportion of the sufferers became paupers as soon as they were disabled), but by the Local Health Authorities, which were to press the patients to apply for the earliest possible treatment, to be supplied gratuitously, in strict secrecy, and without stigma or penalty of any kind. By the action taken in 1917, all the sufferers from this class of disease were accordingly " taken out of the Poor Law ", and given absolutely gratuitous treatment.

[2] Forty-third Annual Report of Local Government Board, 1914, C. F. Roundell's Report, pp. 31-32.

occurrence of these diseases, through a better water supply, improved drainage and stricter sanitary arrangements, so as to diminish its own expenditure on treatment. But heart disease and rheumatism, phthisis and infantile paralysis were, in 1909–1914, still mainly " Poor Law diseases ", though they were aggravated or disseminated by bad environment. " Not only has there been avoidable mortality . . . and presumably prejudice to the health of survivors ", stated one of the Local Government Board Inspectors in 1911 in criticism of a Local Health Authority, " but the Poor Rate has had to pay in expert nursing and maintenance for what was saved to the Sanitary Rates by not providing proper drainage arrangements. Without improved housing and sanitation, there seems little prospect of much further diminution in the bodily and mental unfitness to which so large a proportion of pauperism is due ; and even from the material point of view of the ratepayer there seems a case for expenditure in this direction." [1] The unwisdom of such parsimony might be brought home to a Local Health Authority because it had powers of sanitation. But the Board of Guardians had to stand idly by, and merely receive the expensive patients, without being able to check their multiplication.

Combinations of Unions

The most constant aspiration of Poor Law administration during the years immediately preceding the Great War was, however, a loudly expressed yearning for combinations of Unions to undertake all the various tasks that individual Unions had found beyond their capacity, such as the effective treatment of tuberculosis, of epilepsy or of mental deficiency ; and most intractable of all, the administration of the provision for the standing army of Vagrants.[2] This aspiration towards larger

---

[1] Forty-first Annual Report of Local Government Board, 1912, Report of E. D. Court, p. 91.

[2] For half a century, as we have related (pp. 262-265 of Vol. I.), the Central Authority had tried to induce the Boards of Guardians to combine for the maintenance of Separate Poor Law Schools. Yet it could be said, in 1913, that " In the whole of England and Wales to-day there are only six School Districts, four of which are in the Metropolis ; and the whole six Districts only represent in the aggregate the areas of fifteen Boards of Guardians, of which ten are in the Metropolis. And yet the District School provision was enacted in 1844 that ' Workhouse children ' might be altogether removed from

areas through combinations of Unions was, in fact, an alternative to the proposals of the Majority of the Poor Law Commissioners in favour of transferring all the Poor Law institutions to the Municipal and County Authorities. " As far as one who is not behind the scenes can judge," remarked an Inspector of the Local Government Board in 1911, " the Government are in no hurry to adopt either the Majority or Minority scheme of the Royal Commissioners ; but are leaning more in the direction of the combination of existing areas and the retention of Boards of Guardians. This will suit the views of Guardians much better than any scheme for handing over their powers to County Councils and County Borough Councils ; and if Guardians, especially those representing small country Unions, will recognise that each Union, acting for itself alone, cannot secure the proper care of all the many classes of inmates which Workhouses contain, and that combination or co-operation, in some shape or other, is a necessity, the threatened extinction of Boards of Guardians may be indefinitely postponed." [1]

" A feature of the year 1910 ", stated another Inspector, " was the increased interest shown by Guardians in the principle of institutional treatment for certain diseases of inmates of Workhouses by means of combinations of Boards for the purpose. The classes chiefly considered are those suffering from phthisis, epileptics, feeble-minded and certified inmates generally." [2] " At the same time, if classes of persons now outside the Poor Law are to be brought within its province", urged Sir William Chance, " we must be prepared for the establishment of District Poor Law Authorities, representative of the Boards of Guardians in the district, covering wider areas than the existing Poor Law Unions, so as to enable certain classes of ' dependants ' to be dealt with in a more satisfactory manner than is possible at present. But I believe that very little, if any, legislation is

---

Workhouses ! " (" Co-operation between Boards of Guardians by Joint Committees or otherwise ; the Difficulties in the Way, and their best Solution ", by R. A. Leach, *Poor Law Conferences, 1912–1913*, pp. 540-556). The idea of combination, abandoned with regard to Poor Law schools, was now revived with regard to some other sections of paupers.

[1] *Poor Law Conferences, 1910–1911*, letter from H. Jenner-Fust, who had, until 1906, been a L.G.B. Inspector, p. 249.

[2] Fortieth Annual Report of Local Government Board, 1910, Report of Mr. E. B. Wethered, p. 62.

necessary for this, and that the Local Government Board have full powers to establish such District Boards." [1]

This idea of retaining the *ad hoc* elected Poor Law Authority, whilst extending its area, had been, in fact, as stated by a delegate to the Poor Law Conference, embodied in the proposals laid before the Poor Law Commission by Charles Booth, and strongly supported by Sir Arthur Downes. " The possibilities arising from amalgamation and combination of Unions are immense, both from the point of view of economy, and of efficient administration. Combination would prevent the dissipation of resources in small rural Unions in the laudable attempt to cover the whole field of Poor Law operations, and in these days of easy communication and transit, it is not difficult of accomplishment. The benefits are so obvious as to need no explanation or defence. The only question is as to the powers of Boards of Guardians in this regard. . . . Section 8 of the Poor Law Act, 1879, confers statutory powers on the Local Government Board to make an Order combining two or more Unions, not in the Metropolis, ' for any purpose connected with the administration of the relief of the poor, etc.' Again, Dr. Downes, in his Memorandum, tells us that powers already exist, more elastic and more extensive than the ' proposals of the Report, whereby any necessary extension of area, any combination of local administration, or any classification could be effected '." [2]

In 1909–1913 the idea was taken up with eagerness with a view to providing for the institutional treatment of feebleminded or mentally defective persons. The Local Government Board Inspectors gladly reported the beginnings of combination for this purpose. " There has been for some time a great increase of interest ", stated P. H. Bagenal, " in the care and treatment of the mentally defective under the Poor Law in Yorkshire ; and there is at present some hope that a strong combination of Unions in the West Riding will be formed to deal with the question. On the 27th September 1912 a conference of representatives of the Sheffield, Barnsley, Dewsbury, Doncaster, Eccleshall Bierlow, Halifax, Hemsworth, Huddersfield, Penistone, Pontefract, Wakefield and Wortley Unions met to consider

---

[1] *Poor Law Conferences, 1910–1911,* Paper by Sir William Chance on " Old and New Ideas on Public Relief," pp. 327-328.

[2] *Poor Law Conferences, 1911–1912,* Paper by Rev. W. Morgan, pp. 379-380.

the question at the Union Offices, Westbar, Sheffield ; and some progress has been made by the appointment of a provisional committee." [1]

"The number of mentally defective and epileptic persons chargeable to the Guardians is steadily increasing," reported another Inspector, "and the Guardians are maintaining practically the whole of these cases in institutions specially adapted for them. It is hoped that the scheme proposed with regard to a combination of Boards of Guardians in the county of Suffolk for the care and treatment of feeble-minded and epileptics will be adopted and come into operation at an early date." [2] Some of the necessary Orders were actually prepared. "In matters relating to the care of the feeble-minded", another Inspector observed, "an Order forming a Joint Committee has been issued in draft to the Essex Guardians ; and in Suffolk at a meeting of delegates, held at Ipswich, it was unanimously resolved that the various Boards of Guardians in the county should apply to the Local Government Board for powers to form a joint committee." [3]

But the actual progress was slow. The period under review, it was said of the South-western Counties in 1913, "has been occupied in this district in ' marking time ' so far as concerns the projected provision of accommodation for mental cases by combinations of Boards of Guardians. The check has been mainly caused by the prevailing feeling of uncertainty as to what would be the outcome of the Government's legislation as regards the country generally ; and, so far as regards the south-western counties, of proposals put forward by private individuals, and in addition there have been the usual objections to be met, economic, sentimental, and so on." [4]

---

[1] Forty-second Annual Report of Local Government Board, 1913, Report of P. H. Bagenal, p. 76.

[2] *Ibid.*, Report of G. A. F. Hervey, p. 31.

[3] *Ibid.* p. 33.   [4] *Ibid.*, Report of E. D. Court, p. 43.

The history of this idea of combination among Poor Law Unions, with a survey of the law, and of the difficulties encountered in its application, is given in an able paper by R. A. Leach, Clerk to the Rochdale Union, in 1912. The first provision was made by the Poor Law Amendment Act, 1844 (7 and 8 Victoria, c. 101), "for the combination, by Order of the Central Poor Law Authority, of Unions and single parishes into School Districts for the institutional management of orphan and deserted chargeable children, and for chargeable children in respect of whom the Guardians have the consent of parents, or the surviving parent, or the legal guardian, for institutional

" As a result of the resolution passed last year at Chester," stated Lord Richard Cavendish in his presidential address to a Poor Law Conference in 1913, " at this moment steps have been taken to utilise the Lunesdale Workhouse as a place for the reception of feeble-minded children, and Tarvin Workhouse for adults. . . . The real importance, to my mind," added optimistically the noble President, " is that we have laid the foundation for future joint enterprise on the part of Guardians. If we can combine for such purposes as the care and detention of feeble-minded, surely it is not too much to hope that in the varied work—and it is very varied work which the Poor Law now embraces—it will be possible to arrange for further co-operation. I foresee a great field of usefulness to this and other similar Conferences, because it is only at meetings such as this that we can ventilate our opinions and form the sub-committees by which it is possible to deal with these matters." [1]

Unfortunately all these recommendations, whether by individual members of the Royal Commission of 1905–1909, by the Poor Law Division of the Local Government Board, or by the more progressive members of the Boards of Guardians, were discussed at meetings, and voiced in resolutions at Poor Law Conferences, but not carried out in practice. One of the Local Government Board Inspectors quotes with obvious agreement a description of a Poor Law Conference in 1910. " ' The Conference was hardly distinguishable from similar gatherings at any time for a generation past. The delegates voted, as they have been voting for many years, in favour of powers of detention over feeble-minded persons. They voted, for what seems like the fourteenth millionth time, that " in the opinion of the conference it is desirable that Boards of Guardians in each county

---

management. It is unnecessary to elaborate details. One detail of the provision is that the School District Board of Management are elected, in such proportion and in such manner as the Local Government Board may from time to time direct, by all the Boards of Guardians in the combined district, the chairman of each Board, if he consent thereto, being an *ex-officio* member. The second provision referred to is section 8 of the Poor Law Act, 1879 (41 and 42 Victoria, c. 54), which applies to the provinces only, the Metropolis being dealt with by the Metropolitan Poor Acts " (" Co-operation between Boards of Guardians by Joint Committees or Otherwise ; the Difficulties in the Way, and their best Solution ", by R. A. Leach, *Poor Law Conferences, 1912–1913*, pp. 540-556).

[1] *Poor Law Conferences, 1912–1913*, pp. 490-491.

should take into consideration the desirability of combining for the purpose of the treatment of the feeble-minded ". Should take into consideration ! Why, they have been doing that for years until Guardians seem to have persuaded themselves into the belief that passing resolutions about the matter is the same thing as dealing with it. They say " Hear, Hear " and " No, No ", as they have been saying it for as many years as the memory of the oldest delegate would carry back, when someone read a paper asking, " Was the Workhouse the proper place to bring up children ? " Take it for all in all, the Conference might have been merely a gramophone record of the annual conferences of ten or twenty years ago ! ' " [1]

" Although during the last two or three years ", we are told in Mr. Leach's paper, " Boards of Guardians in many Counties have been discussing combinations for dealing with the feeble-minded and others ", only four Joint Committees have been formed. " Of these four combinations, one is that of the Liverpool, West Derby, and Toxteth Park Boards of Guardians, for a joint hospital for consumptives ; another is that of the Manchester and South Manchester Boards of Guardians, for a colony for epileptics ; another is that of the last two mentioned Boards, for joint Casual Wards ; and the fourth is that—brought into existence last April—of the Amesbury and nine other Boards of Guardians in Wiltshire for a joint home for epileptics and feeble-minded. There was a combination by the Birmingham group of Unions for dealing with epileptics and feeble-minded ; but the Birmingham group have, during the present year, become one Union for all purposes " ; [2] and, it may be added,

---

[1] Fortieth Annual Report of Local Government Board, 1911, G. A. F. Hervey's Report, pp. 49-50.

[2] *Poor Law Conferences, 1912-1913*, pp. 542-543. In 1913, the Mental Deficiency Act (3 and 4 George V. c. 28) recognised the undesirability of continuing to pester Boards of Guardians to supply the treatment required for the mentally defective, and placed the duty upon the Lunacy Authorities. The only separate Poor Law Institutions now (1928) maintained by Boards of Guardians for this class are those at Monyhull and Erdington by the Birmingham Union ; that at Seafield House by the West Derby Union—these two representing former Joint Committees which were merged in complete amalgamations of the combining Unions—those of the Metropolitan Asylums Board, which is an independent Poor Law Authority for this and other purposes ; and two only under Joint Committees, namely, that of Great Barr Park (Walsall and West Bromwich Unions Joint Committee), and that of Prudhoe Hall (Northern Counties Joint Poor Law Committee). See Thirteenth Annual Report of Board of Control, 1927, pp. 39-41, 76.

two of the other instances were also soon merged in the amalgamations of the West Derby (Liverpool) and Manchester Unions.

To remedy this apathy, it was suggested that the Local Government Board should compel Boards of Guardians to combine for specialised institutions. Such a power of compulsion had not been explicitly conferred by the statutes authorising combination ; but the Central Authority, as already mentioned, had power to unite, in Unions for particular purposes, any parishes that it thought fit ; and it was often suggested that, in this or other ways, the necessary joint provision might be made for particular classes. But this notion of compulsion was hotly resented. " It has not been, nor may it ever be expected to be the policy of the Local Government Board, to directly compel co-operation between Boards of Guardians, although it is reasonable, as well as the duty of the Central Authority, to compel defaulting Boards to make good their default. A policy compelling co-operation would be a serious interference with the principle of local self-government ; and Boards of Guardians would not be worth their salt if they were not ready, did need arise, to resist such a policy." [1]

In short, Boards of Guardians nearly always continued to find it impossible or impracticable, as they had done ever since 1834, to combine to establish and administer a joint institution. Neither the Poor Law Commissioners, nor the Poor Law Board, nor the Local Government Board—much as they desired, in different decades, to get such combinations established—had ever provided proper machinery for the purpose. The statutory powers were far from adequate, as they did not extend to raising money by loan, with which to build a common institution, although the Joint Committee could invite its constituent Unions to raise their several shares of the required loan. The Joint Committee could apparently own no real property, which had to remain vested in the constituent Boards of Guardians. Moreover, down to 1910, the members of the Joint Committee, who were termed " Managers ", were habitually appointed at dates not coinciding with the dates at which the electors chose their representatives on the Boards of Guardians, so that the membership and policy of the Joint Committees were practically

[1] *Poor Law Conferences, 1912–1913*, p. 543.

beyond all control by the electorate.[1] " It is more than the play of mere sentiment ", suggested the experienced Clerk to the Rochdale Union, " to contend that the setting up of a local spending Authority, not directly answerable to the ratepayers, is unjustifiable, unless the setting up of the Authority is the only way to secure a paramount public or local advantage. The larger the area for which the joint committees are to act, the more substantial becomes the objection to their creation." [2]

An easier alternative to combinations of Unions, and one often suggested, was that Boards of Guardians might at least make use of each other's institutions. Boards of Guardians had no power actually to provide accommodation for any persons not chargeable to their own Union ; but there had long been nothing to prevent them from receiving, by agreement, in any existing institutions, persons remitted to them by other Boards of Guardians. " Under Section 14 of the Poor Law Amendment Act, 1849, as amended by Section 22 of the Divided Parishes and Poor Law Amendment Act, 1876, the Guardians of any Union may contract to receive in their Workhouse persons chargeable to another Union in any case in which the Local Government Board shall deem it expedient and shall give their consent. There are ", it was said in 1913, " many agreements under this section, generally in respect of particular classes of chargeable persons. This section is only useful when a Union has surplus accommodation." [3] But although this surplus of accommodation existed in many Unions, the objection to pay money outside the Union's area, and thus lose control over its expenditure—often put as an objection to entrusting their own paupers to the care of strangers — prevented this method from being adopted, otherwise than exceptionally, by a number of the Boards of Guardians. Even when no objection was made to the principle, difficulties arose about the amount of the charge made by the receiving Union, especially as the full cost of maintenance per head often seemed to be in excess of the cost per head in the Union from which the persons were to be sent.

---

[1] This defect was not remedied for more than half a century, and then only for the Metropolitan area. In September 1910, the Local Government Board issued an Order providing that, from May 1913, the triennial election of Managers shall take place shortly after the elections of the Guardians of the constituent Unions (Fortieth Annual Report of Local Government Board, 1911, p. lxvi.).

[2] *Poor Law Conferences, 1912–1913*, p. 544.   [3] *Ibid.*, p. 284.

Eventually some of these difficulties were got over (but only within the Metropolis) by the Local Government Board, which (as the Guardians were reminded in 1913) had, under the Metropolitan Poor Act, 1867, " when they are of opinion that the Workhouse (that is, any Poor Law institution) of a Union in the Metropolis is adapted only for the reception of a particular class or classes but is capable of accommodating poor persons of that class or classes from any other Union in the Metropolis, to issue an Order directing the Guardians to receive and maintain in that Workhouse these poor persons. " Orders under this section have been issued recently in two cases : (1) Belmont Workhouse, under the management of the Fulham Guardians, for able-bodied and for epileptics ; (2) Bow Institution, under the management of the City of London Guardians, for adult males suffering or recovering from chronic diseases. In this case adult males who require more skilled nursing than a Workhouse provides and not the expensive treatment of an Infirmary, are received. Male nurses only are to be employed, and the Institution is to provide a long-felt want in the Poor Law service, viz., an institution where male nurses can be trained. The Act referred to should be extended to extra-Metropolitan Unions." [1] This, however, was never done.

Vagrancy

It will be remembered that the Departmental Committee on Vagrancy in 1905 had been so convinced of the inability of the Boards of Guardians to grapple effectively with the problem of Vagrancy that it recommended that the whole of this trouble-some class of men and women, wandering on the roads pro-fessedly in search of employment, should be taken out of the Poor Law, and handed over to the County and Borough police forces : a recommendation which was endorsed by the Majority Com-missioners of 1905–1909. Most of the Boards of Guardians were not particularly willing to let the Vagrants go, and the Home Office refused to plant them on the Watch Committees and Standing Joint Committees which did not want them ; and Poor Law ad-ministrators generally were anxious to prove that Vagrancy could be adequately dealt with by the existing Poor Law Authorities.

---

[1] *Poor Law Conferences, 1912–1913*, p. 284 ; 29 and 30 Victoria, c. 6.

It so happened that, largely owing to the expansion of trade between 1909 and 1914, they were able to show that the particular methods proposed by the Central Authority and adopted by many Boards of Guardians, had, in fact, been coincident with what was counted as success, the number of Vagrants accommodated in Poor Law Institutions on one night of the year dropping from 14,757 in June 1909 to 7719 on January 1, 1914.

The most scandalous manifestation of Vagrancy in 1909, because it came under the direct observation of the wealthy inhabitants of the West End, and the politicians and journalists in particular, were those unfortunate men and women who slept out, night after night, on the Thames Embankment between Chelsea and Blackfriars, or in the open spaces within and adjacent to the Metropolis. Not that there was insufficient accommodation afforded by the Metropolitan Boards of Guardians : many of their Casual Wards were nearly empty night after night. What happened was that the treatment meted out to those who sought these shelters was markedly uneven. It was lax and indulgent in some Unions and harsh and even cruel in others, with the consequence that the Casual Wards in the former became so full that they had to close their doors to the late-comers. " Each Casual Ward in London ", explained an Inspector in 1910, " is under the management of a separate Board of Guardians, and though endeavours have been made to ensure a uniform system of treatment throughout the whole of London, the attempts have proved unsuccessful ; and, it would seem, are likely to continue so, so long as the regulations are interpreted by a different body for each Ward. The Casual Poor Act of 1882 (45 and 46 Victoria, c. 36) provided that, for the purpose of determining the number of admissions of a casual pauper, every Casual Ward in the Metropolis is to be deemed a Casual Ward of the same Union, and it would appear that the only way to insure equality of treatment in the Wards made one for the purposes of detention by this Act is that they should be made one for the purpose of administration. At present the tasks differ, the food differs, and the detention differs, and the habitual Vagrant is the first to discover where he is most comfortable, and to make his arrangements accordingly." [1]

[1] Fortieth Annual Report of Local Government Board, 1911, J. S. Oxley's Report, p. 36.

To remedy this unequal treatment, the obligation and duty to relieve Vagrants, together with all the existing Casual Wards in London, were transferred by the Metropolitan Casual Paupers Order, 1911, and the Metropolitan Casual Wards Transfer Order, 1912, from the 28 Boards of Guardians to the Metropolitan Asylums Board, which was assisted by a voluntary " Houseless Poor Committee ", made up of members of that Board and representatives of charitable agencies. " The result of this change ", we are told in a Circular Letter from the Local Government Board to the London Boards of Guardians, " has been to secure uniformity of treatment in the several Casual Wards, and a more systematic discrimination as regards those resorting to the Wards, while the Managers, as the Authority in charge, have been enabled to co-operate with various charitable organisations in a genuine effort to assist such of those persons coming under their care as appear likely to respond to a helping hand." [1]

Within a couple of years, we find it stated in the Local Government Board Report of 1913–1914 that the new administration had " almost entirely cleared the sleeping-out class from the neighbourhood of the Embankment ",[2] and had actually closed 16 Casual Wards, 12 being found sufficient to accommodate all the houseless poor in the Metropolis having a right to Poor Law relief.

The administration of the Vagrancy Acts by provincial Boards of Guardians was even more chaotic than it had been in the Metropolis, with every degree of penal harshness and sentimental indulgence. Thus the Chairman of the Test House Committee at Nottingham stated that " it was extremely difficult to distinguish between the good and the bad tramp, and that it did not take very long for an honest wayfarer to degenerate into an habitual Vagrant. It largely depended upon the treatment he received, and the treatment in some Unions was scandalous. He was so treated not because he was of the criminal class, but because he was poor. It was not right to treat every tramp as a scamp, and do nothing to assist him on the way. Sending him without a ticket for food, or any help, was

---

[1] Forty-second Annual Report of Local Government Board, 1913, pp. 3 and 4, and J. S. Oxley's Report.

[2] Forty-third Annual Report of Local Government Board, 1914, p. xviii.

putting a premium on begging. . . . The ' work-shy ' preferred prison to the Nottingham Test House, so their treatment
could be imagined, but they gave them something better than
bread and water, namely, gruel and bread and cheese. The
Way-Ticket appeared to be a sort of licence, but the paper
omitted to say whether it was permanent in operation or could
run out." [1] In Lincolnshire, the Prison Commissioners drew
attention to the overcrowding of the Lincoln Gaol by Vagrants,
owing to the absence of any decent Poor Law accommodation
for the men on the road.

On the other hand, a Yorkshire Union suddenly decided to
increase its indulgence of the Vagrant. A better supper was
provided, and " stone-breaking was abolished on the score of
humanity, and only one night's detention was demanded, and
a light task of two hours enforced. Naturally, the Sculcoates
Workhouse became a Mecca for all the ' Vagrom ' men of the
East Riding. The Vagrant Master reported, at the end of the
year, that ' the lighter task induced the same casuals to come
more frequently and at shorter intervals than before '. The
total number of admissions for the last quarter of the year was
586 as compared with 141 for the corresponding quarter of 1909.
The object of the Casual Poor Act of 1882 (45 and 46 Victoria,
c. 36) was to secure uniformity of treatment, particularly with
regard to detention for two nights ; a discipline which when
combined with a task of work would prove most irksome to the
professional tramp. Provision has been made for excusal from
the performance of the task in cases where it is not suited to the
age, strength or capacity of the person detained. The action
of one Union, in altering the treatment without any consideration
for the practice of the neighbouring Unions, can only operate in
favour of the professional roadsters, who are always willing to
vary their route according to the treatment they receive at each
Workhouse. Repressive measures may not be the last word on
Vagrancy, but Guardians would be better advised to combine and
consider a uniform system for a district than to act suddenly
and independently on impulse." [2]

" Anglesey and Carnarvonshire ", reported a medical delegate

[1] *Poor Law Conferences, 1912–1913*, pp. 584-585.
[2] Fortieth Annual Report of Local Government Board, 1911, Report of
P. H. Bagenal, p. 94.

to the North Wales Poor Law Conference in 1912, " seem to be the happy hunting - ground of tramps ; and probably the other counties of North Wales are equally favoured by these undesirable guests. The comfort of Welsh Workhouses is well known ; this led in 1904–1905 to a great influx of the vagrant class into Wales, and the prisons were filled by tramps who rebelled against regulations. To such an extent did this obtain that, ' two or three times a week, batches of tramps had to be removed from the prisons of Carnarvon and Ruthin to Shrewsbury and Knutsford, and even to other gaols in English towns '." [1]

Meanwhile, urged by the Poor Law Division and its Inspectorate, certain provincial Unions had adopted the Bread Ticket System. " The main object of this system ", we are told in the Circular of 4th February 1913, " is to secure co-operation between the several Boards of Guardians in the County, with a view to a more uniform treatment of the casual paupers, while, by means of a voluntary committee, to which the Guardians, with the Board's consent, make contributions, provision is made for securing a midday meal for Vagrants who leave the Casual Wards in the morning. The importance of this midday meal is twofold. It removes the objection, pointed out by the Departmental Committee on Vagrancy, that a Vagrant, after he leaves the Casual Ward, has no means of getting a meal until he arrives at the next Ward. As they say, ' If he is really destitute, and cannot get any work, he is practically bound to beg or steal any meal he gets during the day '. And, secondly, in removing this excuse for begging, it takes away a reason for the indiscriminate giving of alms which is so strong an encouragement to Vagrancy." [2]

A more detailed account of this policy is given by the Inspector of the West Midland Counties, Mr. R. G. Duff (who had been Secretary to the Royal Commission of 1905–1909), which, according to him, consists of three features :

" (1) ' Bread-stations ' are established at convenient distances between the various Casual Wards at which all Vagrants can, on production of a bread-ticket, obtain a midday meal, the object being to do away with the excuse for begging which exists where no mid-day meal is provided.

---

[1] *Poor Law Conferences, 1912–1913*, Paper by Dr. T. W. Clay, p. 421.
[2] Forty-second Annual Report of Local Government Board, 1913, p. 4.

" (2) Each genuine working-man in search of work applying for admission to a Casual Ward is provided with a ' Way-Ticket ' which shows the route the man intends to follow, and as long as he keeps to that route, he is passed on from Casual Ward to Casual Ward as quickly as possible, without having to perform the ' tasks ' prescribed for the ordinary Vagrant.

" (3) The dietary for each class of Vagrants, as well as the nature of the tasks and the period of detention enforced on Vagrants not entitled to Way-Tickets, are supposed to be uniform in all Casual Wards in the area, and Vagrants not entitled to ' Way-Tickets ' are detained for the full period authorised by law." [1]

In order to carry out this system, groups of Boards of Guardians in the same County or adjacent Counties were encouraged to form Joint Vagrancy Committees, with a view to adopting a uniform treatment of Vagrants, based on discriminating between the *bona fide* traveller in search of work and the unemployable man or woman who took to Vagrancy practically as a means of livelihood. According to the Casual Paupers Order, 1913, the old regimen of two nights' detention and a task of work was to be continued for the latter class, whilst the *bona fide* unemployed man or woman honestly seeking work was to be permitted to use the Casual Ward for one night's lodging, and even provided with a ticket which secured a midday meal. " An endeavour is made as far as possible to confine the giving of ' Way-Tickets ' ", reported the Inspector for Essex and Sussex, " to genuine working men who are honestly in search of employment ; and it is therefore a very significant fact, especially in view of the large amount of Unemployment that prevailed during the period covered by these reports, that the proportion of Way-Tickets to the number of male casuals admitted to the Vagrant Wards is so small." On the other hand, he added, " It has been the experience of many of the Workhouse Masters to have the offer of a ' bread ' ticket angrily refused, the refusal being not infrequently accompanied by abuse, one reason for this, amongst others, being that, if found begging whilst in possession of bread tickets, the Vagrant realises that it may be looked upon as an aggravation of the offence." [2]

[1] Forty-third Annual Report of Local Government Board, 1914, Report of R. G. Duff, pp. 56-57.

[2] Thirty-ninth Annual Report of Local Government Board, 1910, p. 25.

" Formerly they begged their way along the road," reported the Inspector for Berks, Bucks and Oxford, " but since the reintroduction of the Way-Ticket System much less is given to the tramps, so now they have to take advantage of the Casual Wards. The increased use of Casual Wards by this class since the Way-Ticket System has been introduced is shown by a slight increase in the number of children, coincident with a considerable reduction in the total number of persons admitted to Casual Wards." [1]

It was hoped, in some quarters, that the establishment of Labour Exchanges in 1909 and of Unemployment Insurance in 1911, would render the Way-Ticket System obsolete. The *bona fide* unemployed man or woman was assumed to obtain from the Labour Exchange a list of all vacancies, and, quite often, he could be provided with a railway fare if he was considered suitable for a job ; whilst insurance provided him (at least if he belonged to the industries most subject to fluctuations) with maintenance during short periods of Unemployment. In 1912, indeed, the general improvement in trade seemed to diminish the number of Vagrants. But to the unscrupulous Vagrant the Insurance Card gave additional claims to unconditional relief. "It is interesting to note that it is reported from 51 Unions that National Health Insurance cards were found in the possession of 4912 men out of a total of about 35,000 admissions to the Casual Wards; but how many of these insured men were *bona fide* cases it is impossible to say, for it has been stated that the wide-awake tramp considers it worth 7d. a week to him to stamp his own card and enjoy the

[1] Forty-third Annual Report of the Local Government Board, 1914, Report of N. Herbert, pp. 25, 48. The futility of the Way-Ticket System, whilst unaccompanied by adequate and suitable treatment of the Vagrant, was represented by many critics. An Inspector, in 1914, was emphatic in his assertion that " The only way to stop this mode of existence is for charitable persons to discontinue giving alms to tramps on the road, and for magistrates to impose sentences which will deter ; but this can scarcely be expected unless the public and magistrates are satisfied that a man on the road can obtain reasonable subsistence without resorting to begging. Of course, the object of Guardians in providing bread-and-water diet is on the theory that it discourages Vagrants ; but the effect is to give, as I have intimated, an excuse for begging which should be removed by a more generous treatment, but not such as would be an encouragement to people to remain on the road and become Vagrants (Forty-third Annual Report of Local Government Board, 1914, Wethered's Report, p. 48). One attempt to provide such treatment was the Training Colony near Wallingford (Berks), established by the National Union for Christian Social Service, with sixty beds (Forty-second Annual Report of Local Government Board, 1913, p. 21).

sweets thereof, by getting let off lightly from the Casual Wards, taskless. The following is, I believe, a true account of the methods adopted by the up-to-date ' Vagrant ' : He no longer cadges from door to door for broken victuals, or money for a night's lodging : instead, he calls at houses in fairly well-to-do neighbourhoods, where servants are kept, and begs an insurance stamp. Few householders can resist the appeal, for it seems so perfectly genuine and straightforward. The beggar produces a partially-stamped Insurance Card, and explains that until he is able to fill up the remaining spaces he cannot hope to obtain work. In nine cases out of ten he gets what he wants, and goes on his way rejoicing, secure in the knowledge that whatever comes he is sure of a week's board and lodging, since in practically all Workhouses it is the custom nowadays, if a tramp produces a stamped Insurance Card, to admit him as a *bona fide* working man. This means that he is not detained, nor made to perform the Labour Test demanded of ordinary casuals, but is provided with a supper and free lodging, and given a meal ticket for his day's journey. So well is this recognised amongst the tramping fraternity that a regular trade in these cards is done during week-ends in the common lodging-houses they frequent. A card fully stamped up-to-date finds ready sale amongst tramps ; and an industrious ' cadger ', gifted with a glib tongue and a fairly decent appearance, finds little difficulty in filling from eight to a dozen cards during a Saturday afternoon and evening, all of them of course being made out in different names." [1]

The Able-bodied Man

A marked feature of the pre-war quinquennium—one which lulled the Poor Law world into a certain complacency—was the numerical dwindling of the pauperism of the healthy able-bodied man. The very category of the Able-bodied, which had held an important place in Poor Law statistics since 1834, was in 1911–1913 wholly abandoned, alike for Outdoor Relief and in Poor Law institutions.[2] Moreover, the Relief

[1] Forty-third Annual Report of the Local Government Board, 1914, Report of G. A. F. Hervey, p. 37.

[2] " Prior to July 1912, it was customary to employ as the main basis of classification of Outdoor paupers the general headings 'Able-bodied' and 'Not able-bodied'. As all reference to this method of grouping was omitted from the

Regulation Order, 1911, whilst in effect continuing the general prohibition of Outdoor Relief to able-bodied men, carefully avoided the use of this term ; and enabled Boards of Guardians, with the tacit concurrence of the Local Government Board, to vary their ordinary procedure in exceptional cases, or in periods of exceptional distress, either by granting Outdoor Relief in return for test work, or by granting Outdoor Relief to the family if the man entered the Workhouse.

There seems to have been little conflict, during this period, between the Boards of Guardians and the Local Government Board. What the Inspectorate had occasion to deprecate was not the granting of Outdoor Relief in the few exceptional cases to which, in nearly all Unions, this was confined, but the opening of the Labour Yard or any other organised provision of " Test Work ". " Many of the men," it was urged, as an argument against opening the Labour Yard as a means of relieving seasonal Unemployment, " when once relieved in this manner, cease to regard a Labour Yard as a means whereby they can tide over periods of temporary distress. Such men yearly become applicants for this mode of relief. The percentage of those who afterwards obtain regular employment is extremely small, whereas a large percentage manage, when the Labour Yard is closed, to subsist by means of casual work." [1] The influence of the Inspectors was largely successful in preventing the opening of the Labour Yard, and in encouraging reliance on organised charity outside the Poor Law.

" Generally speaking it may be said ", reported in 1913 the Inspector for the North-East Coast, " that relief work during this difficult period was characterised as regards the Poor Law

---

regulations contained in the Relief Regulation Order, 1911, a fresh statistical arrangement with regard to Outdoor paupers was adopted in July 1912 " (Forty-second Annual Report of Local Government Board, 1913, p. xiii.).

In the later statistics there is accordingly no mention of the able-bodied, nor of relief on account of Unemployment—a category which had not then appeared in Poor Law administration—the able-bodied, whether male or female, being included under the general head of relieved on account of " other causes " (than sickness, etc.).

With regard to institutional relief, it will be remembered that the abandonment of the old categories of age and diet as a distinction between the Able-bodied and the Non-Able-bodied was definitely effected in the new classificatory scheme provided for by the Poor Law (Institutions) Order of 1913.

[1] Fortieth Annual Report of Local Government Board, 1911, G. Walsh's Report, p. 72.

by a tendency to avoid the introduction of 'test Labour';
and as regards voluntary effort, by a desire to organise (coupled
with a commendable absence of publicity), and by the co-operation of all classes of the community." [1]

But there were exceptions. " Of the two test Labour Yards
still open on January 1st, 1910," the Inspector for the same
district had reported in 1911, " one only, that at Middlesbrough,
continues to exist. The Sunderland Guardians finally closed
their Yard in the late spring, and two great pyramids of broken
stone are still standing to keep alive the memory of that very
expensive undertaking. The position at Middlesbrough is
doubtless affected to some extent by certain peculiarities of local
industry (as the heavy oscillations in the number of able-bodied
paupers from week to week would seem to indicate). Nevertheless, the Guardians' policy of continuing to grant Outdoor Relief
to able-bodied men in a time of reviving trade tends mainly
to the advantage of the inefficient or undeserving, and cannot
be supported." [2]

Under the advice of the Inspectorate the Nottingham Board
of Guardians tried once more the experiment which we have
already described in some detail, of an able-bodied Test Workhouse. The erection of additional premises, it was reported
in 1911, " has enabled the Guardians to set apart one of the
Workhouse blocks for the old and infirm ; and, in addition,
convalescents who were occupying beds in the Infirmary can
now be transferred to wards in the body of the house where
an attendant is on duty. The Test House itself is completely
isolated from the rest of the Workhouse and has its own workshops, etc. The diet, though equally wholesome and sustaining,
is not as attractive as the ordinary workhouse diet. The men
are kept under constant supervision, and, while their quarters
are clean and comfortable, it is felt that the order and discipline

---

[1] Forty-second Annual Report of the Local Government Board, 1913, p. 77,
Report of W. P. Elias.

[2] Fortieth Annual Report of Local Government Board, 1911, Report of
W. P. Elias, p. 97.

Some of the Northumberland and Durham Unions had already become
notorious for their increasing laxity in the relief of able-bodied persons.
" Among such Unions that of Newcastle-upon-Tyne alone shews throughout the
year a consistent and substantial increase in its adult out-pauperism. This
increase is not counterbalanced by any permanent reduction in the number of
the indoor poor, and seems only to be accounted for by a gradual relaxation of
vigilance in the administration of Outdoor Relief " (*Ibid.*).

which is maintained, though certainly not unduly severe, is too irksome to commend itself to those whose independence is not already thoroughly undermined." [1]

Yet, whilst emergencies were met by exceptional treatment, often contrary to the spirit of the Out-Relief Order of 1911, no advance was made towards a solution of the problem of how to provide, both " adequately " and " suitably " for the able-bodied man with more than the smallest number of dependants ; on the one hand without leaving him in idleness, and, on the other, without contravening the paramount injunction that the relief must in all cases be appreciably less than the current wage of the lowest independent labourer. An experienced ex-Chairman of a Board of Guardians declared that the suggestions of the Local Government Board supplied no solution of the problem. It was prescribed by Order, he observed in 1911, that a Board of Guardians could not " relieve an able-bodied man and family without a task of labour. This task, which is to be suitable and adequate, it is not within the power of the Guardians to provide, and the man is expected to go into the House, with its consequent demoralisation. This treatment of the able-bodied is the crux of the situation; the provision of test labour is the hopeless problem. The President of the Local Government Board was recently questioned in the House as to such provision. He is reported to have replied [that] oakum-picking was no longer available or desirable; there was stone-breaking ; but the chief reliance was to be placed on the land ",[2]—upon which we have only to note that the Local Government Board continued consistently to refuse to allow Boards of Guardians to use their statutory powers to obtain land for any such purpose ; powers which were again embodied by Parliament, after they had been omitted, as being obsolete, by the Ministry of Health, in the Poor Law (Consolidation) Act of 1927 (17 and 18 George V. c. 14).

Destitution Resulting from Industrial Disputes

The years immediately preceding the Great War saw, too, the emergence of a still more intractable problem, namely, that

---

[1] Fortieth Annual Report of Local Government Board, 1911, G. Walsh's Report, p. 74.

[2] *Poor Law Conferences, 1911–1912*, Address by Henry J. Manton, p. 3.

of the relief of the destitution resulting directly from Strikes or Lock-outs on a large scale. This problem had been complicated by a decision of the Court of Appeal in 1900, known as the Merthyr Tydfil Judgment,[1] which for the first time declared that it was illegal for the Guardians to give any form of Poor Relief, even on loan, whether Indoor or Outdoor, and with or without a Labour Test, to able-bodied men in health, who could, in fact, obtain employment at wages, but who, for whatever reason, refused or neglected to accept such employment. It was, at the same time, held that the wives and children of such men, if destitute, could lawfully be relieved.

Owing to the industrial circumstances of the time, this momentous decision did not, for more than a decade, appreciably affect Poor Law administration. The years of prosperity with which the century opened made employment abundant, whilst the effect of the Taff Vale Judgment (by which the legal immunity of Trade Unions from actions for damages caused by strikes of their members was destroyed) was practically to prevent strikes on any large scale until the passing of the Trade Disputes Act of 1906, by which that judgment was reversed. In 1912, however, in the extensive and prolonged stoppage of the coal-mining industry, the Inspectors found it necessary to urge the Boards of Guardians in various Unions to open Labour Yards for men thrown out of work by the scarcity of coal.

In the Metropolitan area, many thousands of men were thrown out of work as a result of the dispute at the London Docks in 1912, as well as in consequence of the coal-mining

---

[1] This important judgment, which is often misquoted and misunderstood, demands more minute analysis than we are warranted in inserting at this point ; and such an analysis will be found in the following chapter.

The Taff Vale Judgment (by which the Amalgamated Society of Railway Servants was condemned to pay heavy damages and costs for loss suffered by the Taff Vale Railway Company owing to an entirely peaceful strike) was delivered in 1901 (see Report of Royal Commission on Trade Disputes, Cd. 2825 of 1906; *History of Trade Unionism*, by S. and B. Webb, 1920, pp. 600-608). One of its effects was to paralyse Trade Union activity and greatly to reduce the number of trade disputes, confining these almost entirely to defensive action against employers' attempts to worsen the workmen's conditions. The number of trade disputes known to the Labour Department of the Board of Trade, which had, in the last decade of the nineteenth century, never fallen below 700 in a year, sank in 1903–1905 to half that number, and did not again reach it until 1911. The Trade Disputes Act of 1906, which virtually reversed the Taff Vale Judgment, restored the Trade Union freedom to take concerted action in withdrawing their members' labour.

dispute, and J. S. Oxley, an experienced Poor Law Inspector, observed that " some pressure was brought unofficially with the object of getting the Board to relax the regulations governing the allowance of relief, and to permit the granting of indiscriminate Out-relief, but it was found that the new Relief Regulation Order provided ample powers for coping with the emergency. If it becomes necessary to do more the adoption by the Guardians of Article X. of the Order enables them to give a man institutional relief, and relieve his wife and children outside ; and so a test is provided to show that the relief is really required, and at the same time to ensure that the man is removed from competition in the labour market with those who are not asking for relief, while his family are enabled to keep the home together." [1]

Again, in Walsall in 1913, the Inspector observed that the local strike of unskilled labourers for a minimum wage " is the first important one that has occurred in my district since the issue of the Relief Regulation Order, 1911 ; and it is satisfactory to be able to state that the Guardians of the various Unions concerned were able to deal with the emergency under the powers of that Order without having recourse to any exceptional measures. *Out-relief in kind was given to the families of men thrown out of work by reason of the strike, but not directly to the men themselves*, most of whom were in receipt of strike pay from their Trade Unions." [2]

The attitude of the Local Government Board, in the exceptional Unemployment caused by the dispute in the Coal-mining industry in 1912, is shown by the Circular issued to the Boards of Guardians. This Circular made no allusion to the Merthyr Tydfil Judgment of 1900 ; and clearly indicated the exceptions in the Out-relief Order of 1911 by which the emergency might be met. "It may be expected", said the Circular, "that the class of applicants for relief with whom the Guardians themselves will first have to deal will be composed in the main of those who have already on previous occasions been in receipt of relief, and the Guardians will no doubt consider that it would be imprudent in affording them relief to relax the usual conditions."

[1] Forty-second Annual Report of Local Government Board, 1913, J. S. Oxley's Report, p. 9.
[2] Forty-third Annual Report of Local Government Board, 1914, Report of E. B. Wethered, p. 45.

" The Guardians will remember that the new Relief Regulation Order contains provisions which are specially designed to enable them to vary their ordinary procedure in periods of exceptional distress."

" The powers referred to in Article X. of the Order authorise the Guardians to afford relief other than institutional relief to the wife and family of any person to whom relief is afforded in a Workhouse, and Article XI. enables them to afford relief other than institutional relief to men upon certain conditions, the chief of which is that the men are set to work by the Guardians and kept employed by them and that one-half at least of the relief given shall be relief in kind."

" Although the Order does not come into operation until the beginning of next month, the Board will be prepared to put it in force at once in any Union in which the Guardians think it desirable to exercise the powers above referred to." [1]

The question of the bearing of the Merthyr Tydfil Judgment was, however, not directly raised until the so-called " General Strike " and the prolonged Lock-out in the Coal-mining industry in 1926, to be described subsequently.

Co-operation with Voluntary Agencies

It will be remembered that a prominent feature of the Majority Report of the Poor Law Commission of 1905–1909 was the remarkable, and, as some will think, the exaggerated stress laid on the use of Voluntary Agencies as a sort of superior partner in the Relief of Destitution. " An essential principle ", the Majority Commissioners stated, " to be observed in connection with Home Assistance to the Able-bodied is that it shall be in some way less agreeable than assistance given by the Voluntary Aid Committee." It was explained that, unless the superiority of the assistance afforded by the Voluntary Aid Committee were in some way secured, it was doubtful whether that Committee would be able to collect voluntary subscriptions for the purpose of helping deserving cases of Unemployment. " As we have shown," the Commissioners summed up, " by the inter-action of the Committee of Public Assistance and the Voluntary Aid Committee new forces will be brought into the field ; and *it will*

[1] Circular of March 19, 1912, in Forty-first Annual Report of Local Government Board, 1912, p. 44.

*be the duty of the Public Assistance Committee to deal with no
application that can be dealt with equally well or better by the
Voluntary Aid Committee."* [1]

The recommendation that there should be set up a statutory
organisation of Voluntary Agencies in all Poor Law areas was,
it is needless to say, not carried out by the Government. Nor
did it receive support from the Boards of Guardians. On the
contrary, the proceedings of the Poor Law Conferences from
1909 to 1914 show that any attempt to compel Guardians to use
Voluntary Agencies, still more any suggestion that the Voluntary
Agencies should be given independent or superior powers of
determining how cases should be dealt with, was hotly resented
by practically every Guardian, and was unhesitatingly condemned
by the Inspectorate. The Poor Law Division, in fact, though
pressing the Guardians to make use of certified institutions for
children and mentally defective persons,[2] always objected to
their giving up any part of their responsibility for deciding the
amount and the character of the relief to be given to any case or
class of cases. "Some Boards of Guardians", it was reported
in 1913 by the Inspector for the Midland Counties, "were anxious
during this period [the 1912 Coal Strike] to contribute lump sums
of money to various charitable agencies, to be used by those
agencies at their discretion, and without any control or investigation by the Guardians." [3] Thus, the Chesterfield Board asked
permission to hand over the relief of necessitous children to
certain Voluntary Agencies by making a payment of 3d. per day
for each child so long as it was needed. This proposal was
decisively negatived by the Local Government Board. The only
way of co-operating with Voluntary Agencies was, it was stated,
for the Guardians to allocate, according to their character,
particular cases for relief to the Poor Law or to charity respectively. "It is important for effective co-operation", stated
in 1914 the Inspector for the Metropolis, "that no attempt
should be made to influence or comment on the action of any
body with regard to their method of dealing with any case ;

---

[1] Majority Report of Poor Law Commission, 1909, p. 536.

[2] The law with respect to this form of co-operation, and its history, was
given in an interesting paper by R. A. Leach, Clerk to the Rochdale Board of
Guardians (*Poor Law Conferences, 1910–1911*, p. 416).

[3] Forty-second Annual Report of Local Government Board, 1913, Report
of Gerald Walsh, p. 62.

such interference only tends to cause a withholding of information. The registration should simply be a means of ensuring that all the known facts about any case are available for the information of the co-operating parties. It is especially necessary that the statutory responsibility of Guardians in deciding whether a case is a proper one for relief should not be interfered with." [1]

But there was one function which the Majority Commissioners wished to hand over entirely to the Voluntary Aid Committees —the registration of all cases assisted within the Union, whether this assistance was given out of voluntary funds or out of rate-supported services. The establishment of such a register, for the information alike of the public Authorities and of charitable agencies, was repeatedly recommended. Thus, the Inspector for the Metropolitan area observed in 1914 that "It is most important that every Authority, whether public or voluntary, giving or administering aid, should be kept informed of what is being received from all sources by any individual they propose to aid ; and one of the most helpful forms of co-operation is a registration scheme where all the Authorities and agencies register the names of the persons they help. Such a register would enable any Authority to find out whether a person they are helping, or propose to help, is known to another body or agency, and makes direct communication between these bodies possible. This appears all that is necessary in the majority of cases, but, where a good deal of information is available, a Case Paper of the case might be prepared. If the registration is carried out on the ' card index ' system, the card would merely indicate the various bodies to which the case is known, and, if it is a case for which there is a Case Paper, a number in the corner of the card would be sufficient to indicate the fact." " It will probably be found ", he added, " that the most effective way of bringing about this co-operation is to make use of the existing registration machinery of the Charity Organisation Society, or other society that may have prepared a register of the district." The Inspector did not encourage the Boards of Guardians to make the register themselves. " An undue multiplication of registers ", he said, " might be harmful." [2]

---

[1] Forty-third Annual Report of Local Government Board, 1914, p. 23.
[2] *Ibid.*, Report of J. S. Oxley, pp. 22-23.

The idea of such a Local Register of all persons receiving any form of assistance from the Local Authorities or organised Voluntary Agencies has been constantly in the minds, first of the Charity Organisation Society (which, in 1910, still had branches in 102 places in England and Wales), and then of the Guilds of Help, which subsequently became Councils for Social Service or Citizens' Societies, affiliated to the National Council of Social Service.

Thus we find the Local Government Board, in its Circular on Voluntary Agencies of January 1914, suggesting that the local Authorities, both Health and Poor Law, should co-operate with the Voluntary Agencies in their areas ; and that with this end in view, a local Conference should take place with a view of formulating some scheme of co-operation.[1] We are told, by the Inspector for the Midland Counties, that this proposal had already been carried out in Birmingham by the establishment in 1910 of the Birmingham City Aid Society (now Citizens' Society), which, at the request of the Birmingham Board of Guardians, dealt in the main with Out-Relief cases.[2] The class of cases which were to be visited by the City Aid Society included the following :

" (a) Where children were, or might be, neglected, or their condition and surroundings were capable of improvement ;

" (b) Where children were approaching working ages, with the view of advising the selection of a skilled trade, and if possible of assisting in obtaining such work ;

---

[1] Circular of January 21, 1914, Forty-third Annual Report of Local Government Board, 1914, Part III. p. 21.

[2] For the organisation and working of the Birmingham " Mutual Registration of Assistance ", which was started in 1908, see *Social Service in Birmingham*, by Richard Clements and Agnes Taunton, 1925, pp. 13-14 ; and the successive Annual Reports since 1916 of the Birmingham Citizens' Society. In 1925–26, there were 135,914 notifications filed by 377 different Authorities and Agencies, from which 28,939 reports were made as to assistance being given to the same family by two or more Authorities or Agencies. " Several bad cases of over-lapping have been discovered which could have been avoided had enquiries been made from the Department before assistance was given. In one case a man who had been known to be of unsatisfactory character for the past thirty years obtained loans amounting to £14 in three days " (Tenth Annual Report of the Birmingham Citizens' Society, 1926, pp. 18-19).

Other towns in which a Register was established, with the assistance of the Board of Guardians and the Town Council, were Derby and Cambridge (see *Poor Law Conferences, 1911–1912*, pp. 130-131). Repeated efforts have been made in other towns, with only partial and temporary success.

" (c) Where the destitution was the result of misfortune ;

" (d) Where there was a reasonable prospect of raising the Standard of Life ;

" (e) Pregnant women or widows with babies, with the object of advising as to their proper feeding and care ;

"(f) Where the distress was caused through the want of proper management of the home, and with the view of making the home more attractive and comfortable ;

" (g) Phthisical and other cases, especially children discharged from the Infirmary, where it was of the utmost importance that hygienic treatment should be continued when they returned home."

Another extensive and efficient Register is that established in 1910 by the Liverpool Council of Voluntary Aid, in co-operation with the three Poor Law Authorities then operating within that city, together with the Liverpool Town Council, and subsequently the Bootle Town Council.[1] By 1923 the Clerk to the West Derby Union could report to his Board that " the total number of bodies co-operating with the Central Register is 242 ", the number of cases reported for registration being 31,664 (almost exactly half by the Board of Guardians) ; whilst 8740 of these were reported from the Register for the information of the various relieving agencies (seven-ninths of them to the Board of Guardians). In suggesting some improvement in the working of the system, the Clerk observed that " whilst the usefulness of this exchange of necessary information respecting cases assisted by more than one body or organisation must be readily admitted, it nevertheless remains a fact that in the past a large proportion of the cases reported to the Central Register by the Union Case Paper Department have not been cases in which the information has ultimately proved helpful by reasons of assistance having

---

[1] The West Derby Board of Guardians contributed £300, the Liverpool Select Vestry £185, and the Board of Guardians of the Township of Toxteth Park £90, making a total of £575 a year ; which was continued as a single item by the enlarged West Derby Union on the amalgamation. The Liverpool Town Council contributed £275 per annum, and the Bootle Town Council, which acceded to the scheme later, subscribed £50 per annum. In 1924 the West Derby Board of Guardians got the financial arrangements altered, so that the Liverpool Council of Voluntary Aid should become responsible for the salary of the Registrar (£400), receiving the contributions from the Municipal Councils and Voluntary Agencies ; whilst the West Derby Union found only office accommodation, stationery, subordinate staff and incidental expenses.

been given by more than one organisation." [1] The Poor Law
officials, it seems, were inclined to believe that the Register
was more effective in stopping overlapping among the various
Voluntary Agencies themselves, than as telling the Relieving
Officers of the Poor Law Union much that they had not already
discovered.   In 1926, when the number of co-operating agencies
had risen to 249, no fewer than 88,632 cases were reported for
registration, representing about a third of the entire population
of the area ; whilst 15,140 reports from the Register were issued
for the information of other bodies. [2]

Thus the one recommendation of the Majority Commissioners
relating to Voluntary Agencies which was whole-heartedly
endorsed by Whitehall—the establishment of a voluntary register
of all forms of assistance of the poor—has not been effectively
put in operation except in Birmingham and Liverpool. [3] Even

[1] West Derby Union Clerk's Report for the Co-ordination of the Register
of Assistance . . . with the Case Paper Department of the Board, by G. W.
Coster, 1923.

[2] Annual Report for 1926 of the Liverpool Council of Voluntary Aid (1927).
It may be observed that the Ministers of Health, Labour and Pensions refuse
to register contributory Old Age Pensions, Health and Unemployment Insurance Benefits or War Pensions, as not being of the nature of charitable relief.
On representations being made to the Ministry of Health in 1926, on behalf
of the Birmingham Mutual Registration of Assistance Committee, as to the
desirability of such particulars being included, with special reference to the
Widows, Orphans and Old Age Contributory Pensions Act, 1925, it was replied
that " the Ministry of Health was most sympathetic on the general question
of registration and . . . fully appreciates the advantage, and indeed the
desirability, of communicating the names of beneficiaries to grants under the
Act ; but, in the first place, the records are kept centrally and not territorially,
so that without a great deal of labour it would be impossible to communicate
the names of Birmingham beneficiaries.   In the second place, widows and
orphans move about a great deal, so that there would need to be a constant
revision of the records ; and, thirdly, the Ministry feels strongly that grants
made from a contributory scheme are quite different in character from those
made without any contributions having been made by the recipients.   Such
pensions are, in fact, a right, and as such the Ministry feel that they should not
communicate information in regard to them.   This is indeed a fundamental
principle in their policy, and constitutes, at present, and under existing circumstances, the strongest reason for not agreeing to the proposal that these pensions
should be communicated to Mutual Assistance Societies " (Ministry of Health
to National Council of Social Service ; see Tenth Annual Report of Birmingham
Citizens' Society, 1926, pp. 18-19).

[3] In about a score of English boroughs efforts have been made to establish
a Register of families assisted, and in some of these towns (notably Manchester
and Brighton) a considerable amount of co-operation has been obtained.   In
London the C.O.S. has long striven to maintain such a Register, but this seems
to contain relatively few cases beyond those known to the C.O.S. itself and a
few other charitable agencies.   In a dozen other towns (such as Bournemouth,

in these centres of vigorous philanthropic effort the register established has failed to obtain the co-operation of some of the religious organisations. More serious is the fact that the Government Departments, themselves making extensive domiciliary payments, have not seen their way to communicate them to the Voluntary Aid Council.

At this point it may be useful to summarise the stages in the age-long controversy with regard to the relation between private charity and public assistance in dealing with the problem presented by poverty in the midst of riches. Prior to the Tudor legislation, the " Laws relating to the Poor " were, as we have elsewhere described, exclusively penal in character, concerned with keeping the " Lower Orders " in due subjection to the rule of their rightful masters. The succour of " God's Poor " was left to the Church and the alms of the faithful. The Tudor Poor Laws arose from the failure of this voluntary philanthropy to avert either fraudulent mendicancy and criminal vagrancy or frequent deaths from starvation and exposure. For more than two hundred years, as we have elsewhere described,[1] parish relief and the alms of the charitable then travelled on side by side without any attempt at co-ordination. The Royal Commission of 1832–1834, confronted with the disastrous results of unconditional Outdoor Relief to able-bodied men, and obsessed with the " Principle of Population " and the Wage-Fund Theory —implying the inevitability of periodical mass destitution— invented, for parish relief, the " Principle of Less Eligibility " and the " Workhouse Test " ; and, with strict logic, looked askance at any extensive voluntary charity. With the growth of humanitarianism in the middle of the nineteenth century there arose a new school of " Poor Law orthodoxy ", which sought to define, once and for ever, the right relations between public assistance and private charity. The Poor Law Guardians were, as we have described, advised rigorously to carry out the " Principles of 1834 ", and even to extend them to their treatment of the non-able-bodied. On the other hand, the rich were solemnly adjured to give freely, not only of money but also of personal

---

Bradford, Chester, Halifax, Poole, Reading, Scarborough, Wakefield and Walsall) Registers have been maintained, usually with small contributions from the Boards of Guardians, but with little claim to completeness or permanence.

[1] *The Old Poor Law*, 1927.

service, so that all " deserving " cases should have no need to apply for Poor Relief. All enlightened philanthropy was to be concentrated on the deserving ; and everyone else left to a distinctly penal Poor Law. Needless to say, it very quickly appeared, not only that it was often impracticable to apply the criterion of deserts, but also that private charity anywhere but in the smallest village was both unequipped and insufficient to deal with more than a small proportion of those in need against whom no indictment could be brought. The Charity Organisation Society soon found itself driven to drop the category of the deserving in favour of that of " the helpable ", meaning no more than those selected cases that private persons and voluntary organisations thought themselves able to succour effectually. Thus the most deserving and most severely suffering, just because they were "unhelpable", were relegated, along with the most undeserving, to the tender mercies of a Poor Law which, accordingly, could never, in practice, be made as deterrent as had been intended. The Majority of the Royal Commissioners of 1905–1909 could not bring themselves to recommend a reversion to a rigorously deterrent Poor Law, even in respect of the able-bodied. All public relief of destitution was to be " restorative ", alike of the body and of the mind, designed to improve the patient, and rehabilitate him as an independent citizen. But in order to leave some place for private philanthropy, the Majority Report, as we have mentioned, sought to set up a " Voluntary Aid Committee " which should intercept such cases as it thought fit ; and demanded that it should be made " the duty of the Public Assistance Committee to deal with no application that can be dealt with equally well or better by the Voluntary Aid Committee ".[1] Such a proposal, as we have seen, was decisively negatived, not only by the Boards of Guardians, but also by the Inspectors of the Local Government Board.

Quite another conception of the co-operation between public and private agencies came into view. The Minority Report pointed out that there had grown up a whole system of Public Assistance of the several classes — the sick, the children, the mentally disordered, the aged, and even the unemployed able-bodied—unconnected with the Poor Law, and embodying the

[1] Poor Law Commission, Majority Report, 1909, Part VII. par. 218, p. 97 of 8vo edition.

conception of preventing the continuance and the very occurrence of destitution. This had inaugurated a new relationship between the work of the Public Authority and voluntary philanthropy. The most promising developments of personal service and voluntary assistance—apart from the perennial maintenance of the voluntary hospitals—have been either the supply of voluntary workers to act as " the eyes and ears and fingers " of the Municipal Authority, or the initiation of novel and experimental methods of treatment of particular classes of persons, to be handed over, when proved, to the Public Authorities for permanent maintenance. Thus there were, in 1909, already a thousand or two of unpaid Health Visitors, acting under the direction of the Medical Officers of Health. Another example was afforded by the four or five thousand members of the Children's Care Committees, established in connection with the public elementary schools in the Metropolis, and the analogous committees of the " special schools " of the London County Council. Similar voluntary assistance was being organised in connection with the Local Health Authority and the Local Education Authority in many a district ; and voluntary assistance of a like kind was already beginning to be used in connection with the work of the Local Pension Authority and the Local Authority for the Mentally Defective. During the past twenty years this organisation of voluntary helpers, under the guidance and control of the responsible administrators of the Local Health Authority, the Local Education Authority, the Local Lunacy Authority and the Authorities for War Pensions and the pensions for widows and the aged, has become almost ubiquitous. Most of the provincial Charity Organisation Societies have given place to Guilds of Help and Councils of Social Service,[1] who, not attempting to substitute themselves for the specialised activities of the various parts of the Framework of Prevention that we have described in a previous chapter, are able, by co-operating with the Public Authorities, to render valuable help. But to this co-operation

---

[1] For these organisations see the Local Government Report on Guilds of Help, by G. R. Snowden (Cd. 5664, of 1911) ; the reports of the Social Welfare Association, from 1910 onwards; the paper by R. A. Leach read at the North-Western Poor Law Conference, October 1, 1911 (*Poor Law Conferences, 1911–1912*) ; *Report on a Test of Mutual Registration of Assistance carried on in Halifax, Reading and Liverpool*, 1923 ; and the Reports and other publications of the National Council of Social Service.

of voluntary service with the treatment afforded by the specialised committees and staffs of the County and Borough Councils there is, as all experience shows, one fundamental condition. There must be no giving of alms by the voluntary visitor in the homes that he or she officially visits. On this point the Minority Report was emphatic in its condemnation. " There is, in our judgment, nothing more disastrous, alike to the character of the poor and to the efficiency of the services of public assistance which is at their disposal, than the alms dispensed by well-meaning persons in the mere relief of distress. The distribution of indiscriminate, unconditional and inadequate doles is none the less harmful when it is an adjunct of quite kindly meant district visiting, the official ministrations of religion, or the treatment meted out by a ' medical mission '. Even when such gifts are discreetly dispensed by the most careful visitor, they have the drawback of being given without knowledge of what the other resources of the family may be, without communication to other agencies which may be simultaneously at work, and without power to insist on proper conditions ".[1]   In short, the most noticeable change in the current methods of dealing with the problem of destitution since Victorian times is the extent to which individual almsgiving and the personal visitation of the poor by unorganised philanthropists have faded out of the picture.

There is, be it noted, still the widest possible field for pecuniary donations, to be administered, if desired, under voluntary management. There is of course still much to be done in England in the extension of higher education and the promotion of research. We know enough now to know how supremely important it is to extend our knowledge. But research and experiment in social subjects cost as much as research and experiment in chemistry or electricity ; and the public does not yet realise this fact ! Here, indeed, is a magnificent field for the volunteer worker and for the munificence of many a millionaire. Whether in practical experiment or in pure research, there is no range of work that is more likely to bring about immediate social betterment than this of the various means of preventing destitution and of scientifically treating the cases that occur. But even in the development of the work of Local Authorities there are still many kinds of institutional treatment which the County and

[1] Poor Law Commission, Minority Report, 1909, p. 417 of 8vo edition.

Municipal Authorities are not likely themselves to initiate ; and there are others that they are almost debarred from conducting. There is room for many pioneer experiments in the treatment of almost every type of distressed person. The whole tendency of applied science is to subdivision, and to the breaking-up of old categories into newer specialisations. We cannot expect our elected Councillors to launch out into experiments of this kind. During the past half-century the private experiments in Industrial and Reformatory Schools, Technical Institutes, Farm Colonies, Inebriate Retreats, Rescue Homes, and what not, have greatly advanced the technique of these services. In this field of initiating and developing new institutional treatment—whether it be the provision of perfect almshouses for the aged, or the establishment of holiday camps or open-air schools for the children ; whether it be the enveloping of the morally infirm, or of those who have fallen, in a regenerating atmosphere of religion and love, or the provision of some subtle combination of physical regimen and mental stimulus for the town-bred " hooligan "— very large sums of money can be advantageously used, and are in fact, urgently needed.[1] And not the financing alone, but also the management of such institutions, affords a sphere for unofficial work. Just as no Public Authority can hazard the ratepayers' money in avowedly experimental institutions, so no Public Authority can assume responsibility for the desirable unconventionality of their daily administration. The several Committees of the County and County Borough Councils can make full use of these voluntary institutions, entrusting to their care (with consent) the special types of cases for which they afford appropriate treatment. But for this use there should be two conditions. Any voluntary institution receiving patients from the Local Authority must necessarily place itself under the regular inspection both of that Local Authority and of the National Department having the supervision of the particular service. And if payment for the treatment is required, even without other subsidy, the Local Authority should be given the opportunity of placing its own representatives on the actual governing body of the institution.

[1] " The rôle of the voluntary worker is to initiate and try out new plans, unfettered by legal limitations, make experiments, and, when the work is proved, hand over the results to the organisation of a central department " (*Health Services and the Public*, by Dr. Stella Churchill, 1928, p. 14).

What the munificent private donor, or the charitable public, must not do, either individually or collectively, is, by their generous but altogether inadequate gifts, to stand in the way of the execution of a duty, or the assumption of responsibility, by the Public Authority, or to delay, impede or hamper its action. A glaring instance was afforded, in 1928, by the action taken in the unparalleled distress in the coalfields. With two or three hundred thousand families—more than a million persons—thrown into much more than transient destitution, the starting, in the spring of 1928, of a National Relief Fund, which could not be expected to afford even a week's subsistence to the families in need—and did not, in fact, amount to half that sum—was, to say the least, inept. The hasty generosity of a few thousand donors had no other effect than to prevent the Government from undertaking the necessary task of organising and providing, in the wisest possible way, whatever was required.[1] The only people whom the charitable public relieved were the Members of the Cabinet, who were spared the pain of thought, and the Income-Taxpayers, who escaped the pangs of parting with an additional penny in the pound. In the end, unless the destitute families are left to die, the community as a whole must eventually make whatever provision is necessary. Moreover, quite apart from the uncertainty and inadequacy of a voluntary relief fund, there is the all-important problem of how to distribute with

[1] The later history of this ill-considered philanthropy is instructive. In a whole six months of begging, the Lord Mayor's Fund failed to reach even £200,000 ; and for very shame the Cabinet, in December 1928, had to abandon the refusal of public assistance to which it had been tempted by the promotion of the Fund. The Prime Minister announced that, besides providing £100,000 to assist family migration, the Government would—not through the Local Authorities undertake the work of coping with what amounted to a localised famine—but merely subscribe £150,000 (and thereafter pound for pound) *to the Lord Mayor's Fund.* It then found it indispensable virtually to take over the receipt and transmission of the money by appointing its own officer to take charge ; to widen the scope of the Fund ; to designate a member of the Cabinet to answer for it in the House of Commons ; to send down to the distressed localities " Regional Organisers " ; to supersede the " Lord Mayor's Fund Committee " by two new " National Advisory Committees ", with a joint National Executive Committee, and to set up new Local Committees in the several areas. What is not ensured, even after a repetition of the appeal to the benevolent by the Prince of Wales had doubled the amount of the Fund, is either the discovery of all the quiet or helpless sufferers, or the complete and instantaneous registration of all the agencies distributing assistance in each place, or anything better than indiscriminate, unconditional and inadequate Outdoor Relief.

advantage—and indeed, without positive harm—the money available. It seems common sense that the discovery of the persons in need, the selection to be made among importunate applicants, and the decision as to the most appropriate form of assistance, should be undertaken, not by hastily formed committees, but by responsible agencies already in touch with the poor population of each locality. In every place there are actively at work, not only the Relieving Officers and the Poor Law Guardians knowing all the destitute families ; the school teachers and School Medical Officers, and Children's Care Committees of the Local Education Authority having an almost continuous supervision of the children of school age ; and the rapidly developing organisation of Medical Officers and Health Visitors, and Maternity and Child Welfare Centres of the Local Health Authority. Whatever provision of the necessaries of life the community is called upon to make in exceptional emergencies ought, we suggest, always to be made through already existing responsible Local Authorities, which can be strengthened, practically to any required extent, by such voluntary organisations as the Guilds of Help and Councils of Social Service.

The Growing Pretensions of the Guardians

Whether it was due to the steady shrinkage of able-bodied pauperism, or to a lively sense of " duty performed " in the more humane treatment of the non-able-bodied,[1] or to the vehemently expressed refusal of the President of the Local Government Board (Mr. John Burns) to carry out the unanimous recommendation of the Royal Commission of 1905–1909 that the Boards of Guardians should be abolished, we note, between 1911 and 1914, a rapid growth of self-confidence—even of self-assertion—on the part of Boards of Guardians. " I think it is true to say ", said one leader of the Metropolitan Guardians in 1911, " that the general position of Boards of Guardians to-day is more secure

---

[1] " Notwithstanding these changes, and the feeling of some uncertainty as to the extent of their effect on Poor Law work, Boards of Guardians generally have been commendably active in their *endeavours to improve and widen their administration*. Better provision has in many cases been made for the children and for the sick, and some further improvement has taken place in classification in Poor Law institutions, and in dealing with the question of Vagrancy " (Forty-second Annual Report of Local Government Board, 1913, p. viii.).

than it ever has been. The frontal attack which was made upon us in 1905, and which culminated in the Report of the Royal Commission, has been repelled, and the abolitionists have been completely routed." [1]

The growth of the pretensions of the Boards of Guardians appeared in two directions : the insistence on a wider autonomy, or a greater independence of the Central Authority ; and the demand that all persons requiring any form of maintenance from public funds should be retained in, or returned to, the jurisdiction of the Poor Law.

Over and over again in Poor Law Conferences delegates expressed their irritation at being singled out from other Local Authorities for constant supervision and minute control. Compared with County Councils, Borough Councils, and even Urban and Rural District Councils, Boards of Guardians, stated a delegate who was at once a County Councillor and a Guardian, are "fettered and hampered in every way . . . subjected in almost every item of duty to the consent or otherwise of the Local Government Board. Take, for example, the matter of diet to Workhouse inmates. Surely one would have thought this was a region in which the Local Authority would not need control, but that, with the help of local medical advice, they would have been better able to form a varying scale than a Central Body ; but the cast-iron principle of Uniformity stands in the way, as it does in numberless instances beside. Why should absolute Uniformity obtain in Poor Law administrative circles any more than within the areas and obligations of Municipalities ? Everybody denounces Boards of Guardians and praises County and County Borough Councils. It is the fashion ! That, and that only, is the real reason, but if there be a whit more grit and effectiveness in the proceedings of Councils than of Boards of Guardians, it is because Councils have grown naturally, and have not been checked and deformed by unshapely moulds. In fact, they have been encouraged and stimulated to act for themselves. Any perceiving person must see that, as between the two services, that of Boards of Guardians must suffer materially in point of dignity as compared with the other." "It was this irritating interference", the delegate continued, "which has had its effect in deterring, to some extent, the best minds from

---

[1] *Poor Law Conferences, 1911–1912,* Paper by Rev. P. S. G. Propert, p. 422.

identifying themselves with a system, one of the chief features of which is mistrust and suspicion of those to whom its administration is nominally handed. I am of opinion that Guardians themselves scarcely apprehend the extreme *minutiae* to which this paternal oversight extends." . . . " Even the bulk of the officials are not the exclusive servants of the Guardians, but have an appeal to the Local Government Board, and can only be suspended, not displaced. Take the case of Relieving Officers. How important it is that they should be the servants of the ratepayers through the medium of their representatives. Surely ' those who pay the piper should call the tune '." . . . " Personally, I am of opinion that the Poor Law was launched under unfortunate conditions," sums up the aforementioned delegate, " It would have been better to have laid down a few simple rules, in the form of elementary enactments, as instructions to all local administrators until developments rendered necessary a more complex system and the calling into existence of an *ad hoc* body, whose exclusive public duty it should be to carry into effect the further and complicated details of this department of local self-government. As soon as such separate body in each Union had been set up, or certainly as soon as it had gathered experience, it seems to me the close supervision of the Local Government Board should have ceased, and that Board should have become an *Advisory* rather than a *Supervisory* Authority." [1]

What appeared to Boards of Guardians even more objectionable than the minute supervision of their administration, was the power of the District Auditor to surcharge on individual Guardians, at his own discretion, expenditure which he deemed to be inconsistent with the Orders of the Local Government Board. " That some Boards of Guardians ", stated a delegate to the South Wales and Monmouthshire Poor Law Conference in 1911, " were too free with the public money, was true, but it was for the ratepayers, and not the Local Government Board, to tell the Guardians when they spent too much money. Let those who find the money be the judges, and change their Guardians, if they want to. The ratepayers on the spot were the people who should dictate the policy of the Boards." [2]

[1] *Poor Law Conferences, 1911–1912*, Paper by Alderman F. J. Beavan, South Wales and Monmouthshire District Conference, pp. 77-95.

[2] *Poor Law Conferences, 1911–1912*, Mr. Neville, p. 95. It should be said that the powers of the District Auditor are nominally no greater with regard

And this power of the District Auditor led Relieving Officers and Clerks to Boards of Guardians, who are, it must be remembered, dismissible by the Central Authority, to refuse to carry out the decisions of their ostensible employers. " They had to relieve certain families one morning," stated a clerical Guardian in 1911, " and the Relieving Officer, acting upon advice given him, openly told the Committee that he would not pay the money, unless the Guardians were present at the Relief Committee, and signed the relief book, so that he might hand the names over to the Auditor. Another case was referred to the full Board, and the Relieving Officer declined to pay the relief, and the Board was helpless. In order to get over the difficulty the Guardians passed a resolution instructing the Clerk to pay the relief by cheque every week, and that was done. The case arose in this way. They had granted relief to a widow who lived with her son-in-law in receipt of 37s. a week wages. Because the son-in-law gave a home to his wife's mother, and was in receipt of money, the Guardians were told that the relief was illegal, and the poor woman, in order that she might still enjoy the relief, had to leave her son - in - law's house. Now the Guardians were surcharged ; and he thought that the whole system of surcharge was wrong, and brought discredit upon Guardians who were trying to do their duty to the best of their ability in relieving the necessities of the poor ".[1]

But it was not only increased independence that the Guardians demanded : it was a direct reversal of the steady trend to take one class of pauper after another out of the jurisdiction of a separately elected Poor Law Authority. " Human beings,

---

to Boards of Guardians than with regard to County, District and Parish Councils, although the greater particularity of the Poor Law Orders than the statutes at large may afford him greater opportunity for disallowance.

[1] *Poor Law Conferences, 1911–1912,* Rev. Ll. M. Williams, p. 93. There is evidence that some of the District Auditors took the view that they must necessarily disallow any item that they considered unwarranted by law, in cases in which a warning to the Guardians might have sufficed. The Local Government Board itself observed in 1910, with regard to the Guardians' appeals against these disallowances of Out-relief held to have been unnecessary, " It did not appear to us that, in any of these cases, the circumstances were such as not to justify us in remitting the disallowances or surcharges. In most instances the relief had been discontinued or the Guardians had promised to exercise greater strictness, in future, in administering Out-relief " (Thirty-ninth Annual Report of Local Government Board, 1910, p. lv.).

whether paupers or non-paupers," urged Mr. George Craighill, (Clerk to the Gateshead Union), " should be dealt with by one Authority especially elected for that purpose ; and there was no other Authority they knew of so suitable for that purpose as Boards of Guardians, because they had no extraneous functions to perform, and the subject was of sufficient importance to take all the time of a body specially elected for that purpose ".[1] " Let it go forth ", urged one champion of the Metropolitan Boards of Guardians, " that they believed in a single Authority for the administration of public relief out of public funds. (A Voice : *Ad hoc*). *Ad hoc*, if they liked. What was happening in London ? There they had so many forms of public relief, that a family might be entirely maintained by public money. . . . What they wanted was to extend the circumference of the Poor Law so as to net in all those outside powers of relief, or get Parliament to transfer them back to the Public Relief Authority. Let it go forth, therefore, that they believed in the retention and the extension of their powers ; and secondly—Mr. John Burns had given them the lead—that they were willing to combine with other Authorities for the purpose of better classification in their Workhouses ".[2] . . . " The Guardians know these people personally, they come in contact with them almost daily, they live their lives among the poor, and that is a thing which you cannot over-estimate in practical value. The personal service of the members of Boards of Guardians to the sick and the poor is a matter which ought not to be forgotten. Instead of trying to do away with that, or, by measures like the Insurance Bill, to render the work of Poor Law Guardians less and less— rendering their position less useful and honourable, and creating other Authorities to undertake their legitimate functions—it really ought to be the other way about. I contend that the whole care of the poor in this country chargeable to the public should be in the hands of one Authority." [3]

This aspiration to become the sole Authority dealing with all classes of necessitous persons was emphatically endorsed by Charles Booth in his Presidential Address to the Central

[1] *Poor Law Conferences, 1910–1911* (Northern District Conference), p. 283.
[2] *Poor Law Conferences, 1911–1912*, The Rev. P. S. G. Propert, South-Eastern District Conference, p. 216.
[3] *Poor Law Conferences, 1911–1912*, G. Craighill, Gateshead, Northern District Conference, pp. 302-303.

Poor Law Conference of 1912. "It is essential", stated this experienced philanthropist, "that the elective character of the Boards of Guardians should be retained, and that the authority of the Guardians and their responsibilities should suffer no diminution". . . . He urged the Guardians not to shrink "from any consistent development in the work or its responsibilities; holding that, whatever may be the causes of distress—whether moral, mental or physical, depravity, incompetence, or ill-health, or pure misfortune—its public relief lies within the proper sphere of the Poor Law". . . . "The task to be performed", he said, "is one which absolutely demands the control of an independent Authority. Nothing would be gained by confusing preventive action with the restorative measures properly connected with relief; confusing, that is, the exercise of medical, moral, or economic interference in the conditions of normal citizen life with the public assistance requisite when the normal life is not possible. Hence the importance of specific election for Poor Law purposes. By its means the Guardians are placed in direct touch with their constituents, and in definite relationship to the Local Government Board itself. . . . I hold too", he concluded, "that the adoption of any other course will lead to an undesirable officialism." [1]

Another aspect of this increased self-confidence of the Boards of Guardians was an objection to the great service of the relief of destitution being stowed away as one among many Divisions of the Local Government Board. "The Poor Law", declared the able Clerk to the Wakefield Union, "is a subject of such magnitude that it ought to have a separate Government Department, with a responsible head in one of the Houses of Parliament, and, heresy as it may seem from a political point of view, the sooner the administration of the Poor Law is divorced from the political world, the better for the people." [2]

---

[1] *Poor Law Conferences, 1911-1912*, pp. 682-684.

[2] *Poor Law Conferences, 1910–1911*, Paper by H. Beaumont, p. 764.
  This desire to return to a separate Central Authority, such as the Poor Law Board of 1848–1871 and the Poor Law Commissioners of 1834–1847, was frequently expressed by Poor Law administrators. "The National Committee for the Reform of the Poor Law, of which I have the privilege to be hon. secretary, is strongly of opinion that in consequence of the complexity and development of Poor Law administration in recent years, it would be to the advantage of Boards of Guardians if the Central Authority was again raised

Uncertainty of Creed

Unfortunately these growing pretensions on the part of Boards of Guardians were not accompanied by any clear view of the policy to be pursued in the relief of destitution. Whatever else the Royal Commission of 1905–1909 had done or left undone, it had swept away the " Principles of 1834 ", as they had generally been understood since that date, without converting the country to any alternative policy, or any general principle of reform. " At present there appears to be no one," complained in 1912 a Poor Law administrator of the old school, " whether statesman or political economist, who is able or willing to show us a line of light through them all—a clue to guide us safely out of the labyrinth of conflicting social theories. To the ordinary observer it would appear that there are only two possible alternative policies—the one to adhere to the old policy of independence and depauperisation, and that of throwing the responsibility upon the individual citizen, which is the policy of 1834 ; the other, frankly to abandon this policy, and to accept the Socialist position that it is the duty of the State to take over the whole responsibility for the welfare of its members, and to intervene at every point in their domestic and family life. That is practically the policy recommended by the Minority Report." [1] Nor did the Central Authority seem, to most Guardians, consistent in its Orders and Circulars. " Under one President ", stated in 1911 a Welsh Guardian, " a particular policy has been recommended, whilst, under the next, probably quite another course has been advised, until the Circulars have represented the game of battledore and shuttlecock almost *ad nauseam*. The public, knowing nothing of this fluctuation in the Circulars from the supervising body, have often concluded that Guardians did not know their own minds, and were unequal to the task of forming a definite judgment, and have attributed to them, rather than to the proper quarter, widely divergent if not wholly contradictory policies. Guardians cannot, if they would, pursue a steady and

---

into a separate Government Department, devoted exclusively to the supervision of the Poor Law and the relief of distress. I agree with this proposal because the administration of these laws requires so much special knowledge and such close attention to detail " (*Poor Law Conferences, 1912–1913,* Paper by Rev. P. S. G. Propert, " Poor Law and its Administration since 1870," p. 331).

[1] *Poor Law Conferences, 1911–1912,* Paper by W. A. Bailward, p. 182.

well-thought-out progressive policy. I have been a Guardian for 28 years, and I do not hesitate to say that, if I had my time to go over again, nothing would induce me to work hard and earnestly under a supervision which, as to policy, is unreliable, and, as to some of its details, tantalising and out of date." [1] . . .

" In no other branch of national service ", a leading Midland Guardian and County Councillor observed, " is there so strong a conflict of opinion, so diverse a translation of principle ; so much agreement as to the defence and retention of a system, so much disagreement as to the principle on which that system should operate, [and] which should govern its development." " I feel ", he continued, " that I am right in believing that internal dissensions form the weakness of the position. Internal unity is impossible so long as one section of Guardians insists on Institutional Relief as the remedy for the social problem of pauperism ; another section insists on ' destitution ' being the only qualification for relief or assistance that the law recognises ; a third section urges that Outdoor or Home Assistance is the natural and legal method of treatment, Institutional Relief being the alternative for conditions or circumstances which unfit the applicant for any other treatment. We shall all be agreed that there are such cases where character and conditions point to Institutional Relief as the remedy, but I can confidently argue that there are cases where conditions and character point to Outdoor Relief or Assistance as that form of help which morally and legally meets the case. . . . The difficulty—or the more serious one—between us is this : that we cannot get together in working agreement so long as ' destitution ' is the definition of a claim for relief ; when so large a section of Guardians has in practice, as well as in principle, gone much beyond it ; and refuses to accept ' destitution ' as the only condition under which an appeal for assistance can be dealt with. . . . The Act of 1834 met the social conditions of that day, but the conditions of 1911 have no point of similarity. Reform of the treatment of the poor, in principle or in method, in 1911 cannot be on the same lines. If the principle [of the Statute] of 1834—essentially a rural Act—is still in any sense applicable in rural districts, it cannot by any reasonable argument be held to apply in 1911 to any congested industrial area. . . . The failure to realise these

[1] *Poor Law Conferences, 1911-1912.*

differences between 1834 and 1911, and the acute pressure of these modern conditions, is responsible for the antagonistic spirit which Poor Law experts exhibit towards each other ; for the excited hostility towards the Poor Law system outside ; for the obstacles to progress ; for the difficulty in obtaining from Parliament those extended powers which we are seeking, and which all are agreed are necessary for an increased efficiency." [1]

It was a significant mark of the disintegration of the principles of 1834 that some experienced Guardians suggested that the Poor Law should be extended to the prevention of destitution as distinguished from the relief of destitution.   Thus Dr. Clay affirmed in 1913 that " Boards of Guardians have efficiently in the past carried out what was expected of them in relieving destitution ; but they must in the future, if they wish to continue to exist, take a wider view of their duties by not merely confining their interests to the narrow compass of dealing with destitution when it is thrust upon them, in other words relieving destitution when it is an accomplished fact ; but what is needed, to put it shortly, is to institute a systematic crusade against the several causes of destitution.   Possessing, as they do, all the advantages in the way of information of the various phases, causes, and results of destitution, the voice of the Guardians of the poor should be the loudest, denouncing all that makes for poverty, such as idleness, drunkenness, and immorality, and whilst they should by all means deal energetically and conscientiously with poverty when it exists, they should even put more energy and labour in banishing destitution from the land." [2]

The Increasing Supersession of the Poor Law

Meanwhile, the stream of tendencies flowed on irresistibly. In spite of the hesitation of the Liberal Cabinet, in spite of the growth of ambition on the part of Boards of Guardians, and in spite of the vehement opposition of the Charity Organisation Society and other philanthropists, the ancient institution of the Poor Law, with its concentration on, and limitation to, the one service of relieving destitute persons whilst they were destitute,

[1] *Poor Law Conferences, 1911–1912*, Address by H. J. Manton, pp. 5-7.
[2] *Poor Law Conferences, 1912–1913*, Paper on " The Vagrant and Modern Legislation " by Dr. T. W. Clay, pp. 434-435.

was, in these very years, being increasingly superseded by other public Authorities, central and local, working under diverse statutes, dealing with different classes of poor persons, and all having for their object the prevention of destitution prior to its occurrence. The first step related to the aged poor. " The removal of the pauper disqualification for Old Age pensions at the end of 1910 ", reported an Inspector in 1911, " caused a reduction in the number of persons in receipt of Outdoor Relief in the various Unions amounting to no less than 26 per cent of the whole." [1] " The Old Age Pensions Act ", reported the Inspector for East Anglia in the same year, " has certainly effected a reduction in the number of applicants for Outdoor Relief ; so much so, in fact, that Guardians in many Unions are wondering how they shall fill up the increased spare time of their Relieving Officers. One or two Unions have dispensed with one Relieving Officer, and have reduced the number of relief districts." [2]

After the Aged came the Mentally Defective, who were formally transferred from the Boards of Guardians to the Councils of Counties and County Boroughs by the Mental Deficiency Act of 1913. " The effect of the regulations " [under this Act], we are told in the Local Government Report of 1913–1914, " is that where a Poor Law Authority has reason to believe that a person to whom relief is being given is a defective who is subject to be dealt with under the Act ; and that special reasons exist why the case should be provided for by the Local Authority, a report may be made to us by the Poor Law Authority, and may be transmitted by us to the Board of Control. The Board of Control are then empowered, if they are satisfied that the Local Authority are able and willing to take the case, to issue a certificate which will remove the case from the Poor Law Authority, and place it in the category of cases in respect of whom the County or Borough

---

[1] Fortieth Annual Report of Local Government Board, 1911, J. S. Oxley's Report, p. 33. It was by the Old Age Pensions Act of 1908 (8 Edward VII. c. 40) that the receipt of Poor Relief ceased, on December 31, 1910, to disqualify for the award of an Old Age Pension ; and this fact, together with the further intimation that Old Age pensioners could not receive, in the future, any Poor Relief, other than Medical Relief only, without the value of such relief being counted as income, which might disqualify them for the receipt of their pension, led to the Circular to the Guardians of December 6, 1910 (*Ibid.* pp. lxxiv, 30-31).

[2] *Ibid.*, G. A. F. Hervey's Report, p. 48.

Council have a duty to perform. The initiative in the matter of the transfer of these cases rests with the Poor Law Authority, and we have impressed upon Boards of Guardians the desirability of transferring suitable cases where circumstances render this course expedient. . . . The Poor Law Authorities will continue to be responsible for mentally defective persons chargeable to the Poor Law who are not defective within the meaning of the Act ; and it will often be found expedient that provision should be made for these cases, as well as for sane epileptics, in special institutions." [1]

It is not surprising that the ordinary citizen was puzzled by this new case of overlapping between the Poor Law and the Lunacy Authorities. " The public have had in their minds no clear delimitation of the respective functions of the new County Authorities set up by the Local Government Board ", observes the Inspector for the West Midlands. " Doubts were felt as to whether the two sets of Authorities were meant to be co-operators or rivals. In some areas they have regarded one another with suspicion if not hostility, and there has been a tendency to discourage or even thwart each other's activities. But the recent Circulars of the Local Government Board and the Board of Control should do much to dispel the prevailing confusion. It has now been authoritatively explained that not only have the two Authorities distinct and separate classes of the feeble-minded for which they are responsible, but also that there are many directions in which they can co-operate with one another so as to secure the carrying out of the letter and spirit of the Mental Deficiency Act with the least possible strain on the resources of the ratepayer." [2]

" With a view to avoiding duplication of work and un-necessary expenditure," Boards of Guardians were informed, " it is desirable that where it is proposed to form a combination the Poor Law Authorities concerned should confer with the Local Authorities under the Act before any definite scheme is pro-pounded and that the Joint Committees already constituted should consult with representatives of the Statutory Committee of the County or County Borough Council." [3]

[1] Forty-third Annual Report of Local Government Board, 1914, lxvii.
[2] Forty-third Annual Report of Local Government Board, 1914, R. G. Duff's Report, p. 55.
[3] *Ibid.* p. 15.

Even more bewildering was the coming into force of the National Insurance Act of 1911, with its unprecedented provision for the whole wage-earning class in times of sickness and for large sections in times of Unemployment, not to mention the Maternity Benefit for the wives of insured men, and the prospect of Invalidity Pensions for all. " They could not shut their eyes to the fact ", observed a Yorkshire delegate, " that the position of the Guardians was very much altered by the National Insurance Act with regard to sanatoria. It was true that in many cases the chronic and hopeless cases would have to remain under the care of the Guardians, and the numbers would not be lessened for some time to come, but, after all, what seemed incumbent upon Guardians a year or two ago—to provide sanatoria—would in the near future largely devolve upon the Insurance Committees. Of course the question of sanatoria was again being brought to the notice of Sanitary Authorities because of that wise measure providing for the medical inspection of children, and also by the notification of consumption." [1]

What seemed to add insult to injury was the exclusion of the Poor Law Authority from the grants made from the Exchequer to the Local Health Authority in respect of sanatoria. " Thus the Act ", said a Guardian in 1912, " is against the interests of Guardians in the case of sanatoria. It expressly precludes those sanatoria provided by Boards of Guardians from being subsidised in any way, although they might be a separate institution, and might be away from the ordinary institutions of the Guardians, and on all fours with the sanatoria provided by any other Local Authority. Seeing what Guardians have done in this direction, it does seem hard that our institutions should not be recognised because they are associated with the Poor Law. So that for some time to come we shall have plenty of consumptives to be cared for." [2]

Finally, the national network of Labour Exchanges, established in 1909, coupled with the National System of Unemployment Insurance, inaugurated in 1911, and extended in subsequent years to nearly the whole of the wage-earners, seemed, in those

[1] *Poor Law Conferences, 1912–1913*, p. 288 (Moorhouse).

[2] *Poor Law Conferences, 1912–1913*, Paper by James Blossom (Guardian of the Ecclesall Bierlow Union, Hon. Sec. North Midland Poor Law Conference), pp. 299–300.

years of good trade, to take out of the Poor Law all persons destitute on account of Unemployment.

" The movement known as the Breaking-up of the Poor Law ", wrote in 1912 one of the ablest Poor Law administrators of the old school, " has set in with increasing rapidity within the last few years ; and to-day some four or five different bodies administer public relief where there was one before. . . . The principal Acts by which the ' break-up ' has been effected are the Unemployed Workmen Act of 1905, the Provision of Meals Act of 1906, the Old Age Pensions Act of 1908, and the Education (Administrative Provisions) Act of 1907. An appreciable amount of relief is also administered by Borough Councils under various Acts dealing with Public Health. The Home Office has been making excursions in the same direction through its Reformatories and Industrial Schools ; and the late Home Secretary even proposed to give to the police the duty of seeing to the clothing of ragged children in London, as is already done in several important provincial towns." [1]

" Hitherto ", summed up in 1914 the author of this interesting article, " the course of legislation has followed the lines of the Minority Report rather than those of the Majority. It has extended public relief in most of the directions indicated by the Minority, and has carried into effect many of their recommendations. But one of these recommendations—the only one for introducing some sort of co-ordination and control into this chaos—namely the suggested registration of all forms of public relief, has been ignored altogether. It is rather significant that no one of the signatories of that Report has, as we might have been entitled to expect, raised any sort of protest against the omission. If we are to have the policy of the Minority, we must have it as a whole and not in part." [2]

---

[1] *Some Recent Developments of Poor Relief*, by W. A. Bailward, 1914, pp. 2-3. This had appeared as an article in the *Economic Journal*, December 1912.

This opinion was shared by one of the ablest of the Local Government Board Inspectors, Sir Arthur B. Lowry, C.B., now Chief Inspector. " For instance, he (the reader of the paper) might consider the tendency of modern legislation to transfer the children to the Education Committee, and the tendency to transfer the Able-bodied and Unemployed to a Government Department. When he saw the Majority Commissioners speak of the County Councils' scheme as a compromise it made him wonder ; and he could not help thinking that, when Mr. Sidney Webb read the County Councils' scheme, there must have been a very broad smile upon his face . . ." (*Poor Law Conferences, 1911–1912*, p. 329).

[2] *Some Recent Developments of Poor Relief*, by W. A. Bailward, 1914, p. 44.

The War and the Demobilisation
(1914–1919)

The foregoing description of Poor Law administration, both central and local, between 1909 and 1914, emphasises the strenuous attempt to remedy the defects and to justify the existence of the old idea of a public relief of destitution ; and thus to stop the continuous encroachment on its domain by the newer preventive services. This attempt, it will be noted, was made during " normalcy " ; that is to say, under conditions which might have been expected to continue if it had not been for the outbreak of the Great War. The period (1909–1914) may, we think, be regarded as that in which English Poor Law adminis-tration reached its high-water mark of efficiency, notably as regards all sections of the non-able-bodied—able-bodied pauperism being at the same time at a minimum.

The Suspension during War

So far as the history of the Poor Law is concerned, the next five years proved to be not merely an arrest of development, but a definite stop to departmental reform, and even the beginning of a new and unparalleled increase of pauperism of a specially dangerous kind from which the nation has (1928) not yet re-covered. So long, however, as the war lasted, the unlimited demand for labour, whether in the fighting line, or for the manu-facture of the munitions of war, together with the enormous public expenditure, not only swept away the last remnant of Unemployment and enabled all Outdoor Relief to the able-bodied to be stopped, but even reclaimed for active service about 100,000 of the less impotent of the inmates of the Work-houses, Mental Hospitals and Casual Wards ; [1] including even an unprecedented " mobilisation, in the ranks of labour, of the decrepit and the unfit, the septuagenarian and the child ".[2]

---

[1] " After the panic rise on the outbreak of the War in August 1914, there followed a steady diminution in the volume of relief both indoor and outdoor, which continued uninterrupted year after year throughout the period of hostil-ities down to the end of the year 1918, and was hardly arrested before the end of July 1919 " (First Annual Report of the Ministry of Health, 1920, Part III., Walsh's Report, p. 106).

[2] *Ibid.*, Duff's Report, p. 99.

At the beginning of 1914 the total number of persons of all ages and either sex in Poor Law institutions of all kinds, and of pauper patients in the County

There was a strenuous concentration, upon winning the war, of the thought and attention of the entire public service. Large drafts were made, for the fighting forces, upon the Poor Law establishment, from Relieving Officers and Workhouse Nurses to doctors and the secretariat. As the war proceeded a considerable proportion of the Poor Law institutions were either turned over to the War Office for temporary use, or else made available for the accommodation of wounded officers or men, or of Belgian refugees or German prisoners. By a succession of Circulars during 1915–1917 the Local Government Board drastically cut down the reports, statistics and applications for sanction or approval which had been required from the Boards of Guardians. The records to be kept locally were reduced in number and greatly simplified. For five years all elections were suspended, and vacancies among the elected representatives were filled by co-option.[1] With the successive extensions of control to all kinds of food and fuel, culminating in a universal rationing of the population, the dietaries in the Poor Law institutions were severely curtailed,[2] so as to bring the quantities down to no more than was allowed by the Food Controller ; to such an extent, it was currently reported, as adversely to affect the health, and even to increase the mortality of the aged, the tuberculous and the insane. Inspection and even audit were reduced to a minimum. Up and down the country rules were suspended, the authoritative Orders were only perfunctorily complied with, all sorts of make-shift expedients were resorted to, and it may almost be said that the Boards of Guardians—in many cases the Workhouse Masters—were left to administer as seemed right in their own eyes. " There was," writes an Inspector, " at any rate in the smaller Unions, . . . a retrogression in what was, before the war, a steady, if slow, movement

---

Lunatic Asylums, was 365,233. This number fell steadily, during the next five years, to 266,282 at the end of 1918. The number on Outdoor Relief rose somewhat during 1914, but from January 1, 1915, it fell from 394,707 to 287, 244 at the end of 1918. The numbers in the Casual Wards fell from 7568 on January 1, 1914, to 1091 on December 28, 1918. Thus the aggregate diminution of all classes of paupers during the War (partly by a smaller annual recruitment of the pauper host, and partly by actual transfer from the Institutions and the Out-relief lists to self-support) exceeded 200,000, comprising practically all those between 14 and 70 who were not absolutely incapacitated.

[1] Circular of December 17, 1915, May 26, 1916, December 8, 1916, and December 12, 1917.

[2] Circular of February 28, 1917, and April 8, 1918.

towards realising the principles of ' Classification within the Institution ', and ' Classification by Institutions '. . . . During the war, a combination of causes, such as the paucity of fuel or of staff, the diminishing number of inmates, the difficulties of keeping premises cleaned and in repair, and the overpowering need for economy, have led in many cases to all the men, irrespective of age and character, using one day-room, and all the women another." [1]

The Planning of Reconstruction

Whilst the War Cabinet was stinting all peace-time services in order to win the War, unsystematic but elaborate efforts were being made by the Government for well-planned " reconstruction " whenever Peace should come. Consideration of the subject was begun as early as March 1916, when a Committee of the Cabinet was appointed by the Prime Minister (Asquith), which deputed nine subordinate Committees, not including any members of the Cabinet, to deal with certain important branches of the work.[2] When Mr Lloyd George became Prime Minister, this " First Reconstruction Committee " came to an end in March 1917, leaving its subordinate Committees still at work on their tasks ; and it was replaced by a new Committee, of fourteen members, chosen mainly outside official circles, and presided over by E. S. Montagu, M.P., as Vice-Chairman. This " Second Reconstruction Committee " never assumed control over the Committees appointed by its predecessor ; although one of their reports (the main report of the " Whitley Committee " recommending Joint Industrial Councils), and certain reports from independent Departmental Committees, came formally before the Reconstruction Committee and were, with comments, passed on to the Cabinet. It divided its membership into four " panels ", which were to deal, as

[1] First Annual Report of Ministry of Health, 1920, R. G. Duff's Report, pp. 99-100.
[2] Namely the Acquisition of Powers Committee under Sir George Murray (Cd. 8982) ; Agricultural Policy Committee (under the Earl of Selborne (Cd. 8506, 9079, 9080) ; Exclusion of Aliens Committee, under Sir George Cave ; Coal Conservation Committee, under Viscount Haldane (Cd. 8880, 9084) ; Commercial and Industrial Policy Committee, under Lord Balfour of Burleigh (Cd. 8482, 9032, 9033, 9034, 9035) ; Demobilisation of the Army Committee under E. S. Montagu, M.P. (report not published) ; Forestry Committee under F. D. Acland, M.P. (Cd. 8881) ; Relations between Employers and Employed, under J. H. Whitley, M.P. (Cd. 8606, 9001, 9002, 9085, 9099, 9153) ; Women's Employment Committee under Major J. W. Hills, M.P.

sub-committees, respectively with Wages and Employment, Local Government and Social Services, Industry and Transport, and Education. Meanwhile the various Government Departments, notably the Board of Trade and the Board of Education—perhaps not without some natural resentment at having been ignored—set formal Committees of their own at work upon particular subjects, whilst the War Office and the Ministry of Munitions produced other memoranda. Within eighteen months the "Second Reconstruction Committee" was, in its turn, superseded by the Ministry of Reconstruction under Dr. Addison, M.P., constituted on 21st August 1917, by the New Ministries Act (7 and 8 George V. c. 44). The Minister of Reconstruction appointed, within his first few months of office, more or less formally, more than a dozen additional Committees ; and in January 1918 a large Advisory Council, divided into five sections, with weekly meetings of the ten chairmen and vice-chairmen, as well as a meeting once a week of the women members of the Advisory Council. Altogether, during the three years 1916–1918, the Cabinet sought and obtained, from not far short of a hundred separate Committees and Sub-Committees comprising over 700 separate members, more counsel than it managed to digest, or, as may be suspected, even to read.[1]

[1] Some idea of the multifarious and confused intellectual production of these years may be gained from the List of Commissions and Committees dealing with questions that will arise after the War (Cd. 8916) ; the Statement with regard to Advisory Bodies other than Reporting Committees appointed by the Minister of Reconstruction (Cd. 9195) ; and the Report on the Work of the Ministry of Reconstruction for the period ending December 31, 1918 (Cd. 9231) ; (in addition to the separate reports on particular subjects elsewhere cited) those on Acquisition and Valuation of Land for Public Purposes (Cd. 8998) ; Legal Interpretation of the Term "Period of the War" (Cd. 9100) ; Standardisation of Railway Equipment (Cd. 9193) ; Building Industry after the War (Cd. 9197) ; Currency and Foreign Exchanges after the War (Cd. 9182) ; Financial Facilities (Cd. 9227) ; Financial Risks attaching to holding of Trading Stocks (Cd. 9224) ; the Chemical Trade (Cd. 8882) ; Engineering Trade (New Industries) (Cd. 9226) ; Civil War Workers (Cd. 9117, 9192, 9228) ; Adult Education (Cd. 9107, 9225) ; besides others on Excess Profits, Trusts and Increase of Rent and Mortgage Interest (War Restrictions); and the dozen twopenny "Pamphlets on Reconstruction Problems" published by the Ministry for popular circulation.

Other Committees and Sub-Committees (many of their reports never being published) dealt with Storage and Transit Difficulties ; Civil Workers Resettlement Co-ordination ; Wages Awards ; Training and Machinery of Supply and Distribution of Domestic Servants ; Supply and Allocation of Materials during the Transitional Period ; Legislative Arrangements to prevent Dumping ;

We shall here deal only with four of these inquiries which had an important bearing on the agencies concerned with the prevention or relief of destitution. We may even ignore, as superseded by later developments, the able reports by the Committee on the shortage of dwelling-houses, with the consequent increase in overcrowding and rise in rents, both revealed and accentuated by war-time conditions ; and the comprehensive " Housing Programme " which was prepared, accepting as inevitable the provision of the necessary number of new cottages— both the million urgently required to make good the estimated shortage in 1919, and the seventy or eighty thousand more required annually for the increasing population—as a municipal service, to be liberally aided by Exchequer Grants.[1] Nor need we do more than mention the report by Mr. J. H. Whitley's Committee on the promotion of peace in industry by the establishment of a series of representative joint councils,[2] one in each industrial enterprise and one for each industry as a whole, to be composed of equal numbers of delegates of the " management " and of the manual-working wage-earners respectively, in conjunction with the Employers' Associations on the one side, and the Trade Unions on the other.

Juvenile Employment ; Rural Development, including the Establishment of Information Centres and the Best Method of attracting Returned Soldiers to the Land ; The Vocational Training and Position of Women in various Occupations ; and Subsidiary Health and Kindred Services.

In view of the experience of the past decade, the student will be surprised to find that no Committee or Sub-committee seems to have been appointed specifically to consider the prospect of there being extensive and long-continued Unemployment, as the result of changes in the course of international trade. A proposal (May 9, 1917) to the Second Reconstruction Committee that a Committee should report on " What action should be taken by the Government (i.) immediately, and (ii.) after the conclusion of Peace, in order to prevent the occurrence of any widespread or long-continued involuntary Unemployment " led (in August 1917) to an able survey (by Mr. B. Seebohm Rowntree and Mr. Delisle Burns) of the requirements of the " transitional period " of dislocation upon demobilisation, which does not appear to have been followed up. We are not aware of any systematic consideration in these years of what action would be required if the " transitional period " and the transient boom should be followed by severe and long-continued Unemployment.

[1] See Cd. 9087, 9166, 9223 ; and pamphlets entitled *Housing in England and Wales* and *Housing in Scotland.*

[2] See Cd. 8606, 9001, 9002, 9085, 9099, 9153.

The proposed " Works Councils " never got established ; but Industrial Councils were set up in many branches of industry, some of which are reported to have rendered useful service. Others have proved disappointing to employers and wage-earners alike.

The Extension of the Franchise

Even before the Armistice, however, the Government brought before Parliament, and carried into law—on the main issues, by common consent—an unprecedentedly large widening of the electoral franchise, alike for the House of Commons and for Boards of Guardians among other Local Authorities. It was generally felt that the soldiers who had fought in the War, whether or not they or their dependants had been in receipt of Poor Law relief, could not be denied votes upon the Peace that was to follow ; and hence there was an almost unanimous acceptance of Manhood Suffrage. It seemed, in the emotion of the time, necessary that the service of the women of the country should be similarly recognised ; although it is said to have required an iron determination on the part of the representatives of the Labour Party in the Coalition Government to bring the Cabinet round to this view. Ultimately the feeling of the House of Commons excluded from the franchise all women under 30 years of age, as well as all single women over that age who were not themselves independent occupiers—a departure from the simplicity of Universal Suffrage that was not remedied until the further Representation of the People Act of 1928. It is significant of the widespread public feeling of the time that not only this enormous extension of the franchise, which increased the electorate for the House of Commons [1] from nine to over twenty millions, and that for the Boards of Guardians in nearly the same proportion, but also so dramatic a reversal of policy as the abolition of the disqualification by reason of the receipt of Poor Relief, should have carried in a House of Commons overwhelmingly Conservative and Capitalist in opinion.[2]

[1] For Local Authorities, the electoral franchise was confined to " occupiers " of house or tenement (excluding lodgers and sub-tenants of furnished rooms) ; but the wives (over 30) of male " occupiers " were given votes as if " occupiers " (Representation of the People Act, 1917–1918, 7 and 8 George V. c. 64 ; for the discussions in Committee, see Hansard, vols. 93-99).

[2] Continuance of the pauper disqualification had been recommended by the Speaker's Conference (Resolution 35), on the decisions of which the Bill was framed, and Clause 8 of the Bill embodied this recommendation. Objection in the House of Commons was sufficiently general to cause the Government to withdraw the Clause, and introduce other provisions sweeping away the pauper disqualification for all electoral franchises (Hansard, June 26, 1917, pp. 281-307). Some remnants of pauper disqualification were allowed to remain, partly

The Numbering of the People

A particular reform, which may yet be found an indispensable instrument of our public administration, was not so well received. One of the difficulties met at every turn in the administration of a densely populated nation is the need for an accurate register of the names and addresses, the ages and the marital state of the people for the time being living in each administrative area. Such registers have had to be made, even in England where public sentiment is averse to any " regimentation " ; and the Reconstruction Committee was astonished to find that no fewer than 32 of them were, in fact, compiled and maintained (12 by national and 20 by local departments), at an estimated aggregate expense of something like half a million sterling per annum. But because each of these registers, from the decennial Census down to the School Attendance Officer's list of children to be got to school, is compiled and maintained under separate statutes without reference to any other, without cognisance of births or deaths, and in most cases with newcomers being added without emigrants being taken off, these expensive records are at all times—to use the technical term—" foul ", and statistically inaccurate, leading to fallacious inferences of all sorts, from misleading birth-rates and death-rates, up to fictitiously swollen totals of insured persons in the Ministry of Labour's ledgers or on the Insurance doctors' lists.

A Departmental Committee on National Registration entrusted to an expert Sub-Committee under the Registrar-General (Sir Bernard Mallet), the duty of discovering by what means and at what cost the existing registers could be automatically brought into relation with each other, without imposing any new obligation or any additional restriction on the ordinary citizen, in such a way as to secure a greater degree of constant accuracy. This was found, by the Sub-Committee, in a Central

---

by inadvertence. Thus residence as a pauper or patient in a workhouse, poor-house or any other similar institution is not to be treated as residence for the qualifying period required for insertion in the Voters' List, so that even the briefest institutional treatment may deprive a person of the franchise ; and receipt of Poor Relief within a year still disqualifies a person for being elected or being a member of a Board of Guardians or a Chairman or a Member of an Urban or Rural District Council, as well as of the Metropolitan Asylums Board and some other joint bodies. This disqualification is extended to membership of a County or County Borough Council by the Local Government Act of 1929.

Index Register to be maintained in London, in daily communication with all the Local Authorities, in order to supply each of them with the additions and subtractions required in the local lists. Such a Central Index Register could be maintained, it was found, for £15,000 per annum, being an addition of no more than two or three per cent. to the cost incurred on the present congeries of incorrect registers. Unfortunately, the Government, far from welcoming such a valuable addition to the administrative machinery, failed even to let the report (which had already been printed)[1] be issued for public perusal. No action has been taken on it. The registers accordingly still remain " foul ", and all our statistics, at any rate from Census to Census, continue to suffer from this fundamental inaccuracy.

The Reorganisation of Central Government

It was in connection with governmental structure that the work of these Reconstruction Committees came in the closest connection with the Poor Law and its administration. A special sub-committee under Viscount Haldane was charged with the task of disentangling and rearranging the central organisation for the various functions of National Government, which had become confused and even chaotic. This sub-committee, whose report was published in 1918, sorted out the numerous offshoots and developments of the various Government Departments and rearranged them, according to their essential character and practical relationships, into fourteen Ministries, which (as we have already mentioned) turned out, quite unexpectedly, to resemble those which Bentham, a century before, had forecasted in his Constitutional Code. These Ministries included those of Education, Health and Labour (or Employment), as the three essential Departments of the

---

[1] Departmental Committee on National Registration : Report of Sub-Committee appointed January 17, 1918 (34 pp.).

The result of the failure to put in operation some such plan as that proposed by the Sub-Committee was that, when Unemployment Insurance was, in 1920, made nearly coextensive with the wage-earners, an entirely independent register of over seventeen million people was instituted, without any arrangement for continuous check by the information obtained for all the other registers ; and accordingly without the means of avoiding the accumulation of hundreds of thousands of duplicate entries (by varying or incorrectly reported names), for each of which a separate ledger account has to be maintained.

Framework of Prevention of destitution, covering, respectively, the whole public provision for children and adolescents in normal health from the age for entering the infant school up to that at which the Technical College or the University is left; the whole public provision with regard to maternity and infancy, sickness and infirmity of mind or body, widowhood and Old Age; and the whole public provision with regard to the conditions of employment of the able-bodied, the prevention of Unemployment and the treatment of the Unemployed. It is significant that this highly expert Committee discarded both any Ministry of Local Government as such, and (herein departing from Bentham's vision) any separate Ministry of Poor Relief.[1]

The Ministry of Health

The first step in this rearrangement of Ministries was immediately taken in connection with the Local Government Board itself.[2] Viscount Long, who had enjoyed an exceptionally long tenure of office as President of that Department, had forcibly pressed on the Reconstruction Committee, in 1916, the evil of " the disintegration which has taken place in recent years with the result that there are now various Departments,

---

[1] The Report of the Machinery of Government Committee was published as Cd. 9230; and came in great demand by Political Science students in Europe and America, so that it quickly went out of print.

[2] By the Ministry of Health Act, 1919 (9 and 10 George V. c. 21), the long-disputed question of the proper scope and function of the Local Government Board was determined in the direction desired by Sir John Simon in 1871 (see pp. 197-199). It was to cease to be a Ministry supervising and controlling Local Government as such, which was now seen to be incompatible with the continued existence and development of the Board of Education (as the Ministry for children and adolescents receiving education), or the Ministry of Transport (as that for roads, tramways, omnibuses, ports and harbours, and electricity supply), or the Board of Trade (as the Ministry for gas supply), or the Home Office (as the Ministry for police and justice, and industrial and reformatory schools), all of them supervising the Local Authorities. As part of this sorting out of functions, the supervision of the Local Authorities' work under the Libraries Acts has since been transferred from the Ministry of Health to the Board of Education.

In 1893, as we learn from Sir Charles Dilke's diaries, " it was even proposed [by Sir William Harcourt] at one moment that a Bill should be brought in to give the Local Government Board, for ever, the inspections, such as mines, factories, etc., and the Artizans Dwellings Act, and other matters not connected with Police and Justice; but no legislation took place, as the idea was hotly opposed by the Home Office " (The Life of Sir Charles Dilke, by Stephen Gwynn and Gertrude Tuckwell, 1917, vol. i. p. 507).

each with its expert medical staff, dealing with different aspects of the same question—a system which cannot be economical and which has an obvious tendency towards departmental rivalry and friction. Development of the public health services is almost inevitable in various directions, nursing, diagnosis of disease, medical treatment, and so on, and it is of prime importance that whatever is done should be controlled by one responsible Minister, assisted as far as possible by a single expert staff ".[1]

Practically the whole world of Public Health was united in demanding that there should at last be established a united Ministry of Health. This was done by a Bill prepared by a Sub-Committee, presided over by Dr. Addison, under which the Board of Control (for persons of unsound mind and the mentally defective) and the General Register Office (for the registration of vital statistics) were definitely attached to the new Ministry, in which the Insurance Commissioners and the Local Government Board itself were merged. The Ministry of Health Bill became law in 1918, and the new Ministry started under Dr Addison, appointed as the first Minister of Health, on 1st April 1919.[2]

The Reorganisation of Local Government

The completion of such a scheme of logical reorganisation of Ministries had necessarily to await other changes ; and one of these—the measure of Poor Law Reform advocated both by the Majority and the Minority of the Poor Law Commission of 1905-1909—was tackled by a special sub-committee under Sir Donald Maclean, appointed in July 1917. Among the members of this sub-committee were the Chairman of the Poor Law Commission (Lord George Hamilton) and Sir Samuel Provis, K.C.B., representing the Majority ; and Mrs Sidney Webb representing the Minority, together with experienced representatives and officials of the Local Government Board, the Board of Education, the London County Council and other Local Authorities concerned. The problem was to formulate a scheme

---

[1] Local Government Board to Reconstruction Committee, October 19, 1917.
[2] 9 and 10 George V. c. 21. See " The Ministry of Health Bill ", by J. Allen Battersby, Clerk to the Nottingham Union, in *Poor Law Conferences, 1918-1921*, p. 64 ; " The Passing of the Local Government Board ", in *Local Government Journal*, 1919.

of reform which would bring the essential features of both the Majority and Minority Reports into harmony with each other and with the practical necessities emphasised by the officials of the various Government Departments and Local Authorities. It is a testimony to the influence of the rival Reports of 1909, and to their educational effects during the ensuing decade on officials and the public, that in 1917–1918 such a scheme should have been worked out and unanimously adopted by so representative a body. The Committee fully confirmed the judgment that the overlapping and duplication between the Destitution Authority on the one hand, and the various Authorities dealing with the services preventive of destitution—increased and intensified in the decade that had elapsed since the Report of the Poor Law Commission—constituted a serious evil which had to be brought to an end. The Committee prepared in some detail a complete scheme under which the Local Education, Health and Lunacy Authorities could deal respectively with the children, with the sick and infirm, and with all persons of unsound mind or mentally defective, under the Education, the Public Health and the Lunacy and Mental Deficiency Acts,"suitably extended "; with a Public Assistance Committee of each County and County Borough Council to consider the circumstances of each family as a whole, and maintain a complete register of all forms of Public Assistance ; whilst the general supervision and provision of Grants in Aid from the Exchequer would be undertaken by the Ministries of Education and Health (including the Board of Control). The provision for the able-bodied would be undertaken (herein departing from both Majority and Minority Reports) by the Town and County Councils through committees analogous to the Distress Committees under the Unemployed Workmen Act.[1]

[1] The Report of the " Maclean Committee ", which was published in January 1918, as Cd. 8917, naturally excited widespread interest in the Poor Law world, and led to various comments, among which may be cited *Reconstruction : Local Government*, by Robert J. Parr (National Society for the Prevention of Cruelty to Children, 1918) ; " The Proposed Transfer of Functions of Poor Law Authorities in England and Wales," by Rev. W. Mahon, *Poor Law Conferences, 1918–1921*, p. 30; *Reconstruction of the Poor Law*, etc., by William G. Lewis, 1918 ; and the critical articles in the *Poor Law Officers' Journal* during that year.

In 1925 the House of Commons passed, *nemine contradicente*, a resolution calling for a systematic rehandling of the whole system of public assistance on the lines of the Maclean Report.

" The Maclean Report ", as it was termed, was accepted by the Cabinet in connection with the Ministry of Health Bill ; and, in due course, professedly adopted, at least in principle, by successive Governments, as affording the lines on which Poor Law Reform would, when opportunity could be found, be presented to Parliament.[1] It is, as will be referred to in the Epilogue, professedly followed but very imperfectly carried out in the Local Government Act of 1929, which—to name only two great classes—leaves all the lunatics and all the destitute Unemployed still in the Poor Law, though under the administration of the County and County Borough Councils.

[1] Among other publications of this period may be cited an able and eloquent appeal to the Christian Church, entitled *Your Part in Poverty*, by George Lansbury, 1918 ; *These Things Shall Be*, by the same, 1920 ; *The Slippery Slope* (a collection of articles and addresses), by W. A. Bailward, 1920 ; *The Facts of Poverty*, by H. A. Mess, 1920.

CHAPTER IX

THE RECURRENCE OF ABLE-BODIED PAUPERISM

THE last ten years of the Boards of Guardians coincided with the most important event in English Poor Law history since 1834. The flood of Outdoor Pauperism arising out of the continuous Unemployment of the years 1920–1928 not only transcended every previous record, but also set at naught all accepted Poor Law wisdom, and submerged principles, Orders and Circulars alike.

The temporary boom in trade, following the Armistice of November 1918, lasted little over eighteen months—and this was longer than some economists had expected—to be succeeded, as we have described,[1] by a catastrophic fall of prices and the widespread collapse of capitalist enterprise. The slump quickly produced Unemployment in nearly every industrial area, with results upon Poor Law administration that demand detailed examination.

The Opening of the Floodgates

We can best begin our description by a recital of the Poor Law statistics. The number of persons in receipt of relief in England and Wales, which, when war broke out in August 1914, had been 619,000, had sunk, by the date of the Armistice in November 1918, to no more than 450,000.[2] By April 1, 1920, this number had risen only to 494,000. In October 1920, however, it started to soar, reaching 568,000 on December 31, 1920, and 653,000 on March 31, 1921, the increase being general throughout

---

[1] See Chapter VII., " Unemployment as a Disease of Modern Industry ", pp. 631-715.

[2] These figures are exclusive of the Vagrants, the insane in County asylums, and those in receipt only of domiciliary Medical Relief ; these classes amounting to between 100,000 and 120,000.

the Metropolitan district, most of the provincial cities and many of the populous urban areas.[1] Between April and July 1921, when there was a prolonged dispute in the coal-mining industry, the number rose suddenly to no fewer than 1,363,121, being more than had previously been recorded at any time since 1849, when Poor Law statistics began to be compiled on the present system. What was of serious import was the fact that the reopening of the coal-mines on July 1, 1921, did no more than slightly and temporarily reduce this swollen total, which by November 5 had again risen to 1,519,823. In spite of increases and extensions of the Unemployment Insurance Benefit to hundreds of thousands of claimants, the number in receipt of Poor Law relief on March 31, 1922, stood at 1,490,996 ; or more than twice as many as in the last week of Peace in July 1914.[2] At or about this high level it has stuck. During the past eight years the total has never fallen below a million, whilst at the peak, during the prolonged stoppage of the coal-mines in 1926, it reached just upon two and a half millions, a number enormously in excess of any previous experience in the whole history of the English Poor Law.

This great expansion of pauperism was all the more serious in that it was, for the most part, not among what used to be called " the impotent poor ", but among men ordinarily in wage-earning employment (together with their dependent wives and children)—applicants who, until 1913, would have been classed as " Able-bodied ", and of whom a large proportion had never previously sought Poor Relief. Prior to the war, the relief, through the Poor Law, of able-bodied men in health had been reduced to a minimum. Men wandering on the roads resorted to the Casual Wards to the number of a few thousands on any one night in the whole of the country. A few thousands in each week may have got bread from the couple of thousand or so of Relieving Officers as cases of " sudden or urgent necessity ". A few thou-

---

[1] Second Annual Report of Ministry of Health, 1921, p. 124.

[2] Third Annual Report of Ministry of Health, 1922, pp. 78–80. " About 793,000 of these were persons insured under the Unemployment Insurance Acts, and their wives and families ; and about 65,000 were persons and families ordinarily employed in some regular employment but not so insured." Excluding these two classes, " the number in receipt of relief at the end of March 1922 . . . was 607,000. The total number in receipt of relief at the end of the last financial year before the War was 644,000 " (*ibid.*). The Ministry of Health thus suggested that the whole increase of pauperism in 1922, in comparison with 1913–1914, was of a new kind.

sands more may have been scattered as temporary inmates among the 600 Workhouses. But apart from small doles to meet exceptional family expenses (such as sickness, burial, or some other emergency), the grant of Outdoor Relief to healthy able-bodied men was, in 1913 and during the next seven years, practically unknown.[1]

The new tide of pauperism that set in during 1920–1921 was almost entirely one of Outdoor Relief, of which there came to be, during eight whole years, never less than close upon a million recipients [2] (about one-fourth of them able-bodied men), at a cost from April 1, 1920, to March 31, 1928, of about £122,000,000. Of this vast sum, it can be estimated that at least £60,000,000 may be ascribed to the new category of able-bodied men and their dependants destitute merely on account of Unemployment, representing an average extra Poor Law expenditure, *apart from the normal pauperism,* of £7,500,000 annually.

The new flood of pauperism came upon a limited number of Unions, some two hundred in number, in different parts of the country ; but these Unions included about one-half of the whole population of England and Wales. Whilst the rural districts were scarcely touched, the flood spread over practically all the industrial areas and the seaports, being most serious in those dependent on such industries as coal-mining, iron and steel production, engineering and shipbuilding, and most of the textile manufactures, together with the commercial and shipping centres. The acute depression in these industrial areas has been aggravated, during the past eight years, by two prolonged national stoppages of coal-mining ; by a brief universal stoppage of the railways ; by troubles among the ironfounders and engineers ; by minor disputes in other industries, and by the ten days' " General Strike " of May 1926. On the other hand, employment has been stimulated by the heavily subsidised erection of more than a million dwelling-houses ; by the establishment with Government aid of the sugar-beet industry ; by the State guaranteeing over £70,000,000 of loans raised for industrial extensions and new developments ; and by the continuous growth of the

---

[1] The only exception was the Poplar Union, which, as we have described, began to give Outdoor Relief to the able-bodied Unemployed in 1904 ; and thereafter, as we shall relate, continued it by various evasions of the spirit, if not also of the letter, of the Relief Regulation Order, 1911.

[2] The figure on March 31, 1928, was 959,862.

industries connected with electric light and power, wireless telegraphy, motor transport, the gramophone, and artificial silk. Unemployment has led to vastly increased Poor Relief in industries which have been substantially free from industrial trouble (such as iron and steel and shipbuilding and textiles), as well as in those (such as coal-mining) which have been exceptionally interrupted by trade disputes. It is remarkable how stable, during the past seven or eight years, has been the geographical distribution of the recurrence of Able-bodied Destitution. Nearly all the Poor Law Unions seriously affected by the flood of Unemployment in 1920–1921 were similarly affected, though naturally not exactly to the same extent, in 1927–1928.[1]

The complicated and disordered dispensation of Outdoor Relief by about 230 out of the 630 Boards of Guardians is hard to describe in a way that will leave on the reader's mind any other impression than a senseless confusion of methods and aims. For the first few years of this extraordinary episode in Poor Law history, Boards of Guardians were left, in the main, to meet the emergency in their own ways, without consistent guidance by the Ministry of Health. Incidentally we may note that this new Ministry, created in 1919, with a much larger content than the Local Government Board, relegated, as its name betokened, the Poor Law Division to a back place. Hence we shall, for this period of our history, concentrate first, not, as heretofore, on the policy of the Central Authority, but on the day by day administration of Boards of Guardians which we have reason to think typical of the new and sometimes unauthorised ways of dealing with the problem of Able-bodied Destitution. But before plunging into this maze of seemingly disconnected detail we have to notice three separate happenings, unrelated one to the others, but each having its own distorting effect on the activities of the Boards of Guardians.

---

[1] Of the able-bodied men, with their dependants, who were, in June 1927, in receipt of Outdoor Relief on account of Unemployment, 96,004, being 82 per cent, were in 50 Unions (containing 35 per cent of the total population of England and Wales). About 180 more were supporting the remaining 18 per cent of the destitute Unemployed. On the other hand, 206 Unions had none, and 185 others fewer than 10 each, making 391 practically unaffected (Ninth Annual Report of Ministry of Health, 1928, p. 140).

The Golden Showers

Only a generation ago the provision of maintenance from public funds, and notably any direct payment by the State of household incomes week by week, otherwise than in return for services rendered, was, apart from Poor Relief, so exceptional as to be outside anyone's mind. At Queen Victoria's first Jubilee in 1887 it did not occur to anyone as a possibility that the whole population, or even the whole of any one stratum or section of the population, would be made, by statute, entitled, as of right, and gratuitously, to weekly money payments from the Exchequer. The receipt of Poor Relief by able-bodied men in health was almost universally regarded as a matter of disgrace; and their case was sharply distinguished from those of Old Age infirmity or disabling sickness, or the widowhood or orphanage due to premature death of the bread-winner, or some other overwhelming misfortune, where the receipt of what was regarded as public charity to particular sufferers was excused.

How has this momentous change of opinion come about? We described in a previous chapter (pp. 554-630) how the gradual elaboration of the Framework of Prevention had led, already at the opening of the Poor Law Commission (1905), to an increasing supersession, by other forms of treatment, of the Poor Law provision for the children and the sick. When the Framework of Prevention was widened so as to make it co-extensive with all disabling ill-health and infirmity, the Government did not adopt, for this purpose, the policy of developing the successful work of the Public Health organisation. Parliament decided in 1911 to set up, under the Health Insurance Commissioners for England, Wales, Scotland and Ireland, a separate system of prompt and ubiquitous medical treatment of every ailment, and to couple with this a small weekly payment as an unconditional contribution towards the cost of maintenance of the sick wage-earner. In this way, with the best of intentions, practically the whole wage-earning class was made acquainted with a system of weekly payments from the State. In another field the new policy dropped even any analogue of the " bottle of physic " by which the Insurance Commissioners sought, in the main, to cope with disease, and supplied nothing but the weekly allowance. That is to say, the scheme of Unemployment Insurance gave no treatment to the Unemployed man. It neither " set him to work ", according to the Elizabethan statutes, nor kept him in training for future employment—the modern equivalent—but merely provided him during a limited number of weeks, and practically unconditionally, with a temporary payment confessedly inadequate for full maintenance. In its first form, Unemployment Insurance did no more than afford, for transient periods of Unemployment, to the workers in trades exceptionally liable to the alternating booms and slumps of the " Trade Cycle ", a subvention in aid of savings. Yet already, when the War broke out in 1914, the two Insurance Schemes, both of them still in the earliest stages of development, were distributing over £150,000 per week to about as many households, which were but a shifting sample of nearly the whole of the wage-earners of the Kingdom.

One observation may be permitted upon this policy of a weekly subvention of working-class households, which, during the past twenty years, has been engrafted on the steadily expanding Framework of Prevention. It was not asked for by the wage-earners. It formed no part of the demands of the representative organisations of the wage-earning class. It is, for instance, not to be discovered in the resolutions, during 1900–1910, of the Trades Union Congress or in those of the Annual Conferences of the growing Labour Party. It was not included in the comprehensive programme for dealing with social problems formulated by either the Majority or the Minority of the Poor Law Commission of 1905–1909, which gave no encouragement to any but the most limited schemes of Social Insurance, which were then already adumbrated.[1]

What has been unkindly called the plan of " salving social sores with shillings ", costly as it might prove in cash, was suggested by politicians, and adopted by Cabinets and Parliaments of the middle and upper classes, as an easier alternative, and one

---

[1] We may note that the Minority Report, to the whole scheme of which the Labour Party presently committed itself, found no use for any National Health Insurance, and had quite other plans for preventing sickness and providing those who were sick with all that was required. With regard to Unemployment Insurance, the Report allowed, with some hesitation, State aid to the voluntary provision of Out-of-Work Benefit by the Trade Unions of specially thrifty workmen. But with this partial exception, the Report proposed quite other means for dealing with Unemployment and the Unemployed. For a critical examination of the Government's Insurance Proposals of 1911, and an examination of the place that Insurance may properly claim in Social Reform, see *The Prevention of Destitution*, by S. and B. Webb, 1911.

more likely to win popular approval, than the regulations and reorganisation that were called for. Any such regulations and reorganisation required from the statesman an " intolerable toil of thought ", and might have proved unwelcome, or at least irksome, to the captains of industry. Moreover, the Insurance schemes seemed, to the Income Tax payer, to have the attraction of " making the poor provide their own Poor Rate " !

On the outbreak of the Great War, the governing class was so desperately anxious to ensure success that anything, however costly, was acquiesced in that would maintain the people in their patriotic support of the Nation's struggle, and evoke from them the utmost contribution of men and munitions. Probably in no great European war did any civilian population of a belligerent nation suffer so little economic hardship, whilst the struggle lasted, as that of Great Britain during 1914–1918. The wife and children of every man absorbed into the fighting forces—even the " unmarried wife " and the illegitimate off-spring—were continuously paid substantial " Separation Allow-ances ", which in many cases made them better off than they had been with the bread-winner at home. Every disabled soldier or sailor was either maintained in hospital or else given an immediate pension, and often, in addition, liberal " Treatment Allowances ". The widows and orphans of those who fell, and often also the parents, were instantly awarded provisional pensions, based very largely on the deceased man's unverified statement upon enlistment of what his earnings had been. Meanwhile many of the women and children of the soldiers' families, and occasionally their parents, were engaged in munition work, or as substitutes in other industry, at relatively high wages. The wholesale prices of food were kept from soaring by Govern-ment imports, and in the case of bread the retail price was reduced by a heavy subvention from the Exchequer. All this watchful care for the civilian population, and especially for the families of the enlisted men, undoubtedly " maintained the national spirit", and, by preventing the war from becoming unpopular, may well have contributed as potently to the eventual victory as the multiplication of shells. But it cannot be ignored, after the event, that this prodigious and long-continued distribution of public money, week by week, in millions of poor homes— necessary as it doubtless was to the object that the nation had at heart—accustomed the people to what (if it had been issued by the Poor Law Authorities) would have been called Outdoor Relief. The effect upon the popular imagination was, as we shall relate, seen in future years. Such a shower of domiciliary allowances, even when given in a great national emergency by the War Office, Admiralty and Air Force, or by the Ministry of Pensions, without any connection with the Poor Law, could not be wholly free from the injurious consequences too often resulting from Outdoor Relief. Nor did the payments end with the fighting. Apart from the continuance of the pensions to the wounded, and to the parents, widows and children of the killed, the demobilisation during 1919 was accompanied by a large distribution of money gratuities to both officers and men. On the whole, however, the arrangements for demobilisation were carefully devised from the standpoint of avoiding pauperisation. To the men, only a small part of the gratuity was paid immediately in cash, the balance being placed to each man's credit in the Post Office Savings Bank, the book being handed to him only on arrival at the town or village to which he had elected to proceed, and for which he received a free railway ticket. Elaborate and varied schemes of education were provided for practically all who would accept training, from University courses for officers and others of sufficient previous education, down to workshop instruction in handicrafts and agricultural training on Government farms. Under the Land Settlement (Facilities) Act of 1919, small holdings were provided, primarily for ex-Service men, both by the Ministry of Agriculture and Fisheries and the Scottish Board of Agriculture, and by the County Councils, assisted by exceptionally liberal grants from the Exchequer, either of the capital required, or of the annual charge for interest, or of the loss incurred. In this way, though at an almost disproportionate cost for each successful family, and with many " failures " from one or other cause, a few thousand non-commissioned officers and men were effectually " settled on the land ". But, for the most part, the demobilised men sought to return to their former employments ; and for these what was done (apart from much assistance in directing them to vacancies, and persuading employers to re-engage ex-Service men) was a general provision for Unemployment, to be available, when required, during twelve months from demobilisation.

The plan was to assure to every man or woman who had either served in the Forces, or in the Mercantile Marine, or in the manufacture of any of the munitions or other requisites of war, a special " Out of Work Pay ", irrespective of any contributory insurance scheme, during any week of Unemployment within the year. The amount disbursed under this head in 1919–1920 proved to amount to more than 40 million pounds for the ex-Service men, and more than 21 million pounds for the munition workers [1]—a new form of Outdoor Relief which was by no means free from objectionable features.

During the year of demobilisation, as during the War, there was, in fact (and perhaps inevitably so), an atmosphere of indulgence and generosity towards those who seemed to be pecuniarily suffering in the industrial dislocation that necessarily followed the sudden cessation of war industries.

During the next few years the operations of the Ministry of Pensions became systematised, so that about a million persons were being maintained (often for life) by weekly payments through the Post Office, almost exactly like the Old Age Pensions, and these were themselves doubled in amount, and made available for a constantly increasing number of claimants. In 1925, indeed, Old Age Pensions were made payable, in the majority of new cases, at 65 instead of at 70, in full, and almost without limitations, and extended to widows and orphans. The result is that to-day (1928) nearly every working-class family in Great Britain has, without being fully conscious of the fact, a continuous ledger account with the National Government—in fact, usually three such ledger accounts, for Unemployment, Health and Old Age Insurance respectively, and, in hundreds of thousands of cases, also a fourth at the Ministry of Pensions—from which he or she is legally entitled, whenever the specific cause for claim arises, to demand a weekly income. The total payments into the households of the wage-earners, under these gigantic schemes, to all intents and purposes from " the Government " or " the State ", amount this year (1928) to over two million pounds *per week*. There can hardly be any family of the wage-earning class that does not, *within each year*, draw, as of

---

[1] Statistics relating to Financial Provision for Relief of Unemployment (including Post-War Resettlement of ex-Members of His Majesty's Forces), from the Armistice, Cmd. 2082, 1924.

right, in respect of the sickness, Unemployment, Old Age, widowhood, orphanage, or pensionable disability of one or other of its members, for a longer or shorter period, an unconditional pecuniary subvention towards its housekeeping. But a number of these claimants fail to obtain this payment, they know not why. In fact, the regulations and conditions are so complicated that no workman or workman's wife can possibly distinguish accurately between the cases in which this income is payable, and those in which it has to be refused. Can it be wondered at that it should now be almost universally accepted, not by the wage-earners alone, but also by the class from which the Poor Law Guardians have been mainly drawn, and, indeed, by public opinion generally, that whenever, by no fault of its own, the wage-earner's family is prevented from earning wages, it is the admitted duty of the State (if not through one or other of the Ministries of Pensions, Labour or Health, or through the local Distress Committee, then at least through the Board of Guardians), not merely, in the old phraseology, to "relieve destitution", but actually to supply, irrespective of any service rendered to the community, the "adequate" income of which the innocent family has been by some technicality deprived ? " The recent changes in social and economic conditions ", significantly observed an Inspector in 1919, " have undoubtedly increased the difficulties of dealing adequately with some branches of Poor Law administration ".[1]

The Effect of Domiciliary Payments

To the individual recipients and to the unheeding public, the predominant feature of these millions of cash payments has seemed to be the provision of weekly maintenance, whether partial or com-

[1] First Annual Report of Ministry of Health, 1920, Part III., Duff's Report, p. 99.

Eight years later the same Inspector reported that : " A public opinion has grown up since the War under which many men have come to expect that as soon as they are out of work the public, through the Guardians, will support them, and the Guardians have become accustomed to doing so. There is a tendency for the casual labourer, and for those elderly men who are capable of light work but not of hard work, to expect to get from the Poor Fund what the insured man can claim from the Unemployed Insurance Fund ; and, indeed, for the man approaching pensionable age, to expect support from the Poor Law until he reaches that age. . . . The former unwillingness to accept Poor Relief has been weakened by the coming of these rival forms of public assistance " (Administration of the Poor Law, Stationery Office, 1928, p. 69, W. D. Bushell's report).

plete. But when we examine the effect of these State-provided weekly incomes on the mind and conduct of the recipients, of their neighbours and acquaintances, and of the various classes of potential recipients, discrimination between the several types of payment is fundamental. In this examination the dominating factor is not the payment or the amount of the payment, or even by whom the payment is made, but the conditions on which it is granted, and especially the service to be rendered, or the obligation to be fulfilled, in respect of the payment. It is, for instance, not the intervention of the National Government or the Local Authority that constitutes the crucial distinction between one payment and another. There can be no objection to the National Government paying wages to the postmen or to the shipwrights in the dockyards. No one can demur to the Local Authority paying wages to the scavengers and the road-menders. The Separation Allowances paid to the families of soldiers on active service were, so far as the feelings of the recipients were concerned, analogous to those paid by shipowners to the wives of seamen on voyages. Whether such provision for the wife and family should be given to the man himself, and only diverted by his order ; or issued direct to the wife and mother ; moreover, whether the allowances should form a part of his wages, or take the form of an additional allowance proportionate to the size of the family, are secondary considerations which need not be discussed in this connection.

When we pass to the War Pensions, whether in respect of disability attributable to active service, or in respect of the death either of the bread-winner or of adult sons, the community is but following the practice of Employers' Liability and Workmen's Compensation for accidents and industrial diseases, with the added sentiment of acknowledging the heroism of those who fought for their country. A similar explanation might be given of the transient episode of the gratuities on demobilisation ; and even of the unprecedented distribution of Out of Work Donation to discharged fighters and munition workers whenever, within the ensuing year, they failed to get wage-earning employment. In all these cases it may well be argued that any invidious effects upon mind and conduct were in their nature temporary, not giving rise to expectations of future payments, and commonly regarded as justified by the national emergency.

Passing from the extensive and varied payments due to the War to the more important permanent commitments of the State, we come first to the non-contributory Old Age Pensions payable under the Act of 1908. These payments, though given without exacting in return either the performance of service or the fulfilment of obligations, have been, in our opinion, in their effect on mind and conduct, not only harmless, but actually beneficial. The expectation of a pension could not cause any person to become aged, and the pensions could, as experience has proved, be so safeguarded in administration as to make it unprofitable for any person to divest himself of his property in order to become eligible. No one has suggested that the superannuation allowances to Civil Servants, or those which large commercial undertakings had found it advantageous to give to their own employees, had had any injurious effects on character or on thrift. Moreover, the Old Age Pensions were, in fact, little more than a substitute for the freely given but inadequate doles of Outdoor Relief, which were actually being drawn by a very large proportion of the aged wage-earners or their widows ; and it seems to us that as regards any influence on personal saving, and as regards the effect on mind and conduct generally, this substitution of State Pensions for Poor Relief has been, in fact, beneficial. When, as under the Old Age, Widows' and Orphans' Contributory Pensions Act of 1925, the pension is made payable at sixty-five or on widowhood, instead of at seventy ; when it is avowedly granted in return for at least a partial provision made in the past throughout life and health by the recipient himself ; and, above all, when it is given, as a matter of right, irrespective of the affluence of the recipient and of the kindly succour afforded by his children, the superiority, in the effect upon mind and conduct, of the State Pension over Poor Relief becomes undeniable. Poor Relief necessarily discriminates in favour, not of the most worthy citizens, but of the most unfortunate, the least skilful and self-reliant, and in countless instances even of the idle, the thriftless, and those of the worst conduct. The supreme social advantage of what (like Old Age Pensions) is provided for all, over any form of Poor Relief, is that it leaves unchanged the superiority in advantage of the citizen of good character, worthy conduct, integrity, industry and capacity over the citizen who, from any cause, has led what the community considers a bad life. The addition of any number of equals to unequals leaves these latter no less unequal than before.

The vast systems of Health and Unemployment Insurance, with their colossal aggregates of weekly payments to practically all the wage-earning families, have, as we have already noticed, some invidious features. The adverse psychological effects of these payments are perhaps obviated, and are at least mitigated, by the consciousness of insurance. A very substantial compulsory deduction is now made from wages, to say nothing of what the economists describe as the certain but indefinite drag upon the rate of wages which results from the toll levied on the employer being in proportion, not to his profits, but to the number of wage-earners whom he employs. It must not be forgotten that, even to the extent that the wage-earners have, in these two ways, themselves to pay throughout their working lives for the Benefits they receive in sickness and Unemployment, the transaction is advantageous both for themselves and for the community. Their weekly contributions quickly become a matter of course : as they become accustomed to the burden, and adjust themselves to it, it is less felt. On the other hand, the Benefits, in which eventually they all share, coming to those in exceptional need at the exceptional moment, are of far greater value to the particular recipients than their contributions were. Moreover, at such times of stress, the money is spent on commodities of first necessity rather than on luxuries, drink and gambling. The whole insured population gains an additional security against destitution, whilst the community is relieved from the necessity of making the provision out of the Poor Rate.

These National Insurance schemes concern us here only in so far as they provide Benefits for the able-bodied. It is, indeed, the mass of payments into the homes of the workers under the system of Unemployment Insurance which is open to the most obvious criticism, and which incurs, in its administration, the greatest dangers. Involuntary Unemployment is more easily simulated than sickness ; and the temptation to a life of slackness and spells of complete idleness is, with many natures, great. Those who objected to the institution of any State scheme of Unemployment Insurance (apart from a public subvention to insurance by voluntary associations)—and these included, it may be remembered, both the Majority and the Minority of the Poor

Law Commission, and many Trade Unionists as well as the Charity Organisation Society—had cogent reasons for their opposition. Though the State scheme has averted a social catastrophe and has not yet done all the harm we feared, it still seems to us that its effect upon mind and conduct must become quite seriously bad in those cases in which Unemployment is long-continued. Those psychological advantages of the scheme which offset the evil depend upon maintaining the feeling that it is really one of Insurance. It ought not, in our judgment, to deal with " Uninsurable propositions ". It is, for instance, most properly applicable to accidental or seasonal interruptions of employment, or to those attributable to the trade cycle. It is less easily adapted to stoppages caused by industrial disputes, even after the actual participants in the dispute have been excluded from Benefit. And in our judgment it ought not to be made to cover the Unemployment of persons for whom no situation has been found after years of attempts by the Employment Exchange and by themselves, whether this prolonged Unemployment is attributable to their own incapacity to perform any service that any employer requires, or to any form of misconduct, or of inability to conform to the industrial routine, or to any such general cause as the decay of their industry, or of trade generally. To continue Unemployment Benefit in such uninsurable circumstances is but to give, under a different name, indiscriminate, inadequate and unconditional Outdoor Relief.

We come now to the last kind of domiciliary payment, the only one with which, in this chapter, we are directly concerned : the grant, on a large scale, of unconditional Outdoor Relief to able-bodied destitute adults. And here we recall the fact that it was a like distribution of money in the homes of able-bodied labourers that led to the appointment of the famous Poor Law Commission of 1832–1834 ; to the formulation of the " Principle of Less Eligibility " and the proposal of the " Workhouse Test"; to the passage into law of the Poor Law Amendment Act ; to the establishment of a new Local Authority under the supervision and control of a new National Department ; in fact, to a revolution, not only in the administration of relief but also in the structure of English Government. It is true that the "scandalous " expenditure on Able-bodied Destitution during the first three decades of the nineteenth century had its characteristic form. The " Allowance System ", set up by the Justices in 1795, provided doles of money for agricultural labourers, handloom weavers and others earning insufficient wages, or temporarily unemployed, which were manifestly insufficient for complete maintenance, and were, in fact, usually regarded as a " Rate in Aid of Wages ". The Scales of Relief adopted in many Unions in 1920–1928 were, as we shall presently recount, deliberately calculated to provide " adequate " maintenance according to the size of each family. And although the practice of supplementing earnings to make them up to the Scale has frequently prevailed, it has seldom been avowed and not much advertised, it being, indeed, expressly forbidden by the Central Authority. These differences in detail between the practice of 1795–1834 and that of 1920–1928 do not affect the issue on which the Poor Law Commission of 1832–1834 was so emphatic. Can we afford to make the condition of the healthy able-bodied man other than " less eligible " than that of the man in employment at wages ; and if so, under what conditions ? These two vital questions seem to us to have been decisively answered by the tragic experiences of the past eight years.

The Merthyr Tydfil Judgment

Near the end of the century there came a dispute in the mining valleys of Glamorgan and Monmouth that resulted, on April 1, 1898, in a five-months' stoppage of practically all the collieries in which the rates of wages were governed by the Sliding Scale, and thus exposed to the vicissitudes of the coal-owners' unrestricted competition among themselves to increase their sales by " cutting " prices. Suddenly something like a hundred thousand men working in collieries, or in the iron and steel and tin-plate industries, and others dependent on coal, found themselves wageless, with the scantiest of financial support from their Trade Unions ; and nearly a third of all the population of South Wales, the majority unprovided with any appreciable savings, were, month after month, without income. In many a narrow valley, dependent on a single colliery enterprise, prac-tically the whole of the wage-earning class became destitute. The Guardians of the Merthyr Tydfil and Bedwellty Unions found, over and above their ordinary pauperism, over 40,000 men, women and children on their hands for months together. With the sanction of the Local Government Board, they put the Outdoor Labour Test Order in force by opening Stone-yards, where several thousands of men broke stone that piled up mountains high, in return for £39,000 in Outdoor Relief.[1]

This strike was of historic importance in Poor Law history, because it led to the " Merthyr Tydfil Judgment ", a solemn and authoritative declaration of the law that in later years produced unforeseen and far-reaching results. " In the Merthyr Union ", the Inspector told the Poor Law Commission in 1906, the Guardians " representing the employers for the most part resented strongly the opening of any Labour Yards for men who could, if they chose, obtain work ",[2] if they would but consent to accept the employers' terms. But a refusal of relief to the thousands of families that were plainly destitute would, testified the Inspector, " have entailed a small army of independent Assistant Relieving Officers (who were, by the way, not to be had) ", in order to watch each household almost day by day, so as to dole out food, when the case became one of " urgent necessity ", in time to prevent death or illness from starvation. Hence the Local Government Board did not hesitate to sanction the grant of Outdoor Relief to the men and their families whom the stoppage had rendered destitute, conditionally on the men performing the task of work in the Labour Yard.

In sanctioning the grant of Poor Relief to men on strike, conditionally on the performance of a task of work, the Local Government Board in 1898 were following the established practice. This had been described in detail by J. S. Davy, on behalf of the Local Government Board, to the House of Lords Committee on Poor Relief in 1888. " In the case of a strike, taking first of all the case as affecting the men who actually struck, a great proportion of them would be in receipt, for some time at least, of what is called Strike Pay, and would not be destitute ; but supposing they were destitute, from whatever

---

[1] The Stone-yards had to be opened also in the Abergavenny, Crickhowell and Pontypool Unions, but only for a short time and a small number of men. In the Pontypridd, Newport and Bridgend Unions, where opportunities for alternative employment were not entirely lacking, the numbers were sufficiently small to permit the Guardians to tide over the emergency by various devices and evasions, without opening the Labour Yard.

[2] Poor Law Commission, 1909, Appendix, vol. i. pp. 29-30, 256-257; also vol. iA, p. 33.

cause, and applied to the Guardians for relief, the Guardians are bound to relieve them, and it would not be enough for a Board of Guardians to say, ' You are on strike ; you must go back to work '. In order to be safe, they must show that the men can, by applying at a certain place at a certain time, get work. Now and then an exceptional arrangement is made with the masters, in case of strike, to keep some work going to offer to men who apply to the Guardians, and in that case the men are not destitute ; but as a rule the masters will not open the works to take on a few hands." [1]

This view of the law was now to be tested, with unexpected results. The South Wales coal-owners, and notably the directors of the Powell Dyffryn Steam Coal Company, resented what they regarded as the Guardians' support of the men with whom they had a dispute ; and as soon as this was ended two actions were, in 1898, begun in the High Court against the Merthyr Tydfil Board of Guardians, asking for a declaration that the relief of able-bodied men who might have obtained work at wages, but did not do so, was, even if they became destitute, unauthorised by any statute, and beyond the powers of any Poor Law Authority. The legal points raised evidently puzzled the Judges, and led to long delay in their coming to a decision. In the Chancery Division, Mr. Justice Romer held that the relief was justified as having been given in " sudden and urgent necessity ". The Powell Dyffryn Steam Coal Company would not accept this decision, and took the case to the Court of Appeal. Ultimately, in 1900, the Court allowed the appeal, and declared the law in a long judgment read by the Master of the Rolls (Sir Nathaniel, afterwards Lord Lindley). It will suffice to say that the Court held, without citing any statutory authority for the assertion, that the law provided that " no one who was starving could be lawfully refused relief ", whether he was in that state by his own fault or not. But the Court also held, on this point citing many Acts of Parliament, that the Boards of Guardians had no statutory authority, and that the Local Government Board could give them none by Order or otherwise, to grant Poor Relief in any form, even by mere admission to the Workhouse, to any able-

[1] Evidence of J. S. Davy, Select Committee of House of Lords on Poor Relief, 1888. This view of the law was popularly published for the guidance of the Guardians, even after the objection of the South Wales coal-owners, in *Knight's Guardians' Guide*, by an Official, 1899, pp. 38-39.

bodied man, whether or not he was on strike, who, to the knowledge of the Guardians, could, in fact, then and there obtain
employment at wages sufficient to support himself and his family.
On the other hand, as the punishment for refusing to work was
not death by starvation, the Guardians were legally warranted
in granting such an obstinate man Poor Relief (in any form and
under any conditions that the Local Government Board had
prescribed) if and when he had become " so weak as to be no
longer able to work ". Moreover, the Court's declaration of the
law went on to include a further provision (for which, again, no
statutory authority was cited), which turned out to be of greater
consequence than all the rest of the Judgment, namely, that—
to quote the summary version that became influential in Poor
Law circles—the Guardians " are justified in relieving the wives
and children of such men who are reduced to a state of destitution
by the men refusing to accept work because they are on strike
for higher wages ".[1]

---

[1] We give this in the words in which it was promulgated to the Poor Law
service ; for instance, *The Relieving Officers' Handbook*, by W. H. Dumsday,
1902, p. 65. For the case itself (the Attorney-General *versus* Guardians of the
Merthyr Tydfil Union) see *Law Reports*, 1900, 1 Chancery 516 ; 62 *Law Journal*,
Chancery, 299 ; 82 *Law Times*, New Series, 662 ; 48 *Weekly Reports*, 403 ; 64
Justice of the Peace, 27 ; 16 *Times Law Reports*, 251 ; *Laws of England*, edited by
the Earl of Halsbury ; Minutes of Evidence, Poor Law Commission, Appendix,
vol. i. (Adrian), 146, 205-221, 974-955, 1071-1081 (Bircham), 4945-4956 ; vol.
iii. (Dodd), 25373 (par. 121).

It may be noted that in Scotland the law has, on this point, been differently
interpreted. The Scottish Poor Law does not allow any relief, of any kind, to the
able-bodied person, male or female, or their dependants ; but it does not regard
a woman having dependent children (without a husband making provision for
them) as being, in this sense, able-bodied (see Appendix to this volume). To
meet the requirements of widespread Unemployment, the Poor Law Emergency
Provision (Scotland) Act, 1921, required the Parish Council to provide Poor
Relief to destitute able-bodied persons who satisfy the Council that they are
" destitute and unable to obtain employment ", thus bringing the law into line
with that of England. But on a case being taken to the Court of Session in 1927,
Lord Constable gave the judgment of the Court to the effect that relief to the
dependants of able-bodied men on strike, unless they actually satisfied the
Council in each case that they were unable to obtain employment by accepting
the employers' terms, was, notwithstanding the Act of 1921, still illegal (see
The Maintenance of Strikers or Persons Locked Out and their Dependants, National
Citizens Union, Edinburgh, 1927). In consequence of this decision, all the
payments by the Parish Council to men during trade disputes had to be made
good to the Poor Rate. The issues having been made with the express sanction
of the Scottish Government, and, indeed, often at its instance, the Government
felt bound to obtain a special grant from the Exchequer, which the House of
Commons voted, in order to relieve the Parish Councillors from their liability to
refund the amount.

The Judgment is often misquoted or misrepresented as making illegal any Poor Relief to men " on strike ". This is inaccurate. It was not the act of " striking " at which the Master of the Rolls aimed, but the act of refusing to accept an opportunity of employment at wages sufficient to take the man and his family out of the category of the destitute. The Master of the Rolls summed up by saying : "I draw no distinction between strikers and other able-bodied men who can support themselves but who will not. There is no difference, so far as the Poor Law is concerned, either for better or for worse, between men on strike and other men who can but will not support themselves. To use the rates to support strikers, or any other persons able to support themselves, is, in my opinion, illegal." It will be noted that, to make the relief illegal by English law, the fact has to be proved that the individual applicant for relief, whether or not a " striker ", has actually refused, or neglected to accept, an opportunity of employment, in any capacity, then and there open to him. In most industrial disputes in large-scale industry the mere continuance of the dispute does not, in itself, afford the requisite proof, even with regard to the men participating in the strike. As J. S. Davy had pointed out to the House of Lords Committee in 1888, it is usual during a dispute for the employers' establishments to be entirely closed down ; and for it to be impossible to take on an isolated man, or even a small group of men. The working of a coal mine, a blast furnace, or a cotton factory, cannot practically be resumed until a large proportion of the full complement of workers can be engaged. Moreover, as Davy also pointed out, the Guardians have to deal with individual cases, and cannot properly refuse all relief unless they are reasonably sure that the destitute applicant can obtain immediate employment at some specified place. They must have knowledge, it is suggested, that some employer, within the man's immediate reach, whether in the same or any other industry, is prepared to take at least one man, and such a man as the applicant before them, which is not often the case. The Master of the Rolls of 1900 failed to deal with these actual conditions of administration, which were not argued in the Merthyr Tydfil appeal, in which the facts were admitted.

In 1926, on the occasion of the so-called " General Strike " in conjunction with the simultaneous discharge from employment of all the manual working mine workers (except the " safety men "), what seems to have been a further extension of the scope of the Merthyr Tydfil Judgment was made by the Ministry of Health. The Circular (No. 703) of May 5, 1926, explicitly informed all the Boards of Guardians " that where an applicant for relief is able-bodied, the grant of relief is unlawful if work is available, *or if his position has arisen through his own act or consent.* Provided that relief may be granted when an applicant is no longer physically able to perform work." The words italicised do not occur in the Merthyr Tydfil Judgment, nor were they reproduced in the summary of the Circular included in the Annual Report of the Ministry. We are not aware of any legal authority for the proposition. In the whole history of the English Poor Law it has never before been officially suggested that the legal obligation to relieve Destitution ceases to apply when the able-bodied person has become destitute in consequence of his own previous conduct. Whether so intended or not, the Circular was generally understood by Guardians and their Clerks to declare it to be illegal, so long as the dispute lasted, to grant any form of relief to any able-bodied coal-miners, whether they had individually any opportunity of accepting employment or not. Nor was any inquiry made whether their position had arisen, to use the words of the Ministry, through their own act or consent. In practice no difference was made between miners who were members of the Trade Union and those who were not ; between members of the Union who had voted for any decision by which they might be supposed to have given their " consent " to the step that led to their discharge and those who had voted against it ; or between youths who were of age to cast such a vote and those who were not. Nor did the Circular suggest any such discrimination with regard to the relief of the " women and children " —we do not know why the word " wife " was not used. The amount usually given was even to be increased. " To cases in which under the Merthyr Tydfil Judgment ", stated the Circular, " relief may not lawfully be given to the man, the allowances to the women and children might be increased to amounts not exceeding 12s. for the women and 4s. for each child respectively ".[1]

---

[1] Circular 703 of May 5, 1926 ; Eighth Annual Report of Ministry of Health, 1927, p. 116.

It was, perhaps, merely by an oversight that the Circular omitted that other

Thus it was that, in the Poor Law world, the Master of the Rolls " broke up the family " ! By deciding that relief to the husband and father was illegal, and yet that wife and child had to be relieved, he overruled the principle, to which the Poor Law Authority had clung for three-quarters of a century, that any relief to wife and child must be deemed relief to the head of the family. In practice, the Judgment has proved on this point quite unworkable. No power can prevent the man who is refusing employment from sharing in Outdoor Relief given for the family.[1] In fact, the law laid down by the Master of the Rolls has not been obeyed, either by the Local Government Board (now Ministry of Health) or by the Boards of Guardians. The relief afforded, in cases of Unemployment, even where the able-bodied man is regarded as able, if he chooses, to obtain work at wages, has continued to be given to the man, who alone applies for it, and who is still (as he always has been) registered as a pauper because of this grant of relief. In many cases, indeed, the relief is granted only " on loan ", the loan being expressly made to the man himself, who is required to sign an acknowledgment of having received the amount, and an undertaking to repay it at some future time. Thus the illegality of the grant of any relief to the man, in the cases of refusal to accept employment, has been, in practice, ignored where the man has one or more persons legally dependent on him.

The Judgment has, however, had a distinct result, and one probably quite unforeseen by the Master of the Rolls, in changing the conditions of Outdoor Relief. Down to 1900, when in local emergencies of Unemployment it was necessary to grant this relief to able-bodied men, the Local Government Board had successfully insisted that it should be given only upon performance of a task of work, in the Labour Yard or otherwise. But

---

qualification in the Master of the Rolls' Judgment, which implicitly sanctioned the Relieving Officer's dole of food " in sudden or urgent necessity ", in order to prevent starvation.

[1] The Master of the Rolls, if he really meant to exclude the man from participating, might have proposed some form of communal meals, to which only the wives and children would be admitted ! This was actually suggested to the Boards of Guardians by the Ministry of Health in Circular 703 of May 5, 1926, in connection with the so-called General Strike and the National mining dispute, but was nowhere adopted by the Guardians, though an example had been set them by the South Wales Miners' Federation, which provided communal meals for single men to whom Poor Relief was refused.

now that it has become illegal to relieve the man himself if he can be shown to be able to get employment at wages, especially as it has been assumed by the Ministry and the Clerks to Boards of Guardians that this applies to all men engaged in a trade dispute, Labour Yards have ceased to be opened in industrial disputes. Task-work is not required from women—moreover, it is the husbands who receive the relief, not the wives—and accordingly what the Master of the Rolls did in 1900 was, in effect, to abolish the Labour Test for men engaged in industrial disputes and thus to make unconditional Outdoor Relief to able-bodied men—if only they have dependants—once more familiar to the Poor Law world and the wage-earning class. The effect was seen in 1921, when the coal-mining stoppage, combined with the general slump in trade, suddenly sent up the numbers in receipt of relief by nearly three-quarters of a million ; and still more in the long stoppage of 1926, when the total on Poor Relief came to amount to the amazing number of two and a half millions. In one Yorkshire Union (Hemsworth) more than one-half, and in several other Unions more than one-third, of the Census population were simultaneously receiving Poor Relief.[1]

In other cases, the difficulty presented by the Judgment has been avoided in a different way. The elaborate decision of the Master of the Rolls dealt only with Poor Relief ordered *by the Board of Guardians*, to the exclusion of that relief " in kind " which the Relieving Officer is empowered and required to grant on his own initiative (including, where necessary, shelter as well as food) to any person in " sudden or urgent necessity ", whether or not he is able-bodied, or refusing to work, or otherwise guilty of an offence in failing to maintain himself and his family. The

---

[1] In 1922 the question was raised in the Birmingham Union whether relief should be granted to men who were not on strike, but who had been " locked out " by their employers, in order to bring pressure to bear on other workmen elsewhere, who had " struck ". The Guardians appealed for guidance to the Ministry of Health, and received the following telegraphic reply : " Minister of Health has no authority to determine question whether Merthyr Tydfil judgment affects men at present locked out, or to authorise relief. Minister will not refuse to approve grant of Outdoor Relief if made by the Guardians in cases of destitution and reported under Article XII. of the Relief Regulation Order, thereby removing liability to disallowance so far as Regulations are concerned." The Guardians thereupon granted Outdoor Relief on loan. Subsequently the employers reopened their works, and notified their willingness to re-engage men ; whereupon the Guardians decided to discontinue Poor Relief to any man belonging to the trade who refused or neglected to apply for employment.

Master of the Rolls, who dealt always with the action of the Board of Guardians, cannot have meant to include the quite distinct duty and obligation of the Relieving Officer, who had been explicitly told by Parliament and the Poor Law Board to give the relief in kind that was necessary to prevent starvation.[1] Indeed, the Master of the Rolls himself, in an earlier part of his Judgment, gave, as the very first class for which the Poor Laws had always authorised and required relief, those persons, *without limitation or exception*, who were in danger of starvation. Accordingly, in the prolonged distress associated with the stoppage of the coal-mines in 1926, when over a million men were simultaneously discharged by their employers, the Poor Law Division of the Ministry of Health took the view, at least in private consultation with Guardians and their clerks, that, whilst the Merthyr Tydfil Judgment absolutely forbade the grant of Relief, whether Indoor or Outdoor, by or on behalf of the Board of Guardians, to any able-bodied man who was destitute merely by reason of his failure to agree to work on the employers' terms, as soon as the employers had stated them (unless and until he became so physically weakened as to be unable to work—and thus in fact, ceased to be able-bodied), yet the Relieving Officer could not allow such men to starve, even if they were thereby enabled to stand out longer ; and that he must therefore, irrespective of their strength or weakness, give them food or food tickets (together with shelter if required) when they had been some time—say a whole day—without food, and had no means of immediately obtaining it. It was held that it would be wrong for the Relieving Officer to give at

---

[1] The Poor Law Amendment Act, 1834, Sec. 54, imposed this duty upon the Overseer, but this was soon transferred to the Relieving Officer (as, for instance, by Article 215 of the General Consolidated Order of 1847) ; and the provision was repeated in the Poor Law Act, 1927, Section 35 (1). This "sudden or urgent necessity relief " is given daily, in one or other Union, to able-bodied men among others, merely because of their necessity, irrespective of its cause or of their character or conduct, without objection by the Central Authority, the Inspectors or the District Auditors, or the Courts of Justice.

The phrase used in the Poor Law Amendment Act, 1834, was " sudden and urgent necessity ", so that urgency alone was not sufficient. But the Orders of the Poor Law Commissioners and the Poor Law Board (perhaps, in the earliest instance, accidentally) used the phrase " sudden or urgent necessity ", which greatly widened the scope. Although the Ministry of Health proposed, in its Consolidation Bills of 1926 and 1927, to revert to the phrase of the statute, the House of Commons, in 1927, successfully pressed the Government to alter the phrase to that of the Orders; and it was in this wider form that it became statute law.

once as much as a week's food (as was done in the Kensington Union), but as he could not possibly issue one meal at a time, it was not unreasonable for him to supply enough for a day or two ; or perhaps even to give food tickets twice a week. In some " strict " Unions, this issue of " urgent necessity relief " has, at the instance of the Guardians themselves, and without objection by the Inspector or District Auditor, occasionally been made continuously for months together, to dozens of men, as the least objectionable way of dealing with them.[1]

A more continuous result of the Judgment, though this was not foreseen by the Court, has been to cut down the amount of the relief to the family as a whole. Thus in May 1926, as we have mentioned, on the beginning of the calamitous stoppage of the whole coal-mining industry, the Minister of Health practically directed the Boards of Guardians (by Circular 703), in cases of destitution through Unemployment, irrespective of whether or not the man could get work if he chose to accept the coal-owners' terms, to limit the grant of Outdoor Relief to the amount deemed adequate for the man's dependants alone (the official direction being that this was not to exceed 12s. per week for the wife and 4s. for each child) without anything for the man himself. As the relief is, in fact, shared among the whole household, this device amounted to no more than reducing the amount of relief that would otherwise have been given for that household, by the amount ordinarily allowed for the adult man ; or by 30 to 50 per cent. On this reduced scale, hundreds of thousands of miners having wife or child in 1926 received unconditional Outdoor Relief as long as the dispute lasted. Thus in Northumberland and Durham over 86 per cent of all the married miners, of whom

---

[1] See, for instance, the action of the Kensington Union, described at p. 863. In the Darlington Union, we gather, all the able-bodied applicants are now (1928) left to the Relieving Officers to deal with, and they are relieved from week to week as in " sudden or urgent necessity ". It seems that, to be lawful, this " sudden or urgent necessity " relief must be given by the Relieving Officer himself, not by (or upon the order of) the Guardians ; and he must himself decide upon the necessity, and upon the amount of food required. During the prolonged mining stoppage in 1926, some Boards of Guardians passed resolutions that relief "in trade dispute cases" should be "left in the hands of the Relieving Officers, according to or within the Scale adopted by the Board ". If such a resolution were to be deemed to have instructed the Relieving Officers to give the relief, or to give any particular amount, or to give it continuously week after week, it would probably be held to have unduly influenced the Officer ; and might take any relief so given out of the lawful category of " sudden or urgent necessity ".

some were without dependent children, were relieved in spite of the Merthyr Tydfil Judgment, without disallowance by the District Auditors, and, in fact, in exact accordance with the directions of the Ministry of Health.

But there has been a further development. In South Wales certain "lax" Unions in financial straits, and some "strict" Unions without that excuse, have, on what is called the "principle of the Merthyr Tydfil judgment", latterly adopted a similar device for their relief to able-bodied men with families. Unconditional Outdoor Relief is not refused to the destitute Unemployed, but nothing is allowed for the man, irrespective of whether or not he can get employment if he chooses to do so. He is granted, sometimes on loan, ten shillings per week for a wife, and two or three shillings for each dependent child. This, of course, is in no way warranted by the Merthyr Tydfil Judgment (which applied only to men actually refusing to accept employment); but the device is not objected to by the Inspectors so long as admission to the Workhouse is not refused to the man; and the Guardians have somehow come to believe that it represents the law.[1] The net outcome of the Merthyr Tydfil Judgment during the widespread Unemployment of the last eight years has accordingly been, not an exclusion of even obstinate "strikers" from Poor Relief if they have wife or child, but the discontinuance of the Labour Yard in industrial disputes; and a reduction of the amount granted for each household below any standard of adequacy. In short, the result has been the reintroduction, on an alarming scale, and the official condonation, of "indiscriminate, unconditional and inadequate" Outdoor Relief to the able-bodied !

---

[1] One result of this device is that the man without legal dependants is, merely as such, excluded from Outdoor Relief altogether, whether he is an elderly widower or a young bachelor.

We do not know how far this practice extends, nor what sanction it has. But we learn that a similar device is now used in various Unions of Northumberland and Durham, and it may be employed elsewhere. In the Alnwick and Morpeth Unions no Outdoor Relief is given for an able-bodied man, but it is given, in money or in kind, to the man himself, for his wife and children. In the latter Union the men were for some time regarded as being only "constructively" paupers, so that it has not been thought necessary to report the cases under Article XII., but this is now done. In the Castle Ward and Chester-le-Street Unions a similar device is employed in cases regarded as unsatisfactory, although the formula used is that the man is thought not to be genuinely seeking work; and in the former Union a considerable proportion of them are regarded as in this category ! We gather that all these cases are now regularly reported to the Ministry of Health.

The Advent of "Proletarianism"

The extension, by the Local Government Act of 1894, of the franchise for the Guardians' election, and the abolition of the rating qualification, did not immediately result in any substantial change in Poor Law Administration. Even under the old system popular feeling had brought upon the Boards of a few urban Unions men of outstanding personality who had been manual working wage-earners, such as (at Poplar in 1892) the late William Crooks, M.P., and Mr. George Lansbury, M.P. These were gradually joined, after 1894, and especially during the first decade of the twentieth century, by other workmen, who brought to the task a new spirit, which has stirred deep feelings, on the one side of enthusiastic sympathy, and on the other of the sternest disapproval. We give the new outlook in Mr. Lansbury's own words. "From the first moment I determined to fight for one policy only, and that was decent treatment for the poor people, and hang the rates ! . . . My view of life places money, property and privilege on a much lower scale than human life. I am quite aware that some people are bad and deceitful. I know this because I know myself. I know people drink, gamble, and are often lazy. I also know that, taken in the mass, the poor are just as decent as any other class ; and so, when I stood as a Guardian, I took as my policy that no widow or orphan, no sick, infirm or aged person, should lack proper provision of the needs of life, and able-bodied persons should get work or maintenance. To-day everybody agrees with this policy. I also determined to humanise Poor Law administration. I never could see any difference between Outdoor Relief and a State pension, or between the pension of a widowed Queen and Outdoor Relief for the wife or mother of a worker. The nonsense about the disgrace of the Poor Law I fought against till, at least in London, we killed it for good and all." [1]

The Guardians of this new type were often men of capacity, not without an education of their own. To a practical acquaintance with working-class life they usually added exceptional training in "committee work" in the administration of the Branches or Lodges of Trade Unions and Friendly Societies, or in that of Consumers' Co-operative Societies and (especially in

[1] *My Life*, by George Lansbury, 1928, p. 133.

Wales) of Nonconformist congregations. Such administrators were, in many ways, markedly superior to the small shopkeepers, little builders and beerhouse-keepers, who had, apart from the spasmodic attendances of the relatively few middle-class phil- anthropists and mine-managers, almost monopolised the active membership of the Boards of Guardians in the poorer Unions of the Metropolitan area, in some of the coal-fields, and in various other urban districts. Though hardly ever forming a majority of their Boards—often, indeed, constituting numerically trifling minorities—their greater knowledge of social conditions, their alertness in seizing opportunities, their persuasiveness and readiness of speech, and generally, their " committee efficiency ", usually gave them much more influence than their numbers warranted. Moreover, these " Labour Guardians ", as they came to be called, though they were not always members of the Labour Party, had a common faith, which led them to work together in close co-operation, and a devotion that made them exceptionally regular in attendance and zealous in the performance of their duties. Another respect in which they were superior to many of their colleagues was that they were, in nearly all cases, personally disinterested. Rarely were they seeking contracts for themselves or their friends. Nor were they bent on obtaining illicit per- quisites. The weaker among them were, of course, not free from favouritism. Living as they did among the poor, and excep- tionally exposed to their importunities, the new men could not escape the besetting sin of nearly all Poor Law Guardians, of insisting on deciding on applications for relief according to their own personal knowledge of, and their individual judgment upon, the applicants with whom they happened to be acquainted. Presently they came to feel that they were literally " Guardians of the Poor " ; that they were elected, not so much to adjudicate according to the statutes and Orders, in all the cases brought before them by the Relieving Officers, as to advocate the " claims of the poor " against the Clerk and the majority of the Board ; and that it was positively their duty, within reason, to get as much as possible for their clients, whose circumstances were often heart-breaking.

So far as any common policy can be ascribed to the minorities of " Labour Guardians " on the hundred or more Boards on which they had gained seats prior to the War, it may be described as a complete abandonment of the Poor Law principles of " strict administration ", enforced by the Local Government Board Inspectorate of 1870–1895, and inculcated by the Charity Organisation Society of that period. The new attitude was, in our judgment, in great measure justified as socially advantageous. But at certain points it was obviously dangerous : indeed, as we shall presently describe, it proved, under pressure, disastrous. Thus the Labour Guardians were right, as against many of their older colleagues, in accepting the dramatic reversal of the policy concerning the Outdoor Relief of the aged, and the amenities to be provided for such of them as had to enter the Workhouse, officially promulgated in 1896 and 1900 by the Local Government Board itself, under Henry Chaplin's presidency, and never subsequently modified or retracted. With regard to the grant of Outdoor Relief to the sick and infirm, to widows with children, and even to able-bodied men in such family emergencies as sickness or burial expenses, the Labour Members simply accepted the Local Government Board's dictum that, *wherever Out-Relief was permitted to be granted*, the amount should, in all cases, be " adequate " to the need.[1] They were equally zealous in promoting, according to their knowledge, the continuous improvement of the Poor Law schools ; and (especially in London and other large towns) also of what had been, as long ago as 1870, officially styled " the hospital branch of the Poor Law ", for which the educational and medical experts of the Department had ever since been pressing. So far as the various classes of the non-able-bodied were concerned, this policy of the Labour Guardians received the endorsement of the Poor Law Commission of 1905–1909, Majority and Minority alike.

The trouble came when the Boards of Guardians had to deal with large numbers of men destitute by reason of involuntary Unemployment. It must be remembered that, until the flood came in 1920, little thought had latterly been given by anybody to the problem of Able-bodied Destitution. Whilst Poor Law

---

[1] See the paper on " Relief Scales ", by R. A. Leach, late Clerk to the Rochdale Board of Guardians, Central Poor Law Conference, February 1928, reminding us that this policy had been expressly laid down by the L.G.B. : " It is the plain duty of the Guardians to take precautions to ensure that the relief is adequate, and that the pauper is sufficiently fed, clothed and lodged " (Circular of March 18, 1910).

" orthodoxy " continued to denounce Outdoor Relief to the Able-bodied so effectively that except in one or two Unions it had practically ceased to exist, all the Poor Law alternatives had, as we shall relate at the end of this chapter, become hopelessly discredited by the revelations of the Poor Law Commission of 1905–1909. Confronted with the absence of any commonly accepted policy of relieving the destitution due to Unemployment, the only plan that seemed open to the Guardians, when, by exception, they had to face a crowd of able-bodied applicants for relief who were known to be penniless, was to take advantage of the loopholes which the Local Government Board had left in the Prohibitory Orders, and to stretch them so as to give Outdoor Relief on one or other ground of exception. At first, as we have already described, in Poplar in 1903–1905 the Labour Guardians took this course with reluctance, after appealing in vain to the Local Government Board for some better way of providing for the distress, and practically in despair of any alternative. Nor were the Labour Guardians responsible, as we shall presently show, for the widespread adoption of Scales of Relief, a device that seemed to carry with it implied sanction of Outdoor Relief on account of Unemployment. Once the easy policy had been adopted by any Board of Guardians it was not surprising that the Labour Guardians, living among poverty-stricken electors, many of whom were fellow Trade Unionists as well as neighbours, should be ready to relieve generously all who were unemployed, or only casually employed. Then it was that became glaringly manifest the administrative error—almost universally prevalent in English Poor Law administration—of allowing Guardians to decide on applications from the very Wards or Parishes for which they had been elected. In the discussion the " Principle of Less Eligibility " took on a new aspect. To the Labour Guardian it seemed obvious that Outdoor Relief on the ground of Unemployment ought to be sufficiently " adequate " (to use the word of the Local Government Board's Circular) to prevent the man from accepting it merely as a " Rate in Aid " of surreptitious earnings from odd jobs, and even sufficient to deter him from seeking employment in sweated industries at a wage below the Trade Board Determinations. On the other hand, where the earnings from Casual Labour or in the " sweated " trades were manifestly insufficient for the maintenance of a large family, it seemed pedantic not to " apply the Scale ", and make up the weekly income to the requisite sum, rather than insist on the worker and his whole family entering the Workhouse. And the same sort of class bias, adopting the common conception of widening the area of employment, has often deterred Labour Guardians from " setting the poor to work " in return for their Outdoor Relief ; and even from using the few able-bodied residents in the Workhouse to clean the windows or cultivate the garden, in order that these tasks might serve to keep in employment men at current rates of wages. An even more equivocal result was the spread of a feeling that this generous dispensation of Outdoor Relief afforded a ready means of re-distributing the National Income in such a way as to remedy, in some slight degree, the existing maldistribution of wealth between the rich and the poor. Any or all of these purposes may be socially advantageous, and worthy of promotion. But it may be (and in our judgment it actually is) disastrous to seek to carry them into effect by the grant of unconditional Outdoor Relief to able-bodied workmen. For there *is* a " disease of pauperism " as well as a " disease of involuntary destitution " ; and the former, unlike the latter, is highly contagious. The special evil of systematic and unconditional Outdoor Relief to the able-bodied is that the area over which it is demanded invariably becomes enlarged. New claimants appear with great rapidity. A sheer addition to one's pecuniary income without having to give anything in return is attractive to nearly every-body, and supremely so to the weaker brethren, to whom its receipt would, as all experience shows, be most demoralising. And the contagion increases with the numbers. To give un-conditional Outdoor Relief to one exceptional case may possibly do no harm. To do the same to a hundred cases in one locality would almost certainly be injurious to the character of many of them, and infect many others. When it comes to be a question of thousands, both the individual and the social harmfulness are immeasurably increased. It is this failure to distinguish between the cases in which Outdoor Relief is exceptionally permissible and even desirable, and those in which it is disastrous ; and the refusal to recognise the danger of voluntary and intentional pauperism, that was nicknamed " Poplarism ". We prefer the wider term " Proletarianism ", seeing that the Poplar Board of

Guardians has by no means been the only, or even the worst, offender.[1]

Here it is fair to point out that the part played by " proletarianism " in unduly lavish Outdoor Relief has been exaggerated. It is not true that the practice of indiscriminate and unconditional Outdoor Relief at high rates is peculiar to Unions in which Labour Guardians have been in a majority. The number of Boards of Guardians in which there are or have ever been such majorities is very small : certainly not exceeding 50 out of 625 in all England and Wales. The

[1] It is well to remember, as was pointed out in 1867, that " Proletarianism " is not the only bias prevalent among Poor Law Guardians by which the character of the administration has been affected. Under the Poor Law Amendment Act of 1834, wrote a distinguished critic of public affairs in 1867, " the initiative of administering relief was confided exclusively to the ratepayers, and no distinction was drawn between the willing and the unwilling recipient. The consequence of the first mistake was an administration solely conducted in the interests of the payers without influence from the receivers, a defect shown in the towns by a penuriousness often verging on cruelty—as for example in the treatment of casuals and the sick ; in the country by a use of the law to keep down wages. When all has been said that can be said, the refusal of the Metropolitan Guardians to obey the law about Casuals, and the cruel reluctance to make pauper hospitals decently comfortable, resolve themselves into the ratepayers' dislike to spend money for other people's benefit. Such a feeling is neither unnatural nor unreasonable ; and it may be admitted that no representation of paupers was possible at the Board. But it was quite possible to represent the State as impartial arbiter, and a really sympathetic House of Commons would long since have done it, either directly by appointing good chairmen as executive officers of the Board, or by enabling the ordinary Courts of Justice, on complaint and evidence, to enforce obedience to the intention of the law. As it is, a parish can get its rates by a very swift legal process ; but the poor of the parish cannot in the same way get due hospital accommodation—pillows, for instance, for bedridden old inmates. Parliament has readily consented to establish the jurisdiction most effective for assisting petty traders ; but the pauper is left to the ratepayers, without any trustworthy arbiter between him and them."

" Again, to the Members of Parliament, looking down from their height, one poor man seems much the same as another—a tramp like a labourer, a labourer like an artisan ; and the same system is consequently applied to all— to the decent ploughman who has broken his leg and the ditcher ruined by drink, to the artisan out of employ and the rascal who never will work while anybody will feed him. It is true that the practice of men being often better than their laws, this mistake is in the country remedied by a system of Outdoor Relief, lenient to the very verge of the law, and worked by men who understand individual wants : but in towns it is not remedied, and every period of distress breaks up thousands of decent households, which might have been saved by judicious discrimination such as impartial officers would exercise."

" There is scarcely a defect in the working of the Poor Law which is not traceable to one of these two mistakes, which between them have made a vast national system of charity, such as no other nation possesses, an object of loathing to those who receive its benefits " (*Questions for a Reformed Parliament*, 1867 ; Essay III., "The Poor", pp. 68-91, by Meredith Townsend, afterwards Editor of *The Spectator*).

number of Boards whose scales of Out-Relief are or have been extravagantly high, according to the views of the Ministry of Health, considerably exceed one hundred ; and the number of those whose Outdoor Relief has been at one or other time swollen in the Flood that we shall describe amounts to twice that figure. A large proportion of these, including some of those with the largest expenditure and the most lax administration—we venture to instance the Unions of West Derby (Liverpool) and Manchester —have had, for years, either no " Labour Members " at all, or only tiny minorities with Labour or Socialist sympathies, and have been governed by overwhelming majorities of members representing the Conservative or the Liberal Party, or an anti-Socialist pact. What may be said is that, where " proletarianism " prevails, lavish Outdoor Relief on a generous and sometimes a lavish scale is given *on principle*, and is thus apt to lead to deliberate evasion, and in some cases to actual defiance, of the Orders of the Central Authority. In other Unions at least an equal laxity arises from the very absence of any principle with regard to the relief of destitution ; from a desire to subsidise the rents or increase the purchasing power of constituents who are also tenants or customers ; or merely from the more excusable wish to be re-elected by poverty-stricken districts, or to strengthen a political Party's hold on these. When we remember how specially exasperating " misdoing on principle " has always been (and always will be) to those in authority,[1] it is only human nature if proletarian Boards have found themselves singled out for detailed investigation, public condemnation and exemplary discipline, whilst others, whose sins are in more than one sense unprincipled, have been left unchecked.

How the Flood Came

The flood came so suddenly, and in such force, as to overwhelm, in the Unions concerned, the local Poor Law adminis-

[1] Significant of this dislike of " misdoing on principle " is the following extract from Sir Arthur Lowry's Report on the Sheffield Union : " It is due to them [the Chairman and Clerk], and to the Board of Guardians, to record that, whatever errors there may have been in the administration of the Poor Law since March 1921, they do not appear to have arisen from a desire to advance any political, social or financial theory " (Report to the Ministry of Health upon a Public Inquiry into the Administration of Relief in the Sheffield Union, 1923, p. 8).

tration. In the Sheffield Union, for instance, which was made, in 1923, the subject of a Public Inquiry by the Minister of Health, " trade had begun to decline towards the end of 1920, but the increase in applications had been slight when the estimates . . . were framed, and 20 per cent increase over the amount allowed for Out-Relief in the previous half year was considered sufficient. . . . At that time there was no general realisation that a serious and prolonged depression in the trade of Sheffield was to be anticipated. . . . The general impression on the Guardians' minds was that it would not be their business to undertake the relief to the Unemployed, and the responsibility, if it fell to any Local Authority, would attach to the Corporation. . . . The Guardians, like many other Boards similarly placed, were taken by surprise when the rush of applications came upon them. . . . In no week since the middle of May 1921 has the number of Unemployed men in receipt of relief been lower than 5420 . . . while it has been as high as 17,400. . . . There is now a total staff of 72 engaged on the work of relief to the Unemployed. . . . The strain upon the members of the Boards of Guardians . . . has been very severe. . . . In some weeks these have 24 Committee meetings. . . . The problem they have had to face has been one the nature and extent of which none of them [in 1920] could have conceived to be possible. . . . New methods had to be improvised, and new policies initiated." [1]

The flood seems to have reached the Stoke-on-Trent Union only in May 1921, when severe distress was caused by the stoppage of the mines through the national dispute. All the available staff was concentrated on dealing with the applicants for relief ; but on May 4 " the number of applications to the Relieving Officer of the Fenton district was so great that it was impossible to make proper inquiries into cases before granting assistance. . . . At the close of Saturday, there were several hundred cases which had not been visited. Thereupon an advertisement was issued for temporary Investigators ", and " six men were appointed at £3 per week. . . . The percentage of school children being fed by the Education Committee is rapidly increasing, and on

---

[1] Report to the Minister of Health upon a Public Inquiry into the Administration of Relief in the Sheffield Union (by A. B., now Sir Arthur, Lowry, General, now Chief Inspector), 1923 ; Fourth Annual Report of the Ministry of Health, 1923, p. 83.

Wednesday nearly 8000 meals were provided, as compared with under 4000 daily last week ".[1]

The "New Methods" and the Improvised "New Policies"

The couple of hundred Unions overwhelmed by the flood differed among themselves—to use the words of the Ministry's Chief Inspector—as to the "new methods" that "had to be improvised", and as to the "new policies" that "had to be initiated ".[2] But they nearly all agreed that the old policy and the old methods were inapplicable.

The most startling innovation was the abandonment, by nearly all the Boards of Guardians concerned, and the acquiescence in that abandonment by the Central Authority, of any serious attempt to make the relief to the able-bodied men conditional on a Labour Test, or on the performance of any work— let alone the abandonment of any insistence on the man and his family, or even the man alone, entering the Workhouse. Reviewing the procedure of the preceding five years, the Minister of Health observed in 1926 that it had to be " admitted that . . . Boards of Guardians " have not " generally insisted upon the attachment of conditions, *e.g.* Labour Test or Modified Workhouse Test, to the grant of relief to such persons as claim, or are admitted to be, employable persons. For this omission the numbers involved and the physical difficulties are generally advanced as a sufficient explanation ; but in the absence of such conditions, and of compliance with the law which authorises Guardians only to set able-bodied persons to work, and not to relieve them unconditionally by allowance of cash or kind, it cannot be regarded as proved that unnecessary expenditure of the ratepayers' money is not being incurred." [3]

The Adoption of Scales of Relief

An invariable feature in the Unions in which pauperism has enormously increased has been the avowed adoption of definite Scales of Outdoor Relief, varying according to the size of the

[1] *Staffordshire Advertiser*, May 14, 1921.

[2] Report to the Ministry of Health upon a Public Inquiry into the Administration of Relief in the Sheffield Union, 1923.

[3] Seventh Annual Report of the Ministry of Health, 1926, p. 109.

family.[1] Such Scales, with their uncomfortable resemblance to those initiated at Speenhamland in 1795,[2] had, since 1834, always been strongly objected to by Poor Law "orthodoxy", and practically forbidden by the Central Authority. Indeed, the prohibition of Outdoor Relief to able-bodied men in health, and its substantial limitation to the aged, the widows and the sick, lessened the need for any Scales for the maintenance of an ordinary family. Their use crept in during the last quarter of the nineteenth century, with the elaboration of local Bye-laws relating to Outdoor Relief ; [3] but the Scales were then usually limited to a few normal rates for specified classes, such as the children of widows, etc., and they remained without official sanction. With the growth, in a few Unions, of Outdoor Relief to able-bodied men at the opening of the present century, the use of Scales was again denounced, as by Sir William Chance before the Poor Law Commission of 1905–1909.[4] The view taken was that the circumstances of each case should be narrowly investigated, with a view to discovering (assuming that any Outdoor Relief at all should be given) what was the exact sum that would suffice in the particular case to " relieve destitution " ; and that no more could lawfully be given. Other witnesses, however, including some Poor Law Inspectors, told the Royal Commission in 1906 [5] that any such procedure was impracticable ;

[1] For these Scales, see the paper entitled " Relief Scales " by R. A. Leach, in Report of Central Poor Law Conference, February 1928 ; Memorandum submitted by Sir William Chance to Poor Law Commission, 1905–1909, and Questions 5622, 8509-8510 of Evidence, 1909 ; Report of Meeting of Metropolitan Poor Law Officers' Association, in *Poor Law Officers' Journal*, January 1928 ; and Eighth Annual Report of Ministry of Health, 1927, p. 130.

[2] See Majority Report of Poor Law Commission, 1905–1909, Part III., paragraphs 31-32.

[3] For the early use of the term " Scale " the following quotation may suffice : " The scale of allowances," reported Inspector Culley in 1873, " by which I mean the allowance usually granted in different classes of cases when the relief given by the Guardians is, or is supposed to be, the only source of income, differs to a degree which I think there is nothing in the surrounding circumstances to justify. To take, for example, the important class of able-bodied widows with children as dealt with by the Guardians of contiguous and similar Unions. I know no reason why the Board of Guardians for Berwick Union should give relief in such cases at the rate of 1s. 6d. for each child, if the Glendale Guardians are right in giving only 1s. ; nor why the Guardians for South Shields should give only 1s., if 1s. 6d. is necessary at Teignmouth " (Third Annual Report of Local Government Board, 1874, pp. 73-74, Culley's Report; *The Better Administration of the Poor Law, by* Sir William Chance, 1893, pp. 65-66).

[4] Evidence of Poor Law Commission, 1909, Q. 8509-8510.

[5] *Ibid*, Q. 5622.

and explained that in actual experience it was found better for the Guardians to have a uniform Scale to go by, in order to maintain a common standard in similar cases.

But the very idea of Scales had been anathema alike to the Poor Law Commissioners and to the Poor Law Board, and it long continued to be objectionable also to the Local Government Board. The first official sanction of Scales that we have found comes in 1911, when the new Relief Regulation Order made provision for Outdoor Relief to able-bodied men against a " Labour Test ", whenever the Guardians, under exceptional circumstances, had passed a resolution under Article IX. and reported it to the Local Government Board. The Order required them to submit also the Scale on which they proposed to give the relief.[1]

With the inrushing flood of 1921, all objection to the Guardians' practice was given up. In 1922, as we shall have later to describe, the Minister of Health himself (Sir Alfred Mond, now Lord Melchett) imposed a very elaborate Scale on the London Boards of Guardians in order to prescribe a maximum of the Outdoor Relief that might be charged to the Common Poor Fund.[2] In 1926, on the occasion of the stoppage of the coal-mining industry and the brief " General Strike ", the Minister of Health (Mr. Neville Chamberlain) again prescribed a Scale as a maximum for Outdoor Relief, namely, for persons unconnected with the dispute, 18s. for a man, 5s. for a wife, and 2s. for each child—incidentally, it may be noted, these were the rates of Unemployment Benefit under the State Insurance Scheme [3]—whilst for the wife and children of a miner (who, it was assumed, could not lawfully be given Poor Relief for himself) the maximum was to be 12s. for the woman and 4s. for each son and daughter under 16.[4] In 1927 the Ministry, with some hesitation, gave a general approval to the adoption of Scales in its Eighth Annual Report, when " the aberrations " of many Boards of Guardians were ascribed, not to the Scales themselves, but to their unintelligent use ; and it was explained that a " normal rate of relief " was necessary in order to maintain some uniformity and justice as between the various applicants. In " the larger Unions ", it was said, a

[1] " Relief Scales," by R. A. Leach (Central Poor Law Conference, 1928).
[2] Third Annual Report of Ministry of Health, 1922, p. 91.
[3] Eighth Annual Report of Ministry of Health, 1927, pp. 116-117.
[4] Circular 703 of May 5, 1926, in *ibid.* p. 116.

Scale even "becomes more important", in order to maintain uniformity among the various Relief Committees.[1]

But when the Central Authority reluctantly recognised, and presently more or less explicitly sanctioned, the use of Scales, they were regarded, not as Scales of Relief but as Tables of Resources. The legitimate use of the Scale, it was contended, was as a table of family income, showing the amount which, at current prices, was to be deemed necessary for the " adequate " maintenance of all the members of the household. All the sources of income having been ascertained, their total could, by the grant of relief, be made up to the sum fixed by the Scale. This involved, it will be seen, not only the complete and accurate ascertainment of all the receipts of all the members of the family—no light task—and also (as is usually forgotten) some provision for the variation from week to week of one or other of such receipts, for which such an application of the Scale left no margin, but, in addition, the settlement of many difficult questions as to how much should be included in the assumed income out of such items as sons' or daughters' earnings ; contributions from relations, liable and not liable under the law ; Friendly Society and Health Insurance allowances ; Old Age Pensions ; War Pensions to the man himself or (in case the widow re-marries) the like allowances made specifically for a deceased soldier's orphan children maintained at home ; compensation for industrial accidents; payments by lodgers who are relatives, and lodgers who are not, and so forth. We do not find that definite instructions on the use of the Scale, covering all these points, were ever given. The Guardians in most of the populous industrial Unions have found it easier, and when dealing with thousands of cases, almost unavoidable, to use the Scale as one determining the amount of Outdoor Relief to be given, in cases in which it was asserted that Unemployment was complete, and when no other sources of income had actually been revealed.[2]

---

[1] Eighth Annual Report of the Ministry of Health, 1927, p. 130.

[2] " A special inquiry into 50 Unions of various types revealed the fact that nearly half these Unions treated the Scale as a ' rigid formula ' for ascertaining the appropriate amount of relief, rather than as a guide expressive of the maximum for normal cases " (Fifth Annual Report of the Ministry of Health, 1924, p. 91).

This practice, it was found, could not be stopped. In 1925 it is reported that " the automatic application of Scales still persists in some Unions, and is often accompanied by an unwillingness on the part of the Guardians to take

The Large Amount of Relief

It was the height of the Scale during these years that constituted the most remarkable innovation. In dealing with the workman with a family rendered destitute by Unemployment, most Guardians in 1921–1928 have felt bound, especially during the time of specially high prices, to allow relief—if we may use the new term introduced in 1895 and repeated in 1910 by the Local Government Board itself—" adequate " to the needs of the household.[1] Thus, the Clerk to the Board of Guardians in an efficiently managed Union explained to us in 1928 that their Scale had been " drawn up in accordance " with the following plan : the " number of calories required to keep a man, woman and child in health is known ; the amount of food of various kinds sufficient to give these calories has been calculated and the price determined. That sum forms the basis of the Scale. To this is added the rent, which is not put in the Scale, but is ascertained from each applicant. In the Scale itself is put a weekly sum for clothes, boots, renewals, etc., and when the sums granted are carefully used, the Scale is found to be sufficient to keep the applicant in reasonable comfort."

Whether or not the Guardians have often counted the calories required for healthy subsistence, it seems that, with a very few exceptions, those who had to provide for the Unemployed at a time of exceptionally high prices put their Scales of Relief at

---

into reasonable account, in deciding the amount of relief appropriate to an applicant, the income available to the dependants and other members of the household " (Sixth Annual Report of the Ministry of Health, 1925, p. 106).

In the following year it was stated that " in one large industrial Union it has actually been an instruction to Relief Committees that the fixed amounts of the Scale should be applied in every case. This is clearly a misconception of the function of the Poor Law and of the discretion properly vested in the Poor Law Authorities " (Seventh Annual Report of the Ministry of Health, 1926, p. 112).

[1] See pp. 723-5 of the present work. In the Circular Letter of March 18, 1910, it was laid down that " when Outdoor Relief is given, it should be carefully adapted to the needs of the case *and adequate in amount* " (Thirty-eighth Annual Report of Local Government Board, 1911, p. xix). And by that of October 8, 1914, as to " Relief to Widows and Children ", it was prescribed that " the Guardians should ascertain, by careful enquiry, what is the normal *standard of income on which a woman may reasonably be expected to bring up her family,* regard being had to the cost and general standard of living, rate of wages, etc., in the locality, and should use that standard as a criterion of the needs of the case " (Thirty-ninth Annual Report of Local Government Board, 1915).

a far higher level than had previously prevailed in Poor Law administration. Many examples are cited in other parts of this chapter. It will suffice at this point to say that when for the Metropolis in 1922 the Minister of Health (Sir Alfred Mond, now Lord Melchett) had to draw up the Scale for what could be charged to the Common Poor Fund, it is understood that this was based on the contemporary practice of many of the Boards of Guardians. This "Mond Scale", which had, however, an overriding maximum that was usually forgotten, went up (for man and wife and eight dependent children) to 71s. per week, with an addition for fuel averaging over 2s. per week. Scales on this level, starting from 15s. per week for a single able-bodied man or woman, and 25s. for a childless couple, and rising to as much as 75s. per week for a large family, were not uncommon during the years of specially high prices; and they were not always reduced when the cost of living had fallen to a much lower level.

It must be added that, after very explicitly declaring (1910) that Outdoor Relief must be " adequate " in amount, and (1914) based on what is reasonably required to bring up a family ; and that the Guardians are (1910) to take precautions to ensure, when they give Outdoor Relief, " that the poor person is sufficiently fed, clothed and lodged ", the Central Authority also declared, years afterwards, by its Circular of September 8, 1921, that the relief " should of necessity be calculated on a lower scale than the earnings of the independent workman who is maintaining himself by his labour " (not, be it observed, the " lowest-paid independent labourer ", who used to set the standard). This left the permissible amount very much in doubt ; for how could anyone say what were the earnings of " the independent workman ", of occupation unspecified ? In the " Mond Scale " of 1922 a more precise definition was attempted. The family income was not to be made up, on the lines of the Scale, beyond a sum "less by 10s. a week than the Standard Rate of Wages for the time being recommended for Grade A under the agreement of the London District Council for Non-trading Services (Manual Labour)". This was an " ascertainable sum "—at that date, in fact, 64s. per week, implying an overriding maximum for Outdoor Relief (where there was no other income) of 54s. per week. It must be noted that the accepted wages of these municipal employees were far above the earnings of the lowest-paid independent labourer; and, indeed, above the actual earnings of many thousands of London labourers who were not in receipt of Poor Relief.

The Guardians were, indeed, on the horns of a dilemma. On the one hand they were told by the Ministry of Health, and required by public opinion, to make their Outdoor Relief "adequate" for the healthy maintenance of the family, however numerous it was ; and on the other hand, they were enjoined, with equal emphasis, never to make the relief as much as the wages currently earned by non-pauper labourers. What were they to do when the case before them was that of a man without resources, who had dependent on him a wife and six or even eight young children ? By any standard whatsoever, such a family could not be maintained on a sum no greater than the current wage of the independent unskilled labourer of the district, let alone on any sum markedly less than that wage. The only answer by the Ministry of Health to that question appears to have been that the whole family, man and wife and children, should be taken into the Workhouse—a proposal that public opinion of the present century refuses to sanction.[1]

At a later date the Ministry of Health seems to have begun to assume that Outdoor Relief ought never to exceed the scale of Unemployment Insurance Benefit. Thus, in 1924 the Ministry remarked that, out of 220 Unions using Scales of Relief in 1923, only 20 had Scales at such rates as "to preclude the grant of

---

[1] The same question was raised in another connection when the Guardians of a Union in East Anglia were pressed to grant relief to a farm labourer in regular employment at the full county rate of 30s., who, at the swollen prices of food, found it impossible to maintain his wife and six children on such a sum. The Guardians proposed to grant him Outdoor Relief in respect of some of his children (being those in excess of an average family). But any such flagrant " Relief in Aid of Wages " was immediately stopped by the Ministry of Health, who advised that, if the family was in fact destitute, the man should simply be " offered the House " (Fourth Annual Report of the Ministry of Health, 1923, p. 82). " It is not disputed ", the Minister of Health had observed in 1922, " that in certain cases the net wages earned have been, in fact, insufficient to meet the needs of even a moderate-sized family ; but it remains true that it is better in the long run, and in the interest of the workers themselves, to remove such a worker from the labour market, even if this means throwing the entire cost of his family's maintenance upon the Poor Rate " (Third Annual Report of the Ministry of Health, 1922, p. 86). Such a solution of the problem, suggested, it is fair to say, only for an isolated case, was hardly practicable when the applicants were as numerous as they were in Liverpool or Manchester.

It would have been distinctly contrary to regulations to admit the children in excess of the " normal family " to the Workhouse whilst the father remained working at wages, though this was long the official suggestion in the case of widows burdened with young children.

Outdoor Relief, in the absence of exceptional circumstances, to persons in receipt of Benefit, under the Unemployment Insurance Acts ".[1] This suggestion has been repeated by the Inspectors, as if there were some reason against Poor Relief being greater than Unemployment Benefit. We are unaware of any proposal that Poor Relief should never be greater than the State Sickness Benefit, but this would have been just as plausible. In either case the suggestion is plainly inconsistent with the Central Authority's repeated dictum that Outdoor Relief, *when given at all*, must always be " adequate ". The Unemployment Benefit, which, like the Sickness Benefit, is given *irrespective of the wealth or poverty of the claimant*, has never been imagined to be adequate for maintenance, being avowedly given only as a subvention in aid of other resources (which may, in fact, rightly include Poor Relief).[2]

It has often been stated by experienced officials, alike of the Ministry of Health and of Boards of Guardians, that it is impossible to judge with any fairness the administration of a Poor Law Union by the Scale according to which the Guardians purport to work. With regard to the application of the Scale, there are, as we have seen, infinite possibilities of variation in the manner and extent of taking account of the family circumstances and of the aggregate incomings of the household. Moreover, there are indefinite variations in the degree to which the several Relief Committees regard the Scale as (*a*) merely a general guide ; (*b*) only a maximum to be in no case exceeded ; or (*c*) an arithmetical computation of relief, according to the number of persons to be maintained, to be universally and automatically paid in every case. A wisely directed Board of Guardians may justifiably have a relatively high Scale, for use as a Table of Family Income necessary for adequate subsistence, without implying its use as a Scale of Relief irrespective of all the varied resources of the

---

[1] Fifth Annual Report of Ministry of Health, 1924, p. 91.

[2] This has been repeatedly explained by the Minister of Labour. " The first point ", he wrote in 1928, " I should like to emphasise is that Unemployment Benefit *has never been intended to afford maintenance during Unemployment.* This is a point which I have emphasised over and over again in the House of Commons, and it is laid down by the Blanesburgh Committee as one of the cardinal conditions of a sound contributory scheme of insurance, and reasons for the conclusion are given in detail in their Report. It was for these reasons that the Blanesburgh Committee unanimously recommended a lower rate of Benefit for young persons of 18 to 21 years of age " (Sir Arthur Steel-Maitland, Minister of Labour, to Capt. J. Griffyth Fairfax, M.P., March 31, 1928; see *Poor Law Officers' Journal*, April 6, 1928).

household ; and also without intending that the full amount allowed by the highest figures in the Scale should necessarily be granted in cases in which it may be thought that the applicant cannot be trusted either to make the best use of the relief, or to resist the temptation to settle down to it complacently as a means of livelihood. In short, a Scale may be both a guide to, and a check upon, Relief Committees ; but it is not a substitute for common sense.

The Lack of Uniformity in the Policy of Boards of Guardians

Passing from the general influences which, between 1920 and 1928, affected Poor Law administration, to the day-by-day work of particular Boards of Guardians, our inquiry reveals irreconcilable diversities. These variations in policy between one Board and another, so repugnant to the principles of 1834, appear to have no relation to the conditions of employment, degree of skill, extent of needs or range of opportunities of the able-bodied applicants residing within the several Unions. The diverse policies seem to arise, partly from the relative wealth or poverty of the area concerned, but mainly from the particular social or religious creed, the profession, the interest or the impulse of the men and women who happen to be chosen from time to time as Guardians in the several Unions by the habitually tiny fraction of electors who take the trouble to vote. In order to give the reader some notion of the widely different treatment meted out, sometimes in adjacent Unions, to Unemployed destitute persons, we have selected for description examples of strict and of lax Boards respectively, and also of Boards of inter-mediate or peculiar character, in London and in various other urban areas.

Kensington and Hampstead

In the Royal Borough of Kensington, where the Board of Guardians is dominated by a relatively wealthy class, it has been the practice, throughout all the eight years of Unemployment, for the Board itself, in practically all cases, to refuse Outdoor Relief to able-bodied men in health.[1] When Unemployment

---

[1] For Kensington we have had the advantage of personal information from the Chairman and the Clerk. See also the annual Accounts of the Union.

began to be serious, towards the end of 1920, the Relieving
Officers were instructed to treat the cases under the head of
" sudden or urgent necessity " ; and to use their own discretion
in issuing food tickets, even to the unusual amount of 15s. or 20s.
in each case, to such applicants (whether single or married, with
dependants or without) as seemed genuinely necessitous, even for
weeks or months at a time. In the distress caused by the railway
stoppage in January 1921, and in that due indirectly to the coal-
mining and other stoppages in the latter part of 1921, 1922 and
1923, this provision had to be temporarily stretched to cover
hundreds of cases, some of them continuously for six months or
more, at a cost, in one black week, of no less than £752.[1] In no
case was any money given by the Board ; but in the severe stress
towards the end of 1921 a private fund of about £100 was raised

[1] ADULT ABLE-BODIED MALES RELIEVED IN KIND BY THE RELIEVING OFFICERS
IN THE KENSINGTON UNION, AS CASES OF " SUDDEN OR URGENT NECESSITY "
IN CERTAIN WEEKS :

Week ended	Adult Able-bodied Males Relieved.	Cost of such Relief. £
July 3, 1920	Nil	Nil
December 11, 1920	31	29
January 1, 1921	60	48
January 29, 1921	144	115
July 2, 1921	27	Not stated
August 6, 1921	8	10
September 10, 1921	178	143
September 17, 1921	417	338
November 19, 1921	896	752
December 31, 1921	648	Not stated
July 1, 1922	259	,,
August 26, 1922	160	134
September 16, 1922	207	170
November 28, 1922	286	218
December 31, 1922	190	Not stated
June 30, 1923	70	,,
August 25, 1923	31	34
December 29, 1923	22	30
June 28, 1924	6	Not stated
December 27, 1924	7	10
December 26, 1924	20	31
December 25, 1926	11	16
July 2, 1927	2	Not stated
October 1, 1927	7	2
December 31, 1927	4	1
March 31, 1928	4	2
June 30, 1928	6	2
September 29, 1928	7	3
January 5, 1929	2	$0\frac{3}{4}$

and dispensed by a voluntary committee, in order to enable deserving families to pay their rent. " It was enough for the purpose ", we were informed ; " and it just saved the situation ". It should be added that many children were fed at school by the London County Council ; the Infant Welfare Centres issued tickets for dinners to nursing mothers ; the Relieving Officers' food tickets could be exchanged for any necessaries, including (as is unusual) fresh milk, and special brands of milk for delicate children ; and in some exceptional cases coals and boots were supplied by the Guardians in addition to the Relieving Officers' dole of food. In any case in which an applicant was refused the Relieving Officer's urgency relief, it was always open to him to appeal to the local Relief Committee ; and the Committee very occasionally took a more lenient view, and urged the Relieving Officer to make his usual grant of food. But neither by the Relieving Officers nor by the Relief Committees, so we are informed, has Unemployment been " recognised as a continuing status ; when it degenerates into chronic destitution it is no longer allowed exceptional treatment ; and sooner or later the House is offered "—to all cases " which turn out to be of a chronic nature ". It is stated that only in a very few cases has the offer been accepted.

The policy of the Kensington Board of Guardians during the past eight years, which has had the constant approval of the Ministry of Health, exemplifies, we think, the best that can be done, under the existing law and practice, by an exceptionally favourably situated Destitution Authority. From their policy of " refusing Outdoor Relief " to the able-bodied, the Kensington Guardians resolutely declined to budge, though assailed during 1920–1921 by no fewer than seven successive deputations demanding full maintenance in money, according to a Scale, for all the Unemployed. But it is important to notice that this apparently ruthless policy of refusal included a generous relief of every case that appeared, on prompt inquiry, to be one of genuine distress, by food tickets which, to an unusual degree, covered all necessaries, including fresh milk ; whilst (by what seems to have been an evasion of the law) this relief was given, under the heading of " sudden or urgent necessity ", continuously for weeks, and in some instances even for more than six months. Meanwhile private funds supplied money for the payment of rent, and wide scope was given to the feeding of the school-children, the new-born babies and the nursing mothers. Even so, the infantile death-rate in the poorest wards of Kensington (especially in 1921) was not creditable to that Royal Borough ; in the worst Wards, indeed, in several years it exceeded 100 per 1000, when that for London as a whole never rose above 81.

The example of Kensington indicates, in fact, that even the best administered Union, with the largest staff of Relieving Officers, working under the strictest of Boards, found much that the situation required to be beyond its scope or its reach. It does not seem that the Poor Law Authority afforded any help to regain employment even to those men who were thought to be deserving.[1] The Guardians appear to have had no systematic

---

[1] This has been done, with the approval of the Ministry of Health, in some Unions with a certain measure of success. We append the scheme of the Lambeth Board of Guardians given us by the able Clerk of that Union.

" On application for relief, the man or woman is sent to the Superintendent Relieving Officer who investigated the case, and has available a list of suitable employers who may have work to offer to the persons concerned. Schemes are established in co-operation with several big employers of labour, and by this means able-bodied women are placed into employment at once. In addition to the Employment Exchanges, private employment agencies are utilised, the Guardians having available charitable funds from which they can pay any fee which may be requested by such agencies. If a man or woman fails to comply with the requirements of the Superintendent Relieving Officer, in seeking employment, or of the employer, he or she having been offered employment, the case is at once reported to the Central Relief Committee, who take disciplinary action, and who in certain cases have instituted proceedings under the Vagrancy Act for wilfully refusing and neglecting to work. Under this scheme several employers take practically all their labour from the Guardians.

" The Guardians have carefully investigated the possibility of educational training for young persons applying for relief, either direct or as dependants, and have freely utilised, in the past, continuation schools established by the London County Council. They have been, however, for some time in a position to place into remunerative employment all young persons applying for assistance, and during the past year have frequently had vacancies for young people which they have been unable to fill. All positions found for young men and women are of a character where they can establish themselves in a trade or occupation for life. The Guardians will not agree to any young person being placed in employment in a blind alley occupation. If such a case arises in a new application for relief, steps are at once taken to remove the young person concerned, who is then placed in a suitable occupation which it is hoped will enable him or her to acquire capacity to earn a competence through life. This scheme to help applicants for relief to help themselves has been eminently successful, and has been in operation since 1922, upwards of 2500 persons having been placed into work. It is found that applicants for relief of sound character at once respond to the Guardians' efforts to place them in work. Those who do not respond are readily discovered, and when brought face to face with their delinquencies and the inevitable results, almost invariably commence to redress their faults by a strong effort to get into work. With very few exceptions when the Guardians

consultation with either the Employment Exchange or with local employers. They provided no training even for the young men, and they gave no information as to the possibilities of migration to places where work was to be got. For the crowds of families to which the Relieving Officers' food tickets were refused, or from whom they were sooner or later withdrawn, nothing was done except to make an offer—that of admission to the Workhouse—which, it could be foreseen, would nearly always be refused. When each case, so far as the Guardians were concerned, ended in this withdrawal of all Poor Relief, there does not appear to have been any subsequent investigation or systematic inquiry as to the conditions under which these people were living ; or to what extent they had been (in the absence of Poor Relief) driven to migrate into another Union, or to depend upon the proceeds of begging or stealing ; or as to what kind of " odd jobs " they were existing on ; or whether they had merely recruited the standing army of Vagrants.[1]

---

have informed a man that they intend to prosecute him as an idle and disorderly person, he has at once obtained work on his own account, and has ceased to be chargeable."

Whether it is desirable that Boards of Guardians should act as a Local Labour Exchange is an open question. Such an arrangement seems to give a preference for employment to applicants for Poor Law relief ! For the opinion of the Ministry, see Ninth Annual Report of Ministry of Health, 1928, pp. 147-148.

[1] In Hampstead, with less poverty than Kensington, substantially the same policy in another form can claim equal success. In 1913–1914, and down to September 1921, no Outdoor Relief whatever was given to able-bodied men (apart from cases of family emergency, such as sickness, etc.). The Order of the Ministry of Health of that date, formulating the " Mond Scale ", led to a change of practice ; and the relatively small number of approved cases were relieved according to the Scale. After a year's experience, it was found that relief of this amount discouraged some men from seeking work ; and on the advice of the Relieving Officers a lower Scale (man and wife, 20s. ; children, 5s. ; falling to 3s. 6d. with coals, and part of the rent) was adopted, which still continues, the number of January 1, 1927, being only 16. Cases are not (as at Kensington) left to the Relieving Officers to relieve wholly in kind, as if in " sudden or urgent necessity ", but are dealt with by small Relief Committees, with much personal encouragement and persuasion of each individual by the Guardians, who generally succeed, in the end, in inducing the men to find employment. " Ultimate refusal " of relief is said to be rarely resorted to. " The House " is offered only to men of bad character or criminal record, as the Guardians are very reluctant to send in respectable persons, deeming the General Mixed Workhouse demoralising. Single men in health are relieved only in exceptional cases, and only by the full Board. Some of them are sent to the Hollesley Bay Colony, which is found to benefit them. There are practically no cases of " sudden or urgent necessity " ; in fact, the total pauperism of all kinds is less than one per cent of the population.

The success of the Hampstead Board is attributed to (1) the exceptional

Dudley

We next select for detailed examination the policy of the Dudley Board of Guardians, as one adopted in an industrial Union subjected to periodical Unemployment of an acute character, resulting in widespread destitution. This policy has been substantially adhered to, with minor changes in detail, throughout the whole seven years since 1921. It is regarded officially as having achieved a great measure of success, and it has latterly received high praise from the Government Inspectors, who have commended it for imitation by other Boards of Guardians.[1]

The flood came upon Dudley only in the second quarter of 1921, and the Outdoor Relief to families destitute by reason of Unemployment, rose, for the half-year ended September 30, 1921, to £2053. Eighteen months later it had reached, for the half-year, £9461. Then it was gradually reduced, until, for the half-year to March 31, 1925, it reached only £108. There again ensued a continuous increase, culminating, in the half-year to September 30, 1926, in a disbursement of no less than £12,689, since which there has been a continuous fall, though the total (for the half-year to September 1928) was still as much as £1625.

The policy of the Dudley Board, which has been continuously presided over since 1920 by Mr. Simeon Webb, a local Trade Union official,[2] was based, from the outset, on the expectation that the period of Unemployment would probably be one of considerable length, so that mere emergency devices were inexpedient. There was never any idea of refusing Outdoor Relief

---

character of the district, the least poor of all the London Unions ; (2) a sufficient supply of zealous and well-trained philanthropists to put each case " under the microscope ", and give it individual treatment and continuous attention. (See *The Annual Reports of the Hampstead Board of Guardians* for 1920–1927 ; and compare *Socialism and the Poor Law*, by Rev. H. J. Marshall, ex-Chairman, Hampstead Board of Guardians, 1927 (a virulent indictment of other Metropolitan Unions).

[1] For the Dudley Union we have relied mainly on information personally obtained ; but see also the frequent brief reports in *The Dudley Herald* ; Eighth Annual Report of Ministry of Health, 1927, p. 244 ; and the annual *Statement of Expenditure and Income*, etc., published by the Union, 1922–1928.

[2] Mr. Webb is secretary to the Sheet-Metal and Hollow-Ware Workers' Trade Union.

to a man with a wife or children dependent on him,[1] in any case in which genuine need existed, and in which institutional treatment was not imperatively called for (as by the illness or chronic infirmity of friendless folk).

At the same time every application was rigorously investigated by the Relieving Officers, the Staff being maintained at sufficient strength to enable this to be done, whilst an energetic Superintendent Relieving Officer kept a vigilant eye on the administration. What is perhaps even more important is that the tradition of the Board of Guardians, which the Chairman helps the Clerk to maintain, appears to be to trust to this staff for the investigation of the cases ; and for the Guardians themselves to confine their individual judgments to the uniform maintenance of the policy on which they have, as a Board, already decided in principle. The applicants, in all cases in which their destitution was by reason only of their Unemployment, have been required to appear, not before a sectional sub-committee (which does not exclude the Guardians for the neighbourhood), although these Sub-Committees continue to deal with " the impotent poor " ; but before the Central Relief Committee meeting in Dudley itself (which incidentally necessitated some of the applicants coming a distance of several miles). The Scale of Outdoor Relief, although it has varied in the course of the past seven years, has always been kept relatively low. Nothing has been given to men in receipt of Unemployment Benefit. Except in a few special cases, at first nothing was given in money, but subsequently this was changed to about one-half being given in money. In order to enable rent to be paid, vouchers are sometimes given for the exact amount payable, which the landlords accept, and themselves exchange for money at the Guardians' offices. Maintenance was provided—at first wholly, but subsequently to the extent of about one-half—by food tickets exchangeable for a wide range of commodities at any shop within the Union area (including any branch of the local Co-operative Society) that agreed to come into the arrangement with the Guardians. And though the Scale was always relatively low (and was not suffered to expand, as in other Unions, under popular pressure), it went

---

[1] Able-bodied single men without dependants are usually offered by the Guardians only " the House ". But the Relieving Officers have to give them food in " sudden or urgent necessity " ; and in exceptional cases the Guardians themselves have given 5s. in food tickets.

up to as much as 33s. 6d. per week, but in 1926 only 26s. (in addition to 8s. 6d. rent) for a man and wife and eight children. For man and wife only it was 15s. per week, plus rent. Nothing extra was given for boots or coal, but at Christmas 2s. for each adult and 1s. per child was added. When the Scale was complained of as inadequate, and the Minister of Health sent an Inspector to visit a random selection of cases, he reported that he found among them none of the acute suffering that had been alleged.

What has proved, however, more effective than anything else is the rule, adopted to meet the rush of Unemployed in 1921, that the able-bodied male applicant is invariably to be required, in return for his food tickets and rent vouchers, irrespective of the weekly amount of the relief, to put in three full days' Test Work. This policy was deliberately adopted in order to make Poor Relief less acceptable than employment at wages. Down to that period, respectable married men, in distress owing solely to involuntary Unemployment, especially coal-miners, had been usually allowed Outdoor Relief without a Labour Test, but only on loan ; and repayment was sought, and often obtained, as soon as the men resumed work.[1] Thus Test Work was, prior to 1921, an alternative to Relief on Loan. Since that date all able-bodied men have been required, both to sign an undertaking to repay the amount of their relief, and to perform Test Work. At the outset the Test Work was performed at the Workhouse. Subsequently the Tipton and Coseley District Councils each provided a lengthy task of shifting a large amount of earth in order to level sites for cottage building.

It will be seen from the statistics [2] that this continuous policy of rigorous administration has not prevented (as it was not

---

[1] Many remissions had, however, to be made ; and over £20,000 was written off as irrecoverable.

[2] Amount of Outdoor Relief in respect of Unemployment in the Dudley Union for successive half-years from 1921–1928 (compiled by the Clerk of the Union). Half - year ended : September 1921, £2053 : 14 : 11 ; March 1922, £5423 : 3 : 10 ; September 1922, £8348 : 11 : 0 ; March 1923, £9461 : 5 : 9 ; September 1923, £1301 : 1 : 9 ; March 1924, £1577 : 6 : 6 ; September 1924, £162 : 14 : 0 ; March 1925, £108 : 0 : 6 ; September 1925, £191 : 12 : 1 ; March 1926, £1265 : 19 : 1 ; September 1926, £12,689 : 11 : 6 ; March 1927, £3167 : 10 : 6.

The average weekly number of applications (families), which had been 193 during 1921–1922 and 221 during 1922–1923, sank to 75 during 1923–1924 and to as few as 5 during 1924–1925 ; rising to 29 during 1925–1926, and to no fewer than 348 during 1926–1927.

intended to prevent, in contrast with what would have been enjoined a generation ago) a relatively enormous expansion of Outdoor Relief in the successive periods of extensive Unemployment. Even in the course of the past eight years the total amount of Outdoor Relief has varied, backwards and forwards, from as much as an average of £300 per week in 1922–1923, and even £600 per week in 1925–1926, to as little as £6 per week over eighteen months in 1924–1925. The Dudley Guardians may fairly claim credit for having succeeded in limiting the expansion to the periods of severe distress. They have, in fact, been able to combine a policy of giving relief adequate for bare maintenance, even in cases of large families, to all who needed it, with a policy of making existence on Poor Relief less acceptable than working for wages when employment could be obtained.

Yet the Dudley Guardians have not wholly solved the problem. The requirement of attendance for Test Work was useful, as far as it went, in deterring applicants who were merely idle ; but experience again showed that it failed to stimulate all the men to seek wage-earning employment. As elsewhere, a certain number of men preferred three days' work a week, with a scanty income, to six days' work for wages at the low rates current for unskilled or unspecialised labour. Moreover, as they enjoyed complete freedom for half the week, they were able to pick up odd jobs on their idle days, which brought them in a few sixpences for very short spells of casual work. An investigation in 1926 showed that, with all their care and scrutiny, and notwithstanding the limitation of each grant to a fortnight only, the Dudley Guardians were giving Outdoor Relief to 42 able-bodied men in health, who had been in receipt either of Unemployment Benefit or of Poor Relief, on and off pretty continuously, for between five and six years ; 29 for between six and seven years ; and 10 for upwards of seven years.[1]

The Dudley Guardians accordingly decided, in 1927, to stop Outdoor Relief altogether to able-bodied healthy men under fifty

---

[1] In exactly the same way the Nottingham Board of Guardians had it reported to them in 1927 that 192 men and 6 single women, able-bodied and in health, and between 16 and 65 years of age, had been in receipt of Outdoor Relief, either continuously, or practically continuously, for between one and three years ; 11 men for between three and four years ; 3 men and 1 single woman for between four and five years ; and 2 men and 2 single women for more than five years (Nottingham Union return for week ending June 18, 1927).

who had remained unemployed, off and on, for five years or more. In the course of the fortnight's warning that was given, several such men obtained employment ; but 87 waited to be actually offered orders for admission to the Workhouse for themselves (Modified Workhouse Test), being informed that, if they went in, Outdoor Relief would be continued to their wives and children. Only 19 of them accepted the admission orders ; only 11 actually entered the Workhouse ; and all of these took their discharge within three days, without any further application for Poor Relief being, within the next few weeks, received from any of them.[1] This action of the Guardians was officially regarded as successful, as, indeed, any complete refusal of Poor Relief may be a success from the standpoint of a Destitution Authority. No investigation was made, or even apparently thought of, as to the conditions under which these families lived when relief was stopped. It should be said, however, that a few of the men subsequently entered the Workhouse; and a few others are known to have found employment. But what happened to the bulk of the cases seems to have remained unknown—whether all the men actually obtained employment at wages (which is unlikely) ; whether any of them took to begging or stealing ; whether any members of their families sickened or died ; whether any of them " took to the road ", and with what consequences. We have here the characteristic shortcoming of any administration that is confined to the relief of destitution. It may not have lain within the accepted duties or legal powers of the Dudley Guardians to make any such investigation. But from the standpoint of the community, no confident judgment can be given as to their policy without a knowledge of its effects upon those applicants for Poor Relief whose applications were refused and who abstained from further requests, as well as upon those others whose relief was continued.

Birmingham

We select as an example of the intermediate type of Poor Law administration, neither deliberately deterrent nor carelessly lax, the extensive and populous Union of Birmingham (including the County Boroughs of Birmingham, except Handsworth Parish,

[1] Eighth Annual Report of Ministry of Health, 1927, p. 244.

and Smethwick). When the Flood came, in November 1920, the citizens of this city showed, in a striking way, the public spirit and municipal wisdom for which they have a reputation. A " Lord Mayor's Fund ", which had been inaugurated each winter to provide boots and clothing for the Unemployed, was allowed, as heretofore, to be suspended each Spring,[1] instead of being expanded to meet the new emergency. The duty of relieving the distress of so large a number of people as had then to be dealt with, was seen to be one for the Local Authorities rather than for the charitable. It was thought essential for the administration to be in the hands of the experienced officials of the Board of Guardians and the Municipal Corporation instead of being placed under any hastily improvised organisation. Acting in close co-operation with the City Council, the Birmingham Board of Guardians—predominantly Conservative and " middle class " in membership, with a small but growing group of Labour men [2]—succeeded in coping with the widespread Unemployment of the ensuing eight years by combining a relatively high Scale of Relief with a carefully thought-out use of Municipal Employment.

At the outset of their proceedings, the Guardians decided (December 20, 1920), on the recommendation of their Central Relief Committee, " that the old methods, *i.e.* a Modified Workhouse Test or a Labour Yard, are not suitable to the present time and circumstances ". The Sectional Relief Committees were accordingly authorised to grant unconditional Outdoor Relief, under Article 12 of the Relief Regulation Order of 1911, according to a Scale (used as a Table of Household Income), which ranged from 15s. per week for a single man, up to 50s. for a family of nine or upwards, one-half in kind and one-half in cash. A remarkable provision, which seems directly contrary to both the law and the approved practice of the preceding three-quarters of a century, expressly directed that " in order to provide an incentive to unemployed persons to accept any kind of work that may be available, only one-half of casual or short time

---

[1] In 1925 the Board of Guardians decided, with the sanction of the Minister of Health, to grant to this Fund the sum of £1000, in recoupment of gifts in kind made to recipients of Poor Relief (Minutes of Birmingham Board of Guardians, January 21, 1925).

[2] Out of 52 members, those elected as members of the Labour Party or as Socialists numbered 4 in 1919, 7 in 1922, 12 in 1925, and 15 in 1928.

earnings of the head of the family of not more than 20s. weekly, and three-fourths of the earnings other than the head, shall be reckoned as income ". Similarly, where a recipient of relief sublets any portion of his house, only three-fourths of the rent was to be reckoned as income. And " the Sub-Committee shall ignore 7s. 6d. of any income received by way of Disablement Pension, Friendly Society Benefit, Trade Union Allowance or Health Insurance Benefit "—subject to an overriding maximum for all these deductions and abatements of 15s. per week in any one case.[1]

The Minister of Health appears to have sent word through the Inspector, fifteen months later, that he thought the Scales of Relief were then too high, " having regard to the wages now paid, and to the fall in the cost of living ", and that " the maximum relief to the Unemployed ought to be less by at least 10s. per week than the wages of labourers in the district ". The Inspector is reported to have said that if this new maximum were not adhered to, he feared that the Minister would not sanction any further overdraft. The Guardians, however, definitely refused to make any reduction in their Scale or in its application, but made some slight concessions (an additional cash allowance for fuel was discontinued ; the fraction of the earnings of children to be ignored was reduced to one-fourth ; and the part of a Disability Pension or Friendly Society Sick Pay to be ignored was reduced to 5s.). The Minister was not satisfied, but the Board, whilst revising the details of the relief in kind, continued to refuse to make any reduction in the money payments under the Scale,[2] although by March 1927 the highest figure given in the Scale was 41s. 3d., then given wholly in money, for a man with wife and five children. It is to be noted that the amount for the single man has remained throughout at 15s. per week, apparently without specific official objection.

The Birmingham Guardians, quite logically and, as it seems, lawfully, took the view that the mere receipt of Unemployment

---

[1] The Committee reported that " the Minister of Health has intimated that he will not dissent from relief administered by the Birmingham Board as long as it is administered in accordance with the foregoing proposals ; and that he will be prepared from time to time to consent to the raising of an overdraft or a temporary loan " (Minutes, December 20, 1920). The meals supplied to children at school were presently also ignored (Minutes, November 16, 1921); medical extras, boots and clothing were also additional.

[2] Minutes, July 19, 1922, and May 16, 1923.

Benefit did not disentitle a person to Poor Relief. The Benefit (other than that for a single man or lone woman), even as increased in 1924, fell far short of the Guardians' judgment of what was " adequate " for complete maintenance, as expressed in their Scale. Accordingly, where there was no other income than the Unemployment Benefit, a regular supplement was paid as Poor Relief, according to the size of the family, ranging from 5s. for man and wife up to 7s. 6d. for man and wife and five or more children ; and 11s. for a woman with one child up to 12s. 6d. for a woman with four or more children. Men in receipt of this supplement " may be set to work as a condition of any relief granted to them if there are exceptional circumstances relating to the particular case ".

The second distinctive feature of the Birmingham administration has been the intelligent and varied use made by the Guardians almost continuously of the employment that the City Council was willing to offer to the able-bodied applicants for Poor Relief. This took three forms. At first the Guardians arranged for some of their able-bodied men to be employed at wages on relief work undertaken by the Birmingham and Smethwick Corporations, which took such cases out of the hands of the Guardians for the time being. Because so very few men were employed on these relief works, a second scheme was begun in January 1923. The City Council, at the request of the Guardians, undertook to put in hand work in its parks and cemeteries, such as levelling, making paths, etc., in order to provide a labour test for the able-bodied men receiving Poor Relief. The City Council controlled the work, but the Guardians were responsible for sending and paying the men engaged. The Council agreed to put to work men sent to them by the Guardians, for whatever number of hours was specified. Such work was imposed on the able-bodied recipients of relief according to the Scale, in proportion to the amount granted in each case—for instance, $3\frac{1}{2}$ days a week for 28s., $4\frac{1}{2}$ days a week for 38s., 5 days a week for 45s. The Guardians sought to get the cards of the men working on this " test " scheme stamped for Health and Unemployment Insurance. With some hesitation this was held to be illegal.[1] In communicating this decision

---

[1] " Persons are not insurable unless they are employed under a contract of service. Persons in receipt of relief and required to perform work as a condition of the receipt of that relief are not, in view of the Minister, so employed " (Ministry of Health to Birmingham Board of Guardians, November 19, 1924).

to the Guardians, the Minister of Health drew attention to the
" possibility of an arrangement with the Municipal Corporation
under which the men whom it was desired to treat exceptionally
should be referred to the Corporation for employment by the Corporation, the Guardians making, with the Minister's approval, a
financial contribution towards the expense so incurred by the
Corporation. The Minister would be prepared to approve of such
a contribution, providing it did not exceed the amount which
would be expended on relief in those cases if employment had not
been found for them." [1] This ingenious device was adopted in
January 1925. The City Council, after consideration, agreed to
pay to the men, as wages, the amount of money which they had
hitherto received from the Guardians.[2] The mode of calculating
the hours to be worked remained the same, though the number
was slightly altered. A new Scale was issued whereby the number
of hours which the men had to work was calculated so as to equal
the amount of Poor Relief to which they would have been entitled,
at one shilling and threepence per hour—the Trade Union District
Rate of wages for the kind of work for which they were formally
engaged by the Corporation. This work thus became insurable
employment, the Guardians repaying the Council the amount
of Poor Relief to which the men would otherwise have been
entitled.

There is reason to think that the arrangement by which the
Sectional Relief Committees were always able to direct any
applicant for relief to Corporation employment had a large
measure of success in preventing the liberality of the Guardians
from being improperly taken advantage of. It was an advantage
for an able-bodied man to be found a temporary situation as a
Corporation labourer, at regular wages, entitling him to Health
and Unemployment Insurance, and taking him off the pauper
roll. But out of 1795 men sent to the Corporation between April 1,
1927, and March 31, 1928, just about half found that they pre-

---

[1] Minutes, November 19, 1924.

[2] " The proposal now put forward by the Guardians is that the men recommended by them shall be found employment by the Corporation to an extent
in each case which would entitle a particular man to a wage payment equivalent
to the contribution to which he would otherwise be entitled by way of Poor
Law Relief. The Guardians would then reimburse the Corporation for the total
wage payments so incurred, and the Corporation would therefore bear only the
cost of insurance contributions in respect of these men " (*Report of the City
Council General Purposes Committee*, January 6, 1925).

ferred, in various ways, to do without the opportunity afforded to them. The weak point of the arrangement was that the employment was only between 23 and 34 hours per week. The success of the scheme seems to have depended largely on the way in which the men were selected. Thus, no man was sent to the Corporation, or kept at work by the Corporation, who was below a fairly high standard of physical fitness. Year after year a considerable number of the professedly able-bodied applicants had to be excused from the test, as not physically fit for continuous work as labourers ; and for these men no alternative test was devised. They were simply continued on unconditional Outdoor Relief.

For the unemployed able-bodied women, without husbands or children, another plan was adopted. The Relief Regulation Order of 1911 is silent as to any test for women. The Birmingham Guardians began by allowing them unconditional Outdoor Relief on a special scale.[1] But the Guardians presently set themselves to find these women (for whom the Employment Exchange could discover no vacancies) suitable situations as cleaners, maids, seamstresses or factory hands. During the year 1927 no fewer than 203 such women were, by the co-operation of the voluntary hospitals, charitable institutions and Public Departments within the city, together with a certain number of public-spirited employers, successfully placed in adequately paid situations.

It is, we think, a tribute to the wisdom with which the Birmingham Board—discarding the devices of the Labour Yard and the Modified Workhouse Test—combined its policy of adequate Outdoor Relief with a sensible use of Municipal Employment, that it was able gradually to bring down the total numbers on Poor Relief on account of Unemployment from 77,931 on January 7, 1922, to 16,736 on January 3, 1925 ; and to reduce them to

---

[1] On November 16, 1921, the Central Relief Committee reported as follows : " At the present time any single woman relieved by the Guardians is given relief in kind (on Scale ½) the approximate value of which is 5s., and where there is little or no cash income, cash is granted up to 10s. The question has arisen as to what grant, if any, should be made to single women, not living rent free, in receipt of 12s. Unemployment Benefit and no other income, and the Committee propose that, within their discretion, Sectional Relief Committees may in such cases grant relief in kind upon a scale to be known as Quarter Scale, viz. : weekly—Tea, 2 oz. ; Sugar, ½ lb. ; Rolled Oats, ½ lb. ; Bread, 4 lb. ; Cheese (Colonial or American), ¼ lb. ; Sweetened Condensed Milk, one 7-oz. tin ; Margarine, ¼ lb. ; Loose Cocoa, 1 oz."

8413 on January 5, 1929.[1] The Birmingham policy, relatively successful as it has been, has fallen short—a characteristic of nearly all Poor Law Work—in its failure to provide any treatment of a remedial or restorative character. Whilst a large proportion of the men have been saved, for most of the time, from the demoralisation of complete idleness, it has been a grave defect that where not sent to be employed by the Corporation, and simply put on " test work " by the Guardians, the single men, a majority of whom whom were under twenty-five, seen to have been required to give only 12 hours per week of their time. The Guardians, as it seems, attempted nothing, and accomplished nothing, in the way of training or otherwise improving the wageless men ; not even the considerable proportion of them who, in each year, have been youths under twenty-one, many of them having enjoyed no regular training in any kind of manual labour. Many others, found too weak for the Corporation work, might advantageously have been asked, instead of doing nothing for their Outdoor

[1] OUTDOOR RELIEF ON ACCOUNT OF UNEMPLOYMENT (BIRMINGHAM UNION)

Week ending	Number of Men Relieved.	Number of Individuals (including Dependants).	Total Amount of Relief paid.
January 15, 1921 .	130	704	107
July 2, 1921 .	2,759	14,228	2,328
January 7, 1922 .	17,886	65,661	14,241
July 1, 1922 .	23,053	77,931	22,326
January 6, 1923 .	16,619	59,059	14,114
July 7, 1923 .	10,128	36,166	7,316
January 5, 1924 .	9,590	34,863	8,375
July 5, 1924 .	6,423	22,891	4,188
January 3, 1925 .	4,683	16,736	3,183
July 4, 1923 .	2,849	9,367	2,041
January 2, 1926 .	3,106	10,569	1,980
July 3, 1926 .	3,238	11,717	2,229
January 1, 1927 .	3,750	13,938	2,448
July 2, 1927 .	2,470	11,025	2,241
January 7, 1928 .	2,735	12,654	2,667
July 7, 1928 .	1,815	8,689	1,833
January 5, 1929 .	1,718	8,413	1,528

Relief, to put in so many hours per week at physical training, varied by educational classes of different kinds.[1] The Birmingham Guardians might reply that they were not aware that Boards of Guardians were expected or encouraged to regard such applicants for Poor Relief as patients for treatment ; and we do not find that such a view of their duty was ever suggested to them.

Liverpool and Manchester

The great urban aggregations centred on Liverpool and Manchester respectively, comprising a population approaching three millions, or over 8 per cent of England and Wales, present Poor Law features both like and unlike those of the Unions so far dealt with. As in other Unions, their total pauperism, in comparison with that of 1913–1914, shows a colossal increase, almost wholly in Outdoor Relief. This is accounted for, largely where not entirely, by the new feature of relief granted systematically to able-bodied men, on account of Unemployment, whose numbers run up in a single Union (as at Liverpool) to ten and even fifteen thousand, with three times as many dependants ; whereas in 1913–1914 practically no able-bodied men in health were granted Outdoor Relief. The relief has been, in nearly all cases, unconditional, without Labour Test, granted almost indiscriminately, according to relatively high scales, which do

[1] Training for some of the unemployed women has been provided by voluntary effort, with the co-operation of the Guardians' officers, and with the approval of the Guardians themselves and of the Ministry of Health. Thus it is recorded in 1925 that " for the last eighteen months weekly classes have been held at four centres . . . for the instruction of women in receipt of Outdoor Relief (both ordinary and unemployment cases). The classes have been augmented by the Chief Woman Visitor and her staff, with the co-operation of qualified teachers. The women are instructed in housewifery, cookery, and in simple dressmaking. No expenditure in connection with these classes falls upon the Board. Use of the rooms has been granted without payment, and all other expenses are met from private sources. The attendances at the classes are good, and considerable benefit is derived. The Visitors report that more nourishing and economical dishes are now prepared in the homes, with the resultant improvement in health. The other classes have been equally successful " (Minutes of Central Relief Committee, February 18, 1925). When the Guardians in 1928 desired to make a grant in aid of these classes, the Ministry of Health did not see its way to sanction it, unless the classes were officially under the control of the Guardians. This would be difficult to arrange without losing the assistance given by the Local Education Authority (which provides the teachers) and private philanthropy. The matter is (1929) still under discussion, and it is hoped that the Departmental objection may be overcome.

not exclude from their benefit single men without dependants. This relief has been, in many cases, renewed continuously for years, without the " offer of the House ". The " Workhouse Test " has passed, in fact, along with the Labour Test, into discredit and disuse. This policy was pursued, between 1920 and 1926, practically without any active intervention by the Ministry of Health ; and it still continues, scarcely mitigated by the criticisms and remonstrances of the Inspectors during 1927 and 1928. But there is one significant unlikeness with other Unions with equally swollen Outdoor Relief in the fact that these enjoy a high rateable value, and, after a relatively small indebtedness, have since managed to pay their way by high rates. Another unlikeness is that none of the Boards of Guardians in this area has ever had a majority of Labour Members. The most important Boards have often had no Labour Members whatever, or none until 1925 or even 1928, and then only a tiny minority.[1]

These features are conspicuous in the story, since the Armistice, of the wealthy Union of West Derby, almost the most populous in the Kingdom, which (since July 1922) comprises the whole of the City of Liverpool and the County Borough of Bootle, together with one large rural and four populous urban districts. (Total population of the present Union area of 39,507 acres in 1921, 944,929 ; total assessable value in 1927, £8,221,690.) A conspicuous element in this great port is casual labour in various occupations, a form of employment which is sometimes said to extend to as many as half of all the manual workers. Since the beginning of the slump in the latter part of 1920, its total pauperism has never been less than 30,000, and it has once (in 1922) come near to 70,000. But the greatest variation has been in the numbers granted Outdoor Relief on account merely of Unemployment, which were nil in 1913–1914, and 56,487 on July 1, 1922,[2] one-fourth being adult men, and three-fourths women or children, almost wholly their dependants.

---

[1] Thus, the West Derby Union (including Liverpool and Bootle) has a Board of 106 Guardians, none of whom were " Labour " until the election of 1928, when seven were returned.

[2] The numbers at successive dates were as follows : July 1, 1922, 56,487 ; January 1, 1923, 46,205 ; July 1, 1923, 35,412 ; January 1, 1924, 37,212 ; July 1, 1924, 34,722 ; January 1, 1925, 23,648 ; July 1, 1925, 23,189 ; January 1, 1926, 29,306 ; July 1, 1926, 35,011 ; January 1, 1927, 39,277 ; July 1, 1927,

These seven to fourteen thousand healthy able-bodied men (the variation in the numbers depending largely on contemporary changes in the " gaps " and other restrictions of Unemployment Insurance Benefit) have been, since 1921, usually granted their Poor Relief of between 10s. and 41s. per week, according to the size of their families, without Labour Test, or other conditions. For about six months in 1922 the Guardians sent many of the men to the Municipal Corporation, which found them " test work " for three days at a time, at intervals of six weeks. This pretence at a Labour Test was given up in November 1922. From 1925 onwards the Guardians have sent various numbers of men (up to as many as 550 in some weeks) to three of the Municipal Authorities within the Union, for regular employment at wages, the Union paying these public employers, by way of subsidy, the amount of Poor Relief that would otherwise have been given to the men. This (as at Birmingham) is deemed insurable employment, and the men's Insurance books are duly stamped.[1]

With these relatively small exceptions, the men receive unconditional relief. A unique feature of the West Derby Union is that they are dealt with by separate depôts and staffs, quite distinct from the District Relieving Officers, who confine themselves to the " ordinary cases ". The Scale adopted by the Board on September 26, 1923, allowed 12s. to a single man living away from the home of relatives, and to a man, wife and five children 36s. per week, which was the maximum, except that a " discretionary allowance " of 5s. per week might be added in exceptional instances. This Scale was retained, in spite of the fall in the cost of living, until September 29, 1927, when, on the peremptory demand of the Ministry of Health, it was reduced, but, generally, by no more than one shilling per case. At the same time the rate of such of the unemployed single men as had been continuously chargeable for two years or longer was reduced from 12s. to 10s. per week ; and it was directed that " relief in cash was not to be given to hawkers, pedlars, tatters and all other uninsured persons with any income ". These very

---

38,304 ; January 1, 1928, 43,317 ; July 1, 1928, 33,965 ; January 1, 1929, 35,949.

[1] " The Experience of Recent Years in dealing with the Unemployment Problem," by W. A. Hanlon, Chairman of the West Derby Union (Central Poor Law Conference, 1928).

mild reductions, estimated to save between £40,000 and £50,000 in a year, were only carried after embittered opposition, which ended in the withdrawal of a considerable section of the Guardians—not all of one political Party—leaving the new rates to be carried by only 39 members out of a Board of 106, a number of those remaining not voting.

In this Union the relief is, in the vast majority of cases, given wholly in money. Originally the able-bodied Unemployed were given half their relief in the form of vouchers on the local tradesmen. This was abandoned by the Guardians in 1923, in favour of letting the recipients have their relief wholly in cash, in order, so we are informed, that they might be free to lay out the amount to the best possible advantage ! But " in doubtful cases " the Relief Committee may, if it chooses, still give part of the relief in kind.

It is not to be wondered at that, in this vast host of able-bodied men, many should go on drawing the Guardians' weekly cash for years together. On June 28, 1927, the Guardians reported to the Ministry of Labour that there were, on Outdoor Relief, no fewer than 3541 single men without any dependants ; that, of these, 1246 had been on relief for less than a year ; 1532 for over one year but less than three years ; 450 between three and four years, whilst 313 had drawn this dole continuously for over four years. The proportions were similar with regard to the 7367 with dependent wives and children. Altogether, in more than 8000 cases of healthy adults, comprising over 30,000 persons, unconditional and indiscriminate Outdoor Relief in money had, on June 28, 1927, been drawn continuously for more than a whole year, and in many cases for much more, without any prospect of its coming to an end.

All this is done in Liverpool under Art. XII. of the Relief Regulation Order of 1911, which allows exceptions to be made on condition that the circumstances of each case are promptly reported to the Ministry of Health, which may then disallow any of them. But, with seven to fourteen thousand cases every week, it was found that this " would involve very great labour ". Accordingly, only the total number and the total amount of relief have been reported weekly, and it is on this barefaced evasion of the requirements of the Order that these colossal sums for Outdoor Relief merely on account of Unemployment, running up to half a million or even seven hundred thousand pounds a year, have been passed since 1921 by the District Auditor. We know of no explanation why this predominatingly Conservative Board of Guardians, operating in the second largest Union of the Kingdom, has not been more sharply pulled up by the Ministry of Health.

The great Manchester Union, which, down to the end of 1920, apart from a few exceptional cases in peculiar circumstances, granted no Outdoor Relief to able-bodied men in health, has never found on its hands anything like the number of men claiming to be relieved on account of involuntary wagelessness that we have described in the West Derby Union.[1] But during 1921 the flood of Unemployment equally swept away the Guardians' defences ; and Outdoor Relief has ever since been paid to between two and five thousand such men, with three times that number of dependants. Here, too, the relief has been almost entirely unconditional, the only use of the Labour Test being that in about 6 per cent of the cases men have been required to do work at the Institutions of the Union for a few days or weeks at a time.[2] The Scale, which seems to have been usually applied automatically, has always been relatively high ; and in January 1925 it was substantially raised. For the next three years it gave, to a single unemployed man 10s. per week, together with the rent actually paid up to 6s. per week ; and to a man with dependants from 20s. up to 44s. per week, together with the rent actually paid up to 10s. per week. On the Inspector's

[1] For the Manchester Union (which amalgamated the former Manchester, Chorlton and Prestwich Unions, and now includes in its area of 25,210 acres the whole City of Manchester, but not the Borough of Salford ; and which had, in 1921, a population of 766,030 and had, in 1928, a rateable value of £7,263,045), much information is afforded by the printed copy of Ministry of Health Inspector's Report and Observations of a Special Committee of the Guardians thereon, January 1928 ; see also Hansard, December 7, 1927, and frequent reference in *The Manchester Guardian*, 1927–1928.

[2] The Inspector's Report of November 3, 1927, points out that, out of the 17 Relief Districts : " In 3 Districts there is no Test work ; in 1 District only 1 per cent of the cases are required to perform Test work ; in 2 Districts the proportion is 2 per cent ; in 1, 4 per cent ; in 5 between 5 per cent and 10 per cent ; in 2 between 10 per cent and 20 per cent ; and in 3 from 20 per cent to 29 per cent. The average for the whole Union is 6 per cent . . . even in Districts where a large number of cases are put on Test work, intervals varying from four to six months are the rule. Case 9953 has done 16 weeks' Test work in 4½ years ; 55,121 has done 8 weeks in 6 years. Many similar cases could be quoted " (Copy of Ministry of Health Inspector's Report and Observations of a Special Committee of the Guardians thereon, January 1928).

remonstrances, the rate for a single man was reduced, in November 1927, to 8s. per week, whilst the relief for a family was cut down to 17s. for man and wife, and to a maximum of 28s. in all cases, with the addition of the rent. The Scale for widows with children, and for the aged and infirm, has always been equally liberal. But the main criticism made upon the Manchester administration was that of an irregularly generous laxity of interpretation of the rules. It appears that the seventeen Sub-Committees which, in practice, dealt with the applications for Out-Relief, consisted, even nominally, only of three or four Guardians, who nearly all persisted in acting for the Wards by which they were elected ; and often there would be only one Guardian in attendance. The liberal Scale was, in nearly all the Sub-Committees, liberally interpreted. In estimating the total family income, some of the Sub-Committees habitually ignored the earnings of relatives not legally liable to contribute ; often regarded War pensions as sacrosanct ; and made a generous allowance from the earnings of sons and daughters for the cost of tramway fares and meals taken away from home. It was customary with most Sub-Committees to ignore the value of the school meals enjoyed by the children of parents receiving relief, as well as the meals supplied to the men on Test Work ; and though assistance by other agencies in the form of boots, clothing, etc., was regularly reported through the Mutual Registration Council, the Clerk explained that " it has always been the policy of the Guardians not to take these allowances into account when granting relief ".[1]

Under these conditions the numbers of persons in receipt of Outdoor Relief in Manchester failed to decrease. In fact, from December 1923 to September 1927, notwithstanding falling prices and periodical diminutions in the volume of Unemployment, the total number on Out-Relief (including the impotent and the widows as well as the able-bodied), steadily rose, quarter by quarter, from 3612 cases in December 1923 to 6820 in September 1927 ; representing in 1923 some 15,000 persons and in 1927 some 27,000. Of these, 3692 cases at the earlier date, and 4763 at the later, were those of men or women destitute by reason only of Unemployment, one-fourth of them being single men or women without dependants. In June 1927 it was found that 45 per cent of these merely " Unemployed " paupers had been continuously

[1] *Ibid.* pp. 9, 18.

on Outdoor Relief for more than three years. Notwithstanding vehement protests by a minority of the Guardians,[1] the Board had the grace, in November 1927, after slightly reducing its Scale of Relief, in various ways to tighten up its administration, and especially to make increasing use of a more continuous Labour Test for men without dependants who had been for a long time living on Poor Relief.

It remains to be said that the Manchester Board has at no time been predominantly, or even largely, composed of " Labour Guardians ". Indeed, until 1925, there were hardly any. So far as can be ascertained, a substantial majority of the Guardians during the past decade have belonged to the Conservative Party. At the end of 1927 we found, on personal inquiry, that out of 64 members, 29 were reputed to be Conservatives, 18 to be Liberals (among these were several Roman Catholics) ; 3 were styled Independents, whilst only 14 (being 22 per cent of the Board) were classed as Labour, nearly all these having been elected only in 1925.

Salford

The Salford Board, which happens to have a majority of Labour Guardians,[2] has shown greater resourcefulness in dealing with the Unemployed than its neighbour at Manchester ; and has come out, after various interesting experiments, with a unique scheme of educational training to which, after cautious demur, the Ministry of Health has extended its approval.[3] From the coming upon them of the Flood of Unemployment towards the end of 1921 the Salford Guardians found themselves driven to give unconditional Outdoor Relief to the able-bodied appli-

[1] Hansard, December 7, 1927.

[2] Of the 20 Guardians, 13 are described as " Labour " and 7 as " Independents and Other Parties ".

[3] For Salford we have had the advantage of seeing not only the volume of *Standing Orders, Regulations, Relief Scales, Legal Precedents*, etc., 1925, but also many reports and Minutes of the Board of Guardians : the *Scheme of Employment under the Salford City Council* (May 1926), and the Circular of June 22, 1927, in which the scheme of educational training was first described ; the printed Report of the Sub-Committee on Outdoor Relief Administration of September 16, 1927, embodying the Inspector's critical Report, and the Guardians' reply ; the elaborate pamphlet entitled *Scheme of Work and Training for the Benefit of Unemployed Men in Receipt of Outdoor Relief*, July 1928 ; and *The Observations of the Guardians of the Salford Union on the Provisional Proposals for Poor Law Reform*.

cants ; the numbers rising from next to none in August 1921 to 2091 men (with 6318 dependants) on January 1, 1922, but then gradually falling to 505 (with 2091 dependants) on January 1, 1925. During the prolonged coal-mining stoppage of 1926 the numbers were again trebled ; and during 1927 they remained round about 1250 men (with 4000 dependants). Relief has continued to be granted on a fairly high scale, but with considerable discrimination. There are four Relief Sub-Committees, each of five members, for the four districts of the Union, but the composition of these Sub-Committees is so arranged that no Guardian adjudicates on cases from the district in which he resides, and for which he is elected. The very critical investigation of the Ministry of Health's Inspector in 1927 naturally discovered a certain number of cases in which he thought that the Guardians had been unduly liberal in the exercise of their discretion, but as to which further explanations were afforded. In comparison with the Inspectors' Reports on other Unions that we have seen, the judgment on the shortcomings of the Salford Guardians was only mildly critical. The Guardians were, moreover, continuously struggling with their problem ; and they had put in operation (in July 1926), as an alternative to unconditional Outdoor Relief, a Joint Scheme "under which work is found by the Corporation for men recommended by the Guardians. It provides for the employment of men not in receipt of Unemployment Benefit . . . resident in the Union twelve months . . . on work such as would not ordinarily be carried out at the time ". Each man was "required to put in such number of hours at the rate obtaining in the particular department . . . as will entitle him to wages equivalent to the amount of Relief per Scale. . . . All men for work on the Joint Scheme are chosen by the Relieving Officers from those they consider their most unsatisfactory cases." The Inspector found much to criticise in this attempt of the Guardians to find something better than unconditional Outdoor Relief, notably the employment only in proportion to the amount of relief, and the unsatisfactory discipline enforced by the Corporation over what were doubtless inferior workmen. But neither he nor the Ministry of Health was able to suggest any better device. Meanwhile, however, the Guardians themselves were trying a new experiment, and one that had, we believe, never been officially suggested to any

Board of Guardians, namely, that of exacting, from selected men in receipt of Outdoor Relief, not " work " at all, either at wages or merely as a Test, but attendance at instructional classes. This scheme—an echo of the Cotton Famine of sixty-five years ago—was specially applicable to single young men, whose relief was too small in amount to warrant the exaction of a full week's work. " Since March 1927, the Guardians have required all single men under the age of 35 who pass a medical examination to attend. . . . There are two classes, each in charge of an Instructor. . . . The work of each session is one hour's physical drill, for which vests, shorts and pumps are provided ; and one hour's instruction on general subjects." The Inspector felt able to express only a very guarded opinion on this novel device. Subsequently, however, the Minister of Health gave his approval to the scheme, which the Guardians proceeded to improve and elaborate. The Joint Scheme of employment by the Salford Corporation was continued, under improved conditions, for about 300 men. The simple attendance at instructional class continued to be required from single young men. But for the bulk of the able-bodied men with families a more elaborate " Scheme of Work and Training " was provided. In return for their Outdoor Relief such men are now required to spend normally 30 hours per week (which may be in special circumstances, according to the weather, and to the condition of the men, reduced to 20 hours or increased to 40 hours), partly in working under supervision at digging, levelling, draining, cultivating and generally improving the Guardians' 43 acres of waste land ; and, to the extent of 6 hours a week, in being seriously trained in such handicrafts as wood-carving, picture-framing and sheet-metal work, together with the use of tools and the making of models, as well as of simple household utensils and furniture, the execution of household repairs and decoration and the mending of boots. Men are required to keep up their registration at the local Employment Exchange, and are, by personal co-operation between the Guardians and local employers, assisted in every possible way to obtain situations. On the other hand, those who are apathetic, indolent or refractory, are, after warning, relegated to the Institution, upon the Modified Workhouse Test scheme, under which their dependants may continue to receive Outdoor Relief. In bad cases the whole family is ordered in, preparatory

to the children over three being transferred either to the
Guardians' Cottage Homes or to Certified Schools. The special
point about this scheme is that what it provides is not employment, but physical and technical training. The aim is neither to
punish nor to produce, but to save the men from the demoralisation of idleness, partly by prescribed physical exercise in the
open air, under strict disciplinary supervision (a relatively cheap
form of training) ; and partly by skilled instruction in handicrafts.
Above all, this is offered to the men, not as a punishment, nor
yet as a deterrent to drive them away, but as a help to them
in regaining employment, and as a privilege which they forfeit
unless their conduct is satisfactory. We know of nothing better
done for the Unemployed by any Board of Guardians in England
and Wales. Nevertheless, the Salford Guardians, when considering the Minister of Health's proposals for Poor Law Reform,
specifically recommended the complete transfer of all responsibility for providing for the Unemployed to the Minister of
Labour, his Training Centres and his Employment Exchanges.[1]

The Glamorgan and Monmouthshire Unions

The Poor Law Unions comprising the coal-mining, iron and
steel production and tinplate districts of South Wales and Monmouthshire have many common features ; but under the stress of
the past eight years they have, in regard to able-bodied destitution,
diverged into almost every variety of policy. In some of the
Unions in poverty-stricken mining areas the practice has arisen of
leaving the Unemployed and their families to be dealt with by the
Relieving Officer as in " sudden or urgent necessity ", though this
unconditional Outdoor Relief has been continued, with the tacit
approval of the Guardians, and without objection by the Ministry,
week after week and month after month. On the other hand, the
Cardiff Board of Guardians, until latterly, subsidised Unemployment Benefit almost as a matter of course, and still has a scale
of Outdoor Relief for able-bodied men up to 44s. per week for a
large family ; whilst the Merthyr Tydfil Union goes only up to 35s.
Pontypridd Union follows what it imagines to be the Merthyr
Tydfil Judgment in refusing relief to the able-bodied man,

---

[1] *Provisional Proposals for Poor Law Reform : Observations of the Guardians
of the Salford Union*, 1926, p. 6.

whether or not he can get employment, but nevertheless grants him relief freely on account of his legal dependants. The Abergavenny Union claims to deal with each case on its merits, but seems, in practice, to do the same as Pontypridd.[1]

We can best convey to the reader a sense of the situation by giving, in some detail, the experience during the past fifteen years of the Pontypridd Union, in the Rhondda Valley, the most populous in all Wales (415,642 in 1921). Before the War the Guardians, who were then predominantly small shopkeepers, beerhousekeepers and colliery officials, gave freely small allowances of Outdoor Relief, but almost entirely to the non-able-bodied. Destitution due merely to involuntary Unemployment was practically unknown. If, by exception, an able-bodied man applied for relief, the Guardians could always direct him to a job. When, however, exceptional circumstances justified temporary relief to an ablebodied man, the Guardians did not hesitate, in these isolated cases, to grant Outdoor Relief, and to this, when the cases were promptly reported as exceptions, no objection was taken by the Local Government Board. During the War, and immediately after its close, there was a chronic shortage of labour in the mines. So large a proportion of the miners joined the fighting forces that " men flocked into the coal-fields from almost every part of the country, the major portion of whom either had been rejected or discharged from the Army in consequence of their physical condition ".[2] In fact, almost any man could get taken on at wages ; and when the Pontypridd Union had to relieve a family, 50s. per week was taken as the standard, because it was assumed to be the very lowest wage that the worst man could earn.

---

[1] For the Glamorganshire and Monmouthshire Unions we have relied largely on personal investigation, in which we have received the utmost assistance from officials in all departments, elected Councillors and Guardians, social workers, etc. We may refer also to the illuminating MS. Report which the Superintendent Relieving Officer of Pontypridd Union (D. T. James) presented to the Finance Committee, July 1928 (see MS. Minutes and *Poor Law Officers' Journal*, August 17, 1928) ; Reports and Accounts of Cardiff, Newport and other Unions ; *The Distress in South Wales : Report of Labour Committee of Inquiry*, March 1928 ; three special articles in *The Times*, March 28, 29 and 30, 1928 ; Report of the Appointed Guardians for Bedwellty Union, Cmd. 2976 of 1927 ; Second Report of the same, Cmd. 3141 of 1928 ; Eighth Annual Report of Ministry of Health, 1927, J. Evans' Report, pp. 77 ; Report on . . . South Wales and Monmouthshire, Cmd. 3272 of 1929.

[2] MS. Report of D. T. James, Relieving Officer, Pontypridd, July 1928.

In 1921 came serious trade depression, and a three months' stoppage of all the mines through the great industrial dispute. Although the Board of Guardians was still predominantly middle class in character, with only a minority Labour, it granted Outdoor Relief freely, for the first three weeks of the strike, to all the families who were in distress, irrespective of whether or not the men were participants in the dispute. The aggregate amount thus dispensed presently alarmed the Guardians, who plucked up courage to apply what they were told was the Merthyr Tydfil Judgment—not refusing relief to the participants in the dispute (other than single men), but only cutting down the amount in each case to the sum appropriate to the miner's wife, children, or other legal dependants. This continued on a large scale until the dispute ended, without objection being taken. On the resumption of work there was, for the next few years, comparatively little Unemployment ; and the amount of Outdoor Relief for 1924 and the first part of 1925 fell considerably from the highest previous totals. Later in 1925, there occurred in this Union a local stoppage of the coal-mining industry on a considerable scale, and the numbers on Outdoor Relief went up in some weeks to as much as 30,000. They still numbered about 26,000 in the spring of 1926, when there came the eight months' national stoppage, every man being then actually discharged by the employers, without, at first, any terms being stated on which the colliery companies were prepared to resume work. The Guardians this time, on the instructions of the Ministry of Health's Circular No. 703, applied, from the start, what was represented as the Merthyr Tydfil Judgment, giving the locked-out men—*without inquiry as to whether or not they could obtain employment on any terms*—only relief in kind for wives and children, at the rate, for some time, of 11s. 6d. for the wife and 3s. for each child ; presently reduced to 10s. and 2s. respectively. From May to December in that year the numbers relieved never fell below 76,000, and they reached at the peak no less than 95,000, being not far short of one-fourth of the whole population. In this one Union as much as £21,000 was paid away in Outdoor Relief in a single week.[1] The following

---

[1] All the Unions in Glamorgan and Monmouthshire were severely affected, with some of those in Carmarthenshire, Breconshire and Pembrokeshire. The Unions of Merthyr Tydfil, Bridgend and Cowbridge, and Neath, together with those in Monmouthshire, suffered nearly as much as Pontypridd. Bedwellty Union during one week had 42 per cent of its population on the Out-Relief lists.

report of the Ministry of Health Inspector affords an interesting vision of the official procedure, and of the view of the law to which the Guardians were required to conform.

" In accordance with the Merthyr Tydfil Judgment "—this was how Mr. Evans explained the law—" the miner himself was not entitled to be relieved. I visited ", he reported, " each of the Industrial Boards of Guardians, and discussed with them the requirements of the law in the matter, and particularly the necessity for economy in administration, in view of the fact that practically all these Unions soon found it impossible from their own resources to find the necessary money, and were obliged to obtain the Minister's sanction to overdrafts and loans from the banks and the Goschen Committee, *i.e.* the Exchequer. In the case of some of the Unions (Bedwellty, Bridgend and Cowbridge, Neath and Crickhowell) I also interviewed each Relieving Officer, and in most of the other Unions the Superintendent Relieving Officer. I am glad to be able to say that I found the officers generally were carrying out their onerous duties faithfully and well. The Boards also, though many ingenious arguments were raised by individual members at Board Meetings that I attended, kept themselves, on the whole, within the law. In one instance (Bedwellty), at a meeting at which I was present, the Relieving Officers, through one of their number acting as spokesman, informed the Board that, whatever directions the Guardians might give, they were going to carry out the law strictly. As the dispute proceeded, great pressure was brought to bear on Boards of Guardians and their officers to give relief to single men ; but these efforts were not successful, and, so far as I know, the only cases in which relief was granted were those in which medical certificates were produced showing that the men had been reduced by privation and sickness to such a state that they were physically unable to work. The needs of the single men were met in most cases by communal kitchens set up by the South Wales Miners' Federation. School children were fed in the schools, including Saturdays, Sundays and holidays, under arrangements made by the Local Education Authorities, and under the supervision of the teachers, whose services deserve to be recorded. Deductions of varying amount were made from the Poor Law relief in such cases—at Pontypridd no relief at all was paid to families in respect of children fed at school—and the amount so deducted was in some cases paid by the Guardians to the Education Authorities." [1] After work had been resumed, the same practice was continued to men unemployed from any cause ; and it has been maintained down to the present time, in relation to all applications by able-bodied men in health, irrespective of participation in any dispute. Men without dependants, whether young bachelors or elderly widowers, have been for some time refused Outdoor Relief ; only a very few accept the "offer of the House ", and many tramp away in search of work elsewhere, possibly (though of this we have no evidence) resorting night after night to the different Casual Wards.[2] On the other hand, the Guardians have always tempered their rigour with mercy in exceptionally meritorious cases ; occasionally, we have been told, privately suggesting to the Medical Officer that such and such a man deserved, if only in respect of debility, a medical certificate which would enable him to receive Outdoor Relief on account of sickness. But the generous laxness of administration is now kept within bounds by the fear of bankruptcy. The visitor to the Pontypridd Union, as to Merthyr Tydfil and Bedwellty and others in these mining valleys, finds most conspicuous both the fact, and the general recognition of the fact, of an all but universal insolvency. The proportion of the industrial wage-earners unemployed runs up, in one or other valley, to as much as 80 per cent. The failure of thousands of youths (fourteen to twenty) to get employment at all cuts off an important subsidiary household income. Large withdrawals have been made from the Co-operative Societies. Much of the furniture in the cottages has been sold or pawned. Friendly Society and Industrial Insurance contributions have fallen hopelessly into arrears.[3] Cottages in which the family savings have been invested are now often unsaleable, or go for a few pounds, if not taken over by the mortgagees. Credit can no longer be given by the small shopkeeper, even for a week ; whilst the Co-operative Societies, with debts outstanding to the extent of hundreds of

[1] Eighth Annual Report of the Ministry of Health, 1927, James Evans' Report, p. 76.

[2] Vagrancy in Wales increased by over 41 per cent in 1926 as compared with 1925 (Eighth Annual Report of Ministry of Health, 1927, James Evans' Report, p. 75).

[3] So much is this the case that applications to the Relieving Officer for a pauper funeral—before the War almost unknown—now occur in the Pontypridd Union at the rate of one or two per week (Report of Superintendent Relieving Officer to Pontypridd Board of Guardians, MS. Minutes, July 1928).

thousands of pounds, can now allow no member's indebtedness to exceed his holding of shares. The District Council is unable to collect the whole of the high rates—a burden which the passing out of assessment of closed collieries throws increasingly on the smaller ratepayers—and consequently every district is in arrears with its payment to the County Council. The Local Education Authority did not dare, in the early part of 1928, for fear of bankruptcy, except in a few specially distressed schools, to operate under the Provision of Meals Act. " Medicinal Feeding "—which means cod-liver oil or malt extract ordered by the School Medical Officer for exceptionally ailing children—was accordingly, apparently on the suggestion of the Board of Education, being substituted for the provision of dinners to children found merely hungry by the teachers ! The Boards of Guardians have mostly incurred a relatively gigantic indebtedness on revenue account ; some of them have already had their cheques dishonoured by their bankers ; whilst many of them exist from day to day in chronic apprehension of a complete collapse. It is not too much to say that in the two counties of Glamorgan and Monmouthshire a large part of the population is (December 1927) kept from starvation only by the public administration ; and this, in the mining areas, lives only from hand to mouth at a low level of efficiency. In 1928, the Boards of Guardians having failed to relieve even extreme destitution in a manner adequate to prevent impairment of health, the Government was driven, as we have already mentioned, to permit the starting of a " Lord Mayor's Fund " to save the people from starvation ; and (under the direction of a Cabinet Minister) the public were informed by large posters that " a million of your fellow countrymen are in need of food and clothing ", which, under the instructions of another Cabinet Minister, the local Poor Law Authority was refusing to provide !

Woolwich

We take as an example of an intermediate Union, neither among the nine most " strict " nor among the nine most lax in the Metropolis,[1] but representing, we think, an average ad-

---

[1] In June 1927 the Ministry of Health applied three statistical tests to the Metropolitan Unions with regard to the Unemployed able-bodied persons over sixteen whom they had on Outdoor Relief, namely, the percentage of such per-

ministration, namely, that of Woolwich, in South-East London. This Board of Guardians, which had, in 1919–1922, and after 1925, a majority of Labour Members, with a Conservative minority, has shown itself able to combine a generous treatment of the poor and a high standard in institutional management with some degree of efficiency in the administration of Outdoor Relief on a liberal scale.

Down to nearly the end of 1920 there was no Outdoor Relief of able-bodied men, apart from a few isolated cases of exceptional family circumstances. Even during nearly the whole of 1921, the Unemployed only appeared by dozens. By January 1, 1922, there were 1505 such men on Outdoor Relief (with 3684 dependants). The number rose on July 1, 1922, to its maximum, namely 2443 men ; and fell, gradually, in January 1925 to its minimum during the past seven years, namely 784 men. It rose again during 1926 to 1262 on July 1, and then fell steadily to less than a thousand, of whom about 130 are men without dependants.

The effect of the change, in 1919, from a predominatingly Conservative to an equally predominatingly Labour Board of Guardians has admittedly been considerable ; but it has manifested itself most conspicuously in the administration of the various Institutions of the Union, which have been raised to a relatively high level, both of efficiency and of a wise and prudent humanity. At first, no attempt was made to depart from the rule of refusing Outdoor Relief to able-bodied men in health, unless in exceptional circumstances. On November 25, 1920,

---

sons to the estimated population, the percentage of single persons (without dependants) to the total recipients, and the percentage of recipients who had been on relief for four years or more. A summary was published as Cmd. 3006 of 1927. Omitting the City of London, the 24 other Metropolitan Unions stood as follows. Taking all three tests together, the best five Unions (arranged alphabetically) were Chelsea, Fulham, Hampstead, Kensington and Lambeth ; the next best four (similarly arranged) were Holborn, Marylebone, Wandsworth and Westminster. Seven of these nine pay on balance to the Common Poor Fund, whilst two are, on balance, recipients. The worst five Unions (alphabetically arranged) were Bermondsey, Bethnal Green, Greenwich, Poplar and Shoreditch ; and the next worst four (similarly arranged) were Hammersmith, Islington, Southwark and Stepney. All of these nine Unions are, on balance, recipients from the Common Poor Fund. Between these two sections stood the remaining six Unions, namely Camberwell, Hackney, Lewisham, Paddington, St. Pancras and Woolwich, which, on this combination of tests, may be classed as intermediate. All but one of these six Unions are, on balance, recipients from the Common Fund.

when Unemployment began to become widespread, a resolution was adopted, in accordance with the policy favoured by the Ministry of Health at the moment, authorising the Relief Committees to grant Outdoor Relief to the destitute Unemployed. The "Mond Scale" was adopted in 1922, when prices were exceptionally high ; and down to the end of 1927 it had not been varied. Under this Scale a single man living alone could get 15s. per week ; and a man, wife and six children 53s. 6d. per week, with 1s. 6d. (summer) or 2s. (winter) for fuel, with no other extras, except in sickness. But with the reduction in the cost of living, the Guardians have not found it necessary to give relief up to the maximum amounts provided by the Scale ; and it has been usual, especially where an able-bodied applicant has been for some time in receipt of relief, to reduce the sum. Reliance is, indeed, mainly placed on the vigilant scrutiny of each case by one or other of the four Relief Committees, which each consist of about six members, who do not habitually act for their own districts, but take all districts in turn, each for a period of three months. The Relieving Officers make full personal investigations, and present reports upon every case, each of which is gone into by the Committee, and decided, not by any undiscriminating application of a Scale, or a rigid rule, but " according to its merits ". The applicants are treated with courtesy, and, in contrast with the old Poor Law practice, as far as possible [1] spared personal humiliation. The practice is to allow, for expectant mothers, 2s. per week extra relief. Wives and children are often sent to convalescent homes for treatment and rest ; medical attendance is freely granted and sometimes even proffered in cases in which it seems to be required ; whilst dentures, spectacles and surgical appliances are supplied where necessary, and extra relief is given in many cases of sickness, especially for tuberculosis. In view of its demoralising futility, the " Labour Test " was given up years ago ; and " Institution Orders ", otherwise than for sickness or infirmity, are very sparingly given,

---

[1] This is a matter of importance. " The failure and sorrow and sickness and despair of men and women are not suitable objects for such boisterous mutual recrimination as obtains in certain popularly elected bodies " (Memorandum of the Charity Organisation Society on the Government Proposals for Poor Law Reform, December 21, 1926) ; or, it may be added, for such studied discourtesy and reproach as was frequently characteristic of a stricter Poor Law administration.

usually only to men known or proved to be wastrels or slackers. The majority of cases are said to be those of men getting on in years, often with a record of twenty or more years in Woolwich Arsenal, ended by discharge on reduction of staff, with sometimes no more than a trifling gratuity. Young men, and sometimes others, are frequently sent to the Hollesley Bay Farm Colony, as the most convenient way of providing them both occupation and training. A searching investigation by the Ministry of Health's Inspector in November 1927 resulted in a report which, though naturally critical in tone, made no very serious animadversions, compared with those made in similar reports on other Unions. The cost of the Outdoor Relief amounted to £140,000 a year, or about as much as that of all the Institutions which the Guardians maintained at an unusually high level of efficiency ; and of this Outdoor Relief one-third was to the able-bodied Unemployed,[1] these being, in proportion to population, about one-quarter of the number in Poplar and Bethnal Green, and about one-half the number in Greenwich and Shoreditch, although, naturally, many more than in the West End Unions. The Inspector noted gravely that the great bulk of this relief was without Labour Test or Modified Workhouse Test ; and he objected that the proportion of the relief given in cash was, in the aggregate, rather more than one-half of the total amount. He adduced about a dozen cases in which he thought that the Outdoor Relief had been given too freely, or too continuously, or in too large amounts, or with too little regard for the applicant's bad character. He critised the grant of Outdoor Relief to inmates of common lodging-houses, which the Guardians justified in cases in which the housing shortage had made it impossible for families to find other accommodation. He insisted that some sort of test should be instituted, " by which, in suitable cases, the applicant should be required to perform some task of work, or occupy his time in a beneficial manner ", as a condition of receiving Outdoor Relief. He recognised that the Scale (which had not been reduced since the high cost of living

---

[1] We were informed that in Woolwich, contrary to the practice in various other Unions, each case in which Outdoor Relief is granted in contravention of the Out-Relief Order, 1911, has been week after week individually reported by name to the Ministry of Health, in compliance with Article XII. of that Order, without any disallowance by the Ministry. Nor has the District Auditor made any objection to the grant of Outdoor Relief without Labour Test.

of 1922) was neither indiscriminatingly used as a scale of relief, nor even applied up to its maximum as a table of necessary family resources ; but he asked that it should be reduced by 15 per cent in view of the fall in the cost of living. The Inspector's main criticism of the administration machinery seems to have been that one-third of the Guardians were slack in their attendances —not a failing characteristic of " Labour Guardians "—so that Relief Committees sometimes fell below three in membership ; and that there ought to be a Central Relief Committee to ensure common standards in the District Committees.[1]

The Revolt of Poplar

The difficulties with which the Ministry of Health had to contend, in these years of overwhelming destitution among the Unemployed, and of Cabinet indecision as to how to deal with the crisis, are illustrated by the " Story of Poplar ", which has already been related down to 1906.[2] The Guardians, after reducing by something like one-third the swollen lists of Outdoor Relief that the official inquiry of 1906 had revealed, got the numbers down to one-half that total in the years of good trade, 1911–1914,[3] and to less than one-third by the end of the War. Whilst maintaining efficiently, and even generously, the children, the sick and the aged in their various institutions, the Guardians successfully avoided any increase of the total expenditure until the rise in the cost of living in 1917. But the general slump of

---

[1] Ministry of Health to Clerk to Guardians, Woolwich, November 29, 1927 (printed in Woolwich Union archives).

[2] " The large decrease in Poplar is to some extent accounted for by the fact that all applications by able-bodied men are now dealt with by one special committee instead of by the relief committee of their district, the result being a much greater uniformity in the treatment of cases " (Fortieth Annual Report of Local Government Board, 1911, p. 33).

[3] In 1907 the Poplar Poor Law Union was reconstituted by amalgamating the three constituent parishes of Bow, Bromley and Poplar into a single " parish of Poplar Borough ", with an equalised rate in the pound. For the whole episode see Parish of Poplar Borough : Report of Special Inquiry . . . into the Expenditure of the Guardians (Stationery Office, 1922) ; *The Story of Poplar* (Poplar Borough Municipal Alliance, 1922) ; *The Poplar Case Examined*, by the Editors of the *Poor Law Officers' Journal*, 1923 ; *Guilty and Proud of It*, by the Poplar Board of Guardians, 1923 ; *Can London Climb out of the Slough of Despond* ", by J. C. Pringle, 1927 ; " Poor Relief in London : The Case of Poplar ", by Sir W. Chance, in *The Times*, April 20, 1927 ; *My Life*, by George Lansbury, 1928, chap. viii., Poplarism and Prison, pp. 129-169; and " Poplar and Poplarism ", by Rev. H. J. Marshall, in *Quarterly Review*, January 1929.

1920–1921 hit Poplar as severely as it did other places ; and the numbers on Outdoor Relief rose suddenly, from 4293 on October 30, 1920, to 10,834 on February 26, 1921, and to no fewer than 29,329 on April 22, 1922 ; being nearly twice as many per 1000 inhabitants as in any other Union in London, or as in that of the adjoining Union of West Ham. It was not denied that the distress was met with open-handed liberality. " No attempt was made by the Guardians, even in a modified way, to put in force any Labour Test under the Relief Regulation Order, 1911. . . . In all cases relieved the Guardians grant the full amount according to their Scale," which was at the time one of the highest in the Kingdom, especially in respect of large families. The huge local rate that the emergency threatened to involve was the subject of great discontent ; and this took the form of an organised protest against Poplar, one of the " cities of the poor ", being left, unaided by the " cities of the rich ", to maintain all the Unemployed who happened to live within its boundaries. Poplar was, indeed, not wholly unaided by the other parts of the Metropolis, seeing that its Borough Council received annually from the richer London Boroughs a large sum under the Equalisation of Rates Act of 1893 ; and its Board of Guardians received over £50,000 a year from the London County Council and the Metropolitan Common Fund, in respect, almost entirely, of the cost of maintenance of its Poor Law institutions and their inmates. But the grievance was that these contributions were far too small in proportion to Poplar's heavy burdens ; first, in that the rate per inmate of the institutions had remained for over half a century unchanged at fivepence per day, whereas the total cost had now become (including food, salaries and buildings) nearly ten times that amount ; and, secondly, in that there was no contribution at all in respect of those who were maintained on Outdoor Relief. Nothing was done by the Government to remedy this long-standing grievance, which had become acute, and the dispute was brought to a head in May 1921 by the deliberate and sustained refusal of a majority (24 men and 6 women) of the Poplar Borough Councillors (several of whom were also Poor Law Guardians) to levy the rate required to meet the precepts of the London County Council (May 10, 1921) and the Metropolitan Asylums Board (April 9, 1921). The Borough Council declared that it was financially impracticable to get in the money ; and claimed, in effect, to set off against the precepts the large addition to the subvention from the Common Poor Fund which, as it was urged, was equitably due to the Board of Guardians. This led to a long-drawn-out administrative comedy ! The recalcitrant Councillors were, in due course, haled before the Court of King's Bench and the Court of Appeal, where, in default of submission, they were in due course (August 1921) committed indefinitely to prison for contempt of Court. The 24 male Councillors were accordingly taken to Brixton prison, and the 6 female Councillors to Holloway prison, in both of which their presence, though they were never actually disorderly, was found extremely inconvenient to the prison administration. As unconvicted persons, merely under detention, they had to be allowed all sorts of privileges inconsistent with the common gaol discipline ; they could not be entirely prevented from influencing the ordinary prisoners ; their friends could not be stopped from visiting them, from sending them food and cigarettes and sweets and flowers, and from constantly serenading them under the prison walls, even by the publicly maintained Band of the Poplar Guardians Poor Law School. Meanwhile the Home Secretary was sorely perplexed as to how to bring to an end what had become a public scandal. As no form of submission could be obtained except from the group as a whole, permission had to be granted for the whole Council to meet, the women Councillors being brought to the men's prison for the purpose, and— an event without precedent in British municipal history—a formal meeting of the Poplar Borough Council was held in the prison, with the Mayor presiding, and the Town Clerk in attendance to take the Minutes. Ultimately, on the understanding—not without vigorous opposition from the Metropolitan Boroughs which, as " cities of the rich ", were to be made to pay—that a greatly increased contribution would be given to Poplar and the other poor districts of the Metropolis—an exiguous form of submission was agreed to, and gladly accepted by the Court of King's Bench, when the prisoners were released and conducted to Poplar in a triumphant procession.[1]

---

[1] It is, we think, remarkable that this episode and its sequel should have escaped mention in the Annual Reports of the Ministry of Health. The student must refer to the newspaper reports (see *The Times*, July to October 1921) and to Hansard (vols. 145, 146 and 147) ; as well as to *My Life*, by George Lansbury, 1928, which relates the episode in full. Reports of the legal proceedings will be

The precise method of relieving Poplar and the other poor districts had still to be found. A private and somewhat informal conference of Councillors and Guardians from the various Metropolitan Boroughs and Unions was held at the Ministry of Health. The easiest and least dangerous plan was to increase the levy and distribution under the Equalisation of Rates Act, 1893, which had remained for over a quarter of a century unamended. Such a plan would, however, not have given sufficient help to the Unions where Outdoor Relief on account of Unemployment was most swollen, unless the levy were made so large as to produce a distribution unnecessarily generous to the intermediate districts. Moreover, any increase of the Equalisation Fund was stubbornly resisted by the City and Westminster, and by other districts of high rateable value ; partly because it could be foreseen that such an increase would certainly be permanent. No way out could be seen, when Sir John Hunt, then Town Clerk of Westminster, expressed a willingness to accept, as a strictly temporary measure, the charging of Outdoor Relief to the Common Poor Fund. In despair of any other solution of the immediate difficulty, the representatives of the richer Boroughs and Unions agreed to Sir John Hunt's suggestion. The Minister of Health apparently found no better way of meeting the immediate emergency. He introduced the necessary Bill in the House of Commons on October 20, 1921, and it passed its Third Reading on November 3, 1921, becoming law on November 10, 1921. This measure (The Local Authorities (Financial Provisions) Act [2]) raised the con-

---

found in 1 K.B. 72 ; 91 L.J. (K.B.) 163 ; 126 L.T. 189 ; 85 J.P. 273 ; 37 T.L.R. 963 ; 66 Sol. J. (W.R.) 2 ; 19 L.G.R. 675.

[2] 11 and 12 George V. c. 67 was temporary only, expiring on September 30, 1922 ; but it was continued in 1923 by the Local Authorities (Emergency Provisions) Act (12 and 13 George V. c. 6) which, on the one hand, made the charge in respect of the indoor poor include the inmates of Farm Colonies, but, on the other hand (in substitution for the Mond Scale), limited the charge on the Fund in respect of Outdoor Relief to a maximum of ninepence per head per day (Fourth Annual Report of the Ministry of Health, 1923, p. 89 ; Fifth ditto, 1924, p. 100). The arrangement was again continued for a further period of two years in 1926 ; and further continued for three years by the Local Authorities (Emergency Provisions) Act of 1928 (18 and 19 George V. c. 9), which empowered the Metropolitan Asylums Board to disallow as a charge on the Fund any part of the estimated expenditure to which it objected. This we subsequently describe (p. 916). The Common Poor Fund, and, with it, the above provisions, is abolished by the Local Government Act, 1929.

tribution from the Metropolitan Common Poor Fund, in respect of the inmates of Poor Law Institutions, from fivepence to fifteen-pence per head per day, and also added, as a charge upon the Fund, the interest upon sums borrowed temporarily for the purpose of defraying during each year the expenses repayable out of the Fund after the year had expired. Most momentous of all, for the first time the Act made chargeable to the Fund the whole cost of Outdoor Relief, subject to a scale and conditions to be prescribed by the Minister of Health. On January 4, 1922, the Minister (Sir Alfred Mond, now Lord Melchett) issued the necessary regulations, sanctioning a scale of Outdoor Relief (" the Mond Scale " to which we have already referred) ; on which he had been advised by an informal committee of Metro-politan Guardians, with an overriding maximum, which was, at the moment, as much as 54s. per week, with an additional allowance for fuel averaging over two shillings per week through-out the year.[1] These regulations did not prohibit or make unlawful the use by the Guardians, in their relief of destitution, of any higher scale, but merely limited the amount per person relieved that could be charged to the Common Poor Fund. Under this settlement the amount of Poor Law expenditure charged to the Common Poor Fund, to be shared among all the Metropolitan Unions in proportion to their rateable value, was immediately more than doubled ; and Poplar benefited by its revolt to the extent of over £300,000 a year,[2] or the equivalent of a local rate of six or seven shillings in the pound.

This decision, taken in response to a defiant revolt by a single Local Authority, marks, perhaps, the nadir of weakness of the Government of these years. It had been a cardinal principle of

---

[1] These regulations, and with them the " Mond Scale ", ceased to have effect with the expiry of the Act of 1921 on September 30, 1922. " Experience had shown that control of the charge by reference to a Scale and conditions was cumbrous, and involved a vast amount of clerical work which—apart from the purposes of the Act—was of no substantial value " (Fourth Annual Report of the Ministry of Health, 1923, p. 89). The effect of the " Mond Scale " was, in fact, disastrous, as implicitly sanctioning a Scale of Relief which—automatically applied as it often was—frequently involved making the recipient household better off when the man was unemployed than when he was in full work.

[2] " During the four and a half years ended on the 31st March 1926 . . . a sum of £1,499,000 was received by them [the Poplar Guardians] . . . from the Fund in respect of such expenditure " (on Outdoor Relief) (Eighth Annual Report of the Ministry of Health, 1927, p. 135 ; see also *My Life*, by George Lansbury, 1928, p. 161).

the Metropolitan Common Fund, ever since its establishment in 1867, that nothing should be made chargeable to the Fund, in relief of the rates of the constituent Unions, other than those items of expenditure on which there was little or no temptation to extravagance ; and especially not any forms of relief or other outlay which depended on local policy, which might be such as the Central Authority discouraged. At the very moment of the Government's concession to the rebels of Poplar, the Poor Law Division of the Ministry of Health was begging the Boards of Guardians, in all the Unions in which Unemployment was acute, to refrain from granting Outdoor Relief to the able-bodied without a Labour Test or the Modified Workhouse Test ; abandoning Scales automatically applied to nearly every case, often at rates in excess of the regular wages of those labourers who continued in employment.   The Poplar Guardians were known to be habitually disregarding all these restrictions ; and to be doing so, not merely out of careless laxity of administration, but deliberately on principle.   Yet Poplar, in common with other poor districts of the Metropolis, had a real grievance in the serious inequality of the burden imposed on the ratepayers by the ever-increasing segregation, in the different quarters of the Metropolis, of the rich and the poor—a real grievance which neither the Local Government Board nor the Ministry of Health, during a whole generation, had sought with any determination to remedy.   Mr. Lansbury and other Poplar representatives had, for years, been pressing successive Governments to unify, in one way or another, the Poor Law administration of what is, after all, a single city ; and such a unification, in different forms, under any of which the Poplar Guardians would have lost their autonomy, had, in 1909, formed part of the recommendations of both Majority and Minority Reports of the Poor Law Commission.   But no proposal for this unification in any shape or form had been put forward by any of the nine successive Ministers dealing with the Poor Law between 1909 and 1922, nor, as far as is known, had ever seriously engaged their attention.   The result was a revolt ; an ignominious surrender, and what seems to us, so far as London is concerned, a calamitous further opening of the floodgates that the Poor Law Division had been vainly seeking to close.

The first effect of the success of the Poplar revolt was to cause the Guardians, in January 1922, to consent to raise their Scale of Relief, in compliance with a demand from "an organisation claiming to represent the Unemployed of the parish". This resolution was promptly rescinded on a warning from the Ministry of Health that such an increase would be flagrantly illegal; and on the discovery being made that there would not be sufficient funds to provide the increased outgoings week by week. As the pauperism and expenditure anyhow transcended all the resources of the Union, and necessitated an immediate loan from the Government to avoid bankruptcy, the Minister of Health, in March 1922, ordered a special investigation with a view to securing all the economy compatible with efficient administration. This investigation, which was entrusted to Mr. H. I. Cooper, the experienced Clerk to the Guardians of the Bolton Union, led to a Report in March 1922 which alleged that (in addition to granting Outdoor Relief to the able-bodied on a high Scale, almost automatically applied to every case, sometimes even to the extent of making the man and his household better off than when he and all the members of his family were in full work; and without adequate investigation, without any kind of Labour Test or the exaction of any condition as to work, training or attendance) the Guardians persisted in ignoring various sources of income in the households relieved — not merely the statutory exemptions of Friendly Society or Health Insurance Benefits, but also Old Age Pensions, and the entire earnings of adult sons and daughters living at home—and provided, in addition to the weekly payments, boots, suits of clothes, dresses and underclothing to the extent of no less than £8722 during the preceding twelve months. Moreover, though in the first six months of the year proceedings had been taken in fifty-nine cases in which persons had obtained Outdoor Relief, sometimes for long periods, by flagrantly mis-stating their earnings or concealing other sources of income, no proceedings at all were instituted in the second six months, beginning with the month of the release from prison of the Guardians who had been, as Borough Councillors, committed for contempt; although, as the Special Investigator reported, "a substantial number of such cases have been reported to them since that month"; the Guardians contenting themselves with "cautioning" the delinquents. The various institutions of the Union were reported to be maintained on an equally lavish scale. Various disallowances and surcharges had been made by the District Auditor, and officially confirmed, only to be remitted by the Minister on Appeal, with the result that similar illegalities continued to be committed.[1] The answer of the Guardians to this sweeping indictment was their publication of a pamphlet entitled *Guilty and Proud of It*, in which, whilst a few of the accusations were refuted, the extravagant generosity of the administration was justified on humanitarian grounds.[2] In substance, the necessity was pleaded of raising, by hook or by crook, the Standard of Life of practically all the households of a district of exceptional poverty, which fell below what was assumed to be the prescribed National Minimum of Civilised Life. The Report of the Special Investigator, though officially published, was not presented to Parliament ; and no further proceedings were taken by the Government.

It is difficult not to associate with this victory of " Poplarism ", and with the extraordinary form that the Government gave to the assistance then recognised to have long been due to the poorer districts of the Metropolis, much of the calamitous increase of able-bodied Pauperism that has since marked more than half of the Metropolitan Unions, including certain of those in which the " Labour Guardians " have never been in a majority on their Boards.

The Unemployment Flood may be said to have reached the industrial parts of the Metropolitan area in the autumn of 1920, and by the end of the financial year on March 31, 1921, the total number of persons on Outdoor Relief in the twenty-eight Metropolitan Unions had already risen to twice that reached on the same date in 1920, the increase being almost wholly among the able-bodied men and their dependants. In the course of the following

---

[1] Parish of Poplar Borough : Report of the Special Inquiry . . . into the Expenditure of the Guardians, by H. I. Cooper (Stationery Office, 1922).

One of the extravagances animadverted on in Mr. Cooper's Report was the sending, for a fortnight, of 140 of the Out-Relief children (whom the District Medical Officer had individually certified to be in need of a holiday in the fresh air of the country) to the Guardians' Poor Law School at Shenfield, where two of the houses happened to be empty. The cost in railway fares was £18, and the expenditure was duly reported to the Minister of Health, who did not express any disapproval. By the Special Investigator (Mr. Cooper) this was criticised as " a new departure in the Poor Law ". To instance, among the cases of maladministration, this perfectly lawful and, as we think, entirely desirable action was to weaken the force of the Report.

[2] *Guilty and Proud of It*, by the Poplar Board of Guardians, 1923. A less eloquent but more substantial criticism of the Report of the Special Investigator was published by the Editors of the *Poor Law Officers' Journal* (*The Poplar Case Examined*, 1923).

year, 1921–1922, during which (on October 1, 1921) the Outdoor
Relief began to be placed on the Common Poor Fund, the number
of able-bodied men in health to whom Outdoor Relief was being
paid in the London and certain adjoining Unions was " 14,500
. . . at the beginning of the financial year, 23,000 at the end of
July, 60,000 at the beginning of November, 48,000 at the end of
December, and 56,000 at the end of the year " [1], together with
about three times those numbers of dependants.

By March 1927, following the prolonged coal-mining stoppage,
during which the total pauperism in England and Wales reached
its terrific maximum of $2\frac{1}{2}$ millions, the total number of persons
on Outdoor Relief in the London Unions stood at over seven
times the rate per 10,000 of the population in 1920 ; being more
than double the percentage of increase since 1920 in the aggregate
of other populous Unions of the country, and more than seven
times the percentage of increase for the remaining Unions of
England and Wales.[2]   None of the Boards of Guardians of these
other Unions has had anything equivalent to the right, given
in 1921 to the Metropolitan Boards, of casting upon a Common
Fund a large part of the cost of their distribution of Outdoor
Relief among their own constituents.

The increase was, however, by no means the same in all the
London Unions. A few of them (as we have described in Kensington and Hampstead) steadfastly refused to be influenced in the
direction of increasing Outdoor Relief. Certain others, such as
Westminster, Chelsea, Fulham, Lambeth, Marylebone, Paddington, Wandsworth, Lewisham and Hackney, maintained a relatively strict policy with regard to able-bodied men in health,
and refused to make their Outdoor Relief either unconditional
or lavish. Bethnal Green held out until 1922, but then
succumbed to the prevalent wave of " Proletarianism ". Ever
since 1905, Poplar has enjoyed, year after year, the bad pre-
eminence of having the highest percentage of pauperism to
population, not only in London but also in the whole Kingdom.[3]
The increase in magnitude of its annual distribution of Outdoor
Relief has become portentous. What was £12,395 in 1894–1895

---

[1] Third Annual Report of Ministry of Health, 1922, p. 80.

[2] Eighth Annual Report of Ministry of Health, 1927.

[3] Disregarding the exceptionally swollen pauperism during short spasms of
local Unemployment in particular mining Unions ; brief episodes, which, however, in 1926 lasted in a score of such Unions for as long as several months.

and £24,339 in 1904–1905, became in 1920–1921 £101,643, and (after six years of charging this item to the Common Poor Fund) in 1927–1928, no less than £560,276. The Unions now amalgamated into that of Stepney dispensed in Outdoor Relief in 1920–1921 no more than £28,898, but in 1927–1928 £348,580. Bethnal Green, in 1920–1921 a " strict " Union, giving only £4632 in Outdoor Relief, gave in 1927–1928 £250,460. Bermondsey promptly joined Poplar in an immensely swollen Poor Relief, mainly Outdoor Relief on account of Unemployment, and jumped from £41,707 in 1920–1921 to £345,264 in 1927–1928. Shoreditch went from £29,451 in 1920–1921, to £143,391 in 1927–1928 ; Greenwich from £21,348 in 1920–1921 to £232,880 in 1927–1928 ; and Southwark from £38,639 in 1920–1921 to £181,417 in 1927–1928.

Now it might be urged that the rapid rise in the numbers of the able-bodied on Outdoor Relief between 1921–1922 and 1927–1928 does not, in itself, prove maladministration, as this increase in pauperism may have coincided with an increase in Unemployment and the consequent destitution. But the facts point in the opposite direction. The percentage of Unemployment in the Metropolis as a whole, as revealed for the insured trades in the " Live Registers " of the Employment Exchanges, which was unusually high during 1921–1922, had fallen by 1927–1928 to a rate no greater than has prevailed in normal times. And this marked fall in the registered Unemployed is characteristic alike of the districts in which the numbers on Outdoor Relief have increased, and those others where Outdoor Relief to the able-bodied has not been resorted to, or where the numbers to whom it has been granted have actually been lessened. At the Bermondsey Employment Exchange, which deals with a large part of the area of the Bermondsey Union, the total registered Unemployed have fallen from 7669 in 1921 to no more than 3381 in 1927. In the Bermondsey Union, the able-bodied in receipt of Outdoor Relief rose from 234 in 1921, to 1811 in 1922 and to 3728 in 1927. Other comparisons to like effect might be given.

We have not personally investigated the methods of administration in the Metropolitan Unions addicted to unconditional Outdoor Relief. But the detailed reports of the Ministry of Health Inspectors, many of which we have seen in the Unions concerned, together with the often rebutting information given to us by Guardians and Officials, enable us to give some illuminating specimens. The Scales of Relief were, down to 1927, everywhere high. The total relief allowed to a single man without any resources went up to 18s. per week (Bermondsey), and that for a large family to as much as £3 (Stepney). It has been a feature of the administration that in hardly any case has any use been made of the Labour Test, even where quite suitable opportunities for " testing " selected applicants were ready to hand. Thus one Union, having extensive fields attached to its large Workhouse, preferred permanently to employ men at wages of £3 : 15 : 0 per week to work in the grounds, and spent £400 a year in wages for window-cleaning, rather than utilise the opportunity of imposing these tasks on applicants for Outdoor Relief whom it had reason to suspect of extreme " work-shyness ". Another feature has been the continuity of the relief. The number of cases is large in which men in full vigour have remained on Outdoor Relief continuously for three, four and even six years— some of them marrying on this dole, and getting it increased on the birth of successive children—and not being deprived of it, in certain instances, even when they have been convicted for drunkenness and other offences. In the riverside Unions, in particular, the subvention of Casual Labour has been carried to an outrageous extent. It has been common, for instance, simply to deduct from the total weekly relief for complete Unemployment exactly whatever sums the applicant confesses to have earned by one or two days' employment. Thus, if the dock labourer has earned 10s. 6d. net pay for one day's work in the week, he has received 28s. 6d. Outdoor Relief, making 39s. 2d. per week, which is the income indicated by the Scale for his household if he were entirely unemployed, and without any resources. This is not only a plain subsidy to the employer of Casual Labour, by maintaining his workers whilst they are " waiting " for his next job ; but also a direct encouragement to the labourer not to trouble to secure a job, as he receives as much if he does nothing all the week as if he bestirs himself to get the chance of hard manual toil, under conditions of exposure and risk, in unloading ships. Finally, we note that, owing to the staff of Relieving Officers being chronically overworked by the swollen numbers of applicants, the investigation becomes perfunctory. This aggravates the characteristic defect of all Poor Law administration of there being available no knowledge of the past of those who apply for the first time, and likewise none of the manner of life between the spells of pauperism of the " Ins and Outs ". The inevitable result has been an almost indiscriminate granting of unconditional Outdoor Relief, made more than usually enticing by a Scale which has equalled, and often exceeded, the actual earnings of the household whilst in full work.

The Inaction of the Central Authority

But what—the reader will ask who has followed our account of English Poor Law history—had become of the strong hand and stringent Prohibitory Orders which the Ministry of Health inherited from the Poor Law Commissioners, the Poor Law Board and the Local Government Board? During the second half of the year 1920 the slow but steady rise in Outdoor Relief was watched with anxious eyes by the officials of the Poor Law Division, to whom it seemed caused—less than any exceptional distress—by " the policy adopted by certain Boards of Guardians of affording unconditional relief on fixed Scales to unemployed persons, often persons in receipt of Unemployment Benefit, without adequate discrimination. *This policy appears to have been based on a false analogy between Poor Law relief and the various payments, especially Unemployment Benefit, which are made on a pension basis.*" [1] It seems that only about a score of Unions—scarcely a tenth of the number in which Outdoor Relief was being freely given to the able-bodied unemployed men—had required " the performance " of a Labour Test " by applicants for relief " ; and in London a large proportion of this unconditional Outdoor Relief, and sometimes the whole of it, was being given in money. On the other hand, in three-fifths of all the Unions the Orders were still being complied with ; and in these Unions Outdoor Relief was not increasing. For instance, in London, the Unions of Mile End and Bethnal Green, as well as most of those in the West End, continued for some time to be strictly administered ; and even in some cities where Unemployment became exceptionally acute (such as Nottingham), there was still little or no departure from the Out-Relief Order. The action taken by the Ministry of Health in the course of the year 1920, otherwise than by constant

[1] Second Annual Report of the Ministry of Health, 1921, p. 124.

correspondence and the Inspectors' exhortations, appears to have been confined to the issue of a Circular on December 29, 1920, sent to thirty-six Boards of Guardians only, " by whom Outdoor Relief was known to be freely given, impressing upon them (*not, be it noted, its illegality or even its inexpediency, but*) the necessity for making special examination into each case in which it was proposed to give Out-Relief to an able-bodied applicant on account of Unemployment, and for preventing the overlapping of public assistance. It was indicated that in no circumstances would financial help be afforded by the Government towards the cost of Out-Relief." [1]

It was not until 1921, as we have mentioned, that the flood of Unemployment rose to its full volume ; when the Ministry of Health, with official euphemism, admitted that " the breach with the traditions of the past has been widened, and that in a number of Unions relief has been administered without any Test, and on the almost automatic basis of published Scales of Relief ".[2] In fact, this became, from the middle of 1921, the regular and habitual way in which in some two hundred populous Unions, comprising about one-half of the entire population of England and Wales, more than a million persons, were fed. And, at least from September 8, 1921, it can be claimed by the Guardians that this action had the express sanction of the Minister of Health. " In no other way, it may be said, could the numbers requiring relief on account of the widespread lack of employment have been dealt with." [3] The officials of the Ministry, both the Inspectorate and the Secretariat, continued to strive with all their might, " both by correspondence and through [the visits of] the General Inspectors . . . to keep permanently before the Guardians the principles which should govern their action, and to draw attention to the defects in the local machinery which might lead to unnecessary expenditure ".[4] But the situation was such that the Government avowedly did not think fit, " by any rigid attitude of disapproving departures from the regulations, to fetter the discretion of the Guardians in deciding in what form and subject to what conditions relief which they had determined to be necessary could most properly be administered ". In fact, the Guardians

[1] Second Annual Report of the Ministry of Health, 1921, p. 125.
[2] Third Annual Report of the Ministry of Health, 1922, p. 80.
[3] *Ibid.* p. 80.   [4] *Ibid.* p. 84.

were told, by Circular 240 of September 8, 1921 (as they had
been on a previous occasion nine years before),[1] that the way in
which they could make lawful their practice of granting unconditional Outdoor Relief to able-bodied men, without a Labour
Test, and according to published Scales, was merely to make use
of the exceptions contained in the Out-Relief Order of 1911, and,
on this occasion, especially Article XII., which permits anything
to be done in exceptional cases, subject only to its being reported
within twenty-one days to the Ministry of Health.[2] If the
Ministry does not expressly disapprove the action, the District
Auditor will not, by reason only of its being contrary to the
Order, disallow any such payment. We gather that, from 1921
to 1928, the Clerks to the Guardians in the Unions in which
enormous numbers of able-bodied men were being thus granted
unconditional Outdoor Relief, in most cases simply reported automatically, week by week, *the total numbers thus relieved* (sometimes distinguishing between old and new cases) and the aggregate amount granted, without even specifying the names of the
persons or the particulars of the cases, still less the " exceptional
circumstances " required by the Order. It has been on this
slender basis of legality that something like sixty million pounds
have been disbursed during the past eight years in Outdoor Relief to able-bodied men, without any " Labour Test " ; to be thus
formally reported ; not disallowed ; and accordingly duly passed

[1] On the occasion of the stoppage of the coal-mines in 1912, the Local Government Board Circular of March 19, 1912, indicated to the Guardians the " provisions which are specially designed to enable them to vary their ordinary
procedure in periods of exceptional distress, namely Article X. of the Out-Relief
Order of 1911 (Modified Workhouse Test), and Article XI. (Out-Relief if men
are set to work, and if half the relief is in kind) ". What was novel in the
Circular of September 8, 1921, was the express reference to Article XII., which
related to exceptional contravention of all the provisions of the Order.

[2] This part of the Circular was not included in the reference made to it in
Third Annual Report of Ministry of Health, 1922, p. 84. What is put on record
there is *the other part of the Circular*, in which " emphasis was laid upon three
principles of administration : (1) The Amount of relief given in any case,
while sufficient for the purposes of relieving distress, must of necessity be
calculated on a lower scale than the earnings of the independent workman,
who is maintaining himself by his labour. (2) Relief should not be given without
full investigation of the circumstances of each applicant. (3) The greater
proportion of the relief given in the case of able-bodied applicants should be
given in specified articles of kind, and in suitable cases it should be made a
condition that the relief should be repaid by the applicant."

The Circular will be found printed in full in Appendix III. to *The Third
Winter of Unemployment*, by W. T. Layton and others, 1923, pp. 335-337.

by the District Auditors as payments made in conformity with the Order ! [1]

We are not aware of any official explanation of this policy of the Government in 1920–1922. It is known that the subject had the attention, almost week by week, of a Cabinet Committee, usually presided over by the Minister of Health himself. The secrecy of Cabinet decisions is inviolable ; but we may, as historians, draw our own inference from the known facts of the period. We believe that the Ministers were uncomfortably conscious of their failure to fulfil the expectations that had been aroused, and even the promises that had been made, of social reconstruction after the War, on a higher plane of civilised life for the mass of the working people. Their equanimity had, we gather, been shaken by the Russian Revolution, and it had been quite seriously disturbed, both in the course of the demobilisation and afterwards, by untoward incidents among the troops, carefully concealed from the public, which (although unconnected with any revolutionary movement) seemed to indicate a possibility that the battalions might prove unreliable in the repression of industrial disorder. Moreover, the incessant reports of the Secret Service Departments filled the Ministers' minds week by week (at first accompanied by disquieting bulletins of the Civil War dragging on in Ireland, reporting the horrors of guerilla warfare on both sides), with all sorts of tales of subversive agitation in South Wales and on the Clyde, and among both the Irish and the aliens in the Metropolitan area, agitation which it is always so easy to discover, and of which it is almost impossible for a secret agent not to magnify both the extent and the importance. Moreover, as we have mentioned elsewhere, in these years nearly everyone chose to believe that the serious industrial depression was only transient ; and each successive quarter had its optimistic prophets declaring that they descried already the signs of coming improvement. Under these circumstances the current clamour for a reduction in the aggregate of Government expenditure prevented the adoption of any effective measures for dealing with the Unemployed on a national scale. Poor Relief

[1] We were informed by the Clerk of one extensive Union that the Ministry of Health suggested the procedure . . . [of reporting] " the weekly number of cases of renewal and of new cases respectively, with the amount given in money and kind ; which appears to be the only practicable method in existing circumstances ".

had the advantage that it seemed to cost the Chancellor of the Exchequer nothing, and at any rate involved no Parliamentary vote. Meanwhile the rapid succession of short-lived Ministers of Health [1]—all of them, like their colleagues, thinking about other urgent problems—failed to find any policy by which those members of the huge army of the Unemployed for whom the Unemployment Insurance Acts did not provide (or provided only an inadequate Benefit) could be kept from starvation, without throwing to the winds all the previous century of experience of the Poor Law Division. All that could be attained was in the nature of " face-saving ". The Relief Regulation Order of 1911 was maintained in force ; but only at the cost of condoning the complete evasion of its most important provisions in practically all the Unions to which the flood of Unemployment had extended. The almost automatic application of the Scales to determine the amount of relief in each case was allowed to continue as the only way in which the vast numbers could be dealt with.[2] The loophole in the Order afforded by Article XII. was deliberately enlarged, so as to nullify the whole Order, by the Ministry never disallowing, and for a long time not even questioning, the thousands of " exceptional cases " summarily " reported " week by week by a mere statement of their total number, with the aggregate amount dispensed during the week in cash or in kind ! [3]

[1] There were eight Ministers of Health within six years ; in 1921–1923 alone there were five ! (Sir Auckland Geddes, 1918–1919 ; Dr. Christopher Addison, 1919–1921 ; Sir Alfred Mond, now Lord Melchett, 1921–1922 ; Sir A. Griffith Boscawen, 1922–1923 ; Mr. Neville Chamberlain, 1923 ; Sir W. Joynson-Hicks, 1923–1924 ; Mr. John Wheatley, 1924 ; Mr. Neville Chamberlain, 1924–1929).

For comments on the attitude of the Department, see *The Ministry of Health and the Poor Law*, by Sir W. Chance, 1923.

[2] " Where large numbers of persons have come on the relief lists in the last few years, a Scale of Relief has in practice been necessary to enable Boards of Guardians and their officers to get through their work " (Memorandum from the Ministry of Health, June 1926, in Report of the Unemployment Insurance Committee (Lord Blanesburgh's), vol. ii., 1927, p. 239).

[3] By way of contrast, we append an extract from the local Government Board's Circular of December 2, 1871, stating what would be required in the use of the similar exception in the earlier form of the Order. " The Board will not be prepared to sanction any cases which are not reported within the time limited by the Order, and in which the reports do not contain a detailed statement of the paupers to which they refer, showing the number of their respective families, with the ages and numbers of children employed, amount of wages of the several members of the family at work, cause of destitution, period during which they have been without employment. Amount of relief, if any, given

Strengthening the Powers of the Government

With the collapse of the brief so-called " General Strike " in May 1926, and the marshalling, in July 1926, of the Government forces, both legislative and executive,[1] to suppress any continued resistance of the coal-miners to the coal-owners' demands, the feebleness of the Cabinet in face of the army of applicants for Poor Relief, which had characterised the Government of the greater part of the preceding six years, may be said to have ended. The apprehension, if not of revolution, at least of popular risings, had disappeared. The power of the Trade Unions, at any rate their power for aggression, had suddenly vanished. Even the constitutional progress of the political Labour Party seemed to be arrested. Further, it became at last realised that the depression in the great staple industries, especially in so far as they depended on the export trade, was not merely a transient incident of the usual " trade cycle ", but must be expected to endure for years ; if, indeed, it had not to be regarded as a permanent effect of the dislocations and destructions of the War. It seemed high time for something to be done to " stop the drain " on the national resources represented by an annual expenditure from the rates on Poor Relief that, for Great Britain, in one year reached just upon fifty millions (as compared with less than twenty millions in 1914) ; in addition to a similar amount in Unemployment Benefit from the Unemployment Insurance Fund (as compared with some six millions in 1914), and a further outlay, direct from the Exchequer, in Grants-in-Aid of public improvements of doubtful financial advantage in order to set some of the Unemployed at work for wages. The Treasury put an end, not only to its concessions of guarantees under the Trade Facilities Acts, but also to nearly all its Grants-in-Aid of public works aiming only at an increase of employment ; at the same time

---

previously to the transmission of the report, and what extent of accommodation exists in the workhouse at the time." (First Annual Report of Local Government Board, 1872, p. 67.)

[1] Notably by pressing upon Parliament, at the instance of the coal-owners, the Miners Eight Hours Act (16 & 17 George V., c. 17) ; and—measures never before taken in any trade dispute—in arresting, by a special message from the Prime Minister, the subscription in the United States of voluntary funds in support of families of the locked-out miners ; and by undertaking the State purchase and importation of foreign coal.

threatening a complete arrest of the loans to Boards of Guardians to enable them to meet their current outlay. The Ministry of Labour resolutely set itself, by making Unemployment Benefit depend on more stringent conditions, increasingly strictly administered (and without according facilities or financial assistance for migration on any large scale), by mere pressure to " break up the ice-pack " represented by the congestion of workmen in particular districts where the swollen industries of war-time appeared to have permanently shrunk. The Poor Law Division of the Ministry of Health found itself able gradually to resume its restraining influence on those Boards of Guardians, largely in the same " distressed areas ", which had lapsed into indiscriminate and unconditional Outdoor Relief. The floodgates opened in 1920 could not be immediately or completely closed, or everywhere even simultaneously moved, but some action in that direction could at least be attempted, at one or other point, in one Union after another. Accordingly, from the middle of 1926 onwards—by exhortation and criticism, by the influence of the Inspectors and the District Auditors, and by the Minister's administrative decisions—the influence of the Central Authority was, as we shall describe, increasingly used against the careless or unduly liberal grant of Outdoor Relief.

Additional Statutory Powers

The Ministry of Health presently found that the statutory powers wielded by the Central Poor Law Authority, which had sufficed, in 1834, to revolutionise the whole Poor Law administration, and had been, with unimportant changes, made to suffice for subsequent troubles, were inadequate to cope with the difficulties of 1926. When, under the circumstances that we shall presently describe, a duly elected Board of Guardians, refusing to make the reductions of Outdoor Relief on which the Minister of Health felt bound to insist, had to apply for a further loan which the Government declined to make, the Minister submitted to Parliament a measure for which English Local Government history afforded no precedent.[1]

---

[1] Precedents could be found in the powers of summary supersession conferred on the Local Government Board for Ireland by 1 and 2 Victoria, c. 56, sec. 26, and 10 Victoria, c. 31, sec. 18 ; and in the power of the Board of Supervision in Scotland to present a summary petition to the Court of Session, under

The Board of Guardians (Default) Act, 16 and 17 George V., c. 20, which became law on July 15, 1926, empowers the Minister of Health, when it appears to him that any Board of Guardians has ceased (or is acting in such a manner as will make it unable) to discharge all or any of its functions, summarily to supersede such a Board by his own nominees, who thereupon take over all the powers and duties of the superseded Board. The nominated Guardians may accordingly thereafter administer the institutions of the Union and dispense Outdoor Relief at their discretion, within the limits of the Poor Law statutes and the Orders of the Central Authority ; and they may issue mandatory precepts on the Local Rating Authority for the amount that they from time to time require for their purposes. The Act, as we shall subsequently describe, was immediately put in force in the West Ham Union, and shortly afterwards in the Unions of Chester-le-Street (Durham) and Bedwellty (Glamorganshire).

The expedient of summarily superseding a Board of Guardians and placing in office the Minister's nominees, empowered to levy taxation on the local ratepayers, was, however, designed only for use in extreme cases, and was plainly too drastic for continuously restraining merely lax Boards of Guardians from an unduly liberal interpretation of their discretionary powers. Such a supersession of the elected representatives of the ratepayers could be justified to the House of Commons only when some flagrant and continued defiance of the Minister's orders had taken place, or when the financial position of a Union had become desperate. The more common case in which the Ministry of Health found its powers insufficient was where members of Metropolitan Borough Councils insisted on paying their employees wages far above the market rate ; or where the elected Guardians persisted in putting persons too freely on the Out-Relief lists, or in granting Out-Relief at unduly high rates, or making other illegal payments after warnings from the Inspectors, and even of disallowances and surcharges by the District Auditors. The method of enforcing surcharges on persons who had practically no

---

8 and 9 Victoria, c. 83, sec. 87 (see Majority Report of Poor Law Commission, Part IV. ch. V., sec. 41, p. 129 of vol. i. ; and Appendix I. to this work). The Board of Guardians (Default) Act of 1926 is repealed by the Local Government Act of 1929 ; but its provisions remain in force until 1935 in respect of one of the three Unions in which action has been taken under it (West Ham).

property on which a distraint could be levied, and who did not fear proceedings in bankruptcy, was cumbrous and ineffective. Hence a second measure of coercion was passed into law in 1927.

By the Audit (Local Authorities) Act, 1927, which became law on December 22, 1927, the law as to appeals against disallowances was simplified and strengthened. The Act " abolished the alternative appeal to the High Court or to the Minister. In future all cases may, and certain cases must, go to the former. Where the appeal is taken to the Minister, he may refer questions of law to the High Court and can be obliged to do so." [1] What was expected to be of greater efficacy was the provision that " surcharges of large amount carry with them the additional penalty of disqualification from membership ", not of one Local Authority only, but of any Local Authority whatsoever, for a period of five years ; and, as if in order to increase the menace, this part of the Act was made to come into operation as from October 1, 1927, or nearly three months prior to the measure becoming law. The amount of the surcharge carrying so severe a penalty is placed at £500 or upwards. But as, in practice, the accounts are now audited only once a year—a measure of national economy— instead of once every six months ; and as the District Auditor's surcharge is often formally made months later, what is a matter of less than £10 per week may easily lead to a single surcharge exceeding £500. The effect of so drastic an Act upon Local Government remains to be seen.[2]

[1] Ninth Annual Report of Ministry of Health, 1928, p. xvi.

[2] The imposition (in addition to the enforcement of the surcharge) of the new penalty of five years' disqualification for election to, or services on, any Local Authority whatsoever, appears open to grave objection. The line between a breach of the law and the application of a policy disliked by the District Auditors for the time being may be a narrow one. Whether the lowest tender ought always to be accepted, or the lowest possible wage to be paid ; whether a particular applicant should be granted Outdoor Relief and on what Scale, or merely admitted to the Workhouse, are issues in which economic or political prepossessions will always lead to honest differences of opinion. It is already being said that the new Act so curtailed the discretion *as to policy* of the elected Councillors that " local elections in the future will be a farce, as we shall be bound by Conservative law to exercise Conservative principles as to policy, despite the fact that we have been elected to carry out the administrative programme of the Labour Party ". The worst evil of such legislation is that it tends to reprisals. If a Conservative Parliament sanctions the disqualification of Labour Councillors because of a policy of unduly large expenditure on schools or in relief of the Unemployed, a Labour Parliament may be tempted to disqualify Councillors who exercise their discretion as to policy in such a way as to spend too little : for instance, failing to keep schools in proper repair, or to staff them with certificated teachers ; or failing to enforce the " Fair

In the following session a third measure of repression of lax and extravagant Boards of Guardians was passed into law, this time applicable only to the Metropolitan Unions. The temporary Act of 1923, which authorised the charging upon the Common Poor Fund of the expenditure on Outdoor Relief of the Unions within the Administrative County of London, was due to expire in 1928. The Government had no proposals ready for any more satisfactory arrangement for the admittedly necessary equalisation of the burden of London's poor. But strong objection was taken by those Unions where (as in the City of London and Westminster) the rateable value was exceptionally great ; and by others (as in Kensington and Hampstead) where the pauperism was exceptionally low, all of which had to pay heavily to the Common Poor Fund, to any continuance of a system which enabled the Guardians of such Unions as Poplar, Bermondsey and Bethnal Green, whose extravagance had become notorious, to charge to the Common Poor Fund a large share of the cost incurred in flagrant disregard of the instructions of the Ministry of Health. The only remedy that the Government found immediately applicable was to attach, to the renewal for three more years of the system complained of, a provision requiring the submission by all the London Unions of their estimates of expenditure for the coming half year to the Metropolitan Asylums Board, which was empowered to disallow, not as expenditure by the Guardians, but as charges on the Common Poor Fund, such amounts as might be decided. In this form the Local Authorities (Emergency Provisions) Act of 1928 was passed into law. The Metropolitan Asylums Board, it will be remembered, is composed of representatives of all the Metropolitan Boards of Guardians, 55 in number, together with 18 other persons nominated by the Ministry of Health. Through these nominees, and by its weight with the Metropolitan Asylums Board staff, as well as with some of the other members, the Ministry of Health has always exercised a dominating influence on that Board. Moreover, the representation of the several Unions on the Board is such as to enable the Ministry's nominees to turn the scale in favour of the paying, and against the receiving

---

Wages Clause " or to provide the locally necessary hospital accommodation for the sick. It would seem wise to retain the penalty of disqualification only for electioneering offences—offences in which the rival administrative policies of H.M. Government and H.M. Opposition are not in dispute.

Unions. The measure was therefore universally regarded as one by which " Poplarism " could be more effectively brought under control.

The Poor Law Act, 1927, may also be mentioned in this connection. This was a measure of consolidation, its 246 carefully drafted sections re-enacting the lengthy and often confused provisions of more than a hundred Poor Law statutes extending over three centuries. It did not directly affect the powers of the Ministry ; but by its simplification of the statute law it brought into relief, and made more definite, the relation of subordination in which the Guardians and their officers stand to the Central Poor Law Authority.[1]

A Campaign of Inspection of Outdoor Relief

The legislation of 1927–1928 considerably increased the control over the Boards of Guardians. But it was not upon this legislation that the Poor Law Division had relied when the decision was taken, as we infer, in the latter part of 1926, to bring to an early end the easy tolerance of unconditional Outdoor Relief to the able-bodied Unemployed, which had prevailed since 1920–1921. In the political circumstances of the time this tightening-up of the administration had to be done gently. The Poor Law situation in 1926–1927 was, in some respects, even

---

[1] This Act, professedly one of consolidation only (for which the Majority Report of the Poor Law Commission had pressed in 1909) made two not unimportant changes in the law, and rescued one provision from obsolescence. In order to get rid, once for all, of the complications of the Law of Settlement that might still arise from the very different dates at which alterations had, in the past, been prospectively made, it was enacted that no title to settlement should be deemed ever to have been valid other than those now re-enacted (see p. 433). Moreover, largely owing to the pertinacity of Mr. J. Theodore Dodd, the (probably accidental) divergence between the statutes which referred to " sudden *and* urgent necessity " as a ground for relief in kind by the Relieving Officers, irrespective of any directions of the Boards of Guardians, or even of the Ministry of Health, and the Orders, which mentioned " sudden *or* urgent necessity ", the new Act was made to adopt the wider interpretation. The House of Commons itself persuaded the Government to reinsert in the Bill the provisions of the Acts of 1819 and 1831, which authorised the Local Poor Law Authority to hire land, and to employ labourers to cultivate it at reasonable rates of wages. The Poor Law Commissioners, the Poor Law Board, and the Local Government Board had persistently refused to issue any Order enabling a Board of Guardians to put these provisions in operation ; and the Ministry of Health had been advised by counsel that they might be omitted as obsolete.

worse than it had been in 1834 ; but it could no longer be dealt with by such sweeping peremptory measures as those to which the Poor Law Commissioners had recourse in 1835. The democratically elected Boards of Guardians had acquired, in their ninety years of life, considerable powers of passive resistance, which could not, in face of a greatly enlarged and an easily excitable electorate, be overriden without political danger. Though the policy to be enforced might not be one of stopping all Outdoor Relief to the able-bodied, yet even an intention of insisting upon the principle of Less Eligibility, by the general enforcement of onerous tasks of work or by the application of the Modified Workhouse Test, might not, with political prudence, be publicly avowed. The object of bringing back the Unions, so far as concerned the relief of able-bodied men, to a strict policy of Less Eligibility was therefore not to be attained by Act of Parliament, nor by the issue of any new Order. The change had to be brought about quietly, step by step, in one Union after another, by influencing each Board of Guardians in turn, in order to get enforced just the amount of partial restriction that might be found practicable and acceptable at the particular time and place. It has been to this task that the Poor Law Division has devoted most of its energy for the last two years.

We can imagine the officials at Whitehall congratulating themselves on having succeeded, throughout the five years of severe stress, in maintaining formally intact the Relief Regulation Order of 1911. This Order, which has continued nominally to have the force of law in every Union, definitely prohibits the grant of Outdoor Relief to any persons within the Union, otherwise than on account of sickness or accident or of bodily or mental infirmity, or for the purpose of burying a member of the family, or to a widow or a wife separated from her husband. The Order allows, exceptionally, Outdoor Relief to other persons — that is to say, to able-bodied men in health, apart from exceptional circumstances—only on an onerous Labour Test, or upon the Modified Workhouse Test. The use of the particular loophole, under Article XII., relating to exceptional cases, through which the unconditional Outdoor Relief to the Unemployed, in some two hundred Unions, had burst, is explicitly subject to the specific approval of the Minister of Health, who may at any moment, in any Union, with regard to any case or all the cases, refuse his sanction. Upon this refusal the expenditure thus forbidden stands explicitly pointed to as illegal, so that it would necessarily have to be disallowed by the District Auditor, to be surcharged on, and made payable by, the Guardians who had authorised such payments.

The instrument by which the Boards of Guardians could be influenced gradually to bring back their administration to the lines of the Order of 1911—without obliging the Minister of Health to promulgate any new policy, and without exciting public attention—was found in the Inspectorate. A new vehicle by which the Inspector's influence could be brought to bear on the Guardians was devised in the organisation, for the first time in English Poor Law History,[1] of a general inspection and detailed investigation of the tens of thousands of " case-papers " upon which Outdoor Relief was being paid in each of the hundred or so populous Unions in which extensive unconditional Outdoor Relief in respect of Unemployment still prevailed.

For this considerable work of investigation the General Inspectors engaged in Poor Law work were provided with additional assistance by the concentration, upon this special task, of most of the Assistant General Inspectors of the Ministry. No description of their proceedings has been officially given (apart from slight references in the Ninth Annual Report to their detailed investigations into the Guardians' methods of Out-Relief administration).

---

[1] The Poor Law Commissioners of 1905–1909 found, with some surprise, that there had never been any system of official inspection of the very large part of the Guardians' administration that took the form of granting Outdoor Relief. (" With this part of the work the Inspectors are little in touch " : Majority Report of Poor Law Commission, Part IV., ch. 1, sec. 31, p. 127 of vol. i. " The Local Government Board, for what reason we do not understand, has allowed to continue without any inspection what amounts to one-third of the total Poor Law expenditure, and probably to more than one-third of the work of the Guardians " : Minority Report, p. 368.)

It was inferred that the Local Government Board had continued the policy of the Poor Law Commissioners and the Poor Law Board in ignoring Outdoor Relief, which, throughout the whole of the nineteenth century, it was hoped gradually to extinguish. At the request of the Commissioners, the Local Government Board in 1908 carried out a general inspection of a large number of cases of Outdoor Relief, in many Unions, the reports of which were never published (see references to them in Majority Report of Poor Law Commission, Part IV., ch. 1, sections 263-268, pp. 199-201 of vol. i. ; and in Minority Report, pp. 41-43). We believe that such a general inspection was not repeated ; and that no alteration was made in the instructions to the Inspectors on the subject. In a few Unions, we have been informed that zealous Inspectors had, since 1909, examined in detail a number of the cases of Outdoor Relief.

In the Minutes and Reports of various Boards of Guardians during 1927–1928, we get glimpses of these Inspectors and Assistant Inspectors in some Unions beginning by borrowing for detailed examination all the case-papers of "Unemployment Relief" for the preceding quarter or half year. We hear of them everywhere examining the Relieving Officers as to their knowledge of the circumstances of these families. In some instances the man's employment record, and even his police-court record, is hunted up. The circumstances of the various relatives living in the same household, and even the wages of lodgers, are specially inquired into and recorded. The amount of Outdoor Relief granted in each case, together with the total "money coming into the house", is minutely compared with the Scale upon which the Guardians profess to be working ; and the result is contrasted with the current rate of wages of the poorest unskilled labourers of the locality. The time that each family (and especially each single man) has already continued on Outdoor Relief is carefully tabulated. Separate statistics are compiled of the single men without dependants, of the hawkers or pedlars and others earning no definite wage, of those who avowedly live by casual wage-labour, of the residents in Common Lodging Houses, of the men drawing Unemployment Insurance Benefit, and of any other class for whom the Inspector thinks Outdoor Relief inherently inappropriate. The practice of the Relieving Officers in granting relief in kind (almost exclusively food or food tickets) in " sudden or urgent necessity " is scrutinised and the statistics of its amount, and its continued repetition week after week, are tabulated, particularly where it is known or suspected that the Guardians make use of this form of relief, sometimes by suggestions or requests to the Relieving Officers, as a way of evading the prohibitions of the Order.

The investigation naturally goes beyond the case-papers and the cross-examination of the Relieving Officers. The Assistant Inspector himself visits the homes of selected cases, and pursues his own inquiries. He discovers the dates of marriages, and of successive births in the pauper households. He scrutinises the medical certificates, and makes discreet inquiries of the District Medical Officer, who has sometimes let it be known that the Guardians have not infrequently privately suggested to him that he should give particular men certificates of disability that would make them eligible for relief on the ground of sickness. The Inspector has long and serious conversations with the Clerk to the Guardians, in whom he sometimes confides as another officer of the Ministry, personally responsible for keeping his Board within the limits of the Poor Law statutes and the Minister's Orders. He does not fail to impress on the Clerk the gravity of the situation, and the inevitability of coercive measures if no improvement is effected. He attends himself, not only the Board Meetings, but also the Relief Committees of the Guardians, in order to watch how the cases are dealt with. Contrary to the common practice of the Inspectorate of the past, the Inspector has latterly, we are told, not always refrained from taking part in the Guardians' discussion of particular cases, or from expressing a decided opinion that this or that form of relief ought not to be granted ; or that the Modified Workhouse Test ought to be offered, or the man put to Test Work ; or that the son and daughter or parents of the applicant should be called upon to contribute ; or even that the case is one for prosecution either for fraudulently obtaining relief, or for failing to maintain a family.[1] In the course of the investigation we see the Inspector, in Union after Union, pressing privately upon the Guardians his suggestion of the devices by which they might cope with their swollen lists of Out-Relief cases. Although the " offer of the House " could not, with any plausibility, be made simultaneously to thousands of able-bodied Unemployed, yet this ultimatum might be tendered, it was suggested, to selected cases—perhaps a hundred at a time— choosing first those who had been for years continuously on Outdoor Relief, or at least those among them who were single men, and had no dependants. A like use might be made of the Modified Workhouse Test for the heads of families. Similarly,

---

[1] The Poor Law Amendment Act of 1834 (4 and 5 William IV. c. 76) definitely forbade the Commissioners to interfere in any individual case for the purpose of ordering relief (sec. 16) ; a provision re-enacted in the Poor Law Act, 1927 (17 and 18 George V. c. 14, sec. 1). We have been informed that it has been a tradition among the Inspectors that, according to the spirit of this enactment, it was inadvisable for an Inspector, who might be taken to speak for the Central Authority, when attending a meeting of Guardians, to intervene in the discussion of a particular case, for the purpose of expressing his opinion as to what form of relief should, or should not, be granted. We have also been informed that in some Unions, in recent years, Inspectors have not always refrained from then and there expressing their opinions on particular cases, especially when they have thought it right to warn the Guardians that some suggested decision would be actually contrary to law.

though the Labour Yard could not conveniently be opened for hundreds of men, yet a Labour Test of some sort might be imposed on selected men, whom it was desirable to stimulate to seek employment at wages.

We note here an attempt to make the Labour Test more deterrent than it was before the War. The Poor Law Commission of 1905–1909 found the practice to be that, where the Labour Yard would not accommodate all the able-bodied male applicants for Outdoor Relief, the men were required, in rotation, to work in the Yard for two or three days in each week. This reduced the Labour Test to regularly intermittent employment, which could be fitted in with other odd jobs and thus almost cease to be a deterrent. It might even operate as a distinct subvention towards a demoralising system of Casual Labour. With the advent of Labour Guardians it came to be the practice that the intermittent hours of work in the Yard, or on any other form of Test Work, should be valued at Trade Union rates and set off against the amount of Relief given to each man, according to the Scale in use. The consequent reduction in the duration of the Test made its pretence of deterrence farcical. Against such a use of the Labour Test the Local Government Board was already protesting in 1906.[1]

When the Flood of Unemployment set in, the Guardians seldom " opened the Labour Yard ", which had become thoroughly discredited; and the Inspectors do not appear to have urged it upon them. In those Unions in which nevertheless the Yard was opened, the practice just described, of requiring only such number of hours of work as would " earn ", at the current wage-rate per hour, the Outdoor Relief that the Scale allowed, was adopted.[2] To this no definite objection seems at first to have been made by the Ministry. In 1927 and 1928, however, as part of the

---

[1] " I myself ", Sir James Davy told the Poor Law Commission, " have known men who have been six or seven years in a Stone-yard. The Order says that the man shall be kept on work during the time he is being relieved, which would mean that he ought to be kept on work for six days a week. Now, do what we can—and we have written some very forcible letters on the subject recently —we have the utmost difficulty in preventing Boards of Guardians giving a man one, two or three days a week in the Yard " (Poor Law Commission, Q. 2443, Appendix, vol. i.; Majority Report, 1909, Part IV., ch. 9, sec. 458, p. 265).

[2] Thus the Willesden Guardians in the autumn of 1921 " approached the District Council and asked for their co-operation in a scheme whereby the

Ministerial Campaign to get back to a more strict administration, the Inspectors began everywhere to insist on the fundamental distinction between Test Work of any kind and employment at wages. Test Work, it was explained, was merely an alternative to the enforced residence in the " well-regulated Workhouse " ; and, accordingly, a full week's attendance and labour should be exacted from every recipient of Outdoor Relief, however small the amount. As the Boards of Guardians tended to choose, in particular, the men without dependants as those from whom Test Work should be required ; and as these single men were allowed only 9s. to 15s. per week, half in kind, the disproportion between the Relief and forty-four hours' work per week added

---

Council would provide work for those men sent by the Guardians to the extent in each week of the relief granted.

" At their meeting on September 27, the Council agreed to co-operate in such scheme and gave their instructions for the necessary steps to be taken.

" The Guardians thereupon proceeded to arrange details of scheme, and it was agreed :

" (a) That applications for relief be dealt with in accordance with the scale of relief adopted by the Guardians, but that, in computing the number of days a man shall be set to work, the following scale shall form a basis for arriving at a decision :

						£	s.	d.
8 hours' work in each week @ 1s. 3½d. per hour				.	.	0	10	4
12 ,,	,,	,,	,,	.	.	0	15	6
16 ,,	,,	,,	,,	.	.	1	0	8
20 ,,	,,	,,	,,	.	.	1	5	10
24 ,,	,,	,,	,,	.	.	1	11	0
28 ,,	,,	,,	,,	.	.	1	16	2
32 ,,	,,	,,	,,	.	.	2	1	4
36 ,,	,,	,,	,,	.	.	2	6	6

" The method to be adopted by the Committee in arriving at a decision is to ascertain the amount of relief to be granted on the lines of the existing scale of relief and then to fix the number of hours according to the amount nearest above in the foregoing scale of hours and pay."

This scheme, according to a report from the Clerk of the Willesden Board of Guardians (20/5/27) worked unsatisfactorily. He states that " Owing to unsatisfactory reports respecting certain men in receipt of relief and engaged on the Work Scheme arranged between Guardians and District Council, the question of relief to unemployed persons was carefully gone into.

" As the Engineer of the Council reported unfavourably on the work done by men engaged on the Work Scheme, the Orders for work were withdrawn and the Scheme abandoned.

" It was also ascertained that many men appeared to have ' settled down ' upon the relief given and were not making reasonable effort to obtain work.

" In examining cases it was found that numerous unemployed persons from other Parishes and Unions had obtained furnished rooms or other temporary accommodation in Willesden—ostensibly to participate in the scale of relief granted in this Parish—and the Guardians felt compelled to order the rigid adherence to the law of settlement and removal in all cases."

punishment to penury. The hardship became the more obvious when conditions of the Test Work closely resembled ordinary industrial employment. Thus the Guardians of the Bootle (Cumberland) Union rented, at a royalty of so much per ton, a stone quarry from Lord Lonsdale, to produce stone for sale. The Ministry explicitly insisted that, however small the amount of relief, the recipients should have to work a full week of five and a half days (eight hours a day), and receive in cash only half the amount due to them as relief, the other half being paid in kind. This meant that single men would have to quarry stone in winter weather for forty-four hours, and receive only 4s. 6d. in cash and 4s. 6d. in a food voucher. It was alleged that such an arrangement put the Unemployed men whom the Guardians wished to relieve in a considerably worse position than that of the convicts sentenced to penal servitude in the stone quarries at Portland, who worked for no more hours, in lodgings quite as comfortable, and with a provision of food far more nearly adequate for maintenance in health.[1]

The outcome of this prolonged campaign of the Inspectorate has been, in one Union after another, the presentation to the Guardians of a lengthy, detailed and critical report, mainly concentrated on specifying the various defects in their administration that, in the opinion of the Minister of Health, the Inspector's work has laid bare, together with suggestions for reform. The Minister's letter points out the impropriety, and even the illegality, of the course which the Guardians are taking ; and earnestly begs them to reconsider their policy in order that he may not be driven

---

[1] The requirement that able-bodied men should be compelled to give a full week's work for less than a full week's maintenance has led to acts of defiance. Thus the Wigan Board of Guardians by 18 votes to 13 refused to put into operation the Ministry of Health regulations imposing task work on able-bodied men in receipt of relief. " It is possible ", it was stated, " that the Board may be surcharged, but the chairman and the vice-chairman are to seek an interview with the Ministry. This week no fewer than 368 able-bodied men in the Wigan Union received relief in money and kind amounting to £332, which means £15,600 per annum. This is in addition to 50 able-bodied men who are inmates of the Poor Law institution " (*Manchester Guardian*, Nov. 9, 1928).

In Norwich it was the men who rebelled, and 500 men were suspended, though the families of the married men received relief. It was reported that " the Ministry has laid it down that persons engaged on ' test ' work shall all work the same number of hours daily whatever the amount of relief they receive. To this the men object, stating that, degrading as is test work, the new conditions make it more so. They are quite willing to work for the relief they get " (*Daily Herald*, November 1928).

to take steps to enforce a rigorous compliance with the terms of the 1911 Relief Regulation Order.[1] The Ministry, in all cases, insists on the Board of Guardians making a considered reply to the representations thus addressed to it ; and if the reply does not state definitely that satisfactory reforms are being effected, the Ministry sends a much sharper letter, warning the Guardians that coercive measures will be taken.[2]

The Supersession of the Elected Guardians

The Campaign of Inspection of Outdoor Relief was still being planned, and had scarcely begun, when the powers of the Central Authority over defaulting or rebellious Boards of Guardians were greatly strengthened by the successive statutes of 1926–1927,

[1] The Chairman of the Bermondsey Board of Guardians gave the following account of the proceedings of the Ministry to a public meeting. " He had not come there to excuse anything the Guardians had done," he observed. After giving the old scale of relief, he said: "They were jogging along in their tin-pot way, feeling happy in what they were doing and sure that it was the right thing and that the majority of the recipients of relief were grateful. They were going along all right," he added, " until one day—just after April Fools' Day—there came into their midst a representative from Whitehall. He was not going to say a word against the Inspector personally. The Inspector complained that the scale of relief was too high, and that too much money and too little in kind was allotted. It used to be 95 per cent in money and 5 per cent in kind, and it was gradually altered to 75 per cent and 25 per cent, but that did not satisfy the Ministry. Single men, according to the Ministry, should have two weeks' ' Final ' and then look for work anywhere and anyhow. The Chairman said he would like the Minister to go to the docks and witness the men struggling and fighting for work. He also referred to the letters from Whitehall, and how the Board would have been superseded if they had not fallen into line in some way."

The M.P. for the constituency confirmed what the Chairman of the Board had stated. " In Rotherhithe ", Dr. Salter said, " it was an actual fact that the Bermondsey Guardians had been paying more money in Outdoor Relief than any Board in the country, with two or three exceptions. The Ministry had let it be known perfectly clearly that unless the Board was prepared to take the hint instantly, it would be superseded by Commissioners on November 1. Make no mistake about it, the Ministry had got a case against the Guardians," added Dr. Salter. " The Ministry is by no means satisfied with the cuts we have already made " (*South London Press*, November 4, 1927).

[2] These reports of the Inspectors, with the correspondence upon them between the Ministry and the Board of Guardians in each case, have not, so far, been published by the Ministry ; and it has been indicated, in answer to questions in the House of Commons, that the Ministry preferred, without publicity, to give each Board the opportunity of voluntarily setting its house in order. In most of the Unions copies of the documents have been circulated to all the Guardians ; and lengthy summaries have often appeared in the local newspapers. We have in many Unions been favoured with copies.

which had been, we believe, no part of the Campaign. They were, indeed, hastily devised expedients to meet particular emergencies. But the amplitude of the coercive powers that they established and the drastic action promptly taken against three Unions within half a year, between August 1926 and February 1927, have since been effectively used by the Inspectors, especially in the Unions requiring Government loans, or sanctions for further local borrowing, as warnings of what would happen to other Boards of Guardians if they did not change their ways. The supersession of three Boards of Guardians made an unparalleled sensation in the Poor Law world.

The Bankruptcy of West Ham

One of the Unions in which the distress was greatest— actually one of the three most populous of all the Unions in the Kingdom[1]—was that of West Ham, comprising a vast agglomeration of wage-earning people, adjoining the poorest section of London itself. West Ham forms an integral part of the industrial Metropolis, but being outside the Administrative County of London, is excluded alike from the amenities and advantages of London government, and from any financial assistance in the nature of equalisation of the rates.[2] The district, which had long been above the average in poverty, with a rateable value per head only about one-half that of the other Unions comparable with it in the number to be provided for, had during the preceding twenty years enormously increased in population, almost entirely by a continual influx of wage-earning families who found no room to live in the crowded East End. The slump of 1921, with the

[1] By the census of 1921 it had 738,415 inhabitants, and was still rapidly growing. It is exceeded only by the Birmingham Union (with 969,540 inhabitants) and the Union of West Derby (with 944,922 inhabitants).

[2] For the case of West Ham, see Hansard and *The Times*, July 1926 ; the Boards of Guardians (Default) Act, 1926 (16 and 17 George IV. c. 20) ; *West Ham : an Impartial Study of the Facts*, by the Editor of the *Poor Law Officers' Journal*, 1926 ; *The Boards of Guardians (Default) Act in Operation*, by the same, 1927; *The West Ham Board of Guardians : What the New Board found on taking over, and what they have done since*, by Rev. H. J. Marshall, 1926 ; *Report of the (West Ham) Board of Guardians on their Administration*, July to October 1926 (1926) ; Ditto, November 1926 to May 1927 (1927); Ditto, May to November 1927 (1927) ; Ditto, November 1927 to May 1928 (1928) ; Seventh Annual Report of the Ministry of Health, 1926, p. 113 ; Eighth ditto, 1927, pp. 123-124 ; Ninth ditto, 1928, pp. 151-152.

consequent sudden Unemployment, sent up with a bound the applications for Poor Relief, in West Ham as in Sheffield or West Derby (Liverpool). In West Ham, as in so many other Unions, it seemed both impracticable and inadvisable to do anything but grant Outdoor Relief according to a scale which, though higher than many in use, was not the highest in England, and was indeed lower than that in use at Birmingham. But the West Ham Board of Guardians, like most of the elected bodies within the vast area of this Union, had become composed almost entirely of wage-earning folk ; and at the election of 1921 those belonging to the Labour Party became a Majority on the Board. They were faced with an almost hopeless financial situation, which soon exhausted their credit with their bankers, and drove them, like other distressed Unions, to obtain repeated sanctions for borrowing, and successive loans from the Government through the Committee under Sir Harry Goschen to which the Cabinet had entrusted the administration of this temporary help. By March 31, 1925, the West Ham Guardians had in this way piled up a debt for current outlays of £1,975,000, a colossal sum, even for so gigantic a Union, but not more than 78 per cent of its aggregate rateable value or 15s. 8d. in the pound, proportions which were actually smaller than in several other Unions, including that of Sheffield. The Ministry of Health then called a halt, and refused any further loan except on condition that the Guardians consented to certain new restrictions on the Poor Relief they were giving. The Guardians thereupon refused to agree to what seemed to them an arbitrary reduction of the Poor Relief, dictated, not by any argument that the sum allowed to each poor family was in excess of its needs, but merely by consideration of the poverty of the massed aggregation which had been constituted a separate Union, and excluded from participation in the rateable value of London itself. The Minister, however, was obdurate ; and by the end of September the Guardians found themselves absolutely without funds. The Minister of Health then took a step without precedent in English Poor Law history, and one for which he could cite no statutory authority. To prevent the starvation of the tens of thousands of persons dependent on Poor Relief, the Minister announced that the Government would guarantee payment of the tradesmen's accounts for food supplied to the Guardians for distribution in Outdoor Relief, but only conditionally on the amount supplied to each family being arbitrarily cut down, without further scrutiny of its need, to an amount of food, without anything in money, not exceeding three-fourths of the total in money and food that would have been granted under the Guardians' scale. For four weeks this arrangement was continued, but it became clear that some payments in cash would have to be resumed, if only in order to permit of the payment of rent to the landlords. The Minister therefore intimated that he would have no alternative but to take over, himself, the administration of the Union, superseding altogether the elected Guardians, an unlawful dictatorship for which Parliament would accord him an indemnity. The Guardians thereupon accepted his conditions, and received a further loan.

But matters went from bad to worse. By the 1st of May 1926, the number of persons in receipt of relief had risen to 70,506, or nearly one in ten of the whole population of the Union, a proportion that was already exceeded in half a dozen other Unions. The Unemployment caused by the brief " General Strike " sent up this number to no fewer than 165,217, or over one-fifth of the Union population, a proportion, high as it may seem, which was reached in the course of that summer by more than a score of other Unions, and actually exceeded by over a dozen of them. The Guardians thereupon asked the Government for a further loan of £425,000 in respect of the half-year, being some eleven shillings per head of population. The Minister of Health invited them to a conference, in which the whole range of their administration was discussed. The reports of the District Auditor's examination of their accounts were brought before them, showing many cases of improper relief; and the Guardians were invited to submit their own proposals for drastic reductions so as to avoid constant deficit that bade fair to exceed half a million sterling annually. The Guardians may have urged in reply that their Union had less pauperism in proportion to population than some others, and that their expenditure per head, either of the persons relieved or of the whole population, was also well below that of certain other Unions, so that their condition of indebtedness, which was, proportionally to the rateable value, less extreme than in Sheffield and various other Unions, was due much more to the low rateable value of the Union than to any uniquely excessive expenditure. What is reported is that they refused to admit that their administration of relief was faulty in principle, or open to more than criticism of details ; and they could suggest only some administrative changes that might produce a saving of thirty or forty thousand pounds a year. The Government then took a step never before attempted in connection with the English Poor Law. Local Self-Government was set aside. The Minister of Health pushed through Parliament the peremptory statute that we have already described, empowering him summarily to supersede by his own Order any Board of Guardians that had, in his opinion, become unable to carry out its statutory duties. The Minister immediately superseded the West Ham Guardians, and appointed, at a substantial salary, a retired Civil Servant with two serving Civil Servants at allowances to cover all their expenses, to administer the Union, as from July 20, 1926. By this bureaucratic administration, aided by a carefully selected Advisory Committee of ladies and gentlemen having experience of Poor Law administration (whose names are not published), the Outdoor Relief lists were minutely overhauled and drastically cut down ; the amounts of relief in most of the cases were reduced ; repayment was exacted of relief previously made on loan ; the wages of the institutional staffs were lowered, their number reduced and their hours of work increased, and numerous other economies were effected. In co-operation with a continuous slow improvement in local employment, the financial result has been a reduction of the total number in receipt of Out-Relief from 65,399 on March 27, 1926, to 24,663 on March 31, 1928, and of the weekly expenditure on Outdoor Relief from £27,423 at the earlier date to £6614 at the later ; the average amount per head being thus cut down from 8s. 3d. to 5s. 5d. per week. It is impossible to deny with regard to this bankrupt Union, either the need for financial reform, or the relative success with which it has been carried out. But whether the drastic reduction of Poor Relief has been effected without the infliction of hardship, or without an increase in the sickness and death rates, is not beyond dispute. The problem created by throwing the burden of local-ised Unemployment upon so unfortunately constituted a Union, without any aid from the richer parts of the city of which, industrially, it forms part, remains unsolved.

The Recalcitrancy of Chester-le-Street

The West Ham Guardians were not long alone in their super-session. Within six weeks the same blow fell upon the Guardians of the Union of Chester-le-Street (Durham), not so much because of their bankruptcy, or even of the excessive amount of the Out-Relief, as because of their recalcitrancy in defying the Orders of the Ministry.[1] Among the hundred or so distressed Unions, that of Chester-le-Street had at no time the largest proportion of persons in receipt of Poor Relief, nor was its Scale of Relief the most liberal in the Kingdom, nor did its indebtedness in proportion to rateable value rise to the greatest height. But in this Union —to quote the Department's own Report—" an acute crisis developed. The Board of Guardians had, some twelve months before the year under review, largely increased their Scale of Relief, and had been unable to meet out of current rates the current cost of relief, which had further been swollen by the increase of applications consequent upon the increase of the Scale and the policy adopted by the Guardians in dealing with applications. From time to time they had obtained loan sanc-tions for their current expenditure on condition that the rate of

---

[1] For the case of Chester-le-Street, see Hansard, March 29, 1927 ; Eighth Annual Report of the Ministry of Health, 1927, pp. 120-121 ; Ninth ditto, 1928, p. 152 ; Report of the appointed Guardians of the Union of Chester-le-Street, to December 31, 1926 (Cmd. 2818 of 1927); ditto to June 30, 1927 (Cmd. 2937 of 1927) ; ditto to December 31, 1927 (Cmd. 3072 of 1928).

The Unions in the coal-mining districts had long been notorious—even before their Boards of Guardians had become dominated by majorities belonging to any one political party, or even by working miners—for lax and liberal Poor Relief. Already in 1910 this was commented on, with specific reference to Chester-le-Street, by one of the Inspectors. " The last few years ", observed W. P. Elias in 1910, " have been marked by strong action on the part of the District Auditors in the matter of Out-Relief. In the mining districts of Northumberland and Durham, where wages are good and miners usually enjoy ' free house and coal ', and are accustomed to live in large family groups, the general standard of comfort is a high one. Nevertheless, the early years of the century had witnessed the growth amongst Guardians of a practice of granting Outdoor Relief to old folk in deliberate disregard of their family environment, of the amount jointly earned and expended in the households of which they formed part, and of the question whether or not there was any actual evidence of destitution. This practice was carried to extreme lengths in many instances, and the cost of Out-Relief went up by leaps and bounds. Indeed, the accounts of two wealthy Durham Unions for 1907–1908 show one-half of their expenditure on Poor Law and kindred purposes as made up of payments by way of Out-Relief " (Thirty-ninth Annual Report of Local Government Board, 1910, p. 22).

that expenditure should be reviewed, and that the automatic application of their Scale of Relief should cease. The Guardians had failed to observe these conditions. From the commencement of the [coal-mining] dispute the Chester-le-Street Guardians made a regular practice of relieving unmarried miners "—such relief being regarded, as we think, erroneously, as contrary to the Merthyr Tydfil Judgment, even when given to men discharged by employers who had closed their pits and did not, for some considerable time, even formulate or announce the terms on which work might be resumed. The Guardians " were not only applying for sanction to borrow, but loans had actually to be advanced out of Government funds, since the Guardians' bankers refused any further accommodation. Notwithstanding a nominal acceptance, in order to secure the advances they needed, of the legal limitations of their powers, the Guardians instructed their Relieving Officers to grant relief to miners ; and when the instruction was withdrawn under pressure, it was conveyed to the Relieving Officers that, nevertheless, the Guardians expected them to act as if it was still in force, individual Guardians at public meetings declaring that relief had been ordered. The Relieving Officers were subjected to abuse and even to assault ; and, after repeated negotiations, an instruction was issued by the Department on the 19th August to the Relieving Officers directing them to withhold relief in all circumstances from any miner unless he satisfied the requirements laid down in the Merthyr Tydfil Judgment " [which were to be interpreted, the Minister states, as meaning] " being so reduced by privation as to be physically incapable of work. On the 26th August the Guardians suspended their Relieving Officers because of their compliance with this direction. The suspension of the Officers was at once removed by the Department ; and, since it was impossible in the circumstances to grant further loans to the Guardians, and without such loans the Guardians were unable to exercise their functions, an Order was made on August 30 under the Boards of Guardians (Default) Act, 1926, appointing the General Inspector of the District to be the Board of Guardians in lieu of the elected Guardians. Shortly after, the General Inspector was replaced by three new appointed Guardians " [1]

[1] Eighth Annual Report of the Ministry of Health, 1927, pp. 120-121.

at salaries, by whom the administration is still being conducted.

Whatever may have been the distress in this Union, and under whatever sense of injustice the Guardians may have acted, their disregard of statutory limitations and their defiance of Ministerial injunctions admit, of course, of no excuse. The Minister of Health made it clear in debate that the determining reason for the supersession was the persistence of the Guardians in granting relief to single able-bodied miners, contrary to the law laid down in the Merthyr Tydfil Judgment as interpreted by the Department. Mr. Neville Chamberlain expressly disclaimed the view that his action had any relation to the charges of maladministration subsequently made against the Guardians. He said : " I have heard . . . the general assumption that the supersession of the Guardians has taken place upon the charges that are made in the Report of the Appointed Guardians. . . . We are told that the crime which had been committed by the Guardians, and for which they had been superseded, was that they had given a Scale of Relief to the people in their area, and in particular to the dependants of miners, which was higher than the Ministry of Health was prepared to tolerate. If that be the honest belief of Honourable Members opposite they are entirely mistaken." [1] But the reports issued during 1928 by the " Appointed Guardians " describe (it must be said, with a regrettable lack of impartiality, and with an appearance of an almost malicious bias) a number of malpractices, extending back for several years, of the elected representatives whom they had superseded, some of the allegations being hotly disputed.[2] These reports show also how, with the early termination of the coal-mining dispute and the reopening of the pits, the total number of persons in receipt of relief from the Guardians, as well as the amount granted, fell away to a fourth of what it had been at the height of the distress ; and that they had been further reduced by the end of March 1927, when most of the local collieries were in full work, to something like the normal figures.[3] During the year ending March 1928 no further reduction was effected.

---

[1] Hansard, March 29, 1927.

[2] Report of the Appointed Guardians of Chester-le-Street Union for the period ended December 31, 1926 (Cmd. 2818 of 1927).

[3] Ninth Annual Report of the Ministry of Health, 1928, p. 152.

The Ruin of Bedwellty

There was yet another Union on which the blow fell, namely, that of Bedwellty in South Wales, in a district which has been reduced to absolute financial ruin by the closing of most of the local collieries—a closing directly due, on May 1, 1926, to the dispute, but (as regards most of the pits) made permanent, as has since appeared, owing to the rapid falling away of the export trade. Here, as at West Ham, the default was, in the main, a matter of finance. It was the practice of the Bedwellty Guardians, like so many others in this crisis of Unemployment, " so to interpret their relief regulations as to bring the largest number of persons within their scope, and generally to grant relief on so liberal a scale as to lead to a rate of expenditure which was both unnecessary and extravagant ".[1] Moreover, the Ministry of Health considered that " it was established that the Guardians were not prepared fairly to observe the successive conditions imposed upon them "—not by statute or by the Relief Order of 1911, but specifically as additional conditions on which alone they would be permitted to obtain any further loans. Their real offence was, however, that their indebtedness had become excessive. Among all the 87 Unions for which borrowing had to be sanctioned, Bedwellty was exceeded in the actual amount of its loans only by West Ham, whilst the proportion of the borrowing to rateable value was, in this extremely poor district, actually the highest of all.[2] By September 30, 1926, its total indebtedness was £804,000, and by January 7, 1927, approximately a million sterling, or 35s. 4d. in the pound. An Order was accordingly made in February 1927, under the Default Act, superseding the elected Guardians, first by two of the staff of General Inspectors, and subsequently by three local gentlemen at salaries. Their administration, coinciding with the partial resumption of employment in some parts of the Union, has brought down the numbers relieved from 16,750 on February 5, 1927, to 5062 on March 31,

---

[1] Eighth Annual Report of the Ministry of Health, 1927, pp. 124-125 ; see also Ninth ditto, 1928, p. 153 ; Report on the Administration of Bedwellty Union by the Appointed Guardians to September 30, 1927 (Cmd. 2976 of 1927) ; Second ditto to March 31, 1928 (Cmd. 3141 of 1928) ; *The Distress in South Wales : Report by the Special Committee of the Labour Party*, 1928 ; *Poor Law Officers' Journal*, December 28, 1927.

[2] Eighth Annual Report of Ministry of Health, 1927, p. 140.

1928, and, with this restriction, also reduced the total expenditure; still requiring, however, to meet commitments already entered into, further Government loans to the extent of £75,000, of which only £15,000 has been repaid. " So serious was the financial position of the elected Guardians ", reported the Minister of Health on March 31, 1928, " that, notwithstanding considerable economies, the Appointed Guardians have not yet found it possible to reduce the debt, or to pay interest on it ". A few weeks later, however, the Appointed Guardians paid £15,000 for arrears of interest.[1]

It must be added that every description of Bedwellty that we have read emphasises the fact that throughout the years 1927 and 1928 a considerable amount of destitution has continued to exist there, which the Appointed Guardians do not relieve—if by destitution is to be understood what it has been officially held to mean, an " inadequacy of food, clothing or other necessaries of healthy existence ". So extensive and so serious was the amount of destitution that the Poor Law had failed to relieve, that the state of this Union furnished one of the strongest reasons for the institution, in July 1928, of the Lord Mayor's Fund, to which we have already referred.

The Achievement of the Ministry

The Campaign of Inspection of Outdoor Relief took some time to organise and still longer to put generally in operation, so that the two years that have elapsed since its inception do not show all its results. The problem presented to the Ministry was one of great, and possibly of insuperable difficulty. The continuance of Unemployment to the extent of over a million workers on the " Live Registers " of the Employment Exchanges, and the failure of the Government to devise (or at any rate to erect) anything like an adequate Framework of Prevention—as we have described in Chapter VII.—made it plainly impracticable to bring back Poor Law administration immediately and completely to the restrictions of the Relief Regulation Order of 1911. The most that could be hoped for was to prevent the spread of the evil to the rural Unions ; to stop the worst excesses of the rest; and generally to curb the laxity and extravagance that

[1] Ninth Annual Report of Ministry of Health, 1928, p. 153.

characterised, in so many of the Urban Unions, the administration of what had come to be popularly termed " Unemployment Relief ". On these lines a certain amount of reform had (in 1928) already been accomplished.

The drastic action taken with regard to the three Unions of West Ham, Chester-le-Street and Bedwellty was dramatically successful in reducing the numbers in receipt of Unemployment Relief.[1] In West Ham the total of all sorts of persons on Outdoor Relief had been cut down by the Appointed Guardians from 60,399 on July 17, 1926, to 24,663 on March 31, 1928. In Chester-le-Street the numbers fell from 37,643 on August 28, 1926, when the mining stoppage still continued, to 9735 on December 25, 1926, when the pits had resumed work ; and then were further cut down to 3370 on March 26, 1927. In Bedwellty the reduction was from 16,750 on February 5, 1927, to 5052 on March 31, 1928. Thus, whilst the aggregate number of persons on Outdoor Relief in these three Unions, in the weeks in which the elected Guardians were severally superseded, was 114,792, representing approximately 30,000 families, the aggregate on March 31, 1928, was only 33,244, representing approximately 9000 families. In all three Unions the reduction was very largely, in some parts, we think, almost wholly, in the cases of destitution by reason only of Unemployment. It cannot be gainsaid that after taking into account all criticism, so considerable an elimination must represent the stoppage of a great amount of laxity and extravagance, which were having disastrous effects.

On the other hand, it has to be said that the drastic reductions in Outdoor Relief effected in West Ham and Bedwellty still leave these Unions with far more than the average numbers for England and Wales ; and that their relief lists still include a certain number of able-bodied men receiving Outdoor Relief without the performance of Test Work. In these Unions, as in Chester-le-Street, the effect of the change, as measured by the numbers relieved, appears to have come, at least temporarily, to a standstill. In the Chester-le-Street Union the numbers actually went up between March 1927 and March 1928, from 3370 to 3559. It looks as if the practicable limits of " strict administration " had been reached whilst the goal is still not attained. Yet as a measure of deterrence, the scale of relief has been so drastically reduced that it

[1] Ninth Annual Report of Ministry of Health, 1928, pp. 151-153.

almost seems as if the Appointed Guardians had forgotten the instructions of the Circular of March 18, 1910, that " it is the plain duty of Guardians to take precautions to ensure that the relief is adequate, and that the pauper is sufficiently fed, clothed and lodged ".[1] It would hardly be claimed that the Outdoor Relief to-day in Bedwellty and West Ham allows the thirty thousand persons maintained on it to be " sufficiently " fed, clothed and lodged ".[2] With regard to the still more drastic refusals of Outdoor Relief—even discounting the allegations of serious hardship—it is impossible to be convinced—in face of the very large numbers for whom the local Employment Exchange can find no situations anywhere—that the discontinuance of the relief to some twenty thousand families has, in every case, been followed by the man obtaining employment at wages. The fact that the families have not, except in the rarest of cases, sought admission to the Workhouse, nowadays proves little. We have here an example of the disability under which every Poor Law Authority labours, in being unable to follow those to whom it refuses Outdoor Relief, in order to see what is happening to them. The Relieving Officers may be unaware of any cases of starvation, but the statistics as to infantile mortality, and also as to the rising proportion of claims to Sickness Benefit, are stated to be disquieting, although it is difficult to establish convincing comparisons. What can at least be said is that the wholesale striking off of cases from the Relief List, necessary as it may have been, would be more acceptable and more likely to be copied in other Unions if we had any statistics of how the families lived without relief ; of how many got employment, and after what delay ; of how many families were evicted from their homes for non-payment of rent, and what happened to them ; by how many the great host of vagrants on the roads were recruited ;[3] to what extent

---

[1] Thirty-Ninth Annual Report of Local Government Board, 1910, p. xix ; see *ante*, pp. 723-725.

[2] The Circular of 1910 has of course reference only to the cases in which Outdoor Relief can legally be granted, and these, at its date, included able-bodied men only in exceptional circumstances. But the evil, then recognised, of " inadequacy " of relief is the same whatever may be the status of the families so relieved.

[3] The continued increase in admissions to the Casual Wards of the Metropolis is ominous—from 52,297 in 1925-1926, to 75,869 in 1926-1927, and 80,572 in 1927-1928 (Administration of the Poor Law, Stationery Office, 1928, G. F. Roundell's Report).

private charity had taken over with even less discrimination the work of the Poor Law, and with what results ; and what had been the effect on the volume of mendicancy, petty larceny and prostitution. In the absence of such information, it is to be feared that the example set by the Appointed Guardians in the three Unions for which they are acting will not appreciably affect the administration of other Unions.[1]

In the other Unions, where the elected Boards of Guardians have not been superseded, the achievement of the Ministry during 1927–1928 has varied considerably from place to place. " The chief administrative points to which criticism has been directed " by the Inspectors are stated as follows :

" (a) High Scales of Relief, exceeding or approaching current unskilled wages, or even the wages of skilled men. . . . ."

" (b) The automatic application of such scales without regard to individual circumstances. . . . ."

" (c) Inadequate investigation of the circumstances of applicants. This may be either the cause or the effect of the automatic application of a Scale. If a Scale is automatically applied detailed enquiry may seem unnecessary. If, on the other hand, detailed enquiry is not made, automatic application of the Scale is the possible result. . . . ."

" (d) The grant of Outdoor Relief in unsuitable cases, for example, to persons habitually living in Common Lodging Houses; hawkers and the like, whose earnings and, therefore, whose means, cannot readily be verified, and persons living in unsatisfactory or insanitary homes. . . . ."

" (e) The grant of unconditional Outdoor Relief." [2]

As to the success of the Ministry in getting remedied the defects thus discovered, it is difficult, with regard to these Unions, to come to any assured conclusion. The Minister's own statement in the Annual Report is that " so far as they can be estimated, the results are tangible, if not impressive ". Taking the statistics as a whole, when we exclude the great decrease in West

---

[1] We do not see why the Minister of Health should not put an investigator on the job of looking up all the cases of refusal, to see what has since happened to them. The Poor Law Commission, as we have already mentioned, did this in 1908 (Appendix, vol. xxi., Report of the Effect of the Refusal of Out-Relief on the Applicants for such Relief, by Miss G. Harlock). It is understood that action of this kind is now (1929) under consideration in particular Unions.

[2] Ninth Annual Report of Ministry of Health, 1928, pp. 144-145.

Ham and Bedwellty, it is not easy to trace any considerable achievement elsewhere. Of the total net reduction, between March 1927 and March 1928, of persons " ordinarily employed " and their dependants on Outdoor Relief, of 64,557, we estimate that less than one-half took place in the rest of England and Wales ; and not all of this reduction can be attributed to the Inspectors' Campaign. But a later return published in November 1928 shows that the reduction is still proceeding. The total number in receipt of Unemployment Relief during the week ending June 16, 1928, was only 84,159, as compared with 116,342 during the corresponding week in 1927, showing a net reduction of 32,183. The reduction was most marked in the case of young persons (especially single men). But " the largest proportionate decrease was in the cases of persons over 65 years of age ", which was certainly not due to the Inspectors' Campaign ; and may probably be attributed to the exclusion, not from relief, but from the return, of persons more charitably regarded as unemployable through infirmity.[1]

Occasionally, the Inspectors have found Boards of Guardians prepared cordially to act on their suggestions, and to cut down drastically the Outdoor Relief. " For example, in a Metropolitan Union in which various defects of administration were pointed out, there has been, between April 23, 1927, and April 31, 1928, a decrease in the numbers of able-bodied persons in receipt of domiciliary relief from 3870 to 1898." [2] In the nine Metropolitan Unions, including those in which the administration of Outdoor Relief had been most lax and lavish—all of which were made the subject of the same detailed investigation—a substantial reduction was effected in the course of the year. The Inspector was able to report that, comparing the last week of March 1928 with the corresponding week of March 1927, the number of cases relieved as " departures from the Relief Regulation Order of 1911 " had fallen in every one of them to an extent varying from 10 per cent to as much as 50 per cent ; in the aggregate from 19,398 to 12,791 cases, representing respectively about 75,000 and 47,000 persons.[3]

---

[1] Cmd. 3218 of 1928 : *Labour Gazette*, November 1928, p. 394.
[2] Ninth Annual Report of Ministry of Health, 1928, p. 144.
[3] Administration of the Poor Law, Stationery Office, 1928, G. F. Roundell's Report, p. 41.

Notwithstanding this substantial improvement, in which the Unions of Poplar, Bermondsey and Bethnal Green all shared, the amount of unconditional Outdoor Relief in more than half the Metropolitan Unions on account merely of Unemployment continues to be enormous. As the temporary statute enabling them to charge a large proportion of their Outdoor Relief to the Common Poor Fund had to be renewed in the session of 1928, the opportunity was taken in the Local Authorities (Emergency Provisions) Act of 1928, as we have described, to require them to submit their estimates of expenditure to the Metropolitan Asylums Board. On the first occasion of such submission, in July 1928, the Board, largely by way of warning, exercised its power of disallowing (not as expenditure, but as a charge upon the Common Poor Fund) to the extent of £13,960 in eight Unions, three-fourths of the amount being in Poplar, Bermondsey and Bethnal Green.[1] It remains to be seen what effect this will have upon the policy and administration of the Boards of Guardians in these Unions. The attitude of the majorities on these Boards, not by any means confined to the members of any one political party, has been expressed in an article by Dr. Salter, M.P. for Bermondsey. "For some years past", he wrote in November 1927, "the amount of Out-Relief granted by the Bermondsey Board of Guardians has been higher than that paid by any other Poor Law Authority in the country, with two or three exceptions. The Ministry of Health has now descended on Bermondsey and has demanded drastic reductions in the scale as well as alterations in administrative procedure. The settled policy of the Labour Party has been to give ' adequate ' relief not only to the aged, the sick and to widows with children, but also to genuine able-bodied unemployed who are out of work through no fault of their own. The Party considers that such relief ought not to be so meagre that the persons concerned are kept in a state of chronic semi-starvation, as is the case in many Poor Law areas where the Tories are in power. We believe that the policy hitherto followed in Bermondsey is, generally speaking, just, sound and humane, and that it will be supported by the overwhelming mass of thoughtful people.

[1] Together with smaller amounts in Stepney, Greenwich, Shoreditch, Southwark and Woolwich ; see M. A. B. Minutes, July 1928 ; *Poor Law Officers' Journal*, July 27, 1928.

" Doubtless there have been cases where slackers and wasters have taken money from the rates and have squandered it in drinking, betting, or in other foolish ways. There are almost certainly some cases where impostors have swindled the Guardians and have been given relief to which they were not entitled. Certain men are sufficiently cunning to be able to deceive the most experienced officials of the Board. There are, doubtless, also cases where Weary Willies and Tired Tims have been drawing relief when they might have been and ought to have been at work. No one can defend the retention on the relief lists of people of this description, and it may be that the Guardians have erred in the direction of leniency in handling such cases. After all, however, these people represent only a small minority of the total recipients, and while some tightening up of administration may be desirable it is entirely wrong to make the great mass of innocent people suffer on account of the guilt of the few. That again is the considered view of the Labour Party locally." [1]

In most of the populous Unions which have been put under the microscope of the Inspectors' special investigations, the Guardians have resented the criticisms of their administration, and have yielded to the pressure for reform only unwillingly and, we fear it must be said, not always with sincerity. Some improvement has been effected in the constitution of the Relief Committees. The staff of Relieving Officers has been strengthened ; a Superintendent Relieving Officer has been, here and there, added ; and the Clerk has seen to it that their inquiries have become more nearly invariable, and more searching. Some relatively small reductions have been made in Scales of Relief ; though these have sometimes taken the form of omitting the amounts for the largest families, and leaving such cases to be dealt with outside the Scale. The addition of extra allowances, for coal, boots, clothing, etc., has often become less lavish. But in very few Unions has any considerable use been made of Test Work, and in still fewer of the Modified Workhouse Test.

The Inspectors, for the most part, still believe (though nowadays only for the able-bodied) in the panacea of the "Workhouse Test"—the " offer of the House ", which they think would be almost universally refused ; but they do not manage to convince the Guardians that this virtual abrogation of the system of re-

[1] *Bermondsey Labour Magazine*, November 1927, p. 3.

lieving destitution would be a possible or a desirable end of the cases so disposed of. " Where, however, this test has been imposed," observed the Minister, " the results have been somewhat striking. For example, Mr. Maslin's report gives one instance where admission to the institution was offered in the case of 140 men of whom 30 accepted, and most of the 30 had subsequently left and ceased to be in receipt of relief ; while in another instance, admission orders were given to 84 men of whom only 16 accepted, all the remainder but one having gone off relief altogether. Mr. Batterbury gives an instance in which 62 of 140 cases accepted admission to the institution and only 36 remained there, the remainder apparently having found means of livelihood. The following extract from Mr. Nisbet's report gives an example of the successful application of the Modified Workhouse Test. Eighty married men, who had been " on and off " relief for periods of from one to six years, were offered indoor relief as a condition of continued outdoor relief to their families. The families varied in number from one to eight, over half of the men having three or more children dependent. In 54 cases the offer of a workhouse order was not accepted and no further application for relief was made. In 26 cases the offer was accepted. Thirteen of the men admitted took their discharge within a week, and one on the tenth day after admission. None of these 14 have applied again for relief within five months. Of the remaining 12, only one remained in for more than a week after admission, but all were subsequently re-admitted, seven on four occasions or less, the remaining five from eight to twelve times. Enquiry showed that of the 80 men 35 found regular employment, and 44 were supporting themselves by casual work and by the earnings of other members of the family. In four cases only the man appeared to earn nothing. One man remained in the Workhouse." Similar examples may be found elsewhere in the Inspectors' reports.

Notwithstanding these examples of " clearing the lists ", the Minister of Health had to report " that in many cases the Guardians are particularly reluctant to enforce the institutional test ".[1]

It is only fair to say that one reason for the limited success of the Campaign of the Ministry has been the narrow limits of the

[1] Ninth Annual Report of Ministry of Health, 1928, p. 145.

control over the elected Boards of Guardians that it can practically exercise. The Inspectors may advise and exhort, dissuade and blame ; but the Minister's powers of requirement or of prohibition are small. The drastic new power of superseding the elected Board of Guardians, and replacing them by his own nominees (now repealed by the Local Government Act of 1929), did not extend to any Board, however much the Minister's wishes or recommendations were disregarded, which was both able and willing to go on fulfilling its functions. The District Auditor may disallow and surcharge any expenditure that is flagrantly beyond the statutory powers of the Guardians, or even " unreasonable " in amount ; but he cannot deprive the Guardians of their discretion as to what is needed to " provide such relief as is necessary " for persons " who are poor and not able to work ".[1] It is important to realise the distinction between what is a matter of law and what is only a question of policy. Within the wide ambit of the law (including the Orders in force), the Boards of Guardians enjoy complete autonomy in choosing their own policy. Thus the Minister has no power actually to compel the reduction of any Scale of Relief, within the vague limits of what is reasonable, that the Guardians choose to adopt.[2] He cannot forbid the grant of Outdoor Relief to any section of the non-able-bodied poor who are found, as a matter of fact, to be within the wide category of the destitute. Nor is this all. It has been discovered in practice that, in the British climate, men and women too poor to procure sufficient food, warm clothing and some kind of shelter, are not far off being ill; and a doctor who is either humanely sympathetic with the poor person, or negligently compliant with what he gathers to be the desire of the Guardians, can at once take the case out of the class of the able-bodied by giving a certificate that the applicant, suffering from debility, anæmia or rheumatism, is too weak and ill to get employment— which in the present state of the Labour Market he may easily

---

[1] 43 Elizabeth, sec. 1 (1601) ; 4 and 5 William IV. c. 76, secs. 38 and 54 (1834) ; and 17 and 18 George V. c. 14, sec. 34 (1927).

[2] We are not aware of any instance in which the District Auditors, though they have often protested against the height of some of the Scales, have either disallowed any items of expenditure on relief of destitute persons according to the Scale as unlawful merely because excessive in amount ; or (if any disallowance has been made *on that ground alone*) have had it confirmed on appeal and the surcharge actually enforced.

believe to be not far from the truth![1] Moreover, even with the
Merthyr Tydfil Judgment behind him, the Minister cannot prevent the Guardians from granting Outdoor Relief to the able-
bodied man on behalf of his wife and dependent children ; nor
the Relieving Officer from giving the men themselves " in cases
of sudden or urgent necessity, such temporary relief as each
case may require in articles of absolute necessity, but not in
money ".[2]

The Minister's Campaign has been, in fact, most markedly
successful with those Unions in which the financial position has
put him, irrespective of the Poor Law itself, in a position to dictate
his own terms ; though in some other Unions tangible results
have also been achieved. The Unions which have found themselves compelled to borrow from their bankers, or to obtain a
loan from the Exchequer, can do so only with the Minister's
sanction ; and he can make that sanction conditional on the

---

[1] The investigator into the actual practice of Poor Relief administration
comes across cases in which the applicant himself produces a medical certificate
from his own doctor. More common is it to hear that a sympathetic Guardian—
occasionally even a sympathetic Relief Sub-Committee—has been known to
" pass the word " to the District Medical Officer himself that a particularly
deserving applicant might well be given a certificate that will let him be granted
Out-Relief. In Scotland, prior to 1921, when the law forbade any form of Poor
Relief to the able-bodied man and even to his dependants, the Poor Law Commission found such a " humane " use of medical certificates not infrequent.

[2] 4 and 5 William IV. c. 76, sec. 54 (1834); 17 and 18 George V. c. 14,
sec. 35. It is commonly assumed that the not infrequent practice of repeating
this dole of bread for weeks together to the same person is beyond the legal
power of the Relieving Officer. But the " urgent necessity " of having nothing
to eat may easily recur daily, and equally imperatively require the " temporary
relief " authorised and required by the statute. In fact, there have always
been cases in which obstinate men and women, absolutely destitute, and
becoming daily more and more seriously ill, have refused to enter the Workhouse, or to allow removal from their hovel. In such cases the Relieving
Officer has repeatedly been told that he must " watch the case " and renew
his dole of food indefinitely, as frequently as is required, to prevent death from
actual starvation. Thus there cannot be said to be any legal prohibition of
repeating the dole of food, so long as the " urgent necessity " itself recurs. On
the other hand, it is undoubtedly contrary to the spirit, if not also to the letter
of the law, to use this " sudden or urgent necessity " relief as a substitute for
the grant of Outdoor Relief by the Guardians, as we have described in the
" strict " Union of Kensington (p. 862). This is not infrequently done also
in Unions where unconditional Outdoor Relief to the able-bodied would be
peremptorily stopped by the Ministry. Of some Unions in the South-Western
Counties, it was reported in 1928 that " the Relieving Officer, tacitly or by
direction, gives relief to all able-bodied men, week after week, on the plea of
' sudden and urgent necessity ' ; and the cases never come before the Board
at all, except for confirmation after the event " (Administration of the Poor
Law, Stationery Office, 1928, R. H. A. G. Duff's Report, p. 75).

Board of Guardians adopting whatever reforms in policy as well as in law he chooses to impose. It is by this power that the insolvent Unions—notably those of South Wales and some other coal-mining areas—have been compelled to reform their machinery for administering relief, to reduce their Scales, if not the relief actually granted in the most necessitous cases, to abandon their unconditional Outdoor Relief of this or that section of the able-bodied, to apply in particular instances the Labour Test or the Modified Workhouse Test, and even to refuse Outdoor Relief altogether in some cases, and to offer, instead, the admission of whole families to the Workhouse. Even in these Unions the most drastic prohibitions have sometimes been accepted rather than obeyed, and have failed to prevent the continuance on Outdoor Relief of excessive numbers, and even their increase. The alarming amount of the expenditure on Outdoor Relief, and its growth, with the enormous numbers of persons so relieved, may be due, it seems, more to the willingness of the Guardians to put all and sundry on relief than to the liberality of the Scale according to which the Relief is granted, or to any flagrant breach of the law, or even to the neglect to make thorough inquiry into each case. The amount of the total expenditure of any Board depends mainly on its general attitude towards applicants, with which it is not easy to interfere otherwise than by way of advice. So long as the elected Guardians insist on being sentimentally generous to every family that finds itself pinched, the Minister of Health has practically no means of stopping what may well be a calamitous laxity of administration.

With regard to some Unions in which unconditional Outdoor Relief to the able-bodied Unemployed is conspicuously enormous, but in which the high rateable value enables the Guardians to pay their way without an impossibly heavy rate in the pound, the Ministry has so far found itself unable to achieve its purpose. Even the most strenuous Campaign of Inspection has failed to arrest in certain Unions a further increase during 1927–1928 in the numbers on unconditional Outdoor Relief.[1] The great Union of West Derby (Liverpool), which has now actually a larger

---

[1] The Inspector records also " Very regrettable increases in the Blackburn, Prescot . . . and Wigan Unions ", which are among those in which " investigations of a detailed nature " have been made ; and " communications have in consequence been transmitted to the Board " (Administration of the Poor Law, Stationery Office, 1928, C. J. Maslin's Report, p. 104).

number of persons on Outdoor Relief (60,000) than any other
Union in the country—relieved a pauper host more numerous
than the entire population of the County Boroughs of Oxford or
Exeter or Great Yarmouth. It included a vast number of able-
bodied men engaged in casual labour, hawkers and pedlars, and
residents in Common Lodging Houses ; and it was relieved,
without Labour Test, on a liberal Scale which was, to a great
extent, automatically applied, though during the year 1927–1928
it was actually increasing in number.[1] But after one not very
forcible and only moderately successful attempt, the administration of this Board of Guardians has not been interfered with.

The Growth of Vagrancy

One feature of the past seven years, which cannot be wholly
dissociated from Poor Law policy with regard to the able-bodied
Unemployed, has been the recrudescence of Vagrancy. Almost
immediately after the demobilisation a number of discharged
soldiers began to appear in the Casual Wards, although the
transient expansion of trade for the first few months prevented
any increase in the total on the roads.[2] Special attempts were
made in London and elsewhere to rescue the ex-Service men, by
putting them in the way of obtaining employment ; but it was
usually found that they resented inquiries ; and some of them
appeared, in fact, to be " old tramps who are reverting to their
previous mode of life ".[3] Others, perhaps more numerous, were
discharged soldiers who had learned to prefer an open-air life.
With the coming of the Flood of Unemployment in 1920–1921,
the numbers resorting to the Casual Wards (of whom it was
occasionally found that 25 or 30 per cent were ex-Service men)
rose rapidly and continuously, reaching, on June 9, 1922, no

---

[1] In the West Derby Union, in the last week of March 1928, £16,900 was
given in Outdoor Relief for 59,861 persons, as compared with £16,107 for
56,087 persons in the corresponding week of 1927 (*ibid.* p. 103).

[2] On January 1, 1919, the persons in the Casual Wards sank to the absolute
minimum ever recorded, namely 40 in London and 1011 elsewhere, making a
total of 1051 in England and Wales (First Annual Report of Ministry of Health,
1920, p. 53).

[3] First Annual Report of Ministry of Health, 1920, pp. 56-57; Second ditto,
1921, pp. 139-140 ; Circular of November 24, 1919 : Memorandum to Vagrancy
Committees of March 3, 1920.

fewer than 11,045.[1] During the ensuing three years the numbers fell to a nightly average of round about 8000 ; but they started to rise again in 1926, and reached a total in May 1927 of 12,558—more at any rate than since 1912, but yet fewer than at the high-water mark in 1909, when the total was 14,825.[2] But there is reason to believe that the increase of the number on the roads is greater than is indicated by these figures, and the total in February 1929 is believed to have exceeded 15,000.[3] The admissions to the Casual Wards in the Metropolis have increased in the last two years (1926–1928) by more than 50 per cent ; and those in the South-Eastern Counties by 40 per cent ; whilst those in five Midland Counties are the highest " recorded for 28 years at least ".[4]

The increase will seem all the more alarming if we remember that only a fraction of " the men on the roads " are to be found in the Casual Wards, or even make application for admission on any given night. In 1906 the Departmental Committee on Vagrancy, as we have mentioned, came to the conclusion on the evidence of the police, the Common Lodging Houses, and the vagrants themselves, that this fraction was, roughly, something like one-fourth or one-fifth of the whole moving stream. As there is no reason to think that the proportion has changed, the numbers in the

[1] Fourth Annual Report of Ministry of Health, 1923, p. 91. For instance, the admissions to the Yorkshire Casual Wards rose from 48,634 during 1919–1920 to no less than 115,820 during 1920–1921 ; those to the Casual Wards of the Stafford Union during the second quarter of 1920 were 6040, whilst in the second quarter of 1921 they were 14,739.

[2] Ninth Annual Report of Ministry of Health, 1928, p. 168.

[3] The comparative statistics of Vagrancy, based almost invariably on the number of inmates of the Casual Wards on a single night, habitually understate a general increase in the total Vagrancy, and overstate a decrease. When the total numbers " on the road " rise, there are more Wards in which the insufficiency of the accommodation encourages, and often compels, the abandonment of detention for a second night ; and thus the proportion of admissions to inmates rises. Conversely, when all Wards have vacant beds, the number of detentions increases, and with it the proportion of inmates to admissions. Any change in policy with regard to detention for a second night (such as may accompany an increase in the proportion of men deemed to be genuinely seeking work) acts in the same direction. Moreover, a certain amount of the recruiting of the vagrant host is masked in the statistics by (a) the increased efforts being made, in London and elsewhere, by philanthropic agencies to rescue promising vagrants ; and (b) the operation of the County Vagrancy Committees in getting children " adopted " by Boards of Guardians, and infirm or aged men settled in Workhouses.

[4] Administration of the Poor Law, Stationery Office, 1928, Reports of C. F. Roundell, G. R. Snowden and W. J. T. Turton, pp. 47-49, 60-63, 98-99.

Casual Wards in May 1927 must have represented a much greater host ; on this estimate, indeed, something like fifty or sixty thousand on the roads, a number which, to get the full measure of Unemployment, has to be added to the million or so at that date known to the Employment Exchange. Thus, after three-quarters of a century of incessant experiment with regard to Vagrancy, the nation is still faced with a permanent problem scarcely diminished in magnitude ; and apparently, in the past three years, over large districts actually increasing.

There are, we think, certain novel features characterising the host of possibly fifty or sixty thousand or so, who are now, to the despair of Boards of Guardians and County Vagrancy Committees, drifting backwards and forwards along the roads. In the first place, it has become clear that, contrary to the common impression, a considerable proportion—as it seems, a larger proportion than in past years—of those who are, in the present state of the Labour Market, resorting to the Casual Wards, are not habitual " tramps ", contented to prey upon the community, but involuntarily Unemployed workmen, who, for some unascertained reason, are not in attendance at any Employment Exchange, but are actively, though with very varying degrees of energy and keenness, seeking jobs for themselves. Thus, when on the night of the 10th February 1928, the Ministry of Health caused a simultaneous scrutiny to be made of about one-fourth of the total population of the Casual Wards, in different parts of England and Wales, this official examination indicated that approximately 17 per cent of the men were undoubtedly seeking work, and about 31 per cent were probably of that class ; making nearly one-half who might fairly claim to be of the Unemployed—a much higher proportion than past critics of the floating population of the Casual Wards have usually been willing to allow. On the other hand, about one-third of the whole were unhesitatingly classed as habitual tramps, whilst a further two-fifths were put down as probably of like character.[1] If we may hypothetically take this large sample to be representative of the whole 12,000 ; and the 12,000 found in the Wards on one night to be repre-

---

[1] *Ibid.* p. 169. One Inspector records the opinion of the officers in charge of the Wards that " Of the casuals over 30 years of age, at least half may be classed as certainly or probably habitual Vagrants . . . not more than a quarter can be classified without any doubt as genuinely in search of work " (*ibid.*, G. R. Snowden's Report, p. 62).

sentative of the whole host " on the roads " of possibly something like 50,000 or 60,000, it is tragically illuminating to think that something like 25,000 men actually seeking employment may thus be outside the professedly universal organisation of the National Employment Exchange. It may be equally disquieting that a similar number of men, who are almost certainly committing one or other of the criminal offences punishable under the Vagrancy Acts, should be wandering about the country without the intervention of the police. The Casual Ward, whether lenient or deterrent in its administration, does not appear to be doing what is socially desirable for either the good or the bad wanderer.

The second noticeable feature about the Vagrants of the present day is that they are, on the average, younger than the wandering host of former years. This, at any rate, is the impression reported to us by various observers, alike of the Casual Wards of the Metropolis and of those of the provinces. Whether or not this impression of a fall in the average age would be confirmed by comparative statistics, if such existed, the evidence of to-day proves conclusively that a large proportion are men in the prime of life, many mere youths,[1] strong and vigorous, who, for the sake of social health, quite certainly ought to be either in wage-earning employment or in continuous training.

---

[1] The official scrutiny of February 10, 1928, made it appear that " some three per cent of the Casuals are below the age of 21, 15 per cent between 21 and 30, 46 per cent between 40 and 60, and 15 per cent over 60 years of age " (Ninth Annual Report of Ministry of Health, 1928, p. 169).

Mr. G. E. Usher, M.B.E., the Honorary Secretary of the National Association of Masters and Matrons of Poor-Law Institutions, in a paper on Vagrancy, read at the Northern Poor Law Conference in 1928, drew attention to the increasing number of young men on the road. " In this district ", he said, " about 15 per cent of the Casuals are under 25 years of age. They cannot find work in their own towns, and they go on the road in search of it. Wherever they go, the labour market is flooded and chance of employment remote. They become dispirited and soon deteriorate morally and physically. These young men have never worked for their living. When they set out they were decent youths, but their environment is damning. Not only are they acquiring a taste for the nomadic life, but by contact they are learning the habits of degenerates. In the interests of the country as well as in the interests of these young men, they should be taken off the road at any cost, or the Casual problem will become more acute and of much greater magnitude in the future than it is at the present time. Many of these youths have not learned to work : they have never done any serious work at any time. If the shipyards were in full swing to-morrow, they would be of very little use, any more than they are of use to farmers as farm labourers." Few people realise how quickly a newcomer to " the road " becomes demoralised. In six weeks—some witnesses say a fortnight—character is broken down, and the victim is " in it for life ".

We have gained, too, a more exact vision of the trades to which the Vagrants claim to belong. The Casual Wards, it seems, are habitually used, without any sense of shame or wrong-doing, as " wayfarers' hostels," by almost the main body of one large class of men in fairly frequent (although necessarily discontinuous) employment, on their journeys from one job to another : namely, the " Public Works men ", the contractor's navvies.[1] Much the same is true of a considerable proportion of seafaring folk—sailors, firemen or stokers and cooks—whenever they find themselves stranded with scanty means, and are driven to travel from one port to another in search of work. There is some evidence that something approaching to one-half of all the Vagrants belong to one or other of these two industrial groups, whilst the rest profess to have worked at one or other of some seventy different trades.[2] It was to be expected that none of the men found in the Casual Wards were entitled to Unemployment Benefit. But it seems a matter for consideration by the Ministry of Labour that, in such Casual Wards as take the trouble to record the fact, only a tiny percentage of the Vagrants are in possession of the official receipt for an Unemployment Insurance Book, which ought to be lodged at the Employment Exchange, or of the Book itself, which some of them prefer to keep—though all except agricultural workers and private domestic servants are required to be insured whilst in employment. Complaint is made (a) that the Employment Exchanges are of no use to the

---

[1] As to this class, see the Minority Report of Poor Law Commission, 1909, Part II., ch. iv., pp. 579-584. In the three years 1905-1907, in one Casual Ward the admissions of navvies and general labourers accounted for 60 to 70 of the total, the navvies being considerably more numerous than the general labourers (*ibid.* p. 507). The men's own accounts of their occupations are, of course, by no means always to be trusted, but the evidence as to the navvies and the seafaring folk seems trustworthy. The description of " general labourer " is of much less evidential value.

[2] A detailed inquiry made in a large provincial Union as to all the 8876 Vagrants, who, to the number of about 50 a night, resorted to the Casual Ward during the six months from October 1927 to March 1928, revealed that no fewer than 7559, or seven-eighths of all the men, described themselves as labourers (this including the " public works men ", or navvies), and 488, or over 5 per cent, as seagoing folk, including firemen or cooks, who have a similar habit. The remaining seven or eight hundred belonged to one of no less than seventy different occupations, such as painters, bricklayers, fitters and carpenters ; bootmakers and tailors ; grooms, porters and clerks (Ninth Annual Report of Ministry of Health, 1928, p. 169).

These figures may be usefully compared with those given in the Minority Report of the Poor Law Commission, 1909, Part II., ch. iv., p. 507.

homeless man, who can give no address, and whose admission to the Casual Ward without punitive detention depends on his moving on ; (b) that even the delay involved in claiming and receiving Unemployment Benefit, in the rare cases in which it is payable, has been found to cause men to lose jobs after which they might have gone but for the delay ; (c) that the official receipt for the Unemployment Insurance Book, and even the Book itself, are so flimsy that they soon get worn to pieces ; (d) that they are so easily lost or stolen as to be unconvincing as certificates of the bearer's character ; and (e) that employers of casual labour for brief jobs seek to avoid paying their contributions, and prefer men who do not present Insurance Books to be stamped, whilst the men themselves regard their own contributions as money thrown away.

A third comment to be made upon the present recrudescence of Vagrancy is that the numbers are swollen—to what extent cannot even be estimated—by men to whom Outdoor Relief has been refused, or from whom it has been withdrawn. A certain proportion of the men (either unmarried or widowers) who have been in some Unions, for one reason or another, excluded from Outdoor Relief as having no legal dependants, are reported to have tramped off rather than enter the Workhouse. During the prolonged stoppage in the coal-mining industry in 1926, and in some minor industrial disputes, even admission to the Workhouse has been refused to such men, upon the current interpretation of the Merthyr Tydfil Judgment ; and some, at least, of those are known to have gone " on the road ".[1]

With regard to the administration of the Casual Wards during the past decade, it seems unnecessary to notice the usual instances of alternations of policy among Boards of Guardians, from making the Casual Ward as uncomfortable as possible, with stern detention and task work, followed by a more generous laxity in letting those whom the Superintendent favours leave early on the morning after admission without exacting any work at all. A certain number of Unions have been driven by the

---

[1] We have already mentioned that married men have, in some Unions, latterly been refused Outdoor Relief for themselves, and have been granted only enough for their wives and children.

It was stated in the House of Commons (Hansard, November 15, 1928, pp. 115-118) by Lord Henry Bentinck that " the chairman of a Court of Referees went so far as to advise these young men to go on the tramp in search of work ".

persistent increase of Vagrants to enlarge their Casual Wards or to build new ones, with somewhat improved accommodation for sleeping, bathing and working. There have been the usual transient diversions of the flowing tide. Every change in a Casual Ward causes an alternation of congestion and desertion, as reports of its character circulate among the habitual tramps. On the whole, the accommodation and treatment of the Vagrants have tended slightly both to uniformity and to improvement, especially under the influence of the County Vagrancy Committees, which have come to cover the greater part of the country. Under House of Commons pressure, the Ministry has been insistent (but not always with complete or immediate success) on Boards of Guardians treating all the inmates of the Casual Wards with decent humanity, as manifested in adequate warmth, reasonably confortable bedding, clean water for the bath, nightgowns to sleep in, and so on. The County Vagrancy Committees, to which the Ministry now willingly accords such powers as can be given by Orders, have gradually spread over 30 English and all the 12 Welsh counties, comprising (although some Boards of Guardians stand aloof), with the Metropolitan Asylums Board, over five-sixths of all the Unions in England and Wales, with more than nine-tenths of the population. The Statutory County Vagrancy Committees [1] can now "pool" among their constituent Unions, in proportion to their rateable value, practically all the expenses connected with the relief of the Vagrant. They can thus arrange that only the requisite number of Casual Wards shall remain open throughout the county, and that there shall be no pecuniary inducement to any Union to seek merely to divert the tide of Vagrancy away from its own borders. Any Union that finds in its Casual Ward, either children who ought to be " adopted ", or sick, infirm or aged men or women who ought to settle down in an Institution, can deal with these cases in the most appropriate way at the common charge. Only by some such joint arrangement as to cost can any Board of Guardians be expected to undertake lasting expense in respect of persons not belonging to its own Union. Unfortunately, there are no statistics to show to what extent this scheme has withdrawn

---

[1] The National Association of Vagrancy Committees unofficially seeks to co-ordinate their policy. A Vagrancy Reform Society was established in June 1928.

either children or the infirm from the roads. Unfortunately, too, as one Inspector reports, " A considerable body of Guardians, especially those from rural areas, too often feel that the casuals are not their own people ; that they ought not to be asked to deal with them ; and that, if they do deal with them, it cannot be with sympathy, and should be with a severity proper for a class that mostly consists of incorrigible wastrels ".[1]

Along with the spread of County Vagrancy Committees has gone, during the past decade, the establishment of philanthropic hostels (like that in connection with the Casual Wards under the Metropolitan Asylums Board), and small Training Homes run by individuals or religious communities, which offer to young men chosen from among the inmates of the Casual Wards the opportunity of a period of industrial training in handicrafts or on the land, in order to fit them for wage-earning employment. Of the London hostel it is reported that " during the year now under review (1927–1928), 2119 men were admitted to the hostel and 2120 were discharged. Of the men discharged, 912 were placed in employment, 26 left for emigration (through the ' Morning Post ' Home), 66 were placed in touch with relatives, 175 were transferred to charitable agencies, 380 left at their own request or without notice. The remaining 561 were mostly unsuccessful men, not likely to benefit by a longer stay. During the year, 1369 men who had been at some time or other admitted to the hostel returned to Casual Wards in the Metropolis. *459 of these were men who had left the hostel to take up employment.*" [2] It is only fair to remark that the employment found for the men in many cases was only a temporary job. The evidence appears to indicate that, whilst a certain proportion of these picked men have been thus rescued from Vagrancy, the numbers dealt with have been relatively small, and the percentage of failures is not so much a criticism on the men who are said to have " failed ", as on the system which finds them only temporary jobs, and shows its own failure by providing no adequate industrial training for men who often need restorative treatment.

Thus the problem presented by the wandering host of Vagrants remains unsolved. What has been demonstrated is

[1] Administration of the Poor Law, Stationery Office, 1928, R. H. A. G. Duff's Report, p. 79.
[2] Ninth Annual Report of Ministry of Health, 1928, pp. 170-171.

that its solution is beyond the capacity of any Local Authority, as it is of any voluntary philanthropy. We append, as a piece of illuminating material, a report on Vagrancy Reform by an experienced Vagrant, which we owe to the courtesy of Mrs. Mary Higgs, of Oldham, who is an indefatigable advocate for a systematic treatment of the whole subject.[1]

A Casual's Report on Vagrancy Reform

" You would be astounded if you saw in one mass all the homeless men and youths in the country who, day after day, week after week, travel from Casual Ward to Casual Ward. In some of our larger towns, such as Watford or St. Albans, you can see one hundred, one hundred and fifty, and sometimes as many as two hundred at each place applying for admission to the Casual Wards.

"The Casuals throughout the country form quite a large army, and that army is ever growing larger and larger. I think that it would be good for the Casuals and for the community as a whole if this great army were taken from the road and all Casual Wards closed, and I so think for many reasons, amongst others these :

" (1) The food supplied to the Casual not being ample and varied enough to satisfy, causes the great majority of Casuals to beg from the public for additional food ; for a can of tea, or for dry tea and sugar to make some, or for money to buy same.

" You are creating an army of beggars.

" (2) When begging, the Casual learns to tell the best story or fairy tale, true or otherwise, mostly otherwise, in order to get what he wants. In plain English

" You are creating an army of liars.

---

[1] This able and illuminating report was made in 1926, and represents, we believe, with substantial accuracy, the state of the administration at that date. A number of reforms in matters of detail have since been made, in many of the Casual Wards referred to ; but other Wards seem to have deteriorated under the increased pressure on their accommodation. The general character of the administration does not appear to have materially changed. The writer of the report, whose experience " on the road " was extensive and prolonged, was rescued from Vagrancy by a philanthropic agency, and has proved a steady and trustworthy worker.

For similar testimony as to the Casual Wards in 1928, see the pamphlets, *On the Road : a Description of some Casual Wards in the South-Western Counties* (St. Francis' Home, Batcombe, 1928) ; and its sequel, *On the Road from Reading to York*, with a preface by Mrs. Mary Higgs (Oldham, 1928).

" (3) Hundreds of Casuals are being sent to prison every year for begging, for small petty thefts, for refusing certain classes of work whilst in the Casual Ward, and for various other offences, such, for instance, as making a false statement at the Police Station when applying for a ticket to admit to the Casual Ward. Casuals are often sent to prison for asking for a can of hot water, or for a match, or for trying to sell a post-card. If you were to ask the Governor of some of our Prisons—say Winchester, for instance—how many Casuals passed through his hands during a twelvemonth, you would be surprised at the very large number. Again, when once a Casual has been in prison, he no longer dreads being sent to prison, but returns in many cases again and again. Under the present system

" You are creating a crowd of jail-birds.

" (4) Throughout the country there is a growing objection amongst employers of all classes of Labour to employ Casuals from off the Road, and you must remember that in hundreds of cases, through his clothes, boots and underclothing being worn out, the Casual is not in a position to ask for, or accept, work.

" (5) The homeless Casual on the Road is looked upon by the majority of the public as an outcast, one to be snubbed and slighted, one to be looked upon and treated with contempt.

" (6) The Casual on the Road soon begins to lose his self-respect, and that self-respect becomes less and less the longer he is compelled to remain on the road. He begins to lose all desire to aim after what is highest and best in man. Under the most favourable circumstances it is not an easy matter to be good and to think and do the thing that is right. Above all others the man on the road finds it hard to do what is right, but easy, very easy, to do the things that are wrong. Very seldom is there a hand stretched out to help ; very seldom does he hear a word of encouragement. There are many noble exceptions, I know, but the great majority, alas, are, day by day, drifting away from the Light, drifting away from all that is highest, sweetest, purest and best in life, and drifting further and further away from Heaven and Home, away from the God who loves them and from the Blessed Saviour who died that they might live, and who waits to pardon, to save and to bless them.

" For these and other reasons I would close all Casual Wards, and no longer allow homeless men to travel aimlessly on the road from place to place. It would be better for the Casual, it would be better for the community. (You must not forget that the Casual is human, the same as yourself, and you must remember that the great majority of men on the road joined up and fought like Heroes in the Great War.)

" I would divide the Casuals on the road into three classes— The Old ; The Able-bodied ; The Young.

" The old form but a small percentage of the men on the road. Some of them have done no work for a great number of years, and have no desire for work. Others have worked nearly all their lifetime, work now when they get the opportunity, and would be willing to work. Seeing that there are so many able-bodied and young men to be dealt with, I consider it would be waste of time and energy in trying to obtain work, or to provide work for all the old men. A large number of the old men on the road are between the age of 65 and 70, but are not entitled to a pension until they reach the age of 70, because they have no Insurance Cards with the necessary number of stamps. To remedy that, I would grant the Old Age Pension, stamps or no stamps, to all old men on the road 65 years of age and upwards. The remainder under that age who were unable to maintain themselves should be compelled by law to enter a Poor Law Institution and remain there until they were entitled to a Pension.

" The able-bodied and the young men form the great majority of those who to-day travel the road, and I believe the majority of them would gladly and willingly work if they had the opportunity, providing they had a decent place to live and sleep in. In a lot of public work the one great drawback is the lack of sleeping accommodation. You can hardly expect men to work in all weathers at road construction, road widening, sewer and cable laying, etc., and at the end of the day have to sleep under a tree, hedge, or some such place. For the able-bodied men and the young men I would start a Labour Colony or Colonies in each county into which the able-bodied and young should be invited to enter, and remain and work until such time as suitable work could be provided for them outside. The Labour Colonies at the start would not be self-supporting ; until they became so, seeing that you have done away with the Casual on the road, I suggest that all Unions in each county should by law be compelled to contribute toward the maintenance of the Labour Colony or Colonies in that county a sum per annum equal if necessary to the amount it has cost them for the maintenance of their Casual Wards during the preceding twelve months.

" If such a plan was adopted I do not see that the ratepayers would have any just cause to complain, because they would not be asked to pay a penny more than they are paying now, and gradually, as the Colony became more and more self-supporting, they would be called upon to contribute less and less, and eventually, when the Colony became self-supporting—and I believe in the course of time it would be—they would cease to contribute anything at all. I believe that the amount you would receive for work done, and the contribution you would receive from the Unions, would be sufficient to keep the Colony, or Colonies, going.

" For the starting of each Colony I suggest that you should look to the Government for a Government Grant. I suggest that an order should be asked for calling on all Labour Exchanges, when short of men, to send a list of men wanted to the nearest Labour Colony. I suggest that in each Colony workshops should be erected where you could make most of what is required for the Colony ; such, for instance, as bread, boots, clothing and other things, and in these workshops I would place as many of the youths as I possibly could to learn their trade and become bakers, tailors, shoemakers, etc. I would train as many as possible to understand garden and farm work, and in a very short time you would have quite a large number whom, if work could not be found for here, our Colonies would be glad to welcome and receive.

" In charge of each Colony I would endeavour to place a good, all-round Christian man. What I mean by a good, all-round man I can perhaps best illustrate by relating this story. The Cardinals of the Church of Rome once met to elect a Pope. In the course of their deliberations a certain Cardinal stood up and said : ' If you want a very pious Pope, elect Cardinal So-and-So ; if you want a very learned Pope, elect Cardinal So-and-So ; but if you want a good, all-round Pope, elect me ', which they did, and history records that he made a very popular and successful Pope. That is what you want in charge of a Colony—a good, all-round man, one easy to get at, one with a heart that beats true, one who is not only just, but also kind as well as firm, one who knows how to appeal to what is good and best in men.

" With regard to food and pay, I would treat all in the Labour Colonies until work was found for them in the outside world, in the same way as they are treated here in this Home (St. Francis' Home for Tramps). I think that the System at work here is a most excellent one. I suggest that the good people who have started Homes such as the one here should be requested to still continue their good work.

" I believe that the great majority of men on the road would readily enter a Labour Colony, but there would remain a small minority who have no desire for work, and who would refuse to enter a Labour Colony. To deal with those I suggest that a special Colony, or Colonies, should be started and maintained by the Government into which this small minority should be compelled to enter and work.

" Until some such scheme is put into operation, something ought to be done to improve the treatment meted out to the Casual when he enters many of our Casual Wards.

" (1) Every Casual ought to be supplied with a straw mattress and pillow to lie on at night. This is done in some but not in others. For instance, places like Pewsey in Wilts, Dorchester or Wareham in Dorset, Axbridge or Wells in Somerset, Reading in Berks, supply you with a mattress and, in some cases, a pillow as well. But in places like Henley and Banbury in Oxfordshire; Newbury, Bracknell, Wallingford, Wantage, Hungerford in Berks; Lymington, Lyndhurst, Ringwood, Whitchurch, Winchester in Hants; Lymington in Wiltshire; Poole in Dorset; Taunton in Somerset, you have to lie on the hard board. There are a few Unions such as Chard, Langport, Honiton, Yeovil, where you are supplied with a hammock, but so many of them are torn and broken, and the remainder of them hang so awkwardly, that you cannot lie in comfort in them. In my travels to and fro I have noticed that where there are hammocks the great majority of the Casuals, in order to get a little more sleep, make no attempt to hang them; they prefer to sleep on the floor. The floor in each of the last four Unions I have named is either a stone or concrete one.

" The Unions I have mentioned are not a great distance away from this Home. But if you visited Unions in other parts of the country you would find that the conditions are very similar. For instance, at Staines, a mattress and pillow. At Epsom, hammocks, nearly all torn and broken ; tiled floor ; at Bedford, the hard board ; at Chard, although it is a stone floor, you are only allowed two rugs at night. Two rugs are not sufficient ; the Casual should be allowed three rugs at the least. Just contrast the difference between two Casual Wards—at Christ Church you sleep on a wire bed and are allowed four good, clean rugs ; at Chard, a stone floor, you are only allowed two.

" If ever you visit Langport and enter the Casual Ward the first thing you will notice is the peculiar framework erected to hang the hammocks on ; you will notice how difficult it is to move about ; to get from one end to the other you need to be almost an acrobat, and if you hang one of the hammocks, you will see how useless they are for sleeping purposes.

" I should like to see those Guardians who object to a mattress being supplied to the Casuals enter the Casual Ward and sleep for a week on the hard board or the cold stone. I venture to assert that before the week was half out they would find their bones so sore, and they would have slept so little, that they would be prepared to hold, not one only, but both hands up in favour of the mattress.

" (2) Every Casual on entering a Casual Ward should be provided with a bath and a clean shirt for the night. A number of Unions provide you with a bath and a shirt ; there are others again that make no such provision ; for instance, at Winchester not one in a hundred ever has a bath, and no Casual is supplied with a shirt. At Poole you can have a bath, if you so desire, but very few so desire, because you are not provided with a shirt afterwards. At Taunton, on the night you are admitted, no one is asked to have a bath ; no one is provided with a shirt. In many of the Casual Wards where you are supplied with a shirt it is very often in a torn and dirty condition. At Reading, at Newbury, at Shepton Mallet, the shirts are washed every day and every Casual is supplied after he has had a bath with a clean shirt.

" What these Unions do all others should likewise. It is not right that you should be handed a shirt to wear that is not clean, and not clean because it has been worn by perhaps a dozen or more men without being washed, and it may be that one or even more of these men are suffering from an infectious skin disease.

" (3) Every Casual during the week should have an opportunity of washing his shirt and socks, and by so doing help to keep himself clean. Some Unions give you that opportunity ; others do not. Because of being detained in many Casual Wards for only one night, Sunday is the only day very often that you have the time or opportunity to wash your underclothing. Some Unions, such as Oxford, Devizes, and Dorchester, give you every chance, and are glad to see you trying to keep yourselves clean. There are other Unions who give you no such chance, such, for instance, as Pewsey or Bath, where you are locked up away from the bathroom all day, or such as Chard, where the bathroom is kept locked all day.

" I like the way the Casual is treated at Leicester. Every Sunday all Casuals are invited to wash their underclothes. Those who accept the invitation are lent a shirt, given a piece of soap and a bucket of hot water. When you have finished washing your things they are placed in a drying room, and in the evening you receive them back perfectly dry. It is a great pity that other Unions do not treat the Casual in this respect the same as Leicester does. Under the present system it is absolutely impossible for any Casual to keep himself clean and free from vermin for any length of time.

" With regard to cleanliness the best system that I know of is the one that is in practice in the Casual Wards in London that are under the control of the M.A.B. When a Casual enters one of these wards, whilst he is having a bath his clothes are examined ; if any vermin or sign of vermin are seen they are immediately taken away to be disinfected ; in the afternoon of the next day every Casual whose underclothes are the least dirty is asked to wash them and is provided with soap and hot water. If his clothes are torn he is given a piece of cloth and needle and thread in order to mend them. If his boots require it, he is given leather and the tools to mend them ; if he wants a shave, he is lent a razor to have a shave with. He is lent brushes and given blacking to clean his boots with. Every Casual who enters one of these wards dirty, ragged and verminous, leaves it clean, free from all vermin, and in a presentable condition to look for work. What the M.A.B. does for the Casual, others could. Where there is a will, there is always a way.

" (4) Every Casual who is detained in a Casual Ward for two nights should be allowed to take his tea and sugar, if he has any, in with him. A number of Unions grant you that privilege ; there are others again that do not. Bread and cheese day after day is a very dry meal ; a mug of tea goes a long way towards helping the bread and cheese down. For instance, Newbury, Devizes, Bristol, Bath, Wells, and some other Unions allow you to take tea and sugar in with you. They also provide you with boiling water at dinner-time to make your tea with. On the other hand, there are Unions such as Exeter, Lymington, Axbridge, Yeovil, Shepton Mallet, where they take your little bit of tea and sugar from you on entering, and do not hand it back to you until you are leaving. I would point out that the majority of Casuals work more willingly and do a very great deal more in these Unions where they are permitted to make a mug of tea, than they do in the Unions where their tea and sugar are taken from them. Contrast two Unions again. At Shepton Mallet your tea and sugar is taken from you. At Wells, only five miles away, you take it in, hot water is provided for you at dinner-time and at 2 o'clock (at ten you are given a mug of tea ready made).

" (5) The custom in force in most Unions of discharging men at 11 o'clock should be abolished. It is not right or fair that men should have to walk long distances after that hour. If you have to travel eighteen, twenty or more miles, it is impossible for you during the winter months to reach your destination until long after dark. On the main roads there is such a huge and continuous stream of traffic passing in each direction that it is hardly safe to travel in the daylight ; you can imagine how unsafe it is after darkness has set in. Again, it does not give men the time to seek for work. If there is any work about, the best time to apply for it is in the morning, and not mid-day, or after. The majority of men on the roads want work. The crowds that flock to the pea and the potato fields, the strawberry and hop gardens, the fruit orchards, in the hope of earning a few shillings, convince me that most Casuals would gladly work provided they had the chance."

We leave this illuminating report of actual experience by a competent and trustworthy observer to speak for itself. No more " revealing " document on a social problem, whatever value we may attach to its suggestions for reform, has come to our notice. But there is one factor in the present position of the problem of Vagrancy that it does not mention, and that is the marked diminution, during the past fifteen years, of the provision of Common Lodging Houses, or of other cheap accommodation for the poor traveller of either sex. One of the effects of the War was the discontinuance of a large proportion of the places providing a bed for fourpence or sixpence a night. The subsequent rise in prices made their re-establishment impossible. The increased overcrowding due to the shortage of houses has greatly diminished the chance of finding a vacant room in any habitation. The discontinued Common Lodging Houses, and the other cheap sleeping accommodation, were far from ideal as regards sanitation, decency or comfort. But they met a real need. There is, at present, a serious lack of accommodation for the night for those who cannot afford to pay hotel prices. Yet a large proportion of the wage-earning population must be at least periodically mobile, whether in pursuing work of essentially shifting character (as with the contractor's navvies) ; or in such seasonal employments as the harvesting of various crops (for instance, hop-picking, fruit-picking, potato-digging, or sugar-beet) ; or on work connected with the herring fishery ; or merely in the occasional migrations involved in deaths and other family changes. The people of England become steadily more mobile, not less ; and the community cannot look for Vagrancy Reform along the lines of preventing migration or travelling. It is a drawback, not an advantage, from a public as well as from an individual standpoint, for people to be anchored to one spot, so as to be unable to move to another offering greater economic advantages or superior convenience of family life. Thus the community ought not, in its objection to Vagrancy, or in pursuit of some other advantage, to hamper travelling or migration, *especially among the poorest of the population,* who may be exactly those who ought, in the public interest, to move to new quarters. The Government, national as well as local, is called upon to adapt its arrangements to the needs of a migratory population, instead of seeking to cramp that population to suit official convenience. The organisation of Health and Unemployment Insurance, of the National Employment Exchange, of the Local Health and Education Authorities, and of Poor Relief and Police, ought not to be rendered unnecessarily inconvenient to the traveller and the migrant, who have equal rights to public service with the stay-at-home population. Moreover, if private enterprise cannot or will not provide suitable and inexpensive accommodation for the night, on a profit-making basis, this will certainly have to be furnished as a public service, in England and Wales, as has been done elsewhere. It is already recognised, after a century of experience, that the Casual Ward, unsatisfactory as it is, cannot simply be abolished. It may have to be transformed into a public service of Wayfarers' Hostels,[1] supplying food and bath and comfortable lodging under sanitary and decent conditions, free from any stigma, without expectation of profit, or even necessarily of complete recoupment of cost, on payment of a small minimum charge, for which those without any money may substitute an hour's useful work, not of a punitive character, both after supper on the day of arrival, and after an early breakfast on the day of departure.

The Impotence of the Poor Law Authority in dealing with Able-bodied Destitution

It would be unfair, alike to the Boards of Guardians and to the Poor Law Division of the Ministry of Health, to allow it to be assumed that their shortcomings, in dealing satisfactorily with the Recurrence of Able-bodied Destitution during the past decade, have been, in any appreciable degree, their own fault. In our view, what the record reveals is the impotence of the Board of Guardians, or indeed of any Authority that is confined to the

---

[1] Such a provision of Wayfarers' Hostels would apparently require no fresh legislation. Any Municipal Corporation or Urban District Council has power to provide common lodging houses under the Housing of the Working Classes Act of 1900, section 1, and to equip them with all the requisite furniture, fittings, and conveniences. If the premises are considered too expensive, they may, after seven years, with the permission of the Ministry, be sold.

A certain number of such common lodging houses are maintained by the large towns. The London County Council, for example, maintains three such homes, all for men inmates, which provide a total of 1877 beds. One of these houses is of the type which charge 8d. per night, and the remaining two charge 11d. to 1s. 1d. per night. There are no L.C.C. common lodging houses for women, this need now being met, not quite adequately, by private philanthropy.

Relief of Destitution—that is to say, any Poor Law Authority—to provide for great masses of Unemployed workmen in any way that is, we do not say satisfactory, but other than seriously disadvantageous to the community, and even a peril to the State. If there is any ground for censure of the way in which the Flood of Unemployment has been met, such censure must rest upon those who left the hundreds of local and *ad hoc* elected bodies with strictly limited powers to relieve destitution, and to do nothing else, to meet as best they could this great national emergency : upon the Government which ignored the warnings and the counsels of its chosen advisers, and failed either to prevent or to provide for an eventual Flood of Unemployment that was foreseen.

Let us consider first the difficulties of the existing Boards of Guardians in dealing with the Unemployed. Experience has shown how impossible it is for a body of popularly elected persons to undertake, with any propriety, the distribution of Outdoor Relief to their own constituents. We do not allow the Police Magistrate, or the Judge of any Criminal Court, to be dependent on the popular vote, although the persons accused of crime are not his near neighbours, and constitute only an insignificant fraction of the whole electorate. When, as in recent years, ten or twenty per cent of all the wage-earners in a given locality are involuntarily Unemployed, and almost all the others are apprehensive of Unemployment, it is quite impracticable for members elected by popular vote, and dependent for re-election on that vote, to determine with accurate and unbiassed judgment to which of their constituents they will grant the legal dole that saves the household from dire privation, and from which of them this saving succour shall, on any ground of law or policy, be sternly withheld. The impossibility of an impartial administration of the law—and, what is even more difficult, the maintenance of a scientifically sound policy within the law—is doubtless more evident when the elected member belongs to much the same social stratum as the elector who is himself unemployed, or who fears that at any moment he may become unemployed ; when the representative lives in the same street as his electors, and is personally acquainted with them and their families. It is not that a lax administration of Outdoor Relief is popular among the wage-earners earning good money in regular employment.

On the contrary, such men and their wives are quick to resent the fact that an idle wastrel whom they know has deceived the Relieving Officer and bamboozled the Guardians into giving him a dole that permits him to shirk honest labour. Guardians in close touch with the electors probably receive more private information of such frauds than those who are aloof from the neighbourhood. Nevertheless the electoral pressure in favour of open-handed generosity is real, and not confined to any one political party. As the experience of the Poor Law Guardians of such Unions as West Derby (Liverpool), Manchester and Newcastle-on-Tyne has shown us, even where the elected members are, for the most part, not themselves wage-earners, but shopkeepers, salaried officials and men and women of independent means, the inability to withstand the pressure of the local electorate, when distress is rife, has been almost equally manifest in a lax distribution of Outdoor Relief, as on those few Boards in which the " Labour Guardians " have predominated. It is, indeed, not only the recipients of Outdoor Relief, or the potential recipients, whose pecuniary self-interest is apt to influence the decision. The shopkeepers who supply the poor with food, the licensed victuallers and beerhouse-keepers from whom they purchase alcoholic beverages, the proprietors of the " picture palaces " with whom the workmen's families spend their pennies, even the owners of the cottages to whom they pay rent, have a very tangible interest in all the wage-earners and their wives and children having, not only bread, but also the customary amount of free spending money. Thus the popular pressure in favour of Outdoor Relief to those in real need comes, not from the wage-earners alone, but, in working-class districts, from very nearly the whole electorate. As against this drawback of an elected Authority for Poor Relief are pleaded the personal touch of the relievers with the relieved, the intimate knowledge of local circumstances, the neighbourly sympathy which human-ises the political machine and softens the rigidity of abstract and uniform central regulation. Such considerations carry weight with good-natured people who imagine facts instead of ascertaining them, and imagine them all on one side. They forget that the personal touch calls into play not only the more generous emotions but the class prejudice, the contemptuous dislike of the poor as such, the selfish resolution to keep down the rates at all costs of suffering to others, which, as our instances have shown, are quite as characteristic of Guardian control as the spirit of kindly patronage or even genuine fellowship which offers a straw mattress and a pillow instead of a hard floor to sleep on. The personal touch was Oliver Twist's grievance, not his consolation.

No less crippling as a disability of the Board of Guardians (or any other Local Authority) for dealing with the Unemployed is its very localism. The area of the Union, *or other Local Government district*, cannot coincide, nowadays, with any important industrial region. Industries are carried on, and the applicants for relief have to find their livelihood, entirely irrespective of Local Government boundaries. When massive Unemployment occurs—say on Tyneside, or at Trafford Park or in Bermondsey—wage-earning situations have to be discovered in other areas. This task was recognised to be beyond the capacity even of an Authority acting for the whole of London when the Employment Exchange was established on a national basis. The migration, for which the Central (Unemployed) Body for London tried to arrange in 1906–1909, can be instigated, directed and assisted only on a similar basis. The Boards of Guardians have been, in fact, expressly forbidden to assist applicants for relief to migrate to other parts of England and Wales in which employment might be found ; and they are not even authorised to incur any expenditure from the Poor Rate in making the inquiries that might be useful in this way to the wageless workmen whose destitution they are required to relieve. Moreover, even if the Poor Law Authority were empowered to provide establishments in which suitable men in receipt of Poor Relief could be trained for employment, or even put under training in order to save them from the demoralisation of idleness, such establishments must, to be successful, be specialised in a number of ways, and each of them would require to be recruited, not from a single Union but from a wider area, in order that each kind of establishment might be filled with the selected persons for whom the particular training was appropriate. Such a scheme of training could therefore not be provided by each Union for its own citizens, but must necessarily be organised, irrespective of local boundaries, on a much wider basis ; practically, indeed, on a national scale. Thus, as the Poplar Guardians found when, in 1904, they appealed to the Local Government Board for some better scheme of providing for the Unemployed, rather than put them on Outdoor Relief, all alternatives for dealing wisely with the Unemployed are barred, not only to the Destitution Authority as such, but also to any Local Authority whatsoever. The establishment of the National Employment Exchange in 1909, and the development since 1923 of Training Establishments under the Ministry of Labour, together with the appointment in 1928 of the Industrial Transference Board, and the use for migration of the Minister's Exchanges, manifest the slow and reluctant realisation by the Government of the impotence, in this field of Unemployment, of any branch of Local Government.

A further practical difficulty is presented by the extraordinary inequality in the local incidence of the cost of providing, whether by Outdoor Relief or in Training Establishments, for the tens of thousands of workmen rendered destitute by Unemployment. Industrial depression, as we have seen, lays waste whole districts, but leaves, even at its worst, others entirely unaffected. Half of England has, at the present time, practically no unemployed men to maintain out of the Poor Rate, whilst several scores of populous Unions in other parts of the country are so severely affected as to be driven into an insolvency which not only reduces the ratepayers to despair, but also, by the extraordinary height of the rates, seriously militates against the very recovery of the localised industries that alone can afford a complete solution of the problem. The National Government rightly deems it dangerous to supply subventions from the Exchequer for the Boards of Guardians to expend in the mere relief of destitution, and yet has been driven, if only to stave off a collapse of local government, to make huge loans, almost from month to month, to Local Authorities so hopelessly bankrupt that no banker, or other private capitalist, would extend to them any further credit at any rate of interest whatever. Finally, it must be emphasised that the very inequality between Union and Union, in the incidence of the cost of maintaining those Unemployed for whom the State Insurance Scheme fails to provide, in itself involves the most startling inequality of treatment of similar cases, as between one Union and another. It is bad enough that Boards of Guardians should differ from place to place—whether out of differences in humanity or varieties of policy, or merely shades of caprice—in the succour that it is their duty to afford to those who, from one end of the country to the other, have a common citizenship and equal rights. To secure a national uniformity in Poor Relief, especially as regards the able-bodied, was the most fundamental of all the objects of the Poor Law Inquiry Commission of 1832–1834. But when, as in South Wales and in North-East England, Boards of Guardians find themselves, notwithstanding rates exceeding twenty shillings in the pound, accumulating an indebtedness that runs into hundreds of thousands of pounds, and even into millions, they are driven to such a reduction of the Poor Relief that alone stands between the local population and starvation as to involve a general and prolonged under-nourishment which is plainly undermining the vitality of the community. The Ministry of Health itself has even felt bound, in face of such local insolvency, to ignore its own emphatic dictum [1] that it is the duty of the Guardians " to ensure that the pauper is sufficiently fed, clothed and lodged ", and has insisted, either through the Inspector's pressure or by the peremptory conditions on which alone the Minister will sanction the indispensable loans, on Scales of Relief which—at any rate in such cases as those of large families, and men without legal dependants, and (sometimes) men with families where nothing is granted for the man himself— are plainly inadequate for the maintenance in health of all the members of the household. On the other hand, the workmen destitute through Unemployment in the richer Unions, which are either not suffering from so great a percentage of Unemployment, or else enjoy so high an aggregate rateable value that they find little difficulty in paying their way, can continue to receive Outdoor Relief freely and unconditionally, on a relatively high Scale, without financial stringency, and without the Minister of Health finding it possible, for reasons at which we can only guess, to compel some of these wealthy Boards of Guardians—we may venture to instance that of the great Union of West Derby (Liverpool)—even to bring their practice into conformity with the prescription of the Relief Regulation Order which continues nominally to have the force of law. So great a range of variation in the provision made for workmen of like circumstances, suffering, though in different districts, from one and the same national calamity, cannot be justified or defended.

In short, by reason of all these varied considerations, so over-

---

[1] Circular of March 10, 1910 ; Thirty-ninth Annual Report of Local Government Board, 1910, p. xix.

whelming and conspicuous has been found the disability, and even the impotence, of the Boards of Guardians to cope with the long-continued distress brought about in particular districts by mass Unemployment, that we see Union after Union, and Poor Law Conference after Poor Law Conference [1]—the relatively rich Boards as well as those driven into insolvency—appealing to the Government to relieve the Poor Law Authorities of the whole burden of having to provide for the maintenance of the wageless workmen whose destitution is due to no other cause than the unparalleled Unemployment of the past decade.

We pass now to a more fundamental defect in the existing system of dealing with able-bodied destitution than any particular method of constituting the local relieving Authorities, or any particular area of jurisdiction of the Boards of Guardians—a defect which seems to us irremediable. The Elizabethan Poor Law, as amended in 1834, cannot be considered by any Government responsible to the whole people, four-fifths of whom belong to the manual working and wage-earning class, as a fit agency for dealing with the destitution arising from that most disastrous of all social diseases, the disease of involuntary Unemployment. So long ago as 1884, as we have already mentioned, Joseph Chamberlain perceived this truth, and declared that it was in the highest degree undesirable to familiarise honest and steady workmen, usually in regular employment, with the Poor Law Authorities and Poor

---

[1] We give, as a sample of these resolutions, the one passed by the Northern Poor Law Conference in the autumn of 1927 and reported in the *Poor Law Officers' Journal* for November 4, 1927 :

" That in the opinion of this Conference, representative of Local Authorities in the Counties of Northumberland, Cumberland and Durham, the increase in the number of persons in receipt of Poor Law relief, and the continued growth of a dependent population, are due not to local but to national and even world causes, and demand urgent attention from the Government.

" That the continued and increasing burden of local rates in this area is a serious obstacle to the recovery of trade, increases Unemployment, and is quickly developing a position which may make local administration impossible. This Conference, therefore, calls upon the Government, as a matter of grave urgency, to make the relief of Unemployment a national charge and, pending action in this direction, to take immediate steps to relieve necessitous areas by relaxing the present stringent conditions of the Unemployment Insurance Acts, and thereby assist these areas for the time being. That this Conference appoint a committee representative of the Authorities present, to take such steps as may be deemed necessary to give effect to the foregoing resolution."

We may note that " the tendency to transfer the Able-bodied and Unemployed to a Government Department " was reported by Sir Arthur Lowry (now Chief Inspector) as early as 1911 (*Poor Law Conferences*, 1911–1912, p. 329).

Law relief. And why ? First, because by accepting Poor Law relief they were reduced, through no fault of their own, to the status of paupers : a status which, though no longer accompanied by disfranchisement in Parliamentary and Municipal elections, is still (1929), in substantial matters, below that of full citizenship. Secondly, because an Authority limited to the relief of destitution is unable to afford them what the public interest primarily requires, namely, effective assistance in maintaining character and skill, and opportunity for re-entering the ranks of self-supporting producers. And finally, because, in order to prevent others from voluntarily leaving those ranks and becoming unemployed so as to qualify for relief, any Poor Law Authority finds itself driven, either by experience, or by the regulations imposed by Parliament, or by a Central Authority, to accompany its relief by deterrent and usually dishonouring conditions, in order to " test " the applicant's willingness to work, thereby making its succour so disagreeable that many who ought, in the public interest, to receive it, will be prevented from accepting it. To Joseph Chamberlain this loss of social status, and these deterrent conditions, which might be justified after conviction of some misdemeanour, seemed wholly unwarranted when applied to men and women who were unemployed, not through any misconduct or even any lack of skill, but owing merely to some maladjustment or other shortcoming of the system under which the work of the community is conducted. And he foresaw—what might be more cogent as an argument addressed to the Governing Class—that such a treatment of the Unemployed was calculated to lead to dangerous social discontent. In 1891 he returned to the subject, and admitted " that a stringent administration of the Poor Law ", in its dealings with the Unemployed, " would make a great reduction in the official returns of pauperism ", which would, however, " probably be accompanied by an appreciable increase in the deaths from starvation ". But he added that " a system administered in this spirit would, in a few years, produce a most dangerous reaction ; and would, perhaps, carry us back to all the evils of lax administration which were the cause of the Poor Law of 1834 ". " I have no doubt ", he said, " that in some Unions there is too much laxity, just as in other cases, I think, the law is being administered with too little humanity. I am certain," he concluded, " that an excess of stringency would quickly produce a popular reaction against the whole system." [1]

The Failure of the " Principle of Less Eligibility "

Let us pause to consider whether, and to what extent, the experience of the last forty years has justified Chamberlain's objection to the relegation to the Poor Law of the *bona fide* unemployed workman. For this purpose we must recall to the reader the fundamental principle of English Poor Relief so far as the able-bodied are concerned, which was so sharply enunciated in 1834. " The first and most essential of all conditions," the Commissioners laid down, " a principle which we find universally admitted, even by those whose practice is at variance with it, is that his [the able-bodied person's] situation shall not be made really or apparently so eligible as the situation of the independent labourer of the lowest class. . . . Every penny bestowed that tends to render the condition of the pauper more eligible than that of the independent labourer is a bounty on indolence and vice." Let it be noted, this famous Principle of Less Eligibility was to be applied uniformly throughout the whole country to all able-bodied applicants for relief, whatever the cause of their wagelessness, and whatever the likelihood of their being re-employed in the ordinary course of trade. When we consider the amount of food, clothing and shelter earned in 1834 by " the independent labourer ", whether in agriculture or in the woollen mills, not to mention the stockingers and hand-loom weavers, it is clear that the " Principle of Less Eligibility ", if uniformly applied to the unemployed handicraftsman or mechanic, would lead—and did, in fact, lead—either to such a pittance of Outdoor Relief as barely sufficed to keep body and soul together ; or else to a physiological sufficiency of food and shelter, aggravated by penal conditions of work and discipline. The first of these alternatives was decisively forbidden by the 1832–1834 Commissions for the very good reasons, first, that if the Outdoor pauper died from starvation or exposure, the Overseer (or the Relieving Officer) was criminally responsible ; and secondly,

---

[1] This interesting correspondence between Chamberlain and (Sir) C. S. Loch, Secretary of the Charity Organisation Society, was printed in *The Times*, January 28, 1892; see also *Charity Organisation Review*, No. 86, February 1892.

because the Assistant Commissioners had demonstrated that any such pittance would become, in the majority of cases, what it had always been, a " Rate in Aid of Wages ", operating as a bounty to the irresponsible or inefficient employer. " Whole branches of manufacture," observed the Commissioners, " may thus follow the course, not of coal-mines or of streams, but of pauperism ; may flourish like the funguses that spring from corruption, in consequence of the abuses which are ruining all the other interests of the places in which they are established, and to cease to exist in the better administered districts in consequence of that better administration."

There remained the "Less Eligibility" ensured by "the Workhouse System ". It was this device of confinement, subject to the powers of punishment wielded by the Master of the " well-regulated Workhouse ", that was officially prescribed for the wageless workman, not only by the Report of 1834, but also by the Orders of the Poor Law Commissioners of 1834–1847, the Poor Law Board of 1848–1871, the Local Government Board of 1871–1919, and—by the maintenance in force of the Relief Regulation Order of 1911, which consolidated all the older Orders re-enacting the general prohibition of Outdoor Relief to the able-bodied—by the Ministry of Health down to the present day.

The Failure of the Workhouse Test

There is, we think, no more disheartening episode in English administration than the century-long effort, deliberately planned and persistently pursued by Poor Law administrators, whether Guardians of the Poor, officials of the Central Authority, or successive Ministers of the Crown, to apply the " Principle of Less Eligibility ", as laid down by the Royal Commission of 1834, to the social disease of destitution on account of Unemployment. Let us first recall to the reader the experience with regard to the Workhouse Test—that is, the " offer of the House "—to the able-bodied men and their families ; a device which enlightened opinion in 1834 regarded as a sure method of preventing voluntary Unemployment and the consequent flood of pauperism. The " Principle of Less Eligibility ", as embodied in the Workhouse Test, had, as we have related, one great success : it stopped the agricultural labourers in the South of England from getting Poor

Relief, though how many of them were thereby driven into the towns to intensify the misery of " the hungry 'forties " cannot to-day be ascertained. The General Mixed Workhouse, as established by the Poor Law Commissioners and continued by the Poor Law Board, harbouring indifferently as it did all ages and both sexes, the able-bodied and the impotent, the sane and the feeble-minded, proved, by its companionable promiscuity and its lax regimen, not deterrent at all, but actually attractive, to certain types of men and women, who enjoyed its warmth, its sloth and its shelter. But experience soon indicated that the mixed institution, which always proved too bad for the good, and too good for the bad, was an inevitable result of the mixed Authority. To any Poor Law Authority, however constituted, and for whatever area, if it is burdened with having to provide for the sick and infirm, together with the orphans and the aged (of whom there are always many in chronic pauperism), the ideal of the 1834 Report as regards the able-bodied must appear a fantastic extravagance ; for that ideal is an expensive institution standing always ready but normally empty : a form of relief always on offer but seldom accepted and never long retained. It will always seem more reasonable to admit the one or two able-bodied paupers to the General Mixed Workhouse as exceptions ; with the inevitable result that such men find themselves in conditions certainly more agreeable to the apathetic loafer, if not more " eligible ", than working continuously for long hours at the scanty and intermittent wages of the unskilled labourer. And to him, as to the professional Vagrant, it will always be an additional attraction that the Poor Law is strictly limited to dealing with him *at the crisis of his destitution* ; leaving him free to come and go as he chooses, and to live as he pleases, without even the curb of official cognisance and observation of his doings, whenever he is not actually in receipt of Poor Relief.

Confronted with this failure of the General Mixed Workhouse the Inspectorate of 1871 devised the Able-bodied Test Workhouse, an Institution to be set apart exclusively for the able-bodied, where they could be subjected (to use the words of a leading Inspector) to such a system of labour, discipline and restraint as should be sufficient to outweigh, in the estimation of the inmates, the physical comfort that they enjoyed. As a device for lessening the disease of pauperism these penal establishments were, as we have related, strikingly and almost instantly successful in ridding, *not the community*, but the Poor Law Authority, of the really able-bodied pauper. Unfortunately, even in respect of this limited success, the fact that these penal establishments have been under the jurisdiction of a Destitution Authority, compelled to provide for all the necessitous poor, whether impotent or able-bodied, has always led to their crumbling back into the General Mixed Workhouse as soon as a shortage of room for sick persons or the mentally defective, or for the aged or infirm, compels the Board of Guardians to use their empty accommodation for other classes. And even for the short periods during which Able-bodied Test Workhouses have been reserved for genuinely able-bodied persons, it has, as we have shown, soon become impracticable to enforce the necessary discipline. We doubt whether at the present day any Parliament would knowingly allow even the inmates of an Able-bodied Test Workhouse to be subjected, at the arbitrary will of the Workhouse Master, and without appeal, to compulsory detention for eight days, and even to solitary confinement and starvation diet, as was the practice during the heyday of this experiment. We have described how, in some of the Able-bodied Test Workhouses of the later decades of the nineteenth century, the punishment book reveals that almost every day saw some inmate arbitrarily punished by solitary confinement in the refractory ward on the scantiest possible diet. A Board of Guardians, or other Poor Law Authority, may, or may not, have the machinery for discovering whether a person is destitute, and for affording him the relief that the law requires. It certainly has no machinery for discovering whether or not a person deserves to be subjected to conditions more severe than those of a modern prison. In the past, as we have related, these Poor Law experiments in amateur justice have been more than once brought to an end by the refusal of the magistrates to sentence persons to imprisonment for persistent but often passive resistance to penal tasks. The tragedy of the whole business is that all experience indicates that the Able-bodied Test Workhouse, designed to discipline the wastrel and the loafer, is not in fact applied to them. The persons actually subjected to this stern regimen have not been these men at all, for they seldom stay and never re-enter ; it is the broken-down and the debilitated weakling, the man genuinely without any alternative, the honestly destitute man, often of weak intellect, who is actually forced in by imminent starvation, only to find the conditions unendurable and to claim his discharge, like the wastrel and the loafer. But, unlike these, the " down and out " weakling, who has no alternative, is again and again driven in by dire necessity. Thus, as we have shown, it was the " ins and outs " of the Able-bodied Test Workhouse (as administered between 1871 and 1900) who were subjected to penal discipline ; a depressed, a feeble, but on the whole a docile set of men. But these are just the men who need, if they are to be kept off the rates, not worse than prison tasks and harder than penal servitude, with the sternest discipline on an insufficiently nourishing diet, but a course of quick but restorative mental training, a sufficiency of easily digested food, and progressively graded tasks of work in which they can be taught to take an interest, largely in the open air.

How long it would have been practicable, in face of the rising tide of political Democracy, to continue the Able-bodied Test Workhouse, with its penal conditions for unconvicted persons, we cannot tell. As a matter of history, this particular embodiment of the " Principle of Less Eligibility " was killed dead by the predominatingly Conservative Poor Law Commission of 1905–1909. We need only quote the Majority Report, which was signed without reservations by the then Permanent Head of the Local Government Board (Sir Samuel Provis), as well as by the Secretary of the Charity Organisation Society (Sir Charles Loch), and, on this point, unreservedly concurred in by every member of the Royal Commission. " It does not seem to us," ran this authoritative judgment, " that the maintenance and detention of persons who will not work, or whose recent character and conduct are an insuperable bar to their re-entering industrial life, are within the legitimate functions of a Public Assistance Authority. . . . . Detention Colonies under the control of the Home Office should, in our judgment, be established for the reception of this class." [1] Nor did the Commission stop at a mere condemnation of the Able-bodied Test Workhouse. For all those cases that the Poor Law Authority was to continue to deal with—that is to say, to the exclusion of those who, after judicial conviction, were to be subjected to penal detention—the " Principle of Less Elibigility "

[1] Poor Law Commission, 1909, Majority Report, Part VI., ch. 4, sec. 629, p. 544.

was to be replaced by the " Principle of Restoration ", so that, in the conditions to which they were subjected, " the restoration to independent habits of life should be an ever-present consideration " [1] in the elaboration of the educative, restorative and curative treatment—analogous, we may suggest, to that of the Borstal institution—that was called for.

This decisive condemnation in 1909 of the expedient for which the Local Government Board Inspectorate had been pressing had naturally a damping effect. The story of the only surviving example of the Able-bodied Test Workhouse—that which the Fulham Board of Guardians had, at the instigation of the Local Government Board, established at Belmont in 1908—is full of instruction. As in the previous cases, when Unemployment decreased in severity, the institution started to revert to the General Mixed Workhouse out of which it had sprung. The Metropolitan Boards of Guardians, which had been authorised to send their able-bodied men, began to use Belmont as a " House of Convenience ", upon which they could disburden themselves of any inmates whom they found troublesome. Already prior to the War, we find " a portion of the accommodation set apart for male epileptics from the London Workhouses. . . . Towards the end of 1923 one block was set apart and prepared as a Convalescent Home for men inmates from London (Poor Law) Infirmaries. During 1924, *there being still spare accommodation*, arrangements were made to receive a number of infirm men from Southwark Union ". Naturally, it was presently realised " that Belmont to-day is not carrying out the purpose for which it was devised ". This diversion seemed, to the Guardians, less objectionable because the Institution had been found unsuccessful even with regard to able-bodied men. It neither carried out the " Principle of Less Eligibility " nor the " Principle of Restoration ". It was found that those able-bodied who were admitted to the Institution were neither " deterred " by its regimen from remaining, nor in any way " restored " in character or capacity for independent life.[2] We are not aware what view is to-day taken

---

[1] *Ibid.* sec. 617, p. 541.

[2] In February 1929 the Fulham Guardians issued a circular to the Metropolitan Boards announcing that, with the approval of the Ministry of Health, the use of Belmont as an Able-bodied Test Workhouse was to be abandoned. " The change ", as the *Poor Law Officers' Journal* remarks (February 15, 1929), " is not merely one of name but of ideals and aims ". " The chief end and aim

of this experiment—coming as it does after the experience of the Able-bodied Test Workhouses of Poplar, Birmingham, Manchester and Kensington—by the Minister of Health. But we defy any-one who visited Belmont when it was still an able-bodied Test Workhouse seriously to recommend its revival, or its imitation elsewhere, as a place of internment of the able-bodied paupers for whom the ineptitude of the General Mixed Workhouse has been demonstrated.[1]

The Failure of the Labour Test

Long before the undesirable results of the application of the " Workhouse Test " were realised, it had been found, in practice, impossible to " offer the House " in districts in which widespread

---

of the scheme is to fit each man with a trade, and fit him to take his place in the Labour Market." Workshops are being prepared and instructors are to be engaged, who will undertake the tuition of the men in farm work and gardening, engineering, bricklaying, plastering, bootmaking, upholstery and mattress-making, mat-making and brush-making, cooking and general kitchen work, wood-chopping, bread-making, and concrete block-making. Men are to be encouraged to choose their own trades ; and advice will be given as to their physical fitness for particular occupations. The workers will not receive anything for their work beyond board and lodging. It is apparently hoped to overcome the difficulty of it being practically impossible to dismiss a man whose work or conduct is unsatisfactory by a system of grades. On reception men will enter a middle grade. They may be promoted to a higher grade with privileges of dress, leave, tobacco, travelling fares, etc. The best may even be selected as paid " helpers " at a wage of ten shillings per week in addition to complete maintenance at the highest grade. (These, presumably, will cease to be paupers.) Men found unsatisfactory will be liable to degradation to a lower grade, without privileges, segregated in a separate block, under conditions more rigorous and less inviting, with more arduous work under " intensive supervision ". It is this segregated block which seems to per-petuate the Able-bodied Test Workhouse, and will probably be open to the criticisms that have been made on that institution.

The experience of this novel Poor Law project, in diametrical opposition to all the conceptions of 1834 and 1871, will be watched with interest.

[1] For all this, see the elaborate " Report on the Present Position of the Belmont Institution ", by a Committee of the Fulham Board of Guardians (printed in Minutes of June 7, 1928). The difficulties connected with the ad-ministration as regards the able-bodied inmates are thus summarised : " (*a*) The individual standard of Belmont inmates is low and very mixed, as the sending Boards make a practice of sending only their most difficult cases. (*b*) The structure of Belmont is such that complete classification of the present inmates into the various categories that their different ages, physical, moral and mental capacities would demand is impossible. (*c*) The present limitation of the kinds of work available for the men is a disadvantage, *e.g.* the difficulty during bad weather of finding suitable work for the men on the farm. (*d*) The fact that the men cannot be detained with the object of giving them some

Unemployment had simultaneously reduced to destitution not dozens or scores, but hundreds, and sometimes even thousands, of able-bodied workmen. In these localities, at such times, the " Workhouse Test " was reserved, with the tacit concurrence of the Central Authority and its Inspectors, for those men whom the Guardians chose to consider " bad cases ", whilst Outdoor Relief, with or without conditions, was granted to the mass of able-bodied applicants for whom the Workhouse could find no accommodation. This abrogation of the principles of the 1834 Report —an abrogation not only of the prohibition of Outdoor Relief to the Able-bodied, but also of that of the uniformity of their relief, irrespective of whether they were deserving or undeserving [1]— had been inevitable, on the successive " depressions of trade " in one Union or another, in every decade since 1834, as it was

---

definite training is a pressing problem. (*e*) The lack of outlet for the product of the inmates' labour " (*ibid.*).

It may here be mentioned that, in the impracticability of getting any Able-bodied Test Workhouse, the Central Authority allowed Boards of Guardians to place out some of their able-bodied men at the Hollesley Bay Farm Colony established in 1905 by the Central (Unemployed) Body for the training, not of paupers, but of the Unemployed. From 1921 the Colony has (without becoming a Poor Law Institution) been entirely used for this purpose, on payment by the Guardians of the cost of each man so sent, whilst his wife and children receive Outdoor Relief. This " Test by Rustication " is thus analogous to the Modified Workhouse Test, with the difference that life at Hollesley Bay is healthier, pleasanter and occasionally, perhaps, more " restorative " than life in the General Mixed Workhouse. Hollesley Bay does not seem to have been made the subject of official inspection or report for many years (at least no such report has been published). We gather, however, that it is highly successful in growing fine fruit, for which it gains gold medals ; but that it cannot be said to train its inmates in gardening or agriculture ; or to secure employment for them after their four months' stay, after which, usually improved in physical health, they revert to the London scramble for unskilled employment, and presently reappear as applicants for Outdoor Relief. (Particulars of the Hollesley Bay Farm Colony down to 1909 will be found in the Minority Report of the Poor Law Commission, 1909, pp. 550-558.)

[1] It is not always remembered that the Poor Law Inquiry Commissioners of 1832-1834 laid as much stress on uniformity in the treatment of all able-bodied applicants for Poor Relief, as on " Less Eligibility ". " The bane of all legislation ", they insisted, " has been the legislation for exceptional cases. . . . If merit is to be the condition on which relief is to be given—if such a duty as that of rejecting the claims of the undeserving is to be performed—we see no possibility of finding an adequate number of officers whose character and decisions would obtain sufficient popular confidence to remove the impression of the possible rejection of some deserving cases. . . . When this principle [the Workhouse System] has been introduced, the able-bodied claimant should be entitled to immediate relief on the terms prescribed, wherever he might happen to be ; and *should be received without objection or enquiry* " (Report of Poor Law Inquiry Commission, 1834).

simultaneously inevitable in over a hundred Unions in the unparalleled Unemployment of 1921–1928. For the first three-quarters of a century the approved alternative to the Workhouse Test, when this was impracticable of general application, was, as we have described, the " Opening of the Labour Yard ", where the destitute men could be put to hard and repulsive labour (usually stone-breaking), in return for Outdoor Relief.

This new embodiment of the " Principle of Less Eligibility " had, however, serious disadvantages of its own. Perhaps the least of these was its lack of uniformity, not only among the individuals subjected to it in each Union, but also, arbitrarily, among different Unions. In every decade it could be said that, where the work was most repulsive in character and the relief given was smallest, the task exacted was most severe. What was much worse was that work in the Labour Yard, everywhere and almost universally, had a gravely deteriorating effect on the men on whom it was imposed. Continuous toil could be enforced neither by supervision nor by punishment, whilst every attempt to devise a task which could be accurately defined and universally exacted failed, not only from the difficulty of measuring the exertion exerted by each labourer, but also from the fact that even those who did not complete the amount of work demanded of them could not be dismissed from employment. The work in the Labour Yard on which the Central Authority for three-quarters of a century insisted was, as we have shown, always a sham, and necessarily a demoralising sham. It fostered, in men whom it was important to invigorate, and to inspire with a zest for work, a habit of dull, lethargic loafing, and actually, as one experienced official declared, a continuous overwhelming inertia. Moreover, the Labour Yard failed, in even a majority of cases, to embody the " Principle of Less Eligibility ". Whilst it repelled, from any relief whatever, the temporarily unemployed workman belonging to a skilled craft—to whom, of all others, consideration might have been shown—it proved positively attractive, in the towns, to the large numbers of discontinuously employed unskilled labourers, and especially to those who habitually lived by casual jobs. The Labour Yard came, in fact, even where well administered, to operate as a direct subvention to that great source of chronic pauperism, the demoralising system of Casual Labour, to which it provided, in effect, a " Rate in Aid of Wages ". Finally, the Labour Yard, and with it all forms of Test Work in return for Outdoor Relief, broke down in practice on the impossibility of making any adjustment between the amount of relief and that of the work exacted as a condition of relief. The Guardians could not lawfully give more Outdoor Relief (and they usually insisted on giving less) than would suffice, when added to all the other family resources, just to " relieve destitution ". For this—usually less than full maintenance—they often could not bring themselves to require full-time attendance at the Labour Yard for the entire week, which seemed both to prevent the man from earning something by casual employment, and to stand in his way in diligently seeking regular work.[1] On the other hand, if the Guardians insisted on a full week's work from every man, they felt that they could not refuse him adequate maintenance for himself and his legal dependants, however numerous. Yet Outdoor Relief on any such scale, especially if the family was large, plainly amounted, on any computation, to more than was being earned in the same town by many an honest independent labourer " of the lowest grade ". When, as during the present century, public opinion required the work to be paid for in relief at so much per hour, let alone at " Trade Union rates ", the whole scheme became impracticable. The evidence taken by the Poor Law Commission, and the emphatic condemnation by all its Special Investigators, and both its Reports, brought to an end any credit that the system had enjoyed. The Local Government Board, after 1909, had for some years no need to press for the " opening of the Labour Yard ", and, in these years of abundant employment, actually used its influence against it. To combat the tendency to keep the Labour Yard always open, and, if possible, to get it entirely dispensed with in ordinary times, was, in fact, one of the objects of the language in which the Relief Regulation Order of 1911 was drafted ; at a moment, it must be said, when Able-bodied Destitution was at a minimum. It could not then

---

[1] However logically it was argued by the Ministry of Health and the Inspectorate that relief was not wages ; and that Test Work was not employment, but only the condition on which whatever relief was necessary to supplement the other resources of the family could be granted, the " common sense " of the Guardians refused to insist on equal full-time labour all the week through from the man to whom only five or ten shillings had been granted, and his fellow-labourers whose relief according to the Scale ran up to forty or fifty shillings a week.

have been foreseen that these changes, by which the Labour Yard followed into obsolescence the general application of the Workhouse Test, left the Boards of Guardians no way of meeting the unparalleled Flood of Unemployment of 1920–1921 otherwise than by the grant of unconditional Outdoor Relief.

Meanwhile, the whole conception of Outdoor Relief had itself been changed. Right down to the end of the nineteenth century, destitution had been commonly taken to mean nothing more than the lack of food, shelter, and the minimum of clothing. The relief of destitution, when given as Outdoor Relief, meant, to the average Poor Law Guardian (who was not corrected on this point by the Inspector), no greater sum of money than that on which a family could be kept from actual starvation, without any consideration of the additional needs of the nursing mother and the infant, of the growing children whom an insufficient supply of vitamins would condemn to rickets or tuberculosis, of the wife whom incessant toil and anxiety, combined with continuous under-feeding, would ruin in health or drive out of her mind, or of the able-bodied husband and father whose health and strength could not advantageously be allowed to be undermined by prolonged under-nourishment and exposure in insufficient clothing. But by the end of the nineteenth century, experience had brought the responsible administrators of the Local Government Board to a vastly wider definition of destitution than that of the Poor Law Commissioners three-quarters of a century before. " Destitution ", the Poor Law Commission was told in 1906 by the Legal Adviser to the Local Government Board,[1] " when used to describe the condition of a person as a subject for relief, implies that he is for the time being without material resources (i) directly available, and (ii) appropriate for satisfying his physical needs ; (*a*) whether actually existing, or (*b*) likely to arise immediately. By physical needs in this definition are meant such needs as must be satisfied (i) in order to maintain life, or (ii) *in order to obviate, mitigate, or remove causes endangering life or likely to endanger life, or impair health or bodily fitness for self-support* ". Thus the relief which the Boards of Guardians had to give to the destitute had to be such as to provide, not only against a lack of food sufficient to maintain life from day to day, but also against any

[1] Poor Law Commission ; Evidence of A. D. Adrian, C.B., K.C., Assistant Secretary of the Local Government Board, Q. 973, Appendix, vol. i., 1909, p. 73.

impairment of health and bodily fitness for self-support. It must, in short, as the Local Government Board specifically informed the Guardians in 1910, be " adequate "—adequate, that is, to the particular requirements of the whole family, in each case, for their lasting health and bodily and mental fitness for self-support.[1]

It was, we suggest, to this enlargement of the official conception of what was required for maintenance—this expansion of the meaning of the relief of destitution, entirely in consonance with the teachings of the physiologists and the economists, and with public opinion—that placed the Boards of Guardians, when the Flood of Unemployment came upon them, in a dilemma from which the Ministry of Health never rescued them. On the one hand, they had been repeatedly warned of the social dangers involved in relief that was not adequate—inadequate, that is to say, to the maintenance of the family in health. It was, indeed, plainly uneconomical, as well as cruel, by giving inadequate relief, deliberately to cause the infants to die, the children at school to be hungry and cold, the mother to be driven, by prolonged under-nourishment, into the lunatic asylum, and the husband and father to get so weak as to become incapable of the work that, by great good luck, he presently obtained. When a man and wife and four or five children had to be maintained, " adequate " relief upon post-war prices necessarily went up to a figure never thought possible by the Guardians of the preceding century. Yet it was equally insisted by the Ministry of Health that under no circumstances must the amount of the Outdoor Relief, even for the largest family, come anywhere near the current wages of the lowest grade of independent wage labour— Sir Alfred Mond laid it down officially that it ought not to come within ten shillings of a currently recognised standard wage for unskilled labour. The current wage of the lowest grade of

---

[1] It is sometimes suggested that the Local Government Board's requirement that Outdoor Relief should be adequate had reference only to the non-able-bodied, as these alone were contemplated as being lawfully in receipt of Outdoor Relief. This, however, was not the case, though it may well have been the non-able-bodied whom the draftsman specially had in mind. The able-bodied man was, according to the Orders at that date, as at other times, legally eligible for Outdoor Relief under various circumstances (*e.g.* in case of temporary sickness, or of the sickness of any legal dependant, or for the burial of any member of his family, *as well as in any exceptional case* duly reported to the Central Authority). In all cases his wife and his dependent children, whatever their number, had to be " adequately " relieved, as well as himself.

independent wage labour was barely 30s. per week in the rural districts ; often no more than 35s. per week in the provincial towns ; and scarcely 40s. per week in the Metropolis, at a time when Sir Alfred Mond's maximum for Outdoor Relief in London was 54s. It could not be plausibly asserted that an exceptionally large family could be maintained even upon such a wage ; and few Guardians thought that a normal household could be kept in health on less. At the present day (1929), whilst prices have declined from their highest point, and, with them, the cost of living and the Scales of Relief on which most of the Boards of Guardians are acting, the rates of wages have, in nearly all cases, also been reduced. Thus the dilemma continues. Indeed, so seriously have the earnings been reduced of men working in some of the staple industries, such as coal-mining and certain branches of textile manufacture, in which " short time " prevails, that experienced Poor Law administrators have privately declared that the workmen actually in employment are frequently less able to maintain their families on their actual earnings than those wholly unemployed and fortunate enough to be in receipt either of the State Unemployment Benefit, or the so-called Unemployment Relief of the Board of Guardians.

Can we now sum up the century of experience in the working of the " Principle of Less Eligibility ", or deterrent relief, in dealing with Able-bodied Destitution ? The Poor Law Inquiry Commissioners of 1832–1834 were emphatically right in condemning the unconditional provision of maintenance in their own homes (domiciliary relief) for able-bodied men in health of an age at which they ought to be at work ; whether this Outdoor Relief is adequate or inadequate to physiological requirements, and whether it is merely a subvention of other resources or a complete income for the household. All experience indicates that, in the London or the Liverpool, or the specially necessitous industrial areas of 1928, as in the rural counties of 1832–1840, such Outdoor Relief inevitably operates, if it is not full maintenance, as a Rate in Aid of Wages, subsidising, to their own detriment, decaying trades, inefficient employers and inert or irregular wage-earners, together with all forms of irregular or casual employment. On the other hand, where the maintenance afforded is complete and physiologically adequate, this free and unconditional gift severely tries the virtue of the most industrious recipient, and if it is continued, in most cases insidiously deteriorates his industrial faculty. On all but the best, its influence is disastrous. What is even worse, this reliance on undeterrent Poor Relief is dangerously contagious, leading endless crowds, who have become aware of the " good fortune " of those who have succeeded in obtaining Outdoor Relief, not only to apply for it themselves, but even voluntarily to qualify for it by negligently incurring dismissal from employment, or spontaneously abandoning unpleasant work, or actually resorting to deceit and fraud. In this sense there is a real " disease of pauperism ", the dissemination of which is as fatally easy as it is socially calamitous.

Yet all the alternative forms of relieving destitution as such, to which, as regards able-bodied men who ought to be at work, the Boards of Guardians have been directed—that is to say, all the " tests " in which has been embodied, throughout the century, the principle of making the condition of the pauper " less eligible " than that of the lowest grade of independent labourer—have, in the case of mass Unemployment resulting from depression or dislocation of trade, broken down in practice. Whatever may be said of " deterrence " as, in itself, a remedy for the social disease of pauperism, no one can suggest that it is a remedy for the social disease of involuntary Unemployment. Moreover, it has become impossible to advocate or to justify, as a method of dealing with the necessities of large numbers of unemployed workmen—whose wagelessness is, in the mass, plainly due to no fault of their own, who are of all sorts of industrial faculty and every degree of skill, with widely differing Standards of Life, and needing the most diverse kinds of assistance to rejoin the ranks of productive Labour—the application of any rigidly uniform and almost automatic " test ". It has admittedly been found that any such " test "—whether in the form of the General Mixed or Able-bodied Test Workhouse, or that of the Labour Yard or other Test Work—is " too good for the bad and too bad for the good ". Nor is the difficulty of to-day merely that the application to the Unemployed of any such " test " is, in all its various forms, demonstrably injurious alike to the man who submits to it, and accepts the relief of which it is the condition, and to him who rejects it, and thereby forfeits the assistance that it may be socially advantageous that he should receive. In face of an alert and organised political Democracy, the attempt to deal with the problem of the Unemployed by the application of such a " test " will, as Joseph Chamberlain warned the governing class in 1886 and 1891, inevitably lead to dangerous social discontent ; and, equally certainly, in due course to reaction, and a lax policy of unconditional Outdoor Relief, in the long run even more socially disastrous than its refusal.

The lesson of experience is that provision for the wageless workman, destitute merely through Unemployment, cannot properly or even safely be made, or the problem of Unemployment be dealt with, by any Destitution Authority administering a Poor Law, whatever the area over which it acts, or through the agency of any Local Authority whatever, which will, for this service, be all the more incompetent if it is a popularly elected body.

EPILOGUE

IN the opening chapter of this history of the English Poor Law during the last hundred years we described the establishment of a new and singular type of Local Government. Unlike the ancient Parish and County, which had hitherto been responsible, among other public services, for the relief of the poor, the six hundred and odd Boards of Guardians, designed to cover the whole of England and Wales, were representative bodies elected for one purpose, and one purpose only—the relief of destitution. And these new Local Authorities were, from their very inception, provided with an authoritative rule of conduct—the " Principle of Less Eligibility " embodied in " the Workhouse System ". Moreover, in order to secure, from one end of the Kingdom to the other, both national uniformity and unbroken continuity of administration, the Boards of Guardians were, by a momentous new departure in English Local Government, placed under the Orders, the inspection and the audit of an entirely novel kind of National Department, specialised for the work of interpreting and enforcing the Poor Law as altered by the Poor Law Amendment Act of 1834. In a thousand pages we have followed the doings of these Destitution Authorities, and estimated the successes and failures, from 1834 to 1928, of the deterrent Poor Law that they were set to administer. We are grateful to Mr. Baldwin's Cabinet for enabling us to finish the story with dramatic completeness. For in this Epilogue we recount the sentence of death passed by Parliament in December 1928 on the century-old Boards of Guardians. Is there not also a policy, conscious or unconscious, implicit in this upsetting of existing institutions ? Can it be doubted that the transfer of the obligation to relieve the destitute, from the " Guardians of the Poor " to the Local Authorities primarily concerned, each in its own sphere, with the prevention of destitution, finally disposes of the " Principles of 1834 " ?

The Local Government Act of 1929

Ever since the Government proposals for the abolition of the Boards of Guardians were first published in December 1925, they have been continuously under discussion. They have been vehemently objected to by nearly the whole Poor Law world ; and they were, at first, to say the least, not welcomed by the members of the Councils of the Counties and County Boroughs, to whom the powers and duties of the Guardians were to be transferred. Yet when the Bill came before the House of Commons in November 1928, though many of its provisions aroused deep resentment and were stubbornly resisted, not one member rose to move an amendment to provide for the retention of a separate Destitution Authority. The reasons for uniting the provision for the destitute with the work of the Local Authorities already charged with Public Health and Education, and operating usually over larger areas than those of the Poor Law Unions, were, outside the Boards of Guardians themselves, and because they were indissolubly bound up with the proposals for "de-rating" and the increase in the Exchequer Grants, felt to be irresistible.[1] But although the Boards of Guardians are abolished, the Poor Law formally remains unchanged. The County and County Borough Councils, among which the powers and duties, the assets and liabilities of the 625 Poor Law Unions are to be re-distributed, are directed to appoint Public Assistance Committees, which may include a minority of co-opted members (among whom are to be some women), to which (on the model of the Education Committee instituted by the Education Acts of 1902 and 1903), the work that will remain to be done under the Poor Law Act of 1927 (other than that of levying a rate or borrowing money) will be delegated, subject to such restrictions or instructions as the Council may impose. The Public Assistance Committee, it is provided, shall itself appoint local committees (including members nominated by the local councils, with women and other persons co-opted) by the agency of which, it is contemplated, the work of dealing with

---

[1] We deal here only with the Poor Law provisions of the Local Government Act, omitting consideration of (1) the important alterations of the financial relations between the Local Authorities and the Exchequer (the effect of " de-rating " on Unemployment having been referred to on pp. 701-704); (2) the transfer of the service of Highway Maintenance ; (3) the reorganisation of the service of Registration of Births, Marriages and Deaths (as to which see p. 997) ; and (4) the amendment of the law upon Town Planning.

individual cases of destitution will be performed. So far, it might be said, in the contracted realm of Poor Relief, the reform amounts to little more than the substitution of one board or committee for another. But there are three momentous changes which the new Authorities have to work out. The local committees, unlike the Boards of Guardians, will not be autonomous in their discretion, even within the law, but will necessarily work under the direction and control of the Public Assistance Committee, and indeed, under rules to be made, or confirmed on its recommendation, by the Council of the County or County Borough itself. The Public Assistance Committee will have directly under its own administration and for such rearrangement and specialisation for use by the whole County or Borough as may be decided, such of the Institutions transferred from the Boards of Guardians as the Council may continue to maintain under the Poor Law, whilst the others will be available for assignment by the Council for the use of its Public Health, Education and other Committees. And—most far-reaching of all—the County or County Borough Council is empowered (and intended) to " break up the Poor Law ", at least to the extent of doing exclusively under the Public Health Acts, the Education Acts, the Maternity and Child Welfare Act, and the Blind Persons Act, the very extensive work for the infants under five, the children of school age, the expectant and nursing mothers, the blind, and those persons of all ages who are sick with infectious or other diseases and infirmities (including childbirth), which could hitherto have been done both under the Poor Law in cases of destitution, and under the appropriate Acts irrespective of destitution. Thus the intention of the Ministry of Health is (as rapidly as the County and County Borough Councils can make the necessary arrangements) to end the present duplication and overlap of services, by " taking out of the Poor Law " all the large amount of public assistance, estimated at one-fourth of the whole, that can lawfully be given by the Local Health and Local Education Authorities with their existing powers. This unification, when administratively completed, will leave to an emasculated Poor Law administration under the same Councils (*a*) those wageless workmen who, being unprovided with Unemployment Insurance Benefits, find themselves destitute ; [1] those aged and infirm persons, together with

[1] The Unemployed Workmen Act, 1905, is repealed by this Act of 1929.

those widows and children who, being unprovided with national
pensions, are receiving Outdoor Relief ; (c) the Vagrants resorting
to the Casual Wards; and (d) all those temporarily relieved in kind
on the plea of " sudden or urgent necessity ".[1]

The Special Concession to the London County Council

To the London County Council, on its insistent request, the
Act concedes, by section 17, an important additional option,
which will certainly become a precedent, at least for the County
Boroughs. As such it calls for careful analysis. In London, the
County Council, in taking over the extensive functions of the
Metropolitan Asylums Board in addition to those of the Metropolitan Boards of Guardians and their joint committees, may, at
its discretion, delegate to any of its Committees (and not necessarily to its Public Assistance Committee) any of the new powers
and duties passing to it under the Act. Thus the London County
Council is granted statutory power, so far as administration is
concerned, and subject to the Minister's approval of the administrative scheme that has to be submitted, entirely and completely
to " break up the Poor Law ". The Council may, for instance,
propose to remit to its Education Committee exclusively, the
whole of its powers for dealing with children in attendance at
school, including the maintenance under the Poor Law of those
who are destitute, whether in institutions, or virtually " boarded
out " with their own parents or with others, in addition to all
that it can do for children of school age under the Education
Acts and the Industrial and Reformatory Schools Acts. The
Council may equally remit to the appropriate Committee dealing
with the Public Health Acts (and not to its Public Assistance
Committee) not merely all that it can do under these Acts for
the sick, the infirm and the disabled (including those suffering
from infectious or any other diseases, or merely from pregnancy),
but also all that the Board of Guardians could have done for such

---

[1] The very large number of persons hitherto dealt with by the Boards of
Guardians as lunatics or as mentally deficient persons are not mentioned in this
Act, and they will, for the present, remain paupers. But the Government
promises the early introduction of a Bill embodying, generally, the recom-
mendations of the Royal Commission on Lunacy, and " taking out of the Poor
Law " this whole class of persons, whose treatment will, in future, be given on
Public Health lines,

persons if they had been destitute, including their domiciliary medical treatment and their maintenance on Outdoor Relief. The Council's Committee under the Maternity and Child Welfare Act may be charged, in addition to its present functions, with the exercise of all the powers of assisting destitute mothers, in cash or in kind, before or after childbirth, and all those relating to infants, now exercised by the Board of Guardians. The Council may similarly add, to the functions of its Asylums Committee under the Lunacy and Mental Deficiency Acts, all the powers hitherto exercisable, either by the Boards of Guardians or by the Metropolitan Asylums Board, with regard to persons mentally deficient or certified as of unsound mind. The Council may, if it chooses, delegate all its dealings under the Poor Law with the destitute aged and the prematurely incapacitated, and the destitute widows and orphans, to the Committees that carry out in the Metropolis, under several Government Departments, the various National Pension Acts. The Council, in taking over the Casual Wards maintained by the Metropolitan Asylums Board, may delegate their administration (under the Poor Law and the Orders of the Ministry of Health), not necessarily to its Public Assistance Committee, but to any Committee that it chooses to appoint for the purpose. The Council may even appoint a separate Committee to deal with the destitute Unemployed, under the Poor Law and the Orders of the Ministry of Health, in whatever way the Guardians could have dealt with them, from Outdoor Relief and the Labour Yard up to the Farm Colony and the Able-bodied Test Workhouse, as well as the Council's dealings with them not under the Poor Law, by their employment at wages, along with others not destitute, in the execution of any works that the Council is otherwise empowered to undertake; and in the various ways intended by the Unemployed Workmen Act, in so far as these have been anywhere statutorily authorised. There is accordingly no class or section of persons whose destitution is now being relieved by any of the Boards of Guardians or by the Metropolitan Asylums Board whom the London County Council cannot elect to deal with, under Section 17, through a separate Committee, specialised for treating appropriately that particular class or section, in conjunction with any non-pauper persons of the same class or section whom the Council is, otherwise than under the Poor Law, already empowered to assist or to serve. The Council must, however, appoint a Public Assistance Committee ; and this may possibly find its principal function in supervising the Poor Relief in the form of food or shelter given, on their own statutory responsibility, by the Relieving Officers in cases of sudden or urgent necessity ; and also in directing the prompt transfer, to the appropriate Committees of the Council, of all the applicants for assistance not applying direct to those Committees, but belonging to one or other of the classes or sections for whom specialised treatment is provided. It may possibly also exercise a sort of family guardianship when members of a family are scattered. To that Committee might also be entrusted—to the great relief, as we shall subsequently describe, of the other Committees—the whole duty of " Charge and Recovery " : that is to say, the assessment and collection of the sums which, under the law, the persons responsible for the maintenance of any of the patients treated in the various departments of the Council's present and future work are, in proportion to their means, required to contribute in reimbursement of the expenditure to which the Council is put.

The Administrative Scheme

Much of the success of the Act to which Mr. Neville Chamberlain has given so much thought will depend on the " Administrative Scheme " which, by a bold devolution of confidence, each Council is left to draft for itself. The opportunity which the Act accords to the Councils of deciding to strengthen their Public Assistance Committees by co-opting persons with Poor Law experience (including women), may be expected to be acted on in nearly all cases, because the need for an increased membership will outweigh the theoretical objection to co-option. More likely to create an inconvenient geographical diversity is the decision to be taken (under Section 5) as to the institutions and services to be " taken out of the Poor Law ", and merged in the corresponding branches of administration already within the Council's statutory powers. To some Councils, it is to be feared, especially in the rural areas, it may seem the easiest course simply to take over the functions of the Boards of Guardians as they are, and to delegate them *en bloc* to the Public Assistance Committee. The members and the experienced officials of the Education and

Public Health Committees, even in the most rural of counties, will presumably urge the advantages, both in economy and in efficiency, of concentrating, in a single branch of administration, all that is done at the expense of the rates for each distinct section of the persons assisted. To the extent to which this plan is adopted, the actual pauperism of the County or County Borough will be lessened and its contaminating influence diminished. It is to be noted that the Administrative Scheme to be prepared within six months is not final: it may at any time be amended by a new Scheme. This is a consideration of some importance in making the initial decision. Whatever view may prevail at the outset, it seems certain that the example of the more progressive Councils, and the pressure of public opinion, will, in the long run, compel the " taking out of the Poor Law " of every service that can lawfully be rendered under any other statute. To have one system in one County or County Borough, and another in the adjoining areas, would be not only invidious but also administratively inconvenient to all concerned. The strong pressure which, whilst leaving complete freedom in matters of detail, the Ministry of Health must necessarily exercise in favour of national uniformity in matters of substance, may thus lead to practical unanimity in the decision to be taken under the fifth section of the Act.

Consequential Amendments

Experience warns us that, in English legislation, every great statute is followed, within a very few years, by a series of lesser Acts of amendment or amplification. We need not discuss the minor rectifications to the Act of 1929 that can already be seen to be required. There are, however, in addition to the long-overdue transfer from the Poor Law of everything connected with lunacy, three matters of fundamental importance on which the Act is ambiguous or silent, but which must, we think, be definitely settled by Parliament, in one way or another, before the new organisation of Local Government can be satisfactorily completed. As these three issues may with advantage be borne in mind whilst the new Administrative Schemes are being framed, we deal with them with some particularity.

(a) The Abolition of the Pauper Status

The Act of 1929 does nothing to abolish the pauper status, whilst it restricts its area. Thus the measure not only accepts the political enfranchisement of persons in receipt of any form of Poor Relief which was conferred by the Representation of the People Act of 1918, but also restricts the pauper disqualification for office by specifying particular forms of Poor Relief which are henceforth not to disqualify.[1] Unfortunately the Act makes these restrictions of disqualification in such a way [2] as to leave untouched the status itself which English law affixes to the mere receipt of " parochial relief " ; meaning, not public assistance as such, but assistance given by any Authority by virtue of the Poor Law. This pauper status, whilst affording a definite legal basis for the " stigma of pauperism ", is a matter of greater moment than any sentimental feeling or manifestation of disgrace or disapproval. The person who, however blamelessly, receives Poor Relief in any form, and even for the briefest period, is, by English law, denied or deprived of certain important rights and remedies in invoking the aid of the Courts of Justice which are enjoyed by other citizens and which may be necessary for his protection against serious wrong ; he is subjected to various arbitrary powers from which other citizens are exempt ; [3] he is

---

[1] On the other hand, the Act extends the pauper disqualification for office (which had latterly come to apply only to serving on the Board of Guardians, the District Council and the Parish Council, together with the Metropolitan Asylums Board), in its limited form, to County and County Borough Councils and their Committees.

[2] The Act of 1929 provides that maintenance in a Poor Law institution for the purpose of receiving medical or surgical treatment, or such treatment by itself, or treatment as a certified lunatic, whether of the person concerned or of any dependant, shall not involve disqualification for public offices. If it had been intended to prevent such forms of assistance from carrying with them the degradation to the pauper status, the phrase would have been that used in the Diseases Prevention Act of 1883 and the Public Health (London) Act of 1891, where maintenance and treatment in the infectious disease hospitals of the Metropolitan Asylums Board (a Poor Law Authority) is expressly declared *not to be parochial relief.*

[3] Thus a pauper cannot sue for damages, in respect of wrongs inflicted on him by any non-feasance, even amounting to culpable neglect, either by the Poor Law Authority itself, or by any of its officials or servants. That it is expressly as a pauper he is denied any such right of action is shown by the fact that there is no such deprivation in the case of an inmate in the Public Health or Education institutions. (See the cases cited in *Public Authorities and Legal Liability*, by Gleeson E. Robinson, 1925.) We gather that there is definite authority for saying that the law has not gone so far as to make a Board of

disqualified, merely by reason of past as well as of present pauperism, not only for serving in various offices, but also for receiving various benefits, such as those of many charities under Schemes of the Charity Commissioners. Finally, he is, in certain circumstances, subjected, as a pauper inmate of a Poor Law institution, to arbitrary detention, solitary confinement, diminution of diet, prohibition of smoking, and other punishments, avowedly as punishments, to which the non-pauper inmate in analogous institutions, even if maintained out of public funds, is not sub-

Guardians immune from responsibility for gross violence on the part of its officers or servants. In *Doran* v. *Guardians of Waterford Union* (1901), 1 L.T. Reports, p. 158, an Irish case, the Guardians had to pay damages for physical maltreatment shown by their officers towards two individuals engaged in bringing a pauper to hospital. In the very recent case of *Murray* v. *Wandsworth Guardians* (*Times* newspaper, January 25 and 26, 1929), an English case, a patient who suffered violent assault and false imprisonment at the hands of Poor Law officers, recovered substantial damages from the Guardians. An important distinction must be drawn between malfeasance and non-feasance. The Guardians apparently can be sued for the former in certain circumstances. But they remain immune as regards acts of non-feasance. Negligence is, of course, a form of non-feasance ; and it is in respect of negligence that the pauper suffers most heavily by reason of his inferior status. But he is also under a further disability. If the pauper is set to work, or ordered to do any act in or about a Poor Law institution, and meets with an accident arising out of and in course of such employment, he cannot proceed either under the Workmen's Compensation Acts, the Employers' Liability Acts or at Common Law, because the law has chosen to lay down that there cannot be a " contract of service " between a pauper and the Poor Law Authority or its officials (though the work is exacted in return for relief). Thus the pauper authoritatively set to work, even in so dangerous an occupation as quarrying, gets nothing if he is crippled by an accident. These are Common Law incidents of the pauper status. Parliament itself has added others, by authorising the imposition, without anything like a judicial trial, of specific punishments unknown to the inmates of other public institutions, on pauper inmates whom the Workhouse Master arbitrarily sentences without appeal ; by empowering a local Poor Law Authority, on an arbitrary decision with no more effective appeal than an application to the Justices, involving both more money and more knowledge than the pauper possesses, to take away from their parents, absolutely and for ever, the children of any father and mother in receipt of Poor Relief whom the Poor Law Authority considers unfit to have the custody of their own offspring ; and by enabling any such Authority compulsorily to deport to his " place of settlement " any pauper who has not resided continuously for a year in the place in which he is receiving Poor Relief, together with his wife and dependent children—a peculiarly English form of " exile by administrative order " which is actually suffered each year by literally thousands of poor people. These incidents of the receipt of Poor Relief, which, far from being merely theoretical, occur in thousands of cases annually, cannot, with any candour, be denied to amount to a genuine *capitis minutio*, in comparison with the status of the ordinary citizen, even when he is in receipt of public assistance otherwise than under the Poor Law, and actually is an inmate of a public institution not being a Poor Law institution.

jected ; and this without judicial trial or sentence, and without appeal.[1]

Whatever reason or justification may be pleaded for depriving of some of the rights of complete citizenship the person who voluntarily accepts gratuitous maintenance from public funds, it is, we suggest, impossible to maintain such an inferiority of status only for the person whose maintenance is given under the Poor Law, when assistance of exactly the same nature is given, without any such degradation in status, to even larger numbers of persons in like circumstances, by the very same Local Authority, out of the very same rate, by virtue of such statutes as the Public Health Acts, the Education Acts, the Maternity and Child Welfare Act, and the Blind Persons Act—to say nothing of the gratuitous benefits and pensions dispensed without any pauper status by the Treasury and the Ministries of Pensions, Labour and Health.   The exceptional degradation in legal status inflicted on the " pauper " will become even less defensible when, as may possibly be the case, the Councils of the 150 Counties and County Boroughs are found to adopt Administrative Schemes which differ one from the other as to the institutions and services to continue to be maintained under the Poor Law, and those to be conducted under " the appropriate Acts " not importing the pauper status.   A person who resorts to the local hospital or Maternity Home, or who is maintained when unemployed in an institution where he is instructed or trained, will, in one County or County Borough, retain all the rights and privileges of citizenship.   He who does the same in the adjoining County or County Borough will, because the corresponding institutions are there maintained under the Poor Law, be a pauper, who can (so far as any civil action for damages is concerned) be neglected in the most culpable manner with impunity ; who is liable to be subjected without judicial procedure to arbitrary punishments ; who may have his children taken away from him, without judicial decision, merely because the local Poor Law Authority chooses to con-

---

[1] Let the official or legal reader compare the legal liability to punishment of the pauper inmate of a Workhouse, a Poor Law institution for the Feeble-minded or a Casual Ward, with that of the inmate in a Voluntary Hospital, a Public Health Hospital, a public or voluntary Maternity Home, at the Hollesley Bay Farm Colony of the London Central Unemployed Body, at one of the Ministry of Labour's Training Establishments, or in one of the Homes for the Feeble-minded, whether provided by voluntary funds or by a County or County Borough Council under the Mental Deficiency Act of 1913.

sider him unfit to have their custody ; who may, if he has not resided continuously for twelve months in the County or County Borough in which he has become chargeable, be summarily deported to his " Place of Settlement ", possibly at the other end of the kingdom, which he may not have seen since infancy, quite irrespective of whether or not it is a district in which he can make a livelihood, or, indeed, one in which his state of health will permit him to live at all ; and who will (unlike the convicted criminal) be disqualified for a prolonged period, and in some cases even for life, for offices or benefits open to anyone who has not received " parochial relief ".

Moreover, this degradation in legal status of the person dealt with under the Poor Law is not confined to those who receive the maintenance or other assistance gratuitously. Whatever may happen to the " stigma of pauperism ", the legal pauper status is indelible and irremovable (otherwise than by a special Act of Parliament). *It is not affected by the repayment to the Poor Law Authority of even the full amount of the expense incurred.* A very large proportion of the hundred thousand pauper lunatics in the County Asylums are paid for by their relatives—many of them reimbursing the Poor Law Authorities the whole of the expenses involved—but both these lunatics and the hundred thousand relatives liable for their maintenance are and will continue to be paupers, with all the diminution of status that this implies. Probably few of the sufferers from a road accident who are to-day carried into the nearest institution realise that, when this happens to be a Workhouse, whether or not they are at the time conscious, and whether or not they subsequently send a donation more than covering the entire cost of their treatment, they become legally paupers (and, in strict law, the pauper status once acquired, continues, for some purposes, throughout the whole life of the recipient) ; [1] and their names are irrevocably entered on the pauper roll and included in the statistics of pauperism merely because they have for a short time, whether or not with their assent, in fact received " parochial relief ", which they have subsequently fully repaid.

Finally, it is to be considered that the tendency of modern

---

[1] There are Schemes of the Charity Commissioners, and other instruments, disqualifying all persons who " have received " parochial relief at any previous date.

legislation is not merely to offer public assistance grudgingly and contemptuously to those who, it is assumed, disgrace themselves by asking for it, but to impose it on those who are quite willing to do without it, or even object very strongly to it as an interference with their personal liberty. This is an inevitable consequence of the growing sense that poverty injures the community even when it acts as a deterrent to individual laziness, and, as such, is not to be tolerated even when the sufferer is quite careless : for instance, in matters of sanitation and personal hygiene, or of the proper nourishment of his or her children. In some cases this compulsory public assistance takes the form of Poor Relief. Clearly, when the acceptance of relief is compulsory, it cannot without intolerable oppression be accompanied automatically with the infliction of the pauper status.[1]

(b) *Registration*

The union, under one and the same Council, of all the various branches of Public Assistance in each County and County Borough makes a united register of cases indispensable to administrative efficiency. Such a register, either of persons assisted or of the families to which they belong, at present nowhere exists, though the materials for it are ready to hand. The Local Poor Law Authority is obliged to accumulate an ever-increasing collection of Case-papers relating to all the persons relieved, either in its various kinds of institutions or at their own homes, on account of their destitution. The Local Education Authority has its periodical schedules of children, from those approaching the age of 5 up to those under 14, for whom it is required to ensure education and usually to provide it ; together with its current school registers of enrolment and attendance, its lengthening lists of holders of scholarships and Free Places, its registers of enrolment

---

[1] A wife cannot prevent her husband making her (and their children) paupers, however much she may object to it. If he applies for, and obtains, Poor Relief she (and the children) become paupers. She becomes disqualified for public office ; she becomes liable, if she has any separate estate, to repay what he has received ; if he has not resided continuously for a year in the place where he obtains relief, she (and the children) may be compulsorily removed with him to the place of his settlement ; and because she is deemed to have received Poor Relief through him, she and her children will be disqualified for benefiting from certain charities which exclude those who have ever been paupers—all without her consent and in face of her strenuous protest !

and attendance at classes and lectures, and its more or less scattered records of the children supplied with meals, medical treatment, spectacles, etc. The Local Health Authority has complete lists of patients treated at its various institutions (including those dealing with Tuberculosis and Venereal Disease), either as inmates or as out-patients. The Maternity and Child Welfare Committee has records of all the women and young children whom it assists, either at home or in the institutions that it maintains ; but usually not of those resident within its area who are similarly assisted by voluntary but publicly subsidised organisations of like character, which have hitherto received their grants direct from the Ministry of Health. Each Council's administration of other varieties of Public Assistance, such as those authorised by the Industrial and Reformatory Schools Acts, the Blind Persons Act, and the Midwives Act— now entrusted to different Committees by different Councils—calls for its own special registers. Moreover, all the various departments of the Council's work, whether or not they are governed by separate Committees, have necessarily to keep their own lists of persons on whom they make charges, or from whom they seek to recover payments. Over and above all these lists and records there are the elaborate and complete registers of births, marriages, and deaths, which are now to be kept for the exact area of each Council's administration, by officers who, subject to the direction and control of the Registrar-General, are to become part of its own salaried staff. Finally, it must be noted that the Council's Committee that administers the Old Age Pensions Act necessarily maintains its own record of all the national pensions awarded under this Act to residents within its area at the date of the award.

These varied and extensive local registers, which probably include, in the aggregate, a far greater number of separate entries than there are persons in England and Wales—or, confining ourselves to the present beneficiaries from locally administered Public Assistance of one or other kind, at least ten millions of names— are at present separate from each other, entirely unco-ordinated, and, for the most part, not readily available even for occasional consultation by other branches of what should be a united administration. The result is a certain amount of overlapping by different agencies—even by different Committees of the same Council—due to actual ignorance of what others are doing for

the same family. A more frequent effect of the failure to co-
ordinate all the available information about each case is to make
less perfect than need be the diagnosis of the case, and to lessen
the likelihood of discovering how best to apply the appropriate
remedial treatment. No case, whether of sickness or of Unemployment, of neglected childhood or of adult destitution, can be
assisted to the best advantage without the fullest knowledge not
only of its present family circumstances but also of its past. If
the nation is to continue to provide, as it at present provides, one
or other form of Public Assistance—schooling, training, opportunities for employment or migration, housing, pensions in widowhood or old age, medical treatment from birth to death, not to
mention actual maintenance, institutional or domiciliary, in sickness and unemployment, and whenever destitution occurs—for
three-quarters or more of the whole population (and, in some
forms, potentially for all), it is imperative that the relieving
agency, besides knowing what other agencies are doing, should be
acquainted, not only with the recipient's present circumstances
but also with his record, if any. Throughout the whole history
of the Poor Law, as we have demonstrated in the preceding
pages, nothing has more hampered the Destitution Authority, and
nothing has more prejudiced its action, than the fact that, at any
rate in all the great urban populations, until the applicant made
known his destitution, the Authority from whom he sought relief
usually knew nothing of his life-history ; and that, as soon as
he took his name off the list, he vanished once more into the
unknown. The County and County Borough Councils can start
free from this handicap. Whilst avoiding occasion for delay in
any case of urgency, there ought to be, it is suggested, one comprehensive Case-paper for each family (or rather each family-
household) dealt with in the Council's area, to which there
should invariably be added a record of every step relating to
that family, or any member of it, taken by any branch of the
Council's administration, under whatever statutory or other
authority it is working.[1]

---

[1] Irrespective of any future extension of the Council's work, the mere
union of the existing registers would cover seven-eighths, or even more, of all
the family households within the Council's area. As registration of the potential
applicants is also of considerable value, it is suggested that each Council could,
if desired, after each Census, make its register absolutely co-extensive with the
local population.

It is to be regretted that the Act of 1929 makes no mention of such a registration of cases. But although without legislation there will be no uniformity of procedure, for a mere improvement of each Council's administrative machinery no statutory authority is required. Most of the existing lists and registers have been instituted without specific authorisation ; and their co-ordination and union into a single register would be but incidental to the union of powers and functions effected by the Act. The maintenance of such a comprehensive register could be appropriately provided for in the initial Administrative Scheme. The duty might suitably be delegated to the Public Assistance Committee, which would need to entrust the work to a responsible officer of some standing, for whom a possible title would be that of Registrar of Public Assistance.

It must, however, be added that to permit this local registration to give its full aid to administrative efficiency, the co-operation of the National Government is required. At present more than half the registration that takes place is not geographically coincident with the areas of the Counties and County Boroughs. Thus there are, at-present, long lists of recipients of domiciliary payments with which it is important that the Public Assistance Committees should be acquainted. There are all the Unemployed to whom Insurance Benefit is being paid, or who have been admitted to Training Establishments. There are all the recipients of medical treatment or cash benefits under the Health Insurance Scheme. There are the millions of pensioners under the Old Age or the Widows and Orphans Contributory Pensions Acts, or the War Pension schemes. Information as to these cases in each locality could be automatically distributed week by week to the Councils of Counties and County Boroughs for addition to their local registers, if the Government would include this duty in the work of the Central Index Register, to be maintained by the Registrar-General, as recommended by the Committee on National Registration in 1918.[1]

(c) *Charge and Recovery*

One of the issues left undecided by the Act—though Section 15 refers to the matter in an ambiguous way—is that of Charge and

---

[1] See pp. 815-816 of the present volume.

Recovery. Here there is urgent need for a Parliamentary decision, upon some uniform principle, alike as to the services to be charged for, as to the scale of charges, and as to the persons to be made liable for payment. Only when a clear and definite law has been enacted can we expect to be able to enforce any uniformity of practice.

At present, as was elaborately described in the Minority Report of the Poor Law Commission,[1] to which the student must be referred for fuller details, both the law and the practice are chaotic in their inconsistent diversity. Practically all the Local Authorities affording Public Assistance in any form—Poor Law, Public Health, Education or Police Authorities—have the power, in respect of some of their services, to charge the whole or part of the cost upon the individual benefited or the persons legally liable to pay in respect of him. These powers differ from service to service and from Authority to Authority, alike in the amount or proportion of the expense that is chargeable ; in the discretion allowed to the Authority to charge or not to charge as it sees fit ; in the conditions attached to the charge or exemption from payment ; in the degree of poverty entitling to exemption ; in the degree of relationship entailing payment for dependants, and in the process of recovery and its effectiveness. This chaotic agglomeration of legal powers, conferred on different Authorities at different dates, for different purposes, but all alike entailing on the individual citizen definite financial responsibilities, proceed upon no common principle. Moreover, the practice of the innumerable Authorities concerned, though they be but Committees of the same Council, is even more wanting in principle than the law ; varying, indeed, from systematic omission to charge or recover anything, up to attempts to exact an entirely prohibitive payment for the service performed.

The Poor Law Authority has the widest legal powers of Charge and Recovery ; and usually makes (except in the case of lunatics) less use of them, and recovers a smaller proportion of its expenses, than almost any other Authority. The Board of Guardians has, by a long series of enactments, received power to recover whatever it has expended in relief either (*a*) from the person relieved, or (*b*) from any one of an extensive range of relatives—the grandparents, parents or children, the putative father of an illegitimate

---

[1] Poor Law Commission, Minority Report, 1909, ch. viii. pp. 286-319.

child, and the husband or wife.[1] In practice, most Boards of Guardians make a charge, and enforce payment, chiefly in the cases of : (i) lunatics removed to the County Asylum ; (ii) the putative fathers of illegitimate children ; (iii) the insignificant sums of money found on the persons entering the Workhouse or Casual Ward ; and (iv) the rare instances of a pauper subsequently receiving an inheritance or a legacy, or being discovered to be in possession of a bank balance or similar property.[2]

The Public Health Authority has, under the Public Health Acts, power to recover payment of the expense incurred in the institutional treatment of any person from that person only ; and not from any relative or other person responsible for his maintenance. Moreover, any obligatory charge is excluded throughout the whole Kingdom in the case of treatment for Venereal Disease ; and in the Metropolis also for treatment in the infectious disease Hospitals of the Metropolitan Asylums Board. Elsewhere the practice has, up to the present, varied indefinitely.

[1] These relatives legally liable to *repay what the Board of Guardians has expended* (and subject to the important limitations that (i) they must be of " sufficient ability " to bear the charge and (ii) the person relieved must be incapable of work) should be distinguished from the relatives legally liable *for the maintenance of a person*—a more extensive obligation to which a narrower range of relatives are subjected by Common Law.

[2] These legal provisions are irrespective of the power of the Poor Law Authority (like any other Authority) to enter into a contract with the recipient of relief, by which he voluntarily agrees to repay the amount at a future (unspecified) date. This plan of making relief " on loan " was instituted by the Poor Law Amendment Act of 1834, but was not usually put in operation, as the likelihood of the pauper ever being worth suing is small. Its general adoption was advocated in 1870–1890 by the Inspectors and others who wished to restrict Outdoor Relief, not because it was expected that repayment could often be enforced, but because it was thought that the entering into an express obligation to repay the relief would " deter " persons from applying for it. So it did, and does ; but unfortunately it deters the wrong people. To the thrifty and honest man of character, brought into destitution by ill-fortune, the thought of incurring a load of debt that will keep his wife and family hungry for years, may induce him and his to suffer untold hardship rather than seek the aid which it is in the public interest that he should receive. On the other hand, " relief on loan " has no deterrence for the unthrifty, the dishonest and the wastrel. This well-ascertained fact makes particularly invidious the renewed adoption of Relief on Loan in the Unemployment crisis of 1926–1928. Worst of all is its imposition when Outdoor Relief is given only against an onerous " Labour Test ", so that the work exacted is not even paid for !

Poor Relief " on loan " has to be expressly agreed to by the recipient ; and thus cannot be given when the recipient is unconscious or *non compos mentis*, nor when the actual recipient is a minor. Moreover, " sudden or urgent necessity relief ", given by the Relieving Officer in kind, may not be given on loan.

There are Public Health Hospitals which have made a charge to every patient, even in cases of infectious disease. Most Local Health Authorities have come to recognise the public importance of removing any obstacle or dislike to the prompt and universal use of the Isolation Hospital where any infectious disease is diagnosed or even suspected ; and all attempts to recover the cost of treatment have been, in practice, abandoned. Latterly, the tendency has been to recognise that the public interest in securing the widest possible use of the hospital for all sick persons is not limited to diseases recognised as infectious, the number of which steadily increases. It is no less to the interest of the community as a whole that every sick person should be as quickly as possible restored to health and productiveness ; and it is plainly impossible for any but comparatively well-to-do households to provide the environmental conditions, the nursing, or the medical attendance required for this purpose. Thus the tendency has been not to use any legal powers of recovery of cost ; to ask for no payment from the poorest households ; and to be contented, in any serious case, irrespective of the actual cost of the service rendered to the individual patient, with whatever repayment is voluntarily contracted for by the patient or his relatives. Thus the practice of the Public Health hospitals and Tuberculosis Sanatoria has steadily approximated to that more and more generally adopted by the endowed and voluntary hospitals.

The Local Authority using the Maternity and Child Welfare Act has no statutory power of charging either the patient or her relatives ; but it can, of course, make rules providing that only those patients shall be admitted to its institutions, or otherwise treated, who enter into agreements to repay specified sums. The practice appears to be, alike in Maternity Homes maintained from public funds, and in those dependent partly on voluntary contributions, to require women entering for confinement to pay the whole or a substantial part of the Maternity Benefit to which they may be entitled under the Health Insurance Scheme, and in other cases a sum proportionate, not to the expenses incurred, but to the patient's means.

The Local Education Authority has, under the Education Acts, now that the elementary schools are free, no legal powers of Charge and Recovery ; but it can, of course, and almost invariably does, make a charge (except in so far as scholarships or free places are awarded) to all who voluntarily attend its educational classes or join its educational institutions, or send children to its residential schools. This charge practically never covers the whole cost per student, and is usually a convenient sum fixed for each class of institution, with some regard to the amount that a sufficient number of persons will be prepared to pay, but without assessment according to the means of particular families. Yet when the Local Education Authority maintains schools under the Industrial and Reformatory Schools Acts, it has statutory powers to charge the parents of the pupils committed to these schools a sum assessed in proportion to the parents' means, which is recoverable summarily on pain of imprisonment, even if, as actually occurs in practice, the person charged is in receipt of Poor Relief as being absolutely destitute ! The Local Government Bill, as laid before Parliament, ignored these varieties and inconsistencies of powers and practices in Charge and Recovery ; and contained (in Clause 15) only an ambiguous provision which purported to provide for increased charges without clearly defining what relatives of the patient were to be liable, and without enacting any uniformity of principle or identity of practice.[1]

What the Act will Accomplish

The Act of 1929, for all its length and detail, is more in the nature of an enabling statute, conferring powers to undertake the new work rather than enacting a policy to be adopted. The sudden enlargement of the duties and responsibilities of the County and County Borough Councils is, indeed, colossal. In 1927–1928 the London County Council had to organise and direct works and services costing, apart from expenditure out of loan, no less than thirty millions. To this will now be added the works

[1] As this goes to press, it is still uncertain what form will be given to the provision on the subject made by the Local Government Bill (clause 15). The intention of the Government is believed to be that (1) no payment shall be required or even sought for in cases of infectious disease (including tuberculosis and venereal disease, whether or not in an infectious form) ; (2) in other cases there shall be " one rule for all " public institutions under whatever Committee maintained, approximating to the practice of the voluntary hospitals ; (3) not only the patient himself but anyone liable to maintain him, will be chargeable ; and (4) any charge shall be, within a maximum of the average cost per patient per day of the institution as a whole, in proportion to the means of the household from which the patient comes. It is, however, still unsettled whether the clause will be re-drafted in the House of Lords so as to carry out the Minister's intentions.

and services under the Poor Law in the Metropolis, amounting
to half as much again. The Council has to take over, on the
appointed day, more than 220 separate institutions of the most
diverse kinds, having, in the aggregate, more than a hundred
thousand beds. A like relative expansion of sphere comes to the
County Boroughs and the other County Councils. For years the
Councils and their Committees and Sub-Committees will be hard
at work sorting out their new responsibilities, re-distributing
institutions and services, and necessarily re-organising nearly
every branch of their present administration. For their guidance
in this great task Parliament, whilst imposing some restrictions,
has laid down no principles and given few directions upon the
policy to be pursued. On the passing of the Poor Law Amendment Act of 1834 there was no dubiety as to the policy which the
Boards of Guardians were required to adopt. The passing of the
Local Government Act of 1929 leaves the Councils a large liberty
to determine the structure, the attitude of mind, and the lines of
policy by which they will cope with the diverse and difficult
problems presented by the administration of Public Assistance.
The Government gives the Local Authorities no clear lead. The
Ministry of Health, no less than the Ministries of Education and
Labour, in conjunction with which it has necessarily to work,
appears to speak with two voices. On the one hand the Poor
Law mentality clings, as the only safeguard against extravagant
expenditure, to deterrence, to the maintenance of the stigma of
pauperism, and to the utmost possible enforcement of repayment
of cost. On the other hand, the Public Health and Education
mentality believes in " compelling them to come in "; in fact,
yearning always after universal treatment, in the interest of the
community as a whole, of all diseases and shortcomings of the
individual citizen at the earliest possible stage. For a whole
decade, it may be foreseen, the conflict of principles will continue.
But the issue, in our judgment, is no longer in doubt. The stream
of tendencies which has, during the past thirty or forty years,
built up so extensive a Framework of Prevention in supersession
of the mere relief of destitution, can, with growing knowledge
and a wider electorate, hardly fail to continue. Step by step, in
one locality after another, the Poor Law institutions and services
will yield ever more ground to those of Public Education and
Public Health. The mere logic of facts cannot fail, we think,

increasingly to transform all methods of " relief " into incidents of preventive and restorative treatment.

The Unemployed

The County and County Borough Councils have a real grievance against the Government, in that it has imposed on them, without giving them new powers or even authoritative guidance, the care of the destitute Unemployed. The Act of 1929 does little more than pass over to the Councils the powers that the Boards of Guardians have possessed since 1834. Thus only by methods and devices allowed to the Guardians under the 1911 Relief Regulation Order, to which the Ministry of Health adheres, will the Councils be able to deal with the Unemployed over and above those who are maintained on Unemployment Insurance, and those who may hypothetically be found employment by some addition to the present Municipal enterprises. The Councils, in fact, will find themselves unable to do hardly anything lawfully for the able-bodied wageless workmen whom the Councils cannot themselves employ, except admit them to the Workhouse, or (in the cases and under the conditions permitted by the Ministry of Health) grant them Outdoor Relief, with or without a Labour Test.

The tragedy of the situation is that, as we have described in the preceding chapter, all the varieties of these two alternatives have, after nearly a century of experience, become hopelessly discredited. The most " proletarian " Board of Guardians finds no more plausible justification for unconditional Outdoor Relief to the destitute Unemployed than that, costly and demoralising as it is, it is the only alternative under the Poor Law to the no less demoralising and much more hateful " Workhouse System ". It is equally true that the most convinced believers in the Workhouse Test have only one argument in its favour : harsh and cruel as it may seem, it appeared to be the only expedient for staving off a ruinous flood of applicants for Outdoor Relief, with the consequent spread of one of the worst of social diseases, that of voluntary and intentional Pauperism. It is one or other of these methods of relief that the new Public Assistance Committees will take over from the Boards of Guardians. The three- or four-score Councils of Counties or County Boroughs

that will have to deal with extensive industrial populations
suffering seriously from Unemployment, are not likely to rest
content in this dilemma. Yet, as has been shown in the preceding chapters, there is, in our judgment, no solution to the
problem to be found within the capacity of any Local Authority
whatsoever. What is to be feared is that the pendulum will
swing widely from side to side. Some Councils will insist, after
keenly fought elections, on a policy of Outdoor Relief for which
they will strain all their legal powers, stubbornly withstand the
Inspectors, and set themselves to outwit the District Auditors.
Other Councils will employ the " Workhouse Test ", or insist on a
full week's hard labour for half a week's wage, in order, not to
relieve but to rid themselves of the applicants, in the genuineness
of whose destitution they do not believe—only to find many of
the Unemployed driven over the borders to the adjacent towns,
and others gone " on the road ", whilst mendicancy and petty
larceny have become rife. Here and there the wisest of the
Councils may, at some risk, take upon itself to put the Unemployed into training establishments which may masquerade
as " the Labour Test ". There will be a like see-saw in the
Ministry of Health and in successive Cabinets, for it is a delusion
to imagine that Conservative administrations are strict and severe
and " scientific ", when the Unemployed are clamouring ; or that
a Labour Government is any more likely than its rival to concede
to pressure what is contrary to its convictions. There will be,
as there has been before, an alternation of special Government
Grants in aid of Relief Works, imprudent extensions of Unemployment Insurance Benefit, instructions to the Departments to
turn a blind eye to the resort, by harassed Local Authorities, to
unconditional Outdoor Relief, and all the rest of the relaxations
of 1920–1928 ! Such a policy will not be any the less harmful by
being accompanied, in the swing of the pendulum, by one of
stringent economy with regard to all the social services—cutting
down the Health and Education Estimates, reducing the Government establishments, stopping any extension of the Training
Centres, and postponing the necessary perfecting of the insurance
and pension systems. Indeed, in this way the nation would
" make the worst of both worlds ". It is hard to say which policy
would do the greater harm ; whether the lavish distribution of
Outdoor Relief to the destitute, or the deliberate restriction of the

growing social services, would do most to undermine the character and lessen the productivity of the community, and stir up angry resentment and class-bitterness among all sections of the people. In this brainless rivalry it may be doubted whether Parliamentary institutions and Political Democracy would survive. Which of the two political Parties would be driven to set up a dictatorship might depend only upon accident !

The Need for a Specialised National Authority

We are not pessimists, because we believe that, sooner or later, good feeling and reason will prevail. The step to which the preceding chapters point is the full and complete assumption, by the National Government itself, of the responsibility for dealing with Unemployment and the Unemployed.

Let us consider what such a reform would involve. The conditions require, as has been shown, a distinct and specialised Authority of national scope, charged only with dealing with the problems of Employment, which are difficult and extensive enough to tax the powers of the strongest Government Department. With all its work arising from the regulation of the conditions of employment we are not here concerned. Our interest is in the Disease of Involuntary Unemployment, which, like the disease of cholera or tuberculosis, has to be dealt with on the double lines of prevention and cure. It requires both an alteration in the environment out of which the disease springs, and the appropriate treatment (which, as with the tubercular patient, will usually have to include maintenance) of the individual sufferer. Or, to take another analogy, when the Fen Country, and, indeed, no small part of low-lying England, was subject to widespread and recurrent inundation, it was not sufficient to treat the individual sufferers from rheumatism and malaria, or to relieve the destitution to which they were reduced ; it was eventually recognised as equally incumbent on the community to organise and carry out, as a collective enterprise, the works of embanking and draining by which, with a positive addition to the nation's wealth production, such disease-producing flooding could be prevented. In our chapter on " Unemployment as a Disease of Modern Industry " we have tried to show that the ways of prevention, like those of preventing the occurrence in the individual of physical or mental disease, can be discovered only by skilled and patient research and experiment. The easiest course is not often the appropriate remedy. Thus experience shows that employment on Relief Works (or indeed, any employment at wages) of the Unemployed *as such*, merely because they are unemployed, just where they happen to reside, has the fundamental drawback that the men can practically neither be selected for fitness for the task, nor dismissed for slackness or negligence. On the other hand, any net increase in the aggregate volume of employment for the time being that it is possible to create, by the utilisation, through Government application of the national credit, of plant and machinery standing temporarily idle ; or even by the mere re-distribution of public orders so as to cause a reduction in the swing of the trade cycle, may, if effected through the ordinary channels, afford a real and lasting clearance from the swollen lists of the Unemployed. Moreover, there are ways in which the disastrous incidence of such fluctuations on the wage-earners in particular trades may be mitigated. To mention only one among many, no nation has yet tried to avert the " labour-logged " condition of its decaying industries by removing, through special superannuation allowances, their most aged members, whilst at the same time lessening, by a prolongation of the school years, the general rate of industrial recruiting. Passing from the prevention of Unemployment to the treatment of the Unemployed, the first condition is the fullest use of the instrument of which the nation has already had a couple of decades of experience—the National Employment Exchange, with its 1200 branch offices.[1] It is essential to its highest efficiency that the Exchange should know of all the vacancies that are, even in bad times, daily occurring in industry. At present an employer is under no compulsion to notify either an impending or an actual vacancy ; nor (except in the Mercantile Marine) even to inform any public Department that the vacancy has been filled. The wage-earners are practically compelled to report to the Exchange the fact of their Unemployment. The Exchange should equally be made aware, as a matter of course, of every industrial vacancy, though the employer need be under no obligation to obtain the wage-earners he

---

[1] The admirable account of the organisation and working of this institution, and of its further potentialities—*The British Labour Exchange*, by John Barton Seymour, 1928—has appeared too late for more than this mention.

requires from the Exchange. When no vacancy can anywhere be found, all the unemployed workers must be provided with maintenance. For this purpose the nation has definitely adopted a gigantic scheme of Unemployment Insurance, which in times of stable trade covers nearly the whole field, though with many gaps and omissions. Although this system of Unemployment Insurance has still to be perfected, it has become plain that it cannot, without losing all its virtues, be made to meet the needs of decaying trades, or even of long-continued general stagnation ; whilst to stretch its benefits so as to provide for the victims of a colossal shift of international commerce would be to fall into all the errors of unconditional Outdoor Relief. Thus there will remain, at all times, a greater or smaller number of the Unemployed who have been left outside National Insurance, or who have " run out of benefit ", or whose rate of benefit is insufficient to maintain themselves and their families.

It is not the worklessness but the restoration of these thousands of sufferers in " good times ", and many tens of thousands in bad times, that is the community's real problem. As they are outside or beyond the succour of Insurance, there is, for such of them as are destitute, no common remedy. The treatments they require are as diverse as their several conditions, which vary with age, past record as to health, occupation and skill, and openings available for future employment. For such indispensable individual diagnosis the personal records of health, occupation, periods of employment and public assistance, already kept by the Ministries of Health, Labour, and Pensions, together with those of the various Committees of the Local Authorities, will need to be combined and systematised, so that the *dossier*, or Case-paper, of every person may be promptly accessible.[1] It is to be remembered that the economic objection to Relief Works need not, and should not, stand in the way of there being—if only as an instrument of diagnosis, a means of testing the willingness to work—always some artificial organisation of employment, partly by the Local Authorities aided by national subventions, and partly by the National Government itself.

---

[1] When, as in 1928, it was desired suddenly to send 8000 unemployed men to assist in getting in the Canadian wheat harvest, the lack of such Case-papers made it practically impossible to avoid including in the party a considerable proportion of men whose physical condition, family circumstances or temperament unfitted them for the expedition.

There might even be a Government Labour Corps, waxing and waning in numerical strength, having its own technical officers and under-officers, its own equipment of tools and tents and lorries, which could be sent in detachments, hither and thither, to execute such badly needed works as land drainage and coast defence.[1] Such enterprises would be greatly facilitated if they could be done free of charge to the locality, and in special cases, even to landowners. Among the many methods of treatment there will be some—such, for instance, as emigration on the one hand, and the special preparation for a new industry on the other —which will not only be more " eligible " than employment in the lowest grades of labour, but also more costly than mere Outdoor Relief on the most generous scale yet adopted. On the whole, however, experience points to coupling the provision of maintenance for those among the Unemployed for whom neither work nor Insurance is available, not with artificially stimulated employment, but, *in order primarily to save them from idleness*, deliberately with general training—physical and mental, techno-logical and cultural—with the object, mainly, of their individual improvement. Such a course of training, which should occupy the whole working time of each day continuously for weeks or months, should certainly be imposed on all the younger Unem-ployed, from the very day they are released from school, merely as a condition of receiving Insurance Benefit. It should form the basis of the work of all the various Training Establishments, now steadily increasing in number, in which maintenance is offered to selected men outside the scope of Insurance. Whether the Training Establishment is day or residential, it is found con-venient that those in attendance should be provided with their food on the premises. As a general rule, admission to each of the Government's Training Establishments, like its assistance to migration or emigration, should (except with regard to the young) not be imposed as a condition, but offered as a favour. There will always be plenty of applicants for each specialised form of assistance who will value the privilege ; and who (unlike the recipients of Poor Relief) can therefore be kept up to the mark

---

[1] It is curious to recall that a suggestion of this sort was made in an early pamphlet by the Fabian Society—*The Government Organisation of Unemployed Labour*, 1884—which promptly went out of print. The corps would be most useful for works of which the Government found the entire cost.

by the fear of dismissal. The ingenious may visualise a whole series of kinds of training, and of opportunities of preparation for reinstatement in industrial employment, which might—quite irrespective of whether or not any or all of them are " less eligible " than the worst kind of employment—be offered in succession, to selected men for whom the treatment first chosen had proved unsuited or unsuccessful.[1] Patience and repeated experiments will be as necessary in the treatment of the men suffering from Unemployment as in that of the men suffering from disabling rheumatism. Nor need it be assumed that there will be no room in the treatment for the " Principle of Less Eligibility ". After successive offers of various forms of training and other opportunities, a man found habitually work-shy may have to be offered, merely as a condition of maintenance, a lasting engagement in severe manual toil, or in routine work of any kind suited to his physical capacity. If he throws that up, or refuses to work, he will have to be finally discharged. And if he is thenceforth found committing any offence against the criminal law or the Vagrancy Acts (including that of allowing his wife and dependants to become chargeable to public funds), he may have to be prosecuted, and on conviction committed to a Detention Colony.

With regard to another section of the Unemployed, the fifty or sixty thousand men " on the roads ", of whom a shifting sample numbering some ten or fifteen thousand is to be found, on any one night, in the three or four hundred Casual Wards, the need for a National Authority has long been recognised.[2] It is

---

[1] Such an organisation for the provision of training for unemployed workmen in times of " bad trade " does not involve the permanent maintenance of anything beyond a nucleus staff. When hundreds of thousands of workmen are discharged from their employment, there are also numbers of foremen, assistant managers and skilled craftsmen rendered idle, and premises temporarily available, from empty factories to derelict skating rinks, of which the use, during the period of depression, could be obtained without onerous commitments, possibly by arrangement with big employers or their associations. What would be required at all times would be a few fully staffed Training Establishments, with a small group of researchers working out schemes for expansion, by means of temporarily engaged superintendents and trainers, when the next period of industrial contraction occurred.

[2] Such an Authority was, we believe, in the minds of the highly expert Departmental Committee on Vagrancy in 1906, when they recommended that the Casual Wards should be transferred to the Metropolitan and provincial police forces, who would, it was suggested, follow the instructions of the Home Secretary, and thus maintain that uniformity of treatment which the Local Government Board had failed to secure from the Boards of Guardians.

impossible to persuade any Local Authority that the maintenance of the wandering Vagrants is a legitimate charge on the local rates ; or to ensure, from many scores of separate Authorities, the adoption of that uniform standard of accommodation and treatment which is desirable to prevent the flocking of Vagrants to the Casual Wards in which they are made most comfortable. Still more hopeless is it to expect, from any number of separate Authorities, any common action in the establishment of anything better than the reluctant provision of gratuitous bed and board for this wandering host. Only a National Authority could arrange for a systematic sorting-out of the different classes of which the constantly changing army is composed—the youths just taking to the road ; the men who have been refused Outdoor Relief ; the contractor's navvies tramping from job to job, and the seafaring folk from port to port ; the other genuine seekers for work for which they are daily becoming less fit ; and, finally, the habitual Vagrants, enured to a life of parasitism, for each of which classes some more appropriate treatment might at least be attempted.

There remain to be considered the wives and children of the different sections of wageless workmen for whom provision has to be made. Throughout the nineteenth century any attempt to divest the able-bodied applicant for Poor Relief of the responsibility for personally maintaining his dependants was regarded as sacrilegious. But the Merthyr Tydfil Judgment, which we discussed on pp. 836-845 of the preceding chapter, has removed this difficulty. The Court of Appeal definitely decided that, even when Poor Law Relief could not lawfully be granted to the husband and father, the wife and children with whom he was residing must nevertheless be given Poor Relief. *They are, in fact, in such a case, now treated as if the breadwinner were simply absent.* Under the new arrangements introduced by the Local Government Act it will be both easy and harmless for the Local Health Authority and the Local Education Authority to make the necessary provision, under " the appropriate Acts ", without the stigma or the legal status of pauperism, just as if the men were temporarily absent, for the wives and children of the Unemployed men who have come upon the hands of the National Authority.[1]

---

[1] Already, upon the principle of the Merthyr Tydfil Judgment, over large areas of England and Wales, the Boards of Guardians, with the consent (if not

We claim no expert knowledge for these suggestions of how to prevent Unemployment and how to treat the Unemployed for whom provision has to be made. Here as elsewhere the world will discover the appropriate remedy only by actually attempting to do the job—in short, by the well-worn method of Trial and Error.

The Development of the Ministry of Labour

We are not ourselves sanguine enough to believe that any Cabinet, within the next few years, is likely to adopt, in its entirety, and by one Act of Parliament, any logical and comprehensive scheme of dealing with Unemployment and the Unemployed, though it is just such a scheme that is being asked for, latterly, not only by the Liberal as well as the Labour Party, but also by a considerable proportion of the Boards of Guardians. To the financial advisers of the Government the assumption of responsibility for Unemployment and the Unemployed seems to involve a new financial burden from which the Treasury would never be relieved. What guarantee, it is asked, can be given that all the men whom the Government takes into training will ever find wage-earning employment ? But—although this is not usually a Treasury point of view—it is the burden *on the community* that has to be considered, not that on any particular organ of Government. The obvious answer to the Treasury objection is, that this burden will be, at any rate, neither increased nor perpetuated by the adoption of a method of relief which saves the Unemployed from the deterioration of idleness—a deterioration which, the longer it lasts, renders them ever less likely again to become self-supporting citizens. In fact, whilst the expediency of such an assumption of responsibility by the National Government is being debated, the whole position is being transformed as

---

actually on the suggestion) of the Inspectors of the Ministry of Health, are giving Outdoor Relief for the wives and children of able-bodied men, who (though residing with their families) are themselves regarded as ineligible for relief. Another precedent is afforded by what is known as the Modified Workhouse Test, under which, if the husband and father consents to enter the Workhouse, his wife and children are granted Outdoor Relief.

It may be added that the Board of Guardians of the great Union of West Derby (Liverpool, Bootle, etc.) has, for years, dealt with the applicants for " Unemployment Relief " entirely separately from " the ordinary poor "; providing distinct local offices, with separate staffs, and applying different policies, without objection from the Minister of Health.

the result of a stream of tendencies which no Government has been able to withstand.

Less than forty years ago Gladstone, it has been asserted, expressed the view that for the House of Commons and the Cabinet even to concern themselves about Unemployment and the Unemployed was a constitutional impropriety. Twenty-five years ago the National Government, whilst deigning to gather information about wages and hours of labour, Trade Unions and industrial disputes, still admitted no sort of responsibility for the condition of the wageless workmen, however numerous they might be. Yet for the last eight years the Minister of Labour has con- tinuously paid out, as part of the normal work of his office, the weekly subsistence of over a million workmen, together with their families.[1] Five years ago the Minister of Labour still admitted no responsibility for preserving the wageless workmen in habits of industry, or for fitting them for other employment—none even for saving the younger men among them from the demoralisation of idleness. To-day he is directing and maintaining dozens of Training Establishments of different types, and organising, in conjunction with the Local Education Authorities, scores of Juvenile Employment Centres. Only two years ago the Govern- ment shrank from the responsibility of taking steps to promote any removal of workmen from one part of England to another. To-day the Industrial Transference Board has virtually imposed on the Minister of Labour the task on which the whole available strength of his Department is actively engaged, namely, that of stimulating, organising, directing and financially assisting, at the public expense, the migration of the Unemployed from the distressed districts to areas in which their re-establishment in productive industry seems more practicable. And just as the Industrial Transference Board persuaded the Cabinet that the

---

[1] By way of contrast with this million of unemployed men maintained by the Ministry of Labour (out of the State Insurance Fund, and its borrowings from the Treasury), it may be observed that, in the week ending June 16, 1928, the Poor Law Guardians found, in all England and Wales, only 84,159 men and women to maintain, as Unemployed, on Outdoor Relief—thus indicating that the Ministry of Labour is already performing eleven-twelfths of the whole task. So nearly complete is the range of the provision of the Ministry of Labour that out of 625 Poor Law Unions, no fewer than 230 reported that they had no persons in receipt of relief under the Poor Law on account of Unemployment, whilst 183 more Unions had each fewer than ten. No less than 64,133 un- employed persons out of the total of 84,159 (or over 76 per cent) were relieved in 38 Unions only (*Labour Gazette*, p. 394, November 1928).

severe restriction of many of our export trades was not merely a transient depression, but must be expected to continue, so the economists may be able, one day, to convince the public, if not the Government, that there can never come a time in any industrialised community when there will be no Unemployed requiring the nation's care. It may well be that this or that additional Training Centre, which the Minister of Labour is now (1929) opening every few weeks, will in the course of years be discontinued or reduced ; but it may confidently be predicted that he will henceforth always be supplying training to a greater or smaller number of the Unemployed host. More and more the County and County Borough Councils will find themselves, as regards the Unemployed, working in co-operation with the Ministry of Labour, instead of with the Ministry of Health ; more and more will they be referring to the Government Training Establishments, or perhaps to the Government Labour Corps, the unemployed men for whom such provision is made on a national basis ; and confining their own Public Assistance, no longer under the Poor Law but under "the appropriate Acts", to the mothers and children, the sick and the mentally disordered, the aged and the infirm—for whom alone, it has been contended, and not for the able-bodied Unemployed, the Elizabethan statesmen meant gratuitous maintenance to be provided by the Local Poor Law Authority.

What will remain under the Poor Law

In the second and third chapters of this volume we found ourselves compelled by the facts to diverge from a chronicle of Poor Law administration in order to set forth the slow beginnings and rapid acceleration of a supersession of the Boards of Guardians by new and specialised Authorities, administering separate statutes. In this way the mere relief of destitution has been progressively replaced by a policy of preventive and curative treatment. At the end of our story we may usefully estimate how far—measured by the amount of expenditure and number of persons dealt with—this process of supersession has already gone.

When, after the Poor Law Amendment Act of 1834, the Boards of Guardians took over the relief of the destitute, this service, which was costing nearly £7,000,000 annually, included the whole of the nation's expenditure from public funds upon its poorer citizens, in all their necessities from birth to burial. It represented not quite ten shillings per head of a population in England and Wales of $14\frac{1}{2}$ millions. To-day the nation's annual expenditure, in the way of " social services ", in England and Wales, amounts to more than £335,000,000 ; or over £8 per head of a population of 39 millions. Taking into account the 30 per cent rise in the price level since 1834, the increase per head of population, in the amount of commodities and services annually supplied, may be put as from thirteen shillings to eight pounds. Thus the nation is contributing, collectively, towards the maintenance of its poorer citizens, in commodities and services, over twelve times as much per head of population as a century ago. But so far has the supersession of the Poor Law by the newer services already gone, that less than one-eighth of the enlarged contribution is given by the Poor Law Authorities, whilst more than seven-eighths comes, without the stigma of pauperism, under other Acts, through other channels. The expenditure of the Poor Law Authorities to-day—say £1 per head of the population—is equivalent to no more than fifteen shillings in the money of 1834, when ten shillings per head was being given in Poor Relief. This has therefore been increased by one-half. On the other hand, the annual expenditure per head of population on the other services has grown from nothing to something like seven pounds, or seven times the amount of the Poor Relief. Moreover, whilst the growth of Public Assistance outside the Poor Law has been continuous for three-quarters of a century, it has, during the past twenty years, shown an extraordinary acceleration. In 1907, when its width of range surprised the Poor Law Commission, the total did not exceed forty million pounds. With the adoption of Old Age Pensions (1908), Health and Unemployment Insurance (1911), the rapid widening in range of Public Education (1908–1918), the Maternity and Child Welfare Service (1918–1928), the National Subsidising of Housing (1920–1928), the great extension of Unemployment Insurance (1920–1927) and National Pensions (1924–1925), the total annual expenditure has, since 1908, expanded fivefold ; or more correctly, allowing for the difference in price level, at least threefold. During the last twenty years the " inevitability " of the increase has been more apparent than its " gradualness " !

With regard to the numbers on whom the Public Assistance was bestowed, in 1834 and 1926–1927 respectively, the contrast is no less striking. Though exact statistics are lacking, there is reason to believe that the number of persons simultaneously relieved under the Poor Law in 1834 was about one million, representing a total relieved, at some time in the course of the year, of, probably, between two and three millions, out of a population in England and Wales of 14½ millions (say 17 per cent). In 1926–1927, when the numbers relieved under the Poor Law, even as swollen by Unemployment, were approximately identical with those of 1834, this represented less than 7 per cent of the population. The numbers benefiting by other forms of Public Assistance in 1926–1927 vary according to the service, from at least 85 per cent of all the families in the case of Education and in that of Health Insurance, 70 per cent in that of Unemployment Insurance and in that of Old Age and Widows Pensions, down to a smaller percentage in the Public Health Hospitals and the County Lunatic Asylums, and in the pensions and allowances to the sufferers in the War. So nearly universal has become the provision of the services outside the Poor Law that there can be scarcely a manual-working wage-earning family in the land, and not a very large proportion of those who would rank themselves in the Lower Middle Class, which does not benefit, some time in the course of each year, either from the Public Education or the Public Health service, either from Unemployment or Health Insurance, either from the Old Age or Widows Pensions, or from those in respect of the War.

The Act of 1929 can hardly fail to bring about a further acceleration of the supersession, not merely of the Boards of Guardians, but also of the Poor Law itself. It has, indeed, been estimated that a complete adoption of the principle of union of services, which is embodied in Clause 5, would straightaway relieve the Public Assistance Committees of an expenditure of some ten million pounds a year, thereby lessening by one-fourth the present volume of Poor Relief. The promised measure of Lunacy Law reform will presently take out of the Poor Law the whole treatment of lunacy and mental deficiency. The next amendment of the Pensions Acts may probably transfer from Poor Relief a considerable proportion of the aged and infirm, together with the widows or orphans, now receiving Outdoor

Relief merely by reason of these pensions having been, on one or other technicality, withheld. The continually increasing operations of the Minister of Labour, in opening one additional Training Establishment after another, will take away from the Public Assistance Committees more and more of the able-bodied men now getting " Unemployment Relief ". It may be asked, if all these tendencies continue, will there eventually be anything left of the Poor Law ?

The answer is that there ought still to remain the right to relief accorded by the Elizabethan statutes to every destitute person,[1] in whatever category he may be placed. Moreover, there must always be retained, as experience indicates, the service of granting relief in kind, in the form of doles of food, in cases of " sudden or urgent necessity ". These doles are at present given, on their own responsibility, by the couple of thousand Relieving Officers, who are stationed at suitable intervals throughout the whole country, and who are held responsible for any deaths from starvation which, but for neglect on their part, might have been prevented. We suggest that this service by the Relieving Officers, who will continue to act under the Public Assistance Committee—possibly forming part of the staff of the Registrar of Public Assistance—will constitute the last remnant of the Poor Law administration. With this might be combined, in the district of each Relieving Officer, a small Receiving House—possibly merely the use of one or two rooms at the local Police Station—for the strictly temporary accommodation for the night and " First Aid " treatment of any applicants for assistance who cannot instantly be conveyed to

---

[1] Those who have denied that there is any such right, because no destitute person can sue for the relief that is due to him, may be reminded that the Courts have more than once held that a mandamus may be granted to enforce the performance of the duty of granting relief. In 1864, the Lord Chief Justice is reported as saying, in a case in which Poor Relief had been refused, that " No doubt there ought to be some remedy if a poor person is refused relief ; and an indictment, although a means of punishment, is hardly a remedy. An indictment will not give relief to a destitute person. The remedy by mandamus may be a long way off, but if there is no better it must be resorted to. We cannot say that the Guardians are arbitrarily to refuse relief to a destitute person without just cause, and we must see what that reason may be." (*Ex parte* the Guardians of the Newton and Llanidloes Union, in the *Times* newspaper, November 9, 1804, on an application for mandamus to the Guardians to give relief to an aged woman.) Rule nisi granted—result not stated : see *The General Order . . . relating to the Poor Law*, by W. C. Glen, 11th edition, 1898, p. 217.

the nearest premises of the Local Health, Education, or Lunacy Authority, or admitted to a Training Establishment of the Ministry of Labour.

The passing away of the Boards of Guardians, established nearly a century ago to carry out the " Principles of 1834 ", means more than a reform of Local Government by securing larger areas of administration and better co-ordination of existing services. We hope and believe that it registers at once a change of heart and an advance in knowledge in respect of the problem of persistent poverty in the midst of riches.

The " Principles of 1834 " plainly embodied the doctrine of *laissez-faire*. They assumed the non-responsibility of the community for anything beyond keeping the destitute applicant alive. They relied, for inducing the individual to support himself independently, on the pressure resulting from his being, in the competitive struggle, simply " let alone ". As the only alternative to self-support, there was to be presented to him, uniformly throughout the country, the undeviating regimen of the " well-regulated " Workhouse, with conditions " less eligible " than those of the lowest grade of independent labourer. Behind it all lay the pessimistic conviction that the poverty of the masses was part of the " natural " order of society.

The principles inspiring the Framework of Prevention, which the community has, for three-quarters of a century, been empirically erecting, involve the conception of a mutual obligation between the individual and the community. The universal maintenance of a definite minimum of civilised life—seen to be in the interest of the community no less than in that of the individual—becomes the joint responsibility of an indissoluble partnership. The community recognises a duty in the curative treatment of all who are in need of it ; a duty most clearly seen in the medical treatment of the sick and the education of the children. Once this corporate responsibility is accepted, it becomes a question whether the universal provision of any indispensable common service is not the most advantageous method of making the necessary provision—a method which, unlike any form of relieving the destitute, has, so the classic economists would have argued, the advantage of leaving unimpaired the salutary inequality between the thrifty and the unthrifty. But even in so far as provision is made for all citizens, the indissoluble partnership involves new and enlarged obligations on the individual, unknown in a state of *laissez-faire*, such as the obligation of the parent to keep his children in health, and to send them to school at the time and in the condition insisted upon ; the obligation of the young person to be well-conducted and to learn ; the obligation of the sick to co-operate in their own cure, not to infect their environment, and to submit when required to hospital treatment ; the obligation upon the unemployed workman seeking assistance to respond to the efforts of the Employment Exchange to find him a situation, and when none can be found, to devote himself to the instructional courses provided for him in a Training Establishment. To enforce these obligations— all new since 1834—upon the individual citizen, experience shows that some other pressure on his volition is required than that which results from merely leaving him alone. Hence the community, by the combination of the principles of Curative Treatment, Universal Provision and Fulfilment of Obligations, deliberately " weights " the alternatives, in the guise of a series of experiments upon volition. The individual retains as much freedom of choice as—if not more than—he ever enjoyed before. But the father finds it made more easy for him to get his children educated, and made more disagreeable for him to neglect them. It is made more easy for the mother to keep her infants in health, and more disagreeable for her to let them die. The man suffering from disease finds it made more easy for him to get cured without infecting his neighbours or lowering the general Standard of Life, and made more disagreeable for him not to take all the means of getting back to health. The Employment Exchange and the Training Centres aim at making it more easy for the wageless man to keep fit for employment and to obtain a new situation ; perhaps the reformatory establishment, with powers of detention, is needed to make it more disagreeable for him not to accept and retain that situation when one is found for him. It must be recognised that the ideas inspiring the conception of the Framework of Prevention, to which experience has gradually brought the community in 1929, " hang together ", in theory and practice, no less than did those of 1834.

There is, perhaps, an even wider implication for all the nations of advanced industrial civilisation, to whom the problem of persistent poverty in the midst of riches is common. It may be that the overriding danger of twentieth-century civilisation is the possibility—some would say the probability—of its own self-destruction by war; either a war between nations to alter boundaries or extend trade, or a war between classes within each nation between the "haves" and the "have nots". There looms, indeed, a third kind of war combining the evils of a perverted nationalism with class fanaticism. There are some who discern signs of a recrudescence of Creed Wars, with the difference that the creeds will not be theological and concerned with the next world, but economic or political, insisting on a particular organisation of society; and that the issue will be between nations which practise (or think they practise) equality and those preferring an unequal distribution of riches and personal power. Now the prevention of war between nations is one problem and the prevention of war between social classes is another, though both can be solved only by knowledge and goodwill. Yet the two are not so entirely distinct from each other as might, at first sight, be supposed, for the Creed War of the twentieth century, whether within a nation or between nations, would have, as its exciting cause, the miseries of the poor and the discontent of the "common people". It was no accident that the Dictatorship of the Proletariat, with its imposition of a communistic regimen, has arisen, not, as had been prophesied by Karl Marx, in the most industrialised community, having a comparatively high standard of life for the whole people, but in an almost unorganised and unregulated country, where the mass of the people lived in a state of subjection and subserviency, the victims of every form of destitution. On the other hand, those nations which have equipped themselves, even imperfectly, with a Framework of Prevention against illiteracy, disease and bad conditions of employment have been generally free from revolutionary violence. A "stake in the country" may be given to all men in other ways than by property ownership. The continuance of peaceful evolution depends on an ever-increasing consciousness of security and of advancing opportunity among the great body of the people : security against deprivation of livelihood; security against avoidable accident and preventible disease; security against unmerited destitution in old age or widowhood, together with an equitable share in the opportunities for education, leisure and recreation which the increasing productivity makes possible for all, and which alone give either free choice of occupation or scope for personal advancement. Nor has this policy of the Framework of Prevention and the establishment of a National Minimum of Civilised Life anything to do with the controversy between Individualism and Socialism, or with the concept of Universal Equality. It concerns only the foundation of the social order, compatible with any form of superstructure. It may well be that, without such a foundation, no superstructure, whether Capitalist, Socialist or Communist, can long survive. One thing, however, is clear. Without such a foundation Political Democracy has no future. In short, we are confronted no longer with an appeal to our good nature to relieve destitution, an appeal which we are free to refuse if our hearts are hard enough; but with a stern demonstration that whether we like it or not we must Abolish Mass Destitution or perish as a civilised society. The idols of 1834 have fallen because their clay feet were in the gutter : the ideals of the future must stand on the rock of a general well-being, a deliberately prescribed and effectively enforced National Minimum of Civilised Life.

Finally, as elsewhere, the researcher and experimenter will have to remember that the worst of the evils which he is seeking to overcome is not the material privation or physical suffering that destitution connotes, but the moral degradation with which it is, in the mass, always accompanied. Is there any condition more sordidly tragic than the lot of the youthful Unemployed, to-day counted by the hundred thousand—under-nourished, physically undeveloped, empty-minded, lounging in disconsolate groups at street corners, or aimlessly tramping from one Casual Ward to another—a prey to all evil influences ? Is it seriously contended that by this public neglect the nation is adequately preparing these youths to fulfil their obligations as parents, citizens or producers ? And just as it is the horror of this moral degradation that inspires the work and steels the will of the reformer, so in his selection of means and choice of ends he must incessantly be weighing, not merely the material results to be expected, but also the inevitable psychological reactions in human motive and personal character. It is, indeed, after all, the " Moral Factor " in the problem, whether manifested in the fuller development of individual faculty, the finer tone of family life, or the widening grasp of public spirit, that is and must remain the dominant consideration of every attempt at Social Reconstruction. But noble purpose will not alone suffice. In the latest of the sciences to be developed, that which deals with the art of living in communities, what is required is not only a perpetual widening of the social purpose of the people as a whole, but also a larger and larger measure of foresight, invention and technical efficiency in the specialised groups of brain-workers on whom, for the most part, the execution of this social purpose will necessarily devolve. And it is in the closer communion for the future of these two great forces—the public-spirited citizen exercising his influence and manifesting his will in public opinion, and the specialised investigator and expert administrator supplying the organised knowledge and executing the social purpose—that progress in the Prevention of Destitution, as in all other branches of Social Reform, will, in the main, depend.

APPENDICES

I

A. *The Irish Poor Law*

WE cannot write the history of either the Irish or the Scottish Poor Law, but the former was so closely associated with the English Poor Law Commissioners, and, moreover, gave Sir George Nicholls such a chance of developing his full Poor Law policy, that it requires a brief notice. Ireland had, down to 1838, no public relief of the destitute ; and there was much controversy as to whether or not a Poor Law should be enacted. From 1815 to 1830 the dominant opinion in England was, as we have seen,[1] adverse to any Poor Law ; and Sir James Mackintosh went so far as to declare in the House of Commons in 1825, " that the Poor Law was the only curse which had not been introduced into Ireland, and he trusted that the House would not consent to inflict it upon that country, after the experience it had had of their lamentable consequences in England " (Hansard, March 22, 1825). Nassau Senior himself, as we have mentioned, argued with great force in 1831 against the provision of any system of Poor Relief for Ireland (*Letter to Lord Howick*, etc., 1831). But throughout Ireland there was desperate poverty, with a plague of mendicancy which taxed especially the generosity of the poor peasantry ; and—perhaps the most cogent argument of all—the destitute Irish persisted in swarming across the narrow sea to depress the wages of the English labourers, to demand Poor Relief from the Overseers of the English parishes, and to put the English Counties to heavy costs for their repatriation as vagrants. The steady drain of population from Ireland to England, which Alexander von Humboldt ingeniously computed from the Censuses of 1801–1831 at one million in thirty years, is worth a monograph. (See, besides the Censuses of 1801, 1811, 1821 and 1831, the reports and evidence of the Parliamentary Committees of 1817 and 1818 (Poor Laws) ;

---

[1] Pp. 7-25.

1821 and 1828 (Vagrants) ; 1824 (Labourers' Wages) ; 1825 (Irish Disturbances) ; 1826–1827 (Emigration) ; 1831 (Sabbath Observance) ; 1833 (Agriculture) ; the Royal Commission of 1832–1834 (Poor Law) ; 1834 (Handloom Weaving) ; and Report on the Sanitary Condition of the Labouring Population, by Edwin Chadwick, 1842 ; *A Consideration of the State of Ireland in the Nineteenth Century*, by G. Locker-Lampson, 1907 ; *Economic History of Ireland in the Eighteenth Century*, by G. O'Brien, 1915 ; *London Life in the Eighteenth Century*, by M. D. George, 1925 ; *Rise of the Irish Linen Industry*, by C. Gill, 1925 ; the excellent brief summary in *An Economic History of Modern Britain*, by J. H. Clapham, 1926, pp. 56-63 ; and *Labour Migration in England*, 1800–1850, by Arthur Redford, 1926, especially chap. vii., " The Irish Influx ", pp. 114-129.)

When, in 1830, Lord Grey's Cabinet was thinking of an Irish Coercion Bill, the Lord-Lieutenant (Anglesey) recommended that the boon of a Poor Law should be conceded before coercion was applied ; but in face of the strong opposition of the English theorists this advice was not taken. In 1832, however, when the English Poor Law Inquiry Commission had been appointed, M. T. Sadler (see his *Ireland, its Evils and their Remedies*, 1830, and his biography) and other philanthropists pressed for something to be done for the relief of the Irish poor ; and on September 25, 1833, an Irish Poor Law Commission, with Archbishop Whately as Chairman, was appointed to consider the whole question. This Commission, which worked for nearly three years, began by sending out Assistant Commissioners in couples, an Englishman with an Irishman, to bring back, not as the English Commission had directed, a general view of defects and shortcomings, but an accurate picture of one parish in each of seventeen counties. Its first Report (July 1835) included this survey, and a declaration by the Commissioners, which was in marked contrast with the views of the English Poor Law Inquiry Commissioners. The Irish Commissioners remarked that, " We consider it our duty to endeavour, if possible, to *investigate the causes of the destitution that we discover* ". In the second Report (January 1836) the various charitable and other institutions were described ; and it became known that the opinion of the Commission differed from that expounded in the English Report of 1834. George Nicholls, who was by this time well in his stride as a member of the English Poor Law Commission (which had, up to that date, been markedly successful), thereupon propounded, in a memorandum submitted to Lord John Russell (in January 1836), his own panacea for Irish poverty, which was the establishment of Workhouses on the English model, a free " Offer of the House ", and the absolute prohibition of Outdoor Relief. The Irish Commission, in its third and final Report (1836), argued strongly against Nicholls and the

English Workhouse system, and almost as strongly against making Poor Relief conditional on a mere " Labour Test ". By a large majority the Commission rejected any comprehensive system of relief out of a Poor Rate. Like the Elizabethan legislators, the Commission drew a fundamental distinction between the case of the able-bodied men unable to find wage-earning employment and the various classes of the impotent poor. For the able-bodied men it recommended the establishment of a double national authority (the " Board of Improvement " and the " Board of Works "), which should organise a continuous series of national improvements, many of which were suggested, on which unemployed men could be, without the implication of pauperism, found employment at wages, though at rates below those current in capitalist employment. There was also to be systematic emigration at the public expense for families willing to go to America. For men convicted of vagrancy, stern measures were proposed, including national penitentiaries and compulsory deportation to a new country. Public assistance of the impotent poor was to be put into a different category, and placed under the direction and control of a national Board of Poor Law Commissioners and local Boards of Guardians elected for large districts. It was realised that there would have to be additional institutions, in supplement of those already provided by law and by voluntary charity, for the mentally disordered, for the chronically afflicted, for the sick and for the helpless aged and orphans ; and probably also the provision of necessaries for sick persons in their homes, and other domiciliary assistance. But the Commission recorded its inability to come to any agreement as to whether (as the majority insisted) this provision for the various sections of the impotent poor should be as heretofore entrusted, without any public organisation of Poor Relief out of the rates, to voluntary associations and the alms of the charitable, but helped by grants from both national and local funds ; or whether, as three Commissioners out of eleven urged, the local Boards of Guardians, under the supervision and control of the national Poor Law Commissioners, should, as in England, undertake the task as a whole, supplementing the work of the voluntary organisations by providing under public management whatever else was required, entirely out of the Poor Rate—in short, a general Poor Law, but for the impotent only, parallel with the distinct and exclusively national organisation for the able-bodied men, in which all the Commissioners concurred.

So inconclusive a report, with the Chairman and a large majority violently against any general Poor Relief out of public funds, even for the impotent ; and all the Commissioners in favour of a distinct national authority for the unemployed able-bodied, administering a large scheme of Government intervention in the Labour Market, placed the Whig Ministry in a difficulty. There seemed more to be said, in the English atmosphere of *laissez-faire*, and in the then temper of the House of Commons, for George Nicholls' proposal of an Irish Poor Law on the English model, with the added improvement of a prompt and absolutely universal enforcement of " the Workhouse System ". This appeared all the more plausible as Cornewall Lewis, who had been serving as an Assistant Commissioner to Whately's Commission, put in his own Memorandum to the Government, in which he expressed his disagreement with both sets of the Commission's recommendations, declared his belief in the need for a general Irish Poor Law, and supported the proposals already made by Nicholls. The latter was thereupon despatched to Ireland in September 1836 on a mission of inquiry. He conferred in Dublin with Archbishop Whately, who caustically wrote to Nassau Senior that he had seen the emissary of the Whig Cabinet " who is gone on a tour through Ireland to form the conclusion that Workhouses on a similar plan to those of England will be a safe and effectual remedy for the distresses of Ireland. I do not say that he is not right in this ; I only foretell that he will come back with that conclusion, because he took it out with him, and is not likely to lose it on the way " (Whately to Nassau Senior, October 2, 1836, in *Life of Archbishop Whately*, by E. J. Whately, 1861, vol. i. p. 361). Nicholls raced in two months from one end of Ireland to the other ; and handed his report to the Government on November 15, 1836. He had the satisfaction of seeing it adopted as a whole by the Cabinet, after no more than four weeks' consideration. The Bill was brought in at the opening of the very next session ; and so convincing had been the propaganda, and so successful the first two years' work of the Poor Law Commissioners, that the second reading of the Irish Poor Law Bill was carried without a division. The Bill was, however, lost on the premature prorogation caused by the King's death. Meanwhile the pamphlet controversy grew fast and furious, mostly against the plans of Nicholls and Cornewall Lewis, but evenly divided for and against any general Poor Rate. We can here cite only a few of the mass of pamphlets still extant, namely (in favour of a Poor Law) *Local Disturbances in Ireland*, by Sir G. C. Lewis, 1836 ; and *Evils of the State of Ireland,* by the secretary to the Irish Commission, John Revans, 1837 ; and (against anything like the English Poor Law) *Analysis of the Projects proposed for the Relief of the Poor in Ireland*, by John Pitt Kennedy, 1837 ; *Observations on the State of Ireland*, 1837, and *Observations on the Report of George Nicholls*, etc., 1838, both by Sir F. M. Macnaghten.

In preparation for the reintroduction of the Bill in the ensuing session, Nicholls again rushed through Ireland—this time inside of six weeks—in order to fortify his case, and improve the important measure which, against a great weight of Irish opinion, he was foisting on the nation. In the spring of 1838 the Bill went easily through the House of Commons, but this time in the teeth of strenuous opposition from Daniel O'Connell; and after some modifications in the House of Lords it became law in July 1838 (1 and 2 Vic. c. 56).

The execution of the Irish Poor Law was entrusted, not to any Irish Department but to the English Poor Law Commissioners; and this very heavy task fills a great space in their Annual Reports from 1839 to 1847. Their Chairman, Frankland Lewis, disliked the additional work thus cast upon them, and resigned in 1839, when his son, George Cornewall Lewis, who, with Nicholls, must be deemed jointly responsible for the new measure, was appointed a Commissioner in his father's stead. Nicholls was deputed in July 1839 to proceed to Ireland to put the law in operation; and spent there three busy years. Though every step had nominally to be approved, under the Irish as under the English Act, by the Poor Law Commission as a whole, Nicholls seems to have been given a free hand. He threw his undivided energies into the task, thoroughly enjoying the opportunity of putting into operation, without interference, his own thoroughgoing scheme for dealing with destitution. Nor did he lose any time. Engaging an architect (George Wilkinson), who had built some Workhouses in England, he managed, before returning to London in 1842, to get established 130 Boards of Guardians, and to get erected nearly a hundred new Workhouses— a number presently increased to 115—of the most extreme type of General Mixed Workhouse, which Nassau Senior and Chadwick had tried in vain to avoid for England. In Ireland it was in these institutions alone that the destitute, whether sick or well, able-bodied or impotent, young or old, could obtain any kind of Poor Relief. Minor amendments of the law were obtained without difficulty from Parliament in 1839 (2 Vic. c. 1) and 1843 (6 and 7 Vic. c. 92); but for seven years this rigorous refusal of all Outdoor Relief was maintained. What wrecked the scheme was not the discontent of the Irish people, but the failure of the potato crop. The appalling famine that ensued—a crisis, however, which was rather an exceptionally widespread loss of income (equivalent to what we now term Unemployment) than an absolute lack of food in a country that in fact continued all the time to export some kinds of food—compelled the Government, first to provide employment on inadequate and, indeed, futile public works, which provided scanty wages for three-quarters of a million men; then (under the Temporary Relief Act, 1847, 10 and 11 Vic. c. 7) to organise, through appointed local committees, a free distribution of food to the starving people, largely at the expense of the Poor Rate, the numbers thus fed rising to over three millions; and later, in 1847, to pass into law the Irish Poor Law Extension Act (10 and 11 Vic. c. 31), which excited a renewed storm of controversy (see *Remarks on the Irish Poor Relief Bill*, 1847, and others by G. Poulett Scrope ; *Observations on the Poor Relief Bill for Ireland*, by T. St. Leger Alcock, 1847). This measure, against which Archbishop Whately vainly protested in the House of Lords (Hansard, March 26, 1847), allowed Outdoor Relief, of which there were, within three months, no fewer than 800,000 recipients, a number which had, by the end of 1850, gradually sunk to no more than 2000 (*Edinburgh Review*, vol. xciii. p. 246 ; *Life of Archbishop Whately*, by E. J. Whately, 1866, vol. ii. p. 118). In July 1847 an Act (10 and 11 Vic. c. 90) relieved the English Poor Law Commissioners of their responsibility for the Irish Poor Law, an independent body of " Commissioners for Administering the Law for Relief of the Poor in Ireland " being established, whose proceedings do not concern the subject of this book (see, for the whole episode, *The Irish Crisis*, by Sir Charles Trevelyan, 1848 ; *Cambridge Modern History*, vol. x. ; *History of the Irish Poor Law*, by Sir George Nicholls, 1856).

B. *The Scottish Poor Law*

The connection between the English and the Scottish Poor Laws offers an interest different from that between the English and the Irish. The northern kingdom has had a public organisation for the relief of the Poor as long as England itself. Arising from a like Framework of Repression and entangled in like penal statutes against vagrancy, the early measures of the Scottish Parliament for the relief of the impotent poor are nearly contemporary with the Elizabethan legislation, to which they bear a general resemblance. But there were three outstanding differences. Instead of placing the responsibility for the administration of Poor Relief on the civil organisation of the Parish, under the supervision of the Justices of the Peace, the Scottish law threw it upon the Kirk-Session (the Minister and his Elders), under supervision by the Local Presbytery (one Minister and one Elder from each Kirk-Session). Instead of charging the cost of relief primarily and directly upon a compulsory Poor Rate, the Scottish Law contemplated reliance primarily on voluntary collections in church, together with such parochial endowments as might be available ; and only exceptionally, where such resources proved insufficient, having recourse to a compulsory rate (which in rural parishes was, by custom, levied usually half on owners (the heritors) and half on occupiers). And instead of definitely prescribing the relief (at least by " setting to work ") of the able-bodied, the Scottish statutes left this so vague that the Courts, in 1866, finally held that no Poor Relief whatever, whether by way of residence in a Poorhouse or in the form of Outdoor Relief (domiciliary aliment), could legally be given in Scotland to any able-bodied man or woman, however genuinely and completely destitute.[1]

What first interested English opinion in the Scottish Poor Law was its outstanding preference for voluntary contributions over a compulsory Poor Rate. Not for more than a century after 1579 did even one Scottish parish have recourse to a rate for the poor ; down to 1700 only three parishes had ever done so ; by 1800 the number had risen to 96, by 1817 to 145, and by 1839 to 236, out of a total of nearly a thousand. Dr. Chalmers, as we have seen, carried on a veritable crusade against a " Poor Law "—that is to say, against the establishment, in Scotland as in England, of a public fund, administered by a public body, out of a compulsory rate, from which Outdoor Relief could be given by public officers. He emphasised the superiority, on all counts, of a visitation of the poor by volunteers associated with each church, and the dispensation by these almoners of monies voluntarily contributed for the purpose. The Report on the Poor Laws which the General Assembly of the Church of Scotland supplied to the House of Commons Committee in 1817, together with the continued pleading of Dr. Chalmers (*On the Christian and Civic Economy of Large Towns*, by Rev. Thomas Chalmers, 1823–1826), had a considerable effect on English public opinion ; and may have contributed to the judgment adverse to any Poor Law which Nassau Senior so trenchantly expressed in his *Letter to Lord Howick* of 1831.

Nevertheless the English held, in 1834, to a compulsory Poor Rate, and imposed it on Ireland in 1838 ; whilst Scotland itself, in spite of Dr. Chalmers, accepted the necessity for the same financial device in 1844, just when the troublesome experiences of the English Poor Law Commissioners were seriously exercising the House of Commons. Yet the Scottish system had produced, in 1837, only 80,000 paupers, as compared with more than a million in England and Wales. These Scottish paupers were costing only £155,000 a year, as compared with the English expenditure of four and a half millions. Why was the Scottish financial system abandoned ?

The answer is that it gradually became apparent, not only that the voluntary contributions were, in the populous urban parishes, hopelessly inadequate to the greatly swollen needs, but also that the reluctance of both owners and occupiers to impose upon themselves a new tax was often resulting, in town and country alike, in

[1] Isdale and Jack, 4 M House of Lords, p. 1.

For the extent to which the decision is evaded or disregarded in practice with regard to men see Majority Report of Poor Law Commission, 1909, Part III. chap. 6, pp. 78-83, also Part V. p. 167 ; *Practice of the Scottish Poor Law,* by George A. Mackay, 1907, p. 50. It is also the practice not to regard as able-bodied a woman burdened by young children.

a practical abrogation of the Poor Law itself. Whilst in many rural and scantily peopled parishes, where the landlords were willing to subscribe, and where there was a resident gentry to co-operate, the few deserving poor were perhaps adequately provided for, in the cities where the Irish swarmed, and even in those rural parishes in which the absentee proprietors gave only nominal sums, a large proportion of the destitution simply went unrelieved. This was found to have calamitous results. " Where destitution is not relieved ", summed up Sir George Nicholls (in his *History of the Scottish Poor Law*, 1856, p. 109), " mendicancy must abound, violences will occur, and life and property be insecure. Where destitution is in some degree but not sufficiently relieved, life and property may be less insecure, but mendicancy must still more or less abound ; and the prevalence of a low standard of habits, manners and mode of life . . . will tend to depress the general character of the population ". In 1840 Dr. W. P. Alison, an Edinburgh physician, emphatically demanded an effective Poor Relief, as the first and most indispensable step against the devastating " fevers " of the slums (*Observations on the Management of the Poor in Scotland and its Effects on the Health of the Great Towns*, 1840 ; and *Remarks on the Poor Laws of Scotland*, 1844, both by William Pulteney Alison). " In England ", observed Sir Archibald Alison of his brother's work, " the influence of this important revelation was immense. Its inhabitants had long suffered under the weight of their own Poor Rates, and heard with astonishment, perhaps envy, of a flourishing realm to the north of the Tweed where such burdens were almost unknown, and a frugal educated peasantry maintained their own poor by voluntary contributions, without either desiring or requiring the support of their superiors. It was no small satisfaction to them, therefore, to find these representations were a mere delusion : that the much-vaunted system was nothing but the old plan of starving the poor, veiled under the pretence of a trifling legal and extensive voluntary contribution ; and that nature, in the selfish community which supported it, was avenging its neglected rights, by the spread of typhus fever and other contagious disorders, originating in suffering, but spreading beyond the woe-stricken to the duty-neglecting class " (*Autobiography of Sir Archibald Alison*, 1883, vol. i. pp. 459-460). The severe distress in the manufacturing districts in 1839–1842, and notably that from which the town of Paisley suffered, brought matters to a head. In January 1843 the Government appointed a Royal Commission of seven members—among them Edward Twistleton, who had served as Assistant Commissioner both in England and in Ireland, and who was destined to become in 1847 the Chief Poor Law Commissioner for the latter country—to inquire what alterations in the Scottish Poor Laws were required.

This Commission, reporting in 1844, found that both the relief, and the funds for relief, were, in many parishes, very inadequate to the need ; that it was necessary to set up new machinery, namely a central Board of Supervision and elected Parochial Boards of Management for parishes in which the poor fund was raised by compulsory rate ; and that a Poorhouse should be provided at least in every parish with as many as 5000 inhabitants. Twistleton dissented from the recommendations as inadequate for effective reform. He argued that the obligation to levy a Poor Rate was not sufficiently explicit, whilst the duty to relieve all classes of the destitute out of public funds was only indistinctly expressed ; and in particular that there was no provision made for large bodies of men who were periodically unemployed in the industrial towns. But the Government decided that the Report went as far as Scottish opinion would stand ; and Parliament passed in 1845 the Scottish Poor Law Amendment Act (8 and 9 Vic. c. 83) based on the Commission's recommendations.

We cannot here pursue the development of legislation and administration which gradually brought all the Scottish parishes to compulsory Poor Rates on a uniform system of assessment ; a common organisation of Inspectors of Poor (of superior status and authority to the English Relieving Officers) ; a universal provision of Poorhouses and Lunatic Asylums in combined districts, with a widespread reliance on Outdoor Relief for the aged and infirm, and the widows with families, and boarding out for the orphans, with a nominal refusal of any relief (but usually in practice admission to the Poorhouse) for the able-bodied men and the unencumbered able-bodied women.[1] But we may note in conclusion two important differences between the English and Scottish system which continue to the present day. In the first place the destitute person (not being able-bodied) has, in Scotland, a legal right to Poor Relief, which (unlike the English applicant) he can enforce by a personal appeal to the judiciary. If the Inspector of Poor refuses relief, he is required to give the applicant " a certificate signed by the Inspector, which shall certify the fact, the grounds, and the date of such refusal ". He must at the same time inform the applicant of his right of appeal. The applicant may, then and there, without fee or formality, appeal to the local Sheriff (a stipendiary magistrate), who may issue a peremptory order to grant relief. The system is not, in practice, found very inconvenient, as the Sheriff, to whom appeals are now infrequent, has no power to determine the kind or the adequacy of the relief ; and the Inspector accordingly usually " Offers the House ". There is, however, a further appeal, which

---

[1] Relief to destitute able-bodied persons out of employment was definitely authorised by the Poor Law Emergency Provisions (Scotland) Act, 1921—a temporary Act which is still in operation (1929). But see pp. 838, 943.

is equally strange to English administration. If the Scottish pauper is dissatisfied with the amount or kind of relief afforded to him, or with his treatment in the Poorhouse, he is entitled to appeal direct to the Scottish Health Department (in succession to the Scottish Local Government Board, itself the successor of the Board of Supervision of the Poor). The Inspector of Poor has, on request, to supply a form of appeal, and even to fill it up for the appellant if desired, adding his own remarks in the space provided. The Health Department, which (unlike the English central Poor Law Authority) is not debarred from intervening in individual cases, goes carefully into every such appeal, makes its own inquiries and gives a decision. It is true that the Board is not legally entitled to compel a Parish Council (which has succeeded the Parochial Board of Management) to give relief, or more relief, or another kind of relief, in opposition to the Council's decision ; but the Board will grant to the appellant a certificate entitling him to carry the case to the Court of Session, which can and will order what is required. A number of such appeals are received, investigated and decided in the course of each year. In practice the issue of the certificate referred to has been a rare occurrence, the ground of complaint being usually removed on the central department intimating that the complaint was well-founded.

It is interesting to trace this important difference from the English Poor Law, in giving to the pauper a legal right of appeal, to the influence of Sir Archibald Alison. In writing, in 1840, on " A Legal Provision for the Poor ", he drew attention to the anomaly of leaving the grant of relief to the discretion of persons representing the ratepayers who had to bear the charge. " In this practical working out of a system of relief for the poor, it is of the very highest importance not to lose sight of the principle that the persons who are to be finally entrusted with the right of determining to what parties relief from the public funds should be extended, and what amount of relief they should receive, should not be the persons who are liable to the assessment, nor under their control ; for if they are so, the universal impatience of mankind at taxation is such that, even for the most necessary purposes, or the discharge of the most solemn duties, they will invariably resist the burden or diminish the relief to a ruinously low pittance ; and by their obstinacy in this particular, render abortive the wisest and most benevolent legislative provisions. When the principle is once understood, which lies at the bottom of all sound legislation on this subject, that the claims of the poor for relief are not of the nature of a petition, to be admitted to the benefits of a voluntary donation, but a legal right, founded upon the claim which the destitute and impotent poor in a complicated state of civilised society everywhere have to a reasonable support from the more opulent and fortunate classes of society who have been enriched or maintained by their labour, it becomes sufficiently evident that the duty of determining between the applicants for this relief, and the persons who are entrusted with its distribution, must not be left to the final adjudication of the parties who are to be burdened with the assessment. To do this is nothing less than to entrust one party to a lawsuit with the exclusive right of judging of his opponent's case, a principle universally repudiated by the laws and practice of all civilised nations. What should we say if it were gravely proposed that all claims upon a railway company, or road trustees, or other public incorporation, were to be finally disposed of by a committee of the holders of the stock or the persons liable to assessment to such bodies ? . . . It may readily be conceived, therefore, what reluctance such bodies of men must always feel in augmenting a poor's rate : and how totally inadequate the orphans, aged and destitute, who applied for such relief, must be to maintain the contest with the wealthy bodies on whom the assessment is to be imposed " (*Principles of Population*, by Sir Archibald Alison, 1840, vol. ii. chap. xii., pp. 228-230).

It need only be mentioned that the Local Government (Scotland) Act of 1929 effected a revolution in the Scottish Poor Law administration parallel with that produced in the English Poor Law by the corresponding Act for England and Wales.

See for the whole subject in addition to the works already cited, the Majority and Minority Reports of the Poor Law Commission, 1909 (Scotland) ; *The Law of Scotland relating to the Poor*, by C. S. M. Dunlop (Edinburgh, 1825) ; *The Law of Scotland regarding the Poor*, by Sir John Dunlop (Edinburgh, 1854) ; *The Scottish Poor Laws*, by R. P. Lamont (second Scottish edition, Glasgow, 1892) ; *Pauperism in Scotland—an Inquiry into its Management with Suggestions for its Remedy*, by William Hutchison, 1851 ; *Modern Pauperism and the Scottish Poor Laws*, 1871 ; *Poor Relief in Scotland*, by Sir C. S. Loch, 1898 ; *Poor Relief in Scotland . . . from the Middle Ages to the Present Day*, by Alexander A. Cormack, 1923 ; *An Economic History of Modern Britain*, by J. H. Clapham, 1926, pp. 365-370.

II

WE give in the following pages some statistical tables which afford a view of what is known about the volume of Poor Relief in England and Wales at different dates during the past 250 years. "English Poor Law statistics", said Dr. Aschrott in 1888, " surpass those of all other countries both in their scope and in the time over which they extend ".[1] Compared with the Poor Relief statistics of other countries, whether in Europe or America, this encomium may be merited. But from the standpoint of the modern statistician the statistics of English pauperism are, in many respects, unsatisfying ; and even the elaborate new information for which the Poor Law Commission of 1905–1909 felt obliged to ask, and the additional figures subsequently given, leave, as we shall see, many questions unanswered.[2]

[1] *The English Poor Law System*, by P. F. Aschrott and Herbert Preston-Thomas, 1888, p. 281.

[2] For critical accounts of English Poor Relief Statistics, see the able Appendix II. to *The English Poor Law System*, by P. F. Aschrott and Herbert Preston-Thomas, 1888, pp. 279-304 ; *London Pauperism among Jews and Christians*, by J. H. Stallard, 1867 ; and the address by Sir Robert Giffen in *Poor Law Conferences, 1899–1900*, pp. 458-464.

It may be found convenient to bring together the official sources of statistics of Poor Relief for England and Wales. Those for 1748–1750 and 1776 are in the Second Report of H. of C. Committee on Poor Laws, 1777, and in the Supplementary Report of H. of C. Committee of 1818 ; for 1782–1785, in the Report of H. of C. Committee on Certain Returns relative to the State of the Poor, 1787 ; those for 1802–1803, in the Abstract of Returns relative to the Poor, H.C. 175 of 1804 ; those for 1812–1815, ditto, H.C. 82 of 1818 ; those for 1815–1821, in the Report from H. of C. Committee on Poor Rate Returns, H.C. 556 of 1822 ; those for 1821–1829 in Report from Select Committee on Poor Rate Returns, H.C. 334 of 1825 ; those for 1829–1834 in Poor Rate Returns, H.C. 444 of 1835 ; those for 1834–1836 in Second Annual Report of Poor Law Commissioners ; those for the succeeding years in the successive annual reports of the Poor Law Commissioners (to 1849), of the Poor Law Board (to 1871), of the Local Government Board (to 1919), and thereafter of the Ministry of Health. No official statistics are available for the period before 1748, for 1751–1775, for 1777–1782, for 1786–1802, or for 1804–1812 ; and those prior to 1849 are not comparable with those after that date.

The statistics prior to 1849 may be conveniently found in *History of the*

Of Poor Relief in the sixteenth and seventeenth centuries there are, indeed, no statistics, and for that of the first three-quarters of the eighteenth century there are nothing better than estimates of the total expenditure on relief out of the Poor Rate.[1]

ESTIMATED POPULATION AND POOR RATE IN ENGLAND AND WALES AT VARIOUS DATES FROM 1688 TO 1801.[2]

Year.	Estimated Population.	Estimated Aggregate Amount of Poor Rate.	Approximate Amount per Head of Population.
		£	s. d.
1688	5,500,000	700,000	2 6
1701	5,600,000	900,000	3 2
1714	5,750,000	950,000	3 4
1760	7,000,000	1,250,000	3 6
1776	8,000,000	1,529,780	3 10
1784	8,250,000	2,004,238	5 0
1801	9,172,980	3,750,000	8 3

For the first three decades of the nineteenth century there is somewhat better evidence of the total expenditure on the relief and maintenance of the poor, as well as of the extent of the population; but, as will be explained, few trustworthy statistics as to the numbers of paupers.

[TABLE

English Poor Law, by Sir George Nicholls, 1854, vol. ii. pp. 465-467; *The English Poor Law*, by P. F. Aschrott and H. Preston-Thomas, 1888, p. 296; and in the " Notes by Professor Smart on the Growth of Poor Law Expenditure", in vol. xxv. of Appendix to Report of Poor Law Commission, 1909, pp. 724-726. The greatest mass of figures from 1871 to 1908 will be found in the thick volume last named, which contains a valuable prefatory analysis. Summary Tables for the preceding ten or fifteen years are given in the two valuable annuals, the Statistical Abstract for the United Kingdom (72nd year) and the Abstract of Labour Statistics of the United Kingdom (19th year).

[1] The Bill for a census of the whole population, passed by the House of Commons in 1753, but rejected by the House of Lords, would have provided also for an enumeration of persons in receipt of Poor Relief (*The Economic Development of the Empire*, by Dr. Lilian Knowles, 1924; *Health, Wealth and Population in the Early Days of the Industrial Revolution*, by M. C. Buer, 1926, p. 15).

[2] Compiled from various sources (as to which see our work *The Old Poor Law*, 1926). These estimates are, in most cases, supported by little that can be regarded as evidence. Even the Census figures for 1801 were imperfect.

ESTIMATED POPULATION AND AMOUNT SPENT IN POOR RELIEF
IN ENGLAND AND WALES IN 1803 AND FOR 1813 TO 1834.[1]

Year ended Lady Day.	Estimated Population.	Amount Expended on Poor Relief.	Amount per Head of Population.
		£	*s. d.*
1803	9,210,000	4,077,891	8 11
1813	10,506,000	6,656,106	12 8
1814	...	6,294,581	...
1815	...	5,418,846	...
1816	...	5,724,839	...
1817	...	6,910,925	...
1818	11,876,000	7,870,801	13 3
1819	...	7,516,704	...
1820	...	7,330,254	...
1821	11,978,875	6,959,251	11 7
1822	...	6,358,704	...
1823	...	5,772,962	...
1824	12,517,000	5,736,900	9 2
1825	...	5,786,980	...
1826	...	5,928,502	...
1827	...	6,441,088	...
1828	...	6,298,000	...
1829	...	6,332,410	...
1830	...	6,829,042	...
1831	13,297,187	6,798,889	10 0
1832	14,105,000	7,036,969	10 2
1833	...	6,790,800	9 9
1834	14,372,000	6,317,255	9 1

The year of maximum pauperism (persons relieved as a percentage of the total population) throughout the whole four centuries of English Poor Law history was apparently 1818, when no fewer than 1320 out of every 10,000 of the population received Poor Relief. The year of minimum pauperism was apparently just a century later, 1918, when 123 per 10,000 (during September and October only 119) were relieved.

Under the Poor Law Amendment Act of 1834, the Poor Law Commissioners gradually improved the statistics, though with many deficiencies ; and the changes in population and expenditure acquire greater comparative value.

[1] Compiled from various sources, principally the decennial Census, Thirteenth Annual Report of Poor Law Commissioners, 1847 ; and Nicholls' *History of the English Poor Law*, 1854, p. 466.

ESTIMATED POPULATION AND AMOUNT OF POOR RELIEF IN ENGLAND
AND WALES FROM 1835 TO 1847.[1]

Year ended Lady Day.	Estimated Population.	Amount Expended in Poor Relief.	Approximate Amount per Head per Population.	
		£	s.	d.
1835	14,564,000	5,526,418	7	7
1836	14,758,000	4,717,630	6	5
1837	14,955,000	4,044,741	5	5
1838	15,155,000	4,136,604	5	5
1839	15,357,000	4,406,907	5	9
1840	15,562,000	4,576,965	5	11
1841	15,906,741	4,760,929	6	0
1842	15,981,000	4,911,498	6	2
1843	16,194,000	5,208,027	6	5
1844	16,410,000	4,976,093	6	1
1845	16,629,000	5,039,703	6	1
1846	16,851,000	4,962,026	5	11
1847	17,076,000	5,298,787	6	3

Prior to 1849 the aggregate number of persons relieved can be safely estimated only from the expenditure. Such statistics of numbers of persons as were compiled were usually not collected on a uniform basis all over the country, and (especially prior to 1835) they were, in many parishes and Unions, very imperfectly prepared. A considerable though declining population in various kinds of " extra-parochial places " was not in the returns at all, and may have had no public relief. For the most part the returns represented, not the numbers simultaneously in receipt of relief on any one day, but the total numbers of different persons (sometimes, it may be, of different families or households ; in some places possibly of the same persons, families or households repeatedly applying for relief) during a part (usually a quarter) of the year.[2] In 1849, when the statistics had been put on something like the present basis, it was found that an expenditure of six million pounds in the year represented approximately the relief to one million men, women and children simultaneously maintained ; being about £6 per pauper per annum. The average cost per pauper may well have been greater

---

[1] Compiled principally from the Census and the Registrar-General's estimates, the Annual Reports of the Poor Law Commissioners, 1835–1848 ; Poor Law Commission, 1909, Appendix vol. xxv., p. 724; Aschrott's *English Poor Law System*, 1888, p. 296 ; and Nicholl's *History of the English Poor Law*, 1854, p. 466. The amount per head of population is given differently in different tables according to the estimates made for the population in the inter-Census years.

[2] The total number of persons relieved in the course of the quarter ending Lady Day 1848 was 1,626,201. The total number simultaneously in receipt of relief on July 1, 1848, was 893,743. (Second Annual Report of Poor Law Board, 1849, pp. 8, 10-11.)

in 1849 than in 1835 (when wheat was very cheap, and the Allowance System was being summarily stopped); but it was possibly less than in 1813 when the Allowance System was in full operation and wheat was very dear. If we take it at a constant £6 per head in the first half of the nineteenth century, and £5 per head previously, it is possible to make the following guesses at the numbers simultaneously in receipt of Poor Relief between 1688 and 1850, together with the proportion in each year to the estimated population.

ESTIMATED POPULATION, AGGREGATE AMOUNT OF EXPENDITURE ON POOR RELIEF AND NUMBER OF PERSONS SIMULTANEOUSLY IN RECEIPT OF POOR RELIEF IN VARIOUS YEARS FROM 1688 TO 1847.

Year.	Estimated Population of England and Wales.	Estimated Aggregate amount of Expenditure on Poor Relief.	Estimated Number of persons simultaneously in Receipt of Poor Relief.	Percentage to Population.
1688	5,500,000	£700,000	140,000	2·5
1701	5,600,000	900,000	180,000	3·2
1714	5,750,000	950,000	190,000	3·3
1760	7,000,000	1,250,000	250,000	3·5
1776	8,000,000	1,529,786	306,000	3·8
1784	8,250,000	2,004,238	400,000	4·8
1801	9,172,980	3,750,000	750,000	8·1
1803	9,210,000	4,077,891	800,000	8·6
1813	10,506,000	6,656,106	1,331,000	12·7
1818	11,876,000	7,870,101	1,574,000	13·2
1821	11,978,875	6,959,251	1,400,000	11·7
1824	12,517,000	5,736,900	1,147,000	9·2
1831	13,297,187	6,798,889	1,369,000	10·2
1832	14,105,000	7,036,969	1,400,000	9·9
1834	14,372,000	6,317,255	1,263,000	8·8
1835	14,564,000	5,526,418	1,105,000	7·6
1836	14,758,000	4,717,630	943,000	6·4
1837	14,955,000	4,044,741	809,000	5·4
1841	15,906,741	4,760,929	952,000	5·9
1847	17,076,000	5,298,787	1,059,000	6·2

We do not pretend that this table, depending as it does on an arbitrary combination of several rough guesses, and ignoring changes in the value of money, has any statistical value. But it gives some idea of the relative smallness of the pauper multitude at the end of the seventeenth century ; of its slow increase in the course of the eighteenth century ; [1] of its bound upwards as the century closed ; of its culminating height about 1818 ; of a certain improvement when the Whig Government took office, even before the Poor Law Amend-

[1] The figures lend no support to the assertion, which has several times been made, that there was a positive decrease in aggregate pauperism in the second quarter of the eighteenth century, owing, it has been assumed, to the establishment of Workhouses in a small proportion of the parishes (see *The Old Poor Law*, by S. and B. Webb, 1926, pp. 216, 243-245, 254-256).

ment Act of 1834 ; and of the further reduction that followed that statute.

For the period from 1849 to 1871, representing the administration of the Poor Law Board, and for the period from 1871 to 1908, representing that of the Local Government Board, we may conveniently reproduce the following two tables : [1]

ESTIMATED POPULATION AND MEAN AGGREGATE NUMBER OF PAUPERS IN ENGLAND AND WALES FOR THE PERIOD FROM 1849 TO 1871.

Year ending Lady Day.	Estimated Population of England and Wales.	Mean Aggregate Number of Paupers.	Percentage to Population.
1849	17,356,882	1,088,659	6·3
1850	17,564,656	1,008,700	5·7
1851	17,773,324	941,315	5·3
1852	17,982,849	915,675	5·1
1853	18,193,206	886,362	4·9
1854	18,404,368	864,617	4·7
1855	18,616,310	897,686	4·8
1856	18,829,000	917,084	4·9
1857	19,043,412	885,010	4·6
1858	19,256,516	908,886	4·7
1859	19,471,291	865,446	4·4
1860	19,686,701	844,633	4·3
1861	19,902,713	883,921	4·4
1862	20,119,314	917,142	4·6
1863	20,371,013	1,079,382	5·3
1864	20,625,855	1,014,978	4·9
1865	20,883,889	951,899	4·6
1866	21,145,151	916,152	4·3
1867	21,409,684	931,546	4·3
1868	21,667,525	992,640	4·6
1869	21,948,713	1,018,140	4·6
1870	22,223,299	1,032,800	4·6
1871	22,501,316	1,037,360	4·6

[1] This table is extracted from *History of the English Poor Law*, by P. F. Aschrott and H. Preston-Thomas, 1888, pp. 285-286, where it was reproduced from the official statistics. It contains other statistics as to the numbers of Indoor and Outdoor Paupers, of such of them as were able-bodied and not able-bodied, excluding vagrants, and of the average price of wheat. The " mean number " is the mean of the numbers on January 1 and July 1 in each year. These statistics are not exactly comparable with those for the years prior to 1849.

[TABLE

ESTIMATED POPULATION AND MEAN AGGREGATE NUMBER OF PAUPERS IN
ENGLAND AND WALES FOR THE PERIOD BETWEEN 1872 AND 1908.[1]

Year ended Lady Day.	Estimated Population of England and Wales.	Mean Aggregate Number of Paupers, including Insane and Vagrants.	Percentage to Population.
1872	22,788,594	977,200	4·3
1873	23,096,495	883,688	3·8
1874	23,408,556	827,446	3·5
1875	23,724,834	809,914	3·3
1876	24,045,385	749,476	3·1
1877	24,370,267	719,949	2·9
1878	24,699,539	728,872	2·9
1879	25,033,259	765,455	3·0
1880	25,371,489	808,030	3·1
1881	25,714,288	790,937	3·0
1882	26,046,142	788,289	3·0
1883	26,334,942	782,422	3·0
1884	26,626,949	765,914	2·9
1885	26,922,192	768,938	2·8
1886	27,220,706	780,712	2·8
1887	27,522,532	796,036	2·9
1888	27,827,706	800,484	2·9
1889	28,136,258	795,617	2·8
1890	28,448,239	775,217	2·7
1891	28,763,673	759,730	2·6
1892	29,085,819	744,757	2·5
1893	29,421,392	758,776	2·5
1894	29,760,842	787,933	2·6
1895	30,104,201	796,913	2·6
1896	30,451,528	816,019	2·6
1897	30,802,858	814,887	2·6
1898	31,158,245	813,986	2·6
1899	31,517,725	813,938	2·5
1900	31,881,365	792,367	2·4
1901	32,249,187	781,298	2·4
1902	32,621,263	801,356	2·4
1903	32,997,626	822,786	2·4
1904	33,378,338	837,680	2·5
1905	33,763,434	884,365	2·6
1906	34,152,977	898,259	2·6
1907	34,547,016	893,316	2·6
1908	34,945,600	898,473	2·5

A remarkable feature of these tables is the close approach to uniformity over a long series of years in the percentage of paupers to population. There seems to be no correspondence whatever between the magnitude of the aggregate of persons in receipt of any of the forms of Poor Relief, and what we know to have been the state of trade and the prevalence of Unemployment. Thus, after the boom

[1] This table is extracted from a more detailed table in vol. xxv. of Appendix to Report of Poor Law Commission, 1909, pp. 24/25, which was prepared from the official statistics. The percentage to population is added.

of 1871–1872, trade declined and Unemployment increased, until the black misery of 1879 was reached, when the slump seems to have been the most severe of any between 1841 and 1921. Yet the total number of persons in receipt of Poor Relief was in 1877 and 1878 actually lower than in any year since 1849 ; and even in 1879 the percentage of paupers to population was lower than it had been in any year prior to 1877. The reader of our Chapter IV. (pp. 245-468) will recall that it was in the seventies that took place the energetic campaign of the Inspectorate against Outdoor Relief. It was in these years that " deterrence " was specially emphasised as a necessary feature of efficient Poor Law administration. The successive trade depressions of 1886–1887 and 1893–1895 seem to have had no greater effect on the statistics of aggregate pauperism than that of 1878–1879. Equally, the years of good trade appear to have made little or no impression ; and though the years of bounding commercial prosperity, 1900–1903, saw the percentage of paupers to population at its very lowest in the previous history of the English Poor Law, at any rate since 1688, the reduction compared with the percentage in the years of slump is so small as to be almost inappreciable.

We draw the inference (which has repeatedly been drawn by " Poor Law orthodoxy ") that the pauperism in proportion to the population depends very largely, not on the amount of destitution, but on the forms of relief adopted, or on the policy according to which Relief is granted. If it is desirable that the irreducible minimum of Poor Relief should bear little or no relation to destitution, then the reduction of the percentage of paupers to population between 1872 and 1908 to so low a figure as two or three, and its stabilisation for so many years in good times and bad, may be acclaimed as a triumph for the Local Government Board and the Boards of Guardians.

We have given the preceding figures as the best available statistics. It must, however, be stated that these figures cannot be accepted as completely accurate. In a few cases (stated to amount on January 1, 1907, only to 569 and on July 1, 1908, to 741) persons have actually been entered both as Indoor and Outdoor Paupers.[1] In many more cases the numbers are swollen by persons entered as only " constructively " paupers ; as, for instance, when a child (or other legal dependant) is admitted to a Poor Law institution, or receives

---

[1] When the head of the family alone enters the Workhouse and his dependants receive no Outdoor Relief, he only has been recorded as a pauper. " But if the family (other than the head) receive Outdoor Relief they, or if the relief were specially given for one member only, they or the member relieved, if the relief were specially given for one member only, would be included as Outdoor Paupers, whilst *the head would be counted both as an Indoor Pauper and as an Outdoor Pauper.*" (Poor Law Commission, 1909, Appendix vol. xxv. p. 5.)

domiciliary medical treatment from a Poor Law doctor. In such a case (in addition to the child) the father (or if there is no father living, the mother) is regarded as " constructively " a pauper. Moreover, if the father (or other head of the family) himself receives relief, his wife and dependent children are also included as paupers.[1] Further, the Vagrant leaving one Casual Ward in the morning of January 1 or July 1 and entering another Casual Ward in the evening of the same day, was for a long time recorded as two inmates of the Casual Wards, and consequently as two Indoor Paupers. Finally, it must be said that the practice on all these points has not been uniform in all the Unions, and has also varied in different years in the same Union. Thus, the aggregate totals for the various years can claim no more than approximate accuracy ; and there is no assurance that they can even be closely compared with each other. There is, however, no reason to doubt that, in such a large aggregate as a million or so, these sources of error are of little consequence.

After 1911 the statistics become more accurate, though not all the ambiguities and shortcomings have yet been remedied. We take from the Nineteenth Abstract of Labour Statistics (Cmd. 3140 of 1928) the following more detailed tables :

NUMBER, PER 10,000 OF ESTIMATED POPULATION, OF PERSONS IN RECEIPT OF RELIEF IN ENGLAND AND WALES ON THE LAST SATURDAY IN EACH MONTH IN THE YEARS 1911–1927, AND THE CORRESPONDING NUMBER FOR EACH OF THOSE YEARS CALCULATED FROM THE NUMBERS IN RECEIPT OF RELIEF ON EACH SATURDAY WITHIN THE YEAR.

[*Compiled from the quarterly Statements of the Number of Persons in receipt of Poor Law Relief, supplemented by information specially supplied by the Ministry of Health.*]

Year.	Jan.	Feb.	Mar.	Apr.	May.	June.	July.	Aug.	Sept.	Oct.	Nov.	Dec.	Yearly Average.
1911	193	192	189	183	178	177	174	177	178	179	183	186	181
1912	190	191	203	189	180	179	180	175	175	177	182	183	183
1913	185	183	179	175	171	169	166	167	167	169	172	173	172
1914	177	176	176	172	170	169	167	176	173	172	172	172	172
1915	172	172	170	165	161	158	156	155	153	152	152	153	159
1916	151	151	151	146	144	142	139	138	138	137	138	139	143
1917	139	140	139	136	134	132	131	130	129	127	128	128	133
1918	128	128	126	124	123	121	121	120	119	119	121	122	123
1919	122	124	124	122	121	121	122	124	123	125	127	129	126
1920	131	131	132	132	131	131	131	132	133	137	144	152	134
1921	161	168	174	249	305	345	254	249	328	394	372	360	279
1922	389	389	387	440	455	467	395	374	381	397	371	368	398
1923	369	365	353	355	337	333	344	332	334	335	327	323	342
1924	344	337	319	313	300	297	294	279	270	270	276	277	298
1925	286	287	285	288	282	285	290	309	314	327	334	341	300
1926	333	327	320	316	606	622	635	634	616	579	559	381	494
1927	340	331	319	311	300	300	294	296	294	298	303	316	309

[1] In Scotland the Poor Law Authorities, with greater accuracy, have always recorded the head of the family as the pauper, and have stated separately the numbers of dependants.

Number of Persons (including Dependants) in Receipt of Relief in England and Wales on One Day in Winter and on One Day in Summer, in the Years 1911-1912 to 1926-1927.

[Compiled from the First Annual Report of the Ministry of Health and from later Returns.]

Year.	Persons (other than Lunatics in Asylums, Registered Hospitals and Licensed Houses, and Casuals) Receiving		Lunatics in Asylums, Registered Hospitals and Licensed Houses.	Casuals.	Net Total Number of Persons in Receipt of Relief.*
	Institutional Relief.*	Domiciliary Relief.*			
	(1)	(2)	(3)	(4)	(5)
	On or about the First Day of January.				
1912	279,781	416,532	96,883	9,732	801,881
1913	275,292	410,954	99,262	8,882	794,227
1914	264,292	388,917	100,941	7,568	761,578
1915	258,962	394,843	102,975	5,416	762,060
1916	226,466	354,325	100,182	3,576	684,549
1917	215,283	321,813	97,356	2,875	637,327
1918	198,493	296,104	90,718	1,470	586,785
1919	183,110	287,244	83,172	1,091	554,617
1920†	186,273	305,822	82,288	2,035	576,418
1921†	198,992	376,258	84,333	4,084	663,667
1922†	215,773	1,183,439	87,282	6,572	1,493,066
1923†	217,233	1,222,547	90,582	7,628	1,537,990
1924†	219,245	1,051,276	93,783	7,794	1,372,098
1925†	216,510	886,779	94,314	7,664	1,205,267
1926†	221,986	1,113,019	96,511	8,294	1,439,810
1927†	226,027	1,212,479	99,668	10,737	1,548,911
	On or about the First Day of July.				
1911	255,071	399,680	95,900	9,000	758,777
1912	255,527	412,196	98,020	7,956	773,605
1913	244,956	385,499	99,787	4,310	734,459
1914	246,089	388,987	101,672	5,389	742,021
1915‡	225,068	375,451	101,578‡	4,554	706,651
1916‡	211,612	333,513	98,769‡	3,705	647,599
1917‡	200,350	308,758	94,037‡	2,395	605,540
1918‡	185,224	283,230	86,945‡	1,262	556,661
1919‡	175,581	289,845	82,730‡	1,516	549,672
1920‡	187,146	317,474	83,311‡	2,806	590,737
1921‡	201,989	1,110,386	85,807‡	5,973	1,404,155
1922‡	209,821	1,573,945	88,932	9,999	1,882,697
1923‡	211,709	1,073,528	92,182	8,559	1,385,978
1924‡	209,752	942,718	94,048‡	7,112	1,253,630
1925‡	211,285	908,145	95,413‡	7,351	1,222,194
1926‡	216,321	2,256,871	98,090‡	8,536	2,579,818

* Up to January 1915, persons who received both institutional and domiciliary Relief on the same day are counted both in Col. (1) and in Col. (2) but are counted once only in the Totals shown in Col. (5). From July 1915 onwards such persons are counted once only in Cols. (1) and (2).

† The figures for these dates relate to the numbers in receipt of relief on the *night* of the specified dates.

‡ The numbers of lunatics in Asylums, Registered Hospitals and Licensed Houses on or about the first day of July, were not ascertained for 1915 and subsequent years ; the numbers used in this Table are the means of the ascertained numbers for the preceding and succeeding January 1.

Indoor and Outdoor Relief

Throughout the whole administration since 1834, the greatest importance has been attached, in England and Wales, to one main classification, namely, that of Indoor and Outdoor Relief. The Poor Law Commissioners, who took office in 1834, found, as we have described,[1] somewhat to their surprise, that they quickly had on their hands, as inmates of the new Workhouses for a prolonged stay, nearly one hundred thousand men, women and children, as against (at the outset) nearly ten times that number of recipients of Outdoor Relief. As regards Indoor Pauperism, the total has continued ever since to rise to higher levels, with periodical reductions in decades of good trade, up to 133,513 in 1849 ; 157,740 in 1869 ; 183,872 in 1881 ; 190,347 in 1899 ; 237,549 in 1908, up to the maximum of 279,781 in 1912. The amount of Indoor Relief has, however, little relation to the amount of pauperism ; it has signified, in the main, the steadily increasing utilisation of the Poor Law institutions, not in the way intended by the inventors of the " Workhouse Test ", but as places of refuge for the aged and infirm, and persons mentally disordered or deficient ; as residential schools for children of school age ; and (especially in the past half-century), as hospitals for the sick. After 1912 the aggregate total of inmates started to decline, owing to the successive clearances effected by the Old Age Pensions and Health Insurance Acts, the continued growth of the hospitals and sanatoria of the Local Health Authorities, and the disfavour into which the Poor Law institutions fell as places of residence for the children, for the aged, and for the able-bodied, leading to a preference for domiciliary relief. During the War, in particular, admission to the Poor Law institutions was restricted ; and the total of their inmates had fallen by 1919 to the low figure of 183,110. Since that date there has been, along with the continuous improvement in the specialised Poor Law institutions for the sick, a slow but steady rise in the total of inmates, the figure reaching 226,027 in January 1927.

The statistics of Outdoor Relief are somewhat more significant than those of Indoor Relief as to the contemporary volume of destitution, and they have varied independently of the changes in the extent of institutional treatment. But here again variations in administrative policy are important factors. In some years the aggregate total of recipients of Outdoor Relief has been as low as 400,000. During the War it was exceptionally low, and in 1919 it was only 285,000—the absolute minimum for at least two centuries. On the other hand, the total has often exceeded one million ; rising exceptionally during 1920–1928 to even greater figures, and in 1926 reaching the unprecedented total of two and a half millions. We do not think it worth while to reproduce the lengthy tables that

[1] See p. 132.

would be required to give the exact figures for each of the past eighty years, especially as the basis of calculation has been changed from a " mean " between two counts for each year to an " average " of 52 counts. Moreover, the classification of Indoor and Outdoor Relief has always been arbitrary. It has, for instance, never corresponded exactly with institutional and domiciliary relief. The Indoor Paupers have always included only the inmates of the institutions of the Poor Law Authorities themselves, and that without discriminating between the most diverse kinds of institution, such as General Mixed Workhouses and Able-bodied Test Workhouses, Sick Asylums and Poor Law infirmaries ; homes for the mentally defective, or for the aged ; residential schools, " Cottage Homes " and " Scattered Homes " for the children of school age ; finally the Casual Wards receiving Vagrants. Where the Boards of Guardians had their own Isolation Wards for infectious cases, these persons were counted as Indoor Paupers. Where such pauper patients were sent to the Local Health Authority's hospitals, they have been recorded as Outdoor Paupers. In the Metropolis, when they began to be sent to the hospitals of the Metropolitan Asylums Board, a Poor Law Authority, they were still recorded as Indoor Paupers. In 1883, however, Parliament enacted that treatment in these hospitals should not be deemed Poor Relief, so that, in annually increasing numbers, these patients, though still maintained at the expense of the Poor Rate, disappeared altogether from the statistics of Metropolitan (and therefore also of national) pauperism. On the other hand, paupers sent by the Boards of Guardians to institutions not under their control, and individually paid for out of the Poor Rate—such as those entrusted to certified schools and homes, or to similar philanthropic institutions not certified, and those sent for treatment to hospitals, either under voluntary management or belonging to the Local Health Authorities [1]—have been classified as in receipt of Outdoor Relief. This, too, has been in the past the classification of the steadily increasing number of patients certified as of unsound mind and sent by the Guardians to the County Lunatic Asylums, although the total of such lunatics is now usually given separately. The children " Boarded Out ", either within the Union or without, are to this day merged in the heterogeneous class of Outdoor Paupers. Moreover (as has already been mentioned in connection with the aggregate total of paupers), if one child in a

---

[1] It must be added that if, as has sometimes been the case, a lump sum is paid by the Board of Guardians to a hospital in return for the privilege of sending in paupers who need isolation or special treatment, and no payment per case is made, the persons thus sent to another institution are included neither as Indoor nor as Outdoor Paupers ; and they apparently cease to be paupers at all ! If the method of payment is changed, the status of the patients, and also the total number of paupers, are thereby changed.

family is visited by the District Medical Officer, and, on his order, given medical extras, this counts as two Outdoor Paupers, the father (or other head of the household) being reckoned as " constructively " a pauper.   If, however, the man having a wife and seven children, himself receives the attention of the District Medical Officer, or any other Poor Relief, he is assumed to be counted as nine Outdoor Paupers.   Unfortunately, it seems probable that Unions have from time to time varied in their own practice in this respect, and at any one time have differed from each other to an unascertainable extent— which introduces yet another uncertainty into the recorded classification of Indoor and Outdoor pauperism.

The Able-bodied

From 1834 to 1911 great importance was attached to the classification of the Outdoor Paupers as being either " able-bodied " or " not able-bodied."   Unfortunately, no authoritative definition was given as to the meaning of " able-bodied ", so that the Unions varied indefinitely and unascertainably as to the degree of ability which should require a recipient of relief to be entered in one or other of the two classes.   The apparent intention was to get a separate record of the persons who could reasonably be expected to earn their own living in the competitive Labour Market.   But no limit of age was prescribed, so that Unions varied as to whether to include men of 70 or 80 as able-bodied.[1]   Nothing was said as to physical deficiencies, so that the practice varied as to healthy men with only one arm, or only one leg, or with defective eyesight or hearing. Nothing was prescribed as to mental fitness for employment, so that men subject to occasional epileptic fits, men in different grades of mental deficiency, and men who might have been (but were not) certified as of unsound mind, were entered or not entered as " able-bodied ", according to the way in which the Union's statistical returns were compiled.   The uncertainty was increased by the official direction that men usually able-bodied, but temporarily incapacitated by sickness or accident, were to be recorded as able-bodied ; though it was not stated how it was to be ascertained that the incapacity was only temporary.   The value of the classification was further diminished by the rule that the legal dependants of the head of the family were to be reckoned along with him, so that an able-bodied man with a sick wife and seven young children appeared

[1] J. J. Henley, the Inspector, observed in 1871 that " The term able-bodied is widely construed in different Unions.   In some the age of 60 is sufficient to constitute age, and thus partial infirmity ; in others age without some special infirmity is not deemed sufficient.   I latterly saw a man of between 70 and 80 years of age refused Outdoor Relief on the ground that he was able-bodied " Twenty-third Annual Report of Poor Law Board, 1871, p. 99).

as nine able-bodied paupers![1] Inside the Workhouse the classification was equally uncertain, though in a different way. Men, women and children, however closely related, stood on their own feet. Youth was regarded, but not old age. Women coming in to be confined were usually classed as able-bodied. The mental condition was ignored.[2] The most usual plan seems to have been to classify according to dietary. In many Unions all inmates, male or female, sane or insane, over 16 years of age, who were not on the special diet ordered by the Medical Officer for the sick, were classed as able-bodied. We do not think it necessary to reproduce any statistics so curiously compiled. By the Relief Regulation Order, 1911, this classification was abandoned; and the term " able-bodied " formally went out of use in English Poor Law administration.[3]

The Unemployed.

The class of able-bodied was replaced by that of persons normally in wage-earning employment, or persons insured against Unemployment, or persons destitute merely by reason of Unemployment. These statistics are much more significant than those relating to the able-bodied ; and we append a table of the numbers so recorded in each quarter from 1922 to 1925. Unfortunately, the old Poor Law practice—actually prescribed by the General Order as to Accounts in 1844—of counting the man and his wife, and his children under 16, as all belonging to the same class, namely, that of the head of the family, has not been given up ; so that the numbers contrast very mis-leadingly with those of the Unemployed that are published by the Minister of Labour, where the wives and children for whom Benefit is paid are not included. About three-fourths of the persons in receipt of " Unemployment Relief " from the Poor Rate, as recorded in the following tables, are merely the legal dependants of the Un-employed persons who were " relieved " by the Boards of Guardians.

[1] When it was explained that the merely temporarily sick were entered as able-bodied, it was expressly stated that "if the sick pauper be the male head of the family, the whole family dependent on him are entered in the able-bodied list " (Twenty-second Annual Report of Poor Law Board, 1870, pp. xviii-xix).

[2] " The (Workhouse) Masters do not all adhere to the same definition, many declaring that as regards able-bodied men there were none in the Workhouse. A man subject to fits, or to any other disease which only breaks out occasionally, would be classed in some Workhouses as able-bodied. Women nursing their children would be always entered as able-bodied if not otherwise sick " (Twenty-second Annual Report of Poor Law Board, 1870, p. xix). It was, indeed, admitted that " as evidence of prevalent destitution caused by want of employment or depression of trade, the number of the whole class (of able-bodied) is by no means a true criterion " (ibid.)

[3] Nearly forty years had elapsed since H. (afterwards Sir Henry) Longley, as Inspector, had asked in vain for regulations prescribing a uniform classification (Third Annual Report of Local Government Board, 1874, p. 174).

AVERAGE * NUMBER OF PERSONS (INCLUDING DEPENDANTS) IN RECEIPT OF
DOMICILIARY POOR-LAW RELIEF IN ENGLAND AND WALES, DISTINGUISHING
PERSONS INSURED UNDER THE UNEMPLOYMENT INSURANCE ACTS AND
OTHER PERSONS ORDINARILY ENGAGED IN SOME REGULAR OCCUPATION,
1922–1925.

[*Based upon the quarterly Statements of the Number of Persons in receipt
of Poor-Law Relief, issued by the Ministry of Health.*]

Month.	Persons insured under U.I. Acts (whether in receipt of Unemployment Benefit or not).		Other Persons ordinarily engaged in some regular Occupation.		All other Persons.		Total.	
	Average* Number in Receipt of Relief.	Rate per 10,000 of esti- mated Popula- tion.	Average* Number in Receipt of Relief.	Rate per 10,000 of esti- mated Popula- tion.	Average* Number in Receipt of Relief.	Rate per 10,000 of esti- mated Popula- tion.	Average* Number in Receipt of Relief.	Rate per 10,000 of esti- mated Popula- tion.
1922.								
March .	794,000	210	65,000	17	399,000	105	1,258,000	332
June .	1,090,000	288	63,000	17	411,000	108	1,564,000	413
September	757,000	198	52,000	14	416,000	109	1,225,000	321
December	695,000	182	57,000	15	433,000	114	1,185,000	311
1923.								
March .	636,000	167	67,000	17	438,000	115	1,141,000	299
June .	576,000	151	50,000	13	440,000	115	1,066,000	279
September	551,000	144	47,000	12	435,000	113	1,033,000	269
December	522,000	136	50,000	13	449,000	117	1,021,000	266
1924.								
March .	506,000	132	50,000	13	467,000	121	1,023,000	266
June .	422,000	110	42,000	11	467,000	121	931,000	242
September	328,000	85	38,000	10	466,000	120	832,000	215
December	333,000	87	39,000	10	480,000	125	852,000	222
1925.								
March .	346,000	89	40,000	11	497,000	128	883,000	228
June .	355,000	92	36,000	9	499,000	129	890,000	230
September	438,000	113	36,000	9	513,000	132	987,000	254
December	510,000	131	43,000	11	537,000	138	1,090,000	280

* The averages in this Table are the averages of the numbers in receipt of relief on each .
Saturday in the months shown.

The Duration of Pauperism

An even more important defect in the official statistics than any
yet mentioned is their continued failure to indicate the duration of
the " pauperism " in each case.   To take the most extreme instances,
an able-bodied single man who receives relief for one day only, if the
day happens to be that on which the count is made, is reckoned in
the same way as the microcephalous idiot who has been maintained
in the Workhouse since birth, and may be expected to continue there
until death.   There is plainly an important difference between a
pauperism which is chronic and one which is a momentary, and
perhaps a unique, incident in a working life.   " There appears to be
reason ", Sir Robert Giffen pointed out in 1899, "for having a good

account of pauperism not merely as it exists on one day, but as it has existed during a given period of time ; . . . to introduce a classification . . . according to the length of the period for which relief is given. . . . In this way a distinction would be made . . . between permanents and the others who were relieved for short periods ".[1]

Spasmodic attempts to supply some information as to the average duration of pauperism have been made in the form of a whole year's Census ; that is, a count of all the different individuals who have received Poor Relief at any time during the preceding year.[2] Not until 1892 was any year's count officially made ; and this showed the total to be 1,573,074, as compared with 700,746 on January 1, 1892, or 2·24 times as many.[3] In 1907 the Poor Law Commission asked the Local Government Board to repeat the year's count, when the total was found to be 1,709,436, which was 2·15 times greater than the mean of the day counts of January 1 and July 1, 1907. The ratio seems to have fallen during the past three-quarters of a century.[4] But the " year's count ", no more than the " day's count ", distinguishes between the numbers of the different kinds of paupers whose pauperism is normally of very different duration ; as, for instance, the women coming in for confinement ; the infants under 5 in the Workhouse Nurseries and on Outdoor Relief ; the children of school age in residential Poor Law and other schools, or only boarded and lodged, and sent to the day schools of the Local Education Authority, or merely granted Outdoor Relief ; the Indoor and the Outdoor sick ; the mentally defective or disordered, in Poor Law institutions, in other institutions, or on Outdoor Relief ; the aged and the prematurely incapacitated, whether in institutions or on Outdoor Relief ; and the men and women normally employed and fit for employment, but destitute through Unemployment, either under training or in institutions or on Outdoor Relief.

It is not that there is no information available about most of these classes. At one or other place in the hundreds of official reports

---

[1] Sir Robert Giffen's Address, in *Poor Law Conferences, 1899–1900*, pp. 459-460. This shortcoming in the Poor Law statistics had also been pointed out in *London Pauperism among Jews and Christians*, by J. H. Stallard, 1867, pp. 38-40 ; and also in *The English Poor Law System*, by P. F. Aschrott and H. Preston-Thomas, 1888, p. 282.

[2] Partial calculations on this basis were made in 1850 by Robert Pashley, Q.C. (*Pauperism and Poor Laws*, 1852, pp. 10-12), who found the year's total to be about three times the one-day total; and in 1857 by Frederick Purdy, at that time Principal of the Statistical Department of the Poor Law Board, who made the ratio three and a half. The partial calculation made by Sir Robert Giffen in 1899 indicated that from two-thirds " to four-fifths of the number receiving relief at one time are permanent ", or at least lasting for twelve months, there being no great divergence between Indoor and Outdoor paupers (*Poor Law Conferences, 1899–1900*, p. 461).

[3] Twenty-second Annual Report of Local Government Board, 1893.

[4] Majority Report of Poor Law Commission, 1909, p. 31.

since 1834, scattered figures are to be found by the diligent investigator. What are lacking are consecutive figures for each class of paupers for terms of years, continued in annually lengthening tables, which would reveal the different movements of each section of the pauper host.

On one point of supreme importance to social investigators the Poor Law statistics afford absolutely no information. From 1834 down to the present day there has continuously been a pauper host that has never fallen below half a million. To what extent, if any, have these five hundred thousand people during the past hundred years been, continuously, either the same individuals or the same families ? There were something like one million paupers in 1834 ; and there are much about the same number in the present year. What relationship, if any, is there between these two armies ? We have been told, from time to time, of the large percentage of the boys in Poor Law Schools who have been traced in after life as " making good ". But no one has traced the life-histories of recipients of Outdoor Relief ; nor have we, in this country, any detailed studies of pauper pedigrees.

The Sick

There have been during the past seventy years several attempts to compile statistics as to the paupers who were sick. In the popular agitation of 1865 as to the treatment of the sick poor and the position of Poor Law Medical Officers, the House of Commons ordered a return of the number of sick persons receiving Outdoor Relief in the Metropolitan Unions. Out of 70,889 Outdoor Paupers in London, 10,348, or 13·8 per cent, were then under medical treatment. Four years later a similar return was ordered for England and Wales, and this showed 12·8 per cent of all the Outdoor Paupers were being medically treated. Corresponding returns were made in these years as to the Workhouse inmates who were sick. In 1865, 48 per cent, and in 1869, 39 per cent, of the inmates of Metropolitan Workhouses were under medical treatment. In 1860, Dr. Edward Smith found, in 48 provincial Workhouses, 30 per cent of the inmates sick ; another inspection in 1868 gave 28·2 per cent sick ; and another in 1869 made the percentage 29·7. Here, again, the statistics suffer from a want of clearness of definition. Since 1891–1892, statistics are available of the curious class of " able-bodied sick " ; that is, of those persons classed as able-bodied, who are nevertheless receiving medical treatment as being temporarily sick. The Majority Report of the Poor Law Commission gives the following table.[1]

[1] Poor Law Commission, 1909, Majority Report, p. 68 ; Appendix, vol. xxv. Part I., par. 57.

NUMBER OF ABLE-BODIED PERSONS RELIEVED ON ACCOUNT OF TEMPORARY
SICKNESS FOR CERTAIN YEARS FROM 1891 TO 1900.

Year.	Males.		Females.
	Indoor.	Outdoor.	Indoor only.
1891–1893	7,304	8748	6,923
1895–1896	10,281	8831	8,370
1900–1901	11,449	6950	9,257
1905–1906	15,913	8901	12,187
1906–1907	15,913	9028	12,338
1907–1908	16,061	8569	12,661

The Poor Law Commission, " realising the incompleteness of
this information ", obtained a return—not for the whole of England
and Wales, but—" from 128 Unions, giving statistics of the persons
under medical treatment at noon on April 13, 1907. From this
return we find that nearly one-third of the persons in receipt of
relief are under medical treatment ; and that this proportion rises
to nearly one-half in the case of the indoor poor, and falls to one-
fifth in the case of the outdoor poor. For men under 50 years of age
the proportion reaches three-fifths, and for men of these ages relieved
indoors it rises to two-thirds. The proportion of women under
medical treatment is smaller than that of men, especially in the case
of Out-Relief." [1]

We may accordingly infer that the Minister of Health has under
the care of the Poor Law Medical Staff for which he is responsible,
at all times, something like 300,000 sick persons. There is available
the very minimum of statistical information about this not inconsiderable mass of " clinical material ". There seem to be no mortality
statistics of paupers as a whole, or of any section of them ; and no
" case-rates ". There is only the scantiest information as to the
diseases from which the 300,000 are suffering ; and none at all as to
the changes in incidence from year to year. To the inquisitiveness
of the Poor Law Commission we owe a conspectus of the diseases
under treatment, in 1907, in 128 out of 631 Unions. This showed
that 44 per 1000 of the paupers were suffering from bronchitis or
pneumonia ; 19·9 per 1000 from rheumatism or gout ; 15·8 per 1000
from pulmonary tuberculosis ; and 13·9 per 1000 from heart disease.[2]

[1] Poor Law Commission, 1909, Majority Report, p. 68, and Appendix, vol.
xxv. Part III., pars. 5 and 7.
[2] *Ibid.* These or any other statistics of paupers under medical treatment
plainly need to be taken together with the corresponding statistics of the
patients under treatment by the Medical Officers of the Local Health Authorities and the National Health Insurance Scheme. No such comprehensive
survey appears to have been attempted.

On the important subjects of maternal mortality in childbirth and the infant mortality in the Workhouse Nurseries there are practically no statistics, although every Union keeps exact records of these deaths.

Some Conspicuous Omissions from Poor Law Statistics

It has been suggested that " some record of refusals should also be kept by the Officers of the English Poor Law. A pauper applies to the Relieving Officer and is sent away without relief, and none of the circumstances are either reported or preserved. Even the Board of Guardians should report refusals of relief, for they give some conception of the character of the poor ; and, better still, of the care and discrimination which is exercised in their relief." [1]

There are, at present, no statistics of the occupations, birthplaces, nationalities, races or creeds of either the applicants for, or the recipients of, Poor Relief.

There have been, owing to the absence of the necessary statistics, no extensive studies of particular classes of paupers, the proper treatment of which is still a puzzle to the administrator. Among such classes may be named the " Ins and Outs ", and the Vagrants.

No statistics have been compiled, on a national scale, of some of the incidents of pauperism which are recorded in every Union. We have no figures as to the number of persons relieved each day or month, or during each year, as in " sudden or urgent necessity ". There are no national statistics of pauper funerals, either of Indoor or of Outdoor paupers.[2] Nor do we learn systematically how many

---

[1] *London Pauperism among Jews and Christians*, by J. H. Stallard, 1867, p. 26.

[2] In view of the fact that every Board of Guardians has been, since 1834, continually paying for the burial of deceased paupers, it is remarkable how little information is available about the practice. It has been extremely rarely mentioned in any part of the vast stream of official reports on Poor Law administration.

The practice of parish officers undertaking the duty of burying inmates of the Workhouse, and even recipients of Outdoor Relief, is one of unknown antiquity, which only gradually received a statutory basis. The general obligation to bury any corpse for which no solvent person could be made responsible was imposed on the Churchwardens and Overseers by 48 George III. c. 75 ; but they could recover the cost from the County fund. It was said in 1845 that there was no legal authority for incurring any expense from the Poor Rate in the burial of persons who had been Outdoor paupers ; and this resulted in the express authorisation to undertake the burial of " any poor person belonging to their Parish or Union ", by 7 and 8 Vic. c. 101, sec. 31 (Eleventh Annual Report of Poor Law Commissioners, 1845, pp. 137-138). 28 and 29 Vic. c. 79 made this a Union charge ; see 10 *Official Circular* (N.S.), p. 149. The Local Government Board Circular of March 22, 1882, may also be consulted ; and see *The General Orders relating to the Poor Law*, by W. C. Glen, 11th edition, 1898, p. 420 ; and *The Poor Law Orders*, by H. Jenner-Fust, 1911, pp. 536, 633-640.

children are compulsorily taken away from unfit parents, and "adopted" by the Boards of Guardians.

There has been no attempt at correlation between the pauper class as a whole, or particular sections of it, with the prison population, and especially with the discharged prisoners.

The most important shortcoming of the Poor Law statistics is, however, the failure to collect the available facts, and to survey their connection with regard, not so much to the persons at any one time in receipt of Poor Relief, as to the whole class or stratum of the population from which these persons are drawn. We need, both for diagnosis and treatment, both for prevention and cure, to gain a much more detailed vision of the life prior to obtaining Poor Relief, and after it has come to an end. Pauper recidivism, in particular, calls for further study.

The Future of Public Assistance Statistics

One result of the Local Government Act of 1929, with its revolutionary changes in areas and its extensive transfers from relief under the Poor Law to treatment under "the appropriate Acts", will be to destroy the continuity of practically all the statistics at present compiled by the Ministry of Health. It accordingly becomes imperative to think out the classifications and the tables that the altered circumstances require. It may be suggested that the fullest advantage will not be obtained from the cost and trouble involved in getting statistics on a national scale unless they are obtained with increased precision, in more detail, and, above all, with greater differentiation between distinct classes, than has hitherto been found possible. There should clearly be a close correlation of the statistics relating to particular classes that are compiled by the Ministries of Health, Labour, Education and Pensions, all of which are "relieving" members of the same families. The Unemployed, the Sick, the Children, and the Aged are being dealt with by all of them ; and comprehensive summaries of the statistics for each class could be compiled. The desirability of a Central Index Register, as recommended by the expert Committee in 1918, in order to keep accurate all the separate local registers, becomes more then ever apparent.[1] An addition of great utility would be comparative statistics of all the various institutions, arranged in appropriate classes, and including figures as to cost of maintenance, admissions and discharges, mortality of inmates, etc.

[1] See pp. 815-816.

INDEX OF PERSONS

INDEX OF PLACES

INDEX OF SUBJECTS